THE SIGHTS *of*
BEIJING

北京名胜游览

朱歧新 / 编著

CHINA TRAVEL & TOURISM PRESS

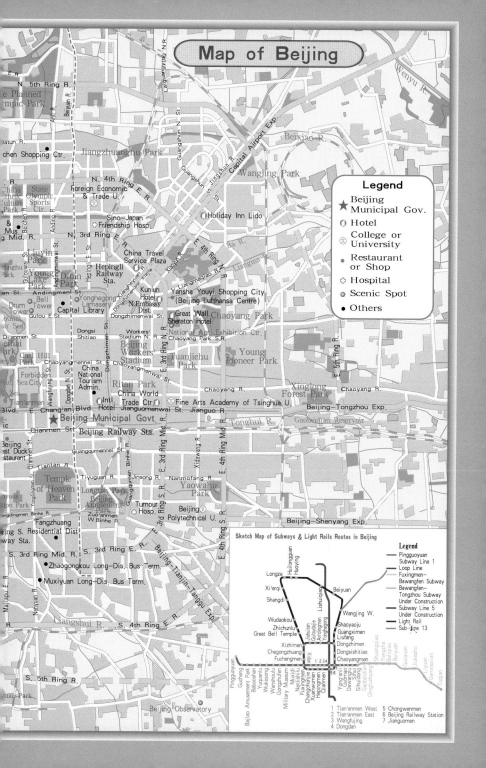

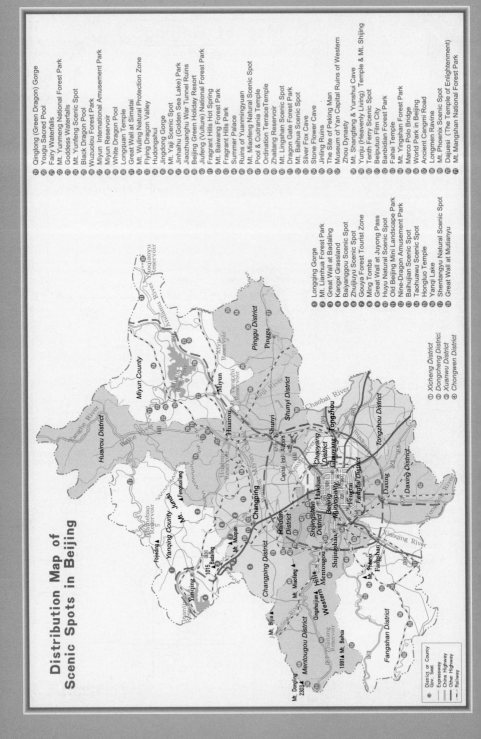

Distribution Map of Scenic Spots in Beijing

① Longqing Gorge
② Mt. Lianhua Forest Park
③ Great Wall at Badaling
④ Kangxi Grassland
⑤ Baiyangpou Scenic Spot
⑥ Zhujiuyu Scenic Spot
⑦ Gouya Forest Tourist Zone
⑧ Ming Tombs
⑨ Great Wall at Juyong Pass
⑩ Huyu Natural Scenic Spot
⑪ Old Beijing Mini Landscape Park
⑫ Nine-Dragon Amusement Park
⑬ Baihujian Scenic Spot
⑭ Taohuawu Scenic Spot
⑮ Hongluo Temple
⑯ Yanqi Lake
⑰ Shentangyu Natural Scenic Spot
⑱ Great Wall at Mutianyu

⑲ Qinglong (Green Dragon) Gorge
⑳ Yougu Sacred Pool
㉑ Fairy Waterfalls
㉒ Mt. Yunmeng National Forest Park
㉓ Goddess Waterfalls
㉔ Mt. Yunfeng Scenic Spot
㉕ Black Dragon Pool
㉖ Wuzuolou Forest Park
㉗ Miyun International Amusement Park
㉘ Miyun Reservoir
㉙ White Dragon Pool
㉚ Longquan Temple
㉛ Great Wall at Simatai
㉜ Mt. Wuling Natural Protection Zone
㉝ Flying Dragon Valley
㉞ Hudongshui
㉟ Jingdong Gorge
㊱ Mt. Yaji Scenic Spot
㊲ Jinhaihu (Golden Sea Lake) Park
㊳ Jiaozhuanghu War Tunnel Ruins
㊴ Beijing Green Holiday Resort
㊵ Jiufeng (Vulture) National Forest Park
㊶ Fragrant Hills Hot Spring
㊷ Mt. Baiwang Forest Park
㊸ Fragrant Hills Park
㊹ Summer Palace
㊺ Ruins of Yuanmingyuan
㊻ Mt. Miaofeng Natural Scenic Spot
㊼ Pool & Cudrania Temple
㊽ Ordination Terrace Temple
㊾ Zhaitang Reservoir
㊿ Mt. Lingshan Scenic Spot
51 Dragon Gate Forest Park
52 Mt. Baihua Scenic Spot
53 Silver Fox Cave
54 Stone Flower Cave
55 Jinling Ruins
56 The Site of Peking Man
57 Museum of Yan Capital Ruins of Western Zhou Dynasty
58 Mt. Shangfang & Yunshui Cave
59 Yunju (Heavenly Living) Temple & Mt. Shijing
60 Tenth Ferry Scenic Spot
61 Beiputuo Film City
62 Banbidian Forest Park
63 Fahai Temple
64 Mt. Yingshan Forest Park
65 Marco Polo Bridge
66 World Park in Beijing
67 Ancient Cangmi Road
68 Longmen Ravine
69 Mt. Phoenix Scenic Spot
70 Dajuesi (The Temple of Enlightenment)
71 Mt. Mangshan National Forest Park

① Xicheng District
② Dongcheng District
③ Xuanwu District
④ Chongwen District

District or County Gov. Seat
Expressway
China Highway
Other Highway
Railway

The Hall of Supreme Harmony

Tian´anmen (Gate of Heavenly Peace)

The Palace of Heavenly Purity

A look down the Forbidden City

Zhongshan Park

The Temple of Heaven

A panoramic view of Beihai Park

The Big Bell Temple

The Lama Temple

The statue of Maitreya in the Lama Temple

Marco Polo Bridge

Red leaves on the Fragrant Hills

The Summer Palace

The Great Wall at Badaling

The Great Wall at Jinshanling

Qianmen (Front Gate)

Deshengmen
(Gate of Virtuous
Triumph)

Beijing Tongrentang Pharmacy

Beijing Ancient Observatory

Wangfujing Church

The Nine-Dragon Wall in Beihai Park

The Ruins of Yuanmingyuan

Beijing Confucius Temple

The statue of Sakyamuni
in the Reclining Buddha
Temple

The Grand View Garden

The Sacred Way of the Ming Tombs

The Underground Palace of Dingling Tomb

The Site of Peking Man at Zhoukoudian

The skull of Peking Man at Zhoukoudian

Yanqing Ancient Cliff

China Millennium Monument

Beijing West Railway Station

The Capital Airport New Terminal

Beijing Subway

The modern appearance of Beijing

Wangfujing Street

A visit to *hutong* (lanes) by pedicabs

Beijing's *siheyuan* (quadrangle---a compound
with houses around a square courtyard)

Liulichang Cultural Street (the
Antique Shops Area)

Sanlitun Bar Street

Peking Opera

Beijing Roast Duck

National Olympic Sports Centre

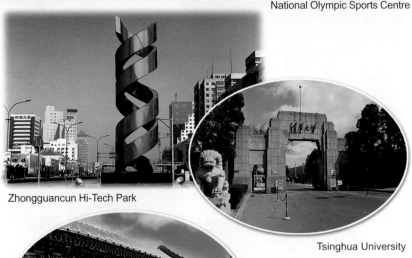

Zhongguancun Hi-Tech Park

Tsinghua University

Peking University

National Library of China

Preface

With the rapid growth of travel and tourism since China's reform and opening-up to the outside world in 1979, particularly the success of Beijing's bid for Olympic Games in 2008 and China's entry into the World Trade Organization (WTO) in 2001, an ever-increasing number of overseas visitors are coming to Beijing.

Beijing is a world-renowned ancient capital, and a famous city of world history and culture as well. Beijing is an ideal place to visit, as well as to invest, and to do business, to shop, to dine or to be entertained. Beijing is both an ancient and a young city. The city is ancient, because it boasts a 500,000-year history of civilization; as a city, Beijing has a history of more than 3,000 years (the city was established in 1045 BC), and as a capital (Jin Dynasty, the first dynasty in the Chinese history, made Beijing its capital in AD 1115), it has a history of nearly 900 years. This ancient city of Beijing is a masterpiece of the longest history and the largest scale in the world and also is the crystallisation of the capital construction in the history of China. Beijing is a young city in terms of vitality and its importance not only in China but also the world over. The reasons why Beijing attracts and pleases people are not hard to discover. To start at the heart of Beijing itself, tourists see the Tian'anmen Square, which is the geographical and emotional centre of the city.

National capitals are always tourist attractions. Most people wish to see their capital city when they begin travelling about their own country. When they go abroad, few neglect to pay at least a cursory call on a country's seat of government.

There is something special about a national capital, and Beijing is no exception. Its eminence among China's tourist attractions is not due solely to its statues as the political and cultural centre of the nation. Beijing is a city of distinction in its own right, a tourist experience of unusual variety and unexpected contrasts.

More than any other city, Beijing offers a splendid microcosm of both modern and traditional China. It contains so many sights within its vicinity that one short visit is insufficient to include them all. "Half a loaf is better than no bread."

The Sights of Beijing, intended both for general readers and for serious students of tourism colleges, tourism universities and tour guide/interpreters, presents very rich, fascinating and balanced pictures of places of interest in Beijing from the geological history of Peking Man's residence site at Zhoukoudian to the present-day in a span of approximately 500,000 years. The author is concerned not only with contents, but with Chinese history, philosophy, religion and the realm of ideas, while he places the contents in their historical, political and social setting. Hence this book is not merely a history of Beijing but, to some degree, a cultural history of Beijing and China as well.

It may also serve as a useful reference book for English-speaking interpreters of government offices and trade corporations who show overseas visitors or business people around from time to time. It may come in handy for overseas tourists who visit Beijing on an individual or family basis. As some sketch maps illustrate it, they may, if they want to, see the sights by themselves without the help of a local guide. China is a relaxed and contented land—and Beijing is the cosmopolitan heart with a great way of life. This book can only be a colourful index to your very special visit. Use it now as a guide then keep it as a fond memory of your all-too-brief stop in Beijing, the capital of the People's Republic of China.

The Sights of Beijing is divided into the following eight different parts. Part One consists of the city sightseeing. Part Two and Part Three contain profiles of the prime sights. Since it is intended both for guide/interpreters and overseas visitors, I try my best to put it in spoken English and follow the routes that include the major spots. Part Four is made up of places to visit. Part Five deals with travel information. Part Six includes some famous scenic spots within one day's journey from Beijing. Part Seven covers Olympics and sports, and Part Eight is concerned with appendix (some important information related to travel). To give readers a sense of reality, the first person is used occasionally in some of the briefings. In terms of contents, *The Sights of Beijing* advances with the times.

The author owes a debt of gratitude to many individuals for their help and support in preparing this book, especially to Professor Jiang Yiqun, the author's wife for her many useful suggestions and for her close scrutiny of the manuscript, and to Zhu Yu and Zhu Li, the author's daughters for their wholehearted participation.

Once more, I would like to express my special thanks to China Travel and Tourism Press and Tan Yan, whose continued general support for my work has helped to make this new, more fully illustrated edition possible.

ZHU QIXIN
May 2002

Development of Travel & Tourism in China and Prerequisites for Being a Quality Tour Guide

Tourism is a comprehensive economic undertaking and it plays a very important role in a country's economic construction; and it is at the same time a part of foreign relations work, as it offers an effective means for people to people diplomacy. Failure or success of tourism industry, therefore, bears on a country's image abroad in terms of its political reputation and of the opportunity of earning foreign exchange for a country's economic construction.

Tourism in China started from scratch, although China surpasses those countries where tourism is well-developed in terms of resources of tourism. China's huge amount of cultural relics, its scenery known far and wide for its quiet beauty, the splendour of its ancient art and culture, its traditional multi-national arts and crafts and food prepared on various local recipes—all these have attracted overseas visitors for a long time. However, as tourism in China has developed since 1980, there aren't sufficient transportation and other facilities. In addition, we still have a lot of problems to be solved in the management of tourism, in tourism infrastructures, in the quality of service and in foreign languages' level of tour guides. With all these problems gradually settled, China's tourism will surely advance to a high stage of development along the pattern uniquely Chinese.

Before 1978, when China launched economic reform, tourism had hardly any standing in the national economy. It was seen only as an element in the reception of overseas friends.

However, travel and tourism in China has achieved much since 1978. More and more people have come to recognize it as an industry. With the development of the modern economy, old industries have declined or even died out because they no longer serve people's needs. But tourism has a very rosy future. It has a unique position in the economy because travelling for sightseeing is something that most people enjoy. Therefore, tourism will rise with the development of the economy. However, it must be made a lucrative industry with low input and high profit. In fact, China National

Tourism Administration is determined to develop tourism with the focus on its economic benefit. It is making an effort to explore world market, improve service quality, increase variety and reduce costs. And it is reforming the old managerial system on the principle of integrating a planned economy with market regulation. The most important thing is for the Chinese Government to adopt a preferential policy for the industry, which will benefit not only the industry itself but also the national economy as a whole.

Unlike other industries, tourism chiefly involves cultural activities. But it is its economic aspect that we must stress now. Tourism can be highly profitable, for it needs less capital investment, energy or raw material than any productive industry. Moreover, it makes money in ready cash, which can be put into circulation immediately.

Domestically, tourism will make the economy safer by drawing off a mint of private deposits, which reached more than 7,400 billion yuan (US\$894.8 billion) by the end of 2001, and getting some of that money into circulation. It can also help to absorb surplus labour.

Since the end of World War II, many countries and regions that geared up their tourism faster than any other industry had got successful economies as a result. When Greece adopted a preferential policy towards tourism, its gross national product (GNP) quadrupled in 19 years, and many other countries such as Spain and the Philippines have made economic progress in the same way.

China already has preferential policies to help certain regions and industries. Now it is time to extend a preferential policy to tourism. At present, China relies chiefly on exports for earning foreign exchange, which is important to the national economy. But foreign trade alone can hardly earn enough on its own. A profitably-run tourism will certainly bring in a big, steady income of foreign exchange.

China has abundant resources for the development of tourism. Unique natural scenery and historical relics on the mainland are highly attractive to foreign tourists and overseas Chinese. Compatriots in Taiwan, Hong Kong and Macao and overseas Chinese will make up the bulk of tourists to the mainland. Japanese people, next-door neighbours, will also come in large numbers.

The centre of the world economy is moving eastwards, and tourism in the Asia-Pacific area is developing rapidly. China could be one of the most competitive nations in the area with a preferential policy, because this would allow the government to concentrate resources on the industry.

Tourism should be developed along with other industries according to e-

2

conomic requirements. Different regions in China, with their own characteristics, advance at different speeds. Regions which possess tourist attractions as well as sufficient facilities in transportation and communications, should give priority to local tourism, for a prosperous tourism will lead to a boom in the whole economy.

In 2001, the number of overseas visitors to the Chinese mainland reached 89. 0129 million, an increase of nearly 46 times the number (1. 8 million) in 1978. Total revenue from the tourism industry (including international and domestic) reached 499. 5 billion yuan (US $60. 4 billion) in 2001, which accounted for 5 per cent of the nation's GDP. The number of stay-over tourists in China in 2001 was listed 5th in the world, up from 18th in 1980. Revenue from overseas tourists is 7th, up from 34th in 1980.

In 2001, China was the 7th in the world's top 10 in the amount of income (US$18 billion) it earned from tourism. Back in 1978, only 760, 000 overseas tourists visited China, which netted only US$260 million in foreign currency ranking 41st in 1979. The booming tourist trade has already turned China into the No. 5 destination spot across the globe. By 2020 China will become the No. 1 destination spot in the world.

By the end of 2000 China had 1, 128 travel agencies engaged in international travel and 7, 725 travel agencies engaged in domestic travel; there are 10, 481 tourist hotels, 6, 029 of which are stared. 5. 6415 million people directly worked in the travel trade, approximately 28 million people were indirect tourism employees, totalling more than 33 million people involved in travel and tourism industry in China. Travel and tourism in China has become a new focus for economic growth, which has propelled the development of the service industry and other related industries.

From the end of 1987, when the state of isolation between the two sides was terminated, to the end of 2001, the number of Taiwan compatriots coming the mainland of China for visiting their relatives, sightseeing, exchanges, investing or doing business reached 23. 802 million by turnstile count.

In fact, quality tour guides are in direct service of overseas visitors (tourists) and their quality and service play a decisive role in the development of tourism industry in China. Their speech and behaviour directly influence overseas tourists' mood in travelling. In a sense, the function of a quality tour guide is similar to that of a diplomat of the people. The quality tour guide's duty is to try his/her utmost to make overseas visitors obtain the maximum enjoyment from the tour in China and at the same time let them understand China's history, geography, people's customs and its cultural tradition better through their interpreting and efforts. Therefore, a quality tour guide's service is the key link of tourism industry. The quality tour guide should be the pioneer of tourism industry, intimate friend of mountains and rivers, envoy of friendship, disseminator of preserving and promoting morals and fine human traditions, and publicity agent of the Chinese culture. If a quality tour guide's service is satisfactory, overseas visitors would have a good impression of China and the Travel Agency, so that they would plan their second trip to China for other sights and furthermore, they would urge others to come along to see China with their own eyes. A Travel Agency would, of course, employ as many such competent and quality tour guides as possible so as to make their business thrive with each passing day.

A quality tour guide should always bear in mind "Three Stresses"三讲, which involve strengthening theoretical study, political awareness, and good conduct 讲学习、讲政治、讲正气 and "Three Represents"三个代表 that the Chinese Communist Party always represents the development requirements of China's advanced social productive forces, the progressive course of China's advanced culture, and the fundamental interests of the overwhelming majority of the Chinese people. 中国共产党要始终代表我国先进生产力的发展要求、中国先进文化的前进方向、代表中国最广大人民的根本利益。Character is the foundation and wealth follows. 德者本也，财者末也。

A quality tour guide should be able to act as an attendant, publicity agent, investigator and defender while accompanying foreign and other overseas tourists. Therefore, the quality tour guide has to have a perfect mastery of the Chinese Communist Party's policies and political ideology, foreign language and knowledge. The guide must be honest and upright, free from corruption, prudent and careful in his/her work, diligent and assiduous in his/her working style.

China's economy has performed remarkable feats since New China was founded in 1949, especially in the last two decades. Economic growth between 1952 and 2001, averaging 7.7 per cent a year, was more than double the 3 per cent recorded by the world economy. This has helped narrow the gap between China's economy and that of developed nations. The economy, worth 9.5933 trillion yuan (US$1.56 trillion) in 2001, ranked the sixth in the world trailing the United States, Japan, Germany, France, and Britain.

Global Concept of Tour Guides Service
导游人员服务的全球概念

The global concept of tour guides service contains 7 meanings represented by the word "SERVICE" with 7 English letters.

1. "S," the first letter stands for SMILE, meaning that tour guides should provide smiling service to tourists. In other words, tour guides are supposed to smile while rendering service to tourists.
2. "E," the second letter represents EXCELLENT, which indicates that service of tour guides should be performed in an excellent way.
3. "R," the third letter symbolizes READY, which shows that tour guides are constantly ready to serve tourists.
4. "V," the fourth letter stands for VIEWING, which indicates that each tourist should be treated as a distinguished guest with his/her special needs.
5. "I," the fifth letter shows INVITING, which means that the tourist will want to return after s/he leaves the city or the country.
6. "C," the sixth letter stands for CREATING, which shows that tour guides should create an amiable and harmonious environment for the guests.
7. "E," the seventh letter indicates EYE, which means that tour guides should pay close attention to tourists with keen observation, anticipate their needs and provide his/her service in time, which makes tourists feel that tour guides carefully and constantly concern them.

Principles of Excellence 上佳服务的原则

Tour guides must:

1. Be knowledgeable about all the tour operation procedures and the areas where you are going to visit.
2. Know how to perform all the duties required of them.
3. Consistently greet every guest with a smile and a warm welcome; practise the spirit of hospitality.
4. Be able to answer all questions posed by tourists.
5. Be neat, clean, and well groomed.
6. Be able to handle all potential problems with tact and skill.
7. Be alert to any guest who needs assistance.
8. Strive for excellence, never be satisfied with "good" enough.

The above-mentioned principles of excellence in operating a tour group or a delegation or a VIP can be summed up by the phrase: "Treat tourists, visitors or guests the way that you would want to be treated if you were a tourist, visitor or guest." 己所不欲,勿施于人。

5

Travel is one of the great sources of knowledge.

旅游是知识的伟大源泉之一。

Tour guides are the path-breakers and vanguards in developing tourism in China.

导游人员是发展中国旅游业的
尖兵和先锋。

Tour guides tend to do those things well, they do often.

导游人员应常做常新。

Talents come from diligence, and knowledge is gained by accumulation.

天才在于勤奋，知识在于积累。

Knowledge is like an ocean, the only way to get to the shore is through hard work.

学海无崖，惟勤是岸。

Listening attentively to elucidation of a scene is more preferable to viewing it in person.

看景不如听景。

Like history itself, the City of Beijing keeps changing with each passing day and growing with the times.

正像历史一样，北京在不断地变化，
并与时俱进。

Managing Editor: Tan Yan
Designer: Wu Tao
Photographers: Wang Wenbo, Xiao Shi and Others

Published and Distributed by China Travel & Tourism Press
Address: A9 Jianguomennei Dajie (Ave.), Beijing 100005, China
Telephone: (0086/010)65201007/65201174/65201180
Printed in the People' s Republic of China

Contents

Part One 第一部分
Beijing and Sightseeing
北京及观光—北京市容市貌游览

City Sightseeing Route C: Dongbianmen Overpass—Chongwenmen—Qianmen Street—Tianningsi (Temple of Heavenly Peace)
线路 C:东便门立交桥—崇文门—前门大街—天宁寺

4

City Sightseeing Route D: Chinese Academy of Sciences (CAS)—The Purple Bamboo Park (Zizhuyuan)—Zhongguancun High-Tech Park—Peking University—The Summer Palace—Fragrant Hills Park
线路 D:中国科学院—紫竹院公园—中关村科技园—北京大学—圆明园遗址—颐和园—香山公园

7

Part Two 第二部分
Profile of the Prime Sights (1)
主要名胜介绍（1）

Part Three 第三部分
Profile of the Prime Sights (2)
主要名胜介绍（2）

9

Part Four 第四部分
Places to Visit 参观单位

Part Five 第五部分
Travel Information 旅游资讯

Dining 珍馐美味

Transportation 交通

Part Six 第六部分
Scenic Spots Within One Day's Journey from Beijing
北京周边地区旅游景点介绍

Part Seven 第七部分
Olympics & Sports
奥林匹克运动会和体育运动

Part Eight 第八部分
Appendix 附录

Part One

BEIJING AND SIGHTSEEING

第一部分　北京及观光—北京市容市貌游览

Ladies and gentlemen:

Welcome to Beijing—the capital of the People's Republic of China! May I introduce my Chinese colleagues to you? This is Mr Wang from CITS (China International Travel Service). He will travel with you throughout the trip in China. This is Mr Yang, our driver. His bus number is × × ×. My name is Zhu. I am from CITS. My job is to smooth your way, care for your welfare, try my best to answer your questions, and be your guide/interpreter during your stay in Beijing. If you have any special interest, please tell your tour leader and s/he will let us know. We'll try our best to make your stay in Beijing a pleasant one. We highly appreciate your understanding and co-operation.

City Sightseeing Route A: Capital Airport—Sanyuan Flyover—Yansha Youyi Shopping City—China World Trade Centre
线路 A:首都机场—三元桥—燕莎购物中心—国贸中心

Capital Airport 首都机场

This is our new airport completed and put into operation in early 1999. Now the civil aviation of China operates more than 1,000 routes, of which 145 are international linking 62 cities in 32 countries and 45 routes linking

Hong Kong and Macao. Beijing has air links with over 150 cities. It is 30 kilometres from town. It will take us about 20 minutes to get there.

Beijing Capital International Airport is the largest international airport at the present time in China with the most advanced facilities and busiest traffic flow, linking in the air with the airports in more than 100 countries and regions in the world. The airport covers a total area of 880 hectares (2,174 acres) and boasts a five-storey satellite style international passenger terminal building covering an area of more than 70,000 square metres.

Encompassing 77,000 square metres, the original terminal building in the west was built in 1980. It was expanded in 1989 and 1992 twice, but it was still unable to meet demand.

Beijing's air traffic control radar covers more of the city's sky to allow more planes to land and leave the Capital International Airport. Starting on January 15, 2001, the advanced, radar-based traffic control system — which means installing the highest technology radar designed and made in the United States—can control more planes within a specified time frame. With the radar-based air control system expanding to cover areas beyond Beijing's air terminal, the airport was capable of handling 1,100 arrivals and departures a day by June 2001. This would enable the airport to accommodate air traffic growth in the coming five years. The punctuality rate of the airport averaged 80 per cent for a number of years—and air traffic control conditions were partly blamed for the flight delays.

The New Terminal Building at the Capital International Airport

Construction of the expansion of the terminal area at the Capital International Airport began in October 1995. It opened to experimental operation on September 20, 1999 to mark the 50th anniversary of the founding of the People's Republic of China. It was officially put into use on November 1, 1999 after the two-month experimental operation. All domestic and international flights are operated in the new building and all passengers board their planes in the new building. The T-shaped new terminal area cost 9.18 billion yuan (US$1.11 billion). It is the largest in China's aviation history in terms of construction size and investment. With the new terminal (the first building to the gate of China 国门第一楼), the airport can handle 35 million passengers by the year 2005, and has the capacity for 190,000 flights, 780,000 tons of freight and airmail to arrive and depart annually. At the new terminal, travellers can check-in for their flights with the help of their family and friends, which was not allowed in the old terminal. The new building to the east of the old terminal is four times as large as the old passenger building.

The huge project included a 335,000-square-metre new terminal, a park-

ing garage which can accommodate more than 5, 167 cars, a freight terminal covering over 20, 000 square metres of space, a 40, 000-square-metre
air park and other supplementary facilities, making it the largest parking
building in Asia. Its advanced facilities include check-in desks, automatic
luggage sorting system, luggage and security check system, departure control system, flight information, broadcasting and clock system, weather
forecast display, inquiry service, inter-communications system and board-
ing bridge, walkways, escalators and elevators. One freight road and two
passenger roads in the terminal area were in operation in 1997. Supplementary facilities, including refrigeration, an air part, a road system, special garage, freight terminal, and heat, water and electricity supplies,
were completed by the end of 1998. The new parking garage, reportedly
the largest in Asia, was completed by the end of 1997. The entire expansion project was completed on October 1, 1999. The terminal showcases
the world's state-of-the-art systems, since all the equipment was procured
through public domestic and international bidding. Pressure on the capital's
airport had been mounted as the old terminal and its facilities could not
cater well to the needs of the ever-increasing number of passengers and
cargo. The number of passengers has been rising at an annual rate of 14. 2
per cent respectively in recent years. In 1998, the airport completed
159, 228 take-offs and landings, transporting 17. 31 million passengers.
However, the old terminal building was just 780, 000 square metres in
area. Airport authorities said the space was insufficient for passengers flying 174 flight routes run by 62 domestic and foreign airlines. Also, the
automatic baggage sorting system will substantially improve and speed up
the baggage claiming process and reduce mistakes.

New Radar System to Ease Bottleneck

China's first radar-based system was installed and put into operation at the
Beijing International Airport by the end of 1997. The advanced radar and
accessories worth nearly 200 million yuan (US $24. 1 million) imported
from Italy, Norway and the United States. The system has alleviated sig-
nificantly the air transport bottleneck in one of China's busiest air terminals and substantially improved the flight punctuality rate, reduced time
between flights and made better use of air space. The technology transportation was part of the expansion project of the airport. Traffic at the
Beijing International Airport had been expanding at a rate of 15 per cent a
year. Arrivals and departures at the airport averaged 403 flights a day in
1996, with a record of 481 on September 1. However, the punctuality rate
of the airport had not gone above 77 per cent for a number of years. Previously all Chinese airports used a procedure-based air control system, with

radar an as auxiliary control means. It lagged far behind systems in developed countries. The Beijing air terminal is operating under radar-based control, the number of planes allowed to land within a specified time frame has doubled.

Following the example of the Beijing International Airport, radar-based air-traffic control systems were also established at Guangzhou Baiyun Airport and Shanghai Hongqiao Airport by the year of 2000. The three airports, whose combined passenger handling capacity accounts for nearly 40 per cent of the country's total, will pilot the system for other places in China.

China's civil aviation business has soared by an average of 20.1 per cent annually for the past 15 years. To facilitate the upgrading to a radar-based system, training of controllers has been prioritized. The best solution for alleviating the aviation bottleneck is to install the radar-based air-traffic control system in all terminals and air routes throughout China.

A new radar-based traffic control system was put into operation at the Capital International Airport on January 15, 2001 to handle increased traffic and enhance flight security. The airport is expected to handle 35 million passengers annually by 2008. The new system will help ease the pressure on air traffic during Spring Festival holidays, an annual transportation peak. It will also serve as a solid trial programme for the planned launch of radar-based traffic control systems for Beijing-Guangzhou, Beijing-Shanghai and Shanghai-Guangzhou routes, which comprise over two-thirds of domestic air traffic. The new radar system, based on the old system launched in 1997, which had an operating radius of only 100 kilometres, covers a total area of over 30,000 square kilometres. The expanded area now under radar control will substantially improve flight punctuality, reduce time between take-offs and landings and make better use of air space. The Capital International Airport has become one of the busiest airports in Asia with an annual expansion rate of 15 per cent. In January 2001, there was an average of 640 flights daily.

Information from the Civil Aviation Administration of China revealed on January 16, 2001, that Beijing Capital International Airport and Tianjin Binhe International Airport have been united under one company. The move aims to help optimize resources at the two airports and enhance competitiveness.

Airport Polishes Hygienic Image

The Beijing Capital International Airport wanted to become a "World Hygienic Airport." Since mid-May 2001, the airport had been strengthening supervision of conditions of food, water and public places to cut down the spread of infectious diseases. Shenzhen and Beijing airports are Asia's only two airports to meet World Health Organization standards and earned the "World Hygienic Airport" title respectively.

The Capital Airport Expressway 首都机场高速公路

This is the new expressway called "the first way to the gate of China 国门第一路." It is 18.735-kilometre long. To meet the needs of increasing flow of both overseas and domestic visitors, construction of the expressway from the Capital Airport to Sanyuan Overpass started on July 2, 1992 and was completed on September 14, 1993.

The expressway is a 34.5-metre wide, six-lane expressway. Speed limit from the expressway is 120 kilometres per hour. Along the expressway there are about 20 crossovers and overpasses including a cloverleaf bridge which occupies an area of 50 hectares (124 acres), the largest of its kind in China. Also there are monitors, a toll gate, traffic and road signs, protective roadside railings and fences, and communication, lighting, dazzle proof and drainage systems. A green project went hand in hand with construction. The completion of the expressway has created favourable conditions for the capital deepening reform and economic development. A grand ceremony at near the Siyuan (Fourth Ring) Overpass on the expressway was held on September 14, 1993. The highway has cut to drive time from the Sanyuan (Third Ring) Overpass to the airport to just 10 minutes. All the road's facilities have been designed to withstand floods or earthquakes. This wide expressway has replaced the one built in 1958, which was only 8 metres wide. From July 2, 1992 to September 14, 1993, about 10,000 builders worked day and night on the construction site. The Capital Airport Expressway Development Corporation contracted to build the road through a bank loan and fund raising. US$172 million were spent on the project. There was no central government investment. The cost of the road will be recouped by tolls which started charges from September 20, 1993 at between 15 yuan (US $2) and 40 yuan (US$5).

The tolls have contributed to other road projects in the Capital City. The ceremony held on September 14, 1993 also marked the opening to traffic of the transformed section of the eastern Third Ring Road of Beijing. The 8.2-kilometre-long-highway starts from the crossing over at Jinsong in the south to Sanyuan Overpass in the north where the road joins with the Airport Expressway. Seven overpasses were constructed on the 8.2-kilometre-long Expressway to ease traffic congestion.

Wenyu River 温榆河

This is Wenyu River, a tributary of Chaobai River. It totals 47. 5 kilometres with a drainage area of 2, 478 square kilometres. There are three major rivers in the Beijing area: the Yongding (Forever Fixed) River totalling 681 kilometres with a drainage area of 50, 800 square kilometres, the Chaobai River (totalling 460 kilometres with a drainage area of 19, 600 square kilometres) and the North Canal (Tongzhou-Tianjin section, with a total length of 180 kilometres).

Trees 树木

Afforestation has been going on on a nationwide scale since 1949. A total of more than 850 million trees have been planted in Beijing alone. Now an average of one million trees are planted each year. March 12th is China's Tree-Planting Day. During the season, people from all walks of life turn out to help.

March 12, 2002 was the 21st National Tree-Planting Day. In the past two decades, each year witnessed a growth of 5. 3 million hectares of trees. Statistics indicate that 90 per cent of the trees are well preserved. According to statistics, 2. 4 billion trees are planted by volunteers each year. China is home to 33. 3 million hectares of human-planted trees, by far the most in the world. There are 137 million hectares of forested land at present, comparing with 115 million hectares at the beginning of 1980s. Forests in China today cover only 13. 92 per cent of the land, a little more than half the average forest coverage in the world. In 1997, the United Nations Food and Agricultural Organization noted in its report on the world forest situation that the world had 3. 454 billion hectares of forests in 1995, which covered 26. 6 per cent of the earth's land area. Three Shelter Forest Projects in Northwest, North and Northeast China and nine other key forestry construction programmes have formed a basic framework for forest expansion. With a forest coverage rate of 13. 92 per cent, China is making greater efforts to make the country greener and more beautiful. Logging workers are encouraged to plant trees rather than to cut them down. Some areas will be classified as welfare forestry, beneficial to the environment, and will be protected from logging. In 1949, the forest coverage in China was only 8. 6 per cent. The success of tree planting should be judged by three standards: to make the land green, rich and beautiful. It is also necessary for China to develop an advanced forestry in future.

Of all the projects, 26, such as the 10. 7-hectare Century Playground in Pinggu District, a 33. 4-hectare green space along Shunyi District's Shunping Avenue, and the 133. 4-hectare forestry park around Niantan Reservoir in Daxing District, have been designated as key or leading projects. It is believed that tree-planting can contribute greatly to protecting Beijing farmlands from wind, curb the development of deserts and green the environment, especially mountainous wilderness areas. Of course, The people of Beijing expect a big direct economic benefit from them. For example, while Fangshan District's focus is on persimmons, Daxing and Shunyi districts on high-quality pears, while Changping District on apples, and Huairou District and Miyun County on cheatnuts, those of Pinggu and Mentougou districts are peaches and walnuts. The Beijing Municipal Government makes special efforts to changing its tree varieties. At present, the main tree varieties in Beijing are the Chinese scholartree, poplar and willow. Although they have taken leading positions in Beijing for a long time, they have long been regarded as not the perfect choices for the Chinese capital. The former easily falls prey to pests, the latter two pollute each spring in Beijing with cotton-like catkins. The Beijing Municipal Forestry Administration expects to have ginkgo trees everywhere in Beijing in ten years.

Beijing is speeding up environmental efforts and the drafting of a sustainable development plan for hosting the 2008 Olympic Games. Beijing plans to increase sewage treatment in the city from the current 42 per cent treated to 90 per cent by 2008. Natural gas usage will also go up from 1 billion cubic metres currently used to 4. 7 billion cubic metres by 2008. In addition, city authorities will try to recycle as much garbage as possible within eight years and increase green areas. More than 240 square kilometres of trees and grass will be planted around Beijing in the next few years. The Beijing 2008 Olympic Games, set up the environmental department, made up of seven officials, Bid Committee in October 2000. Prior to that, the engineering department of the committee conducted work on the environment. An environmental evaluation survey has already been conducted to select sites for the main sporting centres. Beijing has made long-term plans for environmental improvements.

Orchards 果园

The orchards and fields on both sides of the road come under one of the 276 towns and townships in Beijing area. In China, there are more than 19, 341 townships which began to be set up in 1982. Since the break-up of people's commune and adoption of the household contract responsibility system, production has gone up and the living standards of the people have improved. Main crops in Beijing are wheat, maize and rice, with two crops a year. Major fruits include apple, pear, peach and grape.

The Beijing city government invested 15 million yuan (more than US$2. 6 million) in the fall of 1993 and the spring of 1994 to plant fruit trees in its suburban mountainous areas. The money, together with funds raised by the regions, would be used to plant 10, 000 hectares (25, 000 acres) of orchard. This was part of the city's ambitious project to develop another 76, 000 hectares (191, 500 acres) of orchard by the year 2000. The project has provided a bigger variety and quantity of fruit for the city's over 13 million population.

Also the government decided to lease the mountainous land suitable for fruit tree plantation to local residents. The municipal government's policy has stipulated that the contracted plots of land can be transferred or inherited. This policy would help increase the farmers' interest in contracting for the mountainous land for fruit tree planting.

By the end of 2000, Beijing had 474, 000 acres of orchard which not only provides the fruit for the city's markets, but also can export to other provinces and regions.

A Brief Introduction to Beijing 北京概况

Ladies and gentlemen:

To make use of time, I'd like to tell you something about my city.

Beijing, the capital of the People's Republic of China, is the nation's political and cultural centre, as well as a centre of international activity. Some 690, 000 years ago, Peking Man lived at Zhoukoudian, 48 kilometres southwest of Beijing. A small town appeared on the present site of southwestern Beijing in 1045 BC. It was named Ji and then changed to Yan. At the beginning of the 10th century, it was the second capital of the Liao Dynasty. From then on, the city had been the capital of the Jin, Yuan, Ming and Qing dynasties until 1911.

In the early 1920s, Beijing became the cradle of China's new democratic revolution. The May Fourth Movement against imperialism and feudalism began here in 1919.

On October 1, 1949, the late Chairman Mao proclaimed to the whole world the founding of the People's Republic of China.

Beijing is situated at 40 degrees north latitude and 116 degrees east longitude. It is 43 metres above sea level and 183 kilometres from the sea. Beijing encompasses 16, 807 square kilometres, 38% of it is flat land and 62% mountains.

Beijing has a continental climate. According to the data analysis from

1905 to 2001 within 95 years, annual rainfall averaged 620 millimetres, most of it comes in July and August. Winter is dry and cold and has little snow. The frost-free period is 185 days. The best time to visit Beijing is May, September and October, when people enjoy bright sunny sky. Summer is hot. The record highest temperature in mid-June was 42.6℃ and occurred in 1942.

Beijing has a population of 13.819 million, of whom 2.115 million (accounting for 15.6 per cent) live in the city proper 市区 and 6.388 million (account for 47.1 per cent) in the suburbs 近郊区 and 5.067 million (37.3 per cent) on the remote outskirts 远郊区. The municipality of Beijing is divided into 16 districts and 2 counties. The 16 districts are East City, West City, Chongwen, Xuanwu, Chaoyang, Fengtai, Haidian, Shijingshan, Mentougou, Fangshan, Tongzhou, Shunyi, Changping, Pinggu, Huairou and Daxing; the 2 counties are Miyun and Yanqing.

Before 1949, there were only a few small factories and handicraft workshops with hardly any modern equipment. Today, Beijing has industries such as iron and steel, chemical and petroleum, electronic, textile and light industries, with over 4,000 factories and 4.729 million offices and industrial workers.

In the past five decades, public transportation developed rapidly, with over 65,000 vehicles now, as against only 79 buses and 49 tramcars for a city of 2 million people in 1949. In 2002, there are 13,500 public transportation vehicles, embracing over 700 routes with a total route length of 75,000 kilometres. Three subway lines totalling about 53.2 kilometres have been completed and opened to traffic. Before 1949, the total residential building space in Beijing only amounted to 13.5 million square metres. With the growth of production and ever increasing demand on housing space, over 140 million square metres of floor space (from 1949 to 1979, over 30 million square metres of floor space were built; from 1979 to 1999, 110 million square metres of housing space were constructed) have been built in the last 50 years from 1949 to 1999. More than 30,000 high-rise apartments have been built since 1979.

There are 65 institutions of higher learning, over 800 middle schools and about 2,800 primary schools in Beijing, with a total enrollment of over 2 million. Much attention has been paid to special technical schools, such as technical secondary schools (中专), technical schools (技校), vocational senior middle schools (职业高中), vocational middle schools (职业中学), vocational schools (职业学校), with a total about 430 now. Also there are now more than 960 adult schools.

In medical and health care, the city has more than 630 hospitals, 63,000

11

sick beds, with over 117, 000 medical workers.

Now I would like to say a few words about the future development of Beijing. The Party Central Committee and the State Council ratified the Overall Plan for Beijing's Future Development on July 14, 1983. The Beijing Municipal Government started working on the present plan after the 12th National Party Congress in September 1982.

The plan states that, as the capital of socialist China, Beijing should be constructed into a modern city and reflects the rich Chinese culture, history and revolutionary tradition. It envisages updating the old city while maintaining its traditional style. Impressive buildings for State and public use will be erected along Chang'an Boulevard to make a stately and beautiful center for a modern capital. The size and style of new buildings must match nearby ancient ones and no factories or living quarters may be built in scenic spots. The plan also suggests that the Chinese Government put the former imperial city—an area five times the size of the Forbidden City—under special preservation. It calls for gradual dispersion of the population coupled with birth control to keep the city from becoming too crowded.

Four transport corridors will lead to satellite towns in the far suburbs. The plan calls for industrial development to aim at energy and water saving, non pollutant light industries, such as food, textiles, electronics, instrument and metre making, and arts and crafts. Beijing's own rural areas should be its main supplier of vegetables and other non-staple foods.

Now the citizens are redoubling their efforts to build Beijing into a city with high moral standards, fine environment, developed in science and technology and with a thriving economy.

Earlier in 1994, Beijing drafted an urban development plan designed to modernize the city while restoring its image as an historic capital. The master plan for 1991-2010 aims to preserve the traditional architectural style of the city centre, while building around it a modern metropolis with a high quality living environment and modern facilities. The plan stipulates that the old city's 8-kilometre north-south axis shall be protected and expanded. Monotonous modern buildings are banished/disallowed from the area. To preserve the space and historic buildings around the Forbidden City, nearby buildings must remain single storey structures, and buildings within the Second Ring Road must be no more than 30 metres in height. The municipal government has included 25 streets and districts on its protected list. They include the Dazhalan shopping area and Qianhai. These old districts in many ways set the tone of the ancient city. It is important to preserve the tonal atmosphere of a city especially a historic city such as

Beijing. Each city including Beijing is no exception, should have its own aesthetic colour and its sky line should not be cluttered by ill conceived skyscrapers that are disjointed or even opposed to the historic aesthetic ambiance of special places the world over. In this planning mode, Beijing is integrating the positive elements of the concept of socialist central planning with other elements of the move toward modernization and a market economy — and tying all to a rich central architectural and artistic heritage that continues unbroken in the next chapter of the leap forward.

New Metropolis to Be Built

Beijing is to join hands with neighbouring cities in a bid to promote future development and to build a new world metropolis. The long-term Great Beijing Plan, approved by the Ministry of Construction, includes Beijing, Tianjin, and adjacent areas of Hebei Province for development. In Great Beijing, the policy-making in land development, industry distribution and environmental protection will take the whole region into account, instead of Beijing alone. According to the plan, Great Beijing will encompass 70,000 square kilometres with China's two municipalities, Beijing and Tianjin, as its core districts, Tangshan and Baoding of Hebei Province are the key cities that could help form the world metropolis. Sections of some industries and funds in Beijing will be shifted to neighbouring cities and counties, which will help relieve the capital's pressure of economic development and environmental protection, as well as offering job opportunities to underdeveloped areas. Construction of Great Beijing is expected to provide advantages to adjacent cities, and should help avoid the vicious competition in the future. An inter-city traffic network will be constructed to improve transportation. Tianjin is expected to become another communications hub, along the Capital City. The theory of total regional development is wide practiced abroad. London, Paris and New York set good examples for building world metropolis. Experts say that a city relying on its own resources could face restrictions in social development. Building world metropolises is a choice for a country to further its development in the era of globalization.

The Future in Beijing 北京的未来

Beijing has designed a "digital Beijing" centred on the development of Zhongguancun, while Shanghai has put forward the concept of the information port. Guangzhou, capital of South China's Guangdong Province, will provide local people with digital services. In five years' time, more than half of public services will be delivered via the Internet. A multimedia programme base will be completed to provide images, text, languages, movies and software to local residences. People should be aware of the phenomenon of the "digital gap" or digital disparity. Due to different economic and technological development speeds, some developed countries and regions have been dominant in the digital world. Today, developed countries, with only 16 per cent of the global population, account for 90 per cent of the host computer network. The cities of Beijing, Shanghai and Guangzhou have taken up 60 per cent of domain name registration of the whole country. To narrow the digital gap and strive for sustainable and harmonious development, fledgling digitalized cities are encouraged to share resources and provide technical support for lagging cities and regions. Alongside the conference, the China International Exposition on Digital City, (it describes China's coming revolution in urban planning, administration and construction) construction kicked off on September 18, 2001, showcasing the latest technologies and achievements on constructing the digital city, involving 70 Information Technology (IT) firms and research institutes from 20 Chinese cities.

The City of Beijing in Curved Shape "凸"字形的城市

The contour (the shape of the outer limits of an area) of Beijing is largely the same as in the Ming Dynasty (1368-1644). In the centre of the city is a group of palaces in rectangular shape called the Forbidden City (3.42 kilometres in perimeter). A 10-metre-high wall surrounds it with turrets at its four corners. Encircling the wall lies the city moat (52 metres wide). Outside the Forbidden City is the Imperial City, measuring 9 kilometres with symmetrical gates around the city. Twenty kilometres around the Imperial City lies the Inner City in a square, erected in 1397. The rectangular land area south of the Inner City is called the Outer City, built in 1553. The Outer City was constructed for commercial and military use. As a result, the City of Beijing took on a curved shape.

Beijing to Better Manage Migrants

With the highest number of migrant's residents among Chinese cities, and with still more to come in the future, Beijing is being forced to improve its policies to better manage the issue. According to the data on Beijing in the country's Fifth National census in November 2000 which was made public on April 5, 2001, Beijing's permanent population expanded by 27.7 per cent over the past 10 years and four months, increasing from 10.819 million to 13.819 million. The rate is the highest in the country for a city, but as much as 70.4 per cent of the added population is migrant's people from other parts of China. Beijing has the biggest domestic migrant population among all Chinese cities. Since the natural rate of increase will remain low, it is expected that migrants will continue to be a major source of increase in the population of the city for the foreseeable future, if our country economy can still develop fast. Altogether 81, 000 people were born and 70, 000 died between November 1, 1999 and October 31, 2000, a birth rate of 6 per thousand and a death rate of 5. 1 per thousand, leaving a natural population increase rate of 0. 9 per thousand. The census data have drawn much concern from the municipal government. The rapidly expanding population is exerting great pressure on local infrastructure facilities such as transportation and water supply, and the municipal government is therefore stepping up the construction of its 10-odd satellite cities like Daxing and Shunyi. Preferential policies in employment, taxation, and resettlement will be instituted to attract more people out of the city center into the suburbs. In addition, while on the one hand establishing strict controls on domestic migrants with no stable income or fixed residence, Beijing will build more apartments for new residents who contribute to the development of the city, such as high-tech experts, as well as primary and middle schools for their children.

Grand Moving

The Beijing Municipal Government is planning to move the capital city's industrial factories out of the central area to lower the percentage of land occupied by industrial enterprises in the central area from the current 8. 74 per cent to 7 per cent. As the move takes place, the municipal government will restructure the layout of the capital city. The new city plan is expected to include the downtown area, a high-tech industry area and a suburban industrial science and technology park.

There are 14 satellite cities in Beijing. They are Tongzhou 通州, Yizhuang 亦庄, Huangcun 黄村, Liangxiang 良乡, Fangshan 房山 (including Yanhua 含燕化), Changxindian 长辛店, Menchengzhen 门城镇, Shahe 沙河, Changping 昌平 (including Nankou and Niantou 含南口、埝头), Yanqing 延庆, Huairou 怀柔 (including Qiaozi and Miaocheng 含桥梓、庙城), Miyun 密云, Pinggu 平谷 and Shunyi 顺义 (including Niulanshan and Mapo 含牛兰山和马坡).

Localities to Spur Beijing's Economy

The four major economic areas located in Beijing have played a remarkable role in promoting Beijing's economic development and enhancing the capital's image as an international metropolis. It is widely expected that China's entry into the World Trade Organization (WTO) and Beijing's hosting of the 2008 Olympic Games can bring about ample opportunities for Beijing to overtake Shanghai. The reasonable layout of Beijing's four export-orientated economic areas seems to add confidence to investors.

15

In the north is the Zhongguancun Science Park. The park focuses on high-tech development taking advantage of its great number of scientific research institutes, colleges and universities. It has attracted many international corporations like Microsoft to set up research and development organizations in the park. It has also given birth to China's own high-tech giants such as Legend and Founder.

In the east is the Central Business District (CBD). CBD is within a short distance from the Beijing Capital International Airport. Abundant hotels and office buildings are at hand and the embassy area is also nearby. Many multinational corporations have set up the headquarters for their Beijing and Asia-Pacific area operations in the CBD. Motorola, HP, IBM and Nokia all have a presence in the business center.

In the south is the Beijing Economic and Technological Development Area(BDA). BDA is the only State-level development area in Beijing. BDA is advantageous in land resources and location. It is in close proximity to the Beijing-Tianjin-Tanggu Expressway and is situated near the future Fifth Ring Road. Many multinational corporations have set up their pollution-free production bases in BDA.

In the west is the Financial Street. After China's entry into the WTO, the finance, banking and insurance sectors will be gradually opened. This street is expected to welcome more investors then. With the People's Bank of China, China Securities Regulatory Commission and China Insurance Regulatory Commission all located in the area, the street will attract more financial institutions to build itself into a financial centre.

The four economic areas are reasonably distributed and complementary to each other, which have caught the eyes of investors at home and abroad.

Yanxiang Hotel 燕翔饭店

16

Here comes the Yanxiang Hotel (three-star hotel), which is 15 minutes by car to either the Beijing International Airport or Tian'anmen Square, the centre of the city. The hotel occupies 8.75 acres of land. The first phase of the hotel was completed in 1980 and the new building was put into operation in 1984. The hotel has totally 515 guestrooms. It is a modern hotel, an ideal place to stay in.

Yanxiang Philatelic Centre, first of its kind for foreign visitors and stamp collectors, opened on June 18, 1990 on the second floor of the hotel. The Centre offers Chinese stamps from different periods, ranging from the Qing Dynasty(1644-1911) to modern China. It also has collections of foreign stamps, commemorative and first day covers and stamp collecting materials are also available. The Centre is jointly sponsored by the Yanxiang Hotel and Beijing Stamp Company.

Holiday Inn Lido Beijing 北京丽都假日酒店

This is Holiday Inn Lido Beijing (four-star hotel) covering an area of 140, 000 square metres. Completed in 1986, it boasts 997 modern appointed guestrooms, of which 467 are deluxe suites. There are three kinds of apartment blocks providing 318 apartments. In it there is a commercial block which houses a supermarket with overseas management, shops, a Chinese restaurant, a Beijing Duck restaurant, a noodle shop and a delicatessen. The Lido Centre Sports Club has an exclusive club, admission is by membership only. Facilities include indoor and outdoor tennis courts, squash courts, indoor swimming pool and jicuzzi, minigolf, sauna, gymnasium, four bowling lanes, and game rooms. Also there is an international school at the Lido Centre providing larger premises and recreational areas.

It offers an unparalleled range of amenities and facilities to Beijing residents and foreign tourists. In terms of residential accommodation, restaurants, shopping facilities, and sports and recreational amenities, it is the first and only centre of its kind in Beijing.

The area is also known as the electronics city which covers an area of 10. 6 square kilometres.

Siyuan Flyover 四元桥

This is the Siyuan Flyover, occupying an area of 35 hectares and 60, 000 square metres of road space, and it is one of the largest flyovers in Beijing area. Since 1970s, more than 500 flyovers have been built on the main roads of Beijing, whereas the city only had one in 1974.

The Fourth Ring Road 四环路

17

Construction of the Fourth Ring Road started in August 1998 and it was completed and opened to the traffic on June 9, 2001, taking 34 months to complete. The 65. 3-kilometre-long road, the capital's longest transportation artery, can alleviate the city's traffic congestion. The road, which connects almost all the proposed Olympic sites, is dubbed "Olympic Avenue." The road, connecting the Asian Games Village, Zhongguancun, Fengtai Hi-Tech Zone and Beijing Economic Development Area, can also help boost the municipal economy. It is estimated that the expressway will save a total of 45. 1 billion yuan (US$5. 5 billion) by reducing traffic congestion and related costs. Along the road, there are 147 cloverleaves, of which 11 are big or super cloverleaves. Also there are 31 overpasses and

12 underpasses along the road. The expressway cost 7.3 billion yuan (US $881 million), about 5 billion yuan (US$600 million) of which was bank loans. Along most part of eight-lane expressway are 100-metre green belts, which cover an area of 163 hectares (402.77 acres), 10 times the area of the Summer Palace. The road is designed for speeds of 80 to 100 kilometres per hour. The Sihui Cloverleaf 四惠立交桥 (a highway interchange at which two highways crossing each other on different levels are provided with curving access and exit ramps, enabling vehicles to go in any of four directions) occupies an area of 520 mu (34.66 hectares or 85.64 acres) of land. The surface of the bridge covers 78,000 square metres. The bridge has four levels. It is the largest one ever built in Beijing area. In the coming 10 years, about 1.2 million people will live along this road. The road, which connects almost all the proposed Olympic sites, is dubbed "Olympic Avenue."

Beijing International Telecommunications Office
北京国际通讯大楼

Construction of the Beijing International Telecommunications Office (BITO) started on December 2, 1983 and was completed on May 25, 1986. It was officially opened on December 23, 1987.

Covering a floor space of 13,000 square metres, the office provides facilities for over 2,000 international telephones, 12,000 international telex channels another up to date equipment for such services as international telegrams, facsimiles, data transmission, mobile telephones and video conferences.

By the end of 1987, most of the facilities in China's telecommunications services were domestically designed and manufactured. They included a 1,800 channel microwave and a 4,380 channel medium coaxial cable carrier system; optic fibre trunk systems in the local telephone network of some cities; and, newspaper telecommunications throughout the vast country. With the new telecommunications centre in operation, China's links with other countries are greatly expanded. For instance, its international direct dialing (IDD) system permits direct telephone contact with more than 100 countries and regions, as against 19 before the operation of BITO. The project cost 48.42 million yuan, equivalent to US$13 million in 1986.

18

Sanyuan Flyover 三元立交桥

This is Sanyuan Flyover located in northeast of Beijing on the Third Ring Road 三环路 totalling 48 kilometres with 52 cloverleaves on it. The road was opened to traffic in late September 1984 to mark the 35th anniversary of the founding of the People's Republic of China. The three overhead roads occupy more than 350,000 square metres.

Beijing has started building a "beltway" encircling the whole of its urban area. The 200-kilometre-long beltway will pass across Beijing's six counties or districts, as well as join its urban road network and 11 State arterial roads like those connecting Beijing, and Shijiazhuang, Beijing and Shenyang, and Beijing and Kaifeng. Vehicles can run at 100 to 120 kilometres per hour on the expressway. This is its biggest difference from the four ring roads Beijing already has. The road will improve Beijing's traffic flow greatly. When the expressway is put into use, vehicles just passing through Beijing, would not be allowed into the city centre, something that is expected to ease downtown gridlock immensely. Lighter traffic in these areas will also dramatically improve the air quality.

Carrefour 家乐福

It owns 27 stores in 15 Chinese cities. The Qingdao store has registered the largest customer volume of any of Carrefour's Asian outlets since it opened in 1999. There are four such stores in Beijing.

Zuojiazhuang Residential Area 左家庄住宅区

This is Zuojiazhuang Residential Area covering an area of 35.6 hectares (89 acres). There are 74 apartment buildings with 7,000 suites. They can accommodate over 24,000 people in more than 6,800 families. The floor space of the buildings totals 466,000 square metres. There are 76 auxiliary buildings such as grain stores, non-staple food stores, hotels, 2 middle schools, 3 primary schools, 4 kindergartens, 9 car and bicycle parking lots, department stores, markets, post office, bank, book store, hospitals and others. Construction of the buildings started in 1979 and completed in 1984. by the end of 2001, there were 4,706 residential areas with 3.94 million families in Beijing.

Guangming Hotel 光明饭店

This compound known as Guangming Hotel with 136 villas, is located in northeast of Beijing near the Great Wall Sheraton Hotel. Construction of the compound started in the early fall of 1985 and was completed by the end of 1986. The compound covers an area of 4.6 hectares (11.5 acres), including tennis courts, a swimming pool, a children's playground and a 13-storey office building. Seventy per cent of the total investment came from the Tokyo Corporation of Japan. The first 36 villas were constructed in September 1985. The villas are in both Western and Japanese styles. The two-and three-storey designs offer floor spaces ranging from 110 to 140 square metres. The villas were all built with interior components manufactured in Japan. The 10,000-square-metre office building was completed by the end of 1986.

The purpose of building this compound in Beijing was to provide modern conveniences for the increasing number of foreign residents. The compound was built by the Beijing Guangming Industry and Commerce Company Ltd., an equity joint venture between the Tokyo Corporation of Japan and the Beijing General Corporation of Agriculture, Industry and Commerce.

Yansha Youyi Shopping City (Beijing Lufthansa Centre)
燕莎友谊商城

Youyi Shopping City, a part of Beijing Lufthansa Centre—a Sino-German joint venture, is a large international-style luxury shopping centre. It covers an area of 40,000 square metres, 400,000 kinds of imported and domestic high quality commodities are displayed on its six floors and one basement. It is all managed by a computer network. The city is luxuriously and elegantly decorated, equipped with escalators, elevators, central air conditioning, TV monitors and other modern facilities, which provide a pleasant shopping environment. The shopping centre is very conveniently located, 17 kilometres from the Capital Airport and 8 kilometres from the Beijing Railway Station. The business of Youyi Shopping Centre includes retailing, wholesaling, import and export trade, currency exchange, beauty parlour, optician, film processing, seal carving, calligraphy and painting mounting, gift packing, babysitting and repair service. The shopping city also handles mail orders, group service, home delivery and transport service.

Goods on sale include: foods, cereal & oil products, famous tobacco & liquor, rare medicines, leather articles, superior cosmetics, children's articles, high grade toys, cotton & woolen textiles, fashions, high grade suits, shoes & hats, sports goods, body building equipment, high grade furniture, wool & silk fabrics, drawnwork & embroidery, quality brand electric appliances, photo equipment, timepieces & eyeglasses, calligraphy and painting by celebrities, artistic carpets, jewelry & ornaments, ceramics, office equipment, etc.

Landmark Towers 亮马河大厦

This is Landmark Towers, located on North Dong San Huan Road, adjacent to the Great Wall Sheraton Hotel. It was opened to business on July 15, 1990. The complex consists of a 15-storey hotel, a 28-storey office building and a 15-storey apartment building. It has a large shopping centre including a super market, more than 50 small shops selling various commodities, six restaurants offering different cuisine, and a fast-food restaurant. All these facilities are located on the first and second floors of the complex. In addition, the complex has gymnasium, swimming pool, tennis court, entertainment facilities and a business centre.

The Landmark Hotel has 500 guestrooms, and the apartment building has 240 furnished units. The office building has 20,000 square metres for rent.

Great Wall Sheraton Hotel 长城饭店

This is a joint venture hotel. It has over 1,000 rooms, all with modern facilities. The building is made up of three high-rise rectangular guest room wings that radiate from a central service core. The hotel has an atrium tea garden, cafe, specialty restaurant, a night club, a roof top cocktail lounge and a swimming pool. It was completed and opened in December 1983.

Kunlun Hotel 昆仑饭店

Jointly invested and managed, the Kunlun Hotel is situated in the eastern suburbs of the Capital City. It is only 17 kilometres away from the Beijing International Airport. The hotel has 28 storeys above the ground with about 80,000 square metres. It has 853 guestrooms and 74 office suites. The hotel has 28 Chinese and Western restaurants, coffee shops, bars, tea houses, banquet halls, and 20 other convenient service facilities. The hotel has 4 see-through elevators, 4 elevators and 2 escalators for guests. The interior furnishings of the building are exquisite and elegant. The various modern equipment are imported from abroad. The hotel was put into operation in 1986. There is also a revolving restaurant on top of the hotel, with a seating capacity of more than 200 people.

Huadu Hotel 华都饭店

Huadu Hotel, opened in August 1982, is a 6-storey crabshape building with wings on both sides. It occupies a floor space of over 40,000 square metres. The hotel has 541 rooms and complete with cafe, bar, post and telecommunications, hairdresser's, money exchange and other services.

National Agricultural Exhibition Centre 全国农业展览馆

The Agricultural Exhibition Centre, 150 acres in area, was built in 1959, one of the ten major projects completed to mark the 10th anniversary of the founding of the People's Republic of China. In 1978, the first foreign machinery exhibition was held here. It plays an important role in exchanging experience and information on agricultural developments. The National Museum of Agriculture is also housed in one of the halls of this National Agricultural Exhibition Centre. The museum displays about 10, 000 relics showing Chinese agricultural development over the past 8, 000 years. These include fishing tools from the New Stone Age, bronze shovels from the Shang Dynasty (1600 BC-1046 BC), and grain seeds believed to date back to the Han Dynasty (206 BC-AD 220). The museum was opened to the public in September 1986.

Embassy Area 大使馆区

Before 1965, foreign embassies were located in the old "legation quarters" in downtown Beijing. Since 1965, an increasing number of embassy quarters have been built in the east and northeast of Beijing, and almost all of the embassies have been moved to these two areas. China has already established diplomatic relations with more than 160 countries. We have been quite busy with construction of new embassy buildings.

Zhaolong Hotel 兆龙饭店

This is Zhaolong Hotel, which is close to Sanlitun embassy area and Great Wall Sheraton Hotel. It was completed in October 1985. It has 270 guestrooms, including tastefully appointed deluxe suites to accommodate foreign dignitaries and heads of states. The hotel's nine restaurants serve Shandong, Sichuan, Guangdong, and Western cuisine as well.

Named after father of the shipping magnate, Sir Pao Yue-kong who passed away in 1991, Zhaolong Hotel was built with funds provided by the latter plus domestic investment. The hotel's angular shape was selected by the father and the son from three designs submitted by the Beijing Architectural Designing Institute.

Pacific Department Store 太平洋百货北京盈科店

The Pacific Department Store in eastern Beijing, which opened its doors for the first time on October 25, 2001. The store is the first overseas-funded shopping centre and is based in the western part of the Changhong Overpass in Chaoyang District. The store is a six-storey building with 47, 000 square metres of floor space. It was formally opened to the public in November 2001. Another such store will be opened in Xidan, one of the commrecial centres in the Capital City.

Bar Street in Beijing 北京的酒吧街

Located in the northeastern part of Beijing near the diplomatic quarters, Sanlitun Bar Street came into being in 1993 and is now very popular with foreigners and young Chinese. The street, which is known by many Beijingers for its prosperous bars, will become more worthy of its name in two years' time. The current residential area on the street's western side be converted for commercial use from October 2001, with places reserved for more bars and Western-style restaurants. Along the 260-metre-long street there are 19 bars on the eastern side and 7 on the western side. Most bars invite young and energetic bands and singers to put on live shows from 8 pm till midnight throughout the week. When night falls people come to the bars in an endless stream, chatting with friends and enjoying beer and music. Especially in summer, drinkers like to sit at tables outside and talk late into night. They either take taxis or drive their own vehicles and park them along the road, which leads to traffic jams and the sound of honks from impatient drivers. June and July are the best months for the bars. In addition to the noise pollution, security and sanitation are two other problems. Measures have been taken but the effect is small. The street committee decided to co-operate with a real estate company and move the residents out of Sanlitun. Redeveloping this residential area has been on the agenda since early 1990s. The Sanlitun residential area is composed of buildings constructed in the mid-1960s, and they have no gas supply or heating. The redevelopment project began in October 2001. The plan was to build two 10-12 storey high-rises. During the period of construction, all the bars and restaurants will remain open to customers. Sanlitun, the South Gate of Beijing University and Xiyuan Hotel are the three most famous bar streets in Beijing.

Jing Guang Centre 京广中心

23

This is Jing Guang Centre located in the east sector of the city with a 51-storey glass tower above the ground. The total weight of steel structure for the project is 32,000 tons. The tallest part of the centre is 209 metres, which offers a spectacular view of the Capital City. The Centre is the second tallest building in Beijing. The tallest building, located in the western part of the city, is the CCTV Tower with a height of 243 metres.

Three buildings in one, with a floor space of 145,075 square metres, the Centre boasts an equally dynamic combination of facilities and support serves. In addition to more than 20,000 square metres of superbly equipped office space, the complex offers 243 luxuriously furnished apartments and a 452-room first class hotel, also an unequaled range of leisure amenities that includes everything from an indoor pool and a disco to four floors of shops and restaurants. All are conveniently located just moments away from the embassy area. The Centre provides professional management through New World Hotels International. It was put into operation by the end of 1989, the 40th anniversary of the founding of the People's Republic of China.

The 7th storey (23 metres in height) was the highest building in Beijing in 1950s; In 1980s, the tallest building was 53-storey Jingguang Centre (209 metres in height); while in 1990s, CCTV Tower was the tallest building (243 metres tall) in Beijing.

Capital Mansion 京城大厦

Situated on the bank of the Liangma River, the Capital Mansion offers for your enjoyment a new community for work and life in Beijing.

The Capital Mansion features a 52-storey high-rise, multiple low-rises, luxury apartments, ultra modern offices, building automation system, state-of-the-art telecommunications, multifunction conference hall, conference rooms, underground parking area, bank, retail establishments, restaurants, and sports club.

The 183-metre high Capital Mansion is the first super high building of steel structure in China. It has a total floor space of 135,000 square metres, of which 35,000 square metres are for office space. This multi-function complex was built with funds collected from overseas by China International Trust and Investment Corporation(CITIC), which owns and manages the building.

Diplomats' Centre 外交人员中心

On both sides of this avenue is a new set of apartment blocks for foreign diplomats. It is the largest of its kind in China. It is called the Tayuan Centre, situated in the northeast of Beijing. The centre consists of nine apartment buildings with a construction area of 160,000 square metres. It has 540 apartments and service centres, including restaurants and bars. All the buildings in the centre are 16 or 17 storeys high. There is also an underground car parking area for 600 cars.

Pizza Hut 比萨饼屋

Located at Dongzhimenwai Street, a white four-storey pagoda shaped building bears the eye-catching name, Pizza Hut. This Pizza Hut is the first of its kind in this country making China the 58th country in which the American Pepsi Food Service International has opened a Pizza Hut. A joint venture, it opened officially on September 10, 1990. Unlike Kentucky Fried Chicken, also managed by the Pepsi Company, Pizza Hut provides table service. The first and second floors of the building can serve more than 100 customers at one sitting. Customers can also order home delivery by telephone to enjoy steaming pizza without having to go out.

Pizza Hut is a legendary business success. It began in 1958, when Dan and Frank Carney established their pizza business in America with a capital of US$ 600. With the opening of a Pizza Hut in Canada in 1968, their business went international. On September 11, 1990, a Pizza Hut opened in Moscow, making Russia the 59th country to have one of the 7, 000 Pizza Huts. Now a truly world wide industry, the business employs a total of 150, 000 people and is the largest food chain in the world. At present, there are seven outlets in Beijing.

Beijing Workers' Stadium 北京工人体育场

It was built in 1959 in a space of 11 months. It has a seating capacity of 80, 000. Fully packed, it can hold as many as 100, 000 people. Under the stands are living rooms that can accommodate 1, 500 athletes. Attached to the stadium are outdoor and indoor swimming pools and an artificial lake.

The stadium was thoroughly renovated in 1989. The opening and closing ceremonies were held here during the 11th Asian Games in 1990.

Beijing's commitment to host a "Green Olympics" in 2008 have been guaranteed by the introduction of the latest scientific and technological measures. Nanometer materials 纳米材料 have dominated the construction of the Capital Gymnasium, the Olympic Sports Centre Gymnasium and the Workers' Stadium. Thanks to the new nanotechnology, sound-absorbing boards have become water-and-oil-proof and more resistant to distortion. Nano-paint makes floorboards water-resistant, and nano-plastic will stand hard wear and corrosion. In smoking rooms, nano air purifying machines cam turn smoke into harmless air. Nanotechnology refers to technologies that deal with the manipulation of individual atoms and molecules. Materials produced with Nanotechnology demonstrate special physical and chemical properties more suitable for industrial use than ordinary ones, such as nano-material called carbon nanotubes, which is 100 times harder than steel but only one-sixth its weight.

By June 2001, the Capital Gymnasium, the Olympic Sports Centre Gymnasium and the Workers' Stadium completed environmental protection upgrades, a harmonious integration of environmental protection with energy conservation, technology and arts.

The Blue Zoo Beijing, the city's first salt-water aquarium, opened to visitors in November 1997. Covering 7,000 square metres, the aquarium is located in Beijing Workers' Stadium. The aquarium is home to 5,000 fish, including coral reef fish, sharks, rays, eels and crayfish.

New Ways Adopted to Treat Garbage 采取新的办法解决垃圾问题

New garbage disposal methods have been introduced to Beijing to replace traditional disposal measures such as landfills, which took up space and posed a potential threat to underground water resources. Several garbage incineration facilities have been set up in suburban areas of the city in 2001 to help solve the city's garbage headache. Incineration is the most efficient and harmless disposal method at present. The Thermal Energy Department of Tsinghua University designed and helped build a garbage incineration plant at Laiguangying Village in a suburban area of Beijing's Chaoyang District. Thermal energy generated by the disposal process can be used for residential heat or can be turned into electricity. The leftover slag can be made into construction materials such as bricks. Each incinerator made by the department can handle 300 tons of garbage per day and a normal disposal plant will have three or four incinerators. If every major district of Beijing sets up a garbage incineration plant, the city's garbage problem will be solved. By the end of 2005, Beijing's urban household refuse is expected to have been rendered completely harmless, while the integrated utilization of industrial solid waste will reach 90 per cent. At present, more than 80 per cent of the city's urban household waste is being disposed of harmless. But with rapid economic growth and continuing urbanization, the garbage problem is still a major factor threatening the quality of the urban environment and people's health.

Beijing generates more than 8,000 tons of residential garbage every day, or about 3 million tons per year. In most areas of China, however, urban garbage is generally handled in landfills and compound fertilizers are produced from organic waste. But random disposal of garbage takes up large areas of land, and seriously pollutes the air, rivers, lakes and underground water; some cities already have no proper place to put their garbage. The waste-disposal market is big in large cities in China such as Beijing, with the potential for creating highly profitable businesses that at the same time will help protect the environment.

China World Trade Centre 中国国际贸易中心

This is China World Trade Centre (CWTC) occupying an area of 12 hectares (29.65 acres) with a total floor space of 370,000 square metres.

Located at Jianguomenwai, the China World Trade Center is a huge business project which includes a 150-metre high (40 storeys) office tower—the tallest in Beijing—clad in "golden" glass, a fanshaped 70-metre-high international exhibition hall, two 30-storey apartment blocks, a Chinese garden and an underground atrium that connect with the city's subway network. Robert Sober/Emery Roth and Sons of New York, USA, and Nikken Sekkei Ltd. of Japan. designed the project.

The US$ 300 million China World Trade Centre is a joint venture between the China Foreign Economic and Trade Constancy and the Hong Kong Kerry Industrial Company Ltd. owned by the international financial group Kuok Brothers.

The whole complex was completed in 1988. The China World Trade Center completed its new office building—the China World Tower B. Started operation on October 1, 1999, the new edifice was built to celebrate the 50th anniversary of the founding of the People's Republic of China. As the key project of the second phase of the China World Trade Centre, the China World Tower B has a net office area of 54,512 square metres.

The tower is 153 metres high, with 38 storeys above ground and 4 storeys below. The second phase of the China World Trade Centre, started in 1996, also includes parking spaces, an indoor ice-skating rink, a 10,000-square-metre garden, and the China World Shopping Mall. It cost US$150 million.

The China World Complex is recognized as the prime business location in Beijing and this position has been reinforced by the China World Tower B. The entire complex is the core of an emerging central business district and will continue to be the landmark project in Beijing.

China World Trade Centre, Beijing's top multi-functional complex, opened China World Tower B, its latest and most technologically advanced commercial facility. The opening brings the number of fully operational office buildings within the complex to four, making it the world's second largest world trade centre featuring 560,000-square-metre trading area, just behind the New York World Trade Centre in the United States of America. It was destroyed by terror attack on Septemler 11, 2001.

World Trade Centre Third Phase: Located on No 1 Jianguomenwai Avenue, It covers a target area of 500,000 square metres encompassing office buildings, five-star hotels, apartments and business establishments.

City Sightseeing Route B: Jinglun Hotel—International Hotel—Chang'an Boulevard—Xidan—Shougang (Capital

Iron and Steel) Group
线路 B: 京伦饭店—国际饭店—长安街—西单—首钢集团

Jinglun Hotel 京伦饭店

This is Jinglun Hotel (four-star hotel), which lies about four kilometres from Tian'anmen Square, the centre of the capital. Construction of the hotel started in September 1982, and was completed at the end of June 1984. The hotel is a joint venture project.

The white 12-storey hotel has 678 guestrooms, each of them is equipped with individually controlled central air conditioning, colour television, refrigerator, direct dialing phone, automatic alarm system, and mini bar. The hotel has employed Japan Airlines Development Company to manage it. This company has operated over 91 hotels all over the world, with the Jinlun Hotel as the first in China. The hotel has four restaurants specializing in both Chinese and Western cuisine.

Jianguo Hotel 建国饭店

Jianguo Hotel(four-star hotel) has a very good location, close to the embassy area, the International Club and the Friendship Store. It is a joint venture hotel designed by a Chinese American architect after the Holiday Inn in California. The hotel has 528 standard rooms and suites. Its Chinese restaurant serves Cantonese food; its Western restaurant specializes in French and American foods, prepared by Swiss chef and using some imported ingredients.

Guiyou Store 贵友商店

Guiyou Store is a modern shopping centre for overseas tourists, residents, and diplomatic envoys, compatriots from Hong Kong, Macao and Taiwan as well as overseas Chinese. The store has traditional commodities of oriental nationalities. It mainly deals in tourist souvenirs, ready-made traditional Chinese medicine, fur and leather, silk, embroidery, jade articles, antiques, arts and crafts, cloisonné, lacquer ware, porcelain as well as foodstuff, daily-necessities, knitwear, fashionable clothes, household electrical appliance and modern office stationary.

Beijing Arts and Crafts Corporation 北京工艺美术品公司

Beijing Arts and Crafts Corporation, the largest of its kind in China, is a jointly-run industry corporation with more than 60 branches. The corporation has earned an excellent reputation during its long history with over 50

28

of its products winning international and domestic prizes. The corporation has import and export rights and its products sell well in more than 130 countries and regions. Customers are welcome to visit the corporation's display facilities. Its traditional products add beauty to people's homes. Export items include silk and other kinds of carpets, tapestries, palace lanterns, wood carvings, gold inlaid furniture, antique porcelain, enamelware, carved lacquerware, cups and medals, velvet birds, glassware, stage costumes and property, amber, bone carvings, metalwork, leather, embroidered cloth, embroidered hangings, brocade boxes, silk figurines, jade, jewelry, Chinese folk arts and crafts and Chinese paintings as well.

The Silk Market 秀水市场 (Popularly Known to the West as Xiushuijie 秀水街)

Despite its name, the Silk Market has much more than just silk. The Chinese silk products in the market are cheap, but good quality and therefore popular, but there are also lots of cashmere garments, down jackets, leather goods, shoes, hats, watches and some handicrafts and trinkets. The Silk Market basically consists of a long, narrow street (Xiushuijie) crammed with hundreds of stalls. One of the main things about the market is the fact that none of the prices is set. It all depends on your bargaining skills. If you are a proficient bargainer, then you can get great deals on all kinds of clothing, but if you are soft-hearted and don't like confrontation, then you may get taken for a ride. It is often helpful to bring along a Chinese friend who can help you bargain. The way to do it is, look around at all of the stuff and point out to your friend which item you like, without letting the seller know. Then let the Chinese friend go back and bargain for you. Of course not all Chinese people are good bargainers, but at least if they go, the starting price will often be lower than it is for a foreign face. Sometimes the starting price is the same, but the lowest the seller will go will be lower for the Chinese person. If you are a tall person the Silk Market is the best place for you to buy clothes and shoes. Usually the shopping plazas and super-stores do not have really large size. If you are size 12 shoes size or larger, then the only place to really go is to the Silk Market! The silk and cashmere goods are also much cheaper than they would be in other stores or in other countries. These items make great gifts for friends back home, especially the silk Mickey Mouse boxer shorts that you can't get away from. Most of the sellers speak a little English, so you can communicate with these people. It is one of the most popular streets in this Capital City that foreigners either living in Beijing or just tourists would like to go and shop.

CVIK Plaza 赛特购物中心

Here comes the CVIK Plaza. The plaza was completed and opened by the end of 1992. It is a big five-storey building with a total floor space of 12, 000 square metres, including another two floors below ground level. Surrounded by luxury hotels, towering office buildings and other modern tourist facilities, the new plaza contributes greatly to make this area one of the Beijing favourite commercial districts. Besides the shopping centre, it also has dining and recreational facilities. Invested and constructed by Science and Technology Exchange Company, the plaza is jointly managed by China Venturetech Investment Corporation and Yaohan International Company of Japan.

Beijing Friendship Store 北京友谊商店

Located near the embassy area, the Beijing Friendship Store is the largest store in China catering to foreign residents and tourists. It was opened in 1973. The store supplies nearly 100, 000 varieties of goods, ranging from daily necessities to arts and crafts. Both traditional Chinese export commodities and native produce and special products of various places of China are available in this store.

There are some imported items as well as quality domestic produced goods. Since some goods are imported, their prices have to be readjusted frequently according to the fluctuations of the exchange rate.

The Antique Hall is located on the fourth floor of the store. It is a paradise for collectors.

The store also has a florist, laundry, tailoring service, and currency exchange counter. It opens from 9 am to 9: 30 pm.

CITIC Building 中国国际信托投资公司大楼

This is China International Trust and Investment Corporation Building located next to the Friendship Store and only 3 kilometres from Tian'anmen Square. The building is the first of its kind completed in 1985 to provide office and residential space for representatives of foreign business organizations operating in Beijing.

The modern 101-metre high building has 31 storeys, two of them below ground level. Its roof garden offers a panoramic view of the city. The building has a floor space of 50, 000 square metres, with 18, 000 square metres of office space, and 8, 000 square metres of residential space in 105 apartments.

The distinctive, dark building towers majestically over the surrounding light colored edifices. Its upper storeys are lavishly decorated in brown color with gold and they are filled glass mosaic tiles. The windows are of bronze anodized aluminum with double glazed tinted glass. The podium is three-storey high completed with anodized aluminum tinted glass curtain wall and polished black granite faces. With its modern facilities and excellent management, the building offers luxurious and convenient accommodation to users.

The offices and apartments in the building are fully lit, and they are accessible by separate entrances and elevators. Chinese and Western restaurants are located on the top floors. The building accommodated officials of about 90 well-known corporations and financial institutions from 13 countries and regions in Asia, America, Europe and Australia.

Established in 1979, CITIC is a financial, manufacture, trading, and service institution with a four-in-one economic entity. It is a multifunctional corporation with emphasis on investment both at home and abroad. In the mean time, CITIC can also act as agent or trustee of different types on matters relating to business. With further broadening of China's open economic policy, the improvement of China's legal system and with the carrying out of the different reforms under way, economic and technical exchange with foreign countries will be further expanded.

International Club 国际俱乐部

It was built in 1973, a recreation place for foreign diplomats, business people, journalists and exchange students in Beijing. It has a coffee shop and a restaurant serving both Chinese and Western food. Movies are shown in most evenings.

Beijing International Club Hotel 北京国际俱乐部饭店

The Beijing International Club Hotel is ideally located in the centre of Beijing business, shopping and diplomatic precinct, and just a few minutes from Tian'anmen Square, the Forbidden City and the Silk Market. The hotel is neighbouring the historic Beijing International Club established in 1911.

The hotel is 25 minutes from Beijing International Airport. It boasts 287 rooms, including clubrooms, club executive rooms, diplomatic suites, statesman suites, ambassador suites and presidential suites. Room facilities: King-size or double/double bed, private bathroom with separate bath and shower, walking wardrobe, individually controlled air conditioning, remote control colour television with in-house movie channels, CNN and satellite TV, alarm clock, private safe, IDD telephones, personal bar with refrigerator, 220 volt power, in-room facsimile and personal computer outlets, hairdryer, bathrobes, slippers and a deluxe range of bathroom amenities.

The hotel caters for the most prestigious of events with the finest facilities and first class standards of cuisine and service. The splendour of the Great Hall is matched only by the quality of its cuisine, splendid wine list and state-of-the-art audiovisual equipment. It offers a tempting range of banquet styles to choose from, including Western and traditional Chinese. Meetings and conference participants enjoy advanced multi-media presentation and video conferencing facilities. In addition to the Great Hall, there is the Parlour, which is suitable for use as a boardroom, or will host a superb cocktail reception.

US President George W. Bush stayed in this hotel while he paid a state visit to China on February 20 – 21, 2002.

New Buildings Outside Jianguomen (Gate of National Foundation) 建国门外新楼群

These high-rise apartment buildings were completed in 1980. Foreign embassy and business people live in these compounds. This cloverleaf was completed and opened to traffic in 1979.

Overseas Chinese Apartments 华侨公寓

Located in the residential district near the Jianguomen Overpass, just opposite the International Club, the plush Overseas Chinese Apartments consist of six 14-18-storey buildings with a total floor space of more than 51,000 square metres. They are the first group of houses to have been sold directly to returned overseas Chinese, who wished to buy their own houses in Beijing.

The Overseas Chinese Apartments have a total of 282 four-five-and six-room flats plus 18 luxury 8-12 room penthouse apartments. Each apartment has its own telephone, air conditioner (optional) and modern toilet and kitchen equipment imported from abroad.

Another unique feature of the apartments is a three-storey garage, accommodating 140 cars. Within a 1.5-hectare courtyard, there is a spacious paved parking terrace, green areas and a small Chinese garden.

Other facilities include a restaurant, a photo studio, a bank, a florist and a supermarket — all housed in a two-storey annex running along the front of the main block, facing Jianguomenwai Street. The service annex is designed by Hong Kong architects, while the main block is designed by the Beijing Urban Architectural Design Institute.

The whole project was built with a bank loan of 60 million yuan (US$ 22 million) from the Beijing Housing Development and Managing Corporation, which is also responsible for the management and maintenance of the finished apartments and the service facilities.

The corporation, which was set up in March 1983 under the Beijing Municipal Housing and Real Estate Administration, has undertaken the job of developing housing for returned overseas Chinese in answer to their repeated requests.

Earlier December 1984, it refurbished 102 apartments, originally intended for local residents, near the Temple of Heaven and offered them for sale through the Beijing Overseas Chinese Association.

China began selling State-built urban apartments to residents in 1982— first on a trial basis in four cities: Zhengzhou in Henan, Changzhou in Jiangsu, Shashi in Hubei and Siping in Jilin Province. According to the arrangement, the buyer paid only one third of the price, while his employing unit and the State shared the balance equally. The buyer is often allowed to pay his share of the price over a period of five to 20 years in installments.

As a result of the successful experiment, the sale of apartments has now begun throughout China as a major step in reforming the existing housing system, which at present completely depends on State subsidy.

Beijing Ancient Observatory 北京古观象台

Southwest of the flyover is Beijing Ancient Observatory. It dates back to the Ming Dynasty (1368-1644). On the high platform are some large bronze astronomical instruments including an artillery sphere and a celestial globe. The site has been renovated and was reopened in April 1983. It has installed a new reflector, 2.2 metres in diameter, on one of its astronomical telescopes. This new reflector was made of ultra low expansion glass ceramics, a new type of glass developed in the mid 1960s.

Asia Pacific Building 亚太大厦

The Asia Pacific Building welcomes you to the big heart of Beijing. Located just 25 minutes drive from Beijing International Airport and five minutes from Beijing Railway Station, the Asia Pacific Building is within driving distance of the International Club, Friendship Store, embassy area, Wangfujing Street, Tian'anmen Square, and many other exciting Beijing attractions. The Asia Pacific Building is a 15-storey office building with 208 units of offices linked to a 14-storey apartment block with 120 fully serviced and furnished apartments. Amenities in the building include an executive business centre with full secretarial services, well designed offices for rent, and a boardroom fully equipped with the latest in telecommunications. It also offers a 530 square-metre health spa complete with hot and cold water jacuzzis, steam and sauna rooms, a solarium, a gymnasium, and massage rooms, plus a range of support facilities like a squash court, a billiard room, and a video games room, a Chinese and Western restaurant, a cafeteria, a food court serving fast food, a karaoke bar, a supermarket, and other retail establishments, and underground parking adequate for 172 vehicles.

This is the Second Ring Road with a total length of 32.7 kilometres. This Second Ring Road was built and opened to the traffic on September 25, 1992. Underneath it is the second Beijing subway skirting the city built in 1970s and completed and put into operation in 1980s.

The 48-kilometre-long Third Ring Road was completed and opened to the traffic in 1981. And the 65.3-kilometre-long Fourth Ring Road was completed and opened to traffic in June 2001.

Altar of the Sun Park 日坛公园

The Altar of the Sun Park, also known as the Altar of the Rising Sun, was built in 1530. As the name suggests, the altar was the site of imperial sacrifices to the God of the Sun. The park is located in Beijing's diplomatic quarter to the northeast of Chaoyangmen (Facing the Sun Gate). The altar was restored and enlarged during the reign (1736-1795) of Qing Emperor Qianlong. The sacrifice took place from 6 to 8 in the morning. An ox, a sheep and a pig were sacrificed. A square white marble platform once stood in the garden and although it fell into disrepair long time ago, traces of its ruins may still be seen. In 1949, the People's Government began a project of afforestation and converted the area into Ritan Park. In autumn of 1980, construction of a large garden was begun in the southeastern corner of the park. Now the entire area has been turned into a park.

34

China's Manhattan 中国的曼哈顿

Properties along Beijing's Chaoyangmen Street have a huge potential market value because the area is destined to become China's Manhattan.

The 1,050-metre street running from Landao Shopping Centre to the new headquarter of the Ministry of Foreign Affairs will be home to 12 buildings designed as offices, shopping centres and apartment blocks. Ten of the 12 buildings have already been erected or are under development on both sides of the street. The Beijing municipal government plans to build five business centres across the city. Chaoyangmenwai Street is the only one, which has got off the ground so far.

According to the city's overall plan, the four square kilometres area between the Second Ring Road and the Third Ring Road, Chaoyangmen and Jianguomen, is to become China's first Central Business Centre(CBC). Chaoyangmenwai Street today is somewhat like Hong Kong's Causeway Bay, where there is a concentration of offices, shopping centres and apartments.

The business centre will be working in tandem with the Zhongguancun Science Park in the Haidian District in northwestern Beijing, China's "Silicon Valley," to promote the city's economy. The Beijing Municipal Government has decided to focus on high-tech industries in the future. The center will be a window of Beijing to the outside world and will inject more vigor into the city's economy. The State Council approved a plan to establish an integral business centre in the Chaoyang District in 1993. The district is the best place for the business centre to be positioned. The district, which is the largest, richest and most populous area of Beijing, is home to the majority of Beijing's foreign embassies, 60 per cent of more than 3,000 foreign corporate offices and 167 foreign deplomatic organizations. Many State-owned industrial enterprises will move out of the district to create more space for luxury office and apartment buildings, commercial and other public facilities. Construction of the business centre will take many years and involves tens of billions of US dollars.

The Central Business District, Beijing 北京商务中心区

Running from Dongdaqiao Road in the west to Xidawang Road in the east, and from Chaoyang Road in the north to Tonghui River in the south and forming a golden cross in shape, the Central Business District (CBD) aims to become a world-class business community focusing on an outward-looking economy. Experts commented that the CBD programme would greatly propel the capital's social and economic development, along with its successful bid to host the 2008 Olympic Games and China's entry into the World Trade Organization (WTO). According to the final plan, the CBD encompasses 4 square kilometres (400 hectares or 988.4 acres), with the buildings' total floor space less than 10 million square metres. Office buildings will account for about half of the total space, leaving one-quarter to household departments and the remaining quarter to commercial, cultural and entertainment services. The major buildings inside

the CBD will be taller than 100 metres and the height of commercial buildings will vary from 150 to 300 metres. Skyscrapers will mostly gather in
the northeastern part of the district, forming a symbol of the CBD. A green
area in the CBD will reach 33. 39 hectares, nearly 11 per cent of the total
ground space, to ensure an environmentally friendly district. The final
CBD plan also emphasizes the building of an efficient traffic network, pri-
oritizing public transport. Under the traffic scheme, two new subways will
connect to the CBD.

The Beijing municipal government has recently promised to invest a total
of 12 billion yuan (US$ 1. 46 billion) in municipal works in the CBD,
like roads, communication networks and educational facilities. Developers
from both China and abroad will complete a large number of other projects.
The Beijing municipal government noted that the first phase of the CBD
programme, including China World Trade Centre, Phase III, Beijing's
Fortune Plaza and China Central Television, will be completed by the year
2008.

Construction of China World Trade Centre, Phase III alone, is planned
to start soon, with an investment of more than US$ 1. 1 billion.

Chaoyang District is China's richest urban district when it comes to
possessing resources for foreign affairs. The district is home to 136 foreign embassies and three-fifths of the 7, 000 corporate offices in the city.
Four bazaars that are foreigners' favourites for shopping and entertainment in Beijing, such as Xiushui for garments, Panjiayuan for antiques,
and Sanlitun for restaurants and coffee houses, are located in the district. With support of the central and Beijing governments, Chaoyang
District will develop itself into the capital's showcase in foreign relations, economic prosperity, urban amenities and civilization construction.
Chaoyang District is the largest district in the capital and has sufficient
land resources for development. The centre is one of six major opportunities the district should consider leading up to 2010. Other projects include:

(1) A science city, or the east wing of the expected Zhongguancun sili-
    con valley, also planned for the district;

(2) A business expansion, in the capital's northeastern corner, to mainly
    accommodate private and foreign enterprises. It is considered a major
    site for the burgeoning private economy;

(3) Urbanization of the capital's suburbs and construction of satellite
    towns;

(4) An electronics industry zone.

Beijing Intl. Post and Telecommunications Office
北京国际邮局

Located in the eastern side of Jianguomen North Street, the Beijing International Post and Telecommunications Office is a special organization. It deals with international mail matters and telecommunications. It is the only post office, which exchanges international mail matters directly abroad from the Capital City in China.

The office has 20 windows handling international and domestic letters, printed materials, small packets, parcels and E. M. S. (Express Mail Service). They also handle domestic express mails remittance, subscription and retailing periodicals and newspapers. The international insured letters and post retinue items are also delivered here. International and domestic direct long distance calls and telefax are accepted and transmitting day and night.

With the development and improvement, China Post has set up a logistic network accessible to and covering the entire country to provide high quality and efficient service. Booming e-commerce has driven China Post to upgrade its delivery network quickly, laying a sound foundation for its future superior position in the burgeoning e-commerce logistic network. China Post EMS has now established a service relationship with more than 200 countries, opened service in about 2,000 cities across the country, hired a professional delivery group of about 14,000 postal workers and more than 10,000 postal vehicles for collection, delivery and transportation, installed state-of-the-art computers in 201 cities and proactively popularized GPS.

Promptness: The international mail matters which customers post in the Business Hall will reach the sorting centre without any transportation, loading and unloading. And they will be enclosed to the mail bags sending abroad directly. This can increase enormously your working, economic benefit and help customers save time.

Convenience: In the office there is Beijing Customs. It is very convenient for customers to present the international mail matters face to face to the Customs officials. If customers want to mail large quantities of international mail matters they can accept them at any time under an agreement in advance. They can also supply transportation and packing services.

Reliability: This is a special post office, which deals with international mail matters. It is imbued with the characters of well-organized, fine management and high quality of personnel as well as the advantage of high speed and reliability.

Since China began to practice reform and opening up to the outside world in the late 1970s, more than 20 new businesses, which meet the needs of the market and provide conveniences to customers, have been added to the Beijing postal service. The original services include international and domestic letters, printed matters, parcels, remittance, philately, distribution of newspapers and periodicals, and confidential documents. The new businesses include:

(1) Goods Delivery

Beijing postal offices began domestic express mail service in 1984 and postal express delivery in 1987. In 1990, they started international express mail service and in 1992 they began parcel express delivery service from the mainland to Taiwan through non-governmental channels. In 1993, Anbang Express Post started, while in 1997, Beijing post offices launched high-speed express mail service and international and domestic express post services with the addressees in charge of payment, and services of writing letters in reply to international commercial letters. On June 15, 1999 they launched express post within the capital, ensuring that postal matters reach their destinations on the same day they are posted or the next day.

(2) Derived Business from Finance

Postal savings deposit was restored in 1986: service of deposit for payment of monthly telephone fees were offered in 1991; international postal remittance services were provided in 1992; and in 1995, international express money delivery services began.

(3) Etiquette Business

Etiquette telegram services were offered in 1987; etiquette remittance was provided in 1991; etiquette letter services in 1995, and in 1997 international express etiquette were offered on a trial basis.

(4) Business as Agents

In 1995, Beijing post offices were commissioned to sell China Employment Consolation Cards, international consultation cards and football star postcards, register for check inquirers and act as agents to collect postal international travelling fees and pager service fees. In 1997, they started to collect payments for goods for sellers through express mail service.

(5) Services using telecommunication technology. In 1990 phototelegraph service was offered; and in 1992, domestic postal electronic letter service was provided.

With the construction of communication facilities, science and technology as its backbone, the Beijing postal service has expanded its communication capabilities through the use of technology. By the end of 2001, Beijing boasted 611 post offices and post and telecommunications offices, including 147 branch post and telecommunications offices and 19 postal agencies. The total number of computerized post offices reached 271, 45. 9 per cent of all post offices. About 87 per cent of the post offices and post and telecommunications offices in the city were computerized. There were 465 postal savings deposit spots, of which 259 were connected through computer networks. There were 99 automatic teller machines (ATM) in Beijing. There were 499 post offices and post and telecommunications offices with express mail service, 148 with philately service, 7, 913 social newspaper and periodical sales promotion stations, 1, 561 newspaper and periodical retail sales agencies and 2, 548 pillar boxes and letter cases all over the city. By 2001, the total length of Beijing's postal routes reached 101, 715 kilometres, including: 33 air postal routes with a length of 48, 987 kilometers; 13 railway postal routes with a length of 19, 844 kilometres and 486 self-run vehicle postal routes with a length of 31, 094 kilometres. There are 554 postal routes in rural areas with a total length of 18, 084 kilometres.

The Beijing Postal Administration is an organization set up by the State Post Office under the Ministry of Information Industry. It is also the administrative department under the Beijing Municipal Government in charge of postal service and communications in the Beijing area. It has jurisdiction over the Beijing Post Office and its branches include four post offices in urban districts, 10 post offices in suburban counties or districts, seven special post and communications bureaux or companies, two units of scientific research and other affiliated units. Its nearly 20, 000 staff members and workers serve an area of 16, 807 square kilometres with a population of 12. 456 million. It exchanges postal matters with more than 2, 000 domestic cities and counties, delivers newspapers and magazines directly to more than 5, 000 cities and towns, and has direct postal connections with 229 cities in 137 countries and regions in the world. Its major services cover letters, printed matters, parcels, remittance and express mails, money deposits, philately, circulation of newspapers and periodicals, telegrams telephones and agents for many other businesses.

The 22nd Universal Postal Union Congress was held in Beijing, and more than 2, 000 representatives from 189 countries and about 20 international organizations attended the Congress which also marked the 125th anniversary of the establishment of the Universal Postal Union.

Beepers in Beijing One of every 10 Beijing residents has a pager, which means that there are now 1. 5 million of the electronic devices in use in the Chinese capital. Paging services are witnessing a rapid growth in the city. According to the Beijing Radio-Telephone Administrative Bureau, more than 200 pager services are registered in Beijing and the city has established more than 200 pager stations.

By the end of 2001, small phone users reached 140 million in China as against 18, 000 portable phones (mobile phone, hand-held phone) in 1990, surpassing 120. 1 million in the United States of America, ranking the 1st in the world. There were 174. 6 million fixed phone subscribers in China.

Office of General Administration of Customs 中国海关总署

This is the Office of General Administration of Customs done tellingly in the image of a country gate. It was completed in 1990. The building combines traditional style with modern flavour and occupies an area of 26, 000 square metres. It looks dignified with a traditional axial layout. Two buildings topped with two traditional Chinese pavilions are connected and shaped like the English "H" or more to the point the Chinese character for gate, which symbolizes the function of customs. There is thus a harmonization form and function in the aesthetics of this architectural setting. Between the two buildings is an open space. With white granite as its base the building has a strong modern flavour reinforced by the black metal frame around the windows. The 3-metre-high steps in front of the entrance make the building look solemn and regal.

Chinese Academy of Social Sciences 中国社会科学院

The 15-storey building on your right is the Chinese Academy of Social Sciences. The place used to be the site of local examination in the Ming and Qing dynasties. Chinese Academy of Social Sciences was founded in 1977.

Beijing International Hotel 北京国际饭店

Opposite to Beijing Railway Station is the Beijing International Hotel (five-star hotel), which was put into operation in late 1987. Beijing Friendship Store is two blocks away. A comfortable walk will take you to Oriental Plaza, Wangfujing Shopping Centre — the most famous shopping area in Beijing, and Tian'anmen Square — the largest square in the world. Convenient public transportation can whisk you to the Temple of Heaven, the Summer Palace, Beihai Park, Coal Hill Park and other points of interest.

The hotel covers an area of 4. 2 hectares (10. 4 acres). The floor space of the hotel totals 105, 000 square metres with 1, 049 graciously appointed guest rooms and suites. The rooms are all recently renovated, with modern tub/shower bathrooms, colour TV with radio, direct dial telephones, and other amenities.

There are 32 storeys, 29 above the ground and 3 under the ground of the main building of the hotel. The spine of the hotel stands 104. 4 metres high from the ground.

The hotel has a wide range of facilities, such as restaurants, cafe, bar, multifunctional halls, shops, swimming pool, sauna, post office, bank, hairdresser's salons, and taxi inquiry. On the 28th floor with a height of 104 metres, there is a revolving restaurant seating up to 200 people at a time. It takes two hours to make a revolution. Nowadays, there are four revolving restaurants in Beijing. The other three restaurants are at the top of Central Television Tower (80 minutes to make a revolution, with a height of 221 metres), Kunlun Hotel (90 minutes to make a revolution, with a height of 102 metres) and Xiyuan Hotel (150 minutes to make a revolution, with a height of 93 metres).

So if you want classic accommodations with all the modern amenities, check into the Beijing International hotel, a five-star hotel looks forward to welcome you.

China National Tourism Administration 中国国家旅游局

A travel department was set up within the Shanghai Commercial Deposit Bank on August 1, 1923. On June 1, 1927, the Travel Department was upgraded the name to "China Travel Service" and it became the earliest travel agency in China. Its founder was Chen Guangpu, the then general manager of Shanghai Commercial Deposit Bank.

Established in 1949, China Travel Service (China Overseas Travel Service) Head Office was based in Beijing. Its predecessor was Overseas Travel Service. This was the New China's first travel agency, a nationwide travel and tourism enterprise, providing services of entry for compatriots from Hong Kong, Macao, and Taiwan, Chinese foreign nationals, and foreigners and at the same time providing services for returned overseas Chinese, their family members, compatriots from Hong Kong, Macao, and Taiwan and other personnel.

Approved by 124th session of the Standing Committee of the Second National People's Congress, China Travel and Tourism Administration 中国旅行游览事业管理局 was established on July 22, 1964 and was under the direct leadership of the State Council. On April 26, 1978 the name was changed to General Administration of China Travel and Tourism 中国旅行游览事业管理总局 .

On July 17, 1982, China International Travel Service was separated from General Administration of China Travel and Tourism. The 24th Session of the Standing Committee of the Fifth National People's Congress held on

August 23, 1982 decided that General Administration of China Travel and Tourism changed its name to National Tourism Administration of the People's Republic of China 中华人民共和国国家旅游局 (hereafter abbreviated to National Tourism Administration 简称国家旅游局).

Beijing Railway Station 北京火车站

Located at Jianguomen and opposite the Beijing International Hotel, the Beijing Railway Station was built in 1959. At the very beginning, the station could only handle 31 arriving and departing trains with 30,000 passengers a day. Now, with the development of the national economy, the station can handle 80 trains daily serving 130,000 passengers. During holidays, the station can handle 200,000 people.

The main hall of the station has four elevators and four escalators. Domestic passengers depart from the second floor. International passengers depart from the first floor. There are nine waiting rooms for ordinary passengers and six with a floor space of 14,000 square metres, the domestic and international ticket counters are on the first floor. On the second is a restaurant seating 600 persons, a movie house, a recreation room and a reading room. Passengers leave for their trains along the second floor corridors. Those arriving enter the station via underground corridors. The station also has luggage collecting and check-points, stores, restrooms and clinics.

As a first step in keeping up with the increased traffic, ticket handling has been modernized. Fast and efficient automatic machines now deliver tickets for travel from Beijing to 120 other major stations in the country. One of the big bottlenecks in the past was slow ticket service and long lines of worried travelers. There also used to be traffic jams of passengers trying to find their trains. Nowadays, they take escalators to the second floor, where a large multi colored digital sign gives departure times, platforms and locations of the nearest waiting rooms. In the waiting rooms a similar board gives departure times for any train. Radio communications among personnel inside the station helps improve all of this.

For newcomers to Beijing, or anyone with questions, each waiting room and ticket hall has an up-to-date information desk. Checking and getting out luggage, parcels and other items is done with electronic scales and computers to speed weighing, pricing and issuing baggage checks and receipts. Safety and security in the station are handled by a large radio connected staff aided by some 50 TV surveillance cameras covering almost every part of the entire building.

Beijing Railway Station has banned smoking since June 1, 1987. The

measure has improved the badly polluted environment in the railway station, saving about 90, 000 people a day from suffering potential dangers,
and helping keep away fires in the station. Smokers, about one fourth of the
90, 000 in the station each day, can ease their cravings in passageways,
dining halls and the central hall.

"Light Rail" to Be Built from Beijing Railway Station to Beijing West Railway Station

Construction of a light rail will be built from Beijing Railway Station to
Beijing West Railway Station. The total length of the Light Rail is 9. 165
kilometers, of which the tunnel totals 7. 049 kilometres; the width of the
double line is 8 metres, and 6. 05 metres high. The total cost will reach
1. 8 billion yuan (US$217. 5 million). There will be no stop between the
two railway stations.

Beijing has built a park around a part of its ancient wall close to the
Beijing Railway Station. The park has enclosed the last existing section of
the wall, which was built in the Ming Dynasty (1368-1644) between 1531
and 1548 and is about 200 metres long, 2. 7 metres wide and less than 6
metres high. Encompassing 3 hectares, the park is expected to protect the
ruins.

Beijing-Hong Kong Railway 北京—香港铁路

Construction of the Beijing-Hong Kong rail link started on February 20,
1993. The line is the longest and most expensive in China. The government planed to complete the 2, 370-kilometre Beijing-Shenzhen section in
1995 and completed the final Shenzhen-Kowloon section after sovereignty
over Hong Kong reverted to China in 1997 with a total length of 2, 553
kilometres. The railway soaked up a total investment of more than 40 billion yuan (US$ 4. 8 billion).

The line runs between the Beijing-Shanghai railway and the Beijing-Guangzhou railway, and crosses nine provinces and municipalities. It
also connects several major east-west railway lines, including the Beijing-Baotou and Beijing-Qinhuangdao railways in the north, the Lianyun-
gang-Lanzhou railway in Central China and the Hangzhou-Zhuzhou railway
in the southeast. Construction of the railway has greatly eased congestion
in north south transportation, quickened opening to the outside world of
coastal regions and East China, speeded up the development of mountainous areas along the railway, and helped maintain the prosperity and stability of the Hong Kong-Macao region. The railway also runs across various
rivers, including the Yellow and the Yangtze rivers, and vast mountainous
regions. Five extensive bridges and two tunnels at least three kilometers
long were also built.

The Central Government provided the major part of the total investment for the construction. The remainder was provided by provinces along the route, as part of the government's ongoing drive to decentralize transportation construction and financing.

Railway Strategy in China 中国铁路战略

China will open more trunk lines to ease the crowding on rail transportation. At present, 10 key projects are under construction. China's rail transport has restricted economic development. To solve the problem, China is drafting a railway construction strategy. The Chinese Government has made this a priority for development. The strategy actually started in 1991. The first stage ended in 1995, when China should have 6,600 kilometres of new track, 4,100 kilometres of multiple lines and 5,600 kilometres of electrified rail, bringing the total operating lines to some 60,000 kilometres. Efforts are now concentrated on the key projects, including the Beijing-Kowloon line, the largest project in China's railway history, which runs 2,370 kilometres north to south through nine provinces and cities. It opened at the end of 1995. The other nine projects will either add new lines or improve the existing tracks in Northwest, North, Central, East, South and Southwest China.

Between 1996 and 2000, China made concerted efforts to construct a number of large-scale rail corridors. Express rail started to develop, special passenger lines were constructed, railway technologies and equipment improved, and the proportions of multiple and electrified lines increased. During the following decade, railway construction will develop at a higher speed. By 2010, China's total length of track is predicted to exceed 90,000 kilometres. Heavy haul will be adopted for freight transport on most trunk lines, and express passenger transport will meet a shortage of funds. Therefore, a better investment system needs to be established. However, the railway system will further expand its opening to the outside world and introduce overseas funds, advanced technologies and management experience.

By the end of 2001, the total length of railways in operation reached over 70,000 kilometres in China, ranking number one in Asia. There were about 12,000 kilometres of electrified lines, and there were 1,194 pairs of passenger trains on service each day, but the handling capacity can still hardly meet the mounting demand for passengers and cargo transport.

State to Build Key Railways (economic areas to be linked by rail networks)

China is to invest 30 billion yuan (US$3.6 billion) to construct a rail-

44

way network that will run through China's three major economic regions, including the Northeast, Bohai Bay and Yangtze River delta. The railway network is expected to cover 2, 200 kilometres from Harbin, the capital of Heilongjiang Province to Changxing in East China's Zhejiang Province. The railway network will link the Harbin-Dalian railway and a 170-kilometre-long ferry passage from Dalian to Yantai, a coastal city of Shandong Province. It will further extend from Shandong to Zhejiang and wind its way through China's economic hubs including Shanghai and Jiangsu Province. When completed, it will boost the economic development of Northeast China, known for its heavy industry, logging, and grain production. The main part of the project is to accomplish the 170-kilometre-long railway ferry section across the Shandong Peninsula and Liaoning Peninsula. Trains have to make a detour from Northeast China to Shandong Province in order to pass by the C-shaped peninsula of the Bohai Bay. The ferry passage project will need 3. 5 billion yuan(US$ 290 million) with a designed annual transportation capacity of 11 million tons.

The entire project is jointly sponsored by the Ministry of Railway and the provinces of Shandong, and Liaoning. To date, it has received loans from the German Government and the construction work started on January 25, 2002. It is scheduled for completion in 2005. When completed, the project will shorten the distance from Northeast China to South China by 400 to 1, 000 kilometres, and is expected to cut transportation costs by 6 billion yuan(US$ 720 million) annually. Preparatory work was initiated in 1994 when China invested 8 billion yuan(US$ 960 million) to electrify the Harbin-Dalian line.

Sources said that the government is also considering to use the Yantai ferry port as a link to South Korea and Japan's railway network and enable their trains to reach Europe via the new Euro-Asia Continental railway crossing China.

Guang'anmen Railway Station 广安门火车站

Foreign embassies, visitors and overseas Chinese pick up their goods at Guang'anmen (Gate of Universal Peace) Railway Station 3 kilometres away from the Beijing Railway Station. The Guang'anmen Station has experienced a big increase in its work, brought on by the expansion of foreign trade, tourism and the establishment of diplomatic relations with other countries. In 1985, a computer center was installed here to handle the entire process of receiving and shipping, including container freight.

Guang'anmen Station has a perfection shipping record. The staff and personnel work on a responsibility system. Special goods go to special warehouses and are checked by a special staff. For over 30 years the station has served thousands of foreigners from all over the world and people from Hong Kong, and Macao.

South of Beijing, in the town of Fengtai, is one of the biggest freight train marshalling yards in China. Here all shipments to, from or through Beijing, whether domestic or international, are sorted out by freight car and assembled or reassembled into the correct trains. The yard is 8. 5 kilometres long and 4. 5 square kilometres in area. On 69 track lines, it can handle 20, 000 cars a day.

"Humping," or sending cars to their different trains, is completely computerized and automatic, both in general overhead direction and at the hump itself. The yard locomotives are equipped with remote control hitching and unhitching, and speed and stopping points are determined automatically. Computers trace the individual cars. A computer monitoring system oversees the arrival and dispatch of trains and the tracks to be used. All yard information of every kind is fed into central computers, resulting in a completely automated yard.

Chang'an (Everlasting Peace) Boulevard 长安街

The eye-catching Chang'an Boulevard has been extended from the previous 3. 6 kilometres to 46 kilometres with accompanying environmental renovation by the end of 2000. The boulevard, which extended from Xidan to Dongdan, has been stretched from the Capital Iron and Steel Company in Shijingshan District in the west to Tongzhou District in the east. The renovation has expanded 50 to 100 metres on both sides of the boulevard and has included the restoration of municipal infrastructures, service facilities and environmental refinement. The project has maintained the environmental standards of an international metropolis, and it is modeled after the renovation done on Gongzhufen to Dabeiyao. Eight renovation standards for the boulevard have been listed. Besides 310, 000 square metres of new road surface, the list includes the addition of night lighting and cleanup of building signboards. An automatic transportation control system to keep traffic flowing has been set up, and a six-metre-wide green belt has been planned for both sides of the boulevard.

Chang'an Boulevard represents the capital's and China's image. The project also presents the achievements of the capital's modernization construction to the nation and the world. The latest renovation of Chang'an Boulevard took place in 1999.

It is Beijing's main boulevard running east-west through the heart of the city. People can now use integrated cards (IC) to make phone calls in the phone booths installed in early August 1999 along Chang'an Boulevard in Beijing. The Beijing Municipal Government installed 400 such phone booths along this boulevard. The move has made phone use more convenient for both the residents of Beijing and tourists from both at home and abroad.

Chang'an Boulevard starts at Beiyuan, Tongzhou District seat and ends at East Gate of Capital Iron and Steel Company. The boulevard is made up of Jianguomenwai Dajie, Dongchang'an Jie, Xichang'an Jie, Fuxingmennei Dajie etc.

Altogether, 270,000 trees have been planted along Chang'an Boulevard, the city's main artery, and 322,000 square metres of grassy areas have been created along the boulevard.

Dongdan Telephone Exchange 东单电话大楼

This is the Dongdan Telephone Exchange, which was completed by the end of 1984. The new exchange began operation in October 1985 and could provide 10,000 new telephone lines in the East City District of Beijing.

Beijing began an ambitious expansion program of its telephone system in 1985. By the end of 1996, 1,270,032 residential telephones were installed as against 14,006 residential phones in 1987 with a phone in every three families.

Some new equipments have been supplied by foreign manufacturers so as to increase speed and provide a high standard. The Beijing Telecommunications Administration concluded two major business transactions on the supply of telephone equipment with a Swedish and a Belgian firm.

Beijing's telephone system must develop at top speed to meet the demand of the nation's modernization program. In 1984, Beijing installed 10,000 telephones for its urban users, but the waiting list expanded from 10,000 in 1983 to 36,000 by the end of 1984. The capacity will never catch up with the ever-growing demand, until there is a telephone for every 10 Beijing urban residents, but that does not seem possible even by 1995. The existing rate is one phone for every 35 people in urban Beijing. Toady the number of mobile phones chalked up to 32.09 million in China and the mobile phone numbers were upgraded from 10 digits to 11 digits in the first half of 1999.

In Beijing, it took 25 years to upgrade the telephone number from 5 digits into 6 digits and it took 29 years to upgrade the telephone number from 6 digits into 7 digits. The telephone number was upgraded from 7 digits into 8 digits only took 2 years.

Starting May 8, 1996, phone numbers in Beijing were upgraded into eight digits after Paris, Tokyo, Hong Kong, and Shanghai.

Silver Street 银街

The Silver Street refers to the Dongdan North Street (Dongdan Beidajie). All the franchised foreign name-brand shops are located here to give you unsurpassed variety and selection.

The Oriental Plaza 东方广场

Located on East Chang'an Boulevard and adjacent to Tian'anmen Square, with a US$ 2 billion investment, the Oriental Plaza, featuring eight office buildings, a five-star hotel and a conference hall is the largest commercial complex in Asia, and it occupies a site of 100,000 square metres which includes a total floor area of 800,000 square metres. It is a world-class fusion of business, retail, leisure, entertainment and luxury accommodations. The Plaza is served by all modes of transport, including the new Wangfujing Subway Station, which brings international and domestic shoppers directly to the malls. It is a new centre of commercial activities in the heart of the Capital City reflecting the new business and lifestyle trends of the millennium. The Oriental Plaza is the largest and most costly development in the Capital City.

The Oriental Plaza masterfully integrates the concept of traditional Beijing courtyards with modern architectural composition. This exquisite blend of classical eastern charm and modern day refinement are in natural harmony with the capital's grandeur. And the "square beyond circles" configuration, together with its doors beyond doors and towers beyond towers, symbolize infinite opportunities for business. Conceived and designed by world-famous architects. Oriental Plaza is a masterpiece of modern architecture, the Plaza consists of two domains: the "Towers at Oriental Plaza," a self-contained business compound, and the "Malls at Oriental Plaza," with an appealing lifestyle for people of all walks of life.

"The Towers" include office buildings, apartments, a business hotel and a conference exhibition centre. "The Malls" consist of five distinct shopping malls, two landmark fountains, year's round gardens, and one of the world's largest parking area. All the building materials are of world-class quality.

The Plaza was put into operation by the year of 2000.

The eight grade-A office blocks of the Towers offer 2,800 square metres of space on each floor. Some of the floors are equipped with a unique raised floor design, allowing flexible layouts and easy installation of electrical circuits and communication networks.

Besides banking, postal and express delivery services, there are also many high-tech facilities meeting the needs of business tenants. These include a fiber-optic network, a VAST satellite system, multi-media services and in intelligent backbone structure.

Oriental Plaza also attaches great importance to maintaining an inspiring work environment. Large lobbies, nicely fitted senior executive shower rooms contribute to a pleasant and satisfying work environment.

There is also a five-star international business hotel with 600 luxury rooms, a grand ballroom, plentiful meeting rooms, special executive floors and over ten restaurants serving cuisine from around the world. The hotel also has an extra-large swimming pool, a sun deck and a two-storey fully-equipped health club.

There is also a conveniently located, fully equipped conference and exhibition centre.

The world-class serviced apartments at the Towers offer 1,000 fully furnished luxurious apartments for business executives working in Beijing.

The malls at Oriental Plaza comprise five individual and distinct theme shopping malls.

As one of the largest indoor parking area in the world, Oriental Plaza's parking facility includes spaces for 1,800 automobiles and 12,000 bicycles.

Among its neighbours are the General Customs Office, the Ministry of Foreign Trade and Economic Co-operation, the Beijing Municipal Government and the State Council.

The Towers at Oriental Plaza 东方经贸城

- 300,000 square metres of Grade A office space
  30万平方米甲级写字楼
- 1,000 service apartments 一千套酒店式公寓
- An international standard 5-star business hotel 一家国际五星级酒店
- A fully-equipped exhibition and convention centre
  一个设备齐全的会展中心

The Malls at Oriental Plaza 东方新天地

- Five theme shopping and entertainment malls for all lifestyles
  五个风格迥异的主题购物商场
- Four Season ever-green gardens, an urban rarity
  四季盎然的罕见绿化空间
- Three-level car park with 1,800 parking space 三层室内停车场
- Two multi-feature water fountains 五彩激光喷泉点缀身边

The Oriental Plaza, a modern commercial giant next to Wangfujing Street, has challenged its neighbour to become the best shopping district in the capital. On September 15, 2000 the Oriental Plaza revealed its commercial layout, which is a single plaza with two parts — Oriental Economy and Trade City and Oriental New World. The former is for offices, apartments, a business hotel and meeting and exhibition centers. The later, covering more than 100, 000 square metres, is composed of five commercial areas with fountains, gardens, parks, culture exhibition halls, cinemas and gymnasiums. The Oriental New World opened by the end of 2000.

New Museum Construction of Palaeo-anthropological Museum began on February 2, 1999. Occupying more than 400 square metres, the museum is on the third underground floor of the Oriental Plaza's West Third Office Building. On top is a parking lot, while the museum is connected to the subway station on Chang'an Boulevard by a tunnel on the west. The museum is 16. 5 metres under the ground, while the relics were found at 12 and 40 metres south from the relics' original location. The Wangfujing relics are mainly the fossils of homoerectus of Paleolithic Era, as well as fossilized bone fragments of elephant and wild buffalo. The discovery shattered one supposition that humans could not live in Beijing's plain areas at that time. The site of ancient man was discovered towards the end of 1996 during the construction of the plaza.

Ministry of Foreign Trade and Economic Co-operation
对外贸易经济合作部

This is the Ministry of Foreign Trade and Economic Co-operation. By the end of 2001, China already established trade and economic relations with more than 230 countries and regions the world over. In 2001 China climbed past Spain and three of the four "Little Dragons" to become the 10th biggest trader in the world. The country, which was ranked 15th in 1991, generated foreign trade volume of more than US$ 509. 77 billion in 2001. China's import and export volume also surpassed that of Taiwan, South Korea and Singapore, three of Asia's "Four Dragons." China's foreign exchange reserves were US$212. 2 billion by the end of 2001.

On average, the annual growth rate of the gross national product in China increased by 9. 5 per cent between 1979 and 2001, with gross domestic product (GDP) totalling 9. 5933 trillion yuan (US$1. 156 trillion) in 2001, making China the 6th biggest economic power in the world trailing the United States, Japan, Germany, France, and England. The per capital GDP for 2001 was about US$ 1, 000.

With contracted overseas investment of US$ 726 billion in 382, 930 enterprises and actual use of US$ 468. 5 billion from more than 180 countries and regions by the end of 2001, China has become the second largest country the world over in attracting overseas investment.

China is now the largest producer of steel, coal, chemical fibres, fertilizer, TV sets and digital switchboards in the world.

World Trade Organization (WTO)

Chinese entrepreneurs are gearing up increased competition and opportunities after China has joined the World Trade Organization (WTO). The WTO announced on September 17, 2001 that China and its major trading partners reached a formal agreement on the membership of the WTO after 15 years of negotiations. The working party on China's accession formally recommended that the WTO's 142 members welcomed China into their fold at the organization's ministerial conference in Doha, Qatar, from November 9 to 13, 2001. China became a formal member of the World Trade Organization (WTO), the multilateral trade body's 143rd member on December 11, 2001. The close of China's 15-year quest to join the WTO is significant to the country, as well as the world. China's WTO membership is expected to promote the country's own reform, opening up and economic development, boost confidence in the global economic growth and secure the development of the multilateral trade mechanism.

China's entry into the WTO will promote the economic development of China and thus enhance its comprehensive national strength, which to a great extent determines the role that his country could play in the international political arena. A country that has strong comprehensive national strength, adopts independent foreign policies of peace and opposes hegemonism will undoubtedly quicken the world's multi-polarization process. China's entry into the WTO will contribute to the development and stability of East Asia, which suffered severe setback during the 1997 financial crisis. WTO membership will bring China and East Asian countries closer together, and China's stable and high-speed economic growth will quicken the pace of economic recovery in those countries. China's entry into the WTO will also help reform the WTO, and facilitate the establishment of a new world order at large. Until now, the WTO has remained a club dominated by developed nations, adopting regulations and rules sometimes favorable only to the interests of rich countries. Developed countries are in the leading position in the globalization process. Only by integrating themselves into the process of globalization can developing countries obtain opportunities for their own development. Seeking WTO entry is the way for developing countries to better defend their own interests. As the largest developing country with one fifth of the world's population, China boasts the largest potential market in the world. A permanent member to the UN Security Council and also a member to the World Bank and the International Monetary Fund, China's WTO entry as a developing country will definitely be conducive to the establishment of a new international economic and political order.

In addition, China's WTO entry will push forward the diversity of world cultures. Cultural cohesion and attractiveness play an important role in the comprehensive national strength. China's achievement in this regard has been widely acknowledged by the world. After the WTO entry, China will expand its culture exchanges while enhancing economic ties with other countries the world over.

China paid WTO US$ 3 million for membership fee in 2002. The membership fee was worked out on the basis of the proportion of China's foreign trade volume in the total of all numbers. China's imports and exports made up at about 3.5 per cent of the world trade body's 144 members in 2001.

Wangfujing Street 王府井大街

After a construction face-lift, the 700-year-old Wangfujing (the Well of the Prince's Mansion) Street or Golden Street, one of China's oldest and most famous commercial areas, was meant to be well known in the world through the renovation, looked brand new to people on September 11, 1999 when it opened to the public. The Wangfujing Street lives up to its glorious past, but with a new look. To give it a new look they completely got rid of the street's poor infrastructure at a price of over 1 billion yuan (US$ 120.5 million). The new infrastructure can sustain the commercial area of 300 square metres to run smoothly for 50 years, with specially designed supplies of electricity, water, gas, communications and transportation. Along the 810-metre-long street and in an area of about 810 square metres are over 200 shops. A 60-member clean-up team for a single commercial area might have been remarkable in scale in Beijing, but expecting them to keep 500,000 visitors, the estimated average daily volume of visitors in the area, to keep the area clean was just unrealistic. The new street can also provide convenience for pedestrians and motorists alike. Take the transportation as an example. Gone for good are the old days of narrow streets jam-packed with people. The area has no problems at its entry and exit even with a half million people and 1,020 vehicles. Also, in spite of being modern and new, the renovated Wangfujing Street has retained its traditional cultural atmosphere. The street is a kind of beauty perfectly combining tradition, modernity, culture and commerce. With a group of sculptures depicting the lives of Beijingers in the old times was established before the modern Sun Dong An Plaza, a 70-square-metre relief sculpture recalling the operation of the 12 old famous shops in the area was set on the southern wall of the Women's Department Store. Also the ancient well, from which the street got its name, was also symbolically restored.

The street came into being in the Yuan Dynasty (1279-1368) more than 700 years ago. Wangfujing Street is said to have received its name in the Ming Dynasty more than 500 years ago. One of the emperors was said to want all his 10 brothers to build their mansions in the place now known as Wangfujing so as to make it easy for him to keep a wary eye on them for fear that they might pose a direct threat to him. Therefore, the street was then named Shiwangfu, meaning mansions for 10 imperial brothers. Nowadays, the street is one of the busy shopping areas in Beijing. There are more than 200 shops on the 810 metre-long street from Nankou of Wangfujing to Goldfish Kou. Tourists love to go shopping here. Within 8 years from 1992 to 1999, 1 billion yuan (US$120 million) was spent on renovating the whole Wangfujing Street, and shops with more than 1.8 million square metres of all kinds of buildings along the street. According to statistics, before 1992, the highest flow of visitors numbered 450,000 every day in Wangfujing Street. Every day about 200,000 shoppers came to Beijing Department Store, but later, about 50,000 came to do shopping at Beijing Department Store. To change the situation, the Beijing municipal government decided to restore all the shops and the street so that they want to attract more people to come to the street reputed as "a golden street" by the people of Beijing.

Wangfujing Street has presented a shining new face after the second phase of its extension project was completed on September 11, 2000. The traffic conditions in the Wangfujing area have been greatly improved thanks to the construction of new roads, such as the Department Store West Road, running parallel to Wangfujing, and the expansion of old ones like Dengshikou Xijie Street, which runs perpendicular to Wangfujing. More than 330 public and private buildings have been removed to make way for roads, trees and lawns. Donghuamen night fair, the centre of the street, has received a face-lift and serves as a food court for visitors. The newly renovated Wangfujing Roman Catholic Church, originally built in 1905, is now decorated with lights at night. The 340-million-yuan (US$41 million) project aims to make Wangfujing Street the capital's biggest shopping centre. The street has been extended from 810 metres to 1,150 metres (Wangfujing Nankou to Dengshi Xikou), and expanded to include shopping, entertainment, tourism and business. According to the practices of developed countries, places for entertainment and tourism should occupy half of the commercial centre as a whole, Wangfujing was brought up to this standard after renovation. The Jinyu(Goldfish) *Hutong* on the east side of the street has been turned into an avenue of hotels and restaurants, while a back street on the west side has been built into a street of snack bars and was reopened to the public on September 11, 2000.

The Wangfujing area is in the heart of Beijing, next to the Forbidden City, and Tian'anmen Square. Sitting on the north side of Chang'an (Eternal Peace) Boulevard, Wangfujing area is home to the Minstistry of Foreign Trade and Economic Co-operation, the Beijing Municipal Government and many other government offices, making it the city's most strategic location. The commercial history of the Wangfujing area goes back hundreds of years. It became a prosperous commercial area in the later Qing Dynasty (1644-1911). After New China was established, the Wangfujing area gradually became the city's landmark commercial centre. It was well-known all over China for its comprehensiveness, fashion, high quality and sophisticated cultural activities. The area's development entered a new stage in the 1980s. Star-rated hotels such as the Tianlun Dynasty Hotel and Palace Hotel were built, together with Peace Hotel, Taiwan Hotel, Beijing Hotel and the Grand Hotel Beijing. Wangfujing has become the area with the greatest concentration of first-class hotels in Beijing. This has laid a solid foundation for business activities. The opening of the Sun Dong An Plaza and the One World Department Store has helped to attract more visitors to the area—they are now estimated to total 400,000 per day. In the 1990s, China's opening policies have attracted more and more foreign investors to set up offices in Beijing. With its strategic location, business facilities and support services, the Wangfujing area should have been an ideal lo-

Dong'anmen Street

803 103 104 420

Jinyu Hutong

Foreign Languages Book Store

Sun Dong An Plaza

Drugstore Ginseng & Antler

New China Children's Articles Store

Department Store

Wangfujing Famous Watches Store

Daruanfu Hutong

Yanwen Zhai

Quanjude (Repository of All Virtues) Roast Duck Restaurant

Shanghai Yaksi Suit Shop
Daming Spectacles Company

Wangfujing

Datianshuijin Hutong

Youhao Shijie Shop

Shuaifuyuan

Wangfujing Provision Shop

Wangfujing Snack Street

Street

Ruifuxiang

Beijing Painting Shop

Shengxifu Hat Store

Wangfujing Women's Department Shop

Wangfujing Book Store

Dongdan Santiao

Arts & Crafts Store

Chenxi Department Shop

Xiagongfu Street

1 37 52
4 120 420
10 205 802
20 728

Beijing Hotel

Xindongfang Tiandi

E. Chang'an Boulevard

Wangfujing

Wangfujing Mall

cation for many multinational companies. However, due to the shortage of Grade-A office space in the area, many foreign investors had to find offices on the Second and Third Ring roads. The renovation of Wangfujing Street, and especially the completion of the Beijing Oriental Plaza, has met the demand for top-class office space in the area. The Oriental Plaza has eight office buildings, a 600-room five-star hotel, two service-apartment buildings and a 100, 000-square-metre shopping centre. Wangfujing area has become the city's central business district because of its easy access to major roads, high land prices and high density of retail and service business, as well as its high degree of population flow. Nowadays, the Wangfujing area has been formed naturally in the city's centre, in much the same way as most central business districts have sprung up in other international cities.

At present, there are five major commercial areas such as Wangfujing commercial area, Xidan commercial area, Dazhalan commercial area, Longfusi commercial area and Chaoyangmenwai commercial area.

Wangfujing Information Platform

Beijing telecommunications and the digital Wangfujing Technology Company have jointly established the information platform for Wangfujing, the capital city's shopping centre. The project involved information infrastructure construction, government service digitalization, enterprises' online businesses and financial network improvement. Since 2001, an online business group, a public information service platform and a network commercial center have been set in Wangfujing.

Bungee Towers 蹦极

The bungee jumping towers installed in August 2000 in Wangfujing have inspired debate amongst experts and residents. The 30-metre high double towers have been erected opposite a centuries-old Catholic Church, in a little square in front of the Lisheng Sport Shopping Centre near the entrance of the new Wangfujing extension line (the total distance from Wangfujing Beikou to Dengshi Xikou is 430 metres), opened officially on September 11, 2000. Construction of the towers is a part of the second phase of the street's upgrading project.

Beijing Department Store 北京市百货大楼

Founded in 1955, and with an investment of 4. 5 million yuan, Beijing Department Store, the first large-scale shopping mall in Beijing after New China was established in 1949, reopened to the public on August 28, 1999 after a five-month-long massive refurbishment. The department store—the biggest in the retail business sector for decades—has a favourable reputation due to its top-notch service and more than 2, 000 brands in over 70, 000 varieties of goods. The store has made itself known as the place to easily find daily necessities as well as a place the customer can trust.

The Church Restored

Built in 1655, the Catholic Church on Wangfujing Street was revamped in 2000. It is set to be one of the street's main attractions.

Sun Dong An Plaza 新东安商场

Located in the capital's busiest commercial centre of Wangfujing, the Dong'an Bazaar started its renovation on November 18, 1993 and was completed and opened to business on January 18, 1998. The project drew an investment of US$ 386 million (3.2 billion yuan) from Hong Kong Sun Hong Kai Properties LTD and Dong'an Group Company. It is the largest joint venture commercial project in Beijing since it opened to the outside world. The 12-storey new shopping centre can handle 500, 000 customers everyday. The plaza replaced Dong'an Market, which opened in 1903 and was Beijing's first department store. Dong'an Market previously had only 6, 900 square metres. The new complex, which has rejuvenated the Wangfujing area as a forest of shopping malls, has changed the capital's skyline. The project, which began in 1993, was completed by 2000. A station on the central subway line opened in the area by the end of 1999. Sun Dong An Plaza serves as a litmus test to the development of giant commercial complexes in Beijing.

With a total floor space of 220, 000 square metres, the plaza provides comprehensive shopping, offices, restaurants and entertainment centres. It is regarded as the city's first move to update commercial facilities in Wangfujing. The plaza is computerized for quicker sales and inventory. They are also warehouses and cinemas opened in Sun Dong An Plaza later 1998.

The 90-year-old bazaar boasted a sales volume of 442 million yuan (US$ 76 million) in 1992. Though located at Wangfujing, it needed reconstruction because of limited business space and out of date facilities.

"Old Beijing Street" 老北京一条街

People can now experience what the old Beijing looked like and how the people lived in ancient times while shopping in the modern mall of Sun Dong An Plaza on Wangfujing Street in downtown Beijing. The so-called "Old Beijing Street" formally opened on June 28, 2000 and is designed in archaism, displaying the royal court and civilians' town pictures and folk stories during the Ming and Qing dynasties.

There are 60 shops including 40 famous-brand stores and some entertainment and relaxing places such as a food street, a teahouse, a culture street, a magic ancient house and the four-room courtyard.

The street is located on the ground floor of the Sun Dong An Plaza.

New Theatre

Beijing now boasts a new four-screen Cineplex opened by the Beijing Sun Dong An Co Ltd on the fifth floor of its Sun Dong An Plaza on Wangfujing Street. The cinema facilities were imported from the United States. Also, the company opened a paint-ball battlefield in the plaza, which combines military paint-ball sports with amusement.

Beijing Hotel 北京饭店

Beijing Hotel(five-star hotel) is one of the biggest hotels in the city. It consists of three major sections, with over 900 rooms of varying standards. Its new wing, a 17-storey building, was opened in 1974. The middle section was built in 1917 and renovated in 1982, while the western part was constructed in 1955. All the facade of Beijing Hotel was thoroughly renovated in 1999 to mark the 50th anniversary of the founding of the People's Republic of China. The hotel has a very good location.

Grand Hotel Beijing 北京贵宾楼

The finest location of all the hotels in Beijing is undoubtedly that of Grand Hotel (five-star hotel). Not only does it overlook the Forbidden City, but it is only a short stroll down Chang'an Boulevard—the first street in China—to Tian'anmen Square. The important shopping street of Wangfujing is practically next door and the beautiful Beihai Park is a charming walk away.

With 218 luxurious rooms and suites blending the best of ancient Chinese and modern Western decor and furniture, an extensive range of facilities for business and pleasure, a wide choice of restaurants and bars with elegant cuisine, the Grand Hotel Beijing offers the most personalized service. The Grand Hotel Beijing is also one of the leading hotels of the world.

China National Textiles Import and Export Corporation
中国纺织品进出口总公司

Established in November 1951, China National Import and Export Corporation's (CHINATEX) total import and export volume has reached more than US\$100 billion. It has established business relations with about 7,000 clients from more than 170 countries and regions in the world. It is involved in the country's import and export of all sorts of textile materials, semi-finished and finished textile products, garments, knitwear and other

commodities with government approval. Meanwhile Chinatex acts as an a-
gent for the imports and exports of the above businesses. It also engages in
joint-ventures, co-operation, manufacturing with imported materials and
according to customers' designs and samples, sparepart assemblage, import and export of new and advanced technology, re-export, compensation
trade, counter and barter trade. In recent years, Chinatex has diversified
its business to other fields, including high and new technology, project
transfer, enterprise resource planning, intercontinental shipping and cargo
handling, advertising, exhibitions, international trade information and data
service, consultation, labor and service export and technology exchanges.
Similarly, through joint ventures and co-management, Chinatex also participate in domestic wholesale and retail, textiles and garments industries,
restaurants, and hotels and other businesses. However, at the outset of
Chinatex's business, its annual business value was only some ten millions
of US dollars. During the past five decades, in keeping with the enterprises' spirit of unity, creativity, tenacity and practicality and through
painstaking efforts, Chinatex has developed from a traditional foreign trade
company into a world-class diversified conglomerate, contributing much to
the country's foreign trade in textiles. Chinatex is not only dedicated to
developing the country's textile product export but also imports of huge
amounts of textile fiber materials in short supply in China, offering tremendous business opportunities for traders from the international fiber industry.
At present, Chinatex boosts more than 20 subsidiaries directly under itself,
over 20 branches and affiliated enterprises and about 20 overseas enterprises and offices around the world. These organizations form a well-integrated
network. To meet the challenge and opportunities opening up with economic globalization and China's entry into the WTO, Chinatex actively draws
on experiences of prestigious domestic and overseas corporations to further
enhance its competitiveness. Based on its re-devised operation and management system, it has mapped out its long-term development objectives.
Chinatex is willing to join hands with her counterparts throughout the world
in order to make greater contributions to further the enlargement of international exchange.

Shopping Mart 商业区

Located in the city centre north of Beijing Hotel, the Hualong
(Chinese-Dragon) Dining and Shopping Centre opened in Beijing in Octo-
ber 1988 providing tourists with a colourful souvenir hunting environment.
The new complex is comprised of five traditional Chinese-style buildings.
The centre has been built in the shape of a dragon, and the fresh new fa-

cades are likely to make window-shopping almost as much fun as spending money. Covering an area of over 39,000 square metres, the centre has 14 restaurants offering Chinese, Korean, Japanese and Western food. The World Fine Food Centre, where customers can enjoy the famous Kentucky Fried Chicken, is decorated in Hawaiian style. About six large department stores and shops stock daily necessities such as jewelry, medicine, and a variety of imported goods. The centre also has a foreign exchange counter. There are snack bars, cafes, and disco halls where people can relax after meal or shopping trip.

The Imperial City Wall Relics Park 皇城根遗址公园

Also known as the Huangchenggen Relics Park and built in 2001, the park stretches from East Chang'an Boulevard in the south to Ping'an Avenue in the north, totalling 2.4 kilometres in length. The park is only 29 metres in width. Within the park, there are 40,000 square metres of lawn, 44,000 square metres of bushes and 78 varieties of various kinds of plants. It opened to the public in September 2001.

Tian'anmen Square 天安门广场

Tian'anmen Square encompasses 44 hectares (108.7 acres), 880 metres from north to south and 500 metres from east to west, big enough to hold half a million people. The square has witnessed the Chinese people's struggle against foreign aggression and reactionary rule at home.

In 1919, the May 4th Movement broke out in Beijing. Students and residents staged a patriotic demonstration in the square. In 1935, students in Beijing launched the December 9th Movement against the Japanese aggression and Chiang Kai-shek's policy of non-resistance. They held a demonstration in the square.

On April 5, 1976, thousands of people gathered here to commemorate the late premier Zhou Enlai and oppose the "Gang of Four." Many tourists to Tian'anmen Square would like to have their pictures taken in front of the white marble Jinshuiqiao (Golden Water Bridges).

The bridges were named after the Golden Water River they span. Seven bridges, each supported by three arches, cross the Outer Golden Water River in front of Tian'anmen, Zhongshan Park, and the Beijing Working People's Palace of Culture. Five one-arched bridges cross the Inner Golden Water River inside the Forbidden City between Wumen (Meridian Gate) and Taihemen (Gate of Supreme Harmony).

The outer bridges, together with two graceful *Huabiao* (ornamental columns) and two stone lions nearby, set off Tian'anmen, making it look more imposing. The inner bridges make the spacious square look harmonious.

During the Ming and Qing (1368-1911) dynasties, the middle one of the seven outer bridges, which is larger than the others was called Yuluqiao 御路桥 (Bridge of the Imperial Way) and was used exclusively by the Emperor. The two bridges on each side were called Wanggongqiao 王公桥 (Royal Bridges) and were used by the royal family members. The two bridges farther out were the Pinjiqiao 品级桥 (Ranking Bridges) and were used by civil and military officials above the third rank. Those of the fourth rank and below could use only the outer two bridges, which were called Gongshengqiao 公生桥 (Public Bridges).

The Beijing municipal government launched a nine-month project to renovate Tian'anmen Square in the heart of the capital. The reconstruction, started in October 1998 and was completed by June 1999, in time for the grand celebrations to mark the 50th anniversary of the founding of the People's Republic of China on October 1, 1999, improved the worn-out pavement, public address system, and lighting around the periphery of the world's largest square, installing new foundations and repairing underground pipelines. The bricks on the square were replaced with 340,000 pink granite slabs to cover 156,900 square metres (the gradient of the square is 3 per thousand easy for flow of rainwater and each slab is 99.5 cm × 49.5 cm ×15 cm) and shipped in from nearby Hebei Province (they are said to be wear and tear proof and have a more beautiful finish), the public-address system modernized, the low-wattage street lights replaced with more efficient ones, and more decorative lights installed to illuminate the buildings around the square. All these slabs weighed 130,000 tons, with 50,000 cubic metres. Fifty eight spot checks were made during the construction of the whole project. The goal was to create a 21st century style square which reflects China's modernity, and new capital. The first renovation of Tian'anmen Square took place in 1959.

The renovation of the square was part of Beijing's move to improve its appearance for the celebration of the 50th anniversary of the founding of the People's Republic of China.

A grand parade marking the 50th anniversary of the founding of the People's Republic of China (PRC) was staged on the morning of October 1, 1999 in Tian'anmen Square in central Beijing. The square was turned into a huge garden with millions of potted flowers. The five-star red flag—China's national flag—could be seen all over the city. Some 500,000 people, military and civilians, gathered in the square and adjacent streets, in anticipation of the moment they had all been waiting for—the start of the parade at 10: 00 am. President Jiang Zemin and other top officials, reviewed the troops, and military vehicles, missiles and warplanes, most of which were made in China. After the military parade came the turn of civil society with various activities to celebrate the grand occasion, including the performance of a traditional dragon dance. Dozens of specially designated floats featuring China's major social and economic developments during the past five decades thrilled the audience as they passed through the square.

The Grand National Day parade ended with the release of tens of thousands of colorful balloons. Some 50, 000 homing pigeons were also let loose in the skies over the square. New China has staged 13 National Day military parades and celebration activities in Tian'anmen Square since it was founded in 1949.

In the evening of the same day, fireworks lit up the Beijing sky as 100, 000 jubilant Chinese took part in a song and dance extravaganza in Tian'anmen Square to celebrate the 50th anniversary of the founding of the People's Republic of China.

Working People's Palace of Culture 劳动人民文化宫

The Working People's Palace of Culture lies to the east of Tian'anmen. This place used to be the Ancestral Temple in the Ming and Qing dynasties. Now it has become a place where working people in Beijing come to enjoy cultural performances.

Huabiao (White Marble Ornamental Column) 华表

An ornamental column usually made of marble, placed before bridges, palaces, city walls and tombs in ancient times. The stem of the pillar is often carved with coiling dragons and other designs, while near the top a sculptured cloud extends horizontally through the center of the column. A carved stone beast squats in a dish at the top. The finest extant *huabiao* are the two pairs to the south and north of Tian'anmen Gate (Gate of Heavenly Peace).

A "dish for collecting dew" tops *Huabiao* (white marble ornamental column). A carved stone animal known as a "heaven-gazing *hou*" (a small, lion-like legendary creature) squats inside each dish. The purpose of these dishes was to catch the "jade dew" imbibed by the emperor to ensure long life. According to local legend, the "heaven-gazing *hou*" kept watch on the emperor's activities while he was away from the Palace, anxiously awaited his early return and hoped that he would not overindulge in pleasure seeking. If the emperor did not return in good time, the creatures would warn him, "Your majesty, you mustn't spend so much time enjoying yourself. Hurry back and attend to state affairs! Awaiting your return, we've nearly worn our eyes out!" Thus, the pair of "heaven-gazing *hou*" have another name—"Watching for the Monarch's Return," and the ornamental stone columns are known as the "Watching Columns."

Flower Beds 花坛

The four flower beds covering an area of about 5,000 square metres have been laid out in front of Tian'anmen Gate. The flower beds are surrounded by bushes and potted cedars.

Tian'anmen Square Subway Stations and Its Underground Passage 天安门地铁车站及其地下通道

The eastern and western Tian'anmen Square Subway stations were linked up on September 24, 1996. The Tian'anmen section, part of the Fuxingmen-Bawangfen subway project, was built to help ease excess traffic in the downtown area of the City of Beijing. The western station has two levels, one with three entrances and exits. The three-floor eastern station has seven entrances and exits.

The Underground Passage was designed by the Beijing Municipal Designing Institute. Work on the Tian'anmen Underground Passage started in January 1987 and opened to pedestrians on schedule on May 1st of the same year. The passage has six exits and entrances. Its two north-south tunnels and two east-west tunnels are each 12 metres wide and 2.9 metres high. Their total length is 340 metres (including 254-metre-wide slope designed for the disabled).

The tunnels have relieved congestion and improved safety in the square. About 30,000 pedestrians and 6,000 motored vehicles pass Tian'anmen every hour at peak times. There are also 13 bus routes in front of Tian'anmen arches, and about 1 million people flow through the area every day. Beijing is experiencing increasing traffic congestion, with over 10 million bicycles and over 1 million cars and trucks on the streets every day.

The Great Hall of the People 人民大会堂

Located on the west side of Tian'anmen, the Great Hall of the People was built between October 1958 and August 1959. The hall, with a floor space of 171,800 square metres, and propped up using 134 giant columns, is magnificent in architectural style and carries rich national tints. The major conference hall of the Great Hall of the People is large enough to accommodate 10, 000 people, and its banquet hall can hold 5, 000 guests. The Great Hall of the People boasts more than 300 multi-functional feast halls, meeting rooms and offices. They include over 30 meeting lounges named after various provinces, autonomous regions, municipalities directly under the central government and special administrative regions; they reflect the features of these areas and Chinese national style. The Great Hall of the People has become an important venue for China's most important political, economic, cultural and diplomatic activities.

Central and South Seas (Zhongnanhai) 中南海

Now we come to the Central and South Seas or Zhongnanhai in Chinese. It is located on the west of the Forbidden City. The area used to be called "three seas," Western Lake or Pool of Great Secretion 太液池. It covers an area of 100 hectares (247 acres), of which the seas occupy 47 hectares (116 acres). It was first built in Liao (907-1125) and rebuilt in Jin (1115-1234), Yuan (1279-1368), Ming (1368-1644), and Qing (1644-1911) dynasties. The area used to be the travelling palace and a place for tour and banquets for the feudal emperors. After the demise of the Qing Dynasty in 1911, it served as the headquarters of the government of Yuan Shikai.

After the overthrown of the Qing Dynasty in 1911, the Central and South Lakes were turned into a park for a short period of time and served as the headquarters of the government of Yuan Shikai (1859-1916). Since the founding of the People's Republic of China, it has been the headquarters of the Central Committee of. the Chinese Communist Party and the State Council of the People's Republic of China. It is now not only the supreme leading centre for the whole nation, but also one of the important places for both the Chinese people and international friendly intercourse. The late Chairman Mao Zedong (1893-1976) and the late Premier Zhou Enlai (1898-1976) used to live in it.

Ethics Building of Citizens 公民道德建设

The building of a comprehensive moral code began in China during the first year of the 21st century to keep up the country's lasting reputation for virtue. Almost everyone, from top leaders to the man on the street, has taken part in the campaign, which aims to build up "a socialist ethical code" for the development of a market economy with its own characteristics. Early 2001, when the idea of ruling China by law and morality was proposed by President Jiang Zemin, it aroused warm response from the public. In a speech on July 1, 2001 to mark the 80th anniversary of the founding of the Communist Party of China, President Jiang Zemin reiterated his

63

idea by defining ongoing moral development as a crucial part of the nation's task for "developing an advanced socialist culture." The Implementation Outline on Ethics Building of Citizens 公民道德建设实施纲要 issued by the Central Committee of the Communist Party of China, has helped widen and deepen the moral reconstruction campaign. The media has pointed out that these days some Chinese citizens have acted in an immoral way, straying from the country's thousand-year-old valued moral code such as "The benevolent shall love others 仁者爱仁," an instruction given by Chinese philosopher, Confucius more than 2,000 years ago. But today's moral degradation in some aspects has reflected the country's increasing conflict relating to material interests.

With the country's economic transition from central planning to market orientation, new ethical standards like the awareness of competition and working hard to survive have become so pervasive that some people misinterpret them as "profit overrides everything 利润高于一切." Regional disparity in development levels in a modern economy has widened the gap in opportunities and incomes. In the pursuit of fortune and happiness, some people who worship hedonism began to give up traditional moral standards such as tolerance, frugality and modesty to make money in whatever way they could. A lack of moral standards could lead to corruption, could disturb social order, hinder economic reform and finally tarnish China's image in international communities as a virtuous country. Some foreign investors are baffled with China's "red envelope," a euphemism for palm-greasing, and "connections," a euphemism for nepotism "红包"和"关系"分别是向某人行贿和裙带关系的委婉说法.

With China's entry to the World Trade Organization (WTO) and Beijing's successful bid for the 2008 Olympic Games, the Chinese Government has seen the importance of a national ethical code to help social construction. Simply using compulsory legal means will not produce a prosperous and stable China with the ability to follow the fast pace of the global economy. In contrast, developing an ethical code will be more powerful in shaping people's moral outlook as demonstration and persuasion are convincing. Ever since the bid for the 2008 Olympic Games, a nationwide discussion about ethical standards has taken place in China. Confucius's epigram of "learning from moral models" is coming back again. The media has publicized a number of moral heroes from all walks of life. Moral standards proposed by the Implementation Outline on Ethics Building of Citizens such as love of the motherland, abiding by the law, behaving correctly, credibility, honesty, kindness, frugality, and devotion to one's career have become widely recognized. （爱国守法　明礼诚信　团结友善　勤

俭自强 敬业奉献）

Beijing Concert Hall 北京音乐厅

The Beijing Concert Hall is located at Liubukou on West Chang' an (Eternal Peace) Boulevard in Xicheng District. In 1950, the government took over the Central Cinema, renovating it into Beijing's first concert hall to promote the development of New China's music. During the "cultural revolution" from 1966-1976, the concert hall was nearly destroyed. By the end of 1970s with the support of musicians such as Li Delun(1917-2001) (also reputed as a world-famous conductor), the government allocated 9 million yuan (US$ 1. 1 million)to reconstruct and enlarge the hall. Since its grand opening on January 4, 1986 the Beijing Concert Hall has become a renowned venue for professional musicians.

With a seating capacity of more than 1, 100, the Beijing Concert Hall boasts a modern architectural design and facilities that create superb a-coustics; sealed sound-proof doors block out all exterior noise. Capable of holding a 100-piece symphony orchestra or a 100-person chorus, the large stage was designed without a proscenium to bring the performers and audience closer together. A white structure with a black marble base, the concert hall is adorned with a copper-inlaid east wall and an abstract sculpture representing musical scores.

Since its re-opening in 1986, the Beijing Concert Hall has already hosted many world famous musicians, as well as overseas Chinese artists including Tang Muhai, Chen Zuohuang, Hu Yongyan; singers Fu Haijian, Zhu Ailan, Dilibaier, Wang Yanyan and instrumentalists Xu Zhong, Kong Xiangdong, and others.

Telegraph Office 电报大楼

This Telegraph Office was built in 1958. It handles communications by cable, telephone, radio, fax and telex.

Opposite the Telegraph Office is a movie house. In Beijing there are 103 cinemas and more than 60 theatres. Most of the films are produced in China. Sometimes foreign films are also shown.

CAAC Building 民航大楼

This is the office building of the Chinese airline, Civil Aviation Administration of China. The booking office is at Xidan. There are now 23 airlines in China.

Xidan 西单

Xidan commercial street has stretched 880 metres from the Xidan cross-roads to Lingjing Hutong, with a width of 70 metres. A group of corridors has been built between various shops, business centres and office buildings, and has become a hub for clothes vendors, as are the two underground floors in the Xidan subway station. The New Xidan Street is mainly composed of special shops with famous brands and stores for high-tech products, including computers, software and telecommunications-related commodities. The street concentrates on the development of entertainment, recreation, and food, and drinking sectors. It is one of the major shopping centres in the western part of Beijing. What strong appeal Xidan offers to consumers is the bustling commercial atmosphere. The area has been transformed from a traditional commercial marketplace into a comprehensive commercial area bringing catering, entertainment, culture, tourism, finance, hotels, real estate and telecommunications together with commerce at the core. Xidan Food Market, the Snack Centre, the Kangle Sports Centre and the National Product Sales Centre will be built in Xidan commercial area in the next five years.

At present, there are eight large markets in the area, including Xidan market, Xidan CVIK Store, Xidan Shopping Centre, and Zhongyou Department Store. Xidan Market ranked first in Beijing for several years in a row in terms of annual sales. It is one of China's top five large markets in terms of sales volume. Xidan Market received 500,000 consumers during the four holiday weeks of the year.

Picai Hutong

Lingjing Hutong (Lane)

Xidan CVIK Plaza

Xidan Department Store

Xidan Business Office
of China Unicom

Xidan N. Street

Xidan Shopping Centre

Computer Aggregation
of Mobile Phone

808
102 806
105 826
109 726
22   603
     47

Xidan Commercial Street

Huasheng Clothing
Store

Minzu Dashijie

Beijing Book Building

Building of
Bank of China

Zhongyou Store

Cultural
Square

Fuxingmennei Avenue   W. Chang'an Boulevard

Xidan

Beijing Book Building 北京图书大厦

Here comes the Beijing Book Building, and opened to the public on May 18, 1998. The building has 8 floors above the ground and 3 floors underneath, with a total floor space of more than 50, 000 square metres. More than 160, 000 varieties of publications are available for sale. It is one of the largest modern bookstores both in Beijing and in China. On March 9, 1999, it opened a bookstore on Internet and the customer can buy books on the Internet without going to the bookstore. Each year this kind of Internet bookstore can receive one million surfers and purchasers.

Xidan Cultural Square 西单文化广场

Xidan Cultural Square—an Oasis in Busy Shopping Centre 西单文化广场 ——闹市"绿洲"

West of the Beijing Book Building is the Xidan Cultural Square. Encompassing 21, 600 square metres, with a floor space of 35, 000 square metres, the square cost 600 million yuan (US$72.55 million). The West City District Government and Huayang Real Estate Coporation constructed it to mark the 50th anniversary of the founding of the People's Republic of China in 1999.

Construction of the square is divided into the above ground cultural square and commercial and entertainment area, which is connected with the Xidan Subway. Every year lots of recreational and sports activities are organized in the square.

Popular science corridor and the historical scenery sculptures of Xidan area are established along the four directions of the above ground cultural square; commercial and entertainment area includes shops, a cinema, a swimming pool, skating-rink and squash court.

The square acts as an oasis of peace in the midst of a modren metropolis.

67

The Headquarters of Bank of China 中国银行总行大厦

This is the headquarters of Bank of China located in Xidan commercial district. It took 6 years to complete. The 84-year-old Ieoh Ming Pei 贝聿铭, renowned architect, appreciated the design of the Bank of China's headquarters 中国银行总行大厦 in Beijing on June 27, 2001. The building, designed by Pei Partnership Architects 贝氏建筑设计事务所 led by Pei's second son Chien Chune Pei 贝建中, won the 2001 Tucker Award issued by the American Stone Institute 中银大厦获美国石料建筑协会 2001 年的 Tucker 奖.

Cultural Palace for Nationalities 民族文化宫

This is the Cultural Palace for Nationalities designed in traditional Chinese style. It is one of the ten architectural landmarks, including the Great Hall of the People, Beijing Railway Station, Museums of Chinese History and the Chinese Revolution, the Military Museum and others erected in 1959 to commemorate the tenth anniversary of the founding of the People's Republic of China.

The building consists of a central tower and two three-storey wings. The tower, 67 metres high with 13 storeys, was in its time one of Beijing's tallest structures.

The central tower holds 18 exhibition halls and a library. The two wings are devoted to entertainment and recreation, housing an auditorium, a club and a dance dinner hall.

With the development of China's tourism and the increased relations with foreign countries, the 20 well-furnished suites on the third floor are opened for the stay of tourists. They can hold banquets, cocktail parties and tea parties in the dance dinner hall.

After China's Olympic athletes took 15 gold medals in the Los Angeles Games in 1984, the nation's sports enthusiasts were eager to try many other events, including bowling, which is likely to become an Olympic event in the future.

Because bowling requires a large indoor space, it has been regarded in China as a luxurious activity and only a few people have dabbled in it in the past.

Ryonosuke Hasebe, a Japanese businessman, in early 1985 donated bowling equipment to the Palace and helped install it within two weeks. On March 1, 1985 the palace officially opened a four lane alley and held its first bowling match. The bowling lanes are open every evening.

The Cultural Palace for Nationalities was designed in 1956. The designer incorporated the traditional terrace-style used in the three main halls in the Forbidden City, and also in the Hall of Prayer for Good Harvests in the Temple of Heaven. The terrace-style was often used in structures, which reflected solemnity and majesty. The Cultural Palace was designed to have a mixture of entertainment centers and residential apartments, specifically designated for the use of minority groups.

With unity for the country's ethnic groups as its theme, the designer based the main design for the structure on the culture of the Han people. He then added touches of architecture from the minority peoples. The main tower of the Palace stands on two- and three-tier platforms, with the east and west wings in the shape of a U. Typically Chinese with green glazed tiles, the roof is not a copy of any traditional style. Instead, it has several small and large pavilions on top. And the interior of the building has a Tibetan and Islamic decor. The designer was also very concerned about outlines and skylines, which were important elements in traditional architectural designs. The Palace, located along Chang'an (Eternal Peace) Boulevard, is blended in well with the surrounding buildings. It was one of the most distinctive modern classical structures to be constructed in 1959. It occupied relatively little land, yet served several functions.

Ethnic Minorities in China 中国少数民族

With a total population of 108 million China has five autonomous regions, 30 autonomous prefectures and 123 autonomous counties, which occupy 64.3 per cent of the country's total area and they are all rich in natural resources. The system of ethnic regional autonomy is enjoyed by 44 minority nationalities, which comprise roughly 75 per cent of the population of China's minority nationalities.

China has 55 ethnic minority groups, in addition to the Han majority. Since New China was founded in 1949, the Chinese Government has made continous efforts to promote unity among different nationalities and develop new-style socialist relations and communication among nationalities. Strengthening unity among different nationalities and safeguarding the State unity are intimately connected with the fundamental interests of people of every nationality in China. A legal system for minority nationalities has been set up. China promulgated the law on Regional Autonomy for Minority Nationalities in 1984. Since then, it has enacted a set of laws and regulations concerning minority nationalities. To date, 119 autonomous regions, prefectures and counties have formulated regulations on the exercise of autonomy. Some 52 specific regulations on language, culture and education, marriage and family planning have also been published in minority autonomous areas. Meanwhile, the economy in areas inhabited by people of minority nationalities has developed steadily in recent years. The living standards of people in these areas have improved greatly. Statistics show that the gross national product, national income and gross output value of industry and agriculture in the five autonomous regions and three multinational provinces increased.

There are five aspects concerning the country's nationality affairs in this decade which require particular attention.

(1) Economic development in minority regions should be speeded up so as to keep pace with the development in the whole country;

(2) The country should spare no effort to develop social welfare for minority people in minority areas in a bid to promote the overall development of all minority nationalities without discrimination;

(3) China should adhere to its on-going policies of reform and opening to the rest of the world in order to be able to ceaselessly strengthen the ability of the minority ethnic groups and the minority regions to develop under their own steam;

(4) China should continue to constantly adhere to and improve the autonomy system in the minority regions and whole-heartedly carry out the law on regional autonomy for China's minority nationalities;

(5) China should continue to further strengthen the grand unity among all Chinese nationalities as a firm safeguard for the long-term unity of the country and its emergence on equal footing with the modern industrialized nations of the world's internationalized economy.

Minzu (Nationalities) Hotel 民族饭店

This is the Minzu (Nationalities) Hotel (four-star hotel) built in 1959. It has more than 600 rooms.

China is a multi-national unitary state. Apart from the Han people who make up 92% of China's population, there are 55 minority nationalities (108 million people in 2000). The ethnic group people in China account for 8% who inhabit nearly 60% of China's territory. China has 31 administrative divisions, of which 5 are autonomous regions. Minority people usually live in compact communities in border regions or remote areas. Special fund is given to those areas for developing economy and culture.

About 480, 000 ethnic minority people, 3.84 per cent of the population, live in Beijing. The capital is the only Chinese city that has all 55 of the country's minority nationalities living there.

China Industrial and Commercial Bank 中国工商银行

This is China Industrial and Commercial Bank, completed and put into use in 1999. Nineteen Ninety-nine saw two more Chinese mainland firms join the Fortune Global 500 list: the Industrial and Commercial Bank of China (ICBC) and China Petrochemical Corp (Sinopec). The other three mainland firms on the list are the Bank of China(BOC), the China National Chemical Import and Export Corp(Sinochem), and the China National Cereals, Oils and Foodstuff Import and Export Corp(COFCO). Sinopec was ranked 73rd and ICBC 160th on the list. Both companies participated in Fortune's appraisal system held in Shanghai in late September for the first time. BOC, Sinochem and COFCO, ranked 171st, 304th and 362nd on the list. The heads of these Chinese pioneers were convinced that more Chinese companies would join them in the future as China continues to open up and progress.

Industrial and Commercial Bank of China (ICBC) is the largest State-owned commercial bank in China with total assets exceeding RMB 4, 000 billion. It enjoys a leading position in technology among domestic banks and more than 99% of its offices are computer-operated. The annual volume of settlement business conducted by ICBC accounts for more than 50% of that conducted by financial institutions in China. In 2000, ICBC was awarded Bank of the Year 2000 for China and Best Domestic Bank in China by the Banker and Euromoney respectively. ICBC ranks the 7th among the world's top banks in terms of tier one capital, according to The Banker's latest published list of world commercial banks for the years 2001. Since its first participation in the Fortune Global 500 list in 1999, ICBC has ranked 160th, 208th and 213th respectively for the last three years.

Beijing Ocean Plaza (COSCO) 北京远洋大厦

China's Ocean Shipping Companies Group (COSCO), the country's biggest shipping operator, has built its own flagship headquarters on Beijing Finance Street, the city's financial hub. Beijing Ocean Plaza, located, on the other side of the People's Banks of China, has 17 storeys and three basements with a total floor space of nearly 100, 000 square metres. The building design had been modified five times, eventually gathering the strong points from both the domestic construction design agency and partners from the United States. The night scene of the building by installing special lantern decoration to be compatible with the famous Chang' an Boulevard has been cared about.

Beijing Ocean Plaza, with estimated investment of 2. 15 billion yuan (US$259 million) is designated as one of the top 10 projects in the Chinese capital, which contributed to the 50th anniversary of the founding of the People's Republic of China. The materials and equipment used for the building were mostly imported. The plaza also houses an international club to serve the tenants.

Established in 1961, the company is evolving from a traditional ocean-shipping enterprise into a transnational comprehensive logistics provider with a shipping agency, marine bunker supply, road transport, airfreight forwarding and Internet business. COSCO also has expanded its interests in recent years to real estate, industry, international trade and finance.

71

Foreign Sculpture in Beijing

A gorgeous sculpture has found a home in the Chinese capital, the first work by a Western artist to go on permanent display in Beijing. "Just Us," a six-ton stainless steel sculpture designed by British artist Briton Richard Deacon, has been placed in the lobby of Ocean Plaza, a new office building on Chang' an Boulevard. The abstract piece, which is 7.1 metres long, 6.5 metres wide and 4.8 metres high, was purchased at 3 million yuan(US$361,000) by the plaza, which is run by the big-name Chinese shipping company COSCO. The work was produced according to Deacon's design in Beijing under the supervision of sculptor Sui Jianguo, professor and director of the Sculpture Department of the Central Academy of Fine Arts. This is the first time that a Chinese enterprise has purchased a sculpture designed by a leading European sculptor, and it is especially significant given the fact that the piece has been placed in an important venue on Chang' an Boulevard. It indicates China's growing openness to Western modern art, awareness of enterprise culture and the capacity to compete on the international art market.

Beijing Long-Distance Telephone Office
北京长途电话大楼

This building was put up in 1976. It is the largest domestic and international telecommunications network in China. It offers service to more than 100,000 people everyday and has business relations with more than one hundred countries and regions in the world. The use of mobile phones started in 1987. In 1988 there were only more than 3,000 mobile phone users. By the end of 2001 the number of mobile phone users reached 140 million and fixed phones topped 174.6 million. It is estimated that the mobile phone users will reach as many as 250 million by the end of 2004.

72

China International Travel Service (CITS) Head Office
中国国际旅行社总社

This building houses CITS Head Office established in 1954. CITS has its Head Office in Beijing and has more than 160 branch or sub branch offices in all major cities, tourist centres, scenic resorts and ports of entry across the country. CITS is responsible for the reception of overseas tourists in China, outbound travel and domestic travel as well.

The aim of CITS is by means of tourism to expand the ties and contacts between the peoples of China and other countries, promote friendship, exchange culture, and enhance mutual understanding. At present, CITS has established business relations with more than 500 foreign tour operators, friendship organizations, airlines, and shipping companies from scores of countries and regions throughout the world. CITS has a total staff of over 10, 000 including more than 4, 000 professional guide/interpreters who have been well trained.

In addition to branch or sub-branch offices in other parts of the country, CITS has established 14 branch and sub-branch offices in the United States, Japan, France, Sweden, Denmark, and Australia. In Hong Kong, China International Travel Service(CITS) Hong Kong Limited has been established. They provide tourist information and hand out tourist materials on behalf of CITS, and other travel agencies in China. From the establishment of CITS Head Office in 1954 to 1978, it received approximately 355, 000 foreign tourists; from 1978 to 2000, it received totally 7, 395, 500 tourists. In 2000 it received 576, 500 foreign visitors. In 2000, the total revenue from tourism topped 1. 62 billion yuan, net profit reaching 120 million yuan, with a total staff of over 800.

Classification of Tour Guides in China 中国导游分等级

A new system to assess the skills of China's tour guides has already been established. The system is aimed at establishing a market for tour guides, enhancing the quality of guides and improving the management of travel agencies as the country's tourism industry continues to grow at a strong pace. Officials from the Personnel and Education Department of the China National Tourism Administration said that under a pilot program in 15 travel agencies from Beijing, Shanghai and Sichuan Province monitored all those who conducted sightseeing tours in 1994. In 1995, the scheme was extended nationwide on the basis of experience gained in the pilot study.

There are two categories of tour guides according to the language they use: Chinese or foreign languages. Both categories are divided into four classifications: primary, intermediate, senior and superfine. A tour guide may keep a certain classification for five years while working for a travel agency or other tourism bodies. Then the guide must register with the proper authorities and take part in relevant training and examinations.

There are now more than 50, 000 guides of various classifications in China who have formally passed exams and hold certificates. However, most tour guides do not undergo the appraisal system other professions have to assess employee's proficiency.

The new system would judge the guides' language skills, professional knowledge, competence and performance by certain set criteria.

Although China has improved its tourist facilities and made better use of tourism resources, about 60 per cent of complaints from tourists in 2001 focused on the poor service of tour guides, NAC-sponsored China Tourism News reported. Under the planned economy, tour guides were managed as government officials instead of as freelance operators. The traditional system must be reformed to solve some problems that have plagued China's tourism industry for a long time.

Three Types of Travel Agencies In China 中国旅行社分三大类型

The first type of international travel agency handles businesses of foreigners' inbound tours, domestic tour, and Chinese residents' outbound tours: Whose international travel agencies, authorized by China National Tourism Administration(hereafter refer to CNTA), the Ministry of Public Security and Beijing Travel and Tourism Bureau, organize Chinese citizens to travel outside of the Chinese mainland have to submitted a cash deposit of one million yuan (US$120, 482) to CNTA as a guaranty for tourists' rights and interests violated.

The second type of international travel agency deals with foreigners' inbound tours, and domestic tours: Whose international travel agencies authorized by China National Tourism Administration organize foreigners, compatriots from Hong Kong, Macao, and Taiwan to travel within the Chinese mainland have to submit a cash deposit of 600, 000 yuan (US$72, 289) to CNTA as a guaranty for tourists' rights and interests violated.

The third type of travel agency handles domestic tours only. This type of travel agencies has to submit 100, 000 yuan (US$12, 049) to the local travel bureau as a guaranty for tourists' rights and interests violated.

The First Joint Firm for Tourism in China

The first Sino-foreign joint venture business travel service company debuted on January 28, 2002 in Beijing, marking the formal opening of China's travel market after the country's accession to the World Trade Organization (WTO). The joint venture, named CITS American Express Travel Services Ltd, was co-established by the China International Travel Service Corporation (CITS) and the US-based travel management company American Express, with CITS holding a 51 per cent stake.

The joint venture started operating on May 23, 2002, and would provide business travel management services to clients from multinational corporations, large-scale Chinese mainland enterprises and companies in China's Hong Kong, Taiwan and Macao areas.

Specific services include getting visas and booking international and domestic flights and hotel reservations. The joint venture can also arrange business leisure travel for foreign staff with overseas-funded companies in China.

74

China Arts and Crafts Museum 中国工艺品博物馆

This is the China Arts and Crafts Museum which is located on the northeastern side of the Fuxingmen Overpass on the Second Ring Road in west Beijing. Covering an area of 43,000 square metres, the museum is the biggest of its kind ever built in China. Construction of the museum started in 1987 and was completed in October 1989. The Treasure Hall is on the Fifth Floor. China Arts & Crafts Trading Company is on the First and Second Floors. Everyday more than 10,000 people visit the museum to purchase arts and crafts made in China or see the four jadeite carvings—a miniature Taishan Mountain (Mount Tai in Shandong Province), a relief screen of dragons, a chained vase and a perfumer. Those four giant jadeite ornaments are commonly known as the national arts and crafts treasures in China.

The miniature Mt. Taishan is made of a 363.8-kilogram jadeite stone, the largest ever known in China. It shows the majestic frame of Taishan, a sacred mountain in East China. The craftsmen followed the stone's natural shape, veining and bands of colour to create the peak, trees, temple houses, bridges, waterfalls, brooks, 64 figures and 21 animals. The most intricate part of this carving is a glowing sun on the side of the cliff. The sun traced with thin cloud was originally an impurity in the jade. The thoughtful craftsmen carved it into a thin, translucent plaque to reflect its orange colour. Another flaw was turned into a pair of gliding cranes to evoke a famous Tang Dynasty(618-907) poem about Mt. Taishan. The stone's original height was 81 centimetres, while the finished work is 80 centimetres high, indicating the designers' effort to save every modicum of this phenomenal jadeite.

The relief screen of dragons is the most brilliant of the four. It is carved with nine coiling dragons. The jadeite is stunningly beautiful in texture, streaked with dark green, apple green and opal white. To exaggerate the stone's fine quality, the craftsmen sawed the block into four 1.8 centimetre thick slabs and assembled them into one large screen, 146 by 73.5 centimetres. The designers incorporated the stone's nuances of colour to depict the rolling dragons, churning clouds and the turbulent sea. They achieved a vivid, three dimensional picture on a slab. There are four brownish streaks in the screen, which the designers cleverly turned into water jets from the dragons' mouths, thus turning flaws into assets.

The chained vase is a glossy and filled with a dozen species of flowers. The craftsmen succeeded in conjuring up a marvelous vase by hiding the stone's flaws in the complexity of flowers. It is 64 centimetres high, 28 centimetres taller than the original jade. The added height was created by carving 36 interlocked rings out of the same jade piece, thus elongating the jade by hanging the chain on a wooden stand. The craftsmen searched for a pure area of jadeite in which to carve the long chain twisting in and out of the jadeite stone four times. Chain carving is the most challenging part of this work. You must be extremely careful to avoid flaws in the jadeite; otherwise the chain will break and you can never repair it. Using adhesives to fix broken jade is considered dishonest by jade carvers.

The fourth incredible creation is the extravagant looking perfumer in the shape of a two eared cup. The jadeite piece is the second largest of the four, weighing 274.4 kilograms. Because of its enormous size, the designers decided to make it into a perfumer, the state of the art product of the Beijing Jade Carving Factory, the largest in China. The factory is advanced in cutting layers of bowls out of jade, but was nervous with this superb jadeite, so a special rotating cutter machine was built to cut three bowls out of it. The bowls form the base, cup and cover of the perfumer and are screwed together with carved spiral ridges. The 71 centimetre high perfumer is carved with dragons, phoenix, turtles, white tigers, and other significant creatures in Chinese mythology. It also has 10 rings that dangle from carved decorations. Jadeite (imperial jade) is the hard variety of jade. Soft jade is called nephrite, or "mutton fat." Jadeite is finer and rarer than nephrite and mainly comes from northern Myanmar. The four giant jadeite stones, all brought from Myanmar at an unknown date, had been stored at the government treasury since 1949. In 1982, the State Council entrusted the factory to turn the stones into art works. During the next two years, 78 designs were made, involving 32 well-known artists and jade connoisseurs. The carving began in June 1985 and involved some 40 craftsmen working for nearly four years. Polishing took another six months, and the perfumer took even longer.

To the ancient Chinese, jade was the most precious of stones, a sacred material containing the quitessence of virtue, and its use was confined to ceremonial and religious objects, often decorated with elaborately carved designs. The jade pendants and belt buckles of early times were symbolic of the religious and political power of the nobility. In later times, jade came to be used for purely decorative purposes, but the Chinese people have never lost their special reverence for articles made of it.

In his great dictionary, the *Shuo Wen Jie Zi*, the Han scholar, Xu Shen (c. AD 58-AD 147), described that: "Jade is the fairest of stones. It is endowed with five virtues.

Charity is typified by its lustre, bright yet warm; **rectitude** by its translucency, revealing the colour and markings within; **wisdom** by the purity and penetrating quality of its note when the stone is struck; **courage** in that it may be broken, but cannot be bent; **equity**, in that it has sharp angles, which yet injure none. "

While this definition applies essentially to true jade, a word in whose meaning you may include nephrite and jadeite, but it also applies other fine stones such as serpentine, tremolite, hornblende and even marble. (汉朝许慎著的《说文解字》中说,玉石之美有五德:润泽以温仁之方,䚡理自补可以知中义之方,其声舒扬以远闻智之方,不挠而折勇之方,锐廉而不技挈之方。)

Finance Street 金融街

Designed in 1993, after eight years of hard work, a modern financial central area in the southeastern side of the West Second Ring Road has taken shape in 2001. The 103-hectare "golden treasure land" for financial activities dubbed "the Oriental Wall Street," has attracted 13 State-level financial institutions to set up their headquarters and more than 300 non-banking enterprises from across the country to operate there. Construction of the financial street has greatly promoted Xicheng (West City) District's economy. The value added to the district's financial industry reached more than 8.8 billion yuan(US$1 billion) in 2000, making up 45.4 per cent of the district's total gross domestic product. In the period 1996 to 2000, the C and G zones of the street's first phase project, which required a total investment of up to 15 billion yuan (US$1.8 billion), completed construction and have been in operation. Up to 10 large buildings will be erected in the next five years. They will include the International Financial Mansion, the International Financial Convention and Exhibition Centre and the Securities Building. In addition to the construction of a fast-road network and more green areas, financial institutions are encouraged to develop catering, recreational, exhibition, and property and intermediary service industries in the area.

Encompassing 103 hectares (255 acres), Beijing Finance Street is 1,700 metres long from Fuchengmen Inner Avenue in the north to Fuxingmen Inner Avenue in the south, and 600 metres in width. The planned building area will comprise 3.18 million square metres, of which 2.38 million square metres will be above the ground and 800,000 square metres underground. There are more than 40 buildings and two landmark buildings each with a height of 128 metres. It is estimated that all the buildings in the Finance Street will be completed in 2007.

Beijing Finance Street is destined to become China's multi-functional and well-equipped centre for financial management, policy development and information.

The "Big Four" refers to the four major wholly State-owned commecial banks—the Industrial and Commercial Bank of China (ICBC), the Bank of China, the China Construction Bank and the Agricultural Bank of China.

Fuxingmen (Gate of Rejuvenation) Overpass
复兴门立交桥

Fuxingmen Overpass was built and opened to traffic on October 1, 1974. It was the first of its kind ever built in Beijing and has become an important landmark of overpass construction in the city. Since then more than 500 overpasses have been constructed in Beijing.

China Radio International Building 中国国际广播大楼

This is the building for China Radio International (CRI), the only overseas radio broadcaster in the People's Republic of China, built in 1955. China Radio International has grown rapidly since its founding on December 3, 1941, sets correspondent offices and stations covering most provinces, municipalities and autonomous regions, as well as Hong Kong and Macao special administrative regions. Its mission is to enhance friendship and understanding between the Chinese people and people in other countries.

The Radio broadcasts worldwide in 38 foreign languages, as well in standard Chinese and four local Chinese dialects of Guangzhou(Canton), Hakka, Xiamen and Chaozhou for a total of 211 hours daily, covering current affairs and features on politics, economy, culture and science and receives an average of more than 600,000 letters a year from listeners in 200 countries and regions. Many listeners describe CRI as a bridge between China and the rest of the world and one of the most convenient and efficient ways to learn about China. In 1984, CRI opened its first domestic channel, on 91.5FM, offering programs in English and several other languages. This channel became English-only in 1999, when CRI began broadcasting on 88.7FM with programs in Cantonese and eight foreign languages. CRI operates 27 overseas bureaux around the world and many local bureaux across China, including the Hong Kong and Macao, thereby forming comprehensive global news and information networks. CRI also boasts a TV program production center, a newspaper and multi-language website. Since December 26, 1998, CRI's programs have been available on the Internet. Logging on to CRI's website allows one to access CRI services in eight foreign languages as well as Chinese. Since October 6, 1999, CRI has relayed its TV programs focusing on international news to many places via satellite. CRI also runs a Chinese-language newspaper, World News; an English-language publication, The Messenger; and a German-language publication, Information and Echo. In addition, it runs the China International Radio Press and the China International Audio & Video Publishing House. Now, the Radio has become the third largest overseas radio station in the world in terms of the number of languages and the amount of time it broadcasts.

China Radio, Film and Television Group (CRFTG)
中国广播、电影、电视集团

A State media group was launched on December 6, 2001, bringing together the country's top broadcasting, film and TV enterprises in a bid to meet the greater competition that has come with the country's entry into the World Trade Organization (WTO). The new media giant, named the China Radio, Film and Television Group (CRFTG), puts together the country's flagship TV channel, China Central Television, two State radio stations, China National Radio (CNR) and China Radio International (CRI) and some State film and network organs. The new group has fixed assets totaling 21. 4 billion yuan (US$2. 6 billion) and expects annual revenues to exceed 11 billion yuan (US$1. 3 billion). It will have more than 20, 000 employees. China's television and film companies are too scattered and weak and therefore need to join forces to become more competitive. The new group will further strengthen its co-operation with some other domestic and foreign media over the following years to provide better service to its billions of viewers and to let the voice of China be more widely heard throughout the world. China's broadcasting service covers 92 per cent of the country's territory and TV programmes' coverage reaches 93 per cent, and has over 90 million cable television users. The annual revenue of the country's broadcasting, television and film industry amounted to some 43 billion yuan (US$5. 2 billion) in 2000.

Xixiang Road Project 西厢路工程

Construction of the project began in August 1990. and was opened to the traffic in December 1991. It is located in the southwestern part of the city. The 4. 94 kilometre-six-lane highway has five cloverleaves and ten pedestrian overpasses. Traffic can flow through the enclosed lane without any traffic lights. Connecting the north south flow, the project has greatly eased Beijing traffic pressure. The whole project covers an area of 106, 000 square metres, the largest road project in the history of Beijing.

China Council for the Promotion of Intl. Trade
中国国际贸易促进委员会

The China Council for the Promotion of International Trade(CCPIT) has been actively developing non governmental foreign economic and trade relations and technical exchanges since its founding in 1952. CCPIT is influential at home and abroad and, in fact, it performs the functions of the China Chamber of International Commerce. So far, CCPIT has had cooperative ties with chambers of commerce, associations and federations in over 160 countries and regions.

Since 1986 when the CCPIT membership system was adopted, numerous enterprises and organizations (large national enterprises in particular) have been admitted as CCPIT group members. To keep abreast with the situation of deepening reforms and opening wider to the outside world, improve services offered to its members, increase business contacts with overseas chambers of commerce, associations and other economic and trade bodies, and cement cooperative ties with related international organizations, the Council has decided, with the approval of the Chinese Government, to use the name of the China Chamber of International Commerce concurrently as of today.

CCPIT Building 中国国际贸易促进委员会大楼
Completed in 1981, this new building is the seat of China Council for Promotion of International Trade and Arbitration Commission.

Building for China National Chemical Import & Export Corporation 中国化工进出口公司大楼

Established in 1950, China National Chemicals Import & Export Corporation is an international trading conglomerate enjoying high prestige throughout the world, and is well known by the name of "SINOCHEM" among international petrochemical arena. Apart from the import and export, domestic and entrepot trade of oil, fertilizer, rubber, plastics, and chemicals, SINOCHEM has also expanded into other fields like manufacturing, finance, insurance, transportation and ware-housing service. The company boasts to have an operation integrating information flow, cash flow and goods flow. Over the past few years, SINOCHEM has spared no efforts turning itself truly market-oriented and take part in real market competition. The company has implemented new development strategies, enhanced management on a constant basis, improved financial structure, restructured assets, streamlined organizations, developed human resources and further strengthened core business. The company has shifted from attaching importance to business results to the process and sustainability of operation. As the first Chinese foreign trade company to adopt Enterprise Resources Planning(ERP), SINOCHEM regards management improvement as a daily job. As a result of further developing core business, standardizing transaction process and strengthening risk control, the company has remarkably enhanced the safety and profitability of its operation. The IPO of Sinochem International, a breakthrough in the company's capital market.

With the consistent support of friends all over the world, and the unremitting efforts made by the staff of SINOCHEM, the company has topped the list of China 500 largest import and export enterprises for years. It has been ranked among the Fortune 500 largest companies for 11 successive years from 1989 to 1999. It ranked 307th in 1999 and 16th among trading companies. Despite the harsh business environment in 1999, the company achieved satisfactory results due to the joint effort of the entire personnel: the turnover reached US$15. 064 billion, an increase of 9. 2 per cent over the previous year and the net profit stood at US$72 million, increasing 5. 9 per cent. As a result of two years' efforts, the profitability of the company has been greatly improved.

Entering the new century, SINOCHEM has set its long-term strategic goal after analyzing in depth the world economic situation and its own resources: strategically restructuring business configuration in about ten years, shifting from a single import and export company to a trading conglomerate supported by manufacturing power in agricultural materials, and new-type chemicals, capable of providing all-dimensional services to customers. As one of the key State-owned enterprise under the direct leadership of the Chinese central government, SINOCHEM will maintain its main channel role in commodities like petroleum and fertilizer. SINOCHEM sincerely wishes to further its co-operation with business and finance sectors both at home and abroad, improve management on a constant basis, learn from world leading companies, increase corporate value step by step and make bigger contributions to the national economic development.

All-China Trade Unions Federation 中华全国总工会

The All-China Federation of Trade Unions (ACFTU) is a mass organization of the working class formed voluntarily by the Chinese workers and staff members. Established on May 1, 1925, it now has a membership of 103 million in more than 586,000 primary trade union organizations. It is stipulated in the Constitution of the Chinese Trade Unions that membership in trade unions is open to all manual and mental workers in enterprises, undertakings and offices inside China whose wages constitute their principal means of livelihood and who accept the Constitution of the Chinese Trade Unions irrespective of their nationality, race, sex, occupation, religious belief or educational background. The Chinese trade unions apply the organizational principle of combing leadership along industrial lines with that on a locality basis. At present, under the leadership of ACFTU, there are 31 federations of trade unions of provinces, autonomous regions, and municipalities directly under the central government and 16 national industrial unions, namely the Railway Workers' Union, the Civil Aviation Workers' Union, the Seamen's Union, the Postal and Telecommunications Workers' Union, the Machinery and Metallurgical Workers' Union, the Petroleum, Chemical and Pharmaceutical Workers' Union, the Coal Miners' and Geological Workers' Union, the Water Conservancy and Electrical Power Workers' Union, the Construction Workers' Union, the Agricultural and Forestry Workers' Union, the Financial and Commercial Workers' Union, the Banking Workers' Union and the Educational Workers' Union.

The supreme power organ of the Chinese trade unions is the National Congress of Trade Unions. It is convened once every five years. The Chinese trade unions take the Constitution of the People's Republic of China as the fundamental criterion for their activities, conduct their work in an independent way and in accordance with relevant laws and the Constitution of the Chinese Trade Unions, and play an important role in the political, economic and social affairs of the country. The fundamental task of the Chinese trade unions is to carry out the various social functions of the trade unions in line with the guiding principle of reflecting and safeguarding concrete interests of the workers and staff members in a better way while safeguarding the overall interests of the people throughout the whole country, and, united with the broad masses of workers and staff members, strive for the realization of China's socialist modernization. The major social functions of the Chinese trade unions are as follows:

(1) to protect the legitimate interests and democratic rights of the workers and staff members,

(2) to mobilize and organize the workers and staff member to take part in the construction and reform and accomplish the tasks in the economic and social development,

(3) to represent and organize the workers and staff members to take part in the administration of the State and social affairs and to participate in the democratic management of enterprises,

(4) to educate the workers and staff members to constantly improve their ideological and moral qualities and raise their scientific and cultural levels.

82

The basic duty of the Chinese trade unions is to protect the legitimate rights and interests of the workers and staff members. In the course of developing the socialist market economy, the Chinese Labor Law and other relevant laws, actively safeguard workers' political rights, their right to work and their material and cultural interests; participate in coordinating labor relations and regulating social contradictions and make efforts to promote the economic development and a long-term social stability of the country.

In their international affairs, the Chinese trade unions extensively develop friendly relations with the trade union organizations of various countries on the basis of the principles of independence, equality, mutual respect and non-interference in each other's internal affairs and irrespective of the differences in ideology and their international affiliations, for world peace, development, workers' rights and interests as well as social progress together with the workers and trade unions throughout the world. Now the Chinese trade unions have established relations with more than 400 national trade unions centres of more than 130 countries.

New Capital Museum 首都新博物馆

Construction of the new Capital Museum started on December 25, 2001 and will purportedly be the largest cultural building constructed in the city since 1949.

On Baiyun Street, near the western point of Chang'an Boulevard, the new museum aims to become a landmark construction of Beijing in the 21st century. Encompassing more than 60,000 square metres, the seven-storey building will open to the public in early 2005. Involving 780 million yuan (US$94 million), the building itself will be finished by the end of 2003 and work on the interior will last another year. The present Capital Museum opened in 1981 and found a temporary home in the Beijing Confucian Temple in Guozijian Street near the northern section of the Second Ring Road. Due to its limited space and out-of-date equipment, the old Capital Museum is not a proper home for the more than 250,000 cultural exhibits on display and several more pieces in storage. The old Capital Museum will be scrapped and the loaned place will be returned to the Confucian Temple. The new museum will be armed with state-of-the-art technology and equipment. Its aim will be to become one of China's leading museums. Cai Kai, the chief designer and vice-president of the China Architecture Design and Research Group alongside the French AREP Design Corporation designed it. The new museum is designed to have over 10 exhibition halls, covering a total floor space of more than 30,000 square metres.

The museum will be an important base for cultural research and education as well as a venue for leisure and tourism. A 10, 000-square-metre cultural square mixed with green space will be also built near the museum. At present, Beijing now boosts 118 museums, including some private ones. More museums will be built in a few years to better protect and display relics from the ancient city's more than 3, 000 years of history. Beijing plans to increase the number of its museums to 150 by 2008, when the city will host the Olympics.

China Hall of Science and Technology(Hotel and Intl. Convention Centre) 中国科技会堂(饭店及国际会议中心)

China Hall of Science & Technology (Hotel & Intl. Convention Centre) is located in the western part of the city, near the Diaoyutai State Guesthouse, the offices of government and foreign trade corporations. An International conference exhibition hall with a capacity of 600 persons is adjacent to it. All the guestrooms are equipped with air-conditioning, telephone and refrigerator; color TV, central music system, private bath/shower, and bar. The hotel has such facilities as ballroom, health club, beauty salon, hairdresser's, shop, bank, post office and telex, facsimile and e-mail services, taxi, banquet hall, café, 1, 000-square-metre exhibition hall, scientific and technological workers' club and bookstore.

Science and Technology Information Centre
科技信息中心

Located by Bayi(August 1) Lake in the western suburbs of Beijing, China's largest science and technology information centre was completed and commissioned in 1987. It has a total floor space of 64, 000 square metres. The centre has several divisions, including information collection, document processing, computing reading, research, audio visuals, product sampling and cataloguing. The government invested 88 million RMB yuan (about US$ 21 million) in the centre.

Military Museum of the Chinese People's Revolution
中国人民革命军事博物馆

Located in the west sector of the city, the Museum is the largest military museum in the world, which displays rocket missiles, fighter planes, torpedo boats, tanks, and guns.

The Museum opens a two-part exhibition on China's ancient warfare. The first part features weaponry and battle tactics from primitive society to the 1840 Opium War. The second part covers the period from 1840 to

1919, the beginning of modern Chinese history.

Entering the foyer of the exhibition hall, the visitor sees a battle scene on a sweeping, ground to ceiling mural painting. In the middle of the room stands a marble stone inscribed with words from Sun Zi: "War is a matter of vital importance to the State." Alive during the Spring and Autumn Period of China (770 BC-476 BC), Sun Zi has become a world renowned strategist. His book, "Sun Zi's Art of War," is even studied by Japanese business people because it contains many useful tactics and intrigues.

In the main hall, the first thing the visitor sees is a horse-drawn chariot with three life-like warriors on board. Warfare before the Qin and Han (206 BC-AD 220) period, cavalry became popular. This is illustrated by the terracotta army unearthed in Xi'an. Three clay soldiers and their charges were shipped from Xi'an to the museum for permanent display. They are enclosed by glass and a wall of larger than life photographs of the tomb army. The Three Kingdom Period (AD 220-AD 280) saw big developments in war tactics, particularly in battles on water and the use of fire as an offensive weapon. The battles at Guandu, Chibi and Feishui became famous, so did such strategists as Cao Cao and Zhuge Liang. The Sui and Tang dynasties were a time when China was militarily vigorous and campaigned against Koreans, Tibetans and northern nomads. The organizations of the army became more sophisticated, and city defence improved. Gunpowder was invented during this period and was soon applied to war. Song Dynasty (960-1279) was a dynasty full of technological inventions. The Chinese learned to smelt iron and carbonize it to produce steel. Much of the steel went to equip the Song army of over one million. Yet despite the steel arms, the use of catapults, flame throwers and incendiaries, the Chinese were defeated by invaders from the north. On display is a huge replica of a fortified city wall and a variety of weapons and tools used by attackers and defenders, such as a long armed axe mounted on a cart for breaking walls, an armoured mobile shed or sheltering cage that could be hoisted to the top of a mast for observing enemies on the wall. The Yuan Dynasty (1279-1368) was established by the Mongols, who had a superb army in terms of overall direction, organization, toughness and ability in individual combat. These fighters lived in the saddle. They could sleep on horseback. They created the largest empire in world history, stretching from Korea to east Europe. One sand table shows a major battle between the Mongols and the Chinese in 1259. During the Ming and the pre-Opium War Qing dynasties (1368-1840), China's ancient weaponry reached its peak. Artillery and sappers emerged as specialized troops. Improved battle ships equipped with cannons were used to fight the Japanese. One military

85

achievement was the recapture of Taiwan from the Dutch in 1661. The exhibition shows a battleship, one sixth the size of the Ming Dynasty original, which could carry over 100 people. After the 1840 Opium War with Britain, China fell prey to newly industrialized foreign powers, although its troops and people continued to resist the foreign invaders. Meanwhile, there were also constant wars between Qing government forces and peasant rebels.

The exhibition consists of 2, 000 cultural relics selected from museums throughout China. More than 200 historians and military scholars were involved in the preparation of the show, which includes paintings, photographs, replicas, maps, sand tables, wax sculptures, and videos.

Military Ranks in China 中国军衔制

New China installed the military rank system for the first time in 1955 and abolished it in 1965. At that time the ranks also included generalissimo (no one was ever conferred that title), marshal (of which there were ten), and senior captain. The establishment of the military rank system on October 1st, 1988 was required to boost the modernization and standardization of the People's Liberation Army. It would also enhance morale in the armed forces.

The ranks are senior general, general, lieutenant general, major general, senior colonel, colonel, lieutenant colonel, major captain, lieutenant, and second lieutenant.

Three different medals were awarded to the retired veterans in accordance with their contributions to the Chinese revolution. They were the PLA Red Star Medal of Honour, the PLA Independence Medal of Honour, and the Victory Medal of Honour. Mr Deng Xiaoping, the former Chairman of the Military Commission of the Central Committee of the Chinese Communist Party, made the proposal on awarding medals of honour for meritorious services to retired army officers in recognition of wartime service.

The number of years to be served by draftees is: three years for the land force; four years for the air force, the land service forces of the navy and special technical troops of the land force; five years for naval vessel troops and shipping branches of the land force.

Nowadays, the PLA has about 100 military institutions and schools throughout the country, which have provided more than 200, 000 officers in the past five years. The Central Military Commission brought all commanders in the combat troops up to higher education by the year 2000.

Army Uniforms 军制服

October 1st, 1988 was a memorable day for Chinese soldiers, sailors and airmen as they donned smart new uniforms decked with epaulets designating their new system of military ranks. On the Chinese National Day, officers and soldiers began to wear new insignia, epaulets, service badges and symbols officially approved by the Central Military Commission of the Chinese Communist Party. The insignias feature a red star surrounded by patterns of pine leaves, wheat sheaves, machine gears and the Tian'anmen gate tower, with the words "August 1" (Chinese Army Day) at the centre. The red star and the "August 1" legend is also featured in the service branch with symbols and technical officer badges. Naval badges are embossed with an anchor; the new air force insignia includes a wing, and the symbol for technical officers features atomic rings encircling the red star. Officers' epaulets designate three grades and 11 classes and the soft epaulets worn by the soldiers indicates two grades and seven classes of rank. The uniforms are divided into formal evening dress for important ceremonies; day dress for daily use and training dress for combat, training and physical labour. Summer uniforms are open-necked for both officers and soldiers. Male officers wear dark blue ties and female officers wear red ties. And dress uniforms are adorned with collar ornaments. The symbols of rank and new uniforms give the Chinese Army a completely new look.

The Holiday Inn Chang'an West 西长安街假日饭店

Located at the crossroads of the West Chang'an Boulevard and Yongding Road in the Haidian District, the Holiday Inn Chang'an West, a new luxury hotel, officially opened on September 6, 2001 in Beijing. It boasts 248 guest rooms, business function rooms, a large banquet hall and a conference center, which can accommodate 450 people.

China Millennium Monument 中华世纪坛

Located to the west of Chang'an Boulevard, and the Military Museum on the north side of Fuxing Road, the 4.5-hectare area incorporates an elegant dome-shaped structure which is approached along a bronze-clad walk-way through a landscaped square. Within the building structure is a major meeting hall and the memorial site is dotted with special statues and sculptures. Construction of China Millennium Monument began on March 2, 1999, and it was completed by the end of 1999. It was opened to the public on October 1, 2000. The monument is an embodiment of China's splendid national culture and its ancient civilization. It is a centre of patriotic education and international cultural exchange. The monument is also a symbol of the unification of the nation to celebrate the return of Macao. And it is also China's symbolic memorial building to commemorate the 50th anniversary of the founding of the People's Republic of China and greet the new millennium.

Covering a floor space of 30,000 square metres, the monument is made up of nine parts, including the symbolic principal structure, a bronze-paved path leading to the main structure, and an exhibition hall for works of art. Hundreds of architects and artists participated in the design of the project, which was built using modern technology and is quite different from China's traditional commemorative structures. The exhibition hall, built using the most advanced technology and equipment, provides a fine space for art works from the 20th century and other parts of the world.

The monument is a structure combining the spirit of traditional Chinese culture with modern architectural art, and integrating sculpture, mural painting, and other art forms. It represents not only an eternal memory of the turn of the 20th century, but also a centre for cultural, artistic, and scientific exhibitions from home and abroad and, most importantly, an inspiration to patriotism.

Building the monument's foundation, which requires an investment of 200 million yuan (US$24 million), was completed by the turn of the 20th century. The government has announced that the monument is a public welfare project which welcomes donations from overseas Chinese and foreign countries. The committee established a special fund for the public to donate money or materials for the project.

In May 1999, Mr He Hongshen, deputy director of the Preparatory Committee for the Macao Special Administrative Region donated US$3 million at the ceremony in honour of the first donation for the project.

President Jiang Zemin inscribed the name of China's newly completed China Millennium Monument.

In December 1999, a 262-metre-long raised pathway paved with bronze plates will highlight the China Millennium Monument, an altar being constructed in the capital city to commemorate the new millennium. The plate is inscribed with the text of 5,000 years of Chinese history. Of the 262 plates to be placed on the pathway at Yuyuantan Park, the first was installed at 10 am on November 12, 1999. The south end of the path is near Holy Fire Square and ends at the century monument's main structure of the altar. The 180,000-character record covers important events in China's history. The last bronze plate placed in the path will remain blank, pending future historical moments. A unique aspect of the path will be a 5-millimeter-thick stream of water, which will cover the plates year round. Visitors to the monument can walk along the pathway and tread atop the inscriptions covered by a thin shield of water to reach the altar. Visitors can see their shadows in the water, feeling absorbed in the history of our nation. The flowing water and the steps from visitors will not damage the inscriptions, thanks to the special way the plates were designed. The expected life of the inscription is 3, 300 years.

China Central Television 中央电视台

CCTV transmits to every part of the country. It transmits in colour on three channels. The first, beamed to the entire country, broadcasts every day for about fifteen hours, and also on Sunday mornings and afternoons. The second channel transmits only to the Beijing area. CCTV exchanges film programmes with television networks of some 50 countries. The third channel began in January 1986. It offers mainly educational and sports programmes.

In 1982, China had only 15 television stations. By the end of 1994, TV stations at and above county level numbered 982, cable TV networks stations numbered 1, 202, and educational TV stations totaled 941. This was twice the number of stations in the United States and 24 times more than in Japan. As the national TV station of the People's Republic of China, CCTV made its trial transmission on May 1, 1958 and began regular transmission on September 2 of the same year. In the last 40 odd years, Chinese TV has made rapid progress. Nowadays there are more than 600 TV stations, 33, 130 TV transmission stations and relay stations, 41, 469 satellite ground station, 200 million TV sets and more than 800 million TV viewers in China. TV broadcasts reach 81. 3% of the population. Now CCTV has four channels, transmitting more than 60 hours per day. It broadcasts not only to the Chinese mainland, but also, by satellite, to Taiwan, Hongkong, Macao, and more than 60 nations and regions in Asia, Australia, the Commonwealth of Independent States, East Europe and North Africa. CCTV also transmits its TV programmes to North America and Europe.

CCTV is one of the main channels through which the Chinese people may come to know the world. More that 63% of Chinese viewers rely upon CCTV for important news and information. And no less than 70% of Chinese viewers watched the Barcelona Olympic Games in 1992 on television. Chinese television operates as a complete transmission network. CCTV and local TV stations across the country co-operate closely. Half of the programs transmitted by CCTV are produced by local stations. Some highly-influential programmes were jointly produced by CCTV and local TV stations.

In the past few years, CCTV has been co-operating with TV stations in Hongkong, Macao, and Taiwan, and programmes have been exchanged with overseas Chinese language TV stations. These programmes have been well received by local Chinese viewers.

Since the opening of China to the outside world in the 1980s, we have established business relations with over 120 TV stations in more than 80 countries. Through programme exchanges, joint production and other forms of co-operation, many excellent foreign programmes have come to our screen. In order to meet the demands of our viewers as well as to offer through understanding of China, we hope to strengthen our co-operation with TV stations all over the world. We plan to participate in programme exchanges with TV stations of the Asian Broadcasting Union. We also plan to produce more programmes of interest to overseas Chinese and to other people around the world.

China Central Television Station's (CCTV) Overseas Centre launched English Channel in 2000. CCTV used to be English programmes, but never a specific English Channel targeting foreign viewers. The English Channel—also known as CCTV-9—provides English viewers both in China and the rest of the world with news and some other special programmes 24 hours a day. Its feature programmes, documentaries and entertainment programmes offer viewers in-depth reports on China's politics, economy, history, culture and customs. Broadcasting from Beijing and covering 98 per cent of the entire globe via six satellites, the English Channel broadcasts news programmes every hour focusing on the latest national and world news. In the past year, many Chinese families have been able to receive the English Channel through the local cable TV network, and through co-operation with local TV stations. It is broadcast in North and South America, Africa and Europe. Through co-operation with South Africa's MIH, 650,000 families there view English Channel programmes. CCTV's channel 4 relays five hours of English Channel's programmes every day. The programme invites scholars and government officials both from home and abroad to comment on major world events.

New Colour TV Centre 彩电中心

Construction of the New Colour TV Centre was begun in May 1983 and was completed and put into operation in 1987. The 23-storey building covers more than 10,000 square metres. This TV centre is capable of making and showing five sets of colour TV programmes simulaneously with an investment of 230 million RMB yuan. Some provinces, cities and autonomous regions have also built their own colour TV centres. A new television network has been formed with CCTV (China Central Television Station). Cable television in China still lags behind countries with advanced technology. When Beijing Television Station (the former CCTV) was established in May 1958, there were only about 100 black and white TV sets in the capital city. In 1973, China succeeded in putting out colour TV programmes in Beijing, Tianjin and Shanghai. By the end of 1985, 202 TV stations had been opened throughout the county. At present, all the provinces, cities, and autonomous regions can receive programmes from CCTV.

According to a directors' meeting of the national broadcast and television departments and bureau held in October 1988 in Beijing, more than 600 million people watched television in China. In 1988 there were 116 million TV sets in the country, 37 times as many as in 1978. This meant that there was on average one TV set for every 10 people in China in 1988. A spokesman from the Ministry of Radio, Film and Television said that of the families that owned TV sets, 83.5 percent of the people watched them regularly, and the rate of coverage of the daily news programme from the Chinese Central Television Station (CCTV) reached more than 42 percent of the people. He also said that watching TV has become a main source of entertainment and information for the people. Nowadays, there are over 300,000 TV workers and staff in China.

Beijing City and Country Trade Centre 北京城乡贸易中心

Located off the Fuxing Road, adjacent to Colour TV Centre, the Beijing City and Country Trade Centre has a construction area of 36,000 square metres, nearly 20,000 square metres of which is business area. With modern facilities of central airconditioning, escalators and self controlled fire-fighting equipment. The centre is a comfortable and elegant place for customers. In the centre there are more than 30,000 kinds of goods, including foods, cigarettes, wine, sugar, tea, clothes, shoes, gold and silver ornaments, woman necessities, toys, handicrafts, paintings, curiosities, domestic electric apparatuses, hardware and chemical products, etc.

Beijing Sightseeing Tower 北京观光塔（中央电视塔）

Standing 405 metres high with 24 metres underground and covering an area of 15.4 hectares (38 acres) in Yuyuantan Park, the Beijing Sightseeing Tower is the third highest structure in Asia and the fifth highest in the world. It was originally designed as a TV tower for the Chinese Central Television Station. At 240 metres, a three-storey round structure houses a lounge for distinguished guests, a rotating restaurant and balconies. From the top of the tower, visitors can enjoy a bird's-eye view of both old and new Beijing. The tower was built in 1989 before the 11th Asian Games started. There are 1,484 steps leading to the top of the tower.

Located near the China Central Television Tower, the Tai Ping Yang Underwater World opened to the public on May 16, 1998. It embraces about 200 varieties of fish and marine plants and cover 7,000 square metres.

A List of Some Famous TV Towers in the World
世界知名广播电视塔一览

- Toronto Tower, Canada 加拿大多伦多塔
  553.33 metres in height, and was completed in 1976, No. 1 highest in the world.
- Ostankino TV Tower in Moscow, Russia 俄罗斯奥斯坦基诺电视塔
  It is 540 metres in height——the second highest in the world. It is the symbol of Moscow. Part of the tower was unfortunately burned in late August, 2000 and was refurbished again.
- Shanghai East Pearl TV Tower 上海东方明珠广播电视塔
  468 metres in height, the third highest in the world and No. 1 in Asia and in China; opened to the public in 1994.
- Tianjin TV Tower 天津广播电视塔
  It is 415.2 metres in height, the fourth highest in the world, No. 2 in Asia and in China. Construction started in 1988 and was completed in 1991.
- CCTV Tower 中央广播电视塔
  405 metres in height, the fifth highest in the world and No. 3 in Asia and in China and No. 1 in the world in terms of the scope of its construction.
- Berlin TV Tower 柏林电视塔
  It is 368 metres in height, the second highest in Europe. On top of it is installed a 115-metre-high antenna shaped like garden asparagus 顶端有 115 米高的芦笋状天线

- Tokyo Tower, Japan 日本东京塔
  333 metres in height, was completed and put into operation 1958.
- Tour Eiffel in Paris, France 法国埃菲尔铁塔
  320.7 metres in height, and is situated in Paris, France. It was built in the period of 1887 to 1889. It was closed in 1980 for renovation and reopened to the public in August 1982.
- Hubei Guishan (Tortoise Hill) TV Tower 湖北龟山广播电视塔
  221 metres in height and was completed in October 1986.
- Guangdong TV Tower 广东广播电视塔
  200 metres in height and was put into operation in May 1986.
  Note: Tokyo New TV Tower 东京新电视塔

707 metres in height, the highest in the world, will be completed in 2003.

Beijing Cable TV Service 北京有线电视

Beijing Cable TV Service, the first cable television service in China, and the second television station in the capital, started its broadcasting on May 4, 1992. Programmes include famous and new Chinese and foreign films and popular TV dramas, plus criticism of films and television, excerpts from famous films and popular songs from movies and TV dramas. Recently, the demand for multi-channel and high quality television programmes and comprehensive information services has been rising in Beijing because people have more leisure hours and improved standards and there are more tourists from at home and abroad as well. At present, there are more than 2, 000 internal cable TV services in hotels, enterprises and other institutions in Beijing. Viewers were estimated to have exceeded one million.

Nowadays Beijing cable television will charge each of its users a one off installation fee and then six yuan(about US$1) a month for the first channel. Each extra channel costs another two yuan (about 33 US cents). In addition, the sports programme on the cable television serving major external oriented hotels in Beijing is available 24 hours a day.

Beijing West Railway Station 北京西客站

Located in the west of Beijing, the Beijing West Railway Station, the biggest railway station in Asia, opened to the traffic on January 21, 1996. It opened in time for the peak passenger flow period during the Spring Festival. More than 4. 3 billion yuan (US$518 million) has been spent on the 510, 000 square metre station, since construction began in January 1993. At present, the station handles 27 pairs of passenger trains and 4 pairs of freight trains from the Beijing to Guangzhou Railway. The second stage of construction was completed in 2000, the station now can handle up to 90 pairs of trains, and 300, 000 passengers daily, tripling the handling capacity of the old Beijing Railway Station, the largest handling capacity in China. Unlike the old station, the West Railway Station has enormous parking lots, for up to 3, 000 automobiles and tens of thousands of bicycles, both above and below ground. A structure for a double decker subway system was buried under the station, linking the station with the municipal subway system. Bus and taxi service is available in front of the main building. Regarded as the "gateway to the Capital City," the railway station, where the famous 2, 356-kilometre Beijing-Kowloon Railway starts, harmoniously conbines modern science and technology with traditional

Chinese architectural style. There are 99 staircases and elevators and all the facilities are accessible to handicapped people. Also there are 10 large elevated halls, which provide waiting areas, with shops, restaurants, and entertainment. The Beijing West Railway Station occupies a decisive position in Beijing's transportation system, it leads in the business boom, becoming the fourth commercial centre in the city, after Xidan, Qianmen and Wangfujing areas. The south square is the home to a building for attracting investors, a banking centre, an office building, a shopping centre, a restaurant street, and a hotel. These buildings cover a 20-hectare (50 acres) area, have combined floor space of 500, 000 square metres and will require 4 billion yuan (US$481 million) in construction funds. The north square is scheduled to contain five shopping centres in a co-operative deal with Hong Kong business people. With a total floor space of 430, 000 square metres, these projects cost over 3 billion yuan (US$361 million) in construction funds.

The Beijing West Railway Station has installed Asia's largest clock tower, which measures 3. 4 metres in height and weighs 850 kilograms. The clock was installed on April 27, 1998 on the second floor in the central terminal at Beijing's largest station. Japan's Citizen Watch Corporation designed and installed the clock, which has a stainless steel gantry and four faces.

Liuliqiao Bus Hub 六里桥公共汽车枢纽

This is Liuliqiao Bus Terminal, which was jointly built by the Sanbar Development Company of Britain and its local partner, Beijing Haoda Communications Development Company. The terminal cost 130 million yuan (US$15 million). Fifty per cent of the cost was funded by the British Company. Completed in 1995, the terminal has buses running to Beijing suburban counties as well as Henan, Shandong, Shanxi, Jiangsu, Hubei and Hebei provinces. It is designed to move 32, 000 passengers a day and to accommodate 400 coaches at any given time. Liuliqiao is one of the busiest long distance bus centres in the capital city, handling some 19, 300 passengers daily before the hub was built. It now transports 25 million passengers a year.

Shijingshan Gymnasium 石景山体育馆

Located in the west of Beijing, Shijingshan Gymnasium was built in 1989 for the wrestling matches of the 1990 Asian Games. Its eaves are in the triangular shape of airplane wings, and from each of its three sides it looks like a gigantic glider. A concrete bridge rises between the eaves like an airplane's body. Inside the gymnasium the audience's seats are placed in the three corners with a seating capacity of 3,000. The competition area is 44 metres long and 34 metres wide. The area is not right in the centre, but is off to one side to make the building useful for other purposes, such as meetings and performances. The competition court is built 4.5 metres below ground level so the audience can go straight to their seats after entering the hall without walking up and down stairs. The gymansium has skylights in the roof, which make the building well lit.

Shijingshan Amusement Park 石景山游乐园

Situated in the western suburbs of the city, and built in 1968, Shijingshan Amusement Park encompasses approximately 30 hectares (74 acres). The amusement park boasts more than 50 amusement items. Examples of these include Air flight Plane, Atomic Coaster, Brave Turntable, Canyon Driftage, Carrousel, Cinderella Castle, European-style Bridge, Fairy Tales Train, Flying Saucer, Italian Flying Carpet, Love Express, Roller Coaster, Russian-style Door Building, Sounding Rocket, Super Airship, Super Swing and World Film City.

Shijingshan Club Store 石景山专卖店

Wal-Mart 澳尔玛, the world leading retailing enterprise, formally entered the Beijing market on November 7, 2001 after it inked a contract with Beijing Zhongshan Weiye Investment Co Ltd to open its club store in Shijingshan in the west of Beijing. The store is the first chain store for the company in Beijing. Wal-Mart also plans to open another club store and three shopping centres in the capital city within several years. The new stores will be established as joint ventures or co-operation firms. The total investment for the five stores is estimated at US$25 million, US$6.5 million of which will come from foreign partners, and the business areas of the chain stores are to cover 80,000 square metres.

Shougang (Capital Iron and Steel) Group 首钢集团

Located in western Beijing, the Shougang Group was set up in 1919 and has a history of more than eighty years. Before 1949 it was called iron and steel plant, but produced only iron. The total output of pig iron turned out before 1949 came to 286,000 tons, equivalent to less a month's output now. Since the founding of the People's Republic of China, the group has undergone constant expansion and reconstruction, has been gradually turned into a comparatively complete iron and steel complex. Besides steel and iron, the group is involved in 12 other sectors, such as mining, machinery, electronics, building, shipping, foreign trade and finance. The group NEC Electronics Co Ltd, a joint venture between the group and Nippon Electric Co of Japan, manufactures more than 50 million large integrated circuits annually, which help China's electronic technology reach the sub-micron level. The group Motorman Robot Co Ltd was the first of its kind in China to produce large industrial robots.

As immensely large State-owned enterprise and a trial unit for modern enterprise systems, the group was listed in the top 10 iron and steel corporations in China with 8 million tons of steel production annually. It turns out more than 3 million tons of SG-brand wire rods and 2 million tons of screw steels annually, making up one-fourth of China's building steel products market. The company set up a modern enterprise system at the end of 1999, as planned by the Central Party Committee, the State Council and the Beijing Municipal Government. The group will give key emphasis on the development of high-tech industries, while not expanding the iron and steel production in the coming years.

Nowadays, the group has 83 member companies, operating in 18 provinces, municipalities and autonomous regions as well as the Hong Kong Special Administrative Region.

The group has a total of 211, 000 workers and staff members. Its total assets reached 57. 9 billion yuan (US$6. 76 billion).

The group used to be one of the city's major polluters. It has invested a total of 906 million yuan (US$109. 42 million) to carry out 189 environmental improvement projects over the past five years. In the next five years, the funds earmarked for this purpose will reach 1. 25 billion yuan (US$150. 9 million).

In 2001, thousands of visitors thronged to the Beijing Capital Iron and Steel Group, which has transformed itself a heavy polluter to a garden-style manufacturing plant. Visitors can see how iron and steel are produced in an environmentally sound process while enjoying the picturesque location of the factory. This is more persuasive than advertisements.

In 2001 China produced 149 million tons of steel and 157 million tons of steel products respectively.

City Sightseeing Route C: Dongbianmen Overpass—Chongwenmen—Qianmen Street—Tianningsi (Temple of Heavenly Peace)

线路 C:东便门立交桥—崇文门—前门大街—天宁寺

Dongbianmen (East Informal Gate) Overpass
东便门立交桥

Dongbianmen Overpass was completed in December, and opened to traffic on December 25, 1988. It is a new roadway in southeastern part of Beijing, complete with 10 new overpasses. The project was one of the largest undertakings in the city's history and has involved building a road from the Dongbianmen Gate, near the Beijing Railway Station, south to Muxiyuan and Fangzhuang to the Third Ring Road, a distance of 13.4 kilometres. Traffic jams used to be a headache for the residents in this part of the city.

Construction began in August 1987 and more than 20,000 workers, technicians and engineers were involved during the construction. The 10 overpasses are located at Dongbianmen, Guangqumen, Jinsong, Zuo'anmen, Puhuangyu, Liujiayao, Zhaogongkou, Muxiyuan, Dongtiejiangying and Fangzhuang, doubling the number of overpasses that have been built in the city. The Yuting three-level overpass at Puhuangyu is the largest in the city, and one of the largest in China. The project was involved with 821,000 square metres of road surface along with 60 bridges embracing a total length of 97,290 metres. In addition, 102.1 kilometres of pipe were laid.

The road was part of the infrastructure prepared for the 1990 Asian Games in Beijing.

City Wall Relics Park 明城墙遗址公园

As part of the effort to protect Beijing's historical relics, the Ming Dynasty (1368-1644) City Wall Relics Park opened in 2002. The ancient city wall park follows the opening of the Huangchenggen Relics Park in September 2001, also known as the Imperial City Wall Relics Park, in downtown Beijing. The one-kilometre-long Ming Dynasty city wall relics is said to be the last existing part of the third ring of the ancient city wall, which stretches from Chongwenmen to Dongbianmen in eastern Beijing. To make way for the park encompassing 13 hectares (32.12 acres) of land, residents in 1,800 households had to leave. The park cost a whopping 850 million yuan (US$102 million) to build, a large portion of which was used to compensate residents who had to move. More than 120,000 ancient city wall bricks have been collected in the past three years to rebuild the section of the city wall, which dates back to the 14th century. Beijing was once surrounded by four rings of city walls: the Forbidden City wall, the Imperial City wall, the inner city wall and the outer city wall. Broad ring roads were built in the 1950s and 1960s, but the third and fourth rings of the city wall had to be sacrificed.

Beijing Subway 北京地下铁路

The Beijing Subway was opened to traffic in October 1969. The first line, costing 30 million yuan(equivalent to US$ 8. 1 million), runs from Fuxingmen in the east to Pingguoyuan(Apple Orchard) near the Capital Iron and Steel Corporation in the west. The second line, costing 70 million yuan (equivalent to US$18. 9 million) encircles the city and was put into operation in 1984. The total length of the subway is about 40 kilometres.

In the past, the second subway in Beijing could only run a horse-shoe shaped line, and it could carry 50, 000 people a day. To make good use of the second subway in Beijing, a new track at Fuxingmen Station officially went into operation on December 28, 1987. The 358-metre-long new line allows the trains to drop off passengers, so they can change at Fuxingmen from the east-west line to the one going north or south. Passengers are able to travel in a full circle on the subway line, which totals 23. 03 kilometres in length with 18 stations. Every four minutes there is a train and it takes 40 minutes to make a circle on the subway. While the first line is 16. 9 kilometres with 12 stations.

Construction of a 13. 5-kilometre east-west subway from Fuxingmen to Bawangfen started in June 1989. The subway entered trial operation on September 28, 1999, with the first phase of the project, from Fuxingmen to Xidan (1. 81 kilometres) completed in October, 1992.

The subway runs from Pingguoyuan in west Beijing directly to Bawangfen in east Beijing under Chang'an (Eternal Peace) Boulevard, the east-west axis of the city and intersects with the circle line in Fuxingmen and Jianguomen. In 1998 the number of passengers reached 463 millions against 100 million 1984.

The subway, with 11 stops, cost 7. 57 billion yuan (US$ 912 million), connects many important commercial and tourist facilities, such as Tian'anmen Square, the shopping areas of Xidan and Wangfujing, the Oriental Plaza and the World Trade Centre. It took eight years to construct. It stops at downtown shopping centers such as Xidan and Wangfujing, and Fuxingmen where it connects with the loop line. The journey from Xidan to the World Trade Center will take just 25 minutes. Advanced equipment, such as a tunnel excavator, signals and telecommunications system, have been imported for the construction phase.

Beijing's first subway, stretching 23. 6 kilometres from Fuxingmen to Pingguoyuan in western Beijing was opened in October 1969. The second line, the loop line (16. 1 kilometres from the east end of Beijing Railway

Subway Station via Jianguomen to Fuxingmen Subway Station), started operating in the mid-1980s. The new subway line extends the total length of the system to 55. 1 kilometres. A trip on the new line costs 3 yuan (US$0. 36), as elsewhere in the system.

Before the completion of the Fuxingmen to Sihui Subway Line, Beijing had 41. 6 kilometres of metro lines. One line operated from Pingguoyuan to Xidan and the loop line followed the ancient inner wall of the city, which is now the route of Second Ring Road.

The city's subway handles 1. 46 million passengers per day on its 42 kilometres of track and 530 million per year.

Beijing started to construct a new subway line (the 5th line) at the end of 2000. The 27. 7-kilometre line(of which, the underground line totals 14. 88 kilometres, with 15 underground subway stations; overhead railway/elevated railway line total 12. 82 kilometres with 8 overhead railway stations and one ground station) will run north-south through the urban core. It will connect Fengtai District in the south to Chaoyang District in the north. The project will cost 11. 9 billion yuan(US$1. 4 billion) and should be completed in 2006. Foreign capital or loans from the World Bank and other organizations have been used to finance the new line.

The Beijing Municipal Government mapped out in 1992 to construct two more subway lines to ease traffic congestion in the city. First, a 34. 2-kilometre-long subway starts from the Summer Palace and runs via Beijing University to Jiuxianqiao and intersects with the circle line at Xizhimen and Dongsishitiao stations. It has 27 stops. Second, a 24-kilometre-long north-south subway with 17 stops, from Datun in the north to Hongxing in the south suburbs, is at the geological prospecting stage.

Subway Opened in Guangzhou

The first subway line in the capital of South China's Guangdong Province went into operation on June 28, 1999 and cost 12. 7 billion yuan (US$1. 53 billion), making it the fourth city in China to offer subway transportation. The other three lines are in Beijing, Tianjin, and Shanghai. But experts say the Guangzhou metro is the most advanced in the country. Engineering and installations of equipment of the project cost 4. 4 billion yuan (US$530. 12 million). These figures put the cost at 235 million yuan (US$28. 31 million) per kilometre. The per-kilometre cost of the metro line in Guangzhou was lower than similar costs in Hong Kong, and Seoul, the Repullic of Korea.

Currently the metro line is capable of transporting 27, 900 passengers in one direction per hour. In the future, the volume is expected to rise to 55, 800. The 16-station project covers a distance of 18. 48 kilometres.

The metro line links Xilang in the southwest of the city to Guangzhou East Railway Station in the east of the city, where high-speed trains go to and from Beijing, Shanghai, Shenzhen, and Hong Kong. A ride costs 6 yuan (US$0.72) and the 18.48 kilometres journey takes 32 minutes. The trains run at nine-minute intervals during rush hour periods, and every 18 minutes during off-peak periods.

The new metro line's core system includes rolling stocks, signaling, telecommunications, a power supply supervisory control system and a high-medium voltage system, a traction power supply system and depot equipment. All of the features were introduced by German Consortium Guangzhou Metro, which is headed by Siemens. Other facilities, including escalators and fee collection, fire alarm and ventilation systems, were supplied by a global consortia. The 21 six-car trains for Line 1 were manufactured and supplied by Germany-based ABB Daimler-Benz Transportation. Sources say the metro line is the only line in China where financial service is available. China Construction Bank's Guangzhou branches have set up outlets at 16 stations. The metro line is also one of the very few lines where public tele-communications services, including paging services and mobile communications, are available.

Guangzhou Metro Line 2 broke ground in July 1998 and is expected to be completed in 2004. The line will mark the completion of a metro network that runs from south to north as well as from east to west.

Shenzhen Special Economic Zone

It will become the fifth Chinese city to have a subway after Beijing, Tianjin, Shanghai and Guangzhou. The project was approved by the State Council in the first half of 1998.

The first phase of the planned subway includes the eastern section of the No 1 line and the southern section of the No 4 line, with a total length of 14.8 kilometres. There will be 14 stations. Both lines will be connected with ports of entry between Shenzhen and Hong Kong, and railways in Hong Kong. The cost of the first phase is estimated at 6.74 billion yuan (US$812 million).

Chongwenmen (Gate of Exalted Literature) 崇文门

Before 1949, the most popular carts passing Chongwenmen were those carrying liquor, as distilleries were then located in the south and east of the city. Today it is a busy place for traffic from morning till night.

Beijing Tongren Hospital 北京同仁医院

Established in 1886, this general hospital emphasizes ophthalmology and

ear-nose-throat medicine. The hospital's Beijing Research Institute of Ophthalmology houses the blindness Prevention Co-operative Centre of the World
Health Organization. Its ophthalmology department treats ocular diseases
and eye injures, and performs corneal transplants and artificial lens implants. 眼科在眼底病、眼外伤、角膜移植、人工晶体植入及外眼病方面
有较高的诊疗水平。Its ear-nose-throat department has advanced treatments for esophago-tracheal infections, throat cancer and nasal endoscopes
surgery.

Maxim's Cuisine in Beijing 北京马克西姆餐厅

Maxim's, noted as one of the best restaurants, opened a Beijing Branch at
Chongwenmen in September 1983. The restaurant is the first luxuriant
restaurant in China to provide traditional French food. It can accommodate
600 persons.

The project is a joint venture between Pierre Cardin Company and the
Beijing Municipal Government. Each side shares half of the equity capital.
The agreement was signed in Paris in December 1982. The co-operation
lasted for ten years and then the restaurant was turned over to China. The
restaurant includes a bar, two dining halls and three salons for private parties.

Beijing New World Centre 北京新世界中心

It is conveniently located in the city centre, adjacent to Chongwenmen Underground Railway Station. The Twin Office Towers are with ample IDD
phone lines and flexible underfloor trucking system. The Opulently fitted
apartments are from studio suites to deluxe duplex penthouses with full ho-
tel-style services and central air-conditioning. The full club facilities include indoor pool, gymnasium, sauna, billiards, lounge, children's play-
room, business centre, plus an open landscaped garden with jogging trail
and golf putting green. The 70,000-square metres-Beijing New World Shopping Mall is now open to offer a great variety of shopping, dining and entertainment selections. The 300-room New World Courtyard Hotel is managed by the renowned Marriott Hotel Group. Besides, there are ample indoor carparking spaces. The entire complex was completed in 1998.

Capital Hotel 首都大酒店

This is the Capital Hotel (four-star hotel) featuring typical Chinese courtyard style structuers. The construction area of the hotel covers 60,000
square metres. There are 296 guest rooms (243 standard rooms, 41 twin
room suites, 11 deluxe rooms and one presidential suite), 15 restaurants

101

offering different foods, various recreational and sports facilities and a richly stocked shopping and commercial service centre. In addition, there is a building for guests to establish offices and also a commodious underground parking lot. The hotel is ideally located only 10 minutes' walk from Tian'anmen Square.

Apartment Buildings Along Qiansanmen 前三门住宅楼

These apartments were completed in 1979. There are 38 buildings altogether, of which 30 are apartment buildings, which can accommodate 5, 000 families with 20, 000 people. They are complete with electricity, running water, cooking gas, central heating, elevators and other facilities. More than 2, 000 residential areas have been built in Beijing since 1949. The total floor space amounts to over 100 million square metres. To provide larger space for the people, more and more new apartments are under construction both in the city and in the suburbs. People applied for living quarters either through their working units or the housing departments. Rents were very low, about 5% of the family's monthly income. Many factories had their own housing projects and they offered houses at a special low rate. The welfare system for residential housing distribution that operated in China for nearly 5 decades came to an end in 1998 and a new market-oriented system (new system to commercialize urban residential housing) has been established to take its place ever since. By reforming the residential housing policy the Chinese Government is aiming to kill two birds with one stone: cultivating the real estate industry into a new leg of economic growth while solving the housing difficulties of urban residents. The essence of the new housing reform is to replace the system of direct housing distribution with as system of subsidies. Urban residents in China no longer get housing from their work units, but instead they buy houses in the market.

Housing Reform 房改

Since 1950s, China has applied a system of distributing houses to workers at low rent. The welfare housing distribution system played a certain historical role in guaranteeing most workers residences at the time when salaries were low. But the system was unable to meet people's increasing demands for housing, and the low-rent system meant that investment in housing was unable to be refunded for further construction. In other words, building more houses meant that the government had to spend more on subsidies for maintenance, resulting in a bad circulation of funds. The old housing system has seriously impeded the further development of housing. Therefore, it must be reformed.

Deng Xiaoping (1904-1997), chief architect of China's reform and opening-up, was the first in China to propose housing reform in 1980. Pilot projects started in several cities in 1988. But it was not until the last three years (from 1999 to 2001) that the reform spread in urban centres across the country. The traditional welfare allocations finally stopped at the end of 2000. Public servants and employees working in government-funded institutions can buy, at discount prices with government subsidies, an apartment big enough to reach the "comfort level" set by the United Nations, roughly 20 to 30 square-metres per family membre. If they choose to buy a bigger apartment flat than the guideline, they have to pay the market price, about 6,000 yuan (US$720) per square metre on average in Beijing, while the government discount price was 1,450 yuan (US$177) in 1997 and is now 1,560 yuan (US$190). The government agencies and institutes have also started a "housing fund," which is a reserve fund contributed partly by the employees and partly by their employers. The fund usually accounts for 8 per cent to 10 per cent of a worker's monthly salary. Government-owned housing, be it old or new, is sold rather than rented. Low-income residents can afford to rent because they get government subsidies. All the cities in China have begun carrying out the new policy.

The latest trend among an increasing number of young urbanities is becoming "home mortgagors"—buying houses with loans from banks or the "housing accumulation fund." Many commercial banks in China, particularly China Construction Bank, have provided homebuyers a full package of loans. And the home-buyers are even encouraged by some banks and real estate developers to try such novel services as the "zero down payment" loan program in which the mortgagor doesn't have to make the down payment at the time the house is bought. Many people choose the accumulation fund, which is a compulsory saving system. Because it is "taken from the people and used in the interests of the people," it has won general support from the people.

Guang'an (Universal Peace) Avenue 广安大街

Work began on August 26, 2000 on a 4 billion yuan (US$482 million) project to build the third major east-west avenue across Beijing to reduce traffic congestion. Guang'an (Universal Peace) Avenue, south of and parallel to Chang'an (Eternal Peace) Boulevard has given new momentum to plans to develop the southern part of the city. The road is 8.5 kilometres long and has six lanes. It was completed by September 2001. It runs from Guangqumen(Broad Canal Gate) Bridge, in Chongwen District, southeastern Beijing, to Guang'anmen Bridge in Xuanwu District, southwestern Beijing. There are also new facilities, such as shopping malls, built alongside the road. Development in Beijing had not been balanced, with its southern part remaining relatively underdeveloped. But the new road has changed that. The new thoroughfare was built by broadening the old Guang'an Street in Xuanwu District, which was constructed in the 1950s. Guang'an Street was often plagued with traffic jams because it was less than 10 meters wide in most places. About 12,000 households were moved to make way for the new Guang'an Avenue. Cultural relic sites along the new road received protection. The road connected with the Beijing-Shijiazhuang Expressway in the west and the Fourth Ring Road in the east.

Beijing's second major east-west avenue, Ping'an Avenue, was opened to traffic in Autumn 2000. The road, which is parallel to and north of Chang'an Boulevard, has eased the capital's traffic problems.

Yuanlong Embroidery Silk Corporation
元隆丝绸有限公司

With a history of about 100 years and enjoying a high reputation, the Yuanlong (meaning lucky and prosperous in Chinese) Embroidery Silk Store is one of the appointed enterprises of the Beijing Tourism Administration. The store attracts clients and visitors throughout the world. Business lines include embroideries, silk satins, brocade, woolen and fur products, drawnwork products, carpets and tapestries, pearls and diamonds, silver and gold jewelry, traditional Chinese paintings and calligraphy works. The Corporation also offers custom-tailors' services, mail-order services, shipping services and General Preferential Deputy services.

Beijing Amusement Park 北京游乐园

104

Located by Longtan(Dragon Pool) Lake near the Temple of Heaven, the Beijing Amusement Park covers an area of 500,000 square metres, one fifth of which is water. The amusements are on a central island, connected to the surrounding area by 11 bridges.

The amusement facilities include a loop roller coaster, a swing tower, sky jets, a shooting range, a games house, inflated figures, a whirligig, a mini train, sky cycles, a Ferris wheel, merry cups, a water parade, and pedal boats. One of the biggest attractions at night is a new laser fountain. Controlled by music, the colourful laser beams and underwater coloured lights form a great variety of patterns on large water screens. In addition, there is a sports club, a restaurant, a massage parlour and more rides.

Usually, tourists in the capital converge into the north and west of Beijing, where most of the scenic spots are located, such as the Summer Palace, the Fragrant Hills, Beihai Park. However, with the establishment of the amusement park, southeast of the city is beginning to attract Beijing citizens and outsiders.

The amusement park was opened to the public on April 19, 1987. Everyday it receives about 10,000 visitors. And the number is increasing.

The amusement park is a joint venture, run by the Beijing Longtan (Dragon Pool) Tourism Development Company, the Japan-China General Development Company and the Kumagai Gumi Company, with an investment of 6.6 billion Japanese yen equivalent to 172 million RMB yuan (US $36.5 million).

There are another two amusement parks in Beijing, one in Miyun County 80 kilometers away from the city, the other in Shijingshan District west of Beijing, easy access to the park by the subway.

Zhengyangmen or South-Facing Gate (Front Gate)
正阳门(前门)

This is the South-Facing Gate or Front Gate, a 38-metre-high brick structure. It is located at Qianmen (Front Gate), south of Tian'anmen (Gate of Heavenly Peace) Square. It is one of the few remaining gates of the city wall. It was built in 1420 in the early Ming Dynasty and renovated in 1977. In the old days, watchtowers placed at regular intervals around the perimeter guarded the wall. The double gate system played an important role in repulsing enemy attacks. If the first gate was breached, the enemy would still find themselves outside the city wall and would be fired upon from the tower over the inner gate.

The gate is a fortress-like structure, which was built for the city's defense in 1439. It has 94 windows from which archers could shoot arrows. The tower was burned down several times before it was reconstructed in 1914. As a national relic to be protected, it has been renovated according to the 1914 plan. Tourists can visit exhibitions in the three-storey tower. The first storey describes the history of the tower and the second deals with the city gates of ancient Beijing. There are also displays of paintings and the four treasures of study in ancient China — the writing brushes, ink sticks, ink slabs and paper. The tower was opened to the public on January 21st, 1990, adding another scenic spot in Beijing.

Zhengyangmen was the pass the emperor used for travel to the Temple of Heaven for worshipping ceremonies. Only the imperial sedans and carriages were allowed to use the gate, while funeral ceremonies and carriages were forbidden to pass here.

Qianmen Street 前门大街

With the completion of the Guang' an Street expansion project, Qian-men-Dazhalan commercial centre, the oldest such centre in Beijing, has been rebuilt and most of the historical shops, including the Tongshenghe Shoe Store, the Ruifuxiang Cloth Shop, the Duyichu Restaurant and the Tongrentang Pharmacy have been reopened after the completion of the project. The street came into being in the Yuan Dynasty (1279-1368).

Zhengyici Theatre 正乙祠戏楼

The Zhengyici Theatre is situated on a street near Qianmen, south of Tian' anmen Square. The theatre is a wooden structure more than 300 years old. A rich Zhejiang merchant built the guild hall for friends and other people from his home province in 1667 on a piece of land about 1, 000 square metres in size. The theatre can accommodate more than 200 people who can drink tea and eat snacks while appreciating opera shows on stage. Tucked away in a quiet hutong, the Zhengyici Theatre impresses viewers straight away with its crimson gate, pink curtains, whitewashed walls and gray tiles and upturned eaves.

Huguang Guild Hall Theatre 湖广会馆

The two-storey Huguang Guild Hall Theatre, constructed in 1830 and well preserved, has a square stage and more than 1, 000 seats. Many Peking Opera master performers such as Tan Xinpei, Yu Shuyan and Mei Lanfang played there, a theatre where the Kuomintang Party was founded in 1912 with the leadership of Dr Sun Yat-sen. Today' s Huguang Guild Hall has recovered its past grandeur, boasting not only a grand Peking Opera house, but also delicate decorations and winding corridors with good views of the garden. The pavilions near the opera house—Wenchangge and Fengyu Huairenguan—have been turned into a Chinese Drama History Museum and the Sun Yat-sen Studies Museum. The Huguang Guild Hall also offers special snacks from Hunan, Hubei and Beijing, as the word huguang in the Qing Dynasty (1644-1911) referred to the area where today' s Hunan and Hubei provinces are. During the Spring Festival season, rituals are usually held in the hall and, of course, there are Peking Opera performances.

Guangdelou Theatre (Extensive Virtue Playhouse) 广德楼戏园

With a renovated ancient opera house and specially made performances and television programmes, Beijing jubilantly celebrated the 80th anniversary of the Chinese Communist Party, which fell on July 1. Established in 1796, Guangdelou Theatre, the Chinese oldest opera house, has specialized in *quyi* balladry—China's various story-telling and ballad-singing arts with local characteristics. It used to be the most eminent one of its kind in northern China. In contrast to its previous look, Guangdelou today is a richly ornamental building in traditional Chinese style, boasting star-class facilities. *Quyi* balladry is no longer limited to ordinary people but remains a valuable traditional variety of Chinese folk arts. While the re-opening was rushed in order to be presented as a special birthday gift for the 80th anniversary of the founding of the Chinese Communist Party in 2001.

Dazhalan (literally meaning "large wicker gate") 大栅栏

The 270-metre-long Dazhalan Street is one of the shopping centres in Beijing. Along the street are more than 50 units, including a department store, garment shops, a store of traditional Chinese medicine, cinemas and a theater. The street is rather narrow and the houses on either side are closely located, with a huge flow of customers and pedestrians, averaging 80,000 people per day. And the number goes up to 200,000 on holidays. There are about 10,000 people in this street at a given time. Such being the case, to guard against the enemy's surprise attack, we started building the underground defense works by the end of 1969. Extending in every direction, the complex is now linked with various units and is connected with other underground defense tunnels in Beijing. The complex is complete with telephones, wells, first-aid rooms, headquarters and storehouses. Drills proved that all the people in the street succeeded in getting down to the underground in five or six minutes. Five tunnels(passages) have been built to avoid congestion, thus ensuring immediate shelter for the people in good time.

Tong Ren Tang 同仁堂

Established in 1669 and with a history of more than 330 years, Beijing Tong Ren Tang, China's leading producer of traditional Chinese medicine, intend to tap the overseas market. Tong Ren Tang plans to set up 30 joint ventures and 100 pharmacies overseas by the year 2005. It has signed co-operative agreements with firms in Malaysia, Canada, Indonesia and the Republic of Korea recently. And it will open Tong Ren Tang pharmacies in these countries early 2002. At present, Tong Ren Tang has five joint-venture companies overseas to handle local sales as well as several pharmacies in the Hong Kong Special Administrative Region, Britain, the United States, Australia and Thailand. The pharmacy in Thailand, which began a trial operation in February 2001, has been welcomed by Chinese in Southeast Asia and has begun to make a profit. Brisk overseas business has helped the company increase its foreign exchange earnings to more than US$10 million in 2001, compared with US$1. 9 million in 1993, when it began to do overseas trade by itself and the first joint venture was established in Hong Kong. The aim of Tong Ren Tang is by 2005, the sale volume of exported products will amount to 500 million yuan(US$60 million) and foreign exchange earnings will reach US$60 million, with an annual increase of 46. 8 per cent. Tong Ren Tang's existing co-operation with overseas firms largely involves trading. But now it is considering moving into the manufacturing sector. It will first do packing in some areas and then realize the localization of production step by step in two to three years. According to the State Drug Administration, global sales volume of herbal medicines is as high as US$30 billion, increasing 10 per cent yearly basis. Whereas China's products account for only 3 to 5 per cent, and 80 per cent of traditional Chinese medicine traded on the world market is raw materials. The lack of standards and accurate statistics on ingredients and effectiveness is a major factor restricting traditional Chinese medicine from entering the global market. Europe and the United States have set strict restrictions on imports of herbal medicine. Researchers at Tong Ren Tang introduced chromatographic analysis technology to map out components of best quality medicines. Production of medicine must be in accordance with the maps. This will help the company push the products to reach global standards. In addition, Tong Ren Tang is conducting new research on traditional recipes and developing new products to cater to the international market. Despite traditional Chinese medicine like bolus, Tong Ren Tang is now able to manufacture products in many ways, including liquids, tablets, soft and hard capsules, drops and granular preparations, in accordance with customers' demands. Tong Ren Tang medicine is being recognized by more and more Westerners, though its major market is still Asia. It aims to make the reputation of the Tong Ren Tang brand worldwide. It listed in the Shanghai stock market in 1997. Its Technologies Co Ltd listed in the Hong Kong Growth and Enterprise Market in 2000. Manufacturing more than 800 kinds of medicine, Tong Ren Tang had sales volume of 3 billion yuan (US$362 million) in 2001.

Tianqiao (Heavenly Bridge) 天桥

Located in the southern part of Beijing, Tianqiao (Heavenly Bridge) used to be an area where people worked, did their shopping and went for entertainment. Before 1949, Tianqiao exerted tremendous influence on the daily life of the people.

People say that old Tianqiao was a cradle of Beijing folk arts including cross talk, two men comic shows, clapper talk and trick cycling. A large number of folk artists grew up in this area and later became world-famous masters.

In the Yuan Dynasty, what is now the Tianqiao area was then the southern outskirts of the Yuan capital. When the Ming Emperor Yongle moved the capital from Nanjing to Beijing in 1420, the Temple of Heaven and Xiannong Temple (Alter of the God of Agriculture) were set up in this area. Under the reign of Ming Emperor Jiajing (1522-1566), the outer city was built to the south of the inner city, and Tianqiao thus became the centre of the outer city. At that time, beyond the north walls of the Temple of Heaven and Xiannong Temple was a river running from east to west. It was the sole route that the Emperor took from the Forbidden City to the two temples to offer sacrifices to the Gods and ancestors so a magnificent white marble bridge was built over the river. The bridge was named "Heavenly Bridge" because the Emperor was believed to be the Son of Heaven. Only the Emperor could walk on the "Heavenly Bridge," officials and common people had to cross the river on the wooden bridges flanking both sides of the "Heavenly Bridge."

In 1934, when the street from Zhengyang (Facing-Sun) Gate to Yongding (Eternal Stability) Gate was widened, the "Heavenly Bridge" was demolished but the name has been retained until today.

The Tianqiao area used to be a scenic spot in the Ming and Qing dynasties. To meet the needs of increasing flow of visitors, many teahouses, wine shops and restaurants were gradually set up. Entertainment such as shadowboxing, story-telling and ballad-singing were available. The embryo of Tianqiao Fair was thus formed. During Qing Emperor Guangxu's time (1875-1908), the Beijing-Wuhan Railway was built, and the first Beijing Railway Station was established in Majiapu, outside Yongding Gate. Most travellers passing through the gate would stop over at Tianqiao, therefore the fair became more and more prosperous until the Japanese invasion in 1931. When people mentioned old Tianqiao, they had to mention the "Eight Eccentrics"—a group of folk artists who had unique skills but lived "at the bottom of society." The first "Eight Eccentrics" appeared in the late Qing Dynasty; the second "Eight Eccentrics" were active in the early years of the Republic of China (1912-1949); and the third "Eight Eccentrics" referred to the famed folk artists in the 1930s and 1940s. These "eccentrics" made valuable contributions to the development of Chinese folk art. Tianqiao was also a place where various local operas met, including Peking Opera, Pingju Opera and Hebei Bangzi Opera. Another attraction of Old Tianqiao was its more than 100 snacks including *douzhi* (a fermented bean juice), *youcha* (sweetened, fried flour gruel), *guotier* (lightly fried dumpling) and *suanmeitang* (sweet-sour plum juice). Delicious in taste and low in price, the snacks could be bought in any part of Tianqiao.

In modern Chinese history, Tianqiao was also linked with many great names. Li Dazhao(1889-1927) and Chen Duxiu(1880-1942), founders of the Chinese Communist Party, once distributed leaflets here in June 1919 to advocate the revolution against the warlords.

With a history of more than 600 years, Tiaoqiao has left indelible impressions on Beijing citizens. Since the founding of New China in 1949, Tianqiao has witnessed a dramatic change. A lot of new buildings such as Tianqiao Theatre, Tainqiao Bazaar, the Beijing Natural Museum, the Friendship Hospital and Beijing Rainbow Hotel have been constructed. The former local brothels and secret societies have all been cleared away, and most of these places have been turned into residential areas.

In order to inherit and develop the folk arts, a foundation has been set up to help reconstruct the Tianqiao area.

Kentucky Fried Chicken Restaurant 肯德基餐厅

Situated immediately south of Tian' anmen (Gate of Heavenly Peace) Square, the Kentucky Fried Chicken Restaurant was the first of its kind, opened in China by the Beijing Kentucky Company, a joint venture between China and the US Kentucky International Corporation.

With 505 seats, the restaurant is the biggest of all the nearly 9, 000 in the worldwide Colonel Sanders Chain. It was opened on November 12, 1987. When the restaurant opened, many people doubted about its prospects: Would American style fried chicken suit the Chinese palate? Could Chinese get used to the self-help type of service? Would the prices be too high for the average Chinese customers? After a year operation these questions have all been answered. At first, the restaurant estimated an annual turnover of 9 million yuan and a profit of 1. 35 million yuan. However, by the end of October 1988, turnover and profits were already double the planned figures and more. Beijing's Kentucky Fried Chicken Restaurant served nearly one million customers within one year from November 12, 1987 to November 12, 1988.

Kentucky Fried Chicken (KFC) has increased its outlets in 121 cities in China to 475 since its first restaurant opened in Beijing in 1987. By the end of 2001, the Chinese capital alone has over 50 KFC restaurants, employing 26, 000 people, all of whom are Chinese. The remaining outlets scatter in 120 other cities across China. Board chairman of KFC owner

Tricon Global Restaurants Inc, Andrall Pearson, said China's friendly investment environment was paying back. Tricon owns Pizza and Taco Bell as well as KFC.

McDonald's boasts 377 outlets in 67 cities in China.

Fast Food in Beijing 北京的快餐

Fast food operations have mushroomed in Beijing since the first one appeared in the capital in 1984. Beijing now has nearly 300 restaurants that provide quick food and snappy service. And most are repine fairly high profits. Residents in the capital today can sample a wide range of fast food including famed Sichuan snacks, Kentucky Fried Chicken, McDonalds Big Macs and even Pizza Hut fare. Local food industry officials attribute the rapid growth mainly to the changed attitude of local residents, who have quickened their pace of living in recent years.

Fast food restaurants are run by the State, by individuals and by joint ventures, each of which has its own characteristics and advantages. However, Sino foreign joint ventures that offer customers exotic flavors, excellent service and an attractive environment are the most popular. One pioneer, the American Kentucky Fried Chicken(KFC) chain, set up its first joint venture in Beijing's busy Qianmen area in November 1987 with a total investment of US$1 million. Within one year, it recouped its investment, with daily sales hitting a record 140,000 yuan (US$24,137). Nowadays, the Kentucky Fried Chicken has opened six branches in the capital. Sales totalled more than 40 million yuan (US$7 million) in 1992. Other joint ventures that have followed KFC into the Beijing market include Pizza Hut, California Beef Noodle King Company Ltd, Beijing California Roasted Meat Company Ltd. and the International Fast Food City.

Food and Shopping Street

This is the new food and shopping street, which runs 340 meters from Qianmen (Front Gate) to the west and 220 metres from it to the east and occupies a total building area of 24,000 square metres along this wide street.

Businesses or individuals from all parts of the country were offered the chance to rent space on the new street.

This new food and shopping street includes Chinese and Western restaurants, snack shops, delicatessen and other stores. Food and service trades take up more than 60 per cent of the new business area. A green belt taking up 50 per cent of the area gives the new shopping center a pleasant environment and prevents its noise from disturbing Tian'anmen Square. The new street diverts great part of the crowd from the congested Dazhalan Street, which was thronged by a daily crowd of more than 100,000 people.

Lao She Teahouse 老舍茶馆

Located on West Qianmen Street, the Lao She Teahouse is run by the Beijing "Big Bowl Tea" Trade Company. In 1979, Yin Shengxi, the manager of the teahouse, was one of 20 young people selling a bowl of tea for two fen on Qianmen Street—one of the city's busiest shopping areas. Nowadays, Yin has risen above the crowds and made a name for himself operating Beijing's only traditional teahouse.

In old Beijing, there were many teahouses like the one immortalized in Lao She's play "Teahouse." They were ideal places for people to meet, drink and enjoy a performance by a storyteller or a traditional Chinese musician.

Teahouse gradually declined in the late 1950s and vanished completely during the "cultural revolution." Since 1976, they have made a modest comeback, but Yin's is the only one that retains all the traditional features. At the Lao She Teahouse, the waiters are attired in Qing style gowns, while the waitresses wear cheongsam, a close-fitting dress with a high neck and slit skirt.

Tea is poured for the customers from a small brass pot. Sitting around an old fashioned square table facing the stage, customers can enjoy some of China's most famous teas, while nibbling cakes, candied fruits and melon seeds and listening to stories, ballads, comic dialogues and arias from Peking opera. Customers may even go on stage and perform if they wish. Occasionally, Yin himself entertains his customers with an aria from Peking opera, accompanying himself on the *jinghu*, a two-stringed bowed instrument.

Of hundreds of varieties of Chinese tea, there are six major types — green, black, oolong, white, scented tea, and tightly pressed tea lumps. In Lao She Teahouse customers can enjoy some of China's most renowned varieties, including Longjing (Dragon Well) tea from Zhejiang Province, Maojian from Yunnan Province and Zhulan from Guangdong Province.

112

Beijing Emergency Medical Centre 北京急救中心

Located at West Qianmen Street, the Beijing Emergency Medical Centre is one of the finest of the modernized emergency medical centres in China, and is unique.

It was established by the co-operative efforts of the Chinese and Italian governments. At present, it provides prehospital rescue service and shares scientific research and teaching in the field of emergency medicine.

The aim of the centre is to implement timely, effective, and well organized rescue activities and to provide high quality, high level emergency medical care to seriously sick persons, making full use of advanced facilities and modern emergency medical techniques, ensured by correct and decisive direction.

The centre undertakes rescue operations involved in urgent cases and extraordinary accidents and disasters in terms of direction, coordination, statistics, and analyses. It also undertakes to deliver first-aid on the spot, to transport patients and to offer medical monitoring en route. It shares teaching responsibility in the field of emergency medicine, disseminating popular knowledge of emergency medicine, and encouraging medical services at three levels of city, district and grassroots in the conduct of basic and clinical research.

The centre occupies a seven-storey building, with parts ten storeys high, and with a central air-conditioning system built in. The centre has a floor space of 12, 000 square metres. An observation tower and a helicopter platform are on the roof. A modern garage accommodating 40 ambulances with a vehicle control lobby, well-equipped intensive care units, a hyperbaric oxygen chamber, a hemodialysis unit, a CT unit, an angiocardiography room, an X-ray room, an EEG room, an ECG and UCG room, a blood bank, a pharmacy, a medical laboratory, a computer room, operation rooms, information office, research room and a modern communication office are provided for specialized use.

Construction of the centre started in April 1985 and was completed on March 31, 1987. And it was put into operation on April 1, 1988. A national number for emergency call is 120.

In addition to the Beijing centre, there are 7 other emergency medical stations in the city.

Hepingmen Beijing Roast Duck Restaurant 和平门烤鸭店

Hepingmen(Gate of Peace) Beijing Roast Duck Restaurant is one of Beijing's more authentic restaurants for this famous delicacy. Encompassing 15, 000 square metres, this entire building is a roast duck restaurant opened for business in May 1979. The restaurant, the third branch of Quanjude (Repository of All Virtues), boasts 41 dining halls of varying sizes and can serve 3, 000 customers at a time. The banquet hall can seat 400 customers, and more than 1, 000 roast ducks are served each day. Hepingmen is the first restaurant in China, which serves only one main dish to occupy a seven-storey building. The chiefs in the restaurant can make over 30 kinds of cold dishes and more than 50 dishes-all using duck as the main ingredients. The ovens for roasting the ducks have changed from the old hanging type to gas, electric and even automatic machines. Today, a duck order can be roasted automatically in several minutes. The ducks are now sold in halves, thirds or even smaller quantities. Beijing Roast Duck is the real McCoy in Beijing.

Liulichang Cultural Street (the Antique Shops Area)
琉璃厂文化街

(a restored historic area of Beijing noted for antique hunting, arts, handicrafts and other traditional products of China)

This place has a history of about 900 years. After the Yuan Dynasty made Beijing its capital, four big kilns were built in the city. One of them that made glazed tiles for the imperial palaces was located here. Hence the name Liulichang-Glazed Ware Factory.

In the Qing Dynasty (1644-1911), Liulichang became one of the most popular quarters in the city. Now it is noted for antiques, jewellery, ceramics, paintings and rubbings.

West of the street is Rongbaozhai Studio, famous for its woodblock printing and reproductions of traditional Chinese paintings. Most of the shops in the street have been renovated.

Southern Cathedral
南堂—天主教堂

114

This is the Southern Cathedral or Nantang, built in 1703. It was formerly erected on the site of the house where the missionary Matteo Ricco lived. The building standing today is the fourth Southern Cathedral, the other three were destroyed in the past. While in 1979, the Southern Cathedral, or St. Mary of the Immaculate Con-

Liulichang Cultural Street

ception Church, at Xuanwumen, was the only place Beijing Catholics could attend masses, with the biggest attendance being no more than 80. Nowadays, the Eastern Cathedral, the Church of St. Joseph, is also open. The average attendance at the two cathedrals is 400 on weekdays, 2, 000 on Sundays and more than 15, 000 for Easter and Christmas services. The church is now fully functioning. It does baptisms, confessions, Holy Communions, confirmations, weddings, ordinations, and last rites. Every year the church baptizes 300 people, confirms 200, and marries 100 couples. Both people wanting to be married by the church must be Catholics. Catholicism was introduced into China in 1582, during the Ming Dynasty (1368-1644). It began to develop after the Opium War in 1840, and by 1949 there were about 3 million Catholics in China. A Catholic congress was held in Beijing in July 1957, which announced the founding of the China Patriotic Catholic Association.

Nowadays, there are about 40, 000 Catholics, 14 Catholic churches, 22 Catholic priests and 70 other clerics in Beijing. Besides, Beijing has two Catholic colleges with more than 100 students and a convent.

China now has more than 3, 900 churches and places of prayer open to Catholics and over 30 dioceses across the country have self-elected and self-ordained bishops or assistant bishops. Since 1986, national and local Catholic seminaries in China have trained more than 1, 000 priests, some of whom were sent abroad to study. Seminaries have been set up in Beijing, Shanghai, Shenyang, Wuhan, Chengdu, Xi'an and Shijiazhuang. The Theological and Philosophical College of the Catholic Church in China located in Beijing is the highest and most prestigious. At present, there are about 700 students studying in Chinese Catholic colleges and the dioceses of Beijing, Shanghai, Wuhan, Nanjing, Shenyang, Guangzhou and Guizhou have also trained a lot of young sisters. The principle of "independence, self-reliance, and self-administration of churches" is the historical choice and the right of the Chinese Catholic Church. The Chinese Catholic Church used to have a semi-colonial status, as more than 90 per cent of its bishops were foreigners before 1949. This situation didn't change until its patriotic movement in the 1950s. The church should combine protecting its rights and interests with safeguarding national sovereignty and dignity. It should also abide by the Chinese Constitution while praising missionary work. From 1988 to 2001, the Chinese Catholic church received tens of thousands of forgeign friends.

Bishop Zong Huaide, Chairman of the Chinese Catholic Patriotic Association and Acting Director of the Administrative Commission of the Catholic Church in China said: "We will continue to develop friendship with the

Catholics and people of other countries on the basis of mutual respect, e-quality, friendliness and non-interference on each other's internal affairs."

The Cathedrals in Beijing: 天主教堂
- Xuanwumen Southern Cathedral or Nantang 宣武门教堂（南堂）
- Xizhimen Cathedral 西直门教堂（西堂）
- Wangfujing Cathedral 王府井教堂（东堂）
- Xishiku Cathedral 西什库教堂（北堂）
- Dongjiaominxiang Cathedral 东交民巷教堂
- Nangangzi Cathedral 南岗子教堂

The Christian Churches in Beijing: 基督教堂
- Chongwenmen Church 崇文门教堂
- Haidian Church 海淀教堂
- Zhushikou Church 珠市口教堂
- Gangwashi Church 缸瓦市教堂

Beijing to Build Two New Churches

Keeping up the recent momentum of church renovation and construction, Beijing soon will build two new churches. The churches, which will be located in the city's Chaoyang and Fengtai districts, will cost 30 million yuan (US $3.6 million) and each will accommodate about 1,500 worshippers. The churches should be in places with convenient transportation and where a lot of Protestants live. The new churches will be the first for both districts. Protestants who live in these areas now must commute to other districts for religious rites. With the rapid increase of Protestants, the existing churches have become very crowded. Take Gangwashi Church in western Beijing for instance, sometimes five religious rites are performed in a day and the church was always packed with at least 1,000 Protestants for each service. Beijing now has more than 25,000 Protestants, a significant increase over past decades. Most existing churches, boasting a history of more than 100 years, need renovations. The city has spent more than 100 million yuan (US $12 million) in recent years to revamp its Protestant and Catholic churches and cathedrals. Restorations have been already completed on cathedrals in Xuanwumen, Wangfujing, Chognwenmen, Dongjiaominxiang Alley and the Beijing Beitang Catholic Cathedral.

The number of Protestants living in China has surged dramatically in the last two decades. Statistics from the China Christian Council indicate that China now has more than 10 million Protestants, 14 times the figure in 1949. More than 18,000 Protestant clergy are providing services for them. Since the 1980s, an average of some 600 churches have been repaired or built each year. The total number of churches in China now exceeds 12,000.

In addition to these churches, there are about 25, 000 places throughout China where Protestants can hold religious activities. Apart from the Protestant church, Catholicism has also flourished in China. There are about 5 million Catholics, including 1, 400 priests, 2, 000 nuns and more than 70 bishops. Chinese priests have run both the protestant and Catholic churches since the 1950s. There are nearly 6, 000 Catholic churches across China.

Xinhua News Office Building 新华社办公大楼

This is Xinhua News Agency, China's sole official agency. Founded on November 7, 1931, in Ruijin, Jiangxi Province, Xinhua has witnessed fast development and expansion over the past seven decades, establishing a news collecting network covering the country's 31 provinces, municipalities and autonomous regions, the Hong Kong and Macao Special Administrative regions, as well as more than 100 countries and regions the world over. At present, as the country's largest news collection and distribution centre, releases some 1. 8 million words of news in eight languages and 290 news photographs each day to more than 10, 000 domestic and overseas subscribers. Sticking to its work principle of being "true, comprehensive, objective and just," Xinhua News Agency has faithfully recorded the country's evolutionary history and has made China's voice heard throughout the world. Xinhua reporters have covered most key domestic and international events such as the founding of the People's Republic of China in 1949, the restoration of China's lawful seat at the United Nations in 1971, and the terrorist attacks in the United States on September 11, 2001. President Jiang Zeming sent a letter of congratulations on the occasion of the 70th anniversary of its founding, praising Xinhua's continued efforts to offer valuable reference news to the government and precisely voice the country's diplomatic principles and stance in the international community.

Presently, 750, 000 people work in the journalism field across the country. The significance of journalists' role is further acknowledged when they became the third professional group, following teachers and nurses, to have their own festival. It is the media who bring people the latest developments in the world, shrink the planet into a small village and help people communicate with each other. Behind this effort is the hard work, devotion to public service and even sacrifice of journalists. Their pens and microphones touch any place where events occur — in the battlefields, in fire and flood sites, in new progress of human civilization. It is journalists' mission to, from an objective standpoint, faithfully record what has happened. They not only inform the public of any progress in society but also uncover its problems to be solved. In carrying out this mission, Chinese journalists are promoting the country's social and economic progress. It is believed that supervision, an important role of the media, is parallel with legislation, jurisdiction and administration in safeguarding social justice and pushing forward social progress. The media's supervision is making outstanding contributions to building a clean government, to maintaining social stability and a sound economic order and to safeguarding the rights and interests of the public. The special role of the media also sets higher standards for journalists' professional ethics since they are often put under the test of being tempted by material gains. The media should never relax in strengthening self-discipline. While playing society's supervisory role, journalists also subject themselves to the supervision of society.

Journalists' Day

China celebrated its first "Journalists' Day" on November 8, 2000. The celebrations would help the media improve their image as the public watchdog. Premier Zhu Rongji named "Journalists' Day" in 1999. The All-China Journalists' Association chose November 8, the founding date of its predecessor, the China Youth Journalists Association, as the date for the festival. Around 750, 000 journalists work for China's 5, 000 newspapers, magazines, news agencies, and radio and television stations.

Tianningsi (Temple of Heavenly Peace) 天宁寺

This is the Temple of Heavenly Peace located in the southwestern part of the city. In late fifth century, a Buddhist temple stood on this spot. A stone pagoda was added in AD 602 and the name of the temple changed. In the Tang Dynasty (618-907), it was rebuilt and repaired on several occasions. In the early Ming Dynasty it fell into temporary disuse, but its present name was adopted in 1404 in the Ming Dynasty (1368-1644). The pagoda at the temple is now the oldest extant building in Beijing. According to historical records, there was a pagoda here in the Sui Dynasty (581-618). However, the extant pagoda dates from the Liao Dynasty (907-1125), though some of its superficial decorations were added in the Ming(1368-1644) and Qing (1644-1911) dynasties. This octagonal pagoda rests on a large square platform and is clearly divided into three sections: the base, the body and the 13-storey tower. The pagoda is 57. 8 metres high and is constructed entirely of stone bricks. The base is ornamented with a single band of relief-carved arched niches. Above them is a platform with its perimeter decorated with a series of brackets and balusters. This in turn supports three rows of lotus petals and the body of the pagoda itself. The lower part of the pagoda is decorated with large arched openings and numerous relief carvings. Above this, the 13 levels rise in a slightly bowed profile. Bells hanging from each storey tinkle pleasantly in the wind. The uppermost level is surmounted by a pearl-shaped symbol, which stands for the Buddhist faith. In the Liao Dynasty, the temple stood in the most flourishing market district of the imperial city; thus the visitor can imagine the important role it played in embellishing the skyline of ancient Beijing. Nowadays it is an integral part of the city plan.

City Sightseeing Route D: Chinese Academy of Sciences (CAS)—The Purple Bamboo Park (Zizhuyuan)—Zhongguancun High-Tech Park—Peking University—The Summer Palace—Fragrant Hills Park
线路 D:中国科学院—紫竹院公园—中关村科技园—北京大学—圆明园遗址—颐和园—香山公园

Chinese Academy of Sciences (CAS) 中国科学院

Established in November 1949, on the basis of the Former Central Research Institute and Beiping Research Institute, Chinese Academy of Sciences is the highest academic organ of science and technology of the People's Republic of China and is a comprehensive research and development centre of natural science with high technology. It consists of two parts such as CAS departments and research development entity system. The former is the state highest advisory organ in the field of science and technology. Under the advisory organ, there are at present five departments such as mathematics, physics, chemistry, biology, geography and technological science. The later boasts 123 research institutes and more than 20 scientific and research supporting organs of education of higher learning, scientific instrument research and manufacturing, document information, publishing and reprinting. There are over 10 branch academies such as Shanghai and other cities where research institutes are concentrated. Today there are about 16,700 senior researchers and technical personnel. On December 9, 2001, 56 outstanding scientists were elected as CAS academicians, the top honour for a Chinese scientist. This brings the number of CAS academicians to 653. CAS has kicked off five research programs to further its on-going Knowledge Creation Project. The programmes include rice genome sequencing, life science, biological technology, environmental protection and technologies for engineering projects. These programs have strategic significance to the national economy. One of the technologies for the engineering projects, for example, focuses on the interaction between permanent frozen soil and the Qinghai-Tibet Railway Project and its environmental impact. Harsh conditions in the area brought about many engineering problems that need to be tackled by in-depth research. Rice genome sequencing stands out as a new endeavor by Chinese biologists who will decode one of the most important crops in the world following China's successful participation of the Human Genome Project.

Set up in 1994, under the State Council, the Chinese Academy of Engineering 中国工程院 (CAE) has extended membership to 24 overseas experts from the United States, Britain, Germany, Russia, France, Sweden and Japan. These overseas scientists have played a vital role in promoting academic exchanges between China and other countries. Two thousand and one (2001), for the first time, membership offered were expanded to overseas academicians from January to November of every other year. Previously, membership was extended only in June of every other year. On the home front, 81 domestic scientists were granted CAE membership in 2001. They excelled in such fields as engineering, medicine and health, agriculture, textiles and light industry, environment, construction water conservancy, energy and minerals industries, chemical, metallurgical and materials industries, information and electronics sciences and machinery. And for the first time, CAE invited a Taiwanese scientist to join: Zhang Xinshi 张心湜, 59, a urology expert who has made great contributions to the treatment of urological system diseases. The effort to include Taiwan will help expand scientific collaborations between the mainland and Taiwan. To date, the academy has 616 domestic members.

120

Diaoyutai State Guest House 钓鱼台国宾馆

Diaoyutai State Guesthouse is situated in the scenic spot of Old Diaoyutai (Angling Terrace) in the western suburbs of Beijing. This former imperial dwelling place built over 800 years ago is one of the famous gardens in Beijing. In the Jin Dynasty (1115-1234), Emperor Zhang Zong 章宗 had a terrace laid out here for angling. Hence the place came to be known as "Emperor's Angling Terrace." In the early years of the Yuan Dynasty (1279-1368), Prime Minister Lian Xixian 廉希宪(1231-1280) had a villa (Hall of Ten Thousand Willows) constructed here, and the place for a time became a favorite tourist spot. In the Ming Dynasty (1368-1644), the villa was used by eunuchs and imperial kinsmen. In 1774, Emperor Qianlong of the Qing Dynasty had this place turned again into an imperial garden, with the pond dredged and expanded into a lake. Wanghai Terrace rose over the lake, and a poem in the Emperor's handwriting was inscribed on the arch below the terrace. In the period 1909 to 1911, Emperor Puyi bestowed the garden on his tutor and after renovation it was open to the visitor. With vicissitudes of the feudal dynasties over the years, this garden saw both good and bad times. After the establishment of New China, this old garden took on an entirely new look. In 1959, it became the State Guesthouse for heads of state or government, social luminaries and other distinguished guests from various countries. Diaoyutai State Guesthouse represents an enchanting view. Spring water flows from the distant Western Hills into the lake in the Guesthouse compound via Yuyuan(Jade Pool) Lake. The water picks its way southward around pavilions and villas, through groves and under stone bridges, linking the former imperial dwelling place with the new villas. The Guesthouse encompasses more than 400,000 square metres and is one of the grandeur and harmonies in garden architecture.

Skirting the lake of the Guesthouse are 15 villas in different styles constructed in 1959. They are exquisitely arranged, furnished and adorned with many art treasures of different periods. The Guesthouse is a combination of modern amenities and a distinct Chinese style. The former imperial dwelling place remains basically the same as in the days of Emperor Qianlong of the Qing Dynasty. Lake water constitutes the main background of the scenery here as that around the new villas. Each room, hall, pavilion or terrace differs from the others. Yet together they form an integral whole, giving full expression to the unique style in the traditional Chinese garden architecture. Room for Convalescence 养源斋 is surrounded by a corridor, with rockeries zigzagging their way upward and gurgling brooks converging into a lucid pond in front of it. At the time of the founding of the People's Republic of China, the entire area was reduced to desolation. Apart from the Room for Convalescence used by General Fu Zuoyi (1895 – 1974) as a summer villa, there were few dwellings in the area and only a small number of fields and vegetable beds. Today every effort is made to beautify the environment of the Diaoyutai State Guesthouse, improve its facilities and provide the best service possible to make visiting distinguished guests stay pleasant and comfortable.

Xiyuan Hotel 西苑饭店

It is a 27-storey hotel, 92 metres high. On top of the tower is an octagonal revolving dining room, where people can get a panoramic view of the city. It was completed in late 1984.

The Purple Bamboo Park (Zizhuyuan) 紫竹院公园

The Purple Bamboo Park is situated at the southern end of Baishiqiao Road, with its eastern gate directly across the street from the Capital Gymnasium in Haidian District. The park has three connecting lakes, which occupy 27.18 out of the park's 34.59 acres. Earth dredged from the lakes was piled up to form several small hills on the eastern shores to complement the natural hills that line the lakes' western shores. Five bridges connect the lakes, islands, and hills into a single integrated recreational area. On the banks of the lakes and on the islands, flowering shrubs, trees and flowers have been planted with a generous hand. In the 13th century, the lakes of the Purple Bamboo Park served as a reservoir providing an important part of Beijing's water supply. In the late Yuan Dynasty, Guo Shoujing 郭守敬*, an eminent scientist, built a canal along the upper reaches of the Gaoliang River with locks to regulate the water diverted from the Changhe River, the Jade Spring Hill and other nearby waterways. In late years, the canal was neglected and gradually silted up. During the Republican period (1912-1927) it was filled in and rented out as paddy fields. Since 1949, the people's government has transformed the fields into a new park. Through several decades of planting and construction, the park has been provided with lush bamboos and shady trees, small bridges and open-air pavilions. It has become one of popular parks in the city.

Capital Gymnasium 首都体育馆

This is the biggest indoor stadium in China. It was built in 1968, with a seating capacity of 18,000. Table tennis, basketball and volleyball tournaments and gymnastic contests are held here, and even ice hockey and figure skating performances can be organized all the year round.

Rock Climbing 攀岩

The indoor rock-climbing centre of the Capital Gymnasium opened on June 8, 2000 to rock climbing enthusiasts in Beijing. Jointly designed and constructed by the Chinese National Mountaineering Team and the gymnasium, the centre features a 10-metre-high and 14-metre-wide artificial wall. With six routes of different levels of difficulty, the wall is good for both

122

---

* Guo Shoujing 郭守敬 (1231-1316) complied a new calendar called the Time-Telling Calendar (Shou Shi Li 授时历), and also devised a calendar which determined 365.2425 days to be a year, with an error of only 26 seconds. Guo Shoujing played an important role in discovering the water source for Dadu, an old name for Beijing. This eminent scientist also invented many astronomical instruments and made great contributions to the construction of irrigation works.

advanced climbers and beginners. The centre, open year-round, will hold a series of training courses to promote rock climbing in the city.

Big Sports Complex 体育综合馆

The new building located on the east of the Capital Gymnasium is a multi-purpose sports training centre. It was completed in 1985 to host the Fifth World Cup Acrobatic Gymnastic Tournament that year and the World Cup Gymnastic Tournament in 1986. It has two floors, the upper floor is used for gymnastics, basketball, volleyball, badminton, rhythmic gymnastics and fencing training. The lower floor is used for international standard ice hockey rink and also for training purpose in other sports.

The National Library of China 中国国家图书馆

The National Library of China (it got its new name on Febrary 11, 1999), or Beijing Library(Beijing Tushuguan), grows out of the Metropolitan Library of Peking founded in September 1909 at the end of the Qing Dynasty and began serving as de facto State library 1916. In March 1975, under a proposal by the late Premier Zhou Enlai, the State Council agreed to construct a new library building. Construction began in 1983 and was finished in May 1987. It began its operation in October of the same year. The 22-storey library is located north of Purple Bamboo Park in Haidian District in the Capital City. Bestowed with convenient communications and peaceful surroundings, the library covers an area of 7. 4 hectares (18. 3 acres), with 140, 000 square metres of floor space. Including the branch library on Wenjin Street, near the Beihai Park, the National Library of China now has a total floor space of 170, 000 square metres, a shelf capacity of 21. 6 million volumes, 30 odd reading rooms, and more than 3, 000 seats. It is a comprehensive research library with a national general repository of publications.

In fact, the library is now China's best equipped library and Asia's largest storehouse of books, with more than 20 million books and a staff of more than 1, 700. It is equipped with modern facilities such as large-scale computers, book periodical transmission apparatus, microphone duplicators, and carrier document reading devices. The library was opened to the public in October 1987. The library is open to the public from 8 am to 8 pm every day. About half of the reading rooms provide open access service, guaranteeing more convenience for readers. In the Chinese language reading room, for instance, readers can meander between shelves, looking for their favourite books. The library has consultative service desks in some of the reading rooms to answer readers inquiries on the spot. It also provides information service by telephone or by mail. On the first floor, there is a restaurant for readers.

The National Library of China mainly caters to central leading organizations of the Party, government, army, key scientific research institutions and production units. It also opens reading rooms covering certain fields, to the general public, including one exclusively providing books from Hong Kong, Macao and Taiwan. Each day hundreds of people come to get library cards. Sometimes there is a long queue snaking through the library. In library cards are available to any college student. In contrast, the old library provided only grade four college students and above with cards. People from outside Beijing can have access by showing their credentials. Out lending library cards are provided every May beginning in 1988 to scientific researchers, professors and teachers who hold the higher specialized positions, as well as organizations or institutions. With the cards they can borrow books from the lending stack and basic stack rooms. Foreign readers can also use the library after going through certain procedure.

Within library cards they can read in almost all the reading rooms. But out lending cards only go to envoys, counselors and heads of diplomatic missions to China, including the chief representatives of the United Nations and its specialized offices stationed in China.

Embassies along with the United Nations and its specialized offices located in Beijing can apply to the library for out lending cards. According to regulations, an individual out lending card holder can borrow three Chinese books and five foreign books at a time, and card holders from organizations can borrow 10 Chinese books and 15 foreign books. According to agreements signed with foreign countries, the National Library of China will exchange books and periodicals with more than 1,600 libraries and academic research institutions in over 100 countries, including Great Britain, Australia, and Japan. The National Library of China, the largest of its kind in Asia, was in full operation by May 1988. Nowadays, the library is capable of receiving 7,000 to 8,000 readers a day on average. In 2001, it received more than 1.9 million visits.

There have been more than 10 million hits at the library's website, www. nlc. gov. cn, since 1998. Among the site's many features, Internet surfers can read more than 3 million pages of Chinese information on line, which is the equivalent of 20,000 books. By the end of 1999, information equivalent to 150,000 Chinese books was loaded onto the website for readers to browse, free of charge. To speed up downloading time, the National Library of China officials announced on February 11, 1999 implementation of a library LAN(local area work), which uses the most advanced Ethernet networking technology.

The Metropolitan Library of Beijing was built on April 24, 1909. It was only after 1912 that it began to collect publications across the country and made itself known as a national library. After 1949, the library on the old site was expanded several times, but it could not keep up with increasing demands.

China/E. E. C. Symposium on Legal and Practical Aspects of Investment in China was held here in March 1989. Delegates from 18 countries attended the symposium.

On May 18, 1998, the National Library of China opened two reader service centres, where book-worms can get clippings from more than 5,300 newspapers and read books or magazines virtually from any major library in the world.

The 170,000-square-metre library is also simplifying procedures for more library-goers to have wider access to the country's largest treasures trove of knowledge and information. As China's best-equipped national library and Asia's largest storehouse of books with over 20 million books provides the public and the government with a wide range of data, information and references, while serving as the national bibliographic centre. The clipping service centre tracks and processes information from thousands of domestic and foreign newspapers on any topics suggested by readers or enterprises.

A new, 1,400-square-metre open-shelf reading-room offers readers access to books published over the past five years. In the past it took at least 40 minutes for readers to get the books they asked for from the library repository. If a book is not available, it can be borrowed or copied from around 1,000 libraries at home and abroad within a period ranging from a week to a month.

The library has become an easy-to-read "encyclopaedia" thanks to computerized systems that render operations more efficient. The digital library project aims at building a cross-regional information network. Supported by a sophisticated computerized network, the library collects information from libraries, museums, memorial halls, publishers, publicity firms, art institutes, audio, video, film and television programmes, and tourism departments in China. Supplementary databases include historical information on Chinese culture, the Chinese Communist Party and the People's Republic of China, Chinese law and legal systems, education, ethnic group customs, religion, medicine, Chinese contemporary celebrities, economic data, and reports on science and technology. The project broadens the access to culture, especially for citizens living in poor and remote areas where educational conditions are underdeveloped. The digital library means a transfer from traditional paper-documents to pictures, characters and even voices into computerized databases. Networks, no matter where they are located, are able to search these databases anytime as long as they are linked to the National Library of China. The library boasts fast and convenient information transmission and can safeguard intellectual property rights.

Since the United States took the initiative of developing digital libraries in 1991, other developed countries have invested a mint of money to follow suit.

The project was jointly launched by the Ministry of Culture, the National Library of China, The Chinese Academy of Sciences, Qinghua University, and China Posts and Telecommunications Corporation in 1999. China's four major networks—China Net, China Science and Technology Net, China Education and Research Net, and China Golden Bridge Net are all linked to the project. The digital library project uses these networks and other electronic publications to fuel databases.

Meteorological Centre 气象中心

It is a 9-storey silver-grey building. On top of it is a huge radar antenna in search of rainclouds. It also has antennas for collecting data from weather satellites operated by foreign countries. The National Meteorological Centre serves not only as the nation's centre but also as a regional centre in Asia for the world weather watch plan of the WMO. Thanks to a new super computer, and beginning in the fall of 1993, China has been able to forecast global weather changes four to 10 days ahead. This announcement was made by a top official of the China Meteorological Administration to mark the successful trial run of China's latest medium range numerical weather prediction (NWP) system. Establishment of the operational system is one of the major projects in accelerating China's meteorological modernization. The new system is based on the first Chinese made Yinhe 2 (Galaxy 2), a general purpose parallel computation system oriented to large-scale scientific and engineering computation and massive data processing. Developed in November 1992, the computer is widely known as the YH 11 supercomputer. At present, there are only a few countries or regional centres in the world, mostly in Europe, where the medium range NWP have been in operation.

China's first such system, unveiled in 1991, was capable of producing a five day global weather prediction on daily basis. The second NWP system also showed that the process of meteorological modernization in China has reached a new high level. A WMO official, on behalf of the organization's secretary general, said at the ceremony that the role of

China in the WMO is very significant, since it has accepted international responsibilities as one of the WMO's most important regional specialized meteorological centres today and as a regional telecommunication hub in the future. The new computerized system will increase the capabilities in this field.

China has for the first time obtained global meteorological data directly from its Fengyun-1C (FY-1C) sun-synchronous polar orbiting satellite. The satellite, launched on May 10, 1999, on a Long-March 4B rocket at North China's Taiyuan Satellite Launch Centre, makes it possible for China to conduct studies of the 'hottest topics' of meteorology such as the El Nino phenomenon. After the tests conducted between June 24 and July 13, 1999, the results were very successful and the satellite has done what it was designed to do without any breakdown since it was launched. Senior experts engaged in the satellite programme said the quality of the images provided are as good as those provided by a US satellite owned by the National Oceanic and Atmospheric Agency(NOAA). Some technologies used in the FY-1C are of world-advnaced levels and are expected to play a key role in improving the CMA's weather forecasting, China's climate prediction, calamity monitoring and other environmental monitoring programmes. China has succeeded in launching several meteorological satellites, including geostationary and sun-synchronous polar satellites, since the 1980s. Two are still in operation.

At present, there are more than 2,600 meteorological stations with more than 65,000 meteorological workers in China.

New System to Improve Forecast

China has put a medium-range weather prediction system into professional operation by using update powerful high-performance computer Shenwei I (SW-I). The new system can improve the accuracy and extend the time limits of (medium-range predictions) weather changes from 3 to 10 days ahead. The prediction system is one of the world's latest. It is capable of collecting 32 members of ensemble forecasts to reduce possible errors uncertainties. Nowadays, only a few of the developed countries in the world have been able to adopt the system with high-performance computers. The new system will help National Meteorological Centre's (NMC's) weathermen tell the exact areas, hours and intensity of certain kinds of weather changes. The system, which has been on a trial operation since December 1999, is the first and only practical achievement that has been made using SW-I, the Chinese-developed and manufactured super computer with a peak floating speed of about 384 billion times per second.

Peking University School of Stomatology
北京大学口腔医院

Specializing in stomatology, the hospital is famous for trauma, tumour and plastic surgery. Containing many departments, the hospital also houses the Stomatology Research Institute, which researches oral microbes, tooth cavities and other areas. The Office of Beijing Directors Group for the Prevention of Orthodontic Diseases is based in this hospital.

Central University of Nationalities 中央民族大学

This University is mainly for minority students, who study here for four years. Some of the graduates will return to work in their hometowns. Others are assigned jobs according to the needs of the country. It is laid down in the Constitution of the People's Republic of China that all nationalities in China are equal. Discrimination against and oppression of any nationality are prohibited.

Friendship Hotel VIP Beijing 友谊宾馆贵宾楼

The Friendship Hotel was built in 1954. It is the biggest hotel in terms of hotel rooms. There are over 2,000 rooms. Some tourists stay here while they are in Beijing.

The People's University of China 中国人民大学

It is a comprehensive social science university. It was founded on the basis of Huabei University in 1950. It suspended in 1970. In 1978 it was reopened to recruit students. In 1996 the University has 25 departments, 10 colleges, also under the University there is a graduate school.

Theatre of the Central Opera Troupe 中央歌剧院剧场

Construction of the new opera theatre started in October 1986 and theatre was completed in 1989. It covers an area of 18,000 square metres. Its stage can be lifted, lowered, or revolved with all mechanical facilities controlled by computers. It was designed by a design research institute under the Commission of Science, Technology and Industry for National Defence. The Theatre of the Central Opera Troupe was the first modern theatre designed and constructed by China herself.

Oriental Song and Dance Ensemble 东方歌舞团

The Oriental Song and Dance Ensemble was established on January 13, 1962, under the auspices of the late Premier Zhou Enlai(1898-1976) and

Vice-Premier Chen Yi(1901-1972). It has always the mission of this ensemble to introduce traditional Chinese music and dance to the world and, at the same time, to present exotic performances to people at home. During the past 40 years, the troupe has travelled across the country and has visited more than 70 countries and regions. Dozens of popular singers and dancers have grown up here. However, since China began opening up to the outside world in the late 1970s, more and more counterparts have challenged the art troupe. Originally, the troupe was the leading troupe specializing in the performance of Asian, African and Latin American folk songs and dances. As the time passes by, more and more overseas troupes come into China and Chinese theatregoers become much more informed, the troupe has to make all-around improvements to win over audiences.

Zhongguancun and Its Science and Technology Development Park 中关村及其科技园

Sources from the Zhongguancun Science and Technology Park Management Commission said that the government controls big construction projects in the Zhongguancun Park to avoid excessive increases of land transfer fees in this area. The Zhongguancun area is no longer famous for its academic institutes and colleges, but its reputation now standing out, as it grows into one of the most famous high-tech centres in China. It has attracted the attention of many real estate developers since the State Council approved a plan to set up the park in June 1999. A dozen large office buildings are now under construction, and more than 20 apartment buildings are preparing to break ground. Land resources in the Zhongguancun area are becoming increasingly scarce. Sources said the Beijing municipal government has asked related departments to work out a construction plan for the Zhongguancun Science and Technology Park. All the real estate projects of the Zhongguancun area are expecting to be included in it. No new apartment projects will be approved in the core area of Zhongguancun to control the population density of this region.

Zhongguancun Science and Technology Development Park has become a hub for highly trained professionals at home and abroad. About 270, 000 managers and employees worked in the park in 2000 and the figure reached 300, 000 by the end of 2001. Of the present workers there, 7. 7 per cent of the total hold master's degrees or doctorates, and 36. 6 per cent hold bachelor degrees. Preferential government policies put in place in 2000 attracted 204 overseas investors who poured a total of 270. 4 million *yuan* (US$32. 6 million) in new companies in Zhongguancun from July 2000 to February 2001. A remarkable group of skilled employees with

129

modern managing experience and an overall knowledge of the market economy are gathering in Zhongguancun. Zhongguancun mostly needs skilled managers and daring entrepreneurs. Furthermore, more than 60 per cent of high-tech companies in the park regard capital shortages as their most difficult challenge.

The 15 billion yuan (US$1. 8 billion) central park, occupying 51 hectares, is known as the west zone of Zhongguancun and got under way in May 2001. More than 10 million yuan (US$1. 2 million) to protect ancient trees in the west zone of Zhongguancun has been invested. All gingko trees and the Chinese scholar trees with a diameter of over 50 centimetres are being protected. Xiejie Street, the original road travelled by the imperial family members in the Qing Dynasty (1644-1911) to scenic spots, was preserved and even expanded to a central park in the western Zhongguancun. Meanwhile, half the west zone of Zhongguancun will feature grass and trees irrigated with recycled water. The software park also features a 2. 5-hectare lake.

Peking University 北京大学

Peking University was founded in 1898. It specializes in liberal arts and sciences, with an enrollment of over 10, 000 students. About 300 foreign students from over 40 countries are studying in the university. The University has played a very important role in the history of Chinese revolution. There are now in China nearly 1, 100 institutions of higher learning as against 205 in 1949.

The Ruins of Yuanmingyuan 圆明园遗址

Situated on northwestern outskirts of Beijing, Yuanmingyuan or the Garden of Perfection and Brightness is one of the five famous gardens built during the Qing Dynasty (1644-1911). With its charming landscape and numerous springs, the area has always been the site of gardens and parks. Construction of Yuanmingyuan began in 1709, when Emperor Kangxi was in power, and its construction lasted over a period of 150 years. It actually included three separate gardens: the Garden of Perfection and Brightness 圆明园, the Garden of Everlasting Spring 长春园 and the Garden of Eternal Spring 万春园. The three put together encompasses nearly 875 acres. Therefore, the Westerners reputed it as "the garden of the gardens 万园之园." Unfortunately, in 1860 when the Anglo-French Allied Forces invaded Beijing and looted all the precious treasures in it and set fire to it. In 1900, it was again sacked, this time by the Eight Imperialist Powers. Today, it is a place for people both at home and abroad to visit and ruminate over the past. According to the plan, the Ruin Park of Yuanmingyuan will be completed in 2008.

The Summer Palace 颐和园

The Summer Palace has a history of over 800 years. In 1153, when the Jin Dynasty made Beijing (then called Yanjing) its capital, it built an imperial palace. In 1750, Qing Emperor Qianlong spent 4.48 million taels of silver (140,000 kilograms of silver or 140 tons of silver) building the Garden of Clear Ripples in 15 years and changed the name of the hill to Longevity Hill to celebrate his mother's birthday. In 1860, the Anglo-French allied forces invaded Beijing and burned down the palace. In 1888, Empress Dowager Cixi had it restored with the funds of 937 tons of silver intended for the development of the navy and renamed it the Summer Palace. In 1900, it was again plundered by the invading troops of the eight powers. In 1903, Empress Dowager spent a fabulous sum of money to have the palace reconstructed a second time. In 1924, it was turned into a park. The Summer Palace consists of Longevity Hill and Kunming Lake with a total area of 625 acres. It has become one of the most popular parks in Beijing.

The Fragrant Hills Park 香山公园

Encompassing 400 acres, a temple was built in 1186. Terraces, pavilions and pagodas were added by the subsequent dynasties. The area was later turned into a park and renamed the Park of Tranquility & Pleasure 静宜园. The park was twice destroyed in 1860 and 1900. The destruction was so serious that reconstruction efforts made in the later years were never able to restore its original scale and splendor. After 1949, large-scale restoration took place and now the park is a popular place in late autumn for many holidaymakers when the maple leaves redden. Legend has it that a south wind carried the seeds of the red-leaf trees to Beijing. Then the seeds survived, and as years passed they grew into a lovely forest. Another story goes that the sumacs were transplanted to the area by Qing Emperor Qianlong. In November, the frosted leaves of these trees, along with the persimmons and maples, spread over the hills like a thick red blanket. The main attractions include Spectacles Lake, Studio of Tranquil Heart, Bright Temple, Glazed-Tile Pagoda, and the Two Streams Villa.

131

City Sightseeing Route E: Ping'an Avenue—Chaofu Road —Xizhimen Cloverleaf—Beijing Exhibition Hall
线路 E:平安大街—朝阜路—西直门立交桥—北京展览馆

Ping'an Avenue 平安大街

Ping'an Avenue starts at the Dongsishitiao Overpass 东四十条桥 in the east and ends at the Guanyuan Overpass 官园桥 in the west. The avenue is parallel to Chang'an Boulevard. The total length of this avenue is 7,026 metres (7.026 kilometres). Construction of the avenue started on February 28, 1998 and was completed before October 1, 1999 to mark the 50th anniversary of the founding of the People's Republic of China. Its width ranges from 28 metres to 33 metres and 6 to 8 cars can go abreast. This has greatly alleviated traffic congestion in the city. During the construction of the avenue, 3,328 families and 409 units were demolished, 10,627 trees were cut down and 1,758 electric wire posts were removed. All this mentioned above cost 1.8 billion yuan(US$217 million). The construction fee cost 890 million yuan(US$107 million). The total cost of the avenue reached US$ 324 million.

Ping'an avenue is made up of Dongsishitiao 东四十条, Zhangzizhong Road 张自忠路, Di'anmen Dongdajie 地安门东大街, Di'anmen Xidajie 地安门西大街, Ping'anli Xidajie 平安里西大街. The avenue opened to traffic on August 28, 1999.

Chaofu (Chaoyangmen-Fuchengmen) Road 朝阜路

This is Chaofu Road which runs between Chaoyangmen and Fuchengmen. It is one of Beijing's three east-west arteries, along with Chang'an Boulevard and Ping'an Avenue. The eight-kilometre road, linking 40 of Beijing's most important historical and cultural relics—including the Forbidden City, Beihai Park and Guangji Temple—has long been known as the oldest and most beautiful in the city. More than 700 years old, Chaofu Road is lined by royal, classical, folk and religious buildings, as well as many former homes of famous people. With the city's traffic becoming heavier and heavier, the priority of Chang'an Boulevard being political and Ping'an Avenue resembling a river with shacks instead of rocks, people want Chaofu Road to share more of the traffic burden. When six- or four-lane cement roads actually replace two-lane ones, however, many Beijingers are shocked by the sudden loss of culture that accompanies the construction.

The Prime Hotel Beijing 北京华侨大厦

Centrally located within an easy walking distance to the Forbidden City, Tian'anmen Square, and the bustling Wangfujing shopping district, the Prime Hotel Beijing (Hua Qiao Da Sha) has been rebuilt in traditional style and is now a deluxe joint venture hotel.

The Prime Hotel Beijing (five-star hotel) opened in the fall of 1991. The 400-room hotel is an ideally balanced combination of Swedish management and Chinese hospitality in the centre of the capital city, providing guests with its international standard service. The hotel's hospitable staff will make every effort to help guests enjoy their stay in everybody's favourite city. The Prime Hotel Beijing looks forward to welcoming you.

China Art Gallery 中国美术馆

Located on Wusi Street, the China Art Gallery was established in 1962 to exhibit outstanding works of modern Chinese artists. The gallery has 6,000 square metres of exhibition space, which is divided into 14 exhibition halls currently housing 10,000 pieces, not including folk art. The central part of the gallery, with four floors, has an ancient Chinese pavilion typed roof. The surrounding flat roofs have skylights to allow for natural lighting. The building is decorated with glazed tiles, a traditional Chinese construction material. And many of the walls are paved with light yellow ceramic bricks. The designer wanted the building to reflect a ceramic art work. With the development of a commercial economy, traditional donations from fine artists are now being gradually replaced by sales. The gallery gathers works through a variety of channels, which include buying them from national and local exhibitions and offering financial aid to some fine artists, who sell their works to the gallery later. The research staff at the gallery has done a lot of work for the development of the study of fine art, and they have published dozens of articles and papers. From 1962 to 1995, the China Art Gallery organized over 1,000 exhibitions covering everything from photography, calligraphy to stamp collections. Some of the shows were co-ordinated with other galleries such as the China Folk Artistic Work Gallery. From 1962 to 1977, the total budget for the gallery was 2.25 million yuan. The average annual budget since 1978 has increased to 560,000 yuan. With profits from the exhibitions, it has the potential to become the nation's finest art gallery.

Memorial Hall of Beijing New Culture Movement
北京新文化运动纪念馆

This building is the former site of Peking University, built in 1917. Peking University was the cradle of the May 4th Movement in 1919. After 1949, this old building has been listed by the Chinese Government as one of cultural relics to be preserved. Part of the building was damaged in the 1976 Tangshan earthquake. It has been renovated and changed into the Memorial Hall.

Watchtower (Turret) (故宫) 角楼

This is one of the four watchtowers of the Forbidden City, perching on each of the four corners of its surrounding wall. The sophisticated structure consists of a triple-eaved roof, 9 main beams, 18 columns and 72 ridge-pieces. It was a copy of katydid cage. In ancient times, the watchtower was heavily guarded.

Gate of Divine Prowess 神武门

This is the north gate of the Forbidden City. It is a double-eaved structure with yellow glazed-tile roofs, traditionally a symbol of imperial power and grandeur. Visitors usually leave the Forbidden City through this gate.

Jingshan (Coal Hill) Park 景山公园

Coal was once heaped around the foot of the hill, it is therefore known as the Coal Hill. The five pavilions on the ridges were built in 1750. Chongzhen (1628-1644), the last Ming Emperor, hanged himself on one of the locust trees when the peasant rebels broke into Beijing in 1644. On top of the hill, you can get a bird's eye view of the Forbidden City and the city of Beijing.

Beihai Park 北海公园

This is one of the oldest parks in Beijing. The lake and artificial hills were first built in 1179 and additions were made during the successive dynasties. The White Dagoba atop the hill was built in 1651. The halls, pavilions and other buildings are linked together by winding galleries, tunnels, stairways, and footpaths. Among the famous spots in the park are the Nine-Dragon Screen and the Five-Dragon Pavilions. Kublai Khan used to live here.

134

Round City 团城

In front of Beihai Park is a walled compound known as the Round City, 4,553 square metres in area. There are several attractions in it, notably the Hall to Receive the Light with its Jade Buddha and the Jade Jar Pavilion in which stands a large jade jar weighing 3,500 kilos. The jar used to be Kublai Khan's wine vessel.

Shicha* Lake (The Three Rear Lakes 后三海) 什刹海

Located in the southwest of the Drum Tower in beautiful surroundings,

---

* "Shicha" refers to ten temples, which at one time stood on the banks of the lake.

Shicha Lake has a history of about 700 years in the Yuan Dynasty (1279-1368). It assumed its present name in the Ming Dynasty (1368-1644). Strolling along its shoreline, the visitor can appreciate the lake's glimmering blue water, its graceful weeping willows, its twisting railings and the flower-and-tree-covered central island. Pleasure boats are available for rowing and the banks are amply provided with shady places to rest. A swimming area in the lake is open every summer.

Shichahai Scenic Zone, beginning from the Second Ring Road in the north to Ping'an Avenue in the south and from Di'anmenwai Street in the east to Xinjiekou Street in the west, is a paradise for tourists. It encompasses 146.7 hectares (362.5 acres). The Zone is the only area in the city centre where vast open waters, comprised by Xihai (West Lake), Houhai (Back or Rear Lake) and Qianhai (Front Lake) lakes, exist. More than 40 units for protection of historical relics are located there. They include the former residence of honorary president of People's Republic of China Soong Ching Ling (1893-1981); Guo Moruo (1892-1978) Museum, which is devoted to the famous writer, poet and historian; and Guanghua Temple.

Beijing Traffic Control Centre 北京交通控制中心

A computerized traffic control system designed for the central part of Beijing went into operation on March 19, 1988 in the Beijing Traffic Control Centre which was built in late 1987 and is expected to increase traffic efficiency in the downtown business area by about 20 per cent.

The Beijing Urban Traffic Control System (BUTCS), serving all 53 major intersections within the Second Ring Road, is based on redefined and stored signal programmes. These can be adjusted so that traffic lights are timed to co-ordinate the flow of vehicles with minimum delay. A co-operation project with the Iskra Company of Yugoslavia, the system allows groups of vehicles to enter the 45 square kilometre control area at one end and leave it at the other without too many stops.

A main computer control centre, through three zone control centres, monitors the signal lights at 53 intersections and adjusts its control programmes according to the information from traffic volume detectors. Since many pedestrian crossings are equipped with signal lights, the system is expected to make street crossing safer. Pedestrians will have more time to cross because of longer intervals between red and green lights. Bicycle signals are part of the signal switches at some intersections. A green light for cyclists switches off a few seconds before the motor traffic green light to allow enough time for a safe crossing. The new traffic control system is another step forward in the city's efforts to modernize its road traffic facilities. In November 1987, Beijing set up a traffic control system that put 39 intersections in the eastern part of the city under automatic management according to changing traffic flow. The Beijing Municipal Government plans to establish similar advanced traffic control systems in other parts of the city in the next few years. By 2001, Beijing had an advanced traffic information network, including telecommunications, signals, office management and treatment of traffic violation.

Bank of China 中国银行

The new building of the Bank of China located at Fuchengmen (Mound Formed Gate) in Beijing opened for business in early 1987. The bank is directly under the State Council. It is responsible for conducting the entire country's foreign exchange business, including the management of foreign capital, the handling of revenue and the expenditure of foreign exchange (including those in Renminbi which are related to foreign exchange). The bank has already established contacts with over 3,400 branches of 1,200 banks from more than 150 countries and regions. The building is 82 metres high with a total floor space of 27,000 square metres. It has 22 floors on the ground and five floors underground.

Real name required by banks 存款实行实名制

Starting April 1, 2000, Chinese or foreigners who want to open a bank account at any of China's various financial institutions are required to use their real names and present credentials as evidence, the State Council said in a statement on March 31, 2000. Named on identity cards, residence registration forms for people 16 years old and younger, special identity cards for people in the military or police department, passports for foreigners and special passes for residents from the special administrative regions of Hong Kong, Macao or Taiwan are considered real names. The aim of this is to guarantee the reality of savings accounts and protect the interests of depositors.

In the past individuals were not required to prove their identity or use their real name when they opened savings accounts at China's financial institutions. Although only a small portion of depositors used false names, and many problems were exposed. Problems arose when a deposit book was lost or people with the same name came to the bank together. The old practice shielded the corrupt and aided financial fraud, giving rise to calls for a better system using the customer's real name. The China Construction Bank and the peer banks started preparing to use the real name system as early as 1999, upgrading computer systems and taking emergency measures to guarantee a smooth transfer from the old system.

The introduction of the system of using the bank customers' real name should strengthen the social credit system and promote the use of personal checks.

Xizhimen Business Area 西直门商业区

We are now riding on the three-deck Xizhimen Cloverleaf, which was opened to traffic in 1981. It is one of the largest in China, 1, 250 metres north south and 520 meters east west. The Xizhimen Gate was torn down when the subway was built. The subway is running right beneath the cloverleaf.

To meet the needs of developing economy in Beijing, the Xizhimen Cloverleaf was demolished in early 1999 and the cloverleaf was rebuilt that year.

Landmark buildings to rise at Xizhimen hub

Located in the northwestern part of Beijing's Second Ring Road, the Xizhimen area is said to be the last undeveloped "golden corner" on the ring road. Due to its geographic advantage—south of the Zhongguancun Science and Technology Park, north of the Finance Street, which includes dozens of banks and financial institutions, and east of the State executive zone, which is home to several ministries and state committees—the Xizhimen area has become a golden area in the eye of real estate developers.

Construction of a 138-metre-high landmark building, the Crown Tower (a memorial building marking China's entry into the World Trade Organization and symbolizing the bright future of the Chinese economy; From the top of the tower, people can get a bird's-eye view of Zhongguancun, China's high-tech hub in the north, and the Finance Street in the south), will be completed in 2003. Located at the northwestern point of the Second Ring Road, the 60, 000-square-metre building, towering majestically over the Xizhimen Cloverleaf, will be the tallest office building in western Beijing. On top is a crown-shaped four-storey-tall illuminating glass structure, which gives off colourful light at night. A 40-metre wide vegetation belt surrounds Crown Tower. It overlooks the 45-metre wide sightseeing river to the north. The greenery and water enjoyed by the Crown Tower are rarely found in the surroundings of other office towers in the Capital City. Information convenience gives Crown Tower another edge. Crown Tower, the only top-grade office tower in the Xizhimen area, is supported by first-rate digital technologies. Since the construction of the skyscraper began late 2000, three storeys-two storeys underground and one above ground have been built.

As part of the Beijing Xizhimen communications hub, three French-style buildings are expected to be built within three years. The three buildings, one business centre and two residential and business complexes would provide supplementary facilities for the large communications hub in western downtown Beijing. Co-designed by the Construction Designing Academy under the Ministry of Construction and design department of the French State Subway Corporation, construction began by the end of 2001.

The Xizhimen business area is moving towards becoming a "green" business district. First, the transportation network has been improved. The Xizhimen Cloverleaf will be up-graded again. After its completion, the subways, urban light-rail train system and the railway will be linked up. A walk of no more than 150 metres will get people to stations of any of the transportation lines mentioned above. In addition, two major projects have been completed. The first is the widening of the 6.4-kilometre North Xizhimen Avenue, which has become another IT mall in the manner of Zhongguancun. The second is the 6-kilometre Xiwai Avenue, which links up Xizhimen in the east and Zizhu Overpass in the west. These two roads have been listed as an important part of the municipal government's "Urban High-Speed Transportation System." At the same time, the Xizhimen Traffic Hub, which covers an area of 6 hectares, with a total floor space of 290,000 square metres, not only links up the Beijing North Railway Station, the subway (Ring Line, No 3 Line) and the urban light-rail system but also offers 14 bus stops and taxi parking spots. Secondly, by June 2002 when the western section of Beijing's light-rail train system opens, the train station and its supporting business centre will stand in the Xizhimen area. The business centre is a 24-storey French styles building. Thirdly, the old appearance of Beijing as the imperial capital will be restored in this area. The municipal government has decided to turn the covered moat between the Changhe River in the west and Deshengmen in the east an open river. The renovated river will be 15 metres wide and its banks will be lined with large areas of vegetation. In Xizhimen, a sightseeing boat wharf has been built.

138

Xizhimen Light Rail 西直门轻轨铁路

Construction of the Light Rail at Xizhimen started in October 1999 and will be completed in 2005, with a total length of 40 kilometres. The light rail starts at Xizhemen traversing Zhongguancun, Huilongguan, Lishuiqiao, Wangjing and Dongzhimen totaling 16 stations, passing through Qinghua, Beida, Shangdi Industrial Park District, Hangtiancheng and the Future Software Park District. The total cost of the entire project will be 5.8

billion yuan (US$700 million).

Debao Hotel 德宝饭店

Situated in the west of the city proper, Debao Hotel is a 4-star hotel with top-quality facilities and a strong flavor of culture. The hotel caters to the needs of tourists, government officials and business executives.

The hotel has 230 guest rooms and office buildings equipped with IDD/ DDD, 24-hour service satellite TV, 14 meeting halls and 1 Debao ballroom. The ballroom has a capacity of 500 people. It is equipped with facilities for simultaneous interpretation in 6 languages. The various types of restaurants in the hotel offer authentic Chinese and Western foods. It also has in-door swimming pool, keeping-fit massage, steam bath, eddy current bath, sun and moon bar. The hotel keeps its promise of bringing you the finest in comfort, elegance and quality service.

Beijing Exhibition Hall 北京展览馆

Beijing Exhibition Hall is one of China's largest comprehensive exhibition centres. It is well-equipped and employs a knowledgeable staff. In the past four decades, hundreds of Chinese and foreign exhibitions have been held here. It has long been a famous exhibition centre in China. Exhibition space and relevant exhibition stands, exhibition boards, electrical equipment, furniture, flowers, telephones, and tea serving paraphernalia can be supplied. All the exhibition halls are equipped with air-conditioners, electricity and water supplies, public address systems and radio, and fire fighting equipment. They can hoist and transport exhibit items to their proper places in the halls along special railway tracks. They can also supply all kinds of technical and service personnel, arrange exhibitions, do their art design and decorations, and provide photo and videotaping services as well.

Beijing will become a hub for international exhibitions with five to eight years—just in time to attract tourists who will be visiting the city for 2008 Olympic Games. According to the scheme, a group of exhibition centres, each with around 10,000-square metres of floor space, will be built in downtown Beijing, which should be suitable for small and medium-sized exhibitions offering garments and jewellery. Several other centres of between 30,000 to 50,000 square metres will also be built around the city. In rural Beijing, some large and modern exposition centres exceeding 200,000 square metres will be built to cater for business functions and entertainment. The total area set aside for the construction of these exhibition centres is estimated to be between 500,000 to 800,000 square metres.

As the nation's capital and as an international metropolis, Beijing has u-nique advantages and needs to develop its exhibition economy. Up to 2001 there were 12 exhibition halls with a total area of 13,000 square metres in downtown Beijing, which had held 1,251 exhibitions in the period 1996 to 2000. To further promote the development of the exhibi-tion industry, these existing exhibition venues—the Beijing Exhibition Hall, the Exhibition Hall of Beijing Technological Convention and Exhi-bition Centre and the International Trade Centre will be expanded. Some seven new large and medium-sized exposition centres are currently under construction. To date, Beijing's exhibition industry is at the fledgling stage, largely because of its backward facilities, management mechanisms and its immature market environment and because of a shortage of profes-sionals.

Beijing Zoo 北京动物园

Beijing Zoo was first built in 1906 and opened to the public in 1908 with an area of about 10 hectares (24.71 acres) and a few humble pavilions to house the animals. At that time several dozens of species were shown, such as lions, tigers, leopards and monkeys. Today Beijing Zoo covers an area of 90 hectares (222.39 acres). The animal houses and enclosures, with a total floor space of 40,000 square metres, include those for pandas, elephants, brown and polar bears, tigers, hippopotami, rhinoceros, an-telopes, giraffes and reptiles. More than 6,000 animals of over 650 species are on show. Beijing Zoo has become one of ten biggest zoos in the world.

Beijing New Planetarium 北京新天文馆

The old planetarium was opened to public in 1957 at a cost of 2 million yuan. In terms of contents, astronomy develops with the times. Construc-tion of the new planetarium began on December 26, 2001 and will be opened to public in 2003. The 30-metre-high building has seven storeys, two storeys underneath and five storeys above the ground totalling a floor space of more than 20,000 square metres. The entire project cost 240 mil-lion yuan (US$29 million).

Beijing New Century Hotel 北京新世纪饭店

Located in the west of Beijing, each of the five-star Beijing New Century Hotel room is equipped with adjustable air-conditioning, IDD telephone, mini-bar, refrigerator, radio, in-house movie, satellite TV (CNN, NHK and Wowow), private bath/shower. The hotel also offers bar, health, club, tennis courts, indoor swimming pool, blowing, billiards, table tennis, mahjong, sauna, steam bath, and Jacuzzi, karaoke lounge, beauty salon, hairdresser's, massage room, florist, shop, money exchange, post office, ticketing service, banquet hall and 24-hour room service.

Motorola 摩托罗拉

US electronics giant Motorola will keep its title as the biggest foreign investor in China with an accumulated investment of US$10 billion by 2005, company Chairman and President of Chris Galvin announced in Beijing on November 7, 2001. Galvin said Motorola's five-year development strategy in China can be described with three "ten:" US$10 billion in annual production, US$10 billion in local purchasing and US$10 billion in accumulated investment. Motorola will also become the single biggest tax contributor among foreign companies with an accumulated tax payment of US$5. 6 billion in the next five years. The announcement was made after the US firm held its biennial conference of board members in Beijing, the only location outside of the United States to host the conference. The move suggests that Motorola's development focus will further turn to the Asia-Pacific market, especially China. Motorola also announced it will make Beijing one of its major research and development(R&D) centres with an additional investment of more than US$1 billion over the next five years. It currently operates 18 R&D houses in China, which employ over 1, 000 engineers. By 2006, some 5, 000 R&D and software engineers are expected to be working for Motorola in China. Motorola's three major production groups—mobile phones, telecoms network equipment and semi-conductors—all have excellent track records in China. As one of the earliest foreign investors in the Chinese market, Motorola's mobile phone sector is one of the country's biggest players with over 30 per cent of the market share. The country's mobile carriers, China Mobile and China Unicom, which jointly support the largest customer base in the world of 120 million users, have both adopted Motorola's network equipment. The majority of the electronics giant's investment has been directed towards its semi-conductor products, or chips. Its Tianjin wafer fabrication plant has consumed most of Motorola's investment to date. Motorola expects the chips, used in almost all electronic products, to fuel the company's next wave of growth. China's telecoms market has become a haven for investment in the context of worldwide economic downturn. Golva telecoms equipment vendors have all increased their investment in China.

Shangri-La Hotel 香格里拉饭店

Catering to the needs of business and leisure travellers, all the rooms of the hotel provide a wide range of modern amenities. The Horizon Club Floor offers breakfast and cocktails in the evenings, international newspapers, pressing service on arrival, baby-sitting service, handicapped guest rooms, laundry and dry cleaning, facsimile service in the lounge, and full concierge service.

There are 743 guest rooms and 40 suites, all with IDD telephone, colour TV, in-room movie, multi-channel radio, bedside controls, hair-dryer, mini-bar and refrigerator, tea making facilities and individual temperature control.

The hotel is fully equipped with health club with sauna, solariums, massage, gym, indoor swimming pool, two indoor tennis and squash. There is a grand ballroom for 1,000 people plus 13 small function rooms for meetings and interviews.

Located in the west Beijing, the hotel is close to government and business organizations, Silicon Valley, Beijing Gymnasium and Beijing Exhibition Centre.

The five-star Beijing Shangri-La Hotel became the first hotel on China's mainland to win an internationally-protection award. The Certification of China Environmental Management System approved the ISO14001 certificate in early November 1999. All staff at the hotel have undergone training in pollution prevention. To improve the environment, the hotel spent 7.1 million yuan(US$ 855, 420) on changing plastic bags with cloth bags for guests' laundry, recycling paper, saving energy and water resources and reducing water pollution caused by detergents. It has set a good example for other hotels both in Beijing and China to follow.

142

Beijing Dance Academy 北京舞蹈学院

Located at the north of the beautiful Purple Bamboo Garden of Beijing, Beijing Dance Academy is the only place in China that offers higher education in dance. Founded in 1954, Beijing Dance Academy has established ballet, choreography, dance study, national dance drama, folk dance and social dance education departments. The academy has provided numerous dancers, choreographers, dance teachers and dance critics, which earns it the title: "cradle of dancers."

Beijing Experimental Zone for the Development of New Technological Industries 北京高科技技术开发区

Beijing Experimental Zone for the Development of New Technological Industries—China's Silicon Valley—formally began business on August 5, 1988.

Covering an area of 100 square kilometres, the Experimental Zone centres at Zhongguancun in the Haidian District, which is known for its computer and electronics street. The main purpose of this experimental zone is to promote the integration of science and technology with economy and give a boost to the development of China's new technological industries. Approved by the State Council, this is the first technological industries experimental area set up in China. The zone is expected to attract investment and scientific personnel. The scientists are to establish new, high-tech enterprises in the area and build Zhongguancun into an open, outwarding looking technological industries development zone that is influential in the world.

The central authorities have adopted a guideline to support and guide the experimenal zone and grant it preferential policies equivalent to, in some respects, even greater than those for the coastal special economic zones.

Haidian District plans to establish the most updated information network in China, in accordance with a Beijing Municipal Government plan. It will also construct a software park to the west of the Shangdi Information Industrial Base. The district is considered as an engine of China's high-tech industries. It is the home of 378,000 scientists and researchers in more than 230 scientific and research institutes including the Chinese Academy of Sciences. And it boasts more than 50 well-known institutions of higher learning such as Qinghua University and Peking University. National Library of China, the largest one in Asia, and other libraries in the universities and institutes, have made Haidian the biggest information bank in China. Haidian will set up buildings for scientific and technological research and undertake road projects. Efforts will be made to control pollution and protect the environment. In addition, Haidian has established an industrial park for people who have returned China after studying abroad. It will take measures to attract more of them to set up enterprises in the district.

Chinese Office Enters Silicon Valley

The Zhongguancun Science and Technology Park(ZSTP) established a liaison office in Silicon Valley in California on July 1, 2000. This signifies that China's high-tech industry will go to the outside world and merge with the global economy. Introducing technologies and funds was a first step in the development of China's high-tech industry. Next, we should go out to communicate with world leading high-tech giants, promote ourselves and enter the international market. The new economy, typified by high-tech industry, is an an economy characterized by globalization in terms of capital, talent, technology and market. ZSTP, regarded as China's Silicon Valley, located its liaison office in the centre of Silicon Valley, California, the home to world famous high-tech enterprises and research institutes in the United States. The setting up of a Silicon Valley liaison office of the ZSTP will improve communications between Chinese high-tech enterprises and their world-leading counterparts, enhance co-operation between foreign and overseas Chinese experts and promote ZSTP's image in the world.

As the first high-tech park resident institute in a foreign country, the liaison office of ZSTP might play an important role in helping the Chinese high-tech sector catch up with the international high-tech giants. In addition, the office will offer convenient and efficient services for overseas Chinese students who might want to invest, conduct research or study in the ZSTP.

As the first State-level science and technology park in China, the ZSTP was established in 1988 and has created an industrial structure centering on energy-saving and environmentally friendly high-tech industries, involving electronic information, optical-mechanical-electrical integration, spacing, biopharmaceuticals and new materials. Responding to worldwide developments, the ZSTP quickened its pace of internationalization. It now consists not only of a group of domestic enterprises, including Legend, Founder, Stone, Ziguang, but also some world-leading corporations such as Microsoft, IBM, GE, HP, Canon, Hitachi and National. In 1999, with the approval of the State Council, the Beijing municipal government decided to support the ZSTP as a leader of China's high-tech industry and started the construction of "one district with five sub-parks." With Zhonguancun as the dragonhead, construction on the Haidian, Fengtai and Changping sub-parks, and Jiuxianqiao Electronics Town and Beijing Economic and Technological Development Zone are under way.

As of November 2000, 1,682 enterprises had been newly registered in Haidian Park in the Zhongguancun Technological Development Area, bringing the total number of enterprises there to 5,819. The newly registered domestic enterprises had invested 9.1 billion yuan(US$1.1 billion), an increase of 80.4 per cent compared with investment in 1999. Newly registered foreign-funded enterprises had invested US$979 million, up 279 per cent from the previous year's figure.

144

Pagoda of the Temple of Benevolence and Longevity
慈寿寺塔

This pagoda was built during the reign of Ming Emperor Wanli (1573-1620) to celebrate his mother's 60th birthday. There used to be a temple with a surrounding wall. Later the wall and the temple were destroyed, and now only the pagoda is still standing.

Collegiate Gymnasium 大学生体育馆

With a seating capacity of 4,200, the gymnasium is a square with a tower on each of its four corners. The front concrete eaves of the gymnasium's main body are very thick and extend outward. This design stems from traditional Chinese archways.

Built in the Capital Institute of Physical Education 首都体育学院, about 2 kilometres east of the Friendship Hotel and at the northern side of the third ring road, the gymnasium belongs to the institute after the Asian Games. For flexibility of use, the designer made nearly two thirds of the seats removable. All 16 rows of seats on its first and second floors can be slid away like drawers. When the first six rows of seats on the first floor are rolled back, the floor space can be used for handball games or be divided into three basketball courts for the institute's use. When 10 rows of seats on the second floor are rolled back, the space can be made into six badminton courts.

Expansion of Commerce in Store 扩大商业规模

Foreign high street giants are being encouraged to set up shops in Beijing under new plans to expand commerce in the City. The Beijing Municipal Government has listed several commercial fields as priorities for overseas investment, including supermarket chains and shopping centers. Foreign investment is welcome in large multipurpose shopping malls, modern logistics zones, large wholesale enterprises, specialized outlets and chain stores. According to the general plan, four large multi-purpose shopping centres will be built in different styles in the Northwest, Southeast, Northeast and southwest, around Beijing's Fifth Ring Road—each encompassing 200,000 to 300,000 square metres. Transnational companies with rich experience might participate in the design, construction, operation and management of these centers. Three large logistic zones outside central Beijing are expected to be established and global commercial enterprises will be allowed to become involved in the operation and management of the zones. Large supermarkets should be located within the Third Ring Road, while medium-sized supermarkets, chain stores and small discount stores are encouraged in central Beijing to satisfy the daily needs of citizens.

City Sightseeing Route F: Dongzhimen—Lama Temple—Asian Games Village — Changping Satellite City — Beijing-Miyun Canal and Miyun Reservoir
线路 F: 东直门—雍和宫—亚运村—昌平卫星城—京密运河和密云水库

Dongzhimen (Eastern Gate) 东直门

Dongzhimen (Eastern Gate) is one of the two terminal stations of the urban light railway; connect with the ring subway, and many public transportation lines. The planned traffic flow has been more convenient for passengers. Beijing's urban traffic congestion has been greatly eased thanks to the launching of the city's light rail project. The initial tracks of Beijing's first light railway line were laid down on October 1, 2001. Started in October 2000, construction of the light rail began at the Huilongguan (a residential area encompassing 8.5 million square metres and home to 230,000 residents). The light rail stretches from the Huilongguan East Station to Xizhimen (Western Gate) in the west, a communications hub, and Dongzhimen (Eastern Gate), also a communications hub in the east. Construction of the light rail has been divided into two sections. The western section of Beijing's light railway, from Huilongguan to Xizhimen was finished in May 2002 and the eastern section from Huilongguan to Dongzhimen was completed by September 2002. With 16 stations, the 40.9-kilometre light rail opened to traffic before October 2002.

New Visa Centre 新签证中心

The Beijing Public Security Bureau moved its visa centre to a new building on February 1, 1999 near the Lama Temple to better service cross-border travellers. The new visa centre has a hall of more than 1,000 square metres. It can process the border entrance and exit documents of Chinese citizens, Chinese visa and residential documents for foreigners, registering of foreign enterprises and their Beijing representative offices as well as loss of property by overseas visitors and travellers.

Following are the telephone numbers:

64047799 (switch board) 总机

84015300 (duty) 值班

84015292 (inquiry for foreigners' visas) 外国人签证咨询

84015297 (inquiry for outbound of Chinese citizens) 公民出境咨询
84015295 (inquiry for registration on file of foreign organizations) 外商
     机构备案登记咨询
84015316 (people's supervision) 群众监督电话

Lama Temple 雍和宫

Located in the northeastern part of the old city of Beijing, the Lama Temple was a palatial residence constructed in 1694 by Qing Emperor Kangxi (1662-1722) for his fourth son, Prince Yongzheng who later succeeded to the throne. The magnificent temple consists of five main buildings lying on the north-south axis, with annex halls standing on both sides. The temple is listed by the Chinese Government as one of the important historical monuments under special preservation. After the death of his father, Emperor Yongzheng (1723-1735) moved to the Forbidden City. This compound was closed to ordinary people and was renamed Yonghegong(the Palace of Harmony). Yellow roof tiles replaced green ones to suit a monarch's home. In 1744 his successor Emperor Qianlong (1736-1795) converted the palace into a temple. Several renovations have been carried out since 1949. The temple has taken on a completely new look and has been reopened to the public since 1981. It is now not only a functional lama temple, but also a tourist attraction.

White Peacock Art World 白孔雀艺术世界

The White Peacock Art World, one of the biggest arts and crafts centres in China, is situated in the northern suburbs of Beijing, not far from Ditan (Altar of Earth) Park in Beibinhe Road. It was officially established in March 1985 as a division of the Beijing Arts and Crafts Company Department Store. The six-storey building is divided into two sections. On the fourth floors are goods from all over the country, ranging from jewelry and textiles to top quality hardwood furniture. Friendly and helpful services are an important priority, and the sales staff can be easily identified by their traditional dress. The women's cheongsam vary in colour from floor to floor.

    The upper two floors include a duty-free shop, a foreign exchange counter, a massage parlour and a beauty salon. Its basement has been converted into a ballroom and bar as well as a restaurant that serves such famous delicacies as Liu Bang dog meat and beancurd jelly.

Cuishi (Japanese-Style) Garden 翠石花园

Cuishi (Green Rock) Garden, the first Japanese-style garden in China, was completed in Beijing on September 22, 1984. As a part of Shuangxiu Park, which was built in north Beijing, the garden covers 5,500 square metres. It includes artificial rockeries, a waterfall, a wooden arch bridge and Japanese style wooden pavilions. The whole park was jointly built by the Beijing Municipal Bureau of Gardens and Japanese friends Tanimura Chikeo and Nankane Kinsaku. Tanimura Chikeo, president of Tanimura Construction Company of Niigata Prefecture, has donated some 800 tons of rock for the park, as well as the bridge, pavilions, wooden gate and modern Japanese lamps for the garden. The garden was designed by Chikeo's friend Professor Kinsaku of Osaka Art University. Beijing Municipal Bureau of Gardens handled construction. Shuangxiu Park is located some 200 metres east of the Beitaipingzhuang crossing on the south side of the Third Ring Road.

Arrow Castle of Deshengmen (Gate of Virtuous Triumph)
德胜门

Deshengmen, or the Gate of Virtuous Triumph, used to be one of the nine city gates of old Beijing. It was erected in 1439. The arrow castle of this gate is similar to that of the Front Gate. The gate was torn down when the subway was built, but the Arrow Castle remained and was renovated in 1981.

"Desheng" means triumphant return of generals who made brilliant achievements in battlefields. In the Ming and Qing dynasties, troops returned to the city through the Gate of Virtuous Triumph.

Jishuitan Hospital 积水潭医院

A general hospital focused on orthopedic and burn traumas, the Hospital conducts first-class clinical treatment and research of hand surgery and burn medicine. The Beijing Research Institute of Traumatic Orthopedics is set up here.

148

Ring Roads of Beijing 北京环行路

To help facilitate traffic, we have built several ring roads in Beijing. The 33-kilometre-long Second Ring Road, for example, was built along the city wall of old Beijing. The old city wall was torn down as it obstructed traffic while some of the gates and castles have been preserved. A 23.6-kilometer-long loop line subway encircling the city has been completed and is running right beneath it. More than 95 flyovers have been built on the main roads that radiate from the city. About three kilometres away from the Second Ring Road is the 48-kilometre-long Third Ring Road, which was completed and opened to traffic in December 1981. And the 65. 3-kilometre-long Fourth Ring Road was completed and opened to traffic in June 2001. The first segment of the Fifth Ring Road in Beijing opened to traffic on September 22, 2001. The 15. 2-kilometre, six-lane highway, linking expressways leading to the Badaling section of the Great Wall to Capital International Airport, took a year to build and allows cars to travel at speeds of up to 100 kilometres per hour. The northern sections of the Fifth and Fourth Ring roads are in areas where major Olympic gymnasiums and stadiums are planned. Athletes and attendees have been promised they will be able to commute from any one gymnasium to another in 30 minutes or less. The Fifth Ring Road also is the first project in Beijing's major in-frastructure construction plans to hold public hearings to decide fee-collecting methods. Green belts of 100 metres will be planted on each side of the road. The Fifth Ring Road, designed to be 95 kilometres long when completed in 2003, is estimated to cost 13 billion yuan (US$1. 6 billion). The Fifth Ring Road will play a key role in easing downtown traf-fic congestion and promoting the development near the expressways. Bei-jing plans to spend 90 billion yuan (US$10. 9 billion) on a modern trans-portation system that would include expressways, subways, light railways and airport expansions. Beijing has 340 kilometres of expressways, a fig-ure expected to nearly double to 630 kilometres by 2005. And the 188-kilometre-long Sixth Ring Road and the 400-kilometre-long Seventh Ring Road are on the drawing boards.

The Third Ring Road 三环路

About three kilometres away from the Second Ring Road is the 48-kilometre-long Third Ring Road. It was completed and opened to traffic in December 1994.

China International Exhibition Centre 中国国际展览中心

This is China International Exhibition Centre, situated at Jing'anzhuang, Northeast Ring Road, in Chaoyang District. The centre is an enterprise af-filiated with the China Council for the Promotion of International Trade. It covers a gross space of 150, 000 square metres, and an exhibition complex with 75, 000 square metres, and an exhibition complex with 75, 000 square metres.

Construction of CIEC started in early 1984 and the first phase of con-struction was completed in August 1985. The building provides 6 exhibi-tion halls covering more than 40, 000 square metres. At present, the cen-tre is the largest one among the exhibition halls in China.

Anzhen Hospital 安贞医院

A new hospital emphasizing the treatment of cardiovascular diseases, the hospital boasts 750 beds. Active in epidemiological research and community public health, it has monitored over 700, 000 cardiovascular cases in Beijing.

Big Bell Temple Market 大钟寺集贸市场

This is the Big Bell Temple Market, which is a wholesale market for farm and sideline products and it sells more vegetables than any other such market in China. Vegetables sold at the market can feed one fourth of all the people in Beijing all the year round. In 1987, the farmer owned market was still a vegetable field surrounded by tall buildings constructed during the urban development. The market now has four sections—wholesale vegetables, fruit, aquatic products and nonstaple foods. Every day 5, 000 trucks come and an average of 30, 000 sellers and buyers stream through the area. Trade is lively amidst the seeming chaos and hubbub. Sellers at the market are mostly farmers from households specializing in transport and sales, farmers selling surplus produce and private long distance vegetable households.

Buyers are mainly private street stall vegetable sellers and persons buying supplies for organizations, schools and armed forces. The Big Bell Temple Market is a pioneer. In 1985, the Beijing Municipal Government adopted two reform measures — freeing prices of meat, poultry, eggs, aquatic products and vegetables and opening the city's gates to nonstaple foods shipped from all corners of the country.

The market villagers capitalized on their convenient location beside Beijing's Third Ring Road to turn their vegetable field into a marketplace. It opened on January 25, 1985, but at that time the farmers did not have such big ambitions and vision. Nowadays its daily transaction can go as high as 1, 200 tons. The market's trade involves thousands of vegetable peddlers and staff of private, collective and state owned vegetable shops from 600 counties. The market also provides information services.

150

Beijing Hi-Tech Convention and Exhibition Centre
北京科技会展中心

Encompassing 250, 000 square metres and as one of the largest and best quality projects in the centre of the golden axis in the Zhongguancun Sci-tech Park, the Beijing Hi-tech Convention and Exhibition Centre comprises a Cyber Tower, an IT Exhibition Centre, a multi-functional conference centre, an apartment building, service apartment for experts, a shopping centre, and some related facilities. The centre provides an ideal business and residential environment for domestic and foreign high-tech enterprises, finance and telecommunication companies, service agencies and business people as well.

With its 125 metres in height, Cyber Tower 数码大厦 is one of the highest buildings in the northeastern part of Beijing and a proud modern office structure overlooking the city. The tower was completed and put into operation in 2000. It boasts modern facilities, such as digital automatic control systems and a premise distribution system. It also provides comprehensive and quick solutions for telecommunications: network for each enterprise and every eight-square-metre has two information points. The central air-conditioning system consists of a four-pine-fan and cooler system and a fresh air system. The extra wall is made of high-quality materials such as aluminum, metal alloy, and soundproof thermal-insulated hollow double-layer glass. All electrical appliances and the water-supply system are environment-friendly and energy saving.

The three-storey sci-tech expert club on top of the Cyber Tower offers excellent services to domestic and foreign experts and enterprise managers to hold parties, meetings and enjoy entertainment activities. As the main construction of Beijing Hi-Tech Convention and Exhibition Centre, Cyber Tower is the tallest and most technically advanced building complex in Zhongguancun, with its hi-tech style appearance and landmark status.

A sealed overbridge connects Beijing Hi-Tech Convention and Exhibition Center with the superb facilities of Asia's largest garden style hotel—the Friendship Hotel. The combined community covering an area of 600,000 square metres is the hub of Zhongguancun, China's own Silicon Valley.

Corporations located here enjoy preferential policies offered by the State to the Zhongguancun Sci-tech Garden and the mortgage is provided by the Bank of China.

Sino-Japan Friendship Hospital 中日友好医院

Built jointly by the Chinese and Japanese governments in 1981, the Hospital has achieved renown in the research fields of coronary artery disease, artificial pacemaker implants, kidney transplants, laser eye surgery, micro-microsurgery, and lung and esophagus cancer.

The Hospital consists of four parts: a general hospital with 1,000 beds, a recovery ward with 300 beds, a clinical academic institute for 200 researchers, and a nurse school for 300 students. The total floor space of the hospital is nearly 83,000 square metres. The projects produced by Chinese designers and engineers. The project has utilized a variety of local and Japanese materials.

Its architectural design is compatible with Chinese tradition. The general layout is compact, with the main building linked by a central gallery. Ample space has been provided for landscaping and parking facilities.

Foreign Economic and Trade University 对外经济贸易大学

Founded in 1954, the University is China's multi-subject foreign trade university. It was first named Beijing Foreign Trade College. It got its present name in 1984. Under the University, there are five colleges, three directly affiliated departments, two teaching departments, 8 research institutes and 12 training centres.

Asian Games Village 亚运村

Asian Games Village was built for the 11th Asian Games, which was successfully held in Beijing from September 22 to October 7, 1990.

Located in the north of Beijing, the group of buildings in the Asian Games Village occupies an area of 31.5 hectares(78.75 acres). In the centre of the compound is a four-hectare central park in the shape of a semicircle. All the buildings, high and low, are scattered around the park. The buildings include village headquarters, six 13-to 18-storey athletes' apartments, a convention building which housed the games' Information Centre and the Organizing Committee, the Huibin Office Building, the Wuzhou (Intercontinental) Hotel, a recreation palace, shopping centre, restaurant, and a school and kindergarten. Many curves, big and small, can be seen inside and outside the buildings. The curves interact with each other, giving a sense of movement and development. To the southeast of the central part lies to No. 1 Building of the Intercontinental Hotel shaped like an arc. It is similar to the arc in the southeast of the park, and thus creates a certain connection between the building and the park. Few buildings have simple, straight angles. Instead, they have step like tops rising and falling a stark contrast to the rigid, box like buildings that are seen elsewhere, which create a sense of flow and movement. The sense of space comes both from the large open areas between the buildings and the light, soft colors used. Space between buildings not only improves the quality of the air, but also makes people inside feel they have a connection with the outside world. They are not isolated by a dense pack of high-rise buildings. The builders drew inspiration from Chinese painting, where white is often used to symbolize a sense of emptiness.

Beijing International Convention Centre
北京国际会议中心

Located at Anhui Flyover, north 4th Ring (Loop) Road, the Beijing International Convention Centre is an ideal place for tourists, long-term residents, and international and domestic conventions to be held in Beijing.

Conveniently located, well equipped, set in a beautiful environment and elegantly designed, the building complex is novel in style, with a construction area of more than 50,000 square metres. The centre boasts comprehensive facilities for holding conference, exhibitions and other large international and domestic activities. It is complete with scores of meeting rooms able to handle between a dozen to 2,500 people and a 5,000-square-metre of exhibition hall, and a 5,000-square-metre of office building. It is 9 kilometres to the Tian'anmen Square, the centre of the city in the south, 20 kilometres from the Capital International Airport in the east, and 12 kilometres from the Summer Palace in the west; and has access to the Badaling Expressway leading to the world-famous Great Wall and the Ming Tombs Tourist Area in the north. The centre has played host to over 3,000 conferences and exhibitions of varied scales, including the 11th Asian Games, the 14th World Conference on Mining, the 12th Session of the International Measuring Federation, and the 64th International Criminal Police Organization (ICPO-Interpol) General Assembly. The Fourth World Conference for Women, the largest in scale in the history of the United Nations, was also held in this centre. The centre was another main conference venue of the XX UIA (Union of International Architecture) Congress. Whether you are hosting a meeting, working in an office, staying as a guest, or entertaining and shopping, you will surely enjoy the quiet, convenient, comfortable, and fine services. The Convention Centre has everything a traveller needs to feel right at home.

153

National Olympic Sports Centre 国家奥林匹克体育中心

Located in the northern suburbs of Beijing, the National Olympic Sports Centre is the site of a giant indoor swimming pool 110 metres long and 76 metres wide. Construction of the complex began in April 1987 and was completed in December 1989. At a cost of US$ 1.53 million, the swimming pool was the most expensive and most architecturally sophisticated of the new facilities built for 1990 Asian Games. This is the first sports facility in China to adopt the modern architectural design usually used to build bridges. The 177-metre-long steel beam with a square cross section, 1.8 metres on each side is hung by cables tied to the two giant columns standing 60 and 70 metres respectively. It supports a 2,800-ton slope shaped shining roof which features the unique Chinese style for roofs adopted by the imperial palaces in the Forbidden City.

Inside the building is a competition arena with an Olympic sized swimming pool and a diving well. The 10-lane swimming pool is three metres deep. With such modern devices as underwater lighting and audio systems, it can play host to competitive swimming, synchronized swimming and water polo competitions. Also in the arena is a square diving well, 25 metres on each side and 5.5 metres deep. Installed by the poolside are 22 diving springboards and platforms, including 10 fixed platforms. The poolside surface is heated to ensure the comfort of swimmers and divers. The pool water is circulated and is sterilized through a special system using ozone. The 6,000 seat spectator stands are set to the north and south of the arena, with a VIP box and zones reserved for press, competitors and disabled spectators. Under the southern stand is a warm up pool, 50 metres long and 12.5 metres wide with a depth of 1.8 metres, plus a practice pool and locker rooms. Under the southern stand are pressrooms, a medical clinic, the telecommunications centre and rooms for judges and other personnel. Also in the complex are a gymnasium for training divers and swimmers and a hall for synchronized swimmers.

Celebrity International Grand Hotel 名人国际大酒店

Located in the heart of the Asian Games Village, the Celebrity International Grand Hotel (five-star hotel) is just a part of the Celebrity Square, and the apartments and shopping arcade. Surrounding it are notable abodes like the Huiyuan Apartments and Sunshine Plaza. Moreover, middle-class villas are mushrooming on the north. Right at the centre of the business shopping street of the area, the hotel is a place with prime access to wide range of goods—adjunct to the North Star Shopping Centre, Beijing Silk Shop. It is also a street for various Chinese and Western food restaurants, and fast foods like TGI Friday, McDonald's and Mongolian Barbecue. The area is a place of culture as well. Opposite the hotel is Yanhuang Art Museum. To the north is the Chinese Ethnic Cultural Park and to the south the Sports Museum in the Olympic Sports Centre and Beijing Birds Park. Although in the north of Beijing, the brand-new luxury hotel offers easy transport. It is only 10 kilometres away from Tian'anmen Square and a 20-minute ride to the Beijing Capital International Airport. Free shuttle buses are available every day to the airport, shopping and scenic spots in downtown areas. The hotel is ideally located in the business area of the north. Within walking distance is the Beijing International Convention Centre, the largest of its kind in the capital city.

Designed and decorated by famous architects, the hotel includes neo-classic features, representing an ambiance of nobility and dignity. The natural color in the rooms makes guests feel warm and gives a sense of intimacy; the golden lights add a magnificent air. Lamps, art work and other decor take the shape of cups and ribbons, a symbol of honour and achievement. Offering a panoramic view over the city, the 323 rooms and suites are equipped with every modern amenity including an executive-sized desk, IDD telephones, satellite television and in-room movies providing the most comprehensive services of staying, dining, entertainment, and business. Also there is a UFO-shaped club called Celebrity Club on the top of the hotel. It is a meeting place for all notable figures from various fields. At the Fitness Centre, guests can work out on the latest computerized equipment. There are a billiard room, a chess and bridge room, an aerobics studio and a heated indoor swimming pool. After a long day's business or sightseeing around the city, guests can relieve those tired and aching muscles with an invigorating sauna, steam bath or herbal bath. And they can retire to one of the private rooms for a soothing massage.

The hotel tries to meet the demands of guests who hope to find good restaurants and bars. The Chinese Cuisine Restaurant features abalone and shark's fins. It is supported by the Zhongshan Food and Beverage and Entertainment Company. Other specialties include fish lips and baby pigeon. Diners can savour a dazzling array of typical local dishes of each region in China every week. And the Buffet Hall provides the specialties of different countries. The traditional performances will be presented according to the relevant regional foods. The Milky Way Wine Corridor on the second is the most magnificent place in the hotel. Under the glass roof, guests can have a wonderful daytime bask and, in the evening, enjoy the romantic ambiance of a view of the moon and stars, and the glass-framed golden lights. More than 100 kinds of refreshing coffees, wines, and snacks are beautifully served within 24 hours. The Corridor keeps guests entertain with a repertoire of melodious sounds while drinking afternoon tea. In the evening, guests can enjoy a cocktail show and bands.

If guests plan a large-scale business or social activity, the hotel can offer spacious conference and banqueting space. It can accommodate up to 200 people and offer a full range of audio-visual facilities including simultaneous translation. The Grand Ballroom can accommodate 500 guests and there is a choice of multi-function rooms. At the 24-hour Business Centre, the guest will find professional secretarial and other services including translation, fax facilities, private meeting rooms, and offices for rent.

Gymnasium of the Beijing Institute for Physical Education 北京体育学院体育馆

Construction of the project started in November 1986 and was completed in July 1988. The gymnasium is something like a Chinese *Baxianzhuo*, an old-fashioned square table with collapsible leaves that makes it into an octagonal shape. It used to be the site of the boxing tournament of the 11th Asian Games held in the fall of 1990. The gymnasium covers an area of more than 10, 000 square metres and its main competition hall features overhanging steel bars, a red metal roof, white walls, and dark gray glass windows. The building achieves a harmonious combination of strength and beauty. The main gymnasium has a competition arena of 36 by 24 metres for boxing competition. The 2, 050-seat spectator stands flank the arena's northern and southern sides. One third of the seats are removable. It has up to date electronic timing devices and modern lighting and air-conditioning systems. And it is complete with a practice hall, a recuperation centre, a hall for rhythmic gymnastics, a computer centre, drugtesting rooms and a press centre.

It can meet the needs of both international and domestic sports competition and is eminently suitable for high quality television broadcasting. This unique architectural style of the project has won high praise from foreign and domestic architects. The designers and the construction company were invited to build a similar gymnasium in Russia.

China Science and Technology Museum 中国科技博物馆

156

Construction of China's first national science museum started in November 1984, at the junction of Zhongzhu Road and Beisanhuan Road in northern Beijing. The museum stands on 7 hectares, with the buildings occupying 52, 000 square metres. It is divided into eight sections: exhibits and education, laboratories, video training, research and design, information, equipment service, motor station and management. The museum has eight laboratories for experiments in physics, chemistry, electronics, biology, computer, model making, and astronomy. The aim is to develop the ability to solve problems, and to create. It is the biggest science museum in China, and holds exhibitions to introduce modern sciences, organize experiments, hold training activities and have exchanges with science museums in foreign countries. The laboratories are mainly for young people in high schools or elementary schools. The museum will try to rouse children's interest in science while they are young and encourage them to do experiments on their own. There is a combined cinema lecture room with 98 seats and a cyclorama cinema with 500 seats. A library has a reading room and 260, 000 books and hundreds of magazines.

The second phase of the museum's construction started in February 1998 and the project was completed in September 1999 to mark the 50th anniversary of the founding of the People's Republic of China. As the largest one in China, the museum opened to the public early in 2000. With a total investment of 100 million yuan(US$12 million), the construction area of the second stage is 19, 000 square metres, and the exhibition hall covers nearly 10, 000 square metres.

The first stage of the museum, which was completed and opened to the public in 1988, covers an area of 20, 000 square metres, but the space of the three-storey exhibition hall is only 3, 900 square metres. About 300 ancient and modern items are on display. In 1997, the museum received more than 700, 000 visitors. After the second phase of the project was completed, visitors can see more items on display regarding the environment, information technology, life sciences, energy and communications. Some technological advances are also displayed at the hall. And visitor can operate some facilities and do experiments by themselves. The museum co-operates some key national labs and the industrial sector to make the items for display. In the museum, there are a 200-seat lecture hall and two 50-seat lecture halls for scientific discussions and lectures. In addition, visitors have place to eat, rest and entertain themselves.

The 69. 98-Kilometre-Long Badaling Expressway
八达岭高速公路

Construction of 31. 2-kilometre expressway linking Beijing and its suburban county of Changping started in January 1996 and it was completed and opened to traffic in December 1996. The designed speed is 80 to 120 kilometres per hour. There are 31 bridges and 19 overpasses built along the route. The cost of construction totalled 1. 98 billion yuan (US$238 million). The expressway in the only route from the urban districts of Beijing to suburban scenic spots such as the Great Wall and the Ming Tombs.

The 30. 67-kilometre-long extension expressway from Changping to Badaling was built and put into operation on November 8, 1998. Thus the total length of the expressway from the city to the Great Wall is 61. 87 kilometres.

The third stage of 8. 11-kilometre-long extension expressway was completed and opened to traffic in early September 2001. Thus the 69. 98-kilometre-long Badaling Expressway was completed and opened to traffic in September 2001. The expressway links Dandong, Liaoning Province in the east and Lhasa, Tibet Autonomous Region in the south. By the end of 2001, China had more than 19, 000 kilometres of expressways trailing the United States of America, ranking second in the world.

A rough road was formed along the way more than 2, 500 years ago. In the Yuan Dynasty(1279-1368), the old road was used for horse carts to transport provisions(grain), while in the Ming Dynasty(1368-1644) the road was converted into an imperial way leading to the Ming Tombs. Up to the Qing Dynasty(1644-1911), the road was only 5 to 6 metres wide, and it was paved with sand and gravel in 1934, thus a simple highway came into being. After 1949 several renovations and reconstruction were done, but it could not meet the needs of economic and tourism development.

In 1971, an Australian tour group visited Beijing. One of the members in the tour group told the author of the book (then interpreter/tour guide) that she came to Beijing in 1927 while she was very young. She went to the Great Wall by riding a donkey and she stayed in an inn along the road, and the next day she reached the Great Wall. It took her two days to reach the Great Wall. Today, it only takes one hour to arrive at the Wall. What a striking contrast!

Chaozong Bridge and South Big Bridge 朝宗桥及南大桥

On the way to the exciting Great Wall and the Ming Tombs, while passing through Shahe(Sand River) Town, tourists will certainly see two bridges, one is called the South Big Bridge and the other is named the North Big Bridge. In 1449, for the convenience of the Emperor's paying respect to the deceased emperors in the Ming Tombs, Wang Yongshou, minister of the Board of Works, was ordered that he should supervise the construction of the bridges. Then the construction of the North Bridge was presided over by Zhao Chaozong. As he paid great attention to the quality of the bridge building, he delayed the completion of the bridge and was thus executed. The South Big Bridge was constructed ahead of time. Soon afterwards, torrents rushed down the mountain, and the North Big Bridge stood intact, while the South Big Bridge was washed away because of shoddy work. Later on, the royal families learnt that they killed the fine person by mistake. When Emperor Wanli(1573-1620) was in power he ordered that a stone tablet with the name of Chaozong on it be erected at the bridge head as commemoration, and the person who had been persecuted to death was rehabilitated by Ming Emperor Wanli.

Changping District—A Satellite City of Beijing
昌平卫星城

Situated in northern suburbs of Beijing, Changping District is where the Taihang Mountains meet the Yanshan Mountains. The district is encircled by beautiful and magnificent mountains. Changping, 33 kilometres from Beijing, occupies an area of 1,352 square kilometres and has a population of 56,000. Located in a semi-moist monsoon climate area that has a temperate continental climate, the district has four distinct seasons each year, with annual average rainfall of 570 millimetres and a frost free period of 180 to 203 days. The district has a long history. In both the Western Han Dynasty (206 BC-AD 23) and the Ming Dynasty(1368-1644), it was a prefecture. In 1956, it came under the administration of Beijing City. The district has a convenient communications network, with the Beijing-Baotou railway, the Datong-Qinhuangdao railway and the Beijing-Tongliao railway running through the district. There are 345 roads in the area with a total length of 1,569 kilometres. The road network connects the district with all its towns and with neighbouring counties and Beijing. Natural resources are also rich in the district, with proven metal and non-metallic mineral resources totaling 288 kinds. The Xiaotangshan terrestrial heat resources, which are famous in the district, occupy an area of 20 square kilometres. There are also 78 tourist spots in the district. They include the Ming Tombs, and the Juyong Pass of the Great Wall. There are 13 modern tourist spots, including the Nine-Dragon Entertainment Park, the Aviation Museum, the Beifang Shooting Range and the Shenzhou Dog Petting Park. There are also natural scenic spots, such as Gouya and Huyu. They receive about 12 million domestic and overseas visitors annually. The district has a strong science, technology and education work force. Within the district, there are 24 research institutes of the central government and Beijing Municipality and 31 district level research organizations. There are 14 colleges and universities located in the district, including the China Oil University, the China University of Political Science and Law, the Beijing Agriculture College as well as branches of the Qinghua and Beijing universities. A 100,000-line-programme-controlled telephone switching system is now in operation. There are more than 2,700 shops and commercial service spots. Hotels that can receive foreign guests include the Liuting, Yanling, Mingyuan and Zhong'an. In the district, there are more than 2,880 industrial firms, more than 240 foreign funded ventures and more than 110 high and new technology enterprises. They are involved in the fields of metallurgy, building materials, automobiles, chemical, textiles, machinery, garment and handicrafts industries. The establishment of the Changping Science and Technology Area was officially approved by the Beijing Municipal People's Government on November 9, 1991. The area is a base for the development of high and new technology industries and an important part of the Beijing Municipal New Technology Industry Development Zone. Thus, the area enjoys all the State Council approved preferential treatments for the Beijing Municipal New Technology Industry Development Zone. The Changping Science and Technology Area, 30 kilometres north of Beijing, has a space of 40 square kilometres. It is 42 kilometres from the Capital International Airport. Three railways run through the area while road transportation is very convenient. At the same time, the area has abundant supply of electricity and water.

According to the general development plan, 2, 285 square kilometres of land in the area will be the focus for future development. At present, 172 new technology enterprises have been established in the area and their total investment has reached 3 billion yuan (US$517. 2 million). The Changping Science and Technology Area will pay close attention to the development of high and new technology industries, including electronic information laser, photoelectron, new materials, new energy resources and bio-engineering technologies and their products. At the same time, the service industry associated with those high and new technology industries and real estate will also be vigorously developed. To speed up construction of the area and provide a streamlined service to investors, the district has set up a new service system in the area which includes services for industry and commerce administration, taxation, finance, auditing, law, foreign economic co-operation and material supply.

Changping West Ring Interchange 昌平西转盘

The interchange is the largest suburban multi layer overpass. It was built and opened to traffic in June 1987. The interchange is at the junction of three key roads leading respectively to the Badaling pass section of the Great Wall, the Ming Tombs and the Zhangjiakou City of Hebei Province. It was designed to enable a smooth flow of busy suburban traffic, especially during tourist season.

China North International Shooting Range
中国北方国际射击场

Located at Nankou, Changping District, northwest of Beijing proper, a dozen kilometres from the Ming Tombs and the Great Wall, the China North International Shooting Range, a showcase for the country's latest civilian entertainment attraction, opened to Chinese, compatriots from Hong Kong, Macao, and Taiwan, and foreign visitors and tourists in early 1987.

The shooting range provides some 20 kinds of light machinery weapons, all of which are made in China, including pistols, rifles, submachine guns, and light, heavy and wide caliber machine guns and even the 60 mm mortar for marksmen from Hong Kong, Macao, Taiwan and abroad. The range contains over 30 shooting platforms and a foreign guest club, a changing room, a film and video room and a coffee bar. It also provides cable television and automatic scoring facilities. There are mannequins, moving targets, steel plates and simulated defensive shooting. Foreign guests are welcome to use one or more light weapons and hundreds of cartridges for only two or three hundred US dollars.

The range is proud of the variety of machine guns to choose from including the world famous 7. 62 mm calibre AK submachine gun Type 56 and the new light weight submachine gun Type 85 weighing less than two grams. Available at the range is the 7. 62 mm calibre sniper rifle Type 79 which is a favorite of gun lovers for its accuracy. Unlike those at ranges in the United States, Japan and some European countries, all the weapons are real military brands. Sporting guns are also available at the range.

The China North International Shooting Range occupies an area of more than 16. 7 acres of land. It is a military turned civilian project under China's open policy and will continue to expand.

Beijing Shooting Range (Shooting & Recreation City)
北京射击场(射击娱乐城)

Located at the foot of Cuiwei Mountain in the western suburb of Beijing, the Beijing Shooting Range occupies an area of 44 hectares (108. 7 acres). It was first built in 1955 for training national-level athletes. It used to be the cradle of many world-shooting champions. The shooting competition for Asian Games and Inter-continental Shooting Championships were held here. Nowadays, it has become management centre for shooting and archery sports under the leadership of State Physical Culture and Sports Commission, and has been open to the public since December 1997. Apart from afro-mentioned facilities, other amenities include tennis court, singing hall, hotel and other recreational and sports facilities. This place will continue to be the cradle of world champions and at the same time it is a paradise for common people.

161

Beijing-Miyun Canal and Miyun Reservoir
京密运河和密云水库

This canal is 102 kilometres long, completed in 1966. The water comes from Miyun Reservoir, which lies on the northeastern outskirts of Beijing and has a capacity of 4.375 billion million cubic metres. The reservoir encompasses 224 square kilometres and its periphery highway reaches 110 kilometres. Since 1949, 86 reservoirs with varying capacity have been built and thousands of power-operated wells have been sunk in Beijing area. Since 1949, 84,800 reseriors have been built in China.

Construction of the canal has not only relieved the northern part of Beijing from the threat of drought and flood but also ensured water for power stations, afforestation and industrial and household use in the city.

University Regatta 著名大学举行赛艇对抗赛

The first Motorola University Regatta ended on September 23, 2001 with Yale University savouring victory on the Kunyu River in Beijing. Yale University concluded the 6,000-metre course ahead of China's Tsinghua University who claimed second place. Harvard University, who lost to Yale in 2001 in the Harvard-Yale University Regatta, finished third. Showered with champagne, applause and laughter, the cross-continent student sports meet turned into a jubilant gala following the end of fierce competition.

The 8 prestigious universities such as Cambridge University, Oxford University from England, Harvard University, Yale University from the United States, and China's Peking University, Tsinghua University, Fudan University and Shanghai Jiaotong University participated in the fierce competition held from September 22 to 23, 2001.

The Three Green Belts in Beijing 北京三条绿化带

The first green belt will be established in the hilly areas in the western, northern and eastern counties of Beijing, the tree belt will expand the counties' forest coverage to 70 per cent. The second green belt will add 23,000 hectares (56,833 acres) of woodlands along a 200-metre stretch on both sides of the city roads. Green belts along five highways, including the Beijing-Shijiazhuang expressway, will be completed in 2001 with a total area of 7,000 hectares (17,297 acres). The third green belt will be built between Beijing's third and fourth ring roads, and it will cover some 240 square kilometers. In 2000, 2,670 hectares (6,597.6 acres) of trees, shrubs and flowers were planted inside the Fourth Ring Road, exceeding the total for the previous 10 years. Eight "green zones," including fruit gardens and forest parks with a total area of 1, 450 hectares (3, 582. 95 acres), came into being in 2000. Beijing has been working hard in recent years to improve the local environment. The city added nearly 2, 700 hectares (6, 671. 7 acres) of green space in 2000 and planted a total of 112, 000 hectares (276, 752 acres) of forest over the past five years. Within the sandy wasteland areas of the city's major rivers, 57, 000 hectares (140, 847 acres) of trees will be planted to help solve the problem of sandstorms in the capital. These three large-scale green belts will be completed within 5 years from 2001 to 2005 to protect and improve the capital's eco-system.

Amitabha Buddha Near the Great Wall
长城附近的阿弥陀佛像

Ladies and gentlemen, soon we will arrive at the Great Wall. Before you pass through the *Qin*—a seven-stringed plucked instrument in some ways similar to zither Qin Playing Gorge Tunnel, you can see a famous historical site. It is said to be "Wu Lang Figure." Legend has it during the Song Dynasty (960-1279), Yang Wulang, a Song Dynasty general was defeated by the Liao Dynasty soldiers in a fierce battle. He then escaped to Wutai Mountain in Shanxi Province and became a monk. Therefore, this Amitabha Buddha was said to be the image of Yang Wulang to commemorate his deeds. But it is not true.

Why Was Amitabha Buddha Carved on the Cliff Here?
It is said that in the ancient times, this section of the road along Guangou on the way to the Great Wall was the most dangerous. Not far from the Buddha, the three Chinese characters, meaning "Five Ghost Head," are still visible. Legend has it that five ghosts appeared here quite frequently and the people were very scared when they passed by. Therefore, a temple was erected with niches in it. Only in this way could the people be safe while they traveled through here. Later on, the ancient temple was removed because of the construction of Jing-Zhang (Beijing-Zhangjiakou) highway and the railroad. But the carved Amitabha Buddha still remains and is put under better preservation by the local government.

Part Two

PROFILE OF THE PRIME SIGHTS (1)

第二部分　主要名胜介绍 (1)

Principal Sites Around Tian'anmen
天安门及周围主要景点

Tian'anmen (Gate of Heavenly Peace) 天安门

Tian'anmen (Gate of Heavenly Peace) Rostrum was opened to the public for the first time in its history in 1988. From the rostrum of Tian'anmen, the late Chairman Mao Zedong proclaimed the founding of the People's Republic of China on October 1, 1949, and since then it has been the symbol of New China.

In modern Chinese history, several large mass demonstrations have taken place here. The most famous was on May 4th Movement of 1919, when more than 3, 000 students from Beijing schools and universities came to the square to demonstrate against imperialism and the rule of the military leaders. The event was a landmark in modern Chinese history.

The structure was first named Chengtianmen (Gate of Power Endowed from Heaven or Gate of Heavenly Succession) when it was built in 1417 as the main gate of the former Imperial Palace. In 1456 the wooden structure burned down after it was struck by lightning. It was rebuilt in 1651, and renamed Tian'anmen (Gate of Heavenly Peace). In 1644, when the Manchus defeated Li Zicheng, leader of a peasant uprising, he set fire to the building before running away from the city. The building was enlarged when it was rebuilt for the second time in 1651, and this is the structure, which still stands today. The nine-room-wide and five-room-long wooden gate tower was built to reflect the highly exalted status of the emperor. Sixty spherical columns from Indonesia support the entire building. The wood is very hard. To make the columns immortal, the workers scooped out a hole with 10-centimetre in diameter in each column with special bit and tool for injecting insecticide, the prevention and control of plant diseases and e-limination of pests, waterproof and anticorrosive. Each column is 10 metres long and weighs 7 tons.

Located to the north of Tian'anmen Square, the building has red stonewalls, a wooden roof and five entrances—the largest, in the middle, leads to the Forbidden City. The building is surrounded by a moat, Jinshui (Golden Water), which was designed to guard the Imperial Palace. Five marble bridges, the Golden Water Bridges, lead to the five passages of the gate. Two ornamental columns stand in front of the whole complex.

The gate and the square were out of bounds to the public in imperial times. The emperor alone was entitled to pass through the central passage. Before leaving on a journey he would make a sacrifice in front of the gate. At other times imperial edicts were sent down, in a gilded box shaped like a phoenix, to officials kneeling below. Hence the expression: "the Imperial Orders Given by the Gilded Phoenix 金凤颁诏 ." The edict was then taken to the Ministry of Rites 礼部 where copies were made for dispatch to the whole country. It was also the place for the emperor to review royal armies and receive prisoners of war.

Tian'anmen (Gate of Heavenly Peace) is not only the site of the most important gatherings since the founding of the People's Republic of China, but also one of the most valuable historical sites in China. Parades take place here on important days, such as the rallies on May 1, International Labour Day. Before each parade the building is repainted and generally tidied up. The whole tower roof was replaced as part of a large-scale restoration in 1984, following the original line and shape. The balcony is 34.7 metres high, 62.77 metres long and 27.25 metres wide. It can hold 20,000 guests. There are 67 steps leading to the top of the Rostrum of Tian'anmen Gate.

Tian'anmen Square 天安门广场

Tian'anmen Square encompasses 44 hectares (108.7 acres), 880 metres from north to south and 500 metres from east to west, big enough to hold half a million people. The square has witnessed the Chinese people's struggle against foreign aggression and reactionary rule at home.

In 1919, the May 4th Movement broke out in Beijing. Students and residents staged a patriotic demonstration in the square. In 1935, students in Beijing launched the December 9th Movement against the Japanese aggression and Chiang Kai-shek's policy of non-resistance. They held a demonstration in the square.

On April 5, 1976, lots of people gathered here to commemorate Zhou Enlai and oppose the "Gang of Four"—Jiang Qing, Wang Hongwen, Zhang Chunqiao and Yao Wenyuan. Many tourists to Tian'anmen Square would like to have their pictures taken in front of the white marble Jinshuiqiao (Golden Water Bridges).

The bridges were named after the Golden Water River they span. Seven bridges, each supported by three arches, cross the Outer Golden Water River in front of Tian'anmen, Zhongshan Park, and the Beijing Working People's Palace of Culture. Five one-arched bridges cross the Inner Golden Water River inside the Forbidden City between Wumen (Meridian Gate) and Taihemen (Gate of Supreme Harmony).

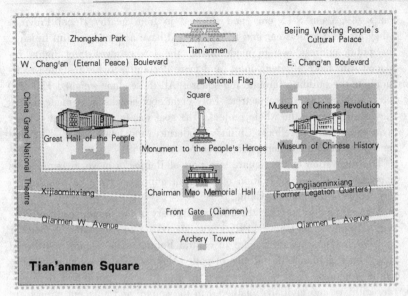

Zhongshan Park

Tian'anmen

Beijing Working People's Cultural Palace

W. Chang'an (Eternal Peace) Boulevard

E. Chang'an Boulevard

National Flag

Square

China Grand National Theatre

Great Hall of the People

Museum of Chinese Revolution

Museum of Chinese History

Monument to the People's Heroes

Xijiaominxiang

Chairman Mao Memorial Hall

Dongjiaominxiang (Former Legation Quarters)

Front Gate (Qianmen)

Qianmen W. Avenue

Qianmen E. Avenue

Archery Tower

Tian'anmen Square

The outer bridges, together with two graceful *Huabiao* (ornamental columns) and two stone lions nearby, set off Tian'anmen, making it look more imposing. The inner bridges make the spacious square look harmonious.

During the Ming and Qing dynasties, the middle one of the seven outer bridges, which is larger than the others was called Bridge of the Imperial Way 御路桥 and was used exclusively by the Emperor. The two bridges on each side were called Royal Bridges 王公桥 and were used by the royal family members. The two bridges farther out were the Ranking Bridges 品级桥 and were used by civil and military officials above the third rank. Those of the fourth rank and below could use only the outer two bridges, which were called Public Bridges 公生桥.

The Beijing Municipal Government launched a nine-month project to renovate Tian'anmen Square in the heart of the capital. Reconstruction started in October 1998 and was completed by June 1999, in time for the grand celebrations to mark the 50th anniversary of the founding of the People's Republic of China on October 1, 1999, improved the worn-out pavement, public address system, and lighting around the periphery of the world's largest square, installing new foundations and repairing underground pipelines. The bricks on the square were replaced with 340,000 pink granite slabs to cover 156,900 square metres (the gradient of the square is 3 per thousand easy for flow of rainwater and each slab is 99.5

cm × 49.5 cm ×15 cm) and shipped in from nearby Hebei Province (they are said to be wear and tear proof and have a more beautiful finish), the public-address system modernized, the low-wattage street lights replaced with more efficient ones, and more decorative lights installed to illuminate the buildings around the square. All these slabs weighed 130,000 tons, with 50,000 cubic metres. Fifty eight spot checks were made during the construction of the whole project. The goal was to create a 21st century style square which reflects China's modernity, and new capital. The first renovation of Tian'anmen Square took place in 1959.

The renovation of the square was part of Beijing's move to improve its appearance for the celebration of the 50th anniversary of the founding of the People's Republic of China.

A grand parade marking the 50th anniversary of the founding of the People's Republic of China (PRC) was staged on the morning of October 1, 1999 in Tian'anmen Square in central Beijing. The square was turned into a huge garden with millions of potted flowers. The five-star red flag—China's national flag—could be seen all over the city. Some 500,000 people, military and civilians, gathered in the square and adjacent streets, in anticipation of the moment they had all been waiting for—the start of the parade at 10:00 am. President Jiang Zemin and other top officials reviewed the troops, and military vehicles, missiles and warplanes, most of which were made in China. After the military parade came the turn of civil society with various activities to celebrate the grand occasion, including the performance of a traditional dragon dance. Dozens of specially designated floats featuring China's major social and economic developments during the past five decades thrilled the audience as they passed through the square.

The Grand National Day parade ended with the release of tens of thousands of colorful balloons. Some 50,000 homing pigeons were also let loose in the skies over the square. New China has staged 13 National Day military parades and celebration activities in Tian'anmen Square since it was founded in 1949.

In the evening of the same day, fireworks lit up the sky as 100,000 jubilant Chinese took part in a song and dance extravaganza in Tian'anmen Square to celebrate the 50th anniversary of the founding of the People's Republic of China.

The eastern and western Tain'anmen Square subway stations were built. The Tian'anmen section, part of the Fuxingmen and Bawangfen subway project, was built to help ease excess traffic in the downtown area of the national capital. The western station has two levels, one with three entrances and exits. The three-floor eastern station has seven entrances and exits.

Chairman Mao Memorial Hall 毛主席纪念堂

South of the Monument to the People's Heroes is Chairman Mao Memorial Hall. The foyer houses a seated figure of Chairman Mao in white marble. Behind it is a 7-by-24-metre needlepoint woolen tapestry "Such a beauty is our motherland." In the second room, Chairman Mao's remains recline in a crystal coffin, with the red flag of the Communist Party of China draped over his body. The building was completed in 1977.

Currently, the remains of late Chairman Mao are mechanically raised from a freezer for viewing, then lowered again at night.

Sculptures 雕塑

The sculpture groups are 6 to 8 metres high and 7 to 15 metres long. The two on the north side are designed on the theme "Great Contributions," representing what the Chinese people achieved in the last half century under the leadership of Chairman Mao. Those on the south side have as their theme "Carry Out Chairman Mao's Behest," expressing the Chinese people's determination to act on his behest and carry the cause of our proletarian revolution through to the end.

Monument to the People's Heroes 人民英雄纪念碑

The Monument to the People's Heroes was built in memory of the martyrs who laid down their lives for the revolutionary struggle of the Chinese people in the past century. It was built in accordance with the resolution of the First Plenary Session of the Chinese People's Political Consultative Conference adopted on November 30, 1949. Chairman Mao and other delegates laid the corner stone for the monument on that afternoon.

The 38-metre-high monument was open on July 1, 1958. It covers an area of 3,000 square metres. The stone tablet is from Qingdao, Shandong Province. On the front is an inscription in Chairman Mao's handwriting: "Eternal glory to the people's heroes!" On the back is the late Premier Zhou Enlai's message: "Eternal glory to the people's heroes who laid down their lives in the War of Liberation in the past three years and the people's revolution in the past three decades! Eternal glory to the people's heroes who laid down their lives in the struggles against foreign and domestic enemies, for national independence and for the people's freedom and happiness from 1840 onward!" At the base of the tablet are eight huge bas relieves carved out of white marble covering the revolutionary episodes.

Burning Opium in the Opium War in 1840 1840 年鸦片战争期间焚烧

鸦片

A revolutionary movement broke out to resist the smuggling of large quantities of opium into China by the British imperialists. In June 1839, altogether 1. 15 million kilograms of opium was destroyed. It showed the Chinese people's determination to struggle against imperialism and marked the beginning of their resistance.

Jintian Village Uprising in Taiping Revolution 太平天国金田村起义

The Taiping Revolution was the biggest and longest revolutionary peasant uprising in the Chinese history. Led by Hong Xiuquan (1814-1864), this great anti-imperialist, anti-feudal peasant movement first broke out in Jintian Village in Guangxi in 1851. The revolutionary flames soon spread to six provinces and the revolutionaries established their capital in Nanjing.

Wuchang Uprising (1911 Revolution) 武昌起义（辛亥革命）

1911 was the year in which the decisive battle against the Manchu Government was fought. Late on the evening of October 10, the revolutionary forces wrecked the cannon in front of the office building of the governor of both Hunan and Hubei provinces, pulled down the royal flag and broke through the gate of the governor's mansion. The first success of the revolution was at Wuhan. The last feudal dynasty collapsed under the fierce attack of the revolutionary torrent on October 10, 1911.

May 4th Movement 五四运动

An anti-imperialist patriotic movement broke out on May 4, 1919 in Beijing. It was the turning point of the Chinese democratic revolution. On that day, several thousand Beijing students held a rally in front of Tian'anmen. A parade followed in which participants held aloft banners inscribed "No signature to the 'peace treaty'!" and distributed the leaflets "Uphold our sovereignty! Punish the traitors!"

May 30th Movement 五卅运动

_172_

A demonstration by Shanghai workers and students on May 30, 1925 ushered in a vigorous anti-imperialist movement. Demonstrators' banners thundered "Down with the imperialists!" and "Revenge Gu Zhenghong, a splendid representative of China's workers shot down by the imperialists!"

Nanchang Uprising 南昌起义

Chiang Kai-shek launched a coup on April 12, 1927 and began slaughtering Communists. To save the revolution and continue struggle, the Chinese Communist Party fired the first shot at the Kuomintang reactionaries in the Nanchang Uprising on August 1, 1927. This was the day the Chinese Communist Party began to lead the revolutionary armed forces independently against the counter-revolutionary armed forces. Hence August 1 is the birthday of the Chinese People's Liberation Army.

War of Resistance Against Japan 抗日战争

Army men and civilians in the revolutionary base areas carried out Chairman Mao's thinking on protracted war. The Chinese Communist Party called on the people's army to go to the enemy's rear to launch guerrilla warfare, mine warfare, etc. War educated the people and the people won the war.

Successful Crossing of the Yangtze River 胜利横渡长江

This was the prelude to the liberation of the whole country. An army one million strong made a forced crossing of the Yangtze River on April 21, 1949 to overthrow the Chiang Kai-shek regime. On the right are the masses helping the PLA men to make the crossing. On the left are the liberated Nanjing people welcoming the entrance of the PLA men. The liberation of the Kuomintang capital heralded the liberation of the whole country.

The Great Hall of the People 人民大会堂

Construction of the Great Hall of the People started in October 1958 and was completed by the end of August 1959, taking ten months altogether.

It has a total floor space of 171, 800 square metres, 20, 000 square metres more than that of the Palace Museum in the neighbourhood. It is 206 metres long and 336 metres wide. Its highest point is 46. 5 metres from the ground. In front of the Great Hall of the People there are 39 steps.

It consists of three major sections: in the north is the Banquet Hall that accommodates 5, 000 people; in the centre is the Grand Auditorium with a seating capacity of 10, 000; offices of the Standing Committee of the National People's Congress are in the south. There are more than 300 reception rooms and conference halls of various sizes. Thirty-four reception rooms are furnished by and named after various provinces, municipalities, autonomous regions and special admininistrative regions.

Each room is featured by its own local style. Today, we'll visit some of them. They are the reception rooms of Taiwan Province, Sichuan Province, Hunan Province, Liaoning Province, Guangdong Province, Shanghai Municipality and Beijing Municipality.

We are now in the central foyer. It's for the people attending meetings to take a rest during intervals. The floor is paved with natural marble and the 20 pillars are made of white marble. Each crystal glass chandelier weighs 1. 2 tons.

The 10, 000-Seat Auditorium 万人礼堂

The auditorium is used for important occasions such as sessions of the National People's Congress, the Party Congress and mass political rallies to support the just struggle of the people of other countries. The massive hall

173

is 76 metres in width, 60 metres in length and 32 metres in height, with a balcony and a gallery. There are 3,600 seats on the ground floor, 3,500 on the balcony and 2,500 on the gallery. The stage can hold a presidium of 300 to 500 people. The total seating capacity is ten thousand. It is also used for festive celebrations and grand stage shows. The proscenium can be converted into an orchestra pit by removing the floor boards.

The seats on the ground floor are equipped with earphones, through which one can hear a simultaneous translation of a speech in any one of 12 different languages. Every two seats share a loudspeaker and every four seats a microphone for extemporaneous speeches. On the ceiling are 500 starlights with an enormous red star in the centre. Seventy light beams radiate in all directions enclosed by a ring of 40 sunflower petals, which in turn is skirted by three layers of hidden lights in the form of expanding waves. This beautiful pattern symbolizes the close unity of the people of the whole country around the Party in their forward march from victory to victory. The ones that have no light are ventilation holes.

The auditorium has three main features: people can evacuate rapidly through its 32 doors; the fan shape hall provides a good view of the presidium from any angle; the acoustics is very good.

Built-in lighting equipment for filming documentaries is set in a crescent shape facing the stage.

Balcony 楼座

The balcony is for non-voting deputies and foreign envoys. A loudspeaker is installed at the back of each seat on the balcony and the gallery. Simultaneous translation in different languages is provided for by block allocation of seats. The volume control is installed on the left arm of the seat.

The Museum of the Chinese Revolution & the Museum of Chinese History 中国革命博物馆和中国历史博物馆

Along the east side of Tian'anmen Square is a cream building with green and yellow eaves, standing 33 metres high; the north wing houses the Museum of the Chinese Revolution and the south wing houses the Museum of Chinese History.

The Museum of the Chinese Revolution contains a two-storey exhibition hall with 4,000 square metres of floor space on each storey. With more than 120,000 relics, the museum is a State museum for revolutionary documents and materials on Party history dating from the May 4th Movement of 1919 and the founding of the Communist Party of China in 1921. The permanent exhibition is devoted to the history of the Communist Party of China up to 1949. The exhibits on Party history in the New Democratic

Revolution are divided into five sections: the founding of the Communist Party of China in 1921; the First Revolutionary Civil War (1924-1927); the Second Revolutionary Civil War (1927-1937); the War of Resistance Against Japan (1937-1945); and the Third Revolutionary Civil War (1945-1949). Over 3, 300 exhibits illustrate the history of the Communist Party of China up to 1949, the founding of the People's Republic of China.

The Museum of Chinese History has a permanent exhibition of over 60, 000 antiques, historical documents and pictures showing the course of Chinese history. It is regarded as a historic vista reviewing the evolution of the Chinese nation. The museum is divided into four sections according to different states in the development of Chinese society: primitive society (from about 600, 000 years ago to the 21st century BC); slave society (the 21st century BC-476 BC); feudal society(475 BC-AD 1840); and the semi-colonial, semi-feudal society of the Period of the Old Democratic Revolution (1840-1919). Exhibits in the first section deals with pre-historic fossils and other relics of Yuanmou Man from Yunnan Province, Lantian Man from Shaanxi Province, and Peking Man from Zhoukoudian, 48 kilometres southwest of Beijing. Other sections contain fine bronze ware, jade and bone implements, drinking vessels and silk fabrics from the slave society; ironwork and farm tools from early feudal society; and the pottery, porcelain and many other objects from the Tang Dynasty (618-907) and after. The four great inventions of ancient China are also on display: gunpowder, printing, the compass and papermaking, along with other achievements in ideology, culture, science and technology. Well-known Chinese statesmen, philosophers, scientists, writers and artists are also shown, and the history of friendly contacts between the Chinese and peoples of other countries is given. There is also a rich collection of historical documents, objects and paintings, which depict peasant uprisings in feudal times and the Chinese people's struggles against invasion in modern times.

175

South-Facing Gate (Zhengyangmen) or Front Gate
正阳门(前门)

This is the South-Facing Gate or Front Gate, a 38-metre-high brick structure. It is located at Qianmen (Front Gate), south of Tian'anmen (Gate of Heavenly Peace) Square. It is one of the few remaining gates of the city wall. It was built in 1420 in the early Ming Dynasty and renovated in 1977. In the old days, watchtowers placed at regular intervals around the perimeter guarded the wall. The double gate system played an important role in repulsing enemy attacks. If the first gate was breached, the enemy would still find themselves outside the city wall and would be fired upon from the tower over the inner gate.

The gate is a fortress-like structure, which was built for the city's defense in 1439. It has 94 windows from which archers could shoot arrows. The tower was burned down several times before it was reconstructed in 1914. As a national relic to be protected, it has been renovated according to the 1914 plan. Tourists can visit exhibitions in the three-storey tower. The first storey describes the history of the tower and the second deals with the city gates of ancient Beijing. There are also displays of paintings and the four treasures of study in ancient China — the writing brushes, ink sticks, ink slabs and paper. The tower was opened to the public on January 21, 1990, adding another scenic spot in Beijing.

The Front Gate was the pass the emperor used for travel to the Temple of Heaven for worshipping ceremonies. Only the imperial sedans and carriages were allowed to use the gate, while funeral ceremonies and carriages were forbidden to pass here.

Working People's Palace of Culture (The Imperial Ancestral Temple) 劳动人民文化宫（太庙）

Also known as the Imperial Ancestral Temple, the Working People's Palace of Culture lies to the east of Tian'anmen. This place used to be the Ancestral Temple in the Ming and Qing dynasties. Now it has become a place where working people in Beijing come to enjoy cultural performances.

The Chinese Harmonious Chimes (*Zhonghua He Zhong*) were installed at the Working People's Palace of Culture on December 27, 1999. The chimes, built and installed in three arrays, 3.8 metres high, 21 metres wide and weighing 17 tons, are the world's largest and feature 108 chimes of various sizes. The upper 34 Niu bells represent the 31 provinces, autonomous regions and municipalities on the Chinese mainland and Hong Kong, Macao, and Taiwan; the middle array is made up of 56 Yong bells standing for the 56 nationalities; the lower layer are 18 Bo bells, with the middle 16 pieces for the 16 historical periods of China and the two on each side for peace and development. They were also used during the gala celebrating the year 2000.

Zhongshan (Dr Sun Yat-sen) Park 中山公园

The park was formerly the Altar of Land and Grain built in 1420. It was opened as a park in 1914 and its name was changed to Zhongshan Park in 1928 in memory of Dr Sun Yat-sen, a great pioneer of the Chinese democratic revolution. Since 1949, the park has taken on a new look after extensive renovations. Cypress, flowers, goldfish, rockeries, ponds and pavilions present a serene and attractive atmosphere. Many large celebrations and meetings for peace and friendship are held there. The bronze statue of Dr Sun Yat-sen, three metres high, stands on a two-metre-high foundation in Zhongshan Park. It depicts Dr Sun in old age. With the support of the Central Committee of the Chinese Communist Party, the project was proposed by a group of 54 members of the Beijing Committee of the Chinese People's Political Consultative Conference (CPPCC). Zeng Zhushao, professor at the Central Academy of Fine Arts, designed the statue and he is also a member of the CPPCC Beijing Committee.

The project was completed by November 12, 1986, the 120th birthday anniversary of the great forerunner of the Chinese democratic revolution.

Zhongshan Concert Hall 中山音乐堂

The renovation of the Zhongshan Concert Hall started in July 1997 and was completed in April 1999 lasting one year and five months and opened to the public on April 26, 1999. The concert hall is gifted with first-class construction norms according to world standards for professional concert halls. It is located in Zhongshan Park (Dr Sun Yat-sen Park, north of Tian'anmen Square, one of Beijing's former imperial gardens and one of the most beautiful parks in the city). It is the first Chinese concert hall to adopt a digital audio-frequency processor. The ups and downs of the concert hall symbolize the development of Beijing's culture. When the People's Republic of China took over the concert hall on January 31, 1949, it was nothing more than an outdoor stage encircled by wires. Later the municipal government built a theatre there. It attracted many famous Chinese musicians and artists. By 1996, it was only used for showing films. The renovation cost more than 80 million yuan (US$9.6 million).

The renovated Zhongshan Concert Hall covers an area of 4,000 square metres, with a total floor space of 11,835 square metres. Its outer appearance looks like a giant fan-shape with a seating capacity of 1,400. Also there are 5 VIP boxes in the hall.

China National Grand Theatre 中国国家大剧院

Construction of controversial China National Grand Theatre officially started on December 12, 2001 after four years preparation and will be completed in 2005. Some revisions have been made to the original plan to reduce costs and construction area. The current estimated cost of the project is 2.688 billion yuan (US$325 million), substantially less than the original 3 billion yuan (US$362 million). The reduction in cost comes mainly from the cancellation of the complex's theatre, which will leave it with a 2,500-seat opera house, mainly receiving world-renowned operas and ballet companies; a 2,000-seat concert hall, the site of concerts of symphony and traditional Chinese music; a 1,200-seat theatre for modern drama, Peking Opera and other local Chinese operas and art galleries. Total construction area has been cut from the original 180,000 square metres to 149,500 square metres, because the 30,000-square-metre parking lot, originally included in the plan, is going to be built separately. This new underground parking lot will provide the entire Tian'anmen Square area with its first major parking lot. When the parking lot is finished, it will be able to accommodate 1,000 vehicles and 1,400 bicycles. Parking will no longer be a headache when there are major activities in the square.

Located on the west side of the Great Hall of the People in downtown Beijing, the theater will be built to a modernistic design by French architect Paul Andreu 保罗·安德鲁. Although the theatre will not be the world's most luxurious, will present "some pleasant surprises:" some of the world's best performance facilities. Departments involved with the building of the theater also solicited opinions from experts and the general public on the design before finalizing the plan.

A domestic contest held in November 1997 attracted eight schemes from five designers. But the authorities then decided to extend participation to overseas companies. The success of foreign-designed projects, such as the Shanghai Grand Opera, has given officials the confidence to award such an important project to a foreign company if it wins the contest. The Proprietor Committee of the Theatre (国家大剧院工程业主委员会) finally selected 21 foreign designers from dozens of applicants. The public bidding of the scheme for the National Grand Theatre attracted 36 architectural design groups. Among these were the SGA Design Group from Italy, which took part in the design of the Sydney Opera House; Wilhelm Holzbauer from Austria, which was the designer of the Amsterdam Municipality Building; and Theatre and Architectural Design Academy of Qinghua University, which designed the original scheme for the National Grand Theatre of China in the 1950s. By July 14, 1998, the participants had submitted 69 schemes for a panel of judges to consider. The panel consisted of renowned architects from both China and abroad, including Fu Xinian, Peng Yigang, Pan Zuyao, Richard Bofill from Spain, Yoshinobu Ashihara from Japan and Arthur Erickson from Canada. The winner was decided and approved by a selection committee of outstanding Chinese and foreign architects. Forty domestic and overseas companies set out on April 13, 1998 to compete for the honour of designing China National Grand Theatre.

None of the 69 designs submitted as part of a competitive bidding process was accepted. Those who assessed the designs decided none of the designs met standards for comprehensiveness or high standards established by the committee, but five of the 69 were allowed to participate in the second round of bidding after revisions were made. The nine new or revised designs were submitted by November 10, 1998. Three were selected from this group for presentation to the Directing Committee, which was then chosen one to further polish, plans and finally implement them in construction. The entire design insisted on the creation theme of "a theatre within the city and a city within the theatre."

The theatre will be China's largest, as well as its first comprehensive and multi-functional theatre. The design should bring home at sight that it is a theater, nothing else, with Chinese characteristics and in harmony with the other buildings on Tian'anmen Square. The building's height shall not exceed 45 metres, keeping it below the height of the Great Hall of the People.

The Great Wall (Badaling, Juyongguan, Mutianyu, Simatai and Gubeikou)
万里长城

Located in Beijing area, the four sections of the Great Walls refer to Badaling in Yanqing County 延庆县的八达岭长城, which is the earliest developed and the most famous both in China and abroad. It is the outstanding representative of the Great Wall and the quintessence of the Ming Dynasty Great Wall. Juyongguan Great Wall in Changping District 昌平区的居庸关长城 features "guancheng culture"关城文化. *Guan* (pass) lies within, while *cheng* (Great Wall) is located outside. "Guan" resembles a supreme headquarters or command post. The other Great Wall has only one section, but Juyongguan Great Wall looks like a complete military castle. The Mutianyu Great Wall in Huairou Dist. 怀柔区慕田峪长城 is surrounded by high mountains and, vegetation rate reaches more than 80 per cent. The watchtowers at Mutianyu are said to have been designed by Qi Jiguang, the Ming general who won many battles in southeast China. A number of his soldiers were from south China, and perhaps they influenced the architectural style of the brick watchtowers—the shape of the lookout openings at the tops of the towers 空心敌楼 greatly resembles a fence design popular in that region. The Simatai Great Wall in Miyun County 密云县的司马台长城 features many aspects, including a strategic pass 险(险隘), being carpeted by a dense growth of foliage 密(树林茂密), strange mirages 奇 (奇特景象), superb craftsmanship excelling nature 巧 (巧夺天工), panorama 全 (全貌) 五大特点, is the only section, which retains the original appearance of the ancient Great Wall. Luo Zhewen 罗哲文, Great Wall expert said: "China's Great Wall is the world's most, but Simatai section of the Great Wall is reputed as the most of China's Great Wall."

The Simatai Great Wall, 110 kilometres northeast of Beijing, has 135 watchtowers. The 19-kilometre wall is dangerous to climb but splendid to view as it meanders up and down the mountain ridges that seem to have been sliced on both sides by a huge axe. The Wangjinglou Watchtower on a steep cliff 986 metres above sea level is the summit of the Simatai Great Wall and also the most dangerous place to reach, because the visitor must walk over some unrepaired paths, including the "scaling ladder" and "overline bridge" before reaching it. The "scaling ladder" is a slope at an angle of 60-70 degrees: the visitor must climb on all fours and be extremely careful. The "overline bridge" is a path about 100 metres long and less than one metre wide which crosses abysses about 500 metres deep. With nothing to hold on to, the slightest wind will make the visitor tremble with fear. Because of the dangers involved in reaching Wangjinglou, only a few people have ever set foot on the tower in modern times.

* * *

The Great Wall, symbolizing China's ancient civilization, is one of the world's most renowned projects. It is a distance of 75 kilometres northwest of Beijing. Its highest point at Badaling is some 800 metres above sea level. A well-known popular saying goes: "He who hasn't been to the Great Wall is not a true man." / "You are not a plucky hero till you climb the Great Wall." Therefore, everyone tries to make it.

Construction of the Wall first began during the period of the Warring States (476 BC-221 BC). Formerly, walls were built at strategic points by different kingdoms to protect their northern territories. In 221 BC after the first Emperor of the Qin Dynasty unified China, he decided to have the walls linked up and extended.

Historical records show that about one million people, one-fifth of China's population at the time, were involved in the project, which took more than ten years. When it was finished we call it "Wan Li Chang Cheng" which means "Ten Thousand *Li* (5,000 kilometres) Long Wall." Now, nature has taken over most of the Great Wall.

The Great Wall, which we are going to visit, was rebuilt during the Ming Dynasty in the 16th century. It extends from Shanhai (mountain and sea) Pass, a seaport along the coast of Bohai Bay, to Jiayu Pass in Gansu Province. Its total length is more than 6, 700 kilometres.

There were many places of strategic importance along the Wall. Fortresses were constructed at strategic points. Beacon towers were built on both sides of the Wall at commanding points. Whenever the enemy was sighted, bonfires were lit on the towers to signal warning messages. Before the Ming Dynasty, the Wall was built mainly of earth and rock. Under the Ming, it was rebuilt in most places with bricks and stones. For instance, the section at Badaling near Beijing was faced with slabs of rock and large bricks and filled with earth and stones. It is 6 to 7 metres high. At regular intervals along the southern side of the Wall, there are gates with stone steps leading to the top of the Wall. The top surface of the wall is paved with three or four layers of large bricks. It is 4 to 5 metres wide, enough for five horsemen to ride abreast. Along the Wall, there are parapets and

Great Wall at Badaling

181

battlements built of bricks and turrets and watchtowers at regular intervals.

The Wall traverses mountains and gullies. It was extremely difficult to build along steep slopes under harsh conditions. Some of the slabs of rock were as long as two meters and weighed as much as one ton. All the rocks, bricks and lime had to be carried up the mountains at the cost of backbreaking labour. The earth and bricks were passed up from hand to hand or carried in baskets by donkeys and goats. The large slabs were moved up slopes by means of rolling rods and hoisting bars. According to rough calculation, the amount of bricks and rock used to build the Wall would have been enough to build a wall five metres high and one metre thick around the world.

The Badaling (Eight Prominent Peaks) section is the best-preserved part of the Wall. Several renovations have taken place since 1949. The Chinese Government has listed the Wall as one of the historical monuments to be preserved. The Great Wall runs 629 kilometres in the Beijing area. More than 100 kilometres are well-preserved and four other sections at Badaling, Juyongguan, Mutianyu, and Simatai have already been renovated for tourists both at home and abroad.

The Great Wall is the great creation of ancient Chinese people. The United Nations' Educational, Scientific and Cultural Organization (UNESCO) listed the Great Wall as one of the World Heritages in 1987.

The earliest part of the Great Wall has been found in Shandong Province, which roughly parallels the ancient Qi Kingdom. The Qi Great Wall started at a small village in Changqing District and ran to the sea near Qingdao, with a total length of 620 kilometres. According to historical records, the Wall had 12 passes, nine gates, 50 castles and barracks and 12 beacon towers. The winding wall comprised the southern fortifications of this strong kingdom. At that time the Qi Kingdom contended with others for hegemony and its king Huangong was one of the five most powerful dukes during the Spring and Autumn Period (770 BC-476 BC). It was extremely difficult for ancient people to build such giant military defenses. The Qi Kingdom's labourers spent 170 years building the wall. Archaeologists recently unearthed cultural ruins and relics near the Zibo sections of the Great Wall, and the new finds will aid in the study on the Qi culture. In the course of Chinese history, more than 20 emperors ordered the building or renovation of the Great Wall, which eventually grew to be more than 5,000 kilometres long. The most famous part of the Great Wall was constructed during the Ming Dynasty (1368-1644).

Note: Whenever you travel to the Great Wall, please wear comfortable shoes with nonslip soles. The climb is steep in parts and sometimes the stones are slippery. If you are going in cooler weather wear more warm clothes; the wind that comes through the mountain in that area will cut right through you.

Special Wall to Inspire Chinese

Erected alongside the Great Wall of China, the inscription telling of the achievements of hundreds of outstanding Chinese, the commemorative wall is 110 metres long, 80 metres high and is composed of 200 pieces of granite. The Outstanding Chinese Declaration Project will more closely unite all Chinese throughout the world. It is the first phase of the project. Organized by the China Cultural Research Society and the Chinese Friendship Union Association, the project was finished by September 2000.

Clock Ticks Millennium Countdown

A millennium countdown clock was erected on March 25, 1998 on the 2,000-year-old Great Wall, one of the world's greatest structures. The clock was set up on the Badaling section of the Great Wall, a popular tourist spot in the northwest of Beijing. An inscription on the timepiece exhorts the nation to "seize the moment to build up the motherland." Erecting a year-2000 countdown clock on the Great Wall was just one of the preparations that Beijing made as it geared up to welcome the 21st century. The white clock is 5.8 metres tall with a red digital display and a base shaped like a part of the Wall. Manufactured by a Chinese high-tech company, the clock has a margin of error of less than one minute for every 30,000 years.

The Remnant Badaling Great Wall or Shixiaguan Great Wall 八达岭残长城或石峡关长城

A section of the Great Wall that has remained unchanged since it was built in the Ming Dynasty was opened to the public on June 18, 2000. The site, called Shixiaguan Pass or the Remnant Badaling Great Wall, 5 kilometres from the existing Badaling section of the Great Wall. As the west gate of the defense system of Badaling Great Wall, it has not been renovated or decorated since it was built. The pass was constructed among lofty and precipitous peaks and the original connecting walls and standing towers still reveal its magnificent grandeur although it is now incomplete and weather-beaten. There are two other areas of archaeological value at the foot of Shixiaguan Pass. One is the ancient quarry used in the construction of the Great Wall, where the split rocks and cutting stones are still quite evident. The other is a part of an original brick kiln, from which all the wall bricks were made by ordinary people hundreds of years ago. With the incomplete beauty of the ancient culture, the Remnant Badaling Great Wall is characterized by its remnant style.

Magnetic Trains Run to Badaling 八达岭将通磁悬浮列车

Tourists to the Badaling section of the Great Wall in 2003 will be able to take a magnetic levitation (maglev) train some of the way. It will be the first medium- and low-speed train of this sort developed in China. The line's first 204 metres were completed in the Changsha-based National Defense Science and Technology University in Hunan Province as part of initial experiments. The 2.2-kilometre maglev line was under construction by the end of 2001. It will take tourists a mere three minutes to arrive at the scenic spot when travelling on the train at a distance of 2.2 kilometres. At cost of 200 million yuan (US$24 million), the line was jointly funded by the Beijing Holdings Ltd., the Beijing Badaling Tourism Development Co. Ltd., and the National Defence Science and Technology University. The line will contribute to reducing traffic and pollution in Beijing, where traffic conditions are becoming increasing chaotic. It can transport about 20,000 tourists per day.

The 30-kilometre long maglev line in Pudong of Shanghai will be completed and put into trial operation by the end of 2002 at a cost of 8.9 billion yuan (US$1.08 billion).

Currently, the number of tourists to Badaling is 4 to 5 million a year; the number will increase greatly by 2008. In order to secure tourists' safety and satisfaction, the Badaling section is aiming to construct a Great Wall museum containing a cultural gallery, a forest of steles, a theatre and an anti-Japanese invasion museum. With greater selection, tourists will be able to visit their favourite places of interest first, leaving the Great Wall less crowded during rush hours. Since 1949, Badaling has attracted 120 million visitors, including over 360 heads of countries and governments in the world, since it was opened to the public in 1952.

New Section of the Great Wall

Chinese archaeologists have discovered a new section of the ancient Great Wall, a structure which dates back over 2,000 years, in North China's Inner Mongolia Autonomous Region. The section of the Great Wall meanders for more than 200 kilometres through sparsely populated areas near the Urad Front Banner of the region. Ancient Chinese used locally quarried black stone to build the wall, which are 5-6 metres high and 3 metres wide. The remoteness of the section has contributed to its remaining virtually intact. The section of the Great Wall features small beacon towers located one kilometre apart, with large beacon towers every 5 kilometres. Archaeological experts pointed out this, one of the most highly preserved sections found in recent years, is a rare historical treasure, which will greatly enhance future research.

Earthquake Leaves Mark on the Great Wall

Even the Great Wall felt the effects of the earthquake, measuring 6. 2 on the Richter scale, in Zhangjiakou, Hebei Province, on January 10, 1998. Cracks appeared on the part of the Wall in Shangyi, Zhangbei and Wanquan counties, which were seriously affected by the earthquake. There are parts of the Great Wall in Zhangjiakou, built mostly during the Ming Dynasty (1368-1644). More than 20 ancient buildings, pagodas and grottoes are located in the quake-hit areas, most dating back to the Ming Dynasty. All the historical sites suffered from the earthquake. Forty-nine people were killed in the quake, over 10, 000 people were injured and 44, 000 people were left homeless. Zhangbei and Shangyi counties suffered losses of about 740 million yuan (US$89 million). The earth-quake-stricken Zhangjiakou will invest total donations of 100 million yuan (US$12 million) and US$20 million of World Bank loans in infrastructure and economic rehabilitation.

Song Dynasty Great Wall

Chinese archaeologists have confirmed after a recent field examination in late 1999 that a 20-kilometre-long section of the Great Wall in North China's Shanxi Province was built in the Song Dynasty (960-1279). This stone-made section of the Great Wall is located in Kelan County in northwestern Shanxi. Sources from local archaeological departments said that about 20 kilometres of the portion of the Great Wall remain intact, though there are longer ruined portions. The discovery disperses experts' doubts that no part of the Great Wall was constructed during the Song Dynasty.

Southern Great Wall Discovered 南方长城被发现

Chinese architect experts have discovered the ruins of the Southern China portion of the Great Wall in Fenghuang County, Central China's Hunan Province. According to historical records, the Ming Dynasty built a 190-kilometre-long sidewall between Tongren County of Guizhou Province and Baojing County of Hunan Province in 1615 to reinforce its control in the area. Local experts said that the ruins of the sidewalls and defensive towers were built in 1797 during the Qing Dynasty.

Juyongguan Section of the Great Wall, Juyong Pass & the Cloud Terrace 居庸关长城、居庸关和云台

Juyong Pass, built in 1368, and together with Zijing Pass and Daoma Pass were called the "Inner Three Passes" along the Great Wall.

Juyong (Dwelling-in-Harmony) Pass, also known as Jundu Pass or Jimen Pass, is an important strategic gateway leading to Inner Mongolia. The slopes on both sides of this narrow pass are carpeted by a dense growth of foliage. It used to be one of the eight famous scenic spots in Beijing. After five years of renovation, the famous Juyongguan section of the Great Wall opened to tourists in late March 1998. A total of 120 million yuan (US$14.4 million) was spent on the renovation of 4,142 metre-long section of the Great Wall. The 20-kilometre-long ravine, so that a few men could hold it against all comers, named Guangou (Pass Ravine), flanked by mountains, was the northern entrance to Beijing in ancient times. The whole area is full of high mountains and narrow passes which are easily defensible. But the cavalrymen of Genghis Khan swept through it in the 13th century. The Yuan emperors had to travel through the ravine every year to their summer resort in Inner Mongolia, staying overnight here at Juyongguan Pass. Entering the Pass, you will see an ancient platform known as Cloud Terrace, built in 1345, and made of marble. It was called the Crossing Street Dagoba, since its arch spanned the main street of the pass. There were formerly three dagobas on the top of the terrace. Unfortunately they collapsed along with the nearby imperial residence and other religious buildings during an early 15th century earthquake. Later on, a new temple was built on the site, but it was also destroyed in the early years of the Qing Dynasty. Now only the terrace remains. The terrace is 9.5 metres high, its width is 26.84 metres and the length of the cave is 17.57 metres.

The half octagonal arch gateway is unique and the Cloud Terrace is renowned fits marvelous artistry. The exquisite relief on the facades and sidewalls of the gateway is most impressive. On both sides of the facades are symmetrically carved crossed pestles of the Buddha's warrior attendants. Above the gateway are images of elephants, lions, serpents and other fabulous beasts.

Engraved on the walls under the arch are daturascrolls, images of Buddha and the four celestial guardians. Their vivid expressions are presented with exquisite workmanship. One shows a furious warrior with a snake wound round his arm. Such grandiose relief works, with several stones pieced together, are rarely seen in ancient Chinese carving. They are undoubtedly brilliant representation of the 13th century sculpture.

These four majestic guardians were said to have magic power against evil emperors. When Ming Emperor Zhengde was passing through the gateway in his sedan chair on a pleasure seeking tour, the horses heading the royal procession were scared by the awe-inspiring images on the Wall and refused to move. At last, one of the court officials had to cover up the terrifying images with a smoke screen.

In this way the terror struck Emperor and his entourage escaped. On the walls of the gateway, there are carvings of Buddhist sutra in Sanskrit (梵文), Tibetan(藏文), Uygur(维吾尔文), New Mongolian(八思巴字亦称蒙古新字或蒙古字), Western Xia(西夏), and Han(汉字) scripts. This is the first time to have ever discovered the six different languages carved on the ancient Chinese stones. They are valuable to the study of Buddhism and ancient languages.

A giant forest park along the Badaling Section of the Great Wall

A giant forest park will be built along the Badaling section of the Great Wall as China steps up efforts to protect the ecological well-being of the nation's top culture relics. The project, which is expected to be completed by 2008, will become a major forest shield against the sandstorms and heavy winds, which have ravaged Beijing and neighbouring areas since 1999. Chinese environmental experts have staked a big interest on the project as a role model for other sections of the Great Wall, which are suffering from global climate changes and the impact of human activities. The park will span about 100 square metres and will be 16. 3 kilometres long and 21. 5 kilometres wide. The project still needs the approval of the State Development Planning Commission to become a national forest park.

It is a part of the nationwide effort to protect the Great Wall, which is more than 6, 700 kilometres long and spans 10 provincial administrations in China. The Great Wall faces such problems as desertification and other climatic changes as well as human activities such as over-exploitation of its tourism potential.

New Park to Enhance the Great Wall

A park will be built at the Badaling section of the Great Wall to help protect the great cultural site. At the inauguration ceremony for the park, named the "International Friendship Forest," held in early June 2001, Phillips China Inc declared that it had joined forces with the Badaling Special Zone Administration and the US-China Environmental Fund to create the project. The petroleum company will invest 5 million yuan (US$600, 000) to initiate the project. According to the plan for the project, the International Friendship Forest will be located along the western edge of the Badaling Great Wall and will cover an area of approximately 40 acres. It will serve as a conservation buffer zone to help protect the natural and cultural resources of the Great Wall. Intensive planting of native trees and plants will help restore the ecology of the area. The park's cultural programme will tell the story of Badaling's past and present. Educational signs will be placed along trails. Guides in traditional costumes will give the history of the area. Visitors will be able to appreciate the beautiful scenery of Badaling while learning about history and culture of the Chinese people and the natural history of the area. The unique park will be a model for how to preserve and promote understanding of China's culture, history and traditions. The Friendship Forest is a key project in the Badaling national park master plan. Badaling section of the Great Wall attracts more than 5 million visitors both from home and abroad. The Forest will be a buffer zone between tourist and business zones of Badaling. It can help to balance economic development and environmental protection in the area. The project was completed in 2002.

Emperor Qin Shihuang (259BC-210 BC) 秦始皇帝

Qin Shihuang was the first Emperor of the Qin Dynasty. Upon the death of his father, he ascended the throne at the age of thirteen. His father's powerful chancellor Lu Buwei served as co-regent until he was 21 years old. He soon forced the former regent into exile and started launching military campaigns to unify the country.

He was known for many contradictory persons, including that of a conqueror, an enlightened leader, a merciless tyrant, a builder and a destroyer. During his 29-year rule, he united the country and transformed the land into what we now call China. He ordered his workers to create thousands of Terracotta Warriors to guard his tomb after his death. The warriors are dressed in armour, carry spears or other weaponry and stand on average at about 1. 9 metres tall. Each wears an army uniform that distinguishes the soldier's rank from bowmen to infantrymen to generals. An archer kneels in the front of the pit, ready to fire volleys to stop the enemy. The accurately proportioned figurines seem so real-to-life, with each having a distinct facial expression. The bodies are said to have been mass-produced, but the hands and heads were made individually, possibly to portray real soldiers of the time.

He spent ten years from 230BC to 221 BC to wipe out all the six different states one after another and established the first centralized feudal state in the Chinese history. He proclaimed himself Qin Shihuang, the first Emperor of the Qin Dynasty, and all the important officials of the central and local governments were to be appointed and dismissed by him. During his reign, he worked out a uniform code of law and standardized currency, weight and measures and even the written language.

He also had the different sections of the walls built by various warring states along their frontiers linked up and had the Great Wall built. All these measures were helpful to the consolidation of unification and promoted economic and cultural development.

The excavation has continued since local farmers digging a well accidentally discovered the terracotta warriors in 1974.

Zhan Tianyou (1861-1919)詹天佑

Zhan Tianyou was a patriotic engineer born in 1861 in Guangdong Province. He was intelligent and interested in machinery when he was a child. At the age of 11, Zhan was accepted to a preparatory class for young people chosen to study abroad. In 1878, he was admitted to Yale University where he majored in civil and railway engineering.

In the early years of the 20th century when the Beijing-Zhangjiakou Railway was built, he took on the responsibility of designing and building the railway, and succeeded in overcoming the gradient problem by switching back the line. The railway was completed in 1909, two years ahead of schedule. It opened a new chapter in the annals of China's railway construction. In memory of his contributions, later, the Chinese Government at Qinglongqiao Railway Station erected a bronze statue of Zhan Tianyou.

President Jiang Zemin spoke highly of the film of "Zhan Tianyou," which premiered in Beijing in late September 2001. The film depicts the moving story of Zhan Tianyou, who spent his entire life working to developing China's railways in the hard years of the late 19th and early 20th centuries. Jiang Zemin said that the film vividly depicts the admirable character of the noble-minded people who struggled for the rejuvenation of the Chinese nation, and that it embodies the Chinese people's patriotic spirit.

Looking-Toward Beijing Rock 望京石

East of Badaling lies a big rock which is called Looking-Toward Beijing Rock. It is seven metres long and two metres high. It is said that Empress Dowager Cixi passed here on her fleeing to the north as the Eight Imperialist Powers were advancing on Beijing in 1900. At this rock she turned to look toward Beijing, thus it is called "Looking-Toward Beijing Rock."

Expressway Tunnel

A 3, 456-metre-long, 13.1-metre-wide highway tunnel with three lanes, Asia widest and the world's fifth widest, was built at Tanyugou near Badaling in early 1998. Drilling through a mountain under the Great Wall, the tunnel was built as part of a new expressway between Beijing and Badaling and was opened to traffic in October 1998.

Guanting Reservoir 官厅水库

Guanting Reservoir is a colossal valley reservoir in China. It stands to the northwest of Beijing on the Yongding River by the Village of Guanting in Huailai County, Hebei Province. The reservoir is effective in the prevention of flood, sand preservation, water storage, generation of electric power and irrigation. The dam of the reservoir is 45 metres in height, 290 metres in length with a storage capacity of 2.27 billion cubic metres of water. Construction of the reservoir started in October 1951 and was completed in the summer of 1954 lasting three and a half years. The reservoir has rendered thousands of inhabitants in Beijing City and in the lower reaches of Yongding River permanently free from disasters wrought by the flood of that river.

The problem of flood disaster had never been solved by the rulers of the past ages for over 670 years—from the Yuan Dynasty to the eve of 1949.

Great Wall at Mutianyu 慕田峪长城

Chinese and foreign tourists are very familiar with the Badaling section of the Great Wall, but not the Mutianyu segment of the wall in Huairou District 79 kilometres away from Beijing proper. The Mutianyu Valley in Huairou District on the outskirts of the capital city was such a strategic point that it was contested again and again through China's history.

The first wall in this area was built some 1, 400 years ago. Construction of the present wall began in the early years of the Ming Dynasty (1368-1644) and was not completed until the 15th century. The mountains around the valley are heavily forested; there are many natural springs and thick, beautiful foliage. In the past, these were important military considerations; today, they make this section of the wall a very pleasant place to visit. The watchtowers at Mutianyu are said to have been designed by Qi Jiguang, the Ming general who won many battles in southeast China. A number of his soldiers were from south China, and perhaps they influenced the architectural style of the brick watchtowers—the shape of the

190

lookout openings at the tops of the towers greatly resembles a fence design popular in that region.

In 1988, Mr Albrecht Woeste, Chairman of the Henkel Shareholders' Committee of Germany donated 300, 000 deutsche marks (US$187, 500) and chemical products worth 200, 000 marks (US$125, 000) to help Beijing to restore the 747-metre Mutianyu section of the Great Wall. It took 5 years and was completed on June 14, 1993. The Beijing Municipal Government gave the Germans an ancient brick of the Great Wall and built a stone-tablet at Mutianyu to commemorate their assistance.

Simatai Great Wall 司马台长城

The Simatai Great Wall, 110 kilometres northeast of Beijing, has 135 watchtowers. The 19-kilometre wall is dangerous to climb but splendid to view as it meanders up and down the mountain ridges that seem to have been sliced on both sides by a huge axe. The Wangjinglou Watchtower on a steep cliff 986 metres above sea level is the summit of the Simatai Great Wall and also the most dangerous place to reach, because the visitor must walk over some unrepaired paths, including the "scaling ladder" and "overline bridge" before reaching it. The "scaling ladder" is a slope at an angle of 60-70 degrees: the visitor must climb on all fours and be extremely careful. The "overline bridge" is a path about 100 metres long and less than one metre wide which crosses abysses about 500 metres deep. With nothing to hold on to, the slightest wind will make the visitor tremble with fear. Because of the dangers involved in reaching Wangjinglou, only a few people have ever set foot on the tower in modern times.

Gubeikou Great Wall 古北口长城

With a total length of 21 kilometres, the Gubeikou Great Wall section is located northeast of Beijing, 128 kilometres from the city centre. The section of the wall was first built in 1368 and expanded in 1567 by a famous general named Qi Jiguang in the Ming Dynasty. It still retains its past magnificence, although it was broken in parts by Japanese shelling during the War of Resistance Against Japan from 1937 to 1945.

This section meanders through mountains 400 to 900 metres high. Unlike other sections, it varies in width, with the widest part able to accommodate five horses walking abreast and the narrowest spot allowing only a single person to pass.

A road leading to the section of the wall has been built for tourists. Many cultural relics have been discovered in the preliminary digging, including arrows, bamboo guns, stone mills and knives. They are exhibited

191

as part of the tourist attraction.

The Great Wall Restoration Committee, jointly sponsored by Beijing's five newspapers and the Badaling Administration Office, was established in Beijing and first launched the drive on July 5, 1984. By September of 1986, Chinese and foreign donors have contributed nearly 10 million yuan (US$2. 7 million) to rebuild the Great Wall. The contributions have come from thousands of people from China's 30 provinces, regions and municipalities and from 26 foreign countries, in response to an open appeal to "Love China and Rebuild the Great Wall. " In addition, many donors have contributed art works such as calligraphy, paintings and sculptures to the drive. As promised by the sponsors in their open appeal, prominent donors will have their names inscribed on plaques which to be erected at the Badaling and Mutianyu Great Wall sites. Out of the contributions one million yuan (US $270, 000) was used to build a Great Wall Museum at Badaling. Construction of monuments to honour individuals and organizations whose donations exceed 500 and 1, 000 yuan respectively was already built. A major monument, with an inscription by Chinese leader Deng Xiaoping in Chinese meaning "Love Our Motherland and Rebuild the Great Wall" has been erected near the entrance to the Great Wall at Badaling. A monument honouring Pakistan Government and other foreign contributions has been erected at Wangjingshi (Looking-Toward Beijing Rock) at Badaling.

Great Wall in Jinshanling of Chengde
河北承德金山岭长城

A Chinese motorcyclist named Yu Shunye 于顺业 set a world record with his two-second flight across the Great Wall one motorcycle with his back facing forward on June 16, 2001. At 11: 58 am, Yu Shunye, a 41-year-old motorcyclist from Dalian in Liaoning Province, started his Jialing-145 bike on the runway platform and made a beautiful curve (a span of 15 metres and 23. 4 metres in drop in elevation 跨度 15 米, 落差 23. 4 米) over the Great Wall in Jinshanling of Chengde, Hebei Province. The morning sun dispersed the heavy clouds left by June 15 night's heavy rain, but the soaked platform was slippery, making his attempt even more difficult. Yu Shunye started his motorcycle feats after leaving the army in 1981. In June 1996, he set his first world record by riding on a motorcycle with his back facing forward and his hands off the handlebars, for 28 kilometres, at a speed of 70 kilometres per hour. Four years later, he set another world record by steering a motor tricycle in its side tram for 4. 8 kilometres.

Great Wall Ruins 长城遗址

Ruins of a section of the Great Wall with more than 2, 200 years old have been discovered in the Yinshan Mountains in north China's Inner Mongolia Autonomous Region. The section of the Great Wall, 5-6 metres high and 3 metres wide, winds through the mountains from east to west for over 200 kilometres. It was constructed in the Qin Dynasty (221 BC-206 BC).

The Great Wall in Linhai, Zhejiang Province

Construction of the Great Wall in Linhai, then called Taizhou Prefecture, dating back about 1, 600 years. In the following Tang, Song, Yuan, Ming and Qing dynasties, expansions and renovations were continuously made. In 1997, a cross section was discovered at the Xingshan Gate of the existing wall. This section of the wall revealed the renovation and expansion process of the Linhai Great Wall. In the Tang Dynasty (618-907), the three-metre-high wall consisted of earth. In the Song Dynasty (960-1279), a layer of bricks was added to it and a one-metre-high stonewall was built along it on the riverside to protect it from floods. During the Ming Dynasty (1368-1644), the height was raised to about five metres and another layer of bricks was added. In the Qing Dynasty (1644-1911), the height was raised again. Both the height and width of the existing wall are greater than 10 metres. It is more than 6, 000 metres long. Several gates still exist, including the Jingyue, Kuocang and Wangjiang gates. In the mid-Ming Dynasty, Japanese pirates invaded the dynasty's southeast coastline, including the Taizhou Prefecture. In 1555, Tan Lun, the local magistrate, began constructing a wall along the border. Two years later, Qi Jiguang, a famous national hero, who fought against Japanese pirates, began his eight-year tour of duty in Taizhou. He renovated the wall, making it thicker and higher, to strengthen its defense capability. Taizhou became a strong fortress against Japanese pirates and Qi and his warriors won nine battles successively in six years. In 1567, the Emperor ordered Tan and Qi to renovate the Great Wall in the north. The Emperor also selected 3, 000 soldiers to participate in the renovation of Taizhou Great Wall to supervise the construction process. The Great Wall in Jixian County of Tianjin and Datong of Shanxi Province was designed and built by Qi Jiguang and his soldiers. The Badaling Great Wall and Mutianyu Great Wall in Beijing were also constructed and renovated by Qi Jiguang and his soldiers. The architectural style was the same as the Taizhou Great Wall. The Great Wall in Linhai is among China's best-preserved historical and cultural relics. Besides the military functions, the Great Wall has another impor-

193

tant function: anti-flooding. The Linhai Great Wall is located at the Lingjiang River's entrance to the sea. River water and seawater join here, and the water often rises to reach the city. To the west of the city is the Kuocang Mountain range. The wall was specially designed to avert the threat of flooding from streams running off the mountain, and walls were built along the south and west of the river. Tourists, who visit the Linhai Great Wall, are amazed by the creativity of its ancestors and the Linhai people's endeavour in preserving this cultural relic. In 1994, the city of Linhai was named Famous Historical Cultural City by the State.

Linhai is located at the middle of Zhejiang Province's coastline. On its east is the East China Sea, on its west the Kuocang Mountain, on its south the Yandang Mountain and on its north the Tiantai Mountain. The city has a 74-kilometre-long coastline.

Legends About the Great Wall 有关长城的传说

There are numerous popular legends and tales in China about the Great Wall. Though many are based on historical facts, they have survived the centuries because they expressed the wisdom and feelings of the ancient Chinese working people.

Brick at Jiayuguan Pass 嘉峪关之砖

Jiayuguan Pass is located at the western end of the Great Wall in Gansu Province and was a strategic point on the ancient Silk Road.

A single gray brick is fixed on the back wall of the western gate tower in the pass. It is said to be a souvenir left from a bet between a craftsman and a supervisor when the Great Wall was being built. A contractor named Yi Kaishan was so good at working out plans he could accurately calculate the number of men and materials needed without any waste.

The supervisor, who bore him a personal grudge, didn't believe him and challenged him with a bet. "I'll allow you just one brick more than you say you need," he said. "If there is one left over, I'll put it on the tower myself to leave a good name for you. If you need more, you'll be punished."

Yi agreed. When the construction was finished, just as he predicted only one brick remained. This can be seen on the gate tower at Jiayuguan Pass today.

A Bird Spirit's Call 燕子之声

In the city of Xiluo near Jiayuguan Pass, the base of the wall is wider than the top for strength and solidity. Strangely, when the high quality bricks of a corner are struck with a stone, a clear and melodious sound like the song of a swallow can be heard. People say that the wall was so heavily guarded that even a swallow could not get through. One evening years ago, a swallow trying to return to its nest was killed when it flew into the wall. Today, the sound is said to be the plaintive voice of the bird's spirit.

The Length of the Great Wall 长城的长度

There are various measurements of the length of the Great Wall because in China's history, more than twenty dynasties and states of dukes or princes built their own walls at different places. Of these, according to historical documents, three exceeded 10,000 *li* (5,000 kilometres). One was built during the reign of Emperor Qin Shihuang, starting from Lintao at the west end to Liaodong at the east end. The second one was built in the Han Dynasty (206 BC-AD 220) from present day Xinjiang to Liaodong, consisting of inner and outer walls with beacon towers and bulwark, measuring over 20,000 *li* (10,000 kilometres) in total. The third, built in the Ming Dynasty (1368-1644), was from Jiayuguan Pass in Gansu at the west end to the Yalu River at the east end. If added together the length of the walls built by various dynasties would amount to 100,000 *li* (50,000 kilometres) or more. The ruins of these walls are scattered over sixteen provinces, cities and autonomous regions. In Inner Mongolia alone, the ruin of the Great Wall extends to 30,000 *li* (15,000 kilometres).

Most of the walls built in the early historical periods are damaged or in a state of decay. Now only the one built in the Ming Dynasty is comparatively well preserved. So, the Great Wall we mention today is the Ming Great Wall which is in total 12,000 *li* (6,000 kilometres). However, this figure is based only on historical records, and, as a matter of fact, in some places double or triple walls were built. With its meandering and loops the actual extent of the structure might be even longer.

Meng Jiangnü 孟姜女

Meng Jiangnü's husband Fan Qiliang was among those conscripted to build the Great Wall. One day while she was in the garden, a man trying to escape from the pressgang labor jumped over the wall and landed at her feet. Her family protected him, and they fell in love and got married.

On the night of their wedding, Fan Qiliang, her husband, was seized by the court officials. Before they parted, Meng took a hairpin of white jade from her head, broke it into two halves and gave one half of it to her husband with the words: "My heart is as white and pure as this jade. Keep this half and you will feel that I am with you."

Fan was forced to work on the Wall. During the construction, thousands upon thousands of laborers died of overwork and maltreatment.

Nothing was known about her husband. When autumn came, the birds began to migrate. She recalled that her husband was wearing only thin

195

clothes. She made some padded clothes and left home to look for her husband.

At last Meng Jiangnü got to the Wall. When she found her husband had died, she was so sad that she cried and cried. Finally, the Wall split open, trapping the cruel officials and soldiers under it and the bodies of million of conscripted labourers were exposed.

Emperor Qin Shihuang got infuriated by what Meng Jiangnü did, but when he saw her beauty, he wanted to make her his concubine. She accepted on the following conditions: a proper burial for her husband, a tomb built for him, and a monument set up for all the labourers who died of hardwork on the Wall. The Emperor himself was to wear mourning as a token of regret for what had been done to the labourers. The Emperor accepted all these. Having avenged herself and putting the Emperor to shame, Meng flung herself into the sea. To commemorate her death, a temple was built at Shanhaiguan Pass near the sea.

In the following verse the unknown folk poet describes how Meng Jiangnü set out:

At the people's festival of the new year
All hang at their doors great lanterns of red;
Faces shining with brightness, husbands look happily
Upon their families; only for me there is bitterness,
For my husband has been taken to build the Great Wall,
Comes early summer and we are all busy
Feeding the silkworms; going arm in arm
Together to pick from mulberry branches;
As we pick we hang the baskets on the trees below us
Falls a tear.
Then autumn through the open door wafts
Scent from the flowering shrub that stands there;
Alone, wild goose flying southward drops from its leg
A letter from my beloved, carrying these words;
Let the loafer spread what rumors they like
About you, my dear, I am sure that you still love me enough
To send me clothes to keep me alive in this cold.
Winter and from the north drive down flying snowflakes,
Yet the girl Meng Jiangnü sets off to carry clothes
To her lover; and in compassion the very ravens
Come down to lead her; weeping with cold and misery
To the Great Wall.

The Great Wall has been called "the longest cemetery in the world" because of the countless workers who died in the building of it.

Great Wall Circle Vision Theatre 长城全周影院

Located at Badaling section of the Great Wall, the Great Wall Circle Vision Theatre was built in September 1990 and put into operation on September 2, 1992. It was a joint venture project managed by Beijing Great Wall Circle Vision Theatre Company—a cooperative enterprise run by Japan's Fukuoka Keizaiboeki Company, Beijing Badaling Tourism Company and CITIC Real Estate Corporation under China International Trust and Investment Corporation (Group).

The movie shows historic relics and landscapes in different seasons along the 6,700 kilometre Great Wall, as well as numerous stories about Great Wall, e.g. the crowning ceremony of the first Emperor of the Qin Dynasty more than 2,000 years ago and the legend of Meng Jiangnü and battlefields to let viewers know the past and present of the Great Wall.

The circle screen movie has used the world's most advanced technology. It is projected at a 360 circular screen with stereo audio effects. In the theatre, the pictures are so vivid as if you were surrounded by the real Great Wall. The historic and natural views of the Great Wall will leave you lots of imagination.

The theatre provides the first rate service facilities and service, including foyers for domestic and foreign viewers and for distinguished guests, air conditioning equipment and shops selling drinks and tourist souvenirs. The theatre has a seating capacity of 500. Business hours are from 9 am to 4 pm (for all seasons). Each film show lasts 15 minutes only with 5 minutes for interval between shows.

Cableway at Badaling Section of the Great Wall
八达岭长城索道

China began to build a cableway at the Badaling section of the Great Wall in 1988. The project is a co-operation between Beijing Badaling Cablecar Ltd. and the Hong Kong Jinhui International Industrial Company. The Hong Kong side invested US$ 4.95 million and bore all the costs of the project. The Beijing Badaling Cablecar Ltd. provided the use of the land, about 10,000 square metres, worth US$ 500,000.

The main reason for building the cableway is to transport visitors to the Wall. In the last couple of years, the number of visitors to the Wall was more than 4.5 million each year. In 1995, the visitors to the Wall reached 6.5 million. At present, there is only a small doorway through which only a bus can pass. Almost 33,000 tourists and 800 cars and buses pass through it daily during the peak season.

The cableway project consists of two parts: a 725-metre northern line with an underground station at the top and a semi underground station at the bottom. The whole cableway is hidden in a valley. A 625-metre southern line was completed above ground and also in a valley. Tourists on the Wall cannot see the cable lines. The equipment is from POMA, a French company. The cableway was completed in 1990, it can transport about one third of the visitors to the further watchtowers. So elderly people and both Chinese and foreign tourists can also get to the top of the Great Wall to enjoy the wonderful scenery.

The Seven Wonders of the World 世界七大奇迹

In ancient times travelers who visited foreign countries generally brought back amazing tales of the wonderful sights they had seen on their holidays. The most famous of these sights became known as the Seven Wonders.
1. *The Pyramids of Egypt* 埃及的金字塔
2. *The Hanging Gardens of Babylon* 巴比伦的空中花园
3. *The Temple of Diana at Ephesus* 以弗非所的阿苔密斯神庙
4. *The Statue of Jupiter at Olympus.* 奥林匹亚的宙斯神像
5. *The Tomb of Mausolus (Mausoleum) at Halicarnassus* 哈利卡纳苏摩 (小亚西亚)素拉斯陵墓
6. *The Colossus at Rhodes* 地中海罗得岛上的太阳神巨像
7. *The Pharos Lighthouse at Alexandria* 亚力山大城(法罗斯岛)上的灯塔
Of the above Seven Wonders of the Ancient World only the Great Pyramids of Egypt survive today.

In the Middle Ages people considered that there existed other sights quite as wonderful and named the following:
1. *The Colosseum of Rome* 罗马斗兽场
2. *The Leaning Tower of Pisa* 比萨斜塔
3. *The Catacombs of Alexandria* 亚力山大里亚地下陵墓
4. *The Great Wall of China* 中国的万里长城
5. *Stonehenge* 石围圈
6. *The Porcelain Tower of Nanking (Nanjing)* 南京的瓷塔 (琉璃塔)
7. *The Mosque of St. Sophia in Constantinople (Istanbul)* 索菲亚大教堂 (又称索菲亚圣殿)

In 1974, the farmers in Lintong, near Xi'an, China, discovered the Terra Cotta Warriors and Horses. People all over the world unanimously considered it the eighth wonder of the world.

Nowadays, it would be impossible to make a completely satisfactory list of Seven Wonders as we have all seen or heard of many amazing man-made structures and scientific marvels.

Bear Zoo at Badaling Great Wall 八达岭长城熊乐园

Sponsored by the Yanbian Dongfang Bear Paradise in Jilin Province and the Beijing Badaling Forestry Centre, the Badaling Bear Zoo, combining wild animal preservation and tourism, opened on June 27, 1993. The zoo covers an area of 2 hectares (5 acres) in the Tianxian Ravine in Badaling. Unlike the wild wolves and foxes that can still be found in the areas, bears are confined in a zoo that consists of 5 sections with 380 in it. The zoo has been expanded into a 40-hectare (98.8 acre-) park for protection of plants and wild animals. The zoo has several sections for bears of different species and ages. Special shows feature tame bears.

The zoo is composed of a group of dark yellow structures designed in harmony with the surroundings. Beginning in 1995, the zoo released some tame bears into forests in Badaling to help restore the area's ecological balance. The zoo has enhanced the Badaling tourism resort, where the famous Badaling section of the Great Wall stands.

Treasures Join World Legacy List
著名风景点加入"世界遗产名录"

The Great Wall (including Badaling, Shanhaiguan, Mutianyu, and Jiayuguan) of China, the only man-made object that can be seen from the Moon has joined the World Heritage List together with 27 other historical sites in China since 1987. Those other 27 historical sites see below. The inscription on the list confirms the sites to be of a universal value, which require protection for the benefit of all humanity. The occasion marked not only a great honor for China but also put a greater demand on our arduous task of protecting these world treasures. The Chinese Government will spare no efforts in protecting more than 500 State level historical places or relic sites. Besides, there are more than 5,192 such places of historical interest at provincial levels. However, some relic sites are suffering natural as well as man-made damages. China will extend international cooperation with other countries and open more joint projects concerning the evaluation and protection of China's vast historical treasures.

China's Contributions to World Heritage
中国已有 28 处自然或人文景观被列入"世界遗产名录"(截止到 2001 年 12 月 14 日)
The United Nations Educational, Scientific and Cultural Organization (UNESCO) has listed 28 sites in China ranking the third trailing Italy, and Spain on its World Heritage List since 1987.

199

The United Nations Educational, Scientific and Cultural Organization (UNESCO) has listed 690 sites in 122 countries on its World Heritage list since 1976.

For years, the United Nations Educational, Scientific and Cultural Organization (UNESCO) has promoted a highly significant international activity involved in preserving the world's cultural and natural properties. In November 1972, the 17th UNESCO Conference adopted the "Preservation of the World Cultural and Natural Heritage Treaty" (known as the World Heritage Treaty), which won international recognition and support. By the end of 2001, 162 countries were accepted as signatories to the treaty.

To ensure the effective implementation of the treaty, UNESCO set up in 1976 the World Heritage Commission—an inter-governmental organization made up of 21 countries chosen by a conference of the signatories. One of its main tasks is to determine, on the basis of the signatories' submission, what should be under the treaty's protection and then included in the "List of World Heritages" those cultural relics and natural sites which are internationally recognized as having outstanding significance and common value. The aim is to place these common heritages of mankind under protection. By the end of 2000, the commission had selected 690 from 122 countries in five continents 五大洲的 122 个国家中的 529 个文化遗产. Among them 529 are cultural values 529 个文化遗产, 138 are natural values 138 个自然遗产, and 23 are both cultural and natural values 23 个文化自然双重遗产. Of the 690, China had 28, including 3 natural values, 21 cultural values and 4 both cultural and natural values.

The World Heritage List has three categories: cultural heritage, natural heritage, and heritage which both cultural and natural.

China's culture dates back 5,000 years and China is a country with a wealth of cultural property and natural scenery. The Chinese Government has always laid stress on the preservation of its culture and has actively supported and participated in international activities organized by UNESCO in this field. In November 1985, the Standing Committee of the National People's Congress of China approved UNESCO's World Heritage Treaty, making China one of its signatories. Since 1986, China has submitted over ten batches of potential world heritage listings for UNESCO's consideration. By December 14, 2001, only 17 years after China began its participation, 28 of the country's cultural relics and sites were included in the "List of World Heritages." As a country with a large number of offerings, China is attracting international attention. China's brilliant ancient culture belongs to the entire Chinese nation. It is also a precious heritage of all of mankind. It is expected that many more cultural and natural properties of

China will be included in UNESCO's "List of World Heritages."

UNESCO adopted the Convention on the Protection of World Cultural and Natural Heritage Sites in 1972, calling for concerted efforts to protect the common history of mankind. One hundred and forty-six countries have signed the convention.

The World Heritage Committee, under UNESCO, each year considers suggestions for listing as World Heritage sites. The international community has listed cultural and natural sites, which are of outstanding significance and universal value, as World Heritage sites for protection.

Nations submit their lists of recommended sites for evaluation by experts from UNESCO's subordinate organizations: for example, the International Centre for the Study of the Preservation and Restoration of Cultural Property (ICCROM). The process takes up three years to complete. Two major criteria are vital when seeking a World Heritage designation—the site's value and status of its preservation. UNESCO has designated 690 properties throughout the world as World Heritage sites till 2001. UNESCO finances training courses for personnel of designated heritage sites.

What is World Heritage?

World Heritage falls into three categories: cultural heritage, natural heritage and mixed heritage. According to the convention of the World Heritage Committee, the following shall be considered as cultural heritages:

Monuments: Architectural works, works of monumental sculpture and painting elements or structure of an archaeological nature, inscriptions and cave dwellings that are of outstanding universal value from the point of view of history, art or science.

Groups of buildings: Groups of separate or connected buildings which, because of their architecture, their homogeneity or their place in the landscape, are of outstanding universal value from the point of view of history, art or science.

Sites' works of man or the combined works of nature and man, and areas which are of outstanding universal value from the historical, aesthetic, ethnological or anthropological point of view.

Other factors considered as <u>natural heritage</u> qualifications:

Natural features consisting of physical and biological formations or groups of such formations are of outstanding universal value from the aesthetic or scientific point of view. Geological and physio-graphical formations and precisely delineated areas which, constitute the habitat of threatened species of animals and plants of outstanding universal value from the point of view of science or conservation. Natural sites or precisely delineated natural areas of outstanding universal value from the point of view of science, conservation or natural beauty. A site that accommodates both the cultural and the natural universal values can be considered as mixed heritage.

China's Contributions to World Heritage List

中国已有28处自然或人文景观被列入"世界遗产名录"

(*C* = *Cultural Heritage* 文化遗产; *N* = *Natural Heritage* 自然遗产; *C* & *N* = *Mixed Heritage* 文化和自然遗产)

1. The Great Wall (Badaling, Shanhaiguan, Mutianyu & Jiayuguan) of China, Beijing (C, 1987) 万里长城（八达岭、山海关、慕田峪、嘉峪关）

2. The Palace Museum in Beijing (C, 1987) 北京故宫

3. Emperor Qin Shi Huang's mausoleum & his terracotta army, Shaanxi Province (C, 1987) 陕西秦始皇陵及兵马俑

4. Mogao Grottoes in Dunhuang, Gansu Province (C, 1987) 甘肃敦煌莫高窟

5. Zhoukoudian—home of Peking Man, Beijing (C, 1987) 周口店北京猿人遗址

6. Taishan Mountain, Shandong Province (C & N, 1987) 山东泰山

7. Huangshan Mountain, Anhui Province (C & N, 1990) 安徽黄山

8. Wulingyuan scenic area, Hunan Province (N, 1992) 湖南武陵源国家级名胜区

9. Jiuzhaigou scenic area, Sichuan Province (N, 1992) 四川九寨沟国家级名胜区

10. Yellow Dragon scenic area, Sichuan Province (N, 1992) 四川黄龙国家级名胜区

11. Potala Palace in Lhasa, Tibet (C, 1994) 西藏拉萨布达拉宫
Jokhong Temple 大昭寺 the extension of Potala Palace (listed in November 2000)
Norbulingka Park 罗布林卡 the extension of Potala Palace (listed in December 2001)

12. Chengde Summer Resort & surrounding temples, Hebei Province (C, 1994) 河北承德避暑山庄及周围寺庙

13. Confucian Temple, Residence and Tomb, Shandong Province (C, 1994) 山东曲阜的孔庙、孔府及孔林

14. Mount Wudang, Hubei Province (C, 1994) 湖北的武当山古建筑群

15. Mount Lushan, Jiangxi Province (C, 1996) 江西庐山风景名胜区

16. Mount E'mei with the Giant Buddha of Leshan (C & N, 1996) 四川峨眉山—乐山风景名胜区

17. The Ancient Town of Lijiang, Yunnan Province (C, 1997) 云南丽江古城

18. The Ancient Town of Pingyao, Shanxi Province (C, 1997) 山西平遥古城

19. Suzhou Classical Gardens, Jiangsu Province (C, 1997) 江苏苏州古典园林 Humble Administrator's Garden 拙政园、Lingering Garden 留园、Garden of Master-of-the-Net 网师园、the Mountain Villa of Secluded Beauty 环秀山庄

    The extensions of Suzhou Classical Gardens include 第二批世界文化遗产的苏州园林包括: Surging Waves Pavilion 沧浪亭、the Lion Grove Garden 狮子林、Yipu 艺圃、Ouyuan Garden 藕园、Tuisi Garden 退思园

20. The Summer Palace in Beijing (C, 1998) 北京颐和园

21. The Temple of Heaven in Beijing (C, 1998) 北京天坛

22. Dazu Grottoes, Chongqing Municipality (C, 1999) 重庆大足石窟

23. Mount Wuyishan, Fujian Province (C & N, 1999) 福建省武夷山

24. The Mount Qingcheng-Dujiangyan Irrigation Project in Sichuan Province (C & N, 2000) 四川青城山和都江堰

25. Longmen Grottoes in Henan Province (C, 2000) 河南洛阳龙门石窟

26. Royal Mausoleums of the Ming and Qing Dynasties—Ming Dynasty Xianling Tomb in Zhongxiang City, Hubei Province and Qing Dynasty Eastern Tombs, in Zunhua City and Qing Dynasty Western Tombs in Yi County, Hebei Province (C, 2000) 明清皇家陵寝:明显陵(湖北钟祥市)、清东陵(河北遵化市)

27. Ancient Villages in Southern Anhui - Xidi and Hongcun (C, 2000) 安徽古村落:西递、宏村(文化遗产, 2000 年 11 月被列入)

28. Yungang Grottoes in Shanxi Province (C. 2001) 山西省云冈石窟(文化遗产,2001 年 12 月被列入)

The following sites already on the List have been extended: the Potala Palace and the Jokhong Temple Monastery, Norbulingka Park (Treasure Garden 宝贝园), Lhasa and the Classical Gardens of Suzhou

The list now has 690 sites of "exceptional universal value" in 122 countries and regions across the world, including 28 Chinese sites.

Cultural sites are required to have historic, artistic, archaeological, scientific and anthropological value, while natural sites must offer distinct ecological and geographical features.

The Convention on the Protection of World Cultural and Natural Heritage, adopted by UNESCO in 1972, requires all its members to preserve listed sites which are protected during times of war. China joined the convention in 1985.

Taiwan Stunt Man Ke Shouliang 台湾特技柯受良

Taiwan stunt man Ke Shouliang flew over the Great Wall on his motor cycle on the morning of November 15, 1992 at the Jinshan Mountain ridge section. He was the first to make the dramatic jump, staking a claim to mention in the Guinness Book of World Records. The stunt biker leaped over the ridge's beacon tower from a 100-metre ramp and landed successfully on the opposite side on another ramp of 50 metres. His distance in the air was about 50 metres.

Wonder of the Great Wall 长城的奇迹

Located about a kilometre northwest to the Shanhaiguan Pass in Hebei Province, the hanging Great Wall was built with rocks blasted from the mountain. It is one of the most spectacular sections of the Great Wall, which was opened in summer 1993 to tourists after several centuries. This Hanging Great Wall tumbles down the cliffs of a big gorge. And from a distance, it looks like a wheeling dragon clinging to the mountainside. This stunning section of the walls is located in a big gorge, which cuts through the Jiaoshan Mountain. Work began simultaneously at the top and bottom of the cliffs and converged half way up. Imposing and magnificent, the Hanging Great Wall also has a delicate flavor especially in the rains. Then the waterfalls flow turbulently down the cliffs, enlivening the quiet of the mountains.

The Giant Dragon Dance at the Great Wall 长城上的巨龙舞

Braving the bitter wind and freezing cold, more than 5,000 young people from Hong Kong, Macao, Taiwan and the Chinese mainland converged atop the Badaling section of the Great Wall to perform dragon dances in celebration of the Lantern Festival, which fell on February 19, 2000, the 15th day of the first month on the Chinese lunar calendar.

The dragon dance, the most symbolic and joyful celebratory event, constituted the major part of the large-scale variety performance. The giant dragon, winding through 12 beacon towers of the Great Wall, which measured 3,048 metres, set a new record in the Guinness Book of World Record. "Dragon Dance at the Great Wall" was part of the youth-supporting project "Dragon at the Great Wall," which was organized by the project's Hong Kong Committee and the All-China Youth Federation. The project was aimed at developing leadership skills and innovative potential and facilitating exchange networks among Chinese youth worldwide.

The dragon weighed 14,460 kilograms and had 1,524 joints. It took 66 experts 69 days to finish the giant dragon.

Genghis Khan （1162-1227） 成吉思汗

Born in 1162 near the Onon River in Mongolia, the Khan-to-be was named Temujin. At that time, feuding Mongol tribes were at each others' throats, killing and looting at will. Simultaneously, the rulers of the Jin Dynasty （1115-1234） in northern China, founded by nomadic Nüzhen people, ruthlessly exploited the Mongol tribes and played them one against the other. The Mongols' common desire to end this age-old vendetta and to free themselves from the Jin rulers set the stage for Temujin's historical mission.

Tempered by harsh life on the steppe, his character was taking shape amid an atmosphere of hatred and a fierce competition for survival. One day an argument about a fish and a bird arose between the 9-year-old Temujin and his brother. The boy who was to become the "universal ruler" of the Mongols cold bloodedly shot his brother to death with an arrow. Temujin laid the foundation of his unprecedented empire by uniting and organizing fragmented Mongol tribes through alliances, marriage, sworn oaths of brotherhood and military annexation. By a combination of discipline, cunning, ruthlessness, superior organization and the ability to attract and retain personal loyalties, he eliminated his enemies and brought under his rule the related Tatar, Kereit, Naiman and Merkit tribes. In 1206, he was named supreme leader of the Mongols in a great assembly called the huraltai. The assembly conferred upon him the title Genghis Khan, meaning "universal ruler." In the same year, Genghis Khan drew up an important legal code, the Great Yasa; in it, he laid down basic rules for the court, army, and nation in civil, criminal and commercial law. Mongol laws and political administration had a strong influence on early Russian institutions, dominated by the Tatars for more than 200 years.

The Mongol society under Genghis Khan was based on a kind of political, economic and military system rolled into one. Breaking down old tribal distinctions, the Khan divided the Mongol empire into 95 Qianhu's （literally 1,000 households in Chinese）, which were in turn subdivided into 10 households. Mongol nobles were placed at each level as political, economic and military chiefs. In these units, Mongols were cavalrymen as well as cowherds. The Mongols paid their taxes to the nobles, herded their animals, milked their cows and made donations of unpaid labor in peace time. However, each Mongol possessed his own horses, bows, spikes and armor and was always ready to turn from a herdsman into a formidable fighter.

Genghis Khan formulated a series of legal and political institutions from which he forged a homogeneous Mongol nation, ethnically, economically, and culturally. This achievement differed from khanates established by Mongol conquerors in West Asia and Russia, which were no more than temporary military administrative amalgamations.

Having united the Mongols, Genghis Khan turned to conquest in 1207. The bloody campaigns resulted in the conquest of the Jin Dynasty, the Muslim kingdom of Khorezm (which now covers northern Iran, Kazakhstan, Uzbekistan and Caucasus) and the kingdom of Xixia established by the Tibetan Tanguts in West China's Gansu and Qinghai provinces. Genghis Khan's strategic talents and his iron will also played a decisive part in the Mongol conquest. He reportedly said "Man's highest joy is in victory to conquer one's enemies, to pursue them, to deprive them of their possessions, to make their beloved weep, to ride on their horses and to embrace their wives and daughters."

Why was Genghis Khan destined to become the master of most of Eurasia? All the Mongol tribes together numbered about one million men, women and children, which afforded Genghis Khan a maximum of 125,000 warriors. How was he able to come literally so close to becoming the "ruler of the universe?"

As a nation set to conquer, the daily life of the Mongols was a continuous rehearsal for war. Clad in leather and furs, leading extra horses as remounts and capable of riding several days and nights in succession with a minimum of rest and food, these warriors introduced "blitzkrieg" into the 13th century world. During a campaign on the plains of Hungary, they are said to have covered 270 miles in three days. They carried leather bags for water, which when empty could be inflated for use in swimming across rivers. Normally, they lived off the countryside, but if necessary they drank the blood of their horses and the milk of their mares.

Mongols were masters of the tactic of feigned retreat, espionage and psychological warfare. Butchering his enemies in cold blood was Genghis Khan's own version of psychological warfare. In addition, the Mongols were quick to adopt new weapons and techniques, many of them learned from the Chinese. These included powerful catapults and battering rams, and the tactics of sappers, who tunneled under walls and blew them up with gunpowder.

Genghis Khan appeared at the right historical moment — a time when China was divided into three fragments with the Jin Dynasty ruling the north, the Song Dynasty the south, and the Tibetan Tanguts ensconced in the northwest. A long period of peace and prosperity had corrupted the rulers and weakened the will of the people. All this lent strength to Genghis Khan and abetted the spread of his empire.

The Palace Museum (Forbidden City)
故宫（紫禁城）

The Palace Museum, known as the Forbidden City in the West, was the imperial palaces of the Ming and Qing dynasties. In early 15th century, large-scale construction involved 100, 000 artisans and one million civilians. The construction took 14 years and was finished in 1420. In the following year, the capital of the Ming Dynasty was moved from Nanjing to Beijing. Twenty-four emperors — "Sons of Heaven" of the Ming and Qing dynasties ruled from the Forbidden City. The last dynasty fell in 1911, but Emperor Puyi still lived in the inner court. It was not until 1925 that the complex was converted into a museum. Since then the palace has been opened to the public. The Forbidden City is a national architectural treasure.

The Palace Museum is located in the centre of Beijing, covering an area of 72 hectares (720, 000 square metres) with more than 90 courtyards of various sizes. It is rectangular in shape, 960 metres long from north to south and 760 metres wide from east to west. There is a 3, 400-metre-long and 10-metre-high wall, encircled by a 3, 800-metre-long and 52-metre wide moat. In the Ming Dynasty, the timber needed for building the palace was brought mostly from Sichuan, Hunan and Guizhou provinces, while in the Qing Dynasty, it was cut from northeast China. Most of the stones were quarried from the suburban district of Fangshan and other districts. Construction of the Forbidden City brought tremendous hardship to the laboring people.

The palace is the largest piece of ancient Chinese architecture still standing. Some of the buildings were damaged by lightning and rebuilt in the Ming and Qing dynasties. The palace had been expanded several times, but the original layout was preserved.

After 1949, some costly renovations were done and the Palace Museum has been listed by the Chinese Government as one of the important historical monuments under special preservation.

Each year the Forbidden City receives about 7 million visitors both from home and abroad. According to 30 yuan per ticket for average, the income of tickets of the Forbidden City would reach US$25. 4 million annually.

The largest restoration project of the Forbidden City began on April 3,

2002. The ground will be renovated to their original look once the project is finished in 2008. It will remain open to tourists during construction. The renovation project will cost 1 billion yuan (US$120. 8 million).

A future target of the Forbidden City, as inscribed in the World Heritage List of the United Nations Educational, Scientific and Cultural Organization (UNESCO) in 1987, is to make the visit as convenient as possible for tourists both at home and abroad. It is the museum's long-term goal for visitors to receive telecommunications service in every part of the Forbidden City. The Forbidden City will increase the number of telephones for visitors, and will invite experts to design the telephone booths using transparent material. These booths will be installed in the corners, so they can stand in harmony with the ancient style of the Forbidden City. From the website, publications, tapes and volunteers, visitors will be well-informed in the Forbidden City. Foreign visitors will meet few language barriers, as brochures will be printed in multi-languages. All toilets will be rebuilt to meet three-star grade that has facilities to wash hands, tissues, hand-dryers and bathrooms specially designed for disabled and elderly people. As a world-class museum, the Forbidden City attracts an average of 25, 000 tourists everyday. Some visitors may, unavoidably, fall ill during their tour. To solve this problem, the museum has two medical teams of five to six full-time doctors to provide medical services. The museum will temporarily invite doctors from other hospitals in the holiday seasons. Therefore, the museum will guarantee a healthier visit to tourists, even if as many as 80, 000 people (the largest number of visitors the museum can accommodate) visit the museum in one single day. For the sake of the security of the historical and cultural treasures, and also for visitors to see the treasures, the museum has to control the number of visitors.

China now boasts 750 key cultural relics protection units.

There are four ancient government offices in feudal China 中国四大古代官衙. They are the Forbidden City in Beijing 北京的故宫, Governor-general Office in Baoding, Hebei Province 河北保定总督署, Huozhou Office built in the Yuan Dynasty (1279-1368) in Shanxi Province 山西霍州署, and Neixiang County Office in Henan Province 河南内乡县衙.

- Kuai Xiang 蒯祥(1377-1461), a native of Wu County, Jiangsu Province, was an outstanding architect in the Ming Dynasty (1368-1644). In 1417 he was in charge of building the imperial palace. In the period 1436 to 1149 he rebuilt the three main halls in the Forbidden City and other key buildings. He was credited as "Master Craftsman Kuai."

- Lu Ban 鲁班—a master craftsman of the Spring and Autumn Period (770 BC-476 BC), since deified as the patron saint of carpenters.

Forbidden City (Palace Museum)

Tongzi River (Moat)   Tongzi River (Moat)

Watchtower (Turret)   Gate of Divine Pride   Watchtower (Turret)
Pavilion of   Gate of   Gate of Purity & Obedience
The Purest Perfumes   Obedience & Purity
Palace of   Palace of ⑬   ④   ⑤ Princes Abodes   Pavilion of
Heroic Splenour   Double Glory   Centuries Imperial   Great Happiness
Hall of Devoted Esteem   Pavilion   Garden   ⑥ Porch of Mingling of Harmonies
Palace of   Gate of Earthly   ⑨ Palace of Southward View ⑭
Universal Happiness ⑮   Tranquility   (Museum of Fabrics)
Palace of   Palace of ㉓   Palace of ⑦   ⑧   ① Treasure Hall
Eternal Longevity   Eternal Spring   Earthly Tranquility   Palace of Eternal Peace
⑲ ㉒ ㉑ Hall of Union   ⑩   ⑯
Hall of Manifest Origin   Palace of   Palace of Charity   Palace of Peaceful
Pavilion of ⑱ Eternal Life   Palace of   (Museum of Bronzes)   Longevity
Rain & Water   Room of Three   Heavenly Purity   Hall of Ultimate
Palace of   Rare Treasures ⑰   ⑫ Museum of Clocks   Greatness
Rear Hall   Princes' Abodes   Gate of   Hall of Abstinence
Palace of   Hall of Great Buddha   Lunar Glory ②   ③   Gate of
Longevity & Health   Gate of Heavenly Purity   Gate for Worship   Peaceful Longevity
Palace of Benevolent Peace ⑪   of Ancestors
Gate of Imperial   Gate of Flourishing   Gate of Ultimate Greatness
Gate of Benevolent Peace   Prosperity   Fortune
Lofty Tower Hall of Preserving   Lofty Tower   Nine-Dragon Wall
Palace of Perfect Peace   Harmony
Hall of Complete   Archery Pavilion
Garden of Benevolent Peace   Harmony
Imperial Kitchen   Princes' Studies
Central-Right Gate   Central-Left Gate
Hall of
Right-Side Gate   Supreme Harmony   Left-Side Gate
Tower of Manifest
Tower of Enhanced   Benevolence
Righteousness   Pavilion of Imperial Library
Hall of Esteem
Deliberation   Qing Dynasty Annals
Tower of
Precious   Hall of Military   Hall of
Accumulation   Prowess   Lofty   Gate of   Lofty Literary Glory   Hall of
) (Tower   Supreme   Tower   Intellectual Honours
Gate of   Harmony
Perfect Peace   Gate of Military Prowess   Gate of Literary Glory   East Flowery Gate
West Flowery   Gate of
Gate   Prosperous Harmony   Gate of Harmony   East Storeroom
South Fragrance Hall   Imperial Archives   Veritable Records Archives
Lantern Storage   Cabinet Hall   South Storeroom
Watchtower (Turret)   Meridian Gate   Watchtower (Turret)

Tongzi River (Moat)   Tongzi River (Moat)

① Hall of Character Cultivation ② Gate of Solar Perfection ③ Hall for Worship of Ancestors
④ Hall of Imperial Peace ⑤ Pavilion of Floating Greenery ⑥ Pavilion of Ten-Thousand Springs
⑦ House of Crimson Snow ⑧ Hall for Carrying Out Imperial Orders
⑨ Palace of Purity in Affection ⑩ Pottery & Porcelain Exhibition Hall ⑪ Office of Grand Council
⑫ Hall of Sincerity & Solemnity ⑬ Pavilion of Propitious Clarity ⑭ Hall of Delight & Longevity
⑮ Palace of Concentrated Beauty ⑯ Pavilion of Melodies Sounds ⑰ Hall of Mental Cultivation
⑱ Hall of Supreme Happiness ⑲ Hall of Manifest Origin ⑳ Hall of Manifest Harmony
㉑ Gate of Intense Happiness ㉒ Queen Consort's Palace

Meridian Gate 午门

This is the main gate of the Purple Forbidden City. The purple colour was symbolically attributed to the North Star, and it was used here to show that the imperial residence was a cosmic centre. The emperor believed that the meridian line went through the city. The gate was also nicknamed the "Five Phoenix Tower," in which drums (on the east) and bells (on the west) were installed. When the emperor went to the Temple of Heaven, bells were struck to celebrate this important occasion. When he went to the Ancestral Temple, it was made known to the public by beating drums.

The gate has five openings. The central passage was reserved for the Emperor alone. High-ranking civil and military officials went in through the side gate on the east and royal family members on the west. The further side gates were for petty officials. Celebrations of victories, ceremonies of "accepting" prisoners of war and announcement of the new calendar all took place here. In the Ming Dynasty, this was also the place where the Emperor punished high officials. The offending officials would be taken out of the gate and beaten with sticks. It was recorded that in 1524, 134 men were beaten on one single occasion and 17 died on the spot.

To get in to the Forbidden City requires a 30 yuan or US$3.75 ticket (50 yuan or US$6.25 for a through ticket). Also, if you purchase the through ticket (or comprehensive ticket), remember to keep your ticket handy for inspection, as you will need to show it upon entering certain different parts of the museum. If you lose the original ticket you will have to buy a new one at each separate section, although these tickets are only about 5 yuan (US$0.6) a piece.

Now we approach the Five Marble Bridges on Golden Water River. The bridges were supposed to represent the five virtues preached by Confucius benevolence, righteousness, rites, intelligence and fidelity. They were shaped like five arrows reporting symbolically to Heaven, because the emperor considered himself the Son of Heaven. In the Forbidden City is the Golden Water River, a second moat; noticeable by the way it meanders through the area. It too is a fire suppression tool, used by the many emperors' forces as a source for water in times of fire.

The buildings on the east were the Imperial Secretariat and the Chronicler's Offices, where daily activities for the emperor were recorded by scholars. The buildings on the west were for translators.

Lucianno Pavarotti, Placido Domingo, and Jose Carreras—Three Tenors Thrilled Beijing

210

Lucianno Pavarotti 帕瓦罗蒂, 66, Placido Domingo 拉希多·多明戈, 60 and Jose Carreras 卡雷拉斯, 55 gathered again for the first time since the 1998 World Cup in Paris, France. The extravaganza was the last one held by the trio. Since 1985, the three artists had visited Beijing separately, but this was their first joint performance. The three artists said that the vitality created by China's reforms and opening up as well as the people enthusiasm for the arts had inspired them to sing in Beijing on June 23, 2001. June 23 is the World Olympic Day. Supported by a symphony orchestra of more than 100 musicians and a chorus of 200 singers, they provided the audience with an unforgettable experience. The concert coincided with the official Olympic Day and formed part of the city's drive to win the bid for the 2008 Olympics. The grand event held in the Wumen Gate (Meridian Gate) Square of the Forbidden City could be regarded as a vote of support for the Olympic Games from all Chinese people and their friends around the world. Over the past three decades, Pavarotti, Domingo and Carreras, have become international stars, captivating audiences and popularizing opera by bringing the gap between classical and popular music. Their rare joint performances were always galas of world operas and modern classics. The world's famous tenors only perform together in aid of sports, charity, environmental protection and world peace 著名的世界三大男高音只为体育、慈善事业、环保、世界和平几个主题唱歌.

Air Quality in the Forbidden City up to Standards

One year-long environmental monitoring project indicates that air quality inside the walls of the Forbidden City, the former residence of emperors, is better than the average level in downtown Beijing. The air quality in the 720, 000-square-metre city meets the State environmental requirements, according to the experts responsible for the monitoring work. The air qaulity over the Forbidden City parallels that in adjacent suburbs and is much better than that in busy streets. As the largest complex structure in China remaining from ancient times, the Forbidden City attracts millions of visitors from all over the world each year. The researchers collected 10 major pollutants, including sulfides, carbon dioxide, carbon monoxide, chlorides, hydrocarbon and total suspended particles, from five locations in the museum in 1999. Most of the pollutants were under the State-designated safety ceiling. However, the hydrocarbon level was comparatively high because of the long-term use of paint used for museum repairs. The Beijing municipal government has worked diligently to fight against pollution, focusing on key sites such as the Forbidden City, which is included on the World Heritage list released by the United Nations Educational, Scientific and Cultural Organization (UNESCO).

BEIJING

Gate of Supreme Harmony 太和门

The gate is guarded by a pair of bronze lions symbolizing the imperial power. In ancient times, lions were supposed to be good doorkeepers and put at the gate to ward off evil spirits. Lions are frequently seen in front of buildings as guardians, one playing with a ball (male) and the other a cub (female). It was considered auspicious. The ball is said to represent imperial treasury or peace. The cub sucks milk from underneath the claw, because the female doesn't have breast.

Now we are at the Gate of Supreme Harmony, the gate leading to the palace court. The emperors of Ming Dynasty attended to state affairs and summoned their ministers for consultations here. In the Qing Dynasty, state affairs were handled in the inner court.

Proceeding to the north, you can see a vast courtyard, 10,000 square metres in area. Flanking the courtyard are 33 room units on each side. They were used as warehouses for storing fur, porcelain, silver, tea, satin and clothes, etc.

In the courtyard there are iron vats for storing water against fire. In the whole complex there are altogether 308 water vats, 18 of them were gilded. Each iron vat weighs 2.2 tons; while each gilded bronze vat weighs 3.4 tons. Most of them were made in the Ming Dynasty. On the roofs of these buildings you can see lightning arresters installed in 1953. [Berjamin Franklin (1706-1790), American statesman, author and scientist invented lightning arrester in 1752] The roofs are of yellow glazed tiles, as yellow was the colour reserved for the emperor. The Forbidden City was heavily guarded, yet the emperor still did not feel secure and was worried that someone might tunnel his way into the palace. So, the ground bricks were laid in a special way: seven layers lengthwise and eight layers crosswise, making up fifteen layers in all.

On the triple marble terrace you find eighteen bronze incense burners. They represented the eighteen provinces in the Qing Dynasty. On this huge terrace stand three big halls: the Hall of Supreme Harmony, the Hall of Complete Harmony and the Hall of Preserving Harmony, all lying on the north-south axis. Each terrace is higher than the other, encircled by marble balustrades carved with dragon and phoenix designs. From the edge of the terraces jut out heads of mythical monsters, totalling 1,142, which serve both as decorations and rainspouts. They stand out as works of art, whether seen from afar or close by.

There are three staircases leading to the Hall of Supreme Harmony, the central one was reserved for the emperor. He was carried in a sedan chair

212

to the marble ramp, which was covered with red carpet on big occasions. The side staircases were for others.

On the terrace in the east stands a sun-dial. It could be used when there was sunlight. People looked at the markings of time on its upper part in summer adorn its lower part in winter. In the west there is a little pavilion in which a copper grain measure is kept. The measure was used as the national standard in the Qing Dynasty, but it was always in favour of the ruling class. The grain measure and the sun dial were symbols of imperial justice and rectitude. The dragon headed tortoises and storks, a pair of each kind, were incense burners. The tortoise was a symbol of longevity and strength while the stork represented longevity.

These are gilded bronze water vats, two on each side. When the Allied Forces of the Eight Powers (Britain, Germany, France, tsarist Russia, the United States, Italy, Japan and Austria) invaded Beijing in 1900, the alien troops scraped the gold off the vats with their bayonets. On the north side underneath the vats (caldrons) are air vents to fan the fires set to keep the water inside from freezing in winter. Looking up, you can see mythical animals (zoomorphic ornaments or *Wenshou* 吻兽 in Chinese) on the upturned eaves of the building. In ancient times, there used to be big wooden nails to prevent the tiles from sliding. They were replaced by glazed tiles which were later shaped into mythical animals, such as *the dragon* 龙, *the phoenix* 凤, *the lion* 狮子, *the heavenly horse* 天马, *the sea horse* 海马, *the Suanni* 狻猊, *the Yayu* 押鱼, *Xiezhi* 獬豸, *Douniu* 斗牛, and *Hangshi* 行什. The dragon and phoenix are symbols of honoured supremacy; the heavenly horse and sea horse stand for Emperor's prestige and morale; *Douniu* and *Yayu* are the strange beasts in the sea. Legend has it that they can make clouds and produce rain to prevent fire from disaster; the lion, king of beasts from foreign lands, is the dominator of the mountains; *Suanni*, a legendary beast of prey, is said to be the beast of eating tiger and leopard. It is the symbol of the unity of the country and the symbol of all beasts following him; *Xiezhi* can distinguish right from wrong. It is the symbol of being open and above board and purity and justice of the royal family; *Hangshi* is symbolic of honour and auspice, prestige and wisdom, and it also implies subduing of evil spirits and getting rid of calamities. Nowadays, these animals are architectural decorations.

The Forbidden City Goes on Line

The Forbidden City, China's largest museum and biggest treasure house has taken its first step into the digital world. In mid-July 2001, the Forbidden City opened its website (http://www.dpm.org.cn) to the public after three years preparation. Co-operating with the Chinese Academy of Science's Sino-soft Group, the museum finally laying optical fibre lines, built a 1,000-MHz LAN computer and developed a software system to manage its collection. The purpose of opening the website is to serve three different groups of people. They include ordinary readers, amateur lovers of cultural relics, and scholars and researchers. The website provides information on 14 major topics and includes an overview of the museum, a guide to Forbidden City, explanations of the relics in the collection and an online museum. The site also offers an "Expert Forum" where scholars can exchange ideas.

The first phase of the website construction involved over 4,000 photographs with 480,000 expository characters and research papers amounting to 5.63 million characters. As the world enters the Internet age, Chinese museums have to face the challenge of changing their old-fashioned manual management strategies. The routine methods that most Chinese museums presently use in the protection, exhibition and study the relics no longer work in modern society. The museum stores nearly 1 million cultural relics. Only 10,000 are displayed for visitors on a year-round basis.

As the largest museum both in China and in the world, with an area of 720,000 square metres, the Forbidden City contains nearly a million art treasures from the past 5,000 years of Chinese culture. Because of this immensity, it is nearly impossible for any visitor to see everything inside the imperial palace. The website is designed to help people work out an ideal route to take through the palace by providing them with information about the different galleries and buildings contained in the palace.

Hall of Supreme Harmony 太和殿

This is the throne hall, built in 1420. It was renovated several times after 1949. It was used for ceremonies which marked great occasions: the Winter Solstice, the Chinese New Year, the Emperor's birthday and enthronement, and the dispatch of generals to battles. On such occasions, there would be an imperial guard of honour standing in front of the hall and extending to the main gate. The hall is 35 metres high, 64 metres long from east to west, and 33 metres wide from north to south, embracing 2,377 square metres. The entire building is supported by 84 giant wooden columns. It is the largest wooden structure in China.

The base and the throne are carved out of sandalwood. The throne was a symbol of imperial power. The floor is paved with bricks. After baking for 136 days they were then immersed in tung oil for a permanent polish.

When you look up you can see "caisson," or covered ceiling. It was placed over the throne and served as architectural decoration. It was designed to create an aura of solemnity and mystery. In the middle of the ceiling is the design of a dragon playing with pearls. They are made of glass, painted with mercury, representing sunlight.

The last Qing Emperor Puyi was born in 1906. He ascended the throne in 1908 at the age of three. He was so scared during the coronation that he kept crying. He shouted: "I don't want to stay here, I want to go home." His cry extremely upset the dignified atmosphere. His father tried to soothe him, saying, "It'll soon be finished, it'll soon be finished." Three years later, the feudal system collapsed that had lasted for more than 2, 000 years. However, he stayed in the palace for another 13 years until 1924 when he was driven out of the palace. The remaining 470 imperial eunuchs and 100 palace maids were freed and he moved into his father's princely mansion with his wife and imperial concubine.

A few months later, he left for Tianjin and disguised himself as a Japanese merchant. After Japanese aggression of northeast China in 1931, Puyi was made a puppet emperor of "Manzhouguo" with Changchun as its capital. He was captured by the Soviet Red Army in 1945 and was sent to China in 1950. He was imprisoned for almost 10 years until 1959 when he was given amnesty.

The former emperor then turned over a new leaf, and was assigned a job in the Institute of Botanical Garden under the Chinese Academy of Sciences in Beijing. He lived 61 years and died of cancer in 1967.

The small holes on the walls in the Forbidden City are used to pour insecticide / pesticide into them for anti-termites, waterproof and anti-rot as well 灌药、防虫、防水、防腐.

Build your own Supreme Harmony

The bright red cover on an elegant packing box is shaped like a palace gate. Through the gate, people seem to enter the Forbidden City. In the box, some 200 wooden fittings are found in five layers lying on royal yellow silk cloth laden with dragon designs. Following the instructions written on a decree-like scroll, people can fit all the wooden pieces together, in hours possibly, to produce the Hall of Supreme Harmony.

Building the hall, major building in the Forbidden City, from these fittings is more than a children's game. Mirroring the richness of Chinese architecture, the wooden pieces teach culture. The miniature Hall of Supreme Harmony gives builders a way to appreciate and explore China's royal architectural art and history.

Produced by Beijing Dragon Seal Museum Company Limited under supervision of the Forbidden City, the model is on a scale of 1:200. Even though the miniature Hall of Supreme Harmony is less than 0.5 metre high and weighs around two kilograms, it took almost a year for researchers from the two museums to finish the dismantling work. Most of the wooden fittings are made in strict accordance with the original architectural elements, with only a few modifications to accommodate the batch production requirement. Tourists can learn more about traditional Chinese culture and history from building the Hall of Supreme Harmony themselves.

The price for the miniature hall is between 2,000 yuan and 3,000 yuan (US$240-360), and available at the Forbidden City and other Beijing's major tourist spots and shops. The company also intends to make build-it-yourself models of other Forbidden City halls—including the Tian' anmen Rostrum—as well as temples, pagodas and ancient residences.

Hall of Complete Harmony 中和殿

This hall is square in shape, with windows on all sides. It served as an antechamber. The emperor came here to make his last minute preparations. Final touches were given to the message to be read in the Ancestral Temple. The seeds intended for spring sowing were also examined here.

The two Qing sedan chairs here were for travelling within the palace. The braziers were for heat, while the four cylindrical burners for sandalwood incense.

Hall of Preserving Harmony 保和殿

Architecturally, this hall has no supporting pillars in its front part, something typical of Ming architecture. In the Qing Dynasty, banquets were given on New Year's Eve in honour of Mongolian princes and high-ranking officials. The imperial examinations were held here. In the Ming and Qing dynasties, there were three levels of exams: the county and prefecture level, the provincial level and the national level. The national level exam was presided over by the emperor. After the imperial examination, three best students from among all the candidates were selected by the emperor. Those three persons were called *Zhuang Yuan* 壮元, *Bang Yan* 榜眼 and *Tan Hua* 探花. *Zhuang Yuan* referred to the "Grand Laurel-Scholar" (the scholar-candidate came first in the palace-examination in old China). Another translation for Zhuang Yuan was a title for people who scored highest on the highest imperial examinations in old China. *Bang Yan* referred to No. 2 "Grand Laurel-Scholar" (the scholar-candidate came second in the palace examination) *Tan Hua* referred to No. 3 "Grand Laurel-scholar" (the scholar-candidate came third in the palace examination) They got promotion and became high officials in the palace court.

The civil service exams in China started in the Han Dynasty. It served the purpose of recruiting Confucian scholars to be ministers and high officials. During the centuries of disunity that followed, the Han Dynasty system of selecting officials by exam went out, and men were appointed, not on merit but by favor and nepotism. The examination system came back and was established again in the Tang Dynasty. It continued until 1905. The Qing Dynasty took over the ancient system of imperial examination. Once every three years, three hundred scholars from all over the country came to Beijing and took the exams for three days and three nights in this hall. The exams were so rigid that competitors sometimes went insane or died of exhaustion. Those who failed sometimes took poison and threw themselves off the high balconies. Those who passed would get honorable titles and become high officials or consort of a princess 驸马 .

Imperial Examination Glossary

Provincial examination 乡试：(under the Ming and Qing civil examination system, the examination for the selection of *juren* 举人 out of *xiucai* 秀才, held trienially in the various provincial capitals)

Metropolitan examination 会试：(under the Ming and Qing civil service examination system, the examination for the selection of *jinshi* 进士 out of *juren* 举人, held triennially in Beijing, the national capital)

The palace examination 殿试：(final imperial examination, presided over by the emperor)

No. 1 at the highest imperial examinations 状元

No. 2 at the highest imperial examinations 榜眼

No. 3 at the highest imperial examinations 探花

Juren 举人：A successful candidate in the imperial examinations at the provincial level in the Ming and Qing dynasties

Jinshi 进士：A successful candidate at the highest imperial examinations

Official Selection Open to Competition

The jobs of Chinese officials are no longer for life, due to the introduction of a competitive mechanism in leading official posts in late 1990s. For many years since 1949, officials in China were selected and appointed in a certain way. Leaders and high-level departments decided which employer would be promoted; this of course sometimes resulted in unhealthy tendencies and corruption in official appointment procedures. To improve the situation, China has begun to reform its government official selection and appointment system. Competing for leading posts has been practiced at many levels, and incompetent official are usually removed. Much has been done in improving checking systems for officials and in strengthening supervision. Laws and regulations have been worked out to create favourable conditions for the promotion of outstanding personnel. Thanks to the new methods, malpractice and corruption in the selection of officials has been greatly reduced. Beijing, the capital of the People's Republic of China, has made a breakthrough in selecting leading officials in an open manner. At an open selection of leading officials at bureau level earlier in 2001, the city municipal government for the first time withdrew the condition that candidates should have registered permanent residence in Beijing. Thus the move is designed to find and recruit outstanding personnel from other areas. The practice of selecting leading officials conforms to reforms towards a market economy and its ultimate goal is to get rid of defects of the old official selection and promotional system, and bring about a more effective and optimized allocation of human resources. Featuring openness, equality, competition and a fair selection of the best person for the job, competition for leading posts involves an open solicitation of candidates, written and oral examinations, discussions and assessment by higher authorities. Selected candidates will then be appointed to leading posts according to set procedures.

Marble Ramp Carved with Cloud & Dragon Designs 浮雕

This is the largest piece of stone carving in the palace, a work of the Ming period. It is 16.57 metres long, 3.07 metres wide and 1.7 metres thick, and weighs about 250 tons. The emperor was carried in a sedan chair over the marble ramp. No one was allowed to set foot on it. Most of the stone used in building the palace was from Fangshan and other counties. It was very difficult to transport such a big piece of stone here. The labouring people were so ingenious that they invented a method of shipping it over ice. Wells were sunk every half a kilometre, and water was brought up and poured on the ground to make a road of ice in winter. Rolling logs were used in summer. Twenty thousand people were involved in shipping this stone all the way from Fangshan Mountains 70 kilometres away from Beijing.

The numerous Ming Dynasty stone carvings in the Forbidden City were transported from Shiwo, a small village in Fangshan District 70 kilometres southwest of Beijing and a place noted for its stone pits as well as craftsmanship.

Marble exploring has been traditional profession in Shiwo Village since the early Tang Dynasty. The Yunju (Heavenly Living) Temple near the village has one of the world's biggest collections of scripture slabs. Making a living from marble for many generations, the village contributed more than their fair share in restoring the country's badly damaged cultural relics. Their work included re-laying the royal square of 3,000 square metres between the Upright Gate or Gate of Correct Demeanour 端门 and the Meridian Gate 午门 in the Palace Museum known as the Forbidden City in the West. In 1985, they carved several columns for a classical Chinese archway, which was set up in Washington, D. C., USA.

Office of the Privy Council 军机处

These rooms used to be the Office of the Privy Council, set up during the reign of Yongzheng (1723-1735), the third Qing Emperor. It assisted the emperor in dealing with routine military and political affairs.

Before entering the Hall of Mental Cultivation, visitors can see a two concentric discs with dragons. It is the mirror of Heaven and Earth, a mirror of all things. The mirror also holds and reflects the rays of the sun, warding off evil and lighting the eternal darkness of the tomb.

Now we come to the Hall of Mental Cultivation 养心殿, which was built in the Ming Dynasty. It served as the living quarters for emperors over many centuries and gained added importance during the reign of Qing emperor Yongzheng (1723-1735) when it became the office where the emperor conducted important affairs of state. It is believed that most of the Qing emperors lived and worked in this hall. The central hall in the Hall of Mental Cultivation was the audience chamber where the emperor read memorials, granted audience to officials and summoned his ministers for consultation. Behind the imperial throne (furnished with yellow satin) is a rosewood tablet engraved with a motto written by the Qing Emperor Qianlong. Over it hangs horizontal tablet bearing the Chinese characters for "just and benevolent" in Emperor Yongzheng's handwriting.

The hall has a magnificent ceiling sculpture of a dragon playing with a huge pearl. The western chamber of the Hall of Mental Cultivation, formerly called Sanxitang (Room of Three Rare Treasures), provides glimpses of the private life of Emperor Qianlong, who was in power from 1736 to 1795. The room bears testimony to his patronage of the classics, calligraphy and painting, and impresses tourists with an air of elegance without being ostentatious. The royal seat is placed behind a small desk for reading and writing, with writing brushes and ink stones arranged along the windowsill to the left. In this room the emperor read reports and discussed military and political affairs with his officials.

The partition in front of the western chamber was to prevent the secret talks between the emperor and ministers from leaking out.

The eastern side room in the Hall of Mental Cultivation is of historical interest because it was here that Empress Dowager Cixi gave audiences behind a screen or controlled power behind the throne for many years, a political phenomenon which was previously unheard of in the annals of the Qing Dynasty. When Emperor Tongzhi ascended the throne in 1862 at the age of six, Empress Dowager Cixi and Ci'an (the first empress of Xianfeng) both sat on a throne in the room, which was separated from the emperor's throne by a screen, to assist him in the conduct of state affairs. This practice continued when Emperor Guangxu succeeded to the throne in 1875 at the age of four. But with the sudden death of Ci'an one morning in 1881, which many people believed was due to an act of intrigue by Empress Dowager Cixi's, state power passed entirely into the hands of the Empress Dowager, known as the "battle axe." She nominally gave up her authority on Guangxu's coming of age in 1890, but later in 1898, became a dictator when she placed Emperor Guangxu under house arrest at Yingtai (Water Terrace Pavilion), an islet in Zhongnanhai (Central South Sea), after she exposed his plans for political reform. A woman with no scruples, Cixi mismanaged the government and indulged in extravagant living for 48 years, plunging China into disasters and humiliations unparalleled in the annals of its history.

The Qing Dynasty, which was the last imperial dynasty in the history of China, was overthrown in the 1911 Revolution let by Dr Sun Yat-sen. Emperor Xuantong (Puyi) was forced to issue an edict in the Hall of Mental Cultivation declaring his abdication and formally recognizing the Republic on February 12, 1912. Under the terms of preferential treatment for the ex-Qing court, Puyi and his family continued to enjoy the privilege of living in the Hall of Mental Cultivation for another 13 years. In 1925, they were forced to move out of the palaces for good.

Behind the Hall of Mental Cultivation is Tishuntang (Hall of Manifesting Obedience). In the courtyard stands a huge piece of crystal, which was supposed to be a symbol of the emperor's character.

The eastern part of the hall used to be Empress Longyu's living room, and is a reminder of a tragedy in the Qing imperial family during the reign of Emperor Guangxu (1875-1908). It is said that Longyu was chosen by Empress Dowager Cixi to be Guangxu's empress against his own wishes. Therefore, he never lived with her except on the night of the wedding, nor did he subsequently visit her room.

Not long afterwards in 1898, Emperor Guangxu became passionately attached to Zhenfei, a favourite concubine who ardently shared his views of political reform. This met with the displeasure of Empress Dowager Cixi.

Deeply jealous of Zhenfei and taking advantage of her disfavour with Empress Dowager Cixi, Longyu spread gossip about her so called infidelity. Longyu is said to have held many secret meetings with the powerful eunuch Li Lianying in the Hall of Mental Cultivation in order to lay plans to persecute Zhenfei.

In 1900, when the Allied Forces of the Eight Foreign Powers were advancing on Beijing, Cixi and her court fled Beijing in panic. On the eve of her flight, Empress Dowager Cixi tried to induce Zhenfei to jump down a well located in the northeastern part of the Forbidden City, which we will see before we leave the palace. When Zhenfei resisted, Empress Dowager Cixi ordered a courtier to push her in. Then the Empress Dowager escaped through a back door of the Forbidden City and headed for Xi'an. The well, named Zhenfei Well in her memory, is today often visited by tourists.

Empress Dowager Cixi (1835-1908) 慈禧太后

Empress Dowager Cixi was born in 1835. Her name was "Little Orchid." Her father was a then a provincial governor from South China. In 1851 she was one of the 28 Manchu girls selected for Emperor Xianfeng because of her good looks, who gave her a new name, Cixi, meaning "Holy Mother." She was made a concubine of the fifth rank when she was seventeen years old. After she gave birth to a son, the only son of the emperor, she was made a concubine of the second rank. Emperor Xianfeng died in 1861 and his six-year-old son succeeded the throne the following year. She was now the empress dowager. She started as a prodigy in the art of intrigue and built power based on the court eunuchs.

While the boy emperor sat in the throne, she sat behind him with a screen in between and told him what to say and what to do. This practice is known in the Chinese history as "giving audience behind a screen" or power behind the throne.

Her son died of small pox at the age of 19. Then she put her sister's 4-year-old son on the throne, whom she dominated and tormented. Empress Dowager Cixi had three ambitions: pleasure, power and luxury. To usurp power she invited Empress Ci'an, the first wife of Emperor Xianfeng, to dinner and poisoned her to death. Others say she died of illness in 1881.

She was then free to enjoy a life of extreme luxury and was free to do whatever she pleased. According to historical records, 6 eunuchs were appointed to take care of her jewelry, shoes, and clothes, which were classified and recorded in a registry. She possessed a huge amount of clothes in

1894 alone, and she ordered 135 suits. Her meals were prepared and
served with the most sophisticated procedure. Each feast contained more
than 100 dishes and all the tableware was made of jade, gold or silver.

In 1898, the Empress Dowager brutally suppressed the 100-Day Reform, a reform movement launched by well-known scholars that won the
support of Emperor Guangxu. She declared that she "would rather lose the
country than carry out the reform." After the failure of the Reform Movement, Emperor Guangxu was put under house arrest. The Empress Dowager died in the Forbidden City at the age of 73. She ruled China for 48
years from 1861 to 1908. Before she died she put Emperor Puyi, another
3-year-old child, on the throne.

The 1911 Revolution led by Dr Sun Yat-sen overthrew the Qing Dynasty
that lasted for 267 years.

Gate of Heavenly Purity 乾清门

This is the gateway leading to the inner court. It was erected in 1429 and
rebuilt in 1655. The Qing emperors sometimes gave audience to government officials here.

On the east were study rooms for the emperor's children. On the west
were offices for guards and eunuchs. In front of the Palace of Heavenly
Purity, there are two small miniature temples, one standing on each side
of the courtyard, and is surmounted by a sort of gilded tabernacle. The
one on the east was called Jiangshan Pavilion representing territorial integrity. The one on the west in Sheji, the God of Land and Grain, a symbol of bumper harvest.

Palace of Heavenly Purity 乾清宫

222

The emperors lived in this palace in the Ming and early Qing dynasties.
After the reign of Emperor Yongzheng, the building was used as an audience chamber for receiving envoys from vassal states, who presented their
tributes to the emperor.

Foreign ambassadors were also received here. The big mirrors and red
candles are all part of the original furniture. The mirror was for vanity purpose and warding off evil spirits. On the west was the emperor's cloak
room. It was also used for holding mourning service before the remains of
his deceased predecessor. The wedding ceremony of the last Emperor Puyi
was held here in 1922.

Far back on the wall you see a plaque bearing an inscription, reading
"Be open and aboveboard," written by the first emperor of the Qing Dynasty. When the peasant insurgents broke into Beijing towards the end of

the Ming Dynasty, the last Ming Emperor Chongzhen fled from here to the Coal Hill Park where he hanged himself.

It was here in 1542 that one of Emperor Jiajing's concubines led a contingent of more than a dozen palace women in an attempt to strangle the emperor in his sleep. Unfortunately, the knot in the noose they brought slipped. For their pains, the gang was executed in public by having their throats cut and the flesh of their limbs sliced off. Following this incident, the emperor spent 20 years cultivating his mind in solitude in a palace in what is now Zhongnanhai (Central South Sea), only returning to the Palace of Heavenly Purity for one day before his death. Emperor Wanli of the Ming Dynasty passed away in the small room on the west side of the Palace, and his son Emperor Taichang only remained on the throne for a month before he died in the palace after taking a double dose of a mysterious medicine.

The plaque inscribed by the first Qing Emperor Shunzi, hangs over the throne in the palace and reads, "Be open and aboveboard." It enumerates with modesty the qualities an ideal Son of Heaven should possess. Beginning in the Qianlong reign, for reasons of security the name of the successor to the throne was not announced publicly, as it had been previously, but was written instead on two pieces of paper, one kept on the emperor's person throughout his reign, and the other placed in a small strongbox that was stored behind this plaque. The box was opened only when the emperor passed away.

Hall of Union and Peace 交泰殿

In this building the Qing emperors conferred honorable titles on their empresses. The empresses also held their birthday celebrations here. Since Emperor Qianlong's reign, 25 jade seals representing imperial authority have been kept in this room. Twenty-five was regarded as a heavenly number.

On the east is a water clock made in 1745. Water clocks had been used for quite a long time before the mechanical clock was introduced into China. The method of keeping time by the method of dripping water was invented by the Chinese people more than 2, 500 years ago. The time piece consists of five bronze vessels. Each vessel has a small hole at the bottom. When the uppermost vessel is filled with water, water begins to drip evenly through the holes. There is a figurine in the lowest container. The calibrated scale in his hands floats with the rising water, and time is indicated on the markings.

To the west is a chiming clock made in 1789 by the Works of Department of the Board of Imperial Household.

The plaque carries two Chinese characters *Wu Wei*. *Wu Wei* is Taoist philosophy, meaning to adapt oneself to the change of nature. Taoist philosophy stressed the oneness and continuity of the material and spiritual worlds. To Taoists, humanity stands midway between heaven and earth. The feudal ruler used this idea to discourage people from taking action.

Palace of Earthly Tranquillity 坤宁宫

The empresses lived here in the Ming Dynasty. The table and the big vats were used for sacrifices to the God of the Kitchen. The room on the eastern side was the wedding chamber. It is entirely painted in red and decorated with "double happiness." The bride and the bridegroom stayed here for two nights and then resided in their living quarters.

A total of 5. 5 million taels* of silver were spent on the wedding of Emperor Guangxu. Puyi, the last Qing Emperor, also got married here.

Double Ninth Festival 重阳节

China's Double Ninth Festival (the 9th day of the 9th lunar month) is also the day when the Chinese people either ascend a height to enjoy a distant view or go to a garden to admire the beauty of chrysanthemum.

The 9th lunar month is also called Chrysanthemum Month. A legend associated with the festival recounts that about 2, 000 years ago there was a scholar named Huan Jing whose teacher was "half celestial." One day, his teacher told him that a misfortune would befall his family on the 9th day of the 9th lunar month and advised his family to ascend a hill and drink chrysanthemum wine. He did what his teacher told him, and escaped the misfortune. However, all his dogs, goats and chickens died since they didn't leave the courtyard. Ever since the Sui Dynasty (581-618), the Chinese people have celebrated the Double Ninth Festival every year. To mark the occasion, poets throughout the ages have written countless verses to praise the proud chrysanthemum.

Clock & Watch Exhibition Hall 钟表馆

Tourists to Beijing from at home and abroad will enjoy a visit to the Palace Museum known as the Forbidden City in the past to see how the royal families and other aristocrats of the Ming and Qing dynasties lived. Of the many rooms and halls, the Clock and Watch Exhibition Hall is one of the most popular.

---

*1 tael is equevilent to 1. 33 ounces of standard silver or 31. 25 grams.

The hall is located in the east of the inner palace outside Jingyunmen (the Gate of Flourishing Fortune). This exhibition hall covers an area of 1, 700 square metres. Inside the hall are 185 rare timepieces selected from the imperial collection of Chinese and foreign clocks and watches.

The first thing visitors see when entering the hall are two timepieces—a bronze water clock and a chime clock. The water clock, the biggest timepiece in China, is made up of four bronze pots arranged vertically. The first three pots have small holes in the bottom. The water in the upper one drops into the second and then to the third and finally to the bottom, in which there is a small float which marks the time. The whole clock is almost 6 metres high. It carries an inscription by the Qing Emperor Jiaqing about its manufacture in 1799.

The chime clock was made in about 1797 by the court clockmakers. It is 5. 85 metres high and stands on a 2. 6-metre square base. The clock strikes hours and quarters and runs for 72 hours after it is wound.

All the other timepieces have been chosen for their superb artistry or unique design. The Chinese-made exhibits include a clock shaped like a seven-tiered pagoda. Each tier slides open while it strikes hours and plays music. There is also a clock shaped like a Chinese gate tower and a table clock with a fairy child, which appears to mark hours. Each of these clocks is based on a Chinese fairy tale.

A video display in the centre of the exhibition hall shows a clock made in the 18th century in Guangzhou. When it is wound, a unicorn with a clock face on its back begins to shake its head and switch its tail. An umbrella and flowers made of precious stones over the clock face revolve and change color. The glass pillars around the clock resemble fountains while they turn. In the middle is a box with three monkeys in it. The two small monkeys kneel in a line, each holding a peach. When the curtain on the box rises, a white monkey comes out with a peach in his hands, kneels down and kowtows. Then he holds the peach up and it opens. After the peach closes, the monkey goes back inside. Music, which sounds like flowing water, comes from a square box at the bottom. This clock is called "White Monkey Offers Birthday Peach." Traditionally, peaches are a symbol of longevity.

More practical clocks can also be seen, such as a clock set into a hat rack, one which is part of a dressing table and a clock with a mirror.

The 51 Chinese clocks on display were all made between the mid-18th century and the early 19th century. At that time, there were famous clockworks in Suzhou and Guangzhou and another group of clockmakers in the imperial court to make special pieces for the royal family and other aristocrats.

Chinese clocks and watches are well-known for their durability and accuracy. A clock made 200 years ago still keeps the right time. A clock made in Guangzhou in the 18th century is astonishingly well manufactured. It shows the positions of all the stars, the tilt of the Earth's axis, the four seasons, and even the first and the 15th day of the lunar month.

Also on exhibition are 83 British clocks and watches made in the 18th century. Some of these have mechanized people, animals or birds who move their limbs, bob up and down or play music. The most attractive is a gold plated bronze clock with a man writing at a desk—a gift given on the emperor's birthday. On top are two people with sticks in their hands. When the clock is wound, they part a streamer to reveal four Chinese characters, *wan shou wu jiang* (wish you a long life). In the centre is the clock face, and atop this stands a person whose head moves to strike hours or to sound music at 3, 6, 9 and 12 o'clock. Under the clock face is a man sitting behind a desk who, when the clock is wound, writes eight Chinese characters *ba fang xiang hui, jiu tu lai wang* (people come from various places to pay their respects to the emperor). All the figures are moved by groups of gear wheels driven by the clockwork spring.

Clocks made in France in the 19th century are also on display. They are distinguished from other European clocks in shape and in drive power. There are clocks shaped like a locomotive, a motor boat, a vase, a screen and a pavilion; clocks equipped with a thermometer, a barometer, a music box, and a compass; and clocks driven by the pressure of a steel ball or by a pendant, instead of a clockwork spring. In one clock the mechanism rolls slowly down an incline at an angle of 10 degrees, while the face remains vertical. The incline is 55 centimetres long and it takes 24 hours for the clock to complete its journey.

Also on display are 18 pocket watches made of silver or gold used by emperors and their empresses. The exhibits are all opulent, unusual, and popular; the exhibition hall receives 3 million visitors a year.

If you go to see the Hall of Ancient Clocks (which has an authentic Chinese water clock!) you will have to buy a pair of "Cultural Relics Protection Shoes," (CRaPS, which are looking florescent orange slippery things that you put on over your shoes. The CRaPS go for a 2 yuan per pair (US$ 0. 25).

Nine-Dragon Screen 九龙壁

"There is a dragon in the ancient East. The dragon's name is China"

The legendary dragon is the symbol of China. It is said that it could dive deep into the sea and fly high to the sky, marshalling clouds to form rain. Never has anyone seen with his own eyes what this creature looks like, but its image has been described and passed on from generation to generation.

This Nine-Dragon Screen was erected in 1773, six metres high and 31 metres long. The dragons romping in the sea are different in colour and posture. A peculiar interest is that a piece of the third dragon from the left is made of wood. The story goes like this: when the Nine-Dragon Screen was completed, a piece of glazed tile fell and was broken. The following day, the ministers in charge were to come for inspection. That was the deadline. It was impossible to make another piece to match it. The craftsmen couldn't do anything about it but asked carpenters to make a wooden one to replace it. During the inspection nothing was found wrong on the screen. That is why this piece of the Nine-Dragon Screen is made of wood. There are four nine-dragon screens in China. The other three: one in Beihai Park, one in Nanning, Guangxi Zhuang Autonomous Region and the other in Datong, Shanxi Province. Nine was regarded as the symbol of supremacy. The Nine-Dragon Screen was used as a decoration and was supposed to ward off evil spirits.

Hall of Imperial Zenith 皇极殿

The whole group of buildings here was built for Qing Emperor Qianlong to relax after abdication. When Emperor Qianlong was 85 years old, his physical condition prevented him from doing the job any longer. One of his sons was over sixty and would soon miss the chance to be emperor. So he decided to let his son try. The old emperor abdicated in 1796 and four years later he died. This hall was left empty almost for a century. After Empress Dowager Cixi came to power, performances by folk opera troupes were given here. Now the building is turned into an exhibition hall. Qing Emperor Qianlong's abdication in 1796 (because he considered it unfilial to occupy the throne longer than his illustrious grandfather—Qing Emperor Kangxi) marked the end of the great days of the Qing Dynasty.

Treasure Halls 珍宝馆

Before seeing the artifacts in the treasure halls you may enjoy the two pinus bungeanes (white bark pines) in the courtyard. They lose their barks all the year round but not their leaves. There are three treasure rooms, one behind the other.

The Third Room 第三展室

These are milk containers. The Manchu drank a lot of milk. These hanging screens are made of gold and precious stones.

227

Others are dinner sets made of gold, silver, jade and crystal. In this showcase are a pair of mythical animals (called *lu* used as incense burners and a pair of column-shaped incense burners. They are made of gold. It is said that the mythical animal could travel 9, 000 kilometres a day and know everything in the world. Usually this kind of incense burner was placed by the side of the throne, and was supposed to be a symbol of the emperor's intelligence.

Here are 16 gold chimes, weighing totally more than 400 kilos. Each weighs differently, so it sends out different tone when struck. In 1924 these chimes were taken to Tianjin. After 1949 they were sent back to Beijing and put on display.

This is a 6. 8-kilogram gold seal conferred by Emperor Guangxu to his favourite concubine Zhenfei. She was also known as the Pearl Consort. The knob of the seal is shaped like the body of a tortoise and the head and tail of a dragon. This kind of tortoise shaped knob was a standard for imperial concubines.

In ancient China, the tortoise was considered an auspicious animal. The dragon was the symbol of imperial power.

Ruyi 如意, a good luck **sceptre***, was developed from a back scratcher, originated from the Eastern Jin Dynasty (AD 317-AD 420). The sceptre is about half a metre long and made of metal, stone, bone, jade, coral or lacquer, etc. It was given as a gift and served as a symbol of good wishes for the prosperity and longevity of the recipient. Ruyi means literally "as you wish." A *ruyi* is a sceptre designed in the shape of a medicinal fungus.

The portable incense burners. When the emperor went out, they were carried by four eunuchs walking ahead and another four behind, keeping the air always pleasant to him. These are sacrificial wine vessels and gold bowls.

Here is a gold tower weighing more than 100 kilos. It was used only to keep the fallen hair of Emperor Qianlong's mother.

This hanging screen is made of gold, showing a cassia tree. The new born prince had his first bath in this gold basin three days after birth. The

---

*Sceptre   The gold and jeweled wand carried by a sovereign as an emblem of royalty; hence, royal authority and dignity. The sceptre of the kings and emperors of Rome was of ivory, bound with gold and surmounted by a golden eagle; the British sceptre is of richly jewelled gold, and bears immediately beneath the cross and ball the great cullinan diamond. Homer says that agamemnon's sceptre was made by vulcan, who gave it to the son of Saturn. It passed successively to Jupiter, Mercury, Pelops, Atreus and Thyestes till it came to Agamemnon. It was looked on with great reverence, and several miracles were attributed to it.

basin has a phoenix design in the middle. This room was formerly the emperor's residence.

The Second Room 第二展室

The jade jar means that the emperor's happiness was as endless as water in the Eastern Sea. The jade mountain means that the emperor's life was as long as the old pine in the Southern Mountain. In the eastern room you will find pavilions, towers and pagodas made of gold, inlaid with precious stones. They were gifts for the concubines. The emperor had many wives, so after he died many of the young women became widows. With nothing to do, they prayed for long life. They were all very particular about the decorations of their own altars.

Here you can see the seven treasures: namely, gold, silver, jade, pearl, seashell, diamond, jadeite: and the eight magic weapons of wheel, spiral shell, umbrella, lid, lotus flower, jar, fish and intestine. They were Buddhist emblems usually found in the lama temples.

Emperor Qianlong wore the dragon robe when he gave an audience. It was woven with peacock feathers adorned with pearls and coral beads.

This is an armor worn by the emperor when he reviewed the military parade. It weighs more than 15 kilograms. The hair pins were for the empresses and concubines. There are the imperial beads and pearls worn by the emperor on big occasions. They originated from the Songhua River in Heilongjiang Province.

Here is a woven ivory mat. The tusk was peeled into thin strips, and it is then softened in some kind of chemical agents before weaving. It is a pity that the method of making was lost! The tusks were gifts from Burma (present-day Myanmar). They are two metres long and weigh 50 kilos each. This is a huge piece of jade carving. It shows how Yu the Great of the Xia Dynasty led the people in their efforts to harness the Yellow River. It weighs more than seven tons and was mined in Xinjiang, Northwest China. The carving has a height of 224 centimetres and a width of 96 centimetres. It was shipped all the way to Beijing and Yangzhou for carving and then shipped back to Beijing again. Mining, transportation and carving took ten years altogether from 1778 to 1788. It is indeed the most significant masterpiece of the ancient Chinese jade art. During Emperor Qianlong's time 3,000 people were involved each year to mine 15,000 kilos of jade for the court.

The daggers in the showcase were used by the emperor for self defence. This room was the place where Emperor Qianlong composed poems and celebrated his birthdays.

229

The First Room 第一展室

Here you see a jade assemblage in the showcase. It was a birthday gift for Empress Dowager Cixi from her ministers. A mint of money was spent on her 60th birthday celebration when China was suffering from the tragic defeat in the Sino Japanese War.

Gold Celestial Globe 金天球仪

This is a gold celestial globe inlaid with pearls. It was manufactured by royal craftsmen during Qing Emperor Qianlong's time (1736-1795). The gold globe has a compass at the South Pole and a plate of the 12 two-hour periods at the North Pole.

On the surface are 3,240 pearls, each symbolizing a star. The base and the stand are both elaborately designed. The stand shows several entwined dragons, while the base has three feet shaped like monsters. It was a favorite possession of Emperor Qianlong, the fourth emperor of the Qing Dynasty.

Zhenfei and the Well of Zhenfei 珍妃和珍妃井

Zhenfei was the daughter of Tatala Zhangxu, an official of the Ministry of Rites in the Qing Dynasty. She was born in 1867, and was the favorite concubine of Qing Emperor Guangxu. In 1888, she was chosen to come to the palace together with her elder sister (later given the honourable title of Jingfei, meaning: the Brilliant Concubine). She was given the honourable title of Zhenfei (Pearl Concubine) in 1894. She was fond of painting and calligraphy and was ambidextrous, able to write with either hand. So she was deeply loved by Emperor Guangxu.

She supported the emperor's political views. Therefore Empress Dowager Cixi constantly persecuted her. Zhenfei was beaten and demoted in 1894, and was put under house arrest in the Forbidden City in 1898 after the Reform Movement was suppressed by the Empress Dowager.

It was at the height of the Boxer Rebellion, on the mid-afternoon of 15th of August 1900. All Peking was in alarm as the foreign armies approached to relieve the besieged legation quarter. In the Forbidden City, the Empress Dowager decided to flee. The murderous Old Buddha, according to legend, had ordered her chief eunuch, Li Lianying, to obtain disguises. She put on the clothes of a peasant, and changed her Manchu hairstyle to Chinese. Carriages waited to spirit them out the back gate, the Gate of Divine Pride, to safety at Xi'an in the west. Informed of her decision to take him along, the young Emperor Guangxu came to plead with her, accompanied by his favorite, the Pearl Concubine. This spirited wisp of a girl, elegantly dressed in layers of embroidered silks, was devoted to the twenty-nine-year-old emperor. But she had never toadied to gain the Old Buddha's favour. Now she prostrated herself and implored the empress dowager to let the emperor remain, to carry out negotiations with the foreign generals. The Pearl Concubine had been a thorn in the Empress Dowager's side, interfering with palace intrigues by giving independent advice to the emperor. It was time to dispose of her. The Empress Dowager bellowed orders. Two eunuchs seized the Pearl Concubine. In terror, the emperor went to his knees and begged for her life. But the eunuchs carried the struggling girl to the narrow well by Leshoutang (the Hall of Pleasure and Longevity) turned her upside down in her shimmering cocoon of silks, and flung her shrieking into its maw. Because the well was so narrow, the eunuchs jumped on her to force her down at the age of 24, hence the name of "Zhenfei Well. "

Gate of Divine Pride (Military Prowess) 神武门

This is the back gate of the Forbidden City. On its tower are bells and drums beaten in the morning and in the evening respectively to mark time. The gate was formerly called Xuanwumen (Universal Prowess) Gate and Emperor Kangxi's name happened to be "Xuanye." Under feudal etiquette, the mention of the emperor's name was a taboo. So it was renamed Shenwumen (Military Prowess) Gate when it was reconstructed in the 17th century.

In China, there are more than 10 million cultural relics in the 1, 331 museums, which are under the administration of the State Bureau of Cultural Relics. Currently, there are more than 2, 000 museums in China. Museums have played a significant role in protecting the country's cultural relics and giving citizens access to various scientific objects.

Foreign Presents on Show 外国礼品展览

More than 680 gifts presented to China by visiting foreign VIPs are put on show in Beijing. The exhibition was officially opened in September 1984 in the Palace Museum. The gifts, including gold and silverware, wood and ivory carvings, paintings, embroidery, lacquerware, glassware and porcelain, are from more than 120 countries.

Among the exhibits is a pair of porcelain swans, presented by former US President Nixon to the late Chairman Mao Zedong. Also on display are statues of Buddha from Southeast Asia, glass vases and plates from Europe, and wood-carvings from Africa.

The exhibition was sponsored by the International Friendship Museum, where more than 6, 000 gifts are kept.

Huabiao (Sculpted White Marble Columns) 华表

Tian'anmen (Gate of Heavenly Peace) is the main gate of the Forbidden City. Before and behind Tian'anmen are pairs of sculpted white marble columns called *huabiao*.

Why were these *huabiao* erected there? What did they signify? The answers go back to time of Shun, legendary monarch some 4,000 years ago.

At that time a *huabiao* was made of wood in the shape of a pillar with a crossbar at the top, and was called *feibangmu or bangmu*, meaning "the wood for commenting upon wrong doings." According to *Huainanzi*, a book compiled in the Western Han Dynasty (206 BC-AD 23), Shun set up *bangmu* at major crossroads so that people could write their criticisms on them. The monarch wanted to show his willingness to accept the views of common people.

Bangmu were also called *biaomu* (wooden sign), and were used as street signs. *Bangmu* were abolished in the Qin Dynasty (221 BC-207 BC) but reappeared in the early Han (206 BC-AD 220). They were then called *huanbiao* and later *huabiao*.

The new *huabiao* tended to be made of stone rather than wood. On top was a *chenglupan* (plate for collecting dew) on which squatted a stone mythological animal called *hou*; the body of the column was elegantly sculptured. *Huabiao* appeared in front of palaces, bridges, city walls, gardens and tombs, thus becoming architectural ornaments.

Splendid examples of their kind, the *huabiao* at Tian'anmen were erected at a time when Chengtianmen, meaning "Gate of Heavenly Succession" (presently Tian'anmen) was built during the reign of the third Ming Emperor (1403-1424). The *hou* (a mythological animal) on the *huabiao* in front of Tian'anmen, facing south, are called *wangjungui*, meaning "awaiting the emperor's return." It was supposed that their duty was to watch over the emperor's behavior when he went on an inspection tour. If he were gone for too long, the *wangjungui* would summon him back to attend to state affairs. The *hou* on the *huabiao* behind Tian'anmen, facing north towards the Forbidden City, are called *wangjunchu*, meaning "awaiting the emperor's emergence." They were to watch over the emperor's behaviour inside the palace. If the emperor spent too much time with his empress and concubines, the *wangjunchu* would call him back to court.

Like the early *bangmu*, the *huabiao* with their *hou* supposed to convince the common people that their emperor was on the job.

Mystery in History of Door Knobs 门钉之谜

Knob—the knobs on the doors in the Forbidden City represent a happy integration of engineering technology and the art of architecture. According to the engineering standards of the Ministry of Works of Qing Dynasty, there were three kinds of arrangements for the gilded ornamental knobs on each of the double doors of the Forbidden City, ranging from 81 (nine rows of nine knobs), 49 (seven rows of seven knobs) to 25 (five rows of five knobs).

These symbolized three ranks, of which nine was the highest. But each door of Donghuamen (East Flowery Gate of the Forbidden City) has 72 knobs (nine row of eight knobs), the only exception. What accounts for this? Explanations differ.

One explanation blames superstition. *Yin* and *yang* are two opposing principles in ancient Chinese philosophy. Ancient Chinese believed that odd numbers and the living belonged to *yang* while even numbers and the dead belonged to *yin*. The funeral processions of the Qing Emperors Shunzhi, Jiaqing and Daoguang went out of the palace through Donghuamen; therefore, the number of knobs there is even.

Another explanation is that Donghuamen originally had 81 knobs. After Li Zicheng, leader of the peasant uprising towards the end of the Ming Dynasty, led peasants to capture Beijing in 1644, the last Ming Emperor Chongzhen, escaped from the Forbidden City through Donghuamen and hanged himself at the Coal Hill (now Jingshan Park). when Donghuamen was restored in the early Qing Dynasty, the landlords, had a line of knobs removed to punish the gate for not blocking the Emperor's way.

Red Walls and Yellow Glazed-Tile Roof
红墙及黄色琉璃瓦屋顶

In China, the colour red has long meant solemnity, happiness, wealth and honor. The Upper Cave Man, a primitive human being who lived near Beijing 10 to 20 thousand years ago, used red colour to decorate their caves. Red painted palaces appeared more than 2, 000 years ago and continued down all the way to the Qing Dynasty. But what about Forbidden City buildings that do not have red walls and yellow glazed tile roofs?

Wenyuange (the Imperial Library) has black glazed tile roofs. This again goes back to the theory of Wuxing (the five elements), in which black represents water. The black roof was supposed to protect the building from fire. Nansansuo, the Qing princes' quarters, has green glazed-tiles on its roofs. According to the rules, green tiles were to be used on princes' residence. Where artisans and chefs worked and lived, the roofs were made of gray tile and the walls were greybrick.

Yellow has long been considered a pure colour in China. It represents the earth among the five elements—metal, wood, water, fire and earth—and indicates the centre and symbolizes dignity.

According to ancient records, the Tang (618-907) emperors adopted the practice of the previous dynasty, and wore yellow robes. Later, they forbade others to dress in yellow. After that, yellow became the symbolic colour of the imperial family.

Yellow glazed-tile roofs were used in the Imperial Palace in the Song Dynasty (960-1279). It was stipulated in the Ming and Qing dynasties that yellow glazed-tiles could be used on imperial palaces and tombs, or on temples built under the orders of the emperor. Those who used them in any other way could be sentenced to death.

Warm as Toast 自然取暖设施

All the important buildings in the Forbidden City face south with their solid back walls to the north. This gives them maximum sunshine and, together with the high enclosure walls, keeps cold northern wind from buffeting the rooms.

Secondly, beneath the floors of the halls were horizontal flues or conduits of heat from fires fed from two manholes under the verandahs. Nowadays, at many halls, such as the Palace of Earthly Tranquility (which was used by emperors Kangxi, Tongzhi, and Guangxu as their bridal chambers), tourists can still see the wooden covers of the manholes, two metres deep in the ground. During the night all the inhabitants of the palace, from the emperor, empresses and imperial concubines down to the maids and eunuchs, slept on kangs—hollow brick beds heated from below in structure very much like the cruder kangs used by the rural people in northern China.

A third source of heat came from braziers. Standing on three (sometimes four) legs, there were burners under perforated covers, elaborately made of gilded bronze or filigree cloisonne. They varied in size. The largest ones, like those still standing in the major halls, could be hundreds of kilograms in weight and more than a metre high. Smaller ones the size of melons were hand or foot warmers. These hand or foot warmers were exclusively used by the members of the imperial family. Fuel for the braziers was best quality charcoal made from hardgrained wood in rural counties around Beijing. In Beijing, the charcoal was delivered to a government organization called Hongluochang in the western part of the old town, where

234

it was cut into specified lengths and, before delivery to the palace, packed into small round wicker baskets painted red. Hence its name "hongluotan" (red-basket charcoal).

Charcoal of this grade was brilliantly black, burnt longer and gave strong fires with very little smoke or smell so that pollution of the ornate halls was cut to the minimum. Large quantities of charcoal were required for the Forbidden City at that time. Daily allotments were dealt out according to rank. For instance, during the reign of Qing Emperor Qianlong, 60 kilograms of charcoal were for the empress dowager, 55 for the empress, 45 for each first grade imperial concubine, 37. 5 for each second grade imperial concubine, 15 for a princess, 10 for a prince, and 5 for a grandson of the emperor.

Administering supplies of firewood and coal to the Forbidden City was a Fuel Department, whose chief during the Ming Dynasty had the privilege of making reports before the emperor in person. During the Qing Dynasty, in addition to serving eunuchs assigned to each hall or establishment, there were three organizations in the palace, each consisting of 25-50 eunuchs, that were charged respectively with the fixing and repairing of stoves and braziers, the storage and distribution of fuels, and the lighting and tending of fires under the floors or brick beds.

Charcoal fires, despite strict regulations for their control, posed a constant threat to the wooden buildings. One serious palace fire was caused by Hao Shitong in 1797, a eunuch in Palace of Heavenly Purity who threw the ashes from a brazier near the foot of a wooden partition. The cinders revived during the night, and set the partition on fire. The flames then spread and burnt down the palace, and three other important buildings in its vicinity. The poor eunuch was sentenced to death and 25 others who were implicated were severely punished.

Preserving the Forbidden City 保护故宫博物院

The Palace Museum, known as the Forbidden City in the Ming and Qing dynasties, is the largest and best preserved ancient structure of its kind in the world. With a total area of 720, 000 square metres, of which 150, 000 square metres are covered by ancient buildings housing one million priceless antiques. The Palace is of great value for scientific research and as well as for tourism.

In the Forbidden City, only part of the grand palace is open to the public. Thousands of unopened rooms are used for storage or remain empty. Of the one million antiques and cultural relics, only 700, 000 are on show, the rest are still to be sorted out. The Forbidden City has had so many visitors that its main paths have been worn three to ten centimetres thinner and some of the famous "golden bricks" in the halls have been worn down by two centimeters. Unfortunately, the technique of producing these "golden bricks" hasn't passed down and, according to experts, it is improbable that modern technology can manufacture exactly the same thing.

Since 1949, the Chinese Government has invested 70 million yuan in the palace, but this has only been enough to pay for part of the renovation work needed, and a large number of buildings and relics are still in a state of disrepair.

With the development of national economy and the policy of opening up to the outside world, the number of visitors has been rising by 10 percent each year during the last few years. In 2001, 16,000,000 people including foreign visitors toured the palace, far exceeding the five million limit considered safe by specialists. In off-season for tourism, the palace receives about 30,000 visitors a day. Effective measures will be worked out to preserve the Forbidden City in the near future.

The Modern Underground Exhibition Hall

A modern underground exhibition hall was built under the Shangsiyuan Courtyard, located in the southeast portion of the Forbidden City (Palace Museum) by the end of 2000. The courtyard covers an area of 10,900 square metres. The aim of building this exhibition hall was to solve several problems including those related to the protection of the existing museum's architecture and the modernization of the museum's exhibition facilities.

The underground exhibition hall is a two-storey structure. The second floor is devoted to the museum's permanent collection of fine art masterpieces collected through the ages. In the new hall, these masterpieces are grouped and displayed according to categories such as painting, calligraphy, bronze ware, pottery, porcelain and jadeware. The first floor exhibits rare and precious cultural relics from royal courts, including goldware, pearls, jadeite and gems.

The Forbidden City had about 1 million relics in its collection, of which only about 8,000 pieces could be displayed at any given time because of current shortage of space before this modern underground exhibition hall was constructed. The overwhelming majority of relics must be stored in warehouses. The situation has been improved after the exhibition hall was finished, allowing a display of 10,000 items.

The exhibition hall is designed and decorated with much respect for the architectural style of the Forbidden City. A combination of modernism and classicism of architecture has been taken into consideration

The new complex has projection rooms, restrooms, a bookstore and sou-venir store. Advanced safety and monitoring equipment and an automated security system is installed in the new structure. Before the exhibition hall was completed, exhibitions were mostly housed in the original palaces, such as the Hall of Paintings, the Hall of Treasures, and the Clock and Watch Exhibition Hall. Although air-conditioners and security sirens were installed in exhibition rooms, modern lighting and audio-video equipment can not be used for fear that a fire could ignite and destroy the wood struc-tures. As precious as they were, the exhibition halls with wooden struc-tures could not protect exhibit items from dust and theft. It was also diffi-cult to keep humidity and temperatures constantly controlled in the old wooden palaces, something crucial for the long-term preservation of histori-cal objects. And the 10 exhibition halls of the Forbidden City were scat-tered throughout the entire complex, which made it difficult to exhibit relics systematically. This was an inconvenience for visitors both from home and abroad. The layout of the modern underground exhibition hall helps solve these problems.

The Shangsiyuan Courtyard, under which the modern underground exhi-bition hall lies, was originally an office of the court, but was abandoned during the Qing Dynasty. Most of the Shangsiyuan Courtyard collapsed in the early 20th century, except for a glazed screen wall.

Geological prospecting and analyses have shown that construction under the courtyard has little effect on the nearby ancient architectural wonders, because soil layers and texture are unevenly distributed and compacted. It is the only open space in the Forbidden City that is suitable for under-ground project.

The Musee du Louvre of France, for example, has an underground exhi-bition hall designed by Ieoh Ming Pei, the master Chinese-American archi-tect.

Two underground cultural relics warehouses with 5,000 square metres and 16,000 square metres were constructed in 1985 and 1999 respectively.

Warehouse in the Forbidden City 紫禁城内仓库

In the Forbidden City, there are more than 930,000 antique treasures (of these antiques, only one-tenth are on display), which have been stored in the old wooden palace buildings for many years without any means of sci-entific protection. Before the warehouse was built, the storage space in the Palace was too overcrowded. The State Administration for the Protection of Cultural Relics allocated 16 million yuan (about US$3.4 million) in 1986 to improve the museum's storage facilities. To preserve the appearance of the Forbidden City, the Museum Administration decided to build an underground warehouse. It was completed in early April 1990.

Located in the southwestern part of the Forbidden City, the warehouse consists of one ground floor and three underground floors with 32 rooms totaling 3,000 square metres. Construction of the warehouse cost 130 million yuan (US$15.7 million).

Entering the warehouse, people have to go through a sterilization chamber first. The idea is to protect the fabrics, paintings, records and other perishable relics from destructive bacteria. The warehouse is equipped with advanced systems for controlling temperature, humidity and ventilation. It also has fire and burglar alarms. The whole structure has double walls filled with flood-proof material. If a sensor detects smoke, the fire extinguishers will emit a substance to douse the flames and the ventilators will automatically shut down to cut off the supply of oxygen. The video monitors along the corridors, the invisible alarms and the 15-centimetre thick iron doors make this warehouse a fortress.

It stores some porcelain ware, jade ware, paintings, woven articles, embroideries and precious classical books totaling over 50,000 volumes.

Sedan Chairs 花轿

The first sedan chair appeared some 3,000 years ago as a vehicle to help people traverse mountains. At first, there was only a single board — no chair — because the chair was not introduced to China until about 1,000 years ago. Sedan chairs became popular during the Tang Dynasty. But they were still of quite open construction. As a result, a Tang Dynasty emperor forbade court ladies from riding in them and exposing themselves to the public. At this time, common people and even merchants were also prohibited from riding in sedan chairs.

Although sedan chairs appeared long ago, imperial courts set strict rules for officials taking sedan chairs. During the early Tang Dynasty, prime ministers traveled on horseback. In 840, the Tang emperor issued an order stipulating that only the prime minister and a few senior men could travel by sedan chairs. Court officials travelling in the provinces who could not ride on horses because of illness, had to obtain court permission to take sedans. Even then, they had to pay the bearers out of their own pockets. In the following years, people added roofs and cloth screens to sedans, turning them into enclosed vehicles for travel. At first, women from rich families were permitted to travel in these sedans.

During the early Northern Song Dynasty (960-1127), some scholarly officials considered riding in a sedan chair immoral because human labour was employed in place of animals. Even with the Emperor's permission, some senior prime ministers refused to take sedans. It was not until the Southern Song Dynasty that emperors began to allow most officials to travel by sedan. At that time court officials usually rode in sedans made of bamboo, while imperial family members had rattan sedan chairs painted in silver and enclosed by felt screens. Rich families would employ two to three sedans. The bride would take a red one and the bridegroom a green one. Guards of honor carrying banners, umbrellas and fans would walk in front of the wedding procession with a team of musicians blowing trumpets and other wind instruments or playing percussion instruments.

Later, by the Southern Song Dynasty (1127-1279), sedan chairs were in popular use, mainly at weddings. Poor families usually hired a single red sedan for the bride.

In the Ming and Qing dynasties, the imperial courts from time to time restricted the use of sedans by officials. Once sedans were identified with the usage of officials, they became symbols of power.

In the Qing Dynasty, the imperial court even set regulations for the colour of the sedan's roof. Gold was for imperial concubines; silver for distant princes, imperial relatives and prime ministers; and tin for lower ranking officials. The number of labourers was also regulated. Ministers travelling inside the capital could use only two bearers, or four, when they left the city. The most grandiose sedan chairs, with a gold circular roof and a yellow silk screen embroidered with dragons, were reserved for the emperor. Often 16 bearers were employed to carry the emperor's sedan. Empress Dowager Cixi of the Qing Dynasty usually rode in a luxurious sedan carried by 24 bearers, all of whom were about the same age and height, and dressed in the same costume.

In feudal China, not even imperial family members dared to violate rules governing sedans. Once a Qing prince was travelling very quickly in a sedan when he saw his brother was in a sedan just in front of him. He immediately shouted at his men not to overtake his brother, but failed to stop them in time. When he returned to his residence, he and his men were beaten as punishment. The following day, the bearers were forced by the prince's brother to walk through the streets of Beijing carrying a sedan loaded with heavy silver ingots. Sedan chairs gradually fell out of use after the 1911 Revolution led by Dr Sun Yat-sen.

239

Jingyang Palace (Palace of the Southward View)景阳宫

At 10 pm on August 23, 1987, the Palace of the Southward was struck by lightning and caught fire. Part of the building collapsed. Renovation work started in early 1989 and was finished, including repainting in 1990. In the Forbidden City, 69 tall buildings have been installed with lightning conductors. The Jingyang Palace was not a tall building, which was why no lightning conductor was fixed to it. At present, some experts suggest that all the buildings in the Forbidden City, no matter how tall, should be installed with lightning conductors. Other specialists argue that if all the buildings are installed with lightning rods they will definitely form a strong magnetic field which may cause more lightning strikes.

Tuned Bells 编钟

Here you can see a set of sixteen bells housed in two large glass cabinets. Cast in gold, these rare treasures weigh 682. 36 kilograms. In 1790, in order to congratulate Qing Emperor Qianlong on his 80th birthday, the viceroys of the various provinces in China collected gold by unfair means in order to cast these 16 bells. This was done to show off the power and wealth of the flourishing age, at the time of his "Longevity Festival." This set of bells was usually placed in the Imperial Ancestral Temple and was taken out and played along with chiming jade, during special audiences, banquets and memorial ceremonies. They are elegant musical instruments and rarely seen in the world because they were cast from gold and can give different tone colors after being struck. The tuned bells were treasures of the imperial family of the Qing Dynasty. After the Revolution of 1911 overthrew the Qing Government, the Qing imperial family remained in the Forbidden City, with a large group of imperial kinsmen still living an isolated and extravagant life, spending an enormous amount of money every year. In 1924, Rong Yuan, the father-in-law of Emperor Pu Yi, the abdicated emperor and others consulted secretly. They decided to borrow 800, 000 yuan from the Salt Industry Bank of Beijing at one per cent month interest, and repayable within one year, by raising a mortgage on a collection of the cultural relics in the Forbidden City (the gold bells were mortgaged for 400, 000 yuan and others for the rest). The limit of one year was set because the Qing imperial family estimated that their restoration to the throne would take place within a year. Unexpectedly, in November of that year, the "National Army" led by Feng Yuxiang drove the imperial family out of the Forbidden City. Restoration became illusion and the borrowed money fell due. The imperial family was unable to redeem the pledge, the Salt Industry Bank having advanced the money foreclosed and thus became the owner of the treasures.

The inside stories of the Forbidden City were usually the gossip of newspapers in those years and this secret bargain was one of them. The bank decided to transfer the treasure to Tianjin for safekeeping in 1932. During the period from 1937 to 1949, the Japanese and Chiang Kai-shek tried in vain to get hold of them. Shortly after 1949, Hu Zhongwen, manager of the local branch of the Savings Association, wrote to the Military Control Commission in Tianjin to present to the nation on behalf of the Salt Industry Bank, the valuable gold bells which he had secretly hidden for nine years. Then they were sent back to Beijing and put on display.

Imperial Garden 御花园

The Imperial Garden was built in 1417 in the Ming Dynasty. It is rectangular in shape with 130 metres from east to west and more than 90 metres from north to south. Its total area covers over 7, 000 square metres, containing more than 20 different styles of architecture with profound palace atmosphere.

In the Imperial Garden, there are two groups of artificial rockeries. One occupies the southeastern part of the garden, stretching to the north and south. Viewed from above, tourists will find that some rocks put together look like many hills attached to each other. Others were arranged in a zigzag pile, appearing as a continuous mountain range. The range is neither very big nor very high, but it still gives visitors the feeling of being in a mountainous region. Climbing up the colourful pebble-paved meandering path leading to the summit, visitors can enjoy various scenes as the vision angles change: The Qin'an (the Imperial Peace) Hall lies among clumps of bamboo and flowers at the heart of the garden.

The Qianqiu, Yanhui pavilions and Yangxing Study are found in the west, north and southwest respectively. Leaning against the western wall and facing eastward, the Yangxing Study (Study of the Cultivation of Nature) is encircled by limestone. The rockeries were arranged to cover up large pieces of plain-looking wall at the lower part of the building. This also creates a tranquil atmosphere. Duixiu (Accumulated Refinement) Hill refers to another group of rockeries at the north gate. It is larger, and the designers piled up the rocks in a vertical manner to reflect the image of natural mountains. The hill was constructed in the shape of a square, to balance with a square pavilion at the other side of the gate. Two stairways spiral up from the south and east sides of the hill to the Yujing (Imperial Viewing) Pavilion on top. A cave was dug through the hill at its centre. In the Qing Dynasty, every emperor would climb up to the Imperial Viewing Pavilion on the Double Ninth Festival (the ninth day of the ninth lunar month) to enjoy the scenery with his consort and concubines. There, look-

241

ing through the Forbidden City, tourists can see the white dagoba on the Qionghua (Jade) Islet in Beihai Park and the Coal Hill in the distance.

At the foot of Duixiu Hill, stand two stone lions each carrying a dragon sprinkling water into the air from its mouth. The two streams of water then drip down along the cliff, join each other and run into a pool with white marble railings at the foot of the hill.

The garden designers believed that water gives "spirit" to the artificial hill. Chinese gardening puts much stress on the effects of water. There is a saying in China: "When water goes around a mountain, the mountain becomes alive."

At the time from two big brown pots in the middle of the hill, the high water pressure caused by the fall would force the water to spurt from dragon's mouths. Now, piped water supplies the fountains.

According to historical records, Duixiu Hill was built in 1538 in the Ming Dynasty on the foundation of the former Guanhua Hall. The rockeries were made in the shapes of 12 animals—depicting the 12 earthly branches, which symbolize the year in which a person is born. Many experts say that this use of animals was not original and was probably made in a later period. This garden was laid out on an invisible axis with the construction on both sides of the axis maintained in balance. The requirement for strict balance and the limited space for construction made it extremely difficult to construct a garden with both harmonious and natural form.

In the long period of Chinese history, gardens and rockeries have been an indispensable part of both private and imperial gardens. The idea of building a mountain with rock occurred at least 2,000 years ago in the Han Dynasty (206 BC-AD 220). After centuries of development, building rockeries in gardens was no longer a simple imitation of natural mountains as it had been in its early stages.

242

Instead, it has been developed into a highly artistic blending of nature and man-made scenery.

Big Stone Pedestal 大石雕像基座

Here you can see a big stone pedestal for a flagpole which stands in front of Qin'an (Imperial Peace) Hall. This pedestal stands on a square stone slab and is made up of two pieces of stone fastened together with a pair of iron hoops. It is 2.1 metres high and each of its four sides is 1.4 metres wide. The flagpole, that used to be on the pedestal, stood high above the Forbidden City and people looking out from the White Dagoba in Beihai Park could easily see the flagpole above the green trees and yellow-glazed tiles of the imperial palaces. It is the only thing that tells people where the imperial garden is located.

The carving on the four sides of the pedestal shows two dragons playing with a pearl. This is the most popular design in the traditional stone carving in China's imperial buildings. The pattern is repeated in the carvings in the stone balustrades around the "Hall of Imperial Peace." Above the dragons and between the two iron hoops, the four sides are carved with mountains and clouds. The two dragons dominate the picture. One of them is heading upwards and the other downwards. They form a circle around the pearl in the centre. In the background, behind the dragon, clouds roll above a turbulent sea.

The stone slab under the pedestal is 16 centimetres thick. The ocean waves carved on its surface appear tranquil. Amid the waves are rocks of various shapes and figures of the spirits and demons of sea animals, such as sea cows, sea horses, snails, walruses, green turtles and crabs. In each of the four corners of the stone slab is a carved whirlpool. A soft shelled turtle emerges from the southeast corner. A fish, a shrimp and a crab emerge from each of the other three corners. Therefore, the carvings of the whole pedestal and the slab under it, present a wonderful scene including the seabed with various demons of the sea, the big waves on the sea, the mountains, and rolling clouds with dancing dragons in them. All these form a fairly world. Legend has it that the dragon is the god of water. The dragons and sea spirits carved here, expressed the emperor's prayers that this god would protect his palaces from fire.

The dragons and the pearls are carved in relief, about 6 to 7 centimetres above the stone surface, while the rocks under the dragon are about 4 centimetres and the rolling clouds and waves are only some 2 centimetres above the surface. The fish, shrimp, turtle and crab in the four corners of the stone slab under the pedestal are also carved in great detail. The fish is arching its body to jump out of the whirlpool. Its scales are carved with an uneven spread according to the form of its body. The small legs and feelers of the shrimp and the fine hairs on the crab are all clearly carved. The turtle appears most interesting. With its neck outstretched, it seems to be struggling with all its might to get rid of the whirlpool. The two legs at its right side have emerged from the water and the foreleg on the other side is half out, while the rear one is still under the surface. The turtle looks as if it has used up all its strength.

The artist used different methods of carving for different objects. The mountains and rocks were carved with rough surfaces. The clouds, sea, dragons and other animals were carved with smooth surfaces which are polished to the touch. This made these figures appear more vivid and added

243

depth to the whole carving. The artistic design of the pedestal and the stone slab under it has been exquisitely expressed through the master's carving techniques. The combination of the artistic design and the wonderful techniques of stone working make the pedestal one of the masterpieces of stone carving left from the Ming Dynasty (1368-1644).

In the Forbidden City, there are 9,999.5 rooms. Why not a round 10,000 ?
在故宫为什么有 9,999.5 间房,而不是 10,000 间房?

Legend has it that the Palace of the Jade Emperor (the Supreme Deity of Taoism) consists of 10,000 rooms. But the emperor in the human world was the son of the emperor in heaven. He could not have the same treatment as the Jade Emperor. The so-called half-room was constructed on the ground floor of the Wenyuange Pavilion (Imperial Library). The small room, which accommodates only a staircase, was built solely for aesthetic layout. If you want to know whether it should be called a room or a half-room, decide for yourself if you have the chance to visit the Forbidden City. With so many rooms in the Forbidden City, if a person changed rooms each night from the day of his birth, he would be 27 years old before he had stayed in every one. To guard against assassins, no one knew in which room the emperor slept at night except his trusted eunuchs.

This is a pair of cypresses grafted together when they were very young. It is said that they planted more than 500 years ago in the Ming Dynasty. When visitors look up, they can distinguish the two different kinds of tree leaves. Towards the end of the Qing Dynasty the last Qing Emperor Puyi and his empress had as a photograph taken in front of the tree. Therefore, the tree is considered as a symbol of unswerving love. Nowadays, many visitors both domestic and foreign would like to take a picture in front of the special tree. Its leaves stay green year round.

What's in a Name? 为什么叫此名?

The full name of the Forbidden City in Chinese should be the Purple Forbidden City. The complex is divided into southern and northern parts. The 24 emperors of the Ming and Qing dynasties used the southern part for imperial affairs of state, while the northern part was reserved for the imperial residence halls. The entire compound is arranged along a central axis which is identifiable with the supposed centre line dividing the earth down the middle, and this line can be clearly seen from the air or from atop the hill in Coal Hill Park just opposite the Museum's back gates.

According to ancient Chinese astrology and some elements of Taoist cosmology and meditation metaphors, the compound's symmetrical arrangement mirrors the mythical "Heavenly Palace", or "Purple Forbidden Enclosure." Legend has it that the centre of the Heavenly Palace was the North Star still depicted above the human head in certain Taoist sacred representations, —the centre of heaven, mirrored again in the microcosm of the human form on earth. The palatial complex is considered to be the earthly incarnation of that celestial palace, the Forbidden City of earth, and hence its full name: Purple Forbidden City. Metaphorically, the palace is an incarnation of heaven just as the human figure is a microcosm of heaven, especially as it roams the rooms and corridors of the Purple City on earth. Purple, along with blue and red, (which together make purple), is also a colour of some significance in esoteric traditions of meditation is Taoist and Indian traditions.

The Imperial Number Nine? 皇家数字"九"

The number "9" received special emphasis in the Forbidden City's design. The houses in the Forbidden City number exactly 9,999.5; the nails on every door are arranged so that each line of nails, vertical to horizontal, contains nine. Why all the nines? Because ancients regarded nine as the largest numeral accessible to man, a number to which only emperors were entitled. The numeral ten (and its multiples) were reserved for true heaven. Also, since in Chinese nine has the same sound as "everlasting," it reflected the emperors' wish that their reign would last forever. The approach to ten indicated by 9 reinforces the image of imperial straining toward the perfection of heaven while maintaining a small margin of reverence for the Heavenly.

Nine, five, three are mystical numbers. Nine consists of a trinity of trinities. According to the Pythagorean man is a full chord, or eight notes, and deity comes next. Three, being the trinity, represents a perfect unity; twice is the perfect dual; and thrice three is the perfect plural. This explains why nine is a mystical number.

From ancient times the number nine has been held of particular significance. Deucalion's ark was tossed about for nine days when it stranded on the top of Mount Parnassus. There are nine Muses, nine Gallicenae, or virgin prientesses of the ancient Gallic Oracle; and lars Porsena swore by nine gods.

Why Yellow? 为什么是黄颜色

The predominant color of the Forbidden City is yellow. Nearly all the houses are roofed with yellow glazed tiles. For the ancient Chinese, the universe was made up of five elements: gold, wood, water, fire, earth, and earth was the most basic of them all. These elements were metaphors in the very ancient philosophies of *Yin Yang* and the Five Agencies and had deeper significance than these associations in nature seem at first to suggest. Yellow, the color of earth, was extensively used for emperors, since they were regarded as the world's supreme rulers and were to imitate and approach heaven as far as reverently possible. The only building in the Forbidden City with a roof of black tiles is Wen Yuan Ge, the royal library. This is because black represents water among the "five elements," and water can overcome fire. Obviously fire was a constant danger for the book collection housed under the library's roof, so the black tiles were a kind of "fire insurance."

Imperial Building Blocks 御砖

All the buildings in the Forbidden City are made of wood or brick, each weighing 24 kilograms. A more compact and higher quality brick of a light golden colour was used to pave the floors of all the halls. Each "golden brick" was made by special order in an imperial kiln no longer in existence. At the prices current during the Ming Dynasty, each brick is estimated to have cost as much as 50 kilograms of rice. This is to say, 600 million kilograms of rice were spent in building the encircling wall of the Forbidden City. A special glue used to hold the bricks and stone slabs in place was made from steamed glutinous rice and egg white. Tens of thousands of huge stone slabs were used to construct the imperial compound. The biggest stone slab, which lies behind the Hall of Preserving Harmony, weighs 250 tons. The slab is 16.57 metres long, 3.07 metres wide and 1.7 metres thick and was hauled some 75 kilometres from Fangshan District in the western suburb of Beijing. The task, which took 28 days, was accomplished by 20,000 labourers and cost 5,500 kilograms of silver. The hauling was done in winter, over an "ice road" specially prepared by the workers along which they ingeniously slid the huge and otherwise immovable slab into place.

For modern tourists, the charm of the Forbidden City lies not only in the massive grandeur of the royal style but also in the City's welter of small yet fascinating details. Take some time to familiarize yourself with the history of the Forbidden City, and your "audience with the Sons of Heaven" is bound to be a rewarding experience.

Semiconductor Lightning Eliminator 半导体避雷针

Two Chinese researchers have invented a semiconductor lightning eliminator (SLE), which is said to be a great leap forward from the lightning rod invented in 1752 by Benjamin Franklin (1706-1790) in America. The SLE device, which was invented by Professor Xie Guangyun and Professor Chen Cixuan from Wuhan University of Hydraulic and Electrical Engineering, is composed of a semiconductor set, grounding wire and grounding installment. Tests have shown that the protective area of SLE is 11 times larger than of the protective area of a common lightning rod. The common lightning rod is a metal strip connected to the earth at its lower end and its upper end to a sharp point attached to the tallest part of a building. The State Commission of Science and Technology and the Ministry of Public Security issued a document in 1992 urging the country to apply the newly invented device in tall buildings.

Many of the treasured buildings in China have been protected by lightning arresters and lightning rods.

Taihu Lake (or Lake Tai) Stones 太湖石

The use of Taihu Lake stones in gardens in China can be traced back to the Tang Dynasty. In the late Song Dynasty, Emperor Huizong, an outstanding painter, calligrapher and gardener, ordered a large imperial garden to be built named Gen Yue in his capital Bianliang (today's Kaifeng, Henan Province). He used a great deal of Taihu Lake stones in the garden and after that the stones became more popular in Chinese gardens and the first choice of Chinese gardeners, especially during the Ming and Qing dynasties. Taihu Lake stones are also popular in the imperial gardens in North China. The using of the stone has two main functions. The first is in construction. They are usually used to block soil and protect slopes. The stones used in these places do not have to be beautifully shaped and their size can also vary. But they should be placed and piled irregularly with twists and turns and rises and falls. The stones are also placed at the edges of flowerbeds, narrow paths with flowers on both sides and on lawns. The second function of the stone is to create scenes in gardens. That means the stone becomes the focus of such scenes. There are various ways of using the stones to create scenes, which are great treasures of China's classical garden art. A main feature in gardens made of Taihu Lake stones is rockery hills. Hills made of Taihu Lake stones are richer in shape than other kinds of stones. The salient feature of the Taihu Lake stones is wrinkles 皱, brightness 透, thinness 瘦 and leak 漏 and sometimes strangeness 怪.

The Five Famous Palaces in the World
世界五大著名宫殿

1. *The Forbidden City in Beijing, China* 中国北京故宫 *built from 1406 to 1420*
2. *Buckingham Palace in England* 英国白金汉宫 *constructed in 1703*
3. *Kremlin in Russia* 俄罗斯克里姆林宫 *erected in 1156*
4. *Chateau de Versailles in France* 法国凡尔赛宫 *completed in 1624*
5. *The White House in America* 美国白宫 *put up from 1792 to 1800*

Emperor Zhu Di (1360-1424) 朱棣皇帝

Zhu Di was born in 1360. He was the fourth son of Zhu Yuanzhang, founder of the Ming Dynasty. His mother used to be one of the ladies-in-waiting.

At his birth, the-lady-in-waiting was raised to Secondary Empress Weng. When Zhu Di reached the age of fifteen, a conspiracy was hatched between Empress Weng and several others of the Court to kill Yun Wen, Zhu Yuanzhang's grandson and the rightful heir to the throne, and attempt to elevate Zhu Di to that position. The conspiracy leaked out, and Zhu Di was arrested and imprisoned for about seven years. In 1390, Zhu Yuanzhang gave him joint command with Prince Kang of Jin to lead an expedition against the North. After the capture of Beijing in 1393, Zhu Yuanzhang appointed him prince of Yan (an old name of Beijing), with full control of the armies of North China. In 1396, the Emperor ordered him to proceed to the frontier and suppress a rising amongst the Mongols and in May of 1398 appointed him to the supreme command of all civil and military affairs of North China.

248

In June of the same year, the Emperor died and was succeeded by Yun Wen under the reign title Jian Wen. The latter's tutor, Fang Xiaoru (1357-1402) who was them a minister of State, persuaded the emperor to reduce his uncle's power. When this movement threatened the Prince of Yan in 1399, he flaunted the banner of protecting the emperor and fought to Nanjing. The second emperor of the Ming Dynasty died of fire in the palace. Others said that he disguised as a monk and escaped from the palace and roamed about. After seizing the throne from his nephew in 1402, Zhu Di became the third emperor of the Ming Dynasty. His reign title was Yongle. Having realized that the capital Nanjing was too far away from northern frontier of China, which was unfavourable for the unity of the country. He decided to change the name Beijing (Northern Peace) to Beijing (Northern Capital) and move the capital from Nanjing to Beijing.

When the reconstruction and modelling of the city, and the construction of the Forbidden City and the Temple of Heaven were completed, and the Grand Canal was dredged for shipping grain from the South to the North, a grand ceremony for moving the capital was held to offer sacrifice to God and Earth at the Temple of Heaven in February 1421. From then on the city of Beijing had become the political, military, economic and cultural centre of China.

Li Zicheng (1606-1645) 李自成

In the early decades of the seventeenth century, the Ming court slowly lost control of its rural bureaucracy and, as a result, of its tax structure. Pressed at the same time for more money to pay and supply the troops needed to counter the attacks of the Nüchen leader Nurhaci in Manchuria, the court both increased extra levies on those populated areas that it still controlled and laid-off-employees in the northwest, where the danger to the State seemed less pressing. One of those laid off in the economy move was a post station attendant from a rural family named Li Zicheng.

Li Zicheng worked previously in a wine shop and as an ironworker's apprentice. In 1630, Li Zicheng enrolled in a military unit in western Shaanxi, but once again the government let him down. Deprived of promised supplies, Li Zicheng and other soldiers mutinied, and over the next few years Li Zicheng slowly emerged as a natural leader among a group of uprooted men that numbered in the thousands, proving himself as intuitively skillful tactician. In 1634 Li Zicheng was captured near the southern Shanxi border by a capable Ming general, who bottled up the rebel forces in a mountain gorges. Li was released after promising that he would take his troops back into the barren northern part of the province, but the agreement fell apart after a local magistrate executed thirty six of the surrendered rebels. Li and his men retaliated by killing the local officials and taking once more to the hills. By 1635 he was stronger than ever, and was a leading representative at an extraordinary conclave of rebel leaders that took place at the town of Rongyang in central Henan Province, just south of the Yellow River.

Finally it was not the Manchus, but the rebel Li Zicheng who brought down the Ming Dynasty. In 1644 Li Zicheng mounted a huge attack on Beijing, moving across north China with hundreds of thousands of troops, sacking the towns that resisted him, and incorporating into his own army the forces of those that surrounded. He waged a skillful propaganda war, pointing to the excesses and cruelties of the Ming regime and promising a new era of peace and prosperity to the exhausted Chinese people. In April

1644 his armies entered Beijing without a fight, the city gates having been treacherously opened at his coming. It is recorded that Emperor Chongzhen, after hearing that the rebels had entered the city, rang a bell to summon his ministers in order to get their advice or assistance. When none of them appeared, the emperor walked to the imperial garden (Coal Hill Park) just outside the walls of the Forbidden City. In this garden was a hill, from the crest of which the emperor and his consorts had been out to look over the panorama of Beijing. This time the Emperor did not mount the hill, but attached a cord to a tree at its foot, and there hanged himself. The last ruler of the Ming Dynasty died. After the collapse of the Ming Dynasty, Li Zicheng called his new kingdom Dashun (the Region of Grand Obedience). At that time, Wu Sangui, one of the Ming generals, stationed at Shanhaiguan Pass. But Li Zicheng held Wu's father as hostage in Beijing. After Wu Sangui threw in his lot with the Manchus, fought off the army that Li Zicheng sent against him, and invited Dorgon, Hong Taiji's younger brother, as a regent to join him in recapturing Beijing. Li Zicheng retaliated by executing Wu Sangui's father and displaying the head on the walls of Beijing. But the morale of Li Zicheng's troops was fading fast, and not even his formal assumption of imperial rank on June 3, 1644, could shore him up. The next day he and his troops weighed down by booty, fled to the west. On the sixth of June, the Manchus and Wu Sangui entered the capital and the boy emperor was enthroned in the Forbidden City with the reign title of Shunzhi. They tried to hunt down and destroy the leading anti-Ming rebels. Li Zicheng was their first target as he fled southwest with his army to Xi'an, where his career as a military rebel had commenced some twenty years earlier. After consolidating their hold on Shanxi Province, the Qing forces, in the spring of 1645, closed in on Li Zicheng with a skillfully executed pincer movement. Forced out of Xi'an, Li fled with a dwindling number of followers southeast along the Han River to Wuchang, crossed the Yangzi, and was finally cornered by the pursuing Manchus in the mountains on the northern border of Jiangxi Province. One source said that he was killed by landlord armed forces at Tongshanjiugong Mountain, Hubei Province; the other source argued that he lived in seclusion at Shimen (Stone Gate), Hunan Province as a monk and died in 1675.

Eunuchs in Feudal China 中国封建王朝的宦官（太监）

Eunuchs were castrated male attendants whose official job was to supervise the management of day to day business in the palace. The practice of using eunuchs in Chinese courts had existed for more than two thousand years, but Ming rulers employed many more than their predecessors, and by the time of Wanli (1573-1620) there were over ten thousand in the capital. Since the emperor would not come out from the inner recesses of the Forbidden City—an area closed to all save the imperial family and their personal attendants—the eunuchs became crucial intermediaries between the outer bureaucratic world and the inner imperial one. Any senior official with business that demanded the emperor's attention had to persuade a eunuch to carry the message for him; the eunuchs, naturally enough, asked for fees in return for such service, and soon the more powerful ones were flattered and bribed by ambitious officials.

In the 1590s, the eunuchs, many of whom were identified with certain court factions, began to play a central role in the political life of the country. Their influence grew as Emperor Wanli assigned them to collect revenues in the provinces. In many cases they acted in a high-handed way, tyrannizing wealthy provincial families, and using an elite group of military guards to enforce their will and to imprison-even torture or kill. The political power of the eunuch was well illustrated in the career of Wei Zhongxian (1568-1627), who cleverly rose to power by obtaining a position as seller of firm of food to the concubine of Emperor Wanli's son, and later, in 1620s, dominated the court life of Wanli's grandson. At the peak of his influence, Wei Zhongxian was able to publish historical works belittling his bureaucratic enemies, and to order that temples in his honour be erected all across China possibly in recompense for the loss of a part of his masculinity.

Tang Tomb 唐墓

A tomb dating from the Tang Dynasty (618-907) has been unearthed in the Forbidden City, the imperial residence of the Ming and Qing dynasties. In 1996 the tomb was discovered during the construction of the world's largest underground storehouse for cultural relics in the Forbidden City. The brick tomb has a gate and a corridor leading to the burial room. A bronze mirror, pieces of gray pottery and part of a gravestone were the only burial objects found in the room, about 4 metres by 4.5 metres, which had been damaged when the Forbidden City was built from 1406 to 1420. Inscriptions on the gravestone show that the tomb was made in AD 799. According to Chinese tradition, burials are never inside the city, therefore, the tomb location indicates that the site of the Forbidden City was outside of the city at that time. Historical documents show that the site was not included in the city until the Yuan Dynasty.

251

Female Emperor Wu Zetain (624-705) 女皇帝武则天

Emperor Wu Zetian was born in 624 and dies in 705. She lived 82 years.

In the more than 2000 years of Chinese feudal history, she was the only female emperor, and in many ways extraordinary.

At the age of 14, she was selected as one of maids serving Taizong (626-649), the second emperor of the Tang Dynasty (618-907). After the emperor passed away, she became a nun for several years. When the third Emperor Gaozong(649-683) of the Tang Dynasty came to power, she was summoned into the court. She scrabbled to survive, to rise above the hundreds of women serving the emperor in his court. With her wisdom, she outwitted all others and became more powerful, and soon afterwards she was conferred empress. From then on she handled the day-to-day affairs of government for the emperor because the emperor was too weak and incompetent. After some time she took charge of state affairs. She became impatient and finally decided to take over. In 690 she proclaimed herself the emperor and established the Zhou Dynasty. She wielded power for another 15 years. She introduced the imperial examination to select personnel to govern the people and tried to entice intellectuals.

Although her obsession with power grew as she grew older, she also came to realize the risk, danger and trouble that came along with the power. She also learned that she, a woman, could not change the imperial patriarchal system, which had already existed for nearly 1,000 years. In her lifetime she exerted power for some 50 years altogether. When she was in power, she was backed by her faithful followers. She climbed to the throne up a ladder of corpses. She killed or persecuted, including two of her sons and a baby daughter. When her other daughter Princess Taiping expressed her desire to follow her mother on the throne, she was turned down. She said to her daughter: "If a man wants to be an emperor, he only has to have one man to work to the bone for him. But when a woman wants to be a ruler, she has to have several people standing behind her." Emperor Wu Zetian knew that Princess Taiping had not had her experience of fighting all the way from being a maid to assuming the throne and was not likely to have the ability to deal with the court conflicts. Under such circumstances, she had, but to handle the throne back to the Li family, the founder of the Tang Dynasty. She was xenophobic, willing to resort to murder to retain power. She became the dictator of a web spun by the wicked palace eunuchs and the huge government bureaucracy.

Even just before her death in 705, the 82-year-old lady tried something innovative. She said to her officials: "My tombstone shall not have an inscription on it. Neither you nor I have the right to comment on my life. Let people in the future do it." She always had her way, and the gravestone in Xi'an has remained blank to this day. Just as she expected, people of later times have never lost interest in commenting on her life.

Dragon 龙

The dragon is a familiar animal to the Chinese people, but nobody has ever seen a real one. At the mention of the word "dragon," the Chinese people definitely think of a gigantic best with the head of an ox, the horns of a deer, the eyes of a shrimp, the claws of a hawk, the body of a snake, the tail of a lion whose whole body is covered by fish scales. In Chinese tradition, 12 animals—rat, buffalo, tiger, rabbit, dragon, snake, horse, goat, monkey, chicken, dog, and pig—are used to represent a cycle of 12 years, in which a person is born. The dragon is the only animal, which is imaginary. However, it is full of power and grandeur. It flew in the clouds, curled up in the fields and dived into the water. In primitive society, it was a totem of many tribes. In the previous dynasties, it was always considered to be "supernatural." Emperors regarded themselves as an incarnation of the dragon. They put on "Dragon robes" and rested their "Dragon bodies" in "Dragon armchairs." In Chinese tradition, the phoenix is also a symbol for good luck. The dragon represents majestic beauty while the phoenix reflects graceful beauty. Therefore, the dragon and phoenix make a perfect match. For thousands of years, the dragon has been the mascot of China. The Chinese people regarded the dragon as a deity with absolute power. In history, emperors always regarded themselves as Zhen Long Tian Zi (sons of the dragon). China was regarded as the land of the dragon and the Chinese as the dragon's descendants.

Tradition has it that the dragon was a benevolent and generally auspicious creature, bringer of rain and emblem of the emperor. Some people say that the flaming ball stands for thunder and lightning, while others think it is surrounded by clouds.

The image of the dragon can be found in ancient buildings, sculptures, clothes, paintings, literature, and mythology. It also appeared on the first Chinese national flag, stamp, silver coin, and bank note.

In the imperial China, the feudal throne was symbolized as a dragon. Legend has it the dragon has nine sons, and each has a strong personality. The nine sons of the dragon are as follows:

1. **Qiuniu** 囚牛 loves music and his figure is a common decoration on the bridge of stringed musical instruments.
2. **Yazi** 睚眦, valiant and bellicose; his image can be found on sword or knife hilts.
3. **Chaofeng** 嘲风, a reckless and adventurous dragon whose image can be seen decorating the eaves of palaces.

4. **Pulao** 蒲牢 is fond of roaring and his figure is carved on bells.

5. **Suanni** 狻猊 is fond of being seated; his likeness can be seen on the lion of seated Buddha.

6. **Baxia** 霸下 is an excellent pack animal whose image decorates many steles.

7. **Bi'an** 狴犴 is good at bringing a case to court, and his image is carved on doors of prisons.

8. **Fuxi** 负屃 is good at literature whose image appeared on panniers of numerous steles.

9. **Chiwen** 螭吻 is a voracious animal whose image can be seen on the ridge of palace.

A song titled "*The Dragon's Descendants*" is as follows:

"*In the ancient East flies a dragon, whose name is China;*
In the ancient East live a host of people,
They are all descendants of the dragon,
Under the dragon's wings we are growing,
Growing as offsprings of the dragon,
With black eyes, black hair and yellow skin,
We remain the dragon's descendants forever…"

Gala Celebrations for New Millennium

Year 2000 happened to be the Year of the Dragon according to the Chinese lunar calendar. According to the calculation that the Year of the Dragon comes once every 300 years as the first year of a century and once every 3,000 years as that of a millennium. This is an auspicious coincidence for China and her people. The dragon is commonly seen as a symbol of Chinese culture. Where there live Chinese people, there spreads the legend of the dragon. And where there is Chinese influence, there exists the dragon culture.

China selected a park designed in the style of ancient Chinese architecture, 50 kilometres away from Beijing, as the site for the country's year 2000 gala activities. The park known as the "The First Town under Heaven," is located in Xianghe County, Hebei Province. The magnificent buildings there are replicas of typical architectural styles which reflect the achievements of Chinese civilization and culture.

Lion 狮子

The lion features predominantly in traditional Chinese sculpture. However, it is interesting to note that the lion lives in Africa and West Asia, but has never been native to China.

According to the "Historical Records, compiled by the famous Han Dy-

254

nasty historian Sima Qian (c. 145-c. 90 BC), the lion first came to China in 138 BC. Emperor Wudi (140 BC-87 BC) of the Han Dynasty sent envoy Zhang Qian to Central Asia to open relations with Central Asian nations and promote trade with them. As a result, the ancient Silk Road was opened, and envoys of Central Asian countries brought lions with them to present as tribute gifts to the Chinese emperor.

By the Eastern Han Dynasty (AD 25-AD 220), a number of lions had been brought to China but very few people in China had actually seen a real one. Therefore, the majority of the artists engaged in lion sculpture had to depend upon their imagination and written and oral descriptions of the lion. Judging from surviving Eastern Han examples, these lion sculptures were used to guard the tombs of emperors, princes and other members of the nobility. The stone lions guarding the Ancestral Shrine of the Wu Family in Jiaxiang County of Shandong Province and those in Lushan County of Sichuan Province are typical examples. Because they were used to exercise evil spirits and fend off disaster, these sculptures emphasized the lion's strength, ferocity and predatory nature. The source of physical features for these lion sculptures was the tiger, which was fairly common in China, so the Chinese lion is essentially a tiger dressed in lion's clothing, with features such as the lion's mane added and often exaggerated for the sake of effect. The result is that the Chinese lion presents an imposing rather than a realistic image. The majority of the sculptured lions are in standing poses and only a very few are in squatting postures.

The lion sculptures in the Southern Dynasties (420-589) were also used to guard the tombs. They generally stand 2 to 3 metres tall and 3 to 4 metres in length. They are sculpted from solid rock, each of them weighing about 15 tons. These lions seem to strut, their heads thrown back proudly. The smooth curves bring out a sense of movement. Linear carving and three-dimensional carving are combined in the process of sculpting these lions. Their bodies and general features are three-dimensional, but details such as the mane and facial features are brought out by delicate line in intaglio, adding a sense of ornateness to the sculpture as a whole.

The lion sculptures of the Northern Dynasties (386-581) are mostly found in Buddhist grottoes, a result of the influence of Buddhism. They are generally carved in relief. They are smaller in size than the lions of the Southern Dynasties and do not look as powerful and militant as the southern ones. Instead, they are like faithful Buddhists safeguarding the Buddhist principles and doctrines. Some lions seem even mild and meek.

The Tang Dynasty lions largely assumed the duty of guarding imperial mausoleums and are in squatting postures. Their pyramid-like bodies are muscular and powerful, exuding an air of gravity. They symbolized the prosperity and stability of the Tang Dynasty. This tallies with the aesthetic standards of that time, which emphasized plump and strong images of human figures and animals in painting. The only difference was that sculpture was capable of a more dramatic expression of power. The lion's mane by Tang Dynasty was covered with small spiral curls of hair, which eventually became one of the most important physical attributes of Chinese lion sculptures. In addition, stone lions during this period began to be sued to carry sculpted Buddhist sages. This tradition lasted until the Yuan Dynasty. Lion sculpture reached its zenith in the Tang Dynasty and many conventions established during that period were to influence lion sculpture in China over the following centuries.

In the Song Dynasty, changes took place in the shape of lion sculpture. The lions, in various postures, were lovely as well as dignified. Figures of frolicking lionesses with cubs began to appear, which symbolized happiness and good luck. At the same time, paired images of lions holding decorative balls and lionesses stroking their cubs began to appear, which was to become a standard image. In addition, lions adorned with necklaces with bells began to appear. This suggests that the sculptured lion was losing its ferocity. Some scholars suggest that such changes reflected political and military weakness and impotence.

The Yuan Dynasty witnessed that the stone lions were no longer used to guard tombs. But the lion as an architectural decorative piece was widely employed in palaces, mansions, residences and houses.

In the Ming Dynasty, lion sculptures were very common decorative pieces in front of the houses of ordinary people as well as before the mansions of officials and the nobility. Lion images began to be widely used to decorate roof ridges, bridge railings and archways as well. Many of the lions in this period are in upright postures. They support their bodies with their forelimbs, which are in turns supported by decorative objects such as balls or lion cubs. The Ming Dynasty lions, which are often in frolicking groups are more pet-like, in variety of gentle postures.

In the Qing Dynasty, lion sculptures were widely used to decorate tombs, palaces, gardens, official mansions, temples and residences of ordinary people. The lions took on more human emotions and feelings, with vivid postures, endearing manners. The dignified air that typified earlier lion sculptures is no. longer in existence. In addition, the pedestal on which the lion was perched became more and more elaborately ornate, with various kinds of meticulous patterns and decorative additions.

Early in the 20th century, many young Chinese artists went abroad to learn foreign arts. When they came back, they brought with them ideas and methods of Western art creation and education. A new style of lion sculpture combining traditional Chinese and contemporary Western styles began to emerge. A number of lion sculptures that retain Chinese characteristics and yet reflect a modern spirit have been created since New China was founded in 1949. They include the piece "Roar! The Lion" in front of the Anti-Japanese War Museum at Lugouqiao in Beijing and the piece of "Nine Lions" in Hefei, capital of Anhui Province.

Lion sculpture has a history of more than 2, 000 years in China. Over the centuries, the Chinese version of the lion image has become so deeply rooted in the minds of the Chinese people and artists that images of real lions have been quite unable to vanquish the traditional conceptual images. The Chinese lion has a life of its own, and has become an integral part of traditional Chinese culture and the Chinese spirit.

Ancient Chinese Treasure Cicadas 宝蝉

Ancient Chinese ate cicadas, wore jade cicadas as ornaments, and even had jade cicadas placed in their mouths when they died. The history of eating cicadas in China can be traced back to the Stone Age, and the habit continued into the Zhou Dynasty (1046 BC-256 BC). In the inscriptions on bones or tortoise shells of the Shang Dynasty (1600 BC-1046 BC), China's earliest characters, there was a special character meaning "roast cicada." Cicada was served as a delicacy at imperial banquets during the Zhou Dynasty. Chinese archaeologists have found seven jade cicadas at a site in Shijiahe, in Central China's Hubei Province. The objects, more than 4, 400 years old, are the earliest cicada ornaments even found in China. The jade cicadas, 2. 5 to 2. 7 centimetres long and 0. 95 to 1. 8 centimetres wide, have small holes in them so that they can be fastened to clothing. Cicada ornaments continued to be popular in the Shang and Zhou dynasties, when they were also used to decorate precious jade and bronze articles. Many cicada ornaments have been discovered in tombs of the Shang and Zhou dynasties. Jade cicadas have also been found in the mouths of the occupants of tombs from the Shang Dynasty to the Western Han Dynasty (206 BC-AD 23).

Jianfu Palace Garden 建福宫花园

Jianfu Palace Garden, also known as the West Garden built in 1740, the second largest garden in the Forbidden City, was just a heap of rubble by fire in 1923, will be restored with money pooled by individuals and international communities. The 4, 000-square-metre garden consists of nine groups of different types of buildings laid out on two north-south axes. Qing Emperor Qianlong liked to stroll in the garden and stayed in a nearby palace, because it was close to where his mother lived. Many of the treasures he collected were stored in a hall inside the garden. The entire garden was destroyed by a big fire in 1923, probably as a cover-up of theft. None of its structures except the plinths and some base stones for columns remain, but they provide a general idea of the garden's layout and dimensions of the buildings.

The project was sponsored by the China Heritage Fund, a non-profitable organization registered in Hong Kong and the United States of America. Working closely with the State Bureau of Cultural Relics and Museums, the foundation plans to donate up to US $4 million for the restoration of cultural relics within China. The restoration of Jianfu Palace Garden is expected to be the first of its projects.

Tumubao Incident & Yu Qian Safeguarded Beijing
土木堡事件和于谦保卫北京

Yu Qian was born in 1398 into a family from Qiantang (today's Hangzhou) in Zhejiang Province, and from his early youth was an avid student. The young Yu Qian greatly admired the conduct of the patriotic statesman Wen Tianxiang 文天祥 (1238-1282). After working his way up through the local and provincial imperial examinations, Yu Qian 于谦 (1398-1457) passed the national palace examination and was assigned to a succession of administrative posts in Shanxi, Jiangxi and other places. His outstanding achievements in office won him the deep affection of the people whom he governed. In the autumn of 1449, the Oyrats took advantage of the seizure of power by the eunuch Wang Zhen (?-1449) 王振 and the resulting political chaos and military corruption to mount a large-scale invasion. Urged on by Wang Zhen, Emperor Zhengtong (reigned 1436-1449 and resumed 1457-1464) gave orders to mount a defensive campaign despite a glaring lack of preparations, and naturally numerous battles were lost. After retreating to Tumubao, near Guanting Reseroir beyond Badaling Great Wall, the emperor was finally besieged by the Oyrats and taken prisoner by the enemy. The defeat at Tumubao threw the Ming Dynasty into unprecedented peril and set off a general panic at the capital. At this critical juncture, Yu Qian took upon himself the task of restoring peace and safety to China. He began by instigating a purge of the government and exposing how Wang Zhen had brought disaster to the country. Next, he took several steps to protect the capital, bringing together the military units from all over the country, recruiting a people's militia and arranging for the transport of grain to feed the army. Military material was repaired, new men were promoted to positions of leadership and defensive units were positioned in outlying regions. In addition, the common people were mobilized to resist the invaders.

On October 11, 1449, the Oyrats, holding Emperor Zhengtong as hostage, advanced on Beijing. Yu Qian engaged them in a fierce battle and after several days of fighting, repulsed the invading army and saved Beijing from falling into enemy's hand. After the victory, Yu Qian was given the honorary title of Shaobao and continued to supervise military affairs as Minister of the Army. He reorganized border defenses and eliminated the threat of enemy troops marauding the outlying areas. The Oyrats suffered heavy losses on several occasions and in 1450 were forced to return the emperor to the Ming court.

After the imprisoned emperor's release, along with Shi Heng, Xu Youzhen, Cao Jixiang and others, formed a conspiracy, and on the 17th day of the first lunar month in 1457 overthrew Emperor Jingtai (reigned 1450-1456) and regained the throne. In order to eliminate all opposition, when Emperor Zhengtong entered the hall to carry out the enthronement ceremonies, his supporters issued a memorial for Yu Qian's arrest. Claiming that Yu Qian had planned to enthrone the son of one of the emperors' brother, they accused him of being a traitor and sentenced him to death. When Yu Qian's property was confiscated it was discovered that his wealth consisted mainly of a large collection of books, as well as a number of gifts from Emperor Jingtai, which demonstrated his loyalty to the Ming court. Yu Qian died on February 16, 1457. It is said that when the news of his death became known, every single woman and child in the capital was moved to tears. In 1466, nine years after his death, Yu Qian was posthumously restored to his former posts by special imperial decree and the site of his old home renamed the Shrine to Loyalty and Integrity 忠节祠. In 1590, a statue of Yu Qian was placed inside the shrine, but this was destroyed along with the rest of the shrine in the early Qing Dynasty.

Museum is a mirror of history, an ocean of knowledge, a paradise of cultural relics and crystallization of wealth 博物馆是历史的镜子, 知识的海洋, 文物的天堂, 财富的结晶。

Functions of the Six Boards of the Ming and Qing Dynasties 明、清两朝六部的作用

(1) Board of Personnel 吏部 It was in charge of selection, examination, appointment and removal, promotion and demotion, transfer and offering merits to official posts. It was similar to the present-day functioning of the Organization Department.

259

(2) Board of Revenue 户部 It was in charge of the State's census register, farmland, currency, and all kinds of taxes and emolument of officials. It was similar to the present-day Ministry of Agriculture and the Ministry of Finance.

(3) Board of Rites 礼部 It was responsible for the court's important ceremonies (such as offering sacrifice to the God of heaven and the God of earth, and offering to the ancestors, etc), imperial examinations, and reception of foreign guests. The Board of Rites was similar to the Ministry of Education and Protocol Department of the Ministry of Foreign Affairs.

(4) Board of War 兵部 It was in charge of officers, military training, arms and weapons and posts (wherez formerly couriers changed horse or rested.) It was similar to the present-day Ministry of National Defence.

(5) Board of Punishment 刑部 It was in charge of the State's justice and administration. It was, by and large, similar to today's Ministry of Justice.

(6) Board of Works 工部 It was in charge of water conservancy projects and the key civil engineering constructions. It was similar to the modern Ministry of Water Conservancy and the Ministry of Building Engineering.

Zhoukoudian—Home of Peking Man, Beijing
周口店"北京猿人"遗址

The Site of Peking Man is located at Zhoukoudian Village, 48 kilometres southwest of Beijing. It is screened by mountains on the northwest with fertile land lying to its southeast. West of the Village stands the Dragon Bone Hill, noted for its large quantities of Chinese medicine dragon bone. Formed by limestone in the Ordovician period, the hill rises 70 metres above the river. It is there that the fossils of the Chinese apeman and their caves were found.

The Chinese apeman, also known as Peking Man, lived some 690,000 years ago, in mid-period of Pleistocene epoch. The first complete skull of Peking Man was discovered in December 1929 by Pei Wenzhong, a Chinese paleoanthropologist. Later, large-scale excavations were done on several occasions, amounting to 25,000 cubic metres of earthwork. Fossils of men and vertebrates were found. Of men fossils alone, a total of 152 pieces were uncovered of skulls, fragments of skulls, facial bones, lower jawbones and teeth belonging to over 40 individuals of different ages and sexes. The findings of 100, 000 pieces of stone implements, charred bones and ashes have proved that Peking Man knew how to use fire and was capable of making production tools. The Site of Peking Man provides not only a valuable scientific basis for the study of the origin and development of mankind but also an important base for research in the origin of human species.

In the cave above that of Peking Man were found fossils of the Upper Cave Man. They lived more than 10, 000 years ago.

The exhibition is established by the Institute of Vertebrate Paleontology and Paleoanthropology of the Chinese Academy of Sciences. On display are: Peking Man material and casts, reconstructed models of human fossils and the fossils of vertebrates discovered in various parts of China since 1949.

New discoveries since 1949 include five teeth, fragments of an upper arm bone and shinbone, a lower jaw bone and a skull cap. The shinbone is the first to have been discovered. Such an abundance of apeman fossils found at a single site is rare in the world.

The exhibition is divided into three sections. The exhibits in the first section show the animal world before man. It depicts the early stage of the earth's existence when there was no living matter and the long process of its emergence from inorganic matter, and the evolution of life from lower to higher stages. The pictures, fossils, casts and reconstructed models trace the history of the animal world with emphasis on the evolution of vertebrates.

In the second section, casts and models of Peking Man, his stone implements and ashes showing the use of fire by apeman explain the origin and development of mankind.

The third section shows the research results in vertebrate paleontology and paleoanthropology. The exhibits include casts of human fossils of the ape-man and later periods excavated in China after 1949. On display are fossils of apeman found at Yuanmou, Yunnan Province and at Lantian, Shaanxi Province; fossils of Mapa Man from Zhujiang County, Guangdong Province, of Changyang Man from Hubei Province; fossils of Ziyang Man from Sichuan Province and of Liujiang Man from Guangxi Zhuang Autonomous Region.

The site was listed by the United Nations' Educational, Scientific, and Cultural Organization (UNESCO) as one of the world's heritages in 1987.

Whereabouts of Peking Man Remains
北京猿人遗骸仍是个谜

Fossil remains of Peking Man and some other higher primates were unearthed from 1927 to 1937, but disappeared during the Anti-Japanese War while they were in the hands of Americans. Their whereabouts is still a mystery.

In 1941, the relationship between Japan and the US was deteriorating. Professor Franz Weidenreich, a well-known anthropologist, decided to continue his study of Peking Man at the New York Natural History Museum. He suggested that the fossils be transferred there for safekeeping. Weidenreich discussed the matter with Professor Pei, saying that the fossils would go to the United States rather than be taken over by the Japanese. Professor Pei suggested that it be made clear that the fossils should be returned to China after the war.

In early December, the Peking Man and Upper Cave Man fossils were placed in two big wooden boxes. The boxes were first moved into a safe room, then into the US Embassy, where they were supposed to be transferred to New York under the protection of the US marines.

After the Pearl Harbor Incident of December 8, 1941, the Peking Union Medical College was taken over by the Japanese troops. Two soldiers with rifles in their hands dashed to the office of Anatomy Section and kept watch over the safes in which the specimens had been kept. The Japanese drove away Weidenreich's typist, an Austrian woman, who had keys to the safes. But inside they found only replicas.

In August 1942, the Japanese newspapers in Beijing and in Japan reported that the Americans had stolen the fossils and taken them to the United States.

262

Two months later, the Japanese said that they had found the Peking Man specimens in Tianjin. Weidenreich's typist was sent to identify them. But when she got off the train in Tianjin, a Japanese stopped her and told her that there had been a mistake.

In November 1945, after the war, a Chinese newspaper reported the missing fossils had been found in Japan. But again they proved to be replicas only.

Professor Pei made further efforts to look for the fossils, but there was no result. The case remains a mystery.

A website on Beijing's Zhoukoudian, www. peking-man. org. cn, a world-known site about the ancient Peking Man, opened to the public on July 6, 1999, heralding the 70th anniversary of the excavation of the first

Peking Man skull. Developed by Netease, an internet service provider and the Beijing Cultural Development Corporation under the Committee of the Zhoukoudian Peking Man Conservation Site, the new website is intended to promote wider understanding of this palaeoanthropological heritage and solicit more support.

The Summer Palace
颐　和　园

The Summer Palace lies about 20 kilometres northwest of Beijing. It consists of Longevity Hill (59 metres high) and Kunming Lake with a total area of 290 hectares (716.6 acres). Longevity Hill is an extension of the Western Hills. Kunming Lake used to be fed by the springs from the Jade Spring Hill lying to its west. Now it has its source from Miyun Reservoir, 102 kilometres northeast of Beijing.

The Summer Palace has a history of over 800 years. In 1153, when the Jin Dynasty made Beijing (then called Yanjing) its capital, it built an imperial palace(the Golden Hill Palace) on the present site of the Summer Palace. In 1750, Emperor Qianlong spent 4.48 million taels of silver (140,000 kilos of silver) building the Garden of Clear Ripples in 15 years and changed the name of the hill to Longevity Hill to celebrate his mother's birthday. He also named the lake Kunming because he wanted to follow the example of Emperor Wudi (156 BC- 87 BC; reigned 140 BC-87 BC) of the Han Dynasty (206 BC-AD 220) who had trained his navy centuries before in Kunming Pool in Chang'an (somewhere near Xi'an today).

In 1860, the Anglo French allied forces invaded Beijing and burned down the palace. In 1888, Empress Dowager Cixi had it restored with the funds (30 million taels* of silver or 937,500 kilograms) intended for the development of the navy and renamed it the Summer Palace. In 1900, it was again plundered, this time by the invading troops of the Eight-Power Allied Forces (Britain, United States, Germany, France, tsarist Russia, Japan, Italy and Austria). The big temples and halls at the back of the Longevity Hill were destroyed. Only one temple remained, the Hall of Sea of Wisdom, a stone structure. In 1903 the Empress Dowager spent a fabulous sum of money to have the palace reconstructed a second time. The Summer Palace of today is more or less the same as the palace rebuilt in 1903. After the last Qing Emperor Puyi was thrown out of the Summer

---

*1 tael is equivalent to $1\frac{1}{3}$ ounces of standard silver or 31.25 grams.

Palace in 1924, this place was turned into a park. But the admission charge was very high, about the price of a bag of wheat flour, equivalent to 60 yuan now.

Since 1949 the Chinese Government has renovated the Summer Palace several times and numerous trees and flowers have been planted. This old imperial garden has taken on a completely new look and become one of the most popular parks in Beijing.

Today, every year the Summer Palace receives 6 to 7 million visitors both from home and abroad. Of whom 70 % are domestic visitors; 20% of them are Beijing residents; 10% are from overseas, and 90% of these overseas visitors are group tourists. In 1980s, the Summer Palace received more than 200, 000 visitors in a single day.

Each year, over 10 million yuan (US$1. 2 million) is spent on renovating the Summer Palace to retain its resplendency and magnificence. Few people know that the Summer Palace has one of the richest collections of cultural relics in China, probably in the world as well. There are nearly 40, 000 relics in collection, including many that are extremely rare. In both historical and artistic value, the collection is the Summer Palace matches the collections of the Forbidden City. The collection includes more than 20, 000 relics that are under special protection as national treasures. These are, in fact, world treasures. To name just two: a bronze tripod belonging to Prince Bai of the State of Gao from the Western Zhou Dynasty (1046 BC-771 BC), and a bronze wine vessel in the shape of three rhinos that dates back to the Shang Dynasty (1600 BC-1046 BC). These cannot be found anywhere else in the world. As part of the cultural treasures, the 400, 000 trees that also crystallize the essence of Chinese culture will be well looked after. Amongst the trees, 1, 600 are more than 200 years old. Every tree has a file and is kept in the garden's database for protection. However, due to a lack of programming, the tree species were not very well selected to plant in the garden in the 20th century. Realizing this, the palace authority plans to plant more pines and cypress trees. In order to restore the original construction, the government has started to move out residents that have occupied the park for many years.

In 1998, the Summer Palace was inscribed as a potent symbol of one of the major world civilizations in the World Heritage List of the United Nations' Educational, Scientific and Cultural Organization.

This is the front courtyard. The annex halls on both sides were used for officials on duty.

This is Taihu rock from Taihu Lake in Jiangsu Province. The rock was formerly located in Prince Morgan's Garden (now the site of Beijing University) and was moved here to provide grand view.

Behind the rock is a bronze *Xuanni*. In ancient Chinese mythology, *Xuanni* was one of the nine sons of the dragon. A point of peculiar interest is that it has the head of a dragon, the antlers of a deer, tail of a lion and hooves of an ox. It was put at the gate because the feudal rulers believed that it could detect any disloyal subject.

These are Tai Ping vats for storing water against fire in the old days. During the war, the Japanese aggressor troops attempted to take them to Japan after they invaded Beijing. After 1945, they were moved back from Tianjin.

The bronze dragons and phoenixes are incense burners. Sandalwood or Tibetan incense was burned when the feudal rulers gave an audience.

Summary Palace

North Palace Gate
Flat-Topped Pavilion
Suzhou Street
Long Bridge   Rear Part of the Lake   Far-Seeing House
West Palace Gate
Pine Grove   Porcelain Pagoda   Hall of Far Vistas
Longevity Hill   of Treasures   Spring-Heralding Hall
Arch Bridge   Stone Bridge   Hall of Buddhist Tenets   Longevity Hall ①
Lake-Boundary Bridge   Temple of   Pavilion of   Know-the-Fish-Bridge
④   Gathering Clouds   Great Happiness   ②
Heart-Purifying   Repository of   Chamber of   Purple Mist
Pavilion   Rambling-   ⑥Buddhist Sutras   Enjoying Prosperity   from the East
Waterside Hall   in-a-Picture   Peony   Beauty Retaining   House of Fragrant Herbs
Welcome-the-Ripple Pavilion   Tower of Terrace   Pavilion   Garden of Virtuous Harmony
Hall of Buddhist Tenets ⑩   Buddhist Incense   Natural Affinity between ⑪ ⑤Life-Prolonging Well
Marble Boat   ⑦   ⑨ ⑧   Water & Woods   Hall of Benevolence
Clear & ③ Limpid Waters   Spring-Heralding Pavilion   & Longevity
Inviting Pavilion   Pavilion   Yeluchucai
Memorial Temple
Pavilion of
Flourishing Culture
Kunming   Lake
⑬
⑭   South Lake Isle
⑮ Spacious⑫   Bronze Ox
(Broad View) Pavilion⑯

①Garden of Harmonious Interest ②Spring-Heralding Pavilion ③Pavilion of Fish & Water Plants
④Cloud-Entertaining Eaves ⑤East Palace Gate ⑥Bronze Pavilion ⑦Hall of Dispelling the Clouds
⑧Enjoy-the-Ripple Pavilion ⑨Long Corridor ⑩Pavilion for Listening to Orioles
⑪ Hall of Jade Ripples ⑫Seventeen-Arch Bridge ⑬Hall of Infinite Space
⑭Dragon King's Temple ⑮Hall of Far Vistas ⑯New Palace Gate

265

Hall of Benevolence and Longevity 仁寿殿

Empress Dowager Cixi and Emperor Guangxu took charge of state affairs and received officials and foreign envoys here. The building was first built in 1750. It was then called the Hall of Industrious Government. In 1860, it was burned down. The present building was rebuilt in 1890.

In the middle of the hall stands a throne carved with a nine dragon design. The nine dragons symbolized the supreme power of the emperor.

By the side of the throne are two big fans made of peacock feathers, put up for dignity purpose. In the Song Dynasty, two fans were held by eunuchs, while in the Qing Dynasty, they were put up by the side of the throne.

There are two column shaped incense burners, one on each side for burning incense on formal occasions.

This is an incense burner assuming the form of a mythological animal, which was supposed to have the power to prevent fire.

The inscription on the tablet says that he who shows benevolence in running the government can live a long life.

The flower basket is made of precious stones in various colors. The base is made of pear wood. On the small table there is a Shang Dynasty bronze mirror over 3,000 years old. On the wall is a scroll with big Chinese character meaning "Longevity." The one hundred bats in the background symbolize happiness and longevity. This big character was written by the Empress Dowager.

This is a lacquer screen inlaid with ivory and green jade, made in Emperor Qianlong's time.

The frame of the big mirror is made of mahogany. It took 3,600-man days or one person ten years to do the job.

A pair of wooden lions is shaped from the roots of birch tree.

The elephant is a symbol of universal peace.

The small chambers on either side were places where the emperor rested and received officials on formal occasions.

Garden of Virtuous Harmony 德和园

It consists of Daxilou (the Theatre Building) and Yiledian (Hall of Pleasure Smile). The theater building was constructed in 1892, at a cost of 1.6 million taels of silver (50,000 kilos of silver). It was the biggest stage in China at the time, with three tiers of tilted eaves. Performances could be staged simultaneously on three levels. (the lower stage was named longevity stage, the middle level was called emolument level, and the top level was a symbol of happiness. Each level has its entrance and exit.) There are trap doors in the ceiling for fairies to descend and on the floor for demons to surface from beneath. A well and five ponds were built under the stage for a good effect. During a performance, a grand water scene could be produced on the stage. Empress Dowager Cixi used to sit on a wooden bed by the window to watch the performances. Emperor Guangxu would sit at the left side of the window outside the door, while the former concubines used to sit at the right side of the window. The aisles of the stage were divided into 12 wings separated by wooden pillars. The east wings were prepared for princess, dukes and ministers. The west wings were for Li Lianying(?-1910), the most favourite superintendent eunuch and the court officials. In the hall there are four screens, representing the four seasons of the year. Peach blossom stands for spring, lotus flower for summer, chrysanthemum autumn and narcissus winter.

Visitors can also see wax models of the Empress Dowager, Emperor Guangxu, his consort, and the palace maids.

Garden of Harmonious Interest 谐趣园

The Garden of Harmonious Interest was originally built in 1751. It was first named Huishan Garden after the Jichang Garden (Garden for Ease of Mind) in Huishan of Wuxi, Jiangsu Province. Jichang Garden used to be the private garden of Qin Jin, minister of the Board of War, towards the end of the Qing Dynasty. Emperor Qianlong of the Qing Dynasty went to South China for inspections and resided there several times. He greatly admired the architectural art for the garden. Later on, he decided to build a similar garden in the Capital City. In 1881, after the Huishan Garden was renovated, Emperor Jiaqing, a son of Emperor Qianlong, renamed it the Garden of Harmonious Interest. In 1860, the garden was burnt down by Anglo French allied forces. It was reconstructed in 1892. When Empress Dowager Cixi lived in the Summer Palace during summer time, she often came to the garden to fish for pleasure. The Hanyuan (Far Vistas) Hall, the main building within the garden, used to be the place where the Empress Dowager relaxed.

In the middle of the garden there is a pond occupying half an acre of land. In the pond there are fish and lotuses. Fish and flowers in the pond, weeping willows along the banks, artificial rockeries by the side of the paths, green pines on the mounds and water pavilions form distinctively different paintings. They ingeniously make up the garden within the garden.

The Garden of Harmonious Interest has eight following "interests:"

1. Interest of the Four Different Seasons ("时"趣)

In spring, water in the pond is as smooth as a mirror with weeping willows wavering in the breeze. In summer, lotuses are in blossom with the flowers sending out a fragrant smell. In autumn, water pavilions and green weeping willows are reflected in the pond. In winter, when snow falls, all the buildings, corridors, water pavilions and weeping willows are heavily covered with snow.

267

2. Interest of Water ("水"趣)

Water for the pond comes from the Rear Lake of the Summer Palace through the bamboo groves. Here there is a "Jade Violin Gorge" which was a copy of the "Eight-Sound Brook" in Jichang Garden in Wuxi.

3. Interest of Bridge ("桥"趣)

In the garden, there are eight small bridges with different styles. The longest bridge is about 10 metres and the shortest being less than 2 metres. The most interesting of all is the bridge known as "Know the Fish Bridge." It is said that more than 2500 years ago during the Warring States Period, two philosophers named Zhuang Zi and Hui Zi had an interesting argument by the side of a pond.

Zhuang said: "Fish swim to and fro in the water. What happy fish!"

Hui asked: "You are not a fish, how do you know they are happy?"

Zhuang replied: "You are not me, how do you know I don't know?"

Hui sighed: "I am not you, therefore, I don't know you. You are not fish, you don't know that fish are happy."

Zhuang said: "You ask me how I know fish are happy. So long as you know that I understand fish are happy, why should you ask me time and again?"

4. Interest of "Calligraphy" ("书"趣)

In the garden there are lots of stone engravings, couplets and poems.

Some of them were written by Emperor Qianlong. People who show great interest in them come here to study the engravings.

5. Interest of Pavilion ("楼"趣)

At northwest corner of the garden, looking eastward from outside the garden, visitors can view a structure with a plaque hanging from it, reading Shu Xin Lou (Fresh View Tower). But the structure is merely an ordinary house with three room units. It is not a building. People would ask why an ordinary house like this was named Fresh View Tower. When visitors step into the garden, looking eastward while standing on the bank of the pond, Shu Xin Lou is not an ordinary house. It looks like a delicate and exquisite two storeyed building. This was created by gardening craftsmen employing topographical advantages and landforms.

6. Interest of Painting ("画"趣)

Within the garden there are hundreds of paintings on the buildings. Some of them are flowers and scenery. Others are paintings based on the figures and historical stories. Flanking the main gate of the garden there is scenery of Guilin in the south; in the north there are a giant panda and a baby panda.

7. Interest of Corridor ("廊"趣)

Around the pond there are structures such as Pavilion for Perceiving the Spring, House of Clear Sky, House of Clear Water and Cool Breeze which are connected by winding corridors. Visitors can enjoy Chinese ancient buildings with unique styles.

8. Interest of Imitation ("仿"趣)

Jichang Garden (Garden of Ease of Mind) used to be the famous private garden of South China, and the Garden of Harmonious Interest was the imperial garden in the ancient Capital City. New creation was made in imitation and new creation didn't betray the original designs. The Garden of Harmonious Interest originated from Jichang Garden in Wuxi, Jiangsu Province, but has exceeded it.

Hall of Happiness and Longevity 乐寿堂

This big rock in its strange shape was discovered in Fangshan Mountains near Beijing. A Ming official named Mi Wanzhong was fond of it and wanted to keep it in his garden inside the present Beijing University. Having spent all his money to ship it he finally gave it up half way and left it by the side of the road near Liangxiang, 30 kilometres southwest of Beijing. Qing Emperor Qianlong saw it on the way back from his tour south of the Yangtze River, and ordered that it be moved to Beijing.

These are bronze vases, vats, deer and storks, two of each kind, symbolizing universal peace. Magnolia, flowering crabapple and peony are grown in this compound. Archaeological finds reveal that 5,000 years ago ancient Chinese regarded spotted deer as the symbol of power, wealth and dignity.

On the left, the deer, especially the spotted variety, is an emblem of longevity, because it is said to be the only animal, which can find the *lingzhi* fungus of immortality.

The hall was Empress Dowager Cixi's residence. After it was rebuilt in 1889, she lived here from May to October every year during the rest of her lifetime.

In the east outer room, she used to have her breakfast and tea.

The east inner room was her dressing room.

The west inner room was her bedroom and in the west outer room she used to read and sign documents.

In the centre of the hall is a large table, at which she had her meals. For each meal, there was a choice of 128 courses and over 50 kinds of rice, bread, noodles and other food. Of porridge alone, there were 30 kinds. The money spent on a single meal would have been enough to feed 5,000 peasants for a day. It is said that there were more than 1,500 sets of gold, silver, jade and ivory tableware in the royal kitchen served only to Empress Dowager Cixi. These gold objects weighed in at 5, 816 taels and the silver at about 10, 590 taels. (a tael is a unit of weight, which is e-quivalent to 31. 25 grams in China)

The big porcelain bowls were used to hold fruit, which was not meant for eating but for smelling. More than one thousand people waited on her in the garden. In this hall alone 28 ladies in waiting and 20 eunuchs attended to her every wish.

The aquariums were used for keeping and showing fish and water plants.

On your right you can see a peacock displaying its full plumage; on your left a phoenix among one hundred birds. It is said that peacock is the most beautiful among all birds while phoenix is the queen of birds. The Empress Dowager compared herself to peacock and phoenix. These two pieces were made in Guangdong Province. There are four famous embroideries in China. The other three are made in Hunan, Suzhou and Sichuan. Guangdong embroidery is noted for mountain, water, flower and bird; Suzhou embroidery is famous for cat and gold fish; Sichuan embroidery is well-known for carp and panda; Hunan embroidery specializes in tiger and lion.

The chandeliers hanging from the ceiling were China's first electric lights installed in 1903. The palace had its own power station.

Yongshou Room (Longevity Room) 永寿斋

Yongshou Room or Longevity Room used to be the residence of court eunuch manager Li Lianying (?-1910) at the end of the Qing Dynasty. The residence has recovered its original decoration after renovation. The most eye-catching features are the chairs covered with yellow silk. It is said that Li dared not sit on the chairs on which Empress Dowager Cixi had sat and therefore he covered them all. A colourful group of sculptures, made up of about 300 clay figurines, shows the guards carrying flags and weapons when Empress Dowager Cixi and Emperor Guangxu went from the Forbidden City to the Summer Palace, vividly exposing the historical facts of how the imperial family put the eunuchs to work.

The exhibitions showing the lives of eunuchs in the Qing Dynasty, for example, generalize the birth, development and decline of the feudal eunuch system and expose its cruelty and savagery.

Li Lianying was born in Hebei Province. When he was young, he was a peddler. Later he was put into prison. After he was released, he changed job, and became a shoe repairer. When Emperor Xianfeng was in power (1851-1861), he castrated himself and worked in the Qing Court. Li Lianying made himself a pet of Empress Dowager Cixi because he was good at inventing distinctive hair styles for the empress. From a eunuch working in Combing Room, he was promoted to the superintendent of all eunuchs in the Forbidden City. In 1886, dispatched by Empress Dowager Cixi, he went to Tianjin together with a prince of the Qing Court to inspect the Navy. Working in the Court for more than 40 years from 1863 to 1910, he meddled in political affairs and accumulated a large sum of money. After Empress Dowager Cixi died 1908, Li Lianying left the Forbidden City and two years later he passed away in 1910 in his residence in Beijing.

Long Corridor 长廊

Along the shore is the famous Long Corridor, next to which is a sign boasts that the Long Corridor was listed in the Guinness Book of World Records as the "longest painted corridor in the world in 1990."

The Long Corridor is one of the most famous garden landscapes in China. It is 728 metres long with 273 sections. The beams of the corridor are painted with more than 8,000 paintings. Some of them are birds and flowers and landscapes of the West Lake in Hangzhou. Others are scenes from literary classics. The Long Corridor was restored in 1959 and retouched in 1979. The Long Corridor was completely renovated in 1999 with a total investment of one million yuan (US$120,000) to mark the 50th anniversary of the founding of the People's Republic of China.

The corridor between the Longevity Hill and Kunming Lake is always crowded and is hard to keep clean. The park management has made it a special sanitation district. Twenty sanitation workers are busy on this road all day long. There are 100 sanitation workers in the whole park.

Hall of Dispelling Clouds 排云殿

It was built in 1750 and rebuilt in 1890. The Empress Dowager used to celebrate her birthday here on the 15th day of the tenth lunar month each year. On that day all the important civil and military officials would stand outside the archway and kowtow to her from here. Most of the things on display were gifts from the ministers for her 70th birthday.

This oil painting was painted by Hobert Vos, a Dutch-American painter, in 1905.

Tower of Buddhist Incense 佛香阁

It is a 3-storey building, 41 metres high, built in 1750. The Empress Dowager Cixi used to worship Gods here on the 1st and 15th day of each lunar month. It was destroyed in 1860 by the Anglo-French Allied Forces and rebuilt in 1889. In 1900, when the eight imperialist powers invaded

Beijing, it was destroyed again and was reconstructed for the second time in 1903. The renovation started in 1987 and was finished in September 1989. The renovation amounted to US$70, 000. The Tower of Buddhist Incense was opened to the public in early October 1989.

According to the original plan for the Garden of Clear Ripple (former name of the Summer Palace), a tower of nine storeys was built on the site of the present building. The tower was designed after the famous Liuhe (Six Harmony) Tower in Hangzhou, Zhejiang Province. During the construction, Emperor Qianlong had inspected the construction site frequently, and wrote several poems extolling the beautiful landscapes and the rising tower. But when the eighth storey of the tower was finished, just before the completion of the whole tower, some of the designers argued over its design. They held that the original plan was effective only in the drawing. The nearby constructed tower did not suit the surrounding hills and lakes or its position on the top of the Longevity Hill. These designers suggested that the high and thin structure be demolished and replaced by a more imposing building. The Emperor accepted their suggestion and the Tower of Buddhist Incense was constructed instead. The results were generally acclaimed. The new building suits its setting far better than a tall, thin tower would have. And Longevity Hill appears much grander.

To the west is Baoyunge (Precious Cloud Pavilion), a pavilion made of bronze, 207 tons in weight. Inside is a bronze table weighing more than 2 tons. All its windows were stolen by the Allied Forces of the Eight Powers. The Japanese aggressors took the bronze table to Tianjin, trying to ship it to Japan. After the war, it was sent back to Beijing.

US Company Helps Return of Lost Relics
美国公司帮助归还丢失的文物

272

A ceremony was held on December 2, 1993 at the Summer Palace celebrating the return of 10 bronze windows that had been taken from the imperial garden nearly a century ago. The service marked the first time a foreign corporation had helped in the return of missing relics from China. In July 1993, the Star Foundation, named after the founder of the American International Assurance Co. Ltd of the United States, purchased the 10 windows from a French collector for US$515, 000. It immediately presented the windows to China, and they were installed in the fall of 1993 in their original locations. The windows had been taken nearly a century ago when Western forces invaded China and desecrated the Summer Palace, an imperial garden built during the 18th century. The windows were part of a famous pavilion called "Baoyunge," which originally had 20 bronze portals. The recovery of these missing relics has always been the cherished desire of generations of the Chinese people. Maurice R. Greenberg, Chairman of the American International Group Inc., said he was proud his corporation had become the first firm to donate missing Chinese relics to their country of origin. As the Chinese saying goes: gold is valuable whereas goodwill is invaluable. Greenberg also expressed hope that others will also return works of art that belong to China so the Chinese people and foreign visitors can enjoy seeing them.

Tingliguan (Pavilion for Listening to Orioles) Restaurant
听鹂馆

The Pavilion for Listening to Orioles Restaurant, the main structure on the western part of Longevity Hill in Beijing's Summer Palace used to be the site where Empress Dowager Cixi of the Qing Dynasty enjoyed opera and music. After the Big Theatre Building was completed, it was used as a residence for imperial concubines. Zhenfei, an imperial concubine and a strong supporter of the 1898 Reform, was put under house arrest here after the failure of the Reform Movement. Opened to the public as a restaurant in 1949, it has become famous for offering dishes in an imperial kitchen style. Encompassing 5, 626 square metres, the restaurant has 10 big and small-size dining halls with a total business area of 1, 784 square metres, able to accommodate 500 diners at a time. Based on the recipes of the Longevity Kitchen of the Qing court, the chefs of the restaurant have developed new dishes including a Manchu-Han feast which combines the best of Manchu and Han cuisine, and can offer foods which are considered nourishing medicinal tonics. There is also a traditional dish of large fresh carp from Kunming Lake, which is a favorite with guests. There are three sittings for lunch in the tourist busy season from April to October each year.

273

Marble Boat 清晏舫 (石舫)

The Marble Boat was first built in 1750. Formerly there was a Chinese style wooden superstructure on the top of it. In 1860, it was burned down by the Anglo-French forces. In 1893, a foreign style superstructure and two wheelers, one on each side, were added to the boat. It was named the Boat for Pure Banquets.

The body, 36 metres long, is built of marble. The superstructure is made of wood, but painted to look like marble. The floor is paved with coloured bricks. All the windows are inlaid with multi coloured glass. There is a drainage system to let rainwater flow down through the four hollow concrete pillars and into the lake by the mouths of the dragon heads.

The boat was used for enjoying the lake scenery and was supposed to be a symbol of stability of the Qing Dynasty.

Hall of Jade Ripples 玉澜堂

The Hall of Jade Ripples lies at the northern corner of Kunming Lake in the Summer Palace. It is noted as having served as the prison of Emperor Guangxu in the late Qing Dynasty.

A courtyard beside the lake contains the main Hall of Jade Ripples, which faces the south, and two side buildings. A back door leads to the Yiyunguan (Chamber of Mortal Beings), the former residence of Guangxu's empress. The annex building on the right (west) is known as Xiagendian (Hall of Coloured Clouds) and the one on the left (east) is called Ouxiangxie (Hall of Lotus Fragrance). Each also has a back door.

In the latter half of the 18th century, Emperor Qianlong (1736-1795) used to spend his leisure hours in the courtyard with his ministers and friends. It became Emperor Guangxu's prison in 1898 when Empress Dowager Cixi learned that her nephew, the young Emperor, was supporting a move for reform of China's feudal system.

She cursed him furiously and had him confined to either Yingtai (Water Terrace Pavilion) in Zhongnanhai (Middle South Sea), the present centre of the Chinese Government near the Forbidden City, or in the Hall of Jade Ripples.

Emperor Guangxu was closely watched, at this hall all the back doors were sealed and a brick wall was put up behind the wooden partition on each side of the two annexes of the courtyard.

Also at the Hall of Jade Ripples, a pair of decorative rocks was erected in the front of the courtyard by Empress Dowager Cixi's order. The rocks resemble a mother and a baby and were meant to symbolize the natural affection between a child and a mother to criticize the emperor for his lack of gratitude.

Relics on display in the hall include a throne, a table, an incense burner and a screen, all made during the reign of Emperor Qianlong. An inscribed board is in the handwriting of Empress Dowager Cixi, reading "The magnificence of the palaces makes the star of moral integrity shine forever." One character has a stroke missing. Some people say Empress Dowager Cixi made the mistake but no one dared to tell her at that time. Actually, it was a common error.

Reform Movement of 1898 戊戌变法

The Reform Movement of 1898 took place at a time when China was in danger of being partitioned by imperialist powers. Whose leading spirits were Kang Youwei 康有为 (1858-1927), Liang Qichao 梁启超 (1873-1929) and Tan Sitong 谭嗣同 (1865-1898), represented the interests of the liberal bourgeoisie and the enlightened landlords. The, movement was favored and supported by Emperor Guangxu (1875-1908), but had no mass basis. Yuan Shikai (1859-1916), who had an army behind him, betrayed the reformers to Empress Dowager Cixi (1835-1908, reigned 1861-1908), the leader of the die-hards. She declared that she "would rather lose the country than carry out the reform." She seized power again and had Emperor Guangxu (1875-1898) imprisoned and Tan Sitong and five others beheaded Lin Xu 林旭 (1875-1898), Yang Rui 杨锐 (1857-1898), Liu Guangdi 刘光第 (1859-1898), Yang Shenxiu 杨深秀 (1849-1898), and Kang Guangren 康广仁 (1867-1898), (younger brother of Kang Youwei). In history, they were called the six gentlemen of the 1898 Reform Movement 史称戊戌六君子. Thus, the 100-Day Reform was nipped in the bud.

Wenchang Courtyard 文昌院

Wenchang Courtyard was recently renovated in which priceless cultural relics are displayed. More than 40,000 relics that were once owned by the Qing Dynasty royal family and widely believed to be among China's most treasured possessions are on show. The display gives an overall view of traditional Chinese artifacts such as jade wares, root carvings and paintings. Authorities believe that the renovation of the ancient courtyard not only provides advanced conservation of the treasures but also gives more Chinese and foreign guests the chance to admire the essence of Chinese culture.

Temple of the Dragon King 龙王庙

Standing in front of the main building in the island, Emperor Qianlong used to review his navy training in the lake. The building is known as the Temple of the Dragon King. The 17-Arch Bridge, 150 metres long, was built after the design of Marco Polo Bridge. It has 544 carved lions in different postures. Seen from a distance, it looks like a rainbow hanging across the water.

Gilt Bronze Ox 铜牛

To the east of the 17-Arch Bridge stands a gilt bronze ox cast in 1755. It is said that in ancient times, ox used to be a symbol of flood control. More than 4,000 years ago in the Xia Dynasty, whenever flood was brought un-

275

der control, people put an iron ox in the river bed. In the Tang Dynasty, instead of putting an iron ox in the river bed, people placed it by the bank of the river. Qing Emperor Qianlong followed the Tang example, and a gilt bronze ox was placed east of Kunming Lake.

Yelu Chucai (1190-1244) Memorial Temple 耶律楚材祠

Yelu Chucai was an advisor to Genghis Khan (1162-1227) and a famous statesman of the Yuan Dynasty. A temple in his honour, located near the Pavilion of Flourishing Culture in the Summer Palace, was opened to public in September 1984.

It is a three-hall temple richly ornamented and surrounded by trees.

The temple consists of Yelu Chucai's coffin chamber, memorial halls and his statue. In addition, a tablet bearing an inscription in the handwriting of Emperor Qianlong (1736-1795) of the Qing Dynasty has been erected. A stone statue placed near the tomb in the court is a relic from the Yuan Dynasty (1279-1368) unearthed in 1979. It is thought to date from the time when Kublai Khan (1215-1294), the grandson of Genghis Khan, built the temple.

The Tomb of Yelu Zhu (1220-1285) 耶律楚材之子耶律铸的墓葬

The tomb of Yelu Zhu, a premier in the Yuan Dynasty, was excavated in autumn, 1998 not far from the temple dedicated to his father, Yelu Chucai, also a Yuan premier. The tomb, found about two metres underground, consists of a tomb gate, an aisle and five coffin chambers. The main chamber was Yelu Zhu's, the others apparently belonged to his wife and concubines. Because the tomb was next to the Temple of Yelu Chucai, the archaeologists believe it is part of a family graves complex. More than 180 precious relics were unearthed, including gold and silver plates and other artifacts, potteryware, and figurines and porcelain. Some were described as period masterpieces. Two round memorial tablets were also found at the same time, which allowed the archaeologists to identify the exact owner of the ancient tomb. Frescoes were also found on the inner walls of two tomb chambers. Unfortunately, most of the frescoes were partly destroyed by air erosion over the centuries. The tomb, whose owner held a high official rank, is the largest tomb from the Yuan Dynasty ever found around Beijing.

Pavilion of Great Happiness 景福阁

The Empress Dowager came here to enjoy the rain and the moon and fete foreign envoys.

Many elderly Beijingers still remembered the day that more than half a century ago the People's Liberation Army (PLA) announced the peaceful liberation of Beijing. It was January 31, 1949. They had been living in fear of approaching battles for a couple of weeks. Beijing, then Beiping, was under the control of Kuomintang army general Fu Zuoyi, who had 250, 000 soldiers stationed in the city. However, the Communist-led PLA was closing in on Fu as well as Beiping. By late December 1948 and early in January 1949, the PLA had successfully captured Xinbao'an, Zhangjia-kou and Tianjin and cut Fu's retreat routes. Most people, from the Communist Party leaders and the PLA generals to common Beiping residents, wanted peace. On January 14, 1949, Chairman Mao Zedong published his communiqué in which he listed eight conditions for the end of the civil war in the whole country. Underground Communists working in the city organized various activities calling on the public to support a peaceful settlement between the PLA and the Kuomintang. The Communists and other far-sighted scholars by the side of Fu, whom included Fu Dongju, Fu's daughter, and Liu Houtong, Fu's senior consultant, lobbied hard. Indeed, battles in Beiping would go down history as a destructive evil. Negotiations between the PLA and Fu's representatives were tough. Having already suffered heavy loses in battles in areas on the outer shirts of Beiping, General Fu was faced with two choices: peace or continuing to fight with the strong possible outcome of defeat. Between the two choices, Fu wisely accepted the first one. On January 16, 1949, PLA representatives Su Jing and Fu's representatives Wang Kejun and Cui Zaizhi signed "The Agreement on the Peaceful Settlement of Beiping's Affairs." Two weeks later, Beiping was under the control of the PLA and subsequently the new people's municipal government was established. Residents had a lot to celebrate for, but above all, they celebrated peace, which guaranteed the preservation of the ancient Chinese capital and marked a good beginning for the city's future development. To commemorate this historical event, the research office of the Party's history in the municipal Party committee in Beijing and the Archives of Beijing compiled an album. More than 300 pictures and 30 files vividly show that eventful and historical moment.

After 1949, Fu Zuoyi was subsequently a Vice Chairman of the Chinese People's Political Consultative Conference, Vice Chairman of the National Defence Council and Minister of Water Conservancy and Power. He died of illness in 1974.

The Summer Palace is home to a variety of waterfowl including ruddy-breasted crakes, found in the reed beds at the south end of the Kunming Lake. There will also be opportunities to observe birds as tourists walk through the restored buildings and pine forests that dot the grounds and to the top of Longevity Hill. A variety of pipits, warblers, buntings, and wagtails are possible here.

Hall of the Sea of Wisdom 智慧海

It was completed in 1750, without a single beam or column used in its structure. So, it was also called "no beam hall." Some of the Buddhist figures on its walls were destroyed in 1900 by the Allied Forces of the Eight Powers.

Naval Academy 海军学院

In 1885, the Qing Government suffered a defeat at sea by France. Three years later, the Kunming Lake Naval Academy was established on the banks of the lake outside the west wall of the present Summer Palace for training navy personnel. Its first enrollment totaled 60 recruits from two firearm battalions of the Eight Banners (the military organization of the Qing Dynasty). The purpose of establishing the Academy by Empress Dowager Cixi was to renovate the Garden of Clear Ripples (presently known as the Summer Palace), which was seriously damaged by the Anglo-French imperialists during the Second Opium War in 1860. Setting up the Naval Academy was a good pretext for Empress Dowager Cixi to raise the funds, which were badly needed for her plan. About 10 million ounces of silver, the greater portion of the money were diverted from the navy's budget to the reconstruction of the garden. The money used for the rebuilding of the garden would have been enough to buy seven major ships. The Chinese Northern Fleet would then have ranked as one of the largest fleets in the world.

Instead, all the Kunming Lake Naval Academy had for training was a little steamer, which was also used to pull the imperial excursion boat around the lake. Only one batch of cadets graduated from the Academy and most of the graduates were from royal families. They played a minor role in the 1894 naval battle between China and Japan.

278

Ancient Archways (*Pailou*) 牌楼

Historical records show there were 57 archways in Beijing near the end of the Qing Dynasty. A lot of these ceremonial archways were built at major crossroads of shopping streets and on long avenues, either to decorate the location or to mark the long streets. At present, Beijing has more than 40 archways. The names of some areas like Dongsi, Xisi, Dongdan and Xidan are derived from the number of archways there. At the beginning of 20th century, there were four archways in the Dongsi area, where the Overseas Chinese Building (presently Overseas Chinese Prime Hotel) and the People's Department Store are now located. Thus the name Dongsi means four archways in the east. Xidan means a single one in the west.

The archways were erected in front of temples, cemeteries, offices, and in gardens.

There is a delicately built stone archway at the end of Know the Fish Bridge in the Garden of Harmonious Interest inside the Summer Palace, a favourite summer resort of Empress Dowager Cixi of the late Qing Dynasty.

Many archways are built of wood. Stone ones are usually in front of tombs and temples, giving a feeling of solemnity and respect. The largest stone archway stands on the way to the Ming Tombs. Built of white marble in 1540, it has five passways. The six pillars were carved with *qilin* (Chinese unicorns), lions, dragons, and other strange animals, all fighting or wriggling in heaven or in the sea.

In ancient times, some archways were built in memory of loyal ministers, dutiful sons or women who sacrificed themselves for their deceased husbands.

But there were exceptions. In the 1901 Treaty signed between the Qing Government and the Eight Power Allied Forces, there was an article ordering that the Chinese Government set up an archway in memory of Ketteler, who was German minister counselor. He beat a Chinese passer by with his stick one day and then dragged the man into the consulate grounds. This incident angered the Chinese people who were already organizing themselves to fight the imperialist invaders. For the foreign diplomats' safety, the Qing Government sent a note, telling the foreign missions to leave Beijing for Tianjin. In defiance of his counterparts in the diplomatic corps, the next day Ketteler drove with his interpreter to the Chinese premier's residence to lodge a protest against the note. He was killed on his way through the archway at Dongdan. The Qing Government submitted to demands of invading foreign forces and erected a marble archway for Ketteler at Dongdan, in addition to an wooden one there. After the First World War (1914-1918), the marble archway was moved to the Zhongshan (Dr Sun Yat-sen) Park and was renamed "Gonglizhansheng" meaning "Justice will always prevail." In 1952, during an Asian Pacific Peace Conference, the name of the archway was changed to "Safeguard Peace." The inscription on it was in late Guo Moruo's handwriting.

Among archways, the ones with glazed tiles were viewed as more important. According to the laws of the Qing Dynasty, only the archways that fronted imperial buildings could have glazed tiles. Today, a few glazed tile archways still remain. There is one in Beihai Park, and in the Imperial Garden in the Forbidden City each.

In the ancient times, ordinary people were not allowed to run through the passageways; they had to slow their steps to a respectful walk. By some archways, there were stone slabs where officials had to step down from their horses or carriages. It was only after the Qing Dynasty was overthrown that rickshaw boys could hurry through the archways.

Archways at the major crossroads have been removed, but archways in front of temples are still considered treasured archways. Most of them were beautifully designed, typical of ancient Beijing architecture.

The People's Government has brought all these archways a new life. Wooden archways have been repainted, while stone archways repaired.

Memorial Archway at the East Gate of the Summer Palace 颐和园东门牌楼

This is the memorial archway, which was repaired and renovated in 1987. On each side of the memorial archway at the east gate of the Summer Palace is an inscription. The one facing the east is "Han Xu," which means containing "emptiness." One meaning of emptiness is water scenery. Therefore, the name tells people that the main scenery in the Summer Palace is a lake. Another meaning is modesty. Chinese people like to modify noble moral character as "to have a mind as open as a valley." Water is almost equal to a mirror, which can reflect things as they are. The Emperors used this to liken their rule to a clear mirror, which is just and objective. On the west side (reverse side) of the archway is "Yan Xiu," which means "collecting excellence." It refers to collecting the most excellent scenery and beauty of ancient and modern times. It also means gathering people of the most extraordinary abilities.

Emperor's Shopping Street 买卖街

Another part of the park, called Suzhou Street, requires a separate ticket, unless you purchase the comprehensive 30 yuan (US$3.75) ticket at the main gate of the Summer Palace. Suzhou Street is supposed to be a model of what the city of Suzhou looked like in the Qing Dynasty.

During his reign (1736-1795), Emperor Qianlong of the Qing Dynasty had made several inspection tours of south China and was impressed by the commercial prosperity. Consequently he had shops built along the imperial resort's Back Lake imitating the shops along the canals in Suzhou, one of the most popular tourist cities in China famous for its waterways and gardens. The imperial resort, including the Emperor's shopping street, was destroyed in 1860 by the Anglo-French Allied Forces. In the late Qing period it was rebuilt as the Summer Palace, but the shopping street was not renovated as there were only holes in the ground where the pillars had once stood.

As part of the renewed effort to return this historical site to its original condition, in 1986 restoration began on the Emperor's shops and was completed in September 1990. The plans for the reconstruction work were drawn by members of the Architecture Department of Qinghua University. Their designs were in strict accordance with the original style based on historical records found in the National Archives of History, the National Library and the Forbidden City. The architectural styles, interior and exterior decorations, and even the shop signs reflect 18th century Chinese social and economic patterns. Located along the northern side of the Longevity Hill, the Emperor's shopping street looks like a scene from a traditional landscape painting of southern China. As part of the restoration project, Huifangtang (The Hall of Painted Flowers) and Jiayinxuan (the Veranda of Fine Shades) above the street on the northern slope of the Longevity Hill have also been revitalized, adding to the depth of the street scene.

The restored street stretches about 300 metres along the edge of the Back Lake.

Construction included more than 60 shop buildings, six bridges, a small temple and nearly 30 wooden archways. The traditional archways are built in front of the shops and decoratively carved and painted in the Qing Dynasty style. All of the buildings are furnished with classical Chinese furniture. The store fronts are trimmed with the traditional sign boards and ornaments.

The shops are distinctive for their historical architecture because many of them represent trades and skills, which no longer exist, such as the incense shops, the dye house and the wooden comb shop. The shopping street also provides visitors with new activities. Jiayinxuan (the Hall of Fine Shades) is reopened as a teahouse and a place where performers will tell traditional stories and sing ballads in the Suzhou dialect. All the shop assistants are dressed in the traditional clothes of the Qing Dynasty. They will also greet visitors in the old way by cupping one hand in the other before their chests. To further attract visitors, each day one shop will hold a traditional opening ceremony. There are five brightly painted pleasure boats of different sizes which visitors can take out to enjoy the lake.

In order to recreate the atmosphere of ancient times, visitors will have the chance to exchange their money for ancient style Chinese coins at the entrance of the street if they wish to spend money in any of the shops or the teahouse or snack counters. The street also opens in the evening when it is lit by old style lanterns hung in every shop.

A New Museum in the Summer Palace (the Underground Cultural Relics Warehouse)

Construction of the museum started in October, 1998 and was completed in September 1999. The museum is built in the style of ancient buildings inside the Summer Palace so that it blends into the surrounding environment. The museum is a two-storey building with an underground storeroom and an exhibition hall, each with 2,800 square metres of floor space. The museum is built at a site 200 metres south of the main palace gate within the royal garden, and in a way that the harmony and symmetry of the whole garden won't be damaged, and tourists can find it easily. The museum may look ancient, but it is equipped with advanced technologies and highly sensitive anti-theft equipment to ensure the safety of these treasures. The museum costs over 60 million yuan equivalent to US$ 7.2 million.

In the museum there are some 40,000 ancient relics on display, including ceramics, bronze wares, paintings and garments from the Qing Dynasty (1644-1911). Some are from the Yuan (1279-1368) and Ming (1368-1644) dynasties. Tourists will be dazzled by these beautiful relics, which are shown for the first time when the museum was opened. Formally, these relics were stored in old warehouses without adequate temperature and humidity control facilities. In order to offset the affect of dramatic weather changes on the relics, which were becoming increasingly fragile, experts had to check them frequently and make repairs. Actually, a small museum in Qinghuaxuan within the palace was set up in 1996 and about 100 relics were on show, but only few tourists seemed to have much interest. This new museum has drawn a larger number of tourists every year.

The Summer Palace, formally named by UNESCO as a World Heritage site in December 1998, is much better known for its beautiful gardens than its rich collection of relics.

Important Elements of the Art & General Conception of the Summer Palace 颐和园艺术及总体概念的重要部分

In speaking of the general conception of the Summer Palace laid out more than 2,000 years ago in the Han Dynasty there appeared then the idea of a layout which incorporated a garden within a palace. According to ancient Chinese mythology, there were three fairy mountains in the Eastern China Sea. They are Penglai, Fangchang and Yingzhou on which many heavenly elixirs grew. Feudal emperors longed for it day and night. South Lake Island, Circle City Island and Seaweed-Viewing Hall Island that dot Kunming Lake in the Summer Palace mimic and symbolize these three fairy mountains. Thus began the tradition of building the imperial garden in ancient China.

The aesthetic standards of Chinese style architectures have long been paying much attention to central axis linking with symmetries on both sides. This is as true of the layout of old Beijing and the Forbidden City as it is of the Summer Palace, which was reserved as a travelling palace. Out of the Empress Dowager's admiration for the gardens of Suzhou and Hangzhou, she had the southern face of Longevity Hill in the Summer Palace laid out in imitation of West Lake in Hangzhou, while the northern face followed the architectural style seen along the canals of Suzhou. Designers tried their best to promote long established traditions of aesthetic feeling in the balance of architecture and is to be felt in a group of buildings arranged around the Tower for Buddhist Incense as a formal point and located at the southern face of Longevity Hill. From the central pier of the northern shore of Kunming Lake, a traveller can pass through 9 structures in order known as Jade like Firmament in Bright Clouds, Cloud-Dispelling Hall, Hall of Virtuous Brilliance, Tower for Buddhist Incense, Multi-Fragrant Boundary, and Sea of Wisdom Temple. Each of the buildings is higher than the previous one above the water surface proceeding to the top of the hill, which also forms a vertical axis with the buildings on both sides strictly symmetrical and well-planned along the axis.

We are now at the Long Corridor totalling 728 metres in length with over 8, 000 paintings on the beams of the corridor. When visitors waltz through they can hardly feel it at all its undulations and turns. In fact, the Long Corridor was built along the rises, falls and turns of the natural terrain in such a way as to deliberately minimize them and appear straight and level. The 4-octagonal pavilions, namely Beauty-Retaining Pavilion (留佳亭), Enjoy-the-Ripple Pavilion(寄澜亭), Autumn Water Pavilion (秋水亭)and Clarity Distance Pavilion(清遥亭)represent the four seasons of a year. They were constructed from rather mysterious principles so that when people walk along the corridor they can't feel the rising and falling of the land. At the same time, tranquil and mood setting scenery on both sides diverts the visitor's visual conception. The floor is in addition uneven, yet you cannot feel it. Similarly, there are turns along the way but visitors cannot feel that it is not straight. This is a magical masterpiece. Where the visitor's awareness is transformed by scenery and technical artistic and engineering device and transported to a plane of relaxed and heavenly wandering.

The largest pavilion ever built in China is located on the east bank of Kunming Lake. It is called fittingly spacious pavilion. The 17-Arch Bridge is the only passage linking the east bank of the lake to South Lake Island. Looking into the distance, west of the bridge visitors can see an island which, were there no spacious pavilion, would monopolize the usual scene and create a feeling of imbalance and heaviness at one end.

Why did the Qing Dynasty build the Three Hills, Five Gardens & the Mountain Summer Resort in Chengde?
为什么清朝建三山、五园和承德避暑山庄

To this interesting question it is said that there are three reasons:

1. The Manchus loved nature. Before they came to Beijing they lived a semi-nomadic life in open spaces amid scenes of natural beauty. After they made Beijing their capital they felt isolated by comparison when in residence in the Forbidden City. Therefore, they began to build gardens and a mountain summer resort to restore a sense of openness, freedom and natural beauty to their lives.

2. Military training and archery practice. After the Manchus occupied Beijing they had a population of 600, 000. For the purpose of military training and archery necessary in those times, they built gardens to house the required activities.

3. Resources sufficient for construction. During the period of Kangxi (1662-1722) and Qianlong (1736-1795), China had rich human and material resources more than sufficient for the construction of gardens of such a scale. The Summer Palace has often been considered the No. 1 imperial garden in China. Construction of the Garden of Clear Ripples began in 1740 and took 15 years to complete. The building of the garden cost 4. 48 million taels of silver. It is said that there were four reasons for Emperor Qianlong to construct the garden. The first was the pretext of showing filial obedience to his mother. The second was to prevent floods by water control and thereby to cherish the people. The third was to unify minority people by building lama temples at the back of Longevity Hill in an area occupying 20, 000 square metres. The fourth was to link the other four imperial gardens namely, Garden of Light Tranquility at Jade Spring Hill, Garden of Peacefulness at Fragrant Hill, Changchunyuan and Yuanmingyuan, together by using the Garden of Clear Ripples as its unifying centre. Thus created, the Summer Palace became the most magnificent imperial garden and is still unparalleled in the world. Since ancient times the Chinese have been keen

on mathematics. Different people have different sayings from 1 to 9. Emperor Qianlong linked three mountains and five gardens together; three plus 5 makes 8, and 8 means "prosperous." Actually, the Garden of Clear Ripples—the Summer Palace, in fact was the last, largest and most prosperous imperial garden.

Architectural Paintings in China 中国建筑绘画

Beams, ceilings, columns and lintels—all pieces of traditional Chinese architecture—are embellished with a variety of paintings. China's ancient architecture holds a unique and important niche in world architecture. Historically, painting has been a major part of architectural decoration in China. The Chinese first painted simple patterns on wooden structure in their homes with mineral paints and tung oil to prevent exposed wooden parts from deteriorating in the wind and rain. The paint also served to prevent termites from eating the wood. Later, more aesthetic elements were added. The painting acquired an artistic form that supplemented the original practical purpose. Before the Warring States Period (475 BC-221 BC), bright primary colours and coloured paintings had already been used on the wooden structures of palaces. The different colours at that time represented different grades of the buildings. In Qin and Han dynasties (221 BC-AD 220), the architectural style of ancient China gradually evolved.

Figures appeared along with geometrical designs, flowers and animals. They were painted, carved and cast on ground bricks, beams, columns, bracket sets, windows, walls ceilings and roofs. New colours were added. Columns of the palaces were painted red, and colored paintings were used in bracket sets, ceilings and tiers; walls were painted blue and purple, and frescoes began to appear on them. Paintings, carvings and Chinese characters were also used to decorated buildings and became dominant elements in architectural decoration. With the introduction of Buddhism into China, decorative patterns in architecture adopted religious themes, in Indian, Persian and Greek styles. Chinese architectural decoration entered its first boom period between AD 265-AD 581. During the period of Sui and Tang dynasties (581-907), colour bleeding was first used in composing architectural paintings, a technique that greatly influenced architectural painting in the Song Dynasty (960-1279). While in the palaces of the Song, Liao and Jin dynasties (960-1279), gold and green were painted under the eaves to sharpen contrast. The colours and patterns of paintings in the Liao and Song dynasties reflected the Tang Dynasty style, with vermilion and yellow the dominant colours, sometimes mixed with green. The Yuan Dynasty (1279-1368) saw multiple religions and cultures add new patterns and colours to the architectural decorations. This paved the way for the development of the architectural decorations in the Ming and Qing dynasty(1368-1644), scroll patterns played a dominant role in architectural paintings, with simple colours in cool tones such as blue and green. The technique of colour bleeding was introduced into the patterns, which, when combining blue and green, conveyed a simple yet elegant tasteful result. Vermilion and gold were occasionally mixed in such patterns to make them look brighter and more vivid. In order to achieve a clear and beautiful contrast of colours, the architectural paintings during this period discarded the traditional technique of the outline drawing with gold and white. The designs were created in two major styles: fine, close lines, or big, unfolding leaves. The creative compositions, the exquisite mixture of colours and the fine drawings all contributed to the greater attractiveness of the architectural paintings to become more attractive. New development occurred in designing patterns and techniques in the Qing Dynasty (1644-1911). Under the feudal hierarchy, with its different grades of buildings, some of the most commonly used styles included imperial-style painting, Suzhou-style painting and scroll pattern painting.

The imperial-style was the highest-grade architectural decoration in the Qing Dynasty. It was used in major imperial palaces and temples where emperors conducted state affairs, offered sacrifices to heaven and the ancestors, or in which they resided. Such paintings usually adopted dragons and phoenixes and dominant images, accompanied by such elements as scroll patterns, lotuses and water chestnut flowers. Gold colouring was used extremely in imperial-style paintings to lend to the palaces a look of majesty and magnificence. Suzhou-style painting was used in gardens, parks and residential buildings. Landscapes, animals and plant as well as historical legends, were all favorite subjects. Compared to the imperial-style, the Suzhou-style was more secular and accessible and therefore more popular.

The scroll pattern of painting could actually be considered a variation on imperial-style painting, distinguished from the latter by its use in minor imperial buildings and temples based on the Ming tradition. It had further developed into eight forms corresponding to the different scales in the buildings. Its designs were evenly laid out with lines closely drawn, using blue and green as the dominant colours, and embellished with black, white and gold, thus creating a grave and solemn tone. Yet another style of architectural painting in the Qing Dynasty that combined Suzhou-style painting with scroll pattern painting to achieve a unique effect of lively composition.

Architectural painting contributes much to the beauty of Chinese architecture in both colour and structure. Take the three major halls in the Forbidden City—the Hall of Supreme Harmony, the Hall of Complete Harmony and the Hall of Preserving Harmony—where vermilion and gold are painted on those parts exposed to the sun so to reflect a dazzling splendour. The hidden parts beneath the double-eaves are painted in cool tones with blue dominant. Thus a sharp contrast adds to the depth and thickness of the projecting eaves. The red columns and the carved, white marble banisters add to the overall harmony, all serving to reflect imperial majesty.

Through thousands of years of architectural practice and development, Chinese architectural painting has developed into a systematic art form with strong national flavour and has lent inspiration to modern architectural decorations. Copying, rather than creating, has been the predominant pattern with contemporary architectural color paintings. They are mainly used for interior decorations on ceilings, beams, columns and lamp sets. The patterns can be found occasionally in exterior decorations. To promote harmony, color designs now employ all the colours used in traditional architecture. In considering the themes of colour paintings, the traditional dragons and phoenixes are to a great extent replaced by plants, animals and geometric figures. Modern architectural colour paintings are greatly influenced by the murals of Dunhuang which merit a separate study. Intermediate colours and warm tones are used instead of the primary colours and cool tones that are found in the colour paintings of Chinese ancient royal palaces. The whole effect of the colours in the newer paintings is warm, elegant and bright.

The Three Hills & the Five Gardens in Beijing 北京的三山和五园

1. *Longevity Hill（万寿山）*
2. *Fragrant Hill（香山）*
3. *Jade Spring Hill（玉泉山）*

1. *Garden of Clear Ripples（清漪园）*
2. *Garden of Everlasting Spring（畅春园）*
3. *Garden of Perfection & Brightness（圆明园）*
4. *Garden of Tranquillity & Brightness（静明园）*
5. *Garden of Tranquillity & Pleasure（静宜园）*

The Four Most Famous Gardens in China 中国最著名的四大园林

1. *The Summer Palace（Park of Nurtured Harmony）was built in 1750 and was completed in 1765.（颐和园）*
2. *The Mountain Hamlet to Flee the Heat（The Imperial Mountain Summer*

Resort）was constructed in 1702 and was finished in 1792.（避暑山庄）

3. *The Humble Administrator's Garden was constructed in 1522.*（拙政园）

4. *The Lingering Garden was built in 1525.*（留园）

There are five aspects for the protection of the Summer Palace:

1. The general layout of the hill and water system—the protection of the Longevity Hill and the Kunming Lake;

2. The protection of the ancient architecture of the palaces, halls, towers, pavilions, corridors, bridges, waterside-pavilions, pagodas, and workshops with a total floor space of 70,000 square metres;

3. The protection of over 400,000 trees within the Summer Palace, of which more than 1,600 trees with over 200 years old;

4. The protection of more than 40,000 cultural relics including bronze wares, ceramics, jade objects, cloisonné used by Empress Dowager Cixi and the protection of ancient books.

5. The protection of view borrowing of the surrounding environment outside the Summer Palace. As the original royal garden, the Summer Palace was not designed for majority people, it was for the service of a few emperors and empresses in feudal China. All the doors and roads were very narrow. In 1950s, some of the palaces and halls were converted into passages. The second door entrance tickets are for control of the flow of visitors.

The Temple of Heaven
天　　坛

The Temple of Heaven is situated in the southern part of the city. It was built in 1420, encompassing 273 hectares (674 acres). The perimeter of the Temple of Heaven is 6,369 metres with 6 metres high.

The temple was the place where the emperors of the Ming and Qing dynasties worshipped heaven and prayed for good harvests. They came here twice a year, on the 15th day of the 1st lunar month and on Winter Solstice. At first, both heaven and earth were worshipped here. After 1530 when the Temple of Earth was built in the northern suburbs, only heaven was worshipped in this temple.

The Temple of Heaven is regarded as one of the greatest architectural structures in the world. Some environmental artists and gardeners describe the temple as a place where people can talk to the heaven. In Beijing, four imperial temples were built during the Ming and Qing dynasties

(1368-1911). At the southern end of the city axis is the Temple of Heaven. It is the most important of the four. The other three are the Altar of the Earth in the north, the Altar of the Moon in the west, and the Altar of the Sun in the east just behind the Beijing Friendship Store. All of them are still standing, but the Temple of Heaven is the largest group of temple buildings of its kind in China, nearly four times larger than the Forbidden City. The whole building complex was designed in a way that makes you feel close to heaven. In making the heaven-like structures, the designers made good use of colour, sound, geometric figures of the circle and the square, and changes in height. The combination of building and garden helps make it appear mysterious and magical.

The temple's architecture has two themes. One is "on the earth," while the other is "in the heaven." The square-shaped palace for fasting in the west of the temple appears like a "forbidden city" in smaller size. The circular shaped Qiniandian (Hall of Prayer for Good Harvests) and Huanqiu (Circular Mound Altar) are thought to have been connected with heaven. This symbolizes the second theme, which dominates the whole temple.

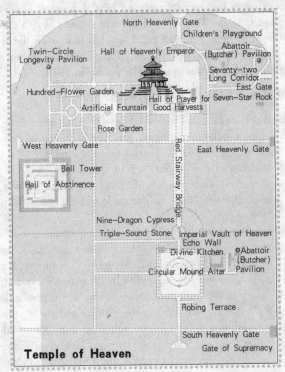

Temple of Heaven

In imperial days, the Chinese people believed that the sky was in circular shape and the earth was square. On the basis of this traditional concept, the circle was widely adopted in the design of the temple's main buildings. It is in accord with people's imagination of heaven.

Nowadays, there are more than 100,000 tress of various kinds, of which 60,000 are evergreen pines. Out of 60,000 pines, 2,566 are ancient cypresses. Of these ancient trees, 100 trees reach the age of more than 1,000 years. The Temple of Heaven has the most ancient trees in Beijing.

After the completion of the Temple of Heaven in 1420 in more than 500 years until the Qing Dynasty, 22 emperors made 654 sacrifices to heaven in the Temple of Heaven.

In ancient China, sacrifice to heaven by people has a history of about 5,000 years. It originated from natural worship. People thought that everything was dominated by heaven due to underdeveloped science in ancient China. Ancient Chinese hoped that heaven could help them by sacrifice. This objectively reflected the people's wishes to nature. But Emperor regarded sacrifice to heaven as his patent and tried to consolidate his rule through sacrifice to heaven. In ancient China dozens of temples of heaven were built and only the Temple of Heaven in Beijing is still standing. It is the largest architectural group of buildings and unique in the world today. The Republic of China (1912-1949) in 1912 abolished the activities of sacrificing to heaven. It was open to the public in 1919.

Hall of Prayer for Good Harvests 祈年殿

This is the Hall of Prayer for Good Harvests, the main building in the compound. It is a lofty cone-shaped structure with triple eaves, and the top is crowned by a gilded ball. The base of the structure is a triple-tiered circular stone terrace over 5,900 square metres in area. Each ring is balustraded in carved white marble. It gives the effect of lace when seen from a distance. The roof of the hall is made of blue glazed tiles, following the colour of the sky.

The building is not only splendid in outer appearance, but also unique in inner frame. Without the use of steel, cement and nails, even without the use of big beams and crossbeams, the entire structure—38 metres high and 30 meters in diametre—is supported by 28 massive wooden pillars and a number of bars, laths, joints and rafters. The four central pillars, called the Dragon-Well Pillars, are 19.2 metres high, and so big that each will take two and a half men to encircle it with their arms stretched out. They represent the four seasons. There are two rings of twelve pillars each, the inner ring symbolizing the twelve months and the outer ring the twelve divisions of the day and night. The pillars, 28 in number also represent the 28 constellations in the sky. The timber for making these pillars was shipped all the way from Yunnan Province in southwest China. The centre of the stone-paved floor is a round marble slab with as a natural pattern of dragon and phoenix. On your right (east) there used to be two sets of screens, two chairs and a long table. The tablets of the Emperor's ancestors were placed on the table, which is now on display. On your left(west) the chair was used by the Emperor to take a rest after the service.

The day before praying for good harvests, the Emperor came to the Hall of Imperial Zenith just behind this hall to present incense and then came here to inspect the tablets. The tablet of the God of Heaven was kept in the shrine while other tablets were placed on the stone platform. He then left by the left side gate for the Storehouse of the Gods to inspect sacrificial articles before he returned to the Hall of Abstinence.

On the day of the prayer, the emperor worshipped the God of Heaven. Fire was built in the oven to usher in the God of Heaven. The Emperor presented white silk and three courses of dishes to the God. Finally, the silk and food were taken away, followed by music and dance.

During the ceremony, the emperor stood on the dragon-and-phoenix marble, delivered a speech and tasted the offering food. The princes stood outside the hall, with the band, the dancers and officials standing on both sides.

The hall has no walls, only partitions of open lattice windows. The ceiling is painted with fine color drawings. It was struck by lightning and burned down. In 1889 and was afterwards rebuilt according to its original design.

Five thousand dragon designs are decorated on the inside and outside of the Hall of Prayer for Good Harvests. They are very sumptuous, and colours are natural and harmonious. They are suited to the occasion.

On each wing of the main hall, there are subsidiary halls in which were worshipped the Gods of the Sun, the Moon and the Stars and the Gods of Wind, Rain, Thunder and Lightning. Now the halls are used as gift shops.

Going out of the gate of the Hall of Prayer for Good Harvests, we come to a raised passage 360 metres long, 30 metres wide and 4 metres high. This broad walk, called Danbiqiao (Red Stairway Bridge) connects the two sets of main buildings in the Temple of Heaven.

In the middle of the passage there is a platform on the eastern side. This is where the emperor changed his clothes before going to worship.

To the south lie the Imperial Vault of Heaven and the Circular Mound

Altar. These three buildings are arranged in a straight line. An aerial view of the enclosure will show that the wall to the south is square while the one to the north is semi-circular. Such a pattern represents the ancient belief that heaven was round and the earth square.

Imperial Vault of Heaven 皇穹宇

This is the Imperial Vault of Heaven, which is a smaller structure. Seen from a distance, it looks like a blue umbrella topped by a gilded ball. This circular building has no crossbeams. Its dome is supported by a complicated span work, which is in complete conformity with the principle of dynamics. It was built in 1530 and rebuilt in 1752. Since 1949 it has been renovated several times. As you can see, its decorative paintings still retain their fresh colors. After the service, the tablets of the Gods of the Sun, the Moon, etc. were placed on the stone platforms.

The building is encircled by a round wall, known as the Echo Wall. A mere whisper at any point close to it will send the sound travelling along the wall so that the echo can be heard clearly at the other end. This is made possible because the wall is round, it has eaves and all the bricks are hermetically laid.

In front of the steps leading down from the hall is the Triple-Sound Stones. If you stand on the first stone and call out, the sound will be echoed once; on the second stone, the sound will be heard twice; and on the third stone, the sound will be repeated three times. This phenomenon is due to the differences in the distance, which the sound waves have to travel from the stone to the Echo Wall. As a result, the sound waves returning at different intervals create different echoes.

Several years ago, a visiting former Democratic German Premier described the Echo Wall as "a microphone of several hundreds years ago!"

292

Circular Mound Altar 圜丘坛

South of the Echo Wall stands the Circular Mound Altar which is wholly built of white marble. The altar is enclosed by two walls, a square wall outside and a round one inside. Its layout forms a geometrical pattern but the structure itself is so designed as to make the most ingenious use of geometry. The altar is 5 metres high. The upper terrace is 30 metres in diameter, the middle terrace 50 metres and the bottom terrace 70 metres. Each terrace has four entrances and a flight of nine steps leading down in every direction. At the centre of the upper terrace lies a round stone surrounded by nine concentric rings of stones. The number of stones in the first ring is 9, in the second 18, and so on, up to 81 in the 9th ring.

The middle and bottom terraces also have 9 rings each. The total number of the marble slabs paved on the altar's surface is 3, 402. Even the numbers of the carved balustrades on these terraces are also the multiples of 9. The number of the balustrades is 360, which stands for the 360 degrees of the circumference of heaven. When you stand in the center of the upper terrace and speak in a low voice, your echo will sound much louder to yourself than to others, as the sound waves are sent back by the marble balustrades to focus at the centre.

The altar was built in 1530, and rebuilt in 1740 in the Qing Dynasty. Although it is over 200 years old, the structure still stands perfectly erect without sagging or cracking.

Every year on Winter Solstice, escorted by soldiers and officials, by musicians and by princes of the royal blood, the emperor would come here to make solemn sacrifice. From the Front Gate to the entrance of the Temple, each gate and every window over-looking his route had to be closed tight. No foreigners were allowed to watch the procession and foreign diplomats were officially advised to stay in their quarters that day. It even happened that the train from Tianjin was forced to stop so as not to disturb the silence of the ceremony

The emperor spent a night of fasting and praying in the temple. The King of Zhou, claiming to be the son of Heaven, made the first offer to Heaven 3, 000 years ago. Yuan Shikai (1859-1916), the head of the Northern warlords in the last years of the Qing Dynasty, made the last sacrifice to Heaven in 1914.

Southeast of the Circular Mound Altar stands an oven built of glazed tiles. It was used as a sacrificial vessel for roasting ox and sheep, etc.

Southwest of the Altar is a lantern-viewing platform, on which a big pole was fixed for hanging big lanterns during ceremonies.

293

How to Offer Sacrifice to the God of Heaven 如何祭天

The official in charge of religious affairs worked out a program of sacrificial ceremony and put it on the table in the Hall of Supreme Harmony for approval by the emperor. Then the prayers were taken to the Hall of Complete Harmony for the emperor to practice. Before the ceremony, the emperor had to wear uniform and ritual hat and fast for two days in the Hall of Abstinence. The day before the ceremony, officials put up a tent near the altar for the emperor to change his clothes and shoes before service. When the emperor left the Hall of Abstinence, the bell started beating until he arrived at the altar. Ovens were lit and the sacrificial ox was roasted. The emperor then led the military and civil officials mounted the altar and offered sacrifices. They looked up to the Heaven to see the God off, and music and dance followed. After the ceremony, the emperor went back to the Hall of Abstinence in the chiming of the bell.

Hall of Abstinence 斋宫

The Hall of Abstinence is located on the western side of the temple. In the Ming and Qing dynasties, emperors and their ministers used to hold three-day fasts there in spring, summer and winter every year before conducting religious rites. In August 1986 the Hall of Abstinence was converted into an exhibition hall containing sacrificial relics. Some 300 relics including utensils and musical instruments, are on display for the first time. Most of these relics are from the Qing Dynasty (1644-1911). They are placed in the original order in which they were used in a sacrificial ceremony.

There are flags used during dances and two sets of percussion instruments called *bianzhong* (a set of bells; chimes) made of bronze, and *bianqing* (a set of musical instruments) made of jade.

Altar of the God of Agriculture 先农坛

The Altar of the God of Agriculture was the site of imperial sacrifices dedicated to the cult of Shennong, the legendary "first farmer" of China. It is located in the souterhn part of the city, directly to the west of the Temple of Heaven, and occupies a total area of three square kilometres. The altar itself, which faces south, is 1.5 metres high and 15 metres long and wide respectively. The hall to the north houses the sacred tablets and is provided with a platform for "observing the harvest."

According to the rites of the Qing Dynasty, on the day of the spring equinox as fixed by the lunar calendar, the emperor would come here to sacrifice to the sacred tablet of Shennong (the Holy Farmer). Following this ceremony, the emperor would plow several furrows of land with his own hands and retire to the observation platform to watch the princes, ministers and a representative group of common people finish the task. It was said that the emperor's plowing "set an example of industry to his subjects, thus dignifying the toil of the meanest agriculture labourer." The area also contains an Altar to the Year God 太岁殿 built in 1532 for carrying out sacrifice to the planet Jupiter and auxiliary halls on the east and west for carrying out sacrifices to the Deities of the 12 Lunar Months (Yuejiangshen).

The Divine Kitchen of Xiannong Altar (Altar of the God of Agriculture 先农坛), an ancient sacrificial site in Beijing, will be renovated with a

US $50, 000 donation from American Express International Inc. Built in 1420, the altar is where the emperors of the Ming and Qing dynasties offered sacrifices to the farming god for bumper harvests. It was destroyed due to natural and man-made causes. More than 80 million yuan(US$9. 6 million) are spent each year in Beijing to restore such sites.

The Ming Tombs (including Dingling, Changling and Zhaoling)

明十三陵（包括定陵、长陵和昭陵）

(about 44 kilometres from the city)

The Ming Dynasty lasted from 1368 to 1644. The first Ming emperor had his tomb built in Nanjing, the town, which he had chosen for his capital. As his eldest son died early, his grandson succeeded the throne, and he became the second emperor.

His fourth son, the Prince of Yan, was guarding the northern frontier near Beijing with an army 100, 000 strong. The second emperor attempted to weaken his forces but was met with counter-attacks. After a 3-year war he was ousted and lost track off completely. So, the fourth son became the third emperor, Emperor Yongle, of the Ming Dynasty.

As a frontier commander, he was deeply aware that a peaceful northern frontier was of great importance to the Ming regime and the unification of the country. Yongle moved the capital to Beijing in early 15th century. Along with the construction of the Imperial Palace, he chose this valley to build his tomb. All his successors followed his example and had their tombs built here, except one who was dethroned and buried in the western suburb. Out of the sixteen emperors, thirteen lie here with their empresses and concubines. The site was chosen with the greatest care, with geomancy (geomancy refers to the superstition that the location of one's ancestors' graves influences one's fortune. The geomancers claim to be able to tell whether a particular site and its surroundings are auspicious) taken into account. The tombs are located about 44 kilometres to the north of Beijing. They are scattered over a basin approximately 40 square kilometres in area, screened by mountains on three sides and open to the Beijing Plain in the south. The road leading to the tombs is guarded by the Tiger Hill on the left and the Dragon Hill on the right. It was a forbidden ground except for those who were officially in charge of its upkeep. It was not allowed to cultivate land, cut wood or to take stones from here. No one could enter it on horseback, even the emperor himself had to dismount at the gate.

Ming Tombs

We are now riding on the road leading to the tombs. The road was opened up in 1979 with the increase in the number of Chinese and foreign visitors. Along the road, we'll find the Memorial Arch, the Big Red Gate, the Tablet House, the stone animals and statues and the Ming Tombs Reservoir. We'll also see a lot of fruit trees planted after the founding of the People's Republic of China.

This road was known as *shendao*, meaning "the way of the spirit." The body of the dead was carried over the route at funeral ceremony. It is 7 kilometres long, from the Memorial Arch to the gate of the main tomb.

The Memorial Arch, built of white marble, was erected in 1540. It is 14 metres high and 28.86 metres wide, and has 5 arches supported by 6 pillars with beautiful bas-relief carvings of lions, dragons and lotus flowers. Double lintels link the six pillars. The roofing is made of round marble tiles, with upturned corners. "The way of the spirit" used to pass beneath the Memorial Arch.

The Big Red Gate was built in 1426. It used to have three huge wooden doors. The central opening was occupied by the deceased emperor alone, and living ministers and imperial family members had to use one of the side openings when they came to pay homage to the deceased emperors.

About 457 metres from the Big Red Gate stands the Tablet House built in 1435. A marble column, known as *huabiao*, stands at each corner of the Tablet House. A huge tablet, 7 metres high, stands in the middle of the house on the back of a tortoise. The front side bears an inscription by the fourth Ming emperor. On the reverse side is an inscription carved during Qing Emperor Qianlong's reign (1736-1795). It described the reconstruction of the Ming Tombs in 1785 and commented on the rules and styles of the Ming Tombs.

Now we come to the famous avenue of stone animals and statues. Stone animals and statues are found at the entrance to imperial tombs from the Han Dynasty onwards, but none of the group is as famous as that of the Ming Tombs.

The avenue starts with two columns, called *wangzhu* in Chinese, one on each side. They are hexagonal, carved with a cloud design, and the top is shaped like a round cylinder. The animals are lions, *Xiezhi* was a mythical beast of the feline family, said to be able to distinguish right and wrong. *Qilin* was a sort of imaginary animal with a scaly body, a cow's tail, deer's hooves and horns on its head.

With "the way of the spirit" turning slightly, the statues appear: two military officers wearing sabers, two civilian officials and two ministers of merit. Six statues on each side and twelve in all.

These animals and statues all date from the 15th century. It is interesting to compare them with those at the tomb of the first Ming Emperor in Nanjing, which are scarcely any older and yet much less fine. They were all meant to serve the dead in the next world. They do give people a sense of solemnity on the way leading to the tombs, don't they?

On your right is the Ming Tombs Reservoir, one of the 17 large and medium-sized reservoirs built in Beijing in the last 50 years. The 627-metre-long and 29 metre-high dam was built in less than five months in 1958. The late Chairman Mao, the late Premier Zhou Enlai and other leading members of the Chinese Government came to join in its construction. During construction, 400,000 volunteers including workers, farmers, business people, students, soldiers, government cadres, foreign diplomats and foreign friends were involved in the project. The reservoir's total area is 300 hectares (750 acres). The project cost 16 million yuan (US$ 1.935 million). It provides water for irrigation in the Beijing area and works the turbines of an hydro-electric power station. It can generate 1.2 billion kilowatt each year. In Beijing area, there are altogether 83 reservoirs with a total capacity of 9.27 billion cubic metres of water.

On your left at the foot of the hill stands the Underground Palace of Dingling amidst pines and cypresses. Dingling is the tomb of Emperor Wanli, the 13th Ming Emperor. He was born in 1563, and was chosen and named crown prince when he was six years old. He ascended the throne at the age of 10 and ruled for 48 years until he died in 1620.

Dingling (Tomb of Security) is the only one of the Ming Tombs excavated so far. Excavation work took more than two years from 1956 to 1958. You may find the following background information interesting.

Emperor Wanli had two wives. The first wife empress Xiaoduan died only a few months before his death. The second wife Empress Xiaojing died in 1612, eight years before and was buried in a nearby tomb reserved for imperial concubines.

The first wife had no son while the second wife had one. He succeeded Emperor Wanli and died 29 days after his succession. He left the throne to his son. As Xiaojing was the second wife, she was not entitled to the privilege of sharing the emperor's tomb. When her grandson became emperor, she was promoted to the rank of empress dowager, and it was decided that her body be moved into the tomb.

Construction of the tomb and the underground palace started in 1584 when Emperor Wanli was only 22 years old. Eighteen years and 8 million taels of silver (250,000 kilos of silver) were spent on it. The bricks were brought from Shandong Province, the stone from the nearby district of Fangshan, and the wood from the southern provinces.

In 1644 when the Ming Dynasty collapsed, the buildings were damaged in a peasant uprising and were not restored until the reign of Qing Emperor Qianlong. They were burned down again at the beginning of the 20th century.

In 1956, a decision was made by the Chinese Government to open up the tomb. It was the first time that an imperial tomb was excavated in China in a scientific way.

Dingling is now a museum made up of three sections: the Underground Palace and two exhibition rooms. The objects on display are mostly originals. The trip to the Ming Tombs certainly gives us a better understanding of the Ming Dynasty art, the tomb structure and the emperor's extravagance in building the tomb.

I'll tell you more as I show you round. Thank you for your attention. Here are two sketch maps. One shows the Underground Palace of Dingling and the other gives you a panorama of the 13 Ming tombs.

We just passed through the gate of Dingling. We are now here at the sketch maps. The two exhibition rooms are here, one on each side. That's the soul tower; behind it is the tomb mound. Beneath the mound lies the Underground Palace totalling 87 metres in length.

This map shows the 13 Ming tombs in this area. The soul towers show the location of the tombs. This one is Dingling and that one is Changling, the first Ming tomb built in Beijing for the third Emperor, but not yet opened up.

When you pay a visit to the Ming Tombs area you will definitely be impressed by the beauty of the location and the tranquillity of the surroundings. It is now a favourite picnic spot for foreign residents in Beijing, and if you go there on a weekend you will find many families sitting on the grass under the old pine trees that dot the grounds.

Souvenir Shop. The Ming Tombs Tour Area near Beijing witnessed the opening of its first souvenir shopping centre in late 1999. The store is located on the southern side of the square out of Dingling. Near the tomb of Emperor Wanli (1573-1620), a business area of 1, 100 square metres carries furniture, carpets, arts and crafts (stones, paintings, carvings, and cloisonné), clothing items, fabrics, Chinese medicines and souvenirs from the area.

The First Exhibition Room 第一展室

1. The Model of the Tomb Mound 墓型

In May 1956, an archaeological team started excavating Dingling. It took them one year to uncover three deep tunnels and find the exact entrance to the Underground Palace. Some decayed bricks at the southwestern end of the surrounding wall showed that there had been an archway. The team later found a narrow, brick walled tunnel, which runs zigzag to the back of the mound.

In opening up the second tunnel, a stone slab was uncovered on which the inscription reads: 48. 8 metres further and 10. 7 metres deep to the "diamond wall," the sealing wall of the Underground Palace. This tablet provided important clue to the further excavation of the Underground Palace. Archaeologists said that the tablet was meant to guide the builders who might need it for reopening the tomb.

2. Jade Belt 玉带

Jade belt used to be one of the decorative objects on the emperor's robe. In the Ming Dynasty, a limited number of ministers also wore such belts, as grants from the emperor. The belt is made of gold and gems linked together by a leather belt. The gems are transparent and beautiful, like pomegranate seeds. They are products of South China Sea islands and reflect friendly exchanges between China and the southeast Asian countries during the Ming periods.

3. Gold Coins 金币

These gold coins, each weighing 38.5 grams, were minted specially for the dead. They bear characters that read: "Longevity and away with misfortune." Lots of porcelain wares uncovered from Dingling are blue and white porcelain. They are bright and clear, pretty and artistic. They were not only used in the court in large number, but were also one of the major export commodities of the time.

4. Silk Fabrics 丝绸织品

A large quantity of silk fabrics was uncovered from Dingling. Here on display is a piece of gold thread gauze with a rabbit design and a piece of figured satin with a design of lotus and Buddhist emblem swastika. They show the level of textiles in those days.

5. Jade Objects 玉饰

These jade objects were unearthed from the underground. The carving is intricate and delicate. They show the exquisite workmanship of jade carving in the Ming Dynasty.

6. Helmet and Sword 盔甲和宝刀

These are helmet, sword and armor worn by Emperor Wanli. The originals had decayed. They are reproductions.

7. Funerary Objects and Wooden Figurines 殉葬品和木俑

The funerary objects were symbolic utensils made specially for the dead. Slaves were buried alive with their deceased masters. Wooden figurines were later used as burial objects to replace human sacrifice.

8. Gold Crown 金冠 (本名翼善冠)

The gold crown, for the emperor, is woven with extremely thin gold wire. The weaving is done from top to bottom. The tiny holes must be the same in size. It is neat and graceful, displaying the high artistry in arts and crafts in the Ming Dynasty.

9. "Pi Bian" 皮弁

The emperor wore the "Pi Bian" when he issued imperial decrees, worshipped gods and received tributes.

10. "Mian" (Heavenly Hat) 冕

The emperor wore the hat when he went to worship Heaven, the Earth or his ancestors.

The Second Exhibition Room 第二展室

1. Phoenix Crowns 凤冠

The empresses wore the phoenix crowns on big occasions. Here on display is the crown (the crown is emblematic of the power of a king) with 12 dragons and 9 phoenixes. The other one has 6 dragons and 3 phoenixes. Each phoenix crown has over 5,000 pearls and more than 150 gems of different colours.

2. Silverware 银器

The silverware unearthed from the tomb was mostly used by the emperors and empresses during their lifetime. They are valuable material for the study of court life in the Ming Dynasty.

3. Silver Ingots 银元宝

Silver ingots, each weighing 1.9 kilos, were the type of money in use at the time. They were land tax collected from Zhejiang Province.

4. Gold Ingots 金元宝

These gold ingots uncovered from Dingling weigh 385 grams each, marked with the name of the place they came from, date of collection, name of the official in charge as well as their weight and purity.

5. Jewelry 首饰

Over 200 pieces of jewelry were unearthed from the tomb. They are in the shape of plum blossom, lotus flower, peony, turtle, phoenix, rabbit and butterfly, patterns symbolizing happiness and good luck.

6. Jade Pendants 玉垂

These jade pendants are made of pearls and small jade pieces, carved into the shape of dragon amidst clouds, tree leaves, fish and cicadas. The jade pieces are linked together by a length of silk thread. They were to hang on both sides of the waist. When the wearer moved, they dangled and sent out clear and pleasing sound.

7. Dressing Articles 梳妆用品

Here on display are dressing articles used by the emperors and empresses. The shape and style can still be seen. They had decayed though.

8. *Yu Bi* (Jade Piece) and Beads 玉璧及珠

Yu Bi is a round flat piece of jade with a hole at its centre, used by aristocrats for ceremonial purposes in ancient China.

Buddhist monks used the beads when they chanted Buddhist sutras. In the Ming Dynasty most of the emperors believed in Buddhism or Taoism. So the beads were also brought to their tombs.

301

Soul Tower (Tower of Brightness) 明楼

The Soul Tower (also known as an open stela tower erected in front of a royal tomb. The stela inside the tower is engraved with the entombed monarch's name, title and accomplishments) is a square double-eave structure towering in front of the tomb mound. The plaque bears the name Dingling, meaning the Tomb of Security.

The whole building is of stone and brick. The four corner stones are made of whole pieces of marble, and the rafters and brackets are carved out of stone and painted with green and blue floral patterns. The tower is beautiful and solemn, strong in structure, with no damage from erosion by rain and wind in the past four hundred years.

Inside the tower is a huge stone tablet inscribed in regular script "The Mausoleum of Emperor Shenzong (posthumous title) of the Great Ming." The top of the tablet has an intertwined dragon design. The base is square, carved with designs of sea waves, mountain cliffs and dragon amidst clouds. The carving is exquisitely done and better than that of other tombs.

The wall surrounding the tomb mound is known as "precious citadel," about 750 metres in length. Its two ends are connected with the left and right outlets.

The wall has indented parapets and is filled with earth. Pines and cypresses grow on the mound, known as the "precious top," under which lies the Underground Palace.

Underground Palace 地下宫殿

Here at the location of the white brick, the stone slab showing the whereabouts of the Underground Palace was found, about one foot below the surface.

Construction of the tomb started in 1584 and it took six years to complete, with a total cost of 8 million taels of silver (250,000 kilos of silver). The emperor died in 1620 and was buried here with his two empresses.

The excavation started in May 1956 and was finished in July 1958. A winding staircase of 160 steps leads down to the Underground Palace. Those who find it inconvenient to take so many steps down may walk slowly back to the bus.

This is a part of the polished porphyritic rocks. They have been preserved to show how they looked like before.

Here is a sketch map of the Underground Palace, with a total floor space of 1, 195 square metres. It is divided into 5 chambers, the front chamber, the middle chamber, the rear chamber and the left and right annex chambers.

This is the Diamond Wall, the sealing wall leading to the Underground Palace. It consists of 23 layers of large bricks. They are preserved this way especially for visitors.

As you can see, this part is new and the iron-gate was added after the excavation.

Reign title 年号

A designation for the years when an emperor was on the throne, e. g. *Kaiyuan* 开元, the title of the second of the three reign periods of Emperor Xuanzong of the Tang Dynasty 唐玄宗; the Ming and Qing emperors, who as a rule used just one reign title throughout the years when they were in power, are sometimes referred to by the titles of their reign periods instead of their temple titles 庙号, e. g. Emperor Shenzu of the Qing Dynasty 清圣祖, better known as Emperor Kangxi 康熙 after the title of his single reign period.

Temple title 庙号

A title, usually with a *zu* 祖 "founder" or a *zong* "ancestor," given to an emperor posthumously when his spirit tablet was established in the imperial ancestral temple 太庙; e. g. Han Gaozu or Emperor Gaozu of the Han Dynasty 汉高祖, Song Huizong or Emperor Huizong of the Song Dynasty 宋徽宗.

"Shi" title "谥"号

A posthumous title (formerly bestowed on a ruler, a nobleman, or an eminent official; chosen as appropriate to the life and moral qualities of the deceased; e. g. the *Wu* 武 "Mighty" of Han Wu Di 汉武帝):诸葛亮"忠武" Zhuge Liang was given the posthumous title of "Loyally Martial." Or Zhuge Liang was canonized as "Loyally Martial."

Tomb title 陵号

A respectful title conferred on deceased emperor's tomb (mausoleum)

Tomb (mausoleum) 陵

Respectful title of address or honorific title

1. Front Chamber 前殿   The stone gate is made of marble, 3. 3 metres high and 1. 7 metres wide. Each door slab weighs 4 tons. On it are 81 round studs and a door ring carved with the facial design of a mythological guardian known as *Pu Shou* 铺首 . The door slab is thicker at the hinges, 40 cm, but tapers off toward the middle, thus lessening the weight and relieving pressure on the pivots. This makes the whole thing easy to open. To secure the huge stone gate, a bronze cross-beam weighing about

303

10 tons was installed on the top.

The stone block, known as "self-acting stone," is a slab to shut the gate from behind. It is 1.6 metres high, and a little wider at the two ends carved with lotus petal design. When the stone gate is closed, the lower end of the slab is fitted into a hole cut into the ground while its upper end leans against the back of the gate. You can't open from outside. To open the gate, the people doing excavation work fitted in a wire through the 4 cm wide gap between the two door slabs, turned it around to hold the stone block and then pushed back the block with a plank. The stone gate was thus opened. The first stone block bears ink-writing in regular script: "The self-acting stones of seven gates in the palace are not yet tested." Hence the name "self-acting stone."

2. Middle Chamber 中殿　　In the front part of the middle chamber stand two marble thrones, both carved with phoenix heads on their arms. They were for Empress Xiaoduan and Empress Xiaojing. Further down the chamber, there is another marble throne carved with dragon-head design on the back and on its arms. That was for Emperor Wanli.

In front of each throne are five glazed pottery altar pieces: an incense burner, two candle sticks and two beakers, and a blue and white porcelain jar with a cloud and dragon design. The jars were originally filled with sesame oil and had each a copper tube with a wick inside. It is called "Everlasting Lamp," lit when the coffins were brought in. After the tomb was covered up, the light naturally went out due to lack of oxygen.

3. Rear Chamber 后殿　　The rear chamber is 30.1 metres long, 9.1 metres wide and 9.5 metres high. The floor is paved with polished porphyritic rocks. In the middle of the platform is placed the coffin of the emperor. On its left is the coffin of his first wife, Empress Xiaoduan. On its right is the coffin of Empress Xiaojing. Her title was conferred posthumously. The emperor died in July 1620 and his first wife died in April the same year. His second wife died eight years before and was buried at the East Pit—a burial ground reserved for imperial concubines. When the Emperor and Empress Xiaoduan were buried, the coffin of Empress Xiaojing was moved here from the East Pit to join them. Around the three coffins are 26 red-lacquered chests containing the funerary objects and some pieces of uncut jade. Sandalwood and blue and white porcelain vases have been taken away. The historical relics are now put on display after sorting and cleaning.

The original coffins and chests already decayed. The ones you see here are reproductions. More than 3,000 artifacts were unearthed from the tomb.

The charts and pictures on the walls show the amount of money and labor spent on construction, sixty five million man days were spent, with 30,000 people working everyday.

A span of six years and 8 million taels of silver were spent. That amount would have been enough to feed one million peasants for six years and a half.

4. Left and Right Annex Chambers 左右配殿   The left and right annex chambers are two symmetrical structures. Each is 26 metres long, 7.1 metres wide and 7.4 metres high. In the middle of each chamber close to the wall is a coffin platform, which is framed with white marble and paved with "Gold Bricks." Right in the centre is a square hole filled with loess linking the coffin with the ground. It is known as "Gold Well." There is an old Chinese saying: buried with jade on a "Gold Well." The "Gold Well" refers to the square hole, and the jade was supposed to have the power to prevent the body from decomposing. That's why uncut jade was found around the coffin, as you saw in the rear chamber. To the west of the platform are the entrance and a section of the underground passage. According to the Ming funerary institution, the coffins of the empresses were to be brought in through the left and right passages and placed on the platforms. When the Underground Palace was opened up in 1958, these two annex chambers were empty. The coffin of the Emperor and those of the empresses as well as funerary objects were all kept in the rear chamber. Presumably there was not enough time to open up the passages leading to the annex chambers. All the three coffins were brought in through the front entrance. But the doorways of the annex chambers were too narrow, so they could only be placed in the rear chamber.

Strict System for Designating Graves in China's Feudal Society
中国封建社会规定坟墓的严格制度

China's feudal society had a strict system for designating graves, stipulating that the tomb for emperors was to be called *ling* 陵 (mausoleum); for princes and noblemen, *zhong* 冢 (tomb); for sages, *lin* 林 (forest) and for common people, *fen* 坟 (grave).

Since Confucius was respected as a scholar sage and Guan Yu known as a military sage, their tombs were respectively called Konglin (the Forest of Confucius) and Guanlin (the Forest of Guan Yu). The Forest of Confucius was also the private burial ground of Confucius and members of the Confucian clan. Though not as grand and heavily guarded as the tombs of the emperors, the Forest of Confucius had been well preserved over time. Although the tombs of emperors were often magnificent to behold, with the ravages of time they were often neglected or forgotten by the people. Many were even burned or robbed.

In contrast, Confucius' modest tomb was enlarged to a forest area encompassing 200 hectares (494. 2 acres). This is because unlike the emperors, Confucius has been continually revered.

Changling 长陵

Changling is the tomb for Emperor Yongle, the third Ming Emperor, and his wife Empress Xu. He ruled for 22 years and made some achievements in political, military, economic, cultural and diplomatic fields.

Changling is located at the foot of Tianshoushan Mountain and is the first and the largest of the Ming Tombs. The tomb was constructed in 1409 and completed in 1427. It took almost 18 years.

In architectural design, it is square in the front and round in the rear, and is divided into three courtyards. The main buildings on the central axis are still standing.

Ling'en Hall, or the Hall of Eminent Favour, is grand and magnificent. It is 66. 67 metres long from east to west and 19. 31 metres wide from north to south. It is supported by 32 gigantic columns of *nanmu*, a kind of cedar. The four columns in the middle are the biggest, 1. 17 metres in diameter and 14. 3 metres in height. Each is made of a whole trunk. This kind of valuable timber came from southwest China. The hall was used by later emperors for offering sacrifices to their ancestors.

According to historical records, 16 imperial concubines were buried alive with the third Ming emperor, as imperial concubines were not allowed to be buried in the tomb of the emperor, various tomb grounds known as "pits" were built on either side of Changling. They were called pits because they were vertical shafts without horizontal tunnels.

Human sacrifice was a common practice in the slaveowning society. From the Qin and Han dynasties onwards, wooden or earthen human figures were used instead, like the ones in Dingling. The first Ming emperor restored the old system. Those buried alive were granted honorable titles and their family members were usually assigned official posts.

This practice came to an end when the sixth Ming emperor made an edict in mid 15th century to abolish the system of human sacrifice.

A bronze seated statue of Zhu Di, the third emperor of the Ming Dynasty, was designed by Miao Xintian, a sculptor in Shanxi Province and manufactured by the Dalian Daqing Metal Company Ltd., was placed in Changling Tomb. The statue is 2. 75 metres long, 3. 18 metres wide, and the total height is 4. 08 metres, weighing 5. 6 tons. A ceremony for placing the statue was held in Changling Tomb on September 18, 1999.

Stone Tortoise Bearing Inscribed Stele 海兽驮碑

The stone tablets along the passage to the ancient tombs are usually composed of three parts: the top, the body and the base. The one erected in front of the tomb is imposing. The crown of the tablet is perfectly round, free from any edges and corners and decorated with a pair of coiling dragons. On the top of the tablet is chiseled a hole, through which was slung a rope holding a coffin when it was being lowered into the grave (a practice in ancient times in which normally two tablets were used). The base of the tablet is the form of a tortoise with its head lifted high. This tortoise is said to be the ninth son of the dragon, named *bixi*. Strong and powerful, it could carry heavy loads over long distances. This tortoise was first made by Emperor Yu, reputed founder of the Xia Dynasty (2070 BC-1600 BC) to bear on its back a stone tablet with inscriptions in praise of his merits and achievements in harnessing the rivers prevent to floods. This practice was handed down from generation to generation.

Super-sized Charm

A huge *bixi*, which was used in ancient times to drive away evil spirits and demons, was unearthed in 2000 in Zhengding County of Hebei Province. The relic, 8. 4 metres long, 3. 2 metres wide and 2. 6 metres high, and weighing 107 tons, is at least 1, 000 years old. The discovery of the relic is of great importance to the study of cultural heritage in ancient China.

Tortoise: from Totem to Evil Thing

For quite a long time, the tortoise was reckoned as a sacred animal, which came from the supernatural domain and could bring people good fortune. The worship of tortoises originated thousands of years ago and formed a special "tortoise culture" in ancient China. This permeated social life, in the fields of the economy, political, military affairs, astronomy, geography, mathematics, medicine, ideology and customs. Much earlier than human beings appeared on the earth, tortoises were already in existence. Primitive men appeared so weak and fragile in the face of serious diseases, lack of food and shelter and treacherous weather before they became civilized. They could not understand the reason for certain natural phenomena, such as thunder, wind, rain, and lightning and death. Nor could they know how to deal with the harsh natural environment. In their eyes, all these phenomena were produced by immortals. Therefore, the worship of nature, animals and vegetation, ghosts, ancestors and totems were all very popular at that time. The tortoise was one of the common animals used as a totem by primitive tribes. There is a widely shared belief that all Chinese people are descendants of the legendary Huangdi Emperor of the prehistoric period. According to historical records, the tortoise was the totem of the tribe he ruled. And the emperor himself was said to be the incarnation of a big tortoise sent to earth from heaven. Chinese ancestors held a deep respect for tortoises. The body of a tortoise was considered as a small but precise resemblance of the universe. Ancient Chinese believed that through careful study of a tortoise, its shell in particular, they could possibly tell certain mysteries of nature and foresee the future. They used tortoises to practice divination in peace or in war. Pre-historic tales that have been handed down through many generations say that the tortoise played an important role in human life. For instance, tortoises were said to have helped Cangji, a legendary figure, invented the first Chinese characters and helped Dayu (Yu the Great), a king in folk tales, harness the floods. The worship of the tortoise also involved fertility symbols. The tortoise earned a niche on a family's incense burner table—where people put offerings for ancestors and gods since the Han Dynasty (206 BC-AD 220)—as it resembled the male sex organ and suggested fertility. At first, people worshipped tortoises in the hope that it might do good in their daily life and that of their offspring. Further people hoped that the tortoise could bring the whole family blessings and could prevent them from any illnesses, disasters or misfortunes. Ancient people also hoped that the worship of the tortoise might secure them a long life and bring them opportunities to make big money or achieve great success in the political arena. The tortoise was worshipped as the God of Wealth for quite a long time before it was replaced by General Zhao Gongming, another figure in folk tales, who changed the fortunes of families. Among the Han people, the tortoise was once depicted as sacred animal, which often helped people who got lost, kept evil and ghosts from people, or even in some folk tales, brought the dead back to life. In order to add to the atmosphere, daily articles including pots, lamps and paper cuttings featuring the shape of tortoises were widely used on festive occasions such as wedding ceremonies, parties to celebrate new babies or when officials were promoted.

In ancient China, people laid great importance upon the geomantic features of the location where they were to build their residential complexes. If the residents wanted to lead a peaceful and happy life, their houses should always be constructed with their backs to the north; the god of that direction was Xuanwu, meaning "the Black Warrior—the guardian spirit of the north in Taoism." The other three directions—east, south and west—were said to be ruled respectively by the gods Qinglong (the Green Dragon—the guardian spirit of the east in Taoism), Zhuque (the Scarlet Bird—

the guardian spirit of the south in Taoism), and Baihu (the White Tiger—the guardian spirit of the west in Taoism). Ancient people also held that Xuanwu (the Black Warrior) was in charge of the weather. The Taoists preached the idea and temples to Xuanwu were built across the nation.· People prayed, presented sacrifices to the god and asked for his blessing. The connotations and extension of tortoise worship in ancient China evolved as times changed. Ancient people worshipped the tortoise for the sake of longevity and the way of life of the animal was even seen as a lofty moral principle. Intellectuals considered it a model for them to follow as how to conduct themselves in society. The tortoise also played a part in deci-sion-making process of the rulers of ancient China.

According to historical materials, a special tortoise hall called " *gui gong*" was created in the royal palace and an official was assigned to take care of divination practices during the Zhou Dynasty (1046 BC-221 BC). The official, who was called " *gui ren,* " could accompany the kings or em-perors and had immediate influence upon them in making important deci-sions. While in the Han Dynasty (206 BC-AD 220), tortoise enjoyed the same respect as the ancestors of the emperors. Seen as an embodiment of the spirit of the ancestors, it was put alongside the memorial tablets of the emperors' ancestors in the royal memorial hall.

In the Tang Dynasty (618-907), the worship of the tortoise by the royal court came to its climax. At that time, the tortoise was vested with enor-mous functions in the country's political life. Before the Tang Dynasty, the generals got " *hu fu,* " a tiger-shaped tally from the emperor as the im-perial authorization for troop deployment. But the Tang emperors changed the tally into a tortoise-shaped one. The Tang garrisons at its remote fron-tiers, once called " *du hu fu*" were call " *gui lin fu*" which literally meant "regions guarded by powerful tortoise. " The Tang imperial court stipulated that some officers and officials with unusual merits were entitled to pin a decorative tortoise made of jade or metal on the breast as a sign of glory. After their death, their tombstones could be constructed with a huge stone tortoise underneath as the pedestal. Song Dynasty (960-1279) witnessed the popular worship of the tortoise. The tortoise was often a subject of lit-erary works in the Song Dynasty as it was a symbol of longevity, wisdom, noble character and sterling integrity in everyone's eyes. The tortoise was adored as a symbol for mild-temper, patience, intelligence and great strength. Before each battle, the armies on both sides would practice div-ination with the shell of a tortoise and the generals would pray for the blessing and protection of the tortoise. Each troop had a flag with the pic-ture of a tortoise. Many military equipment in some way bore the shape of a tortoise such as the shield, the helmet, the armour. The were robes of the ordinary soldiers were embroidered with black lines similar to those on the shell of a tortoise. As a sign of good omen, the word "*gui*" (tortoise) and the image of the tortoise were used in many ways. Places, rivers, lakes and mountains were for a time named with the Chinese character "*gui*" (tortoise). These areas were worshipped and visited as great attractions. Even today, there are 24 mountains in China named after the word "*gui*." Between the Qin(221 BC-206 BC) and the Northern Wei (AD 386-AD 534) dynasties, some feudal emperors named the years under their reign with the word "*gui*." "*Gui*" was also a favourite word used in the names of many prestigious literary and political figures in the Han, Tang and Song dynasties. For a long time, things sacred and precious were named with the word "*gui*." In the Tang Dynasty, the ceremonies to offer sacrifices to ancestors were called "*gui ji*." The wine bowls used in the ceremonies were called "*gui he*." The tripod ding in the royal palace, which symbolized the supreme power of the Emperor was called "*gui ding*." Many things featured the shape of a tortoise, from the handle of the official seals to oil lamps, candlesticks and tea pots. People who led a healthy and long life had a "*gui ling*" which meant "living as long as a sacred tortoise." The age-old bronze mirrors (*jian*) were called "*gui jian*." Mathematical methods were called "*gui suan*." Old coins were called "*gui bei*." Books used in divine activities were called "*gui jing*." In ancient China, Confucianism, Taoism and Buddhism had close ties with tortoise worship.

Tortoises were classified into 10 categories and praised for their virtues. Famous Confucian scholars before the Song Dynasty were all pious worshippers of tortoises. In today's residential complex, temples and tombs of the Confucian family in Qufu, Shandong Province, all the numerous stone tablets were constructed on tortoise-shaped pedestals. Taoists developed a special set of breathing exercises, like the popular *qigong*, which imitates the acts of the tortoise. Content about tortoises is an important part of the Taoist classic "*Bao Pu Zi*." According to the Buddhist scriptures, those who are practicing Buddhism should learn from the tortoise—should stand aloof from worldly strife and give way to avoid trouble, just as the tortoises seemed to be doing to survive in the wild. Traditionally, Chinese cooks used to make dishes with sea cucumbers, snakes, shark's fin, turtles... But no dishes were made with tortoise, according to historical records, though the slow-moving amphibian are easy to capture. Nor are dishes made with the meat of tortoise to be found in cookery books of traditional Chinese dishes. On the contrary, there are plenty of stories, folk tales preaching that people let tortoises go when they were angling, or released tortoises caught by mistake, or bought tortoises from the catcher's hands and set them free. Some tales tell that kind-hearted people who helped tortoises in danger were rewarded while those who harmed tortoises were punished.

Unfortunately, the status of the tortoise began to decline quickly after the late Southern Song (1127-1279) and the Yuan (1279-1368) dynasties. The Mongolian nomads loved birds with colorful plumage, which flew freely in the sky. The tortoise was never mentioned in ancient Mongolian historical records. Nor was it a major character in Mongolian folk tales. In the Yuan Dynasty tortoise's worship declined. The tortoise was no longer used in royal ritual activities, political life, military affairs or in common people's houses as decorations. The tortoise was reduced to something evil in the Yuan Dynasty.

The Han rulers of the Ming Dynasty (1368-1644) did not restore the custom of tortoise worship. Instead, they followed the convention of the Mongolian rulers of the Yuan Dynasty. As a result, tortoise worship was totally terminated in the Ming Dynasty. According to the Ming custom, if a wife was not loyal to her husband and had an affair, her husband was called by name as a "tortoise." Since then tortoise has become a synonym for someone who tolerates his wife having inappropriate relationships. And the word "*gui*" tortoise was also used as curse equal to "bastard."

Golf Course 高尔夫球场

This is the first golf course in Beijing. It was built and put into operation in 1986. It was founded by the Japan Golf Promotion Inc. and is now run jointly with Changping's Foreign Trade Company.

The course covers an area of one million square meters. It's part of the city's plans to turn the area into a modern tourist resort. It should partially appease those who have complained about a shortage of amusement centers in the capital.

The 18-hole course cost about 30 million yuan and was used for the Asian Games in 1990.

Submerged Palace 水下宫殿

Construction of an underwater amusement palace started in April 1985 in the Ming Tombs Reservoir. The Palace of the Dragon King was built ten meters under the surface of the reservoir. It was completed in September 1986. The project cost US$ 33 million.

A contract to build the project was signed in February 1985 between the Ming Tombs Reservoir Development Company and the Japan China Development Company Ltd. of Japan.

The Ming Tombs Recreation Centre also includes a 350-room hotel as well as shops and cafes.

Dragon Boat Race

The dragon boat race is a popular folk sport for Chinese people living alongside rivers, lakes and reservoirs. The earliest dragon boat race emerged in the mid-stage of the Warring States Period (475 BC-221 BC), according to the ancient document "Tales of Mu Tianzi Heavenly Son." The race was later associated with Qu Yuan (c. 340-c. 278 BC), the great ancient Chinese poet and minister of the Chu Kingdom during the Warring States Period. Qu Yuan cherished his state and the Chu people. But the fatuous king and other corrupt ministers prevented Qu Yuan from fulfilling his social ideals. When the invading Qin army captured Chu capital Ying, Qu Yuan, in despair, drowned himself in the Miluo River, a tributary of the Yangtze River on Lunar May 5, later known as Duanwu Festival or Dragon Boat Festival. Since then, to commemorate the death of the patriotic poet, every year people living in the Yangtze River Valley hold dragon boat race and eat *zongzi*, a pyramid-shaped dumpling made of glutinous rice wrapped in reed leaves (eaten during the Dragon Boat Festival), on the day when Qu Yuan was dead. Nowadays, the dragon boat race has spread to other areas outside the Yangtze River Valley. People in the Pearl River Delta, in South China's Guangdong Province, also hold an annual dragon boat race but add some local flavor to the folk sport form.

Usually, the dragon boats, made of wood, are buried in mud all the year round and are only taken out for use for the Dragon Boat Festival, according to the local people. Every rural village along the Pearl River has at least four to five dragon boats. The red-painted dragon boats, however, are usually 1. 5 metres wide and 40 metres long with 42 racers on board. Among them, 19 pairs work as oarsmen, one man at the prow shouts slogans to synchronize the oarsmen's pace, one holds the team flag, one beats a big drum and one man at the stern operates the rudder. Neighbouring villagers take turns hosting the race every year. The host village offers a feast for the guest racers and their families along the riverbank. Audiences watch on the banks or in small boats moored to the banks, blowing buglers, beating gongs and cheering for their team. The winning teams take home a roasted pig—a symbol of youth and strength—as prize.

Ming Tombs Area Modernized 明十三陵区进行改造

Beijing decided to expand the Ming Tombs area into a modernized tourist resort while maintaining the ancient relics and historic treasures in the area. This was approved by the municipal government. The project includes renovation of relics, measures to protect the environment, and establishment of parks, hotels, and entertainment centers. In the project, the whole area has been divided into four parts: tombs area, reservoir area, transitional area, and transport.

The 800-metre-long road (the Sacred Road) leading to the Dragon and Phoenix Gate are turned into a stone pavement while cars and buses are replaced by Ming Dynasty style horse drawn carriages.

New constructions in the area also include a museum, a golf course, a conservatory, an amusement centre, clubs, swimming pools, camping and picnic areas, fishing wharf by the side of the reservoir, caves, hotels, and Mongolian yurts. An aquarium was built completely of glass.

Other tourist facilities are special regions for skiing, shooting, horse racing and archery. A fountain about 200 metres high has been completed.

To ease the traffic to the area, minibuses are available, the main road has been improved and a highway from the city to the tombs has been built.

Friendship Forest 友谊林

The Friendship Forest near the Ming Tombs was designed in 1984, following a suggestion by some foreign residents in Beijing that they should plant trees as a sign of friendship as a contribution to China's nation-wide afforestation drive.

It covers an area of 133 hectares (332.5 acres). Up to 2001, more than 7,000 foreigners, including diplomats, experts, students and businessmen had planted pines and cypresses there. Mr Yuan Xiaoyuan, a member of the Chinese People's Political Consultative Conference who returned from the United States in 1985 donated 20,000 yuan for the Friendship Forest. The Friendship Forest was completed in 1988.

Zhaoling Tomb 昭陵

Zhaoling Tomb, the ninth of the 13 Ming Tombs in Beijing's Changping District, was restored and opened to the public on November 1, 1989. This is the third Ming tomb to have been restored in the Imperial Ming Tombs Valley. The other two tombs are Dingling and Changling which were opened to the public in the late 1960.

The restoration of the tomb by the Beijing Cultural Relics Bureau started in 1985 and it was completed in October 1989. The tomb was built in the 16th century. Damaged in wars and eroded by 400 years of wind and rain, most of the above ground structures of the tomb have been destroyed or fallen into disrepair. The restoration of the main buildings of Zhaoling— Ling'en (Eminent Favour) Hall and Ling'en (Eminent Favour) Gate—required a large quantity of 12 to 14 metres long and one-metre-diametre giant logs for their columns and cross beams.

However, these large-sized logs were not available in China.

Learning of this particular requirement, ITT Rayonier, a subsidiary of ITT Corporation of the United States offered to donate lumber to the restoration. Today, 144 Douglas fir and hemlock trees more than 300 years old from the Pacific coast of the United States were used for the project. The Wood Import and Export Company of the China National Native Produce and Animal By-products Import and Export Corporation offered to transport those "friendship logs" free of charge.

To honour the generous contributions to the Zhaoling restoration project by ITT Rayonier and China TUHSU, the Beijing Cultural Relics Bureau and the Imperial Ming Tombs Special Zone Office have erected a monument facing the tomb to commemorate the friendship between the peoples of China and the United States.

The Zhaoling Tomb was built for Emperor Longqing who was enthroned in 1567 and died in 1572. The emperor and three empresses were buried here.

The Thirteen Imperial Tombs of the Ming Dynasty

Tomb	Emperor	Reign Title	Reign Period
Changling	Zhu Di	Yongle 永乐	1403-1424
Xianling	Zhu Gaochi	Hongxi 洪熙	1425
Jingling	Zhu Zhanji	Xuande 宣德	1426-1435
Yuling	Zhu Qizhen	Zhengtong 正统	1436-1449
(resumed)		Tianshun 天顺	1457-1464
Maoling	Zhu Jianshen	Chenghua 成化	1465-1487
Tailing	Zhu Youcheng	Hongzhi 弘治	1488-1505
Kangling	Zhu Houzhao	Zhengde 正德	1506-1521
Yongling	Zhu Houzong	Jiajing 嘉靖	1522-1566
Zhaoling	Zhu Zaihou	Longqing 隆庆	1567-1572
Dingling	Zhu Yijun	Wanli 万历	1573-1620
Qingling	Zhu Changluo	Taichang 泰昌	1620 (29 days)
Deling	Zhu Youxiao	Tianqi 天启	1621-1627
Siling	Zhu Youjian	Chongzhen 崇祯	1628-1644

Note:

1. The cruel practice of burying the living with the dead was carried out in the first three Ming tombs, the Changling (Emperor Zhu Di's tomb), the Xianling (Emperor Zhu Gaochi's tomb) and the Jingling (Zhu Zhanji's tomb). The emperors' concubines and female attendants were first forced to commit suicide, then buried in a brick pit called "well." The East and West wells can still be seen in the tombs area. This practice did not end until the death of Zhu Qizhen, the 6th emperor, who left instructions for its abolition.

2. Zhu Qiyu (the 7th emperor of the Ming Dynasty), who reigned between 1450 and 1456 when his brother Zhu Qizhen was a prisoner of war, was deposed and later buried at Jin Hill on the western outskirts of Beijing. The other 13 Ming emperors from Zhu Di to Zhu Youjian were all entombed at the foot of Tianshou (Heaven and Longevity) Mountain.

Beijing Zoo
北 京 动 物 园

Beijing Zoo was built in 1906 and opened to the public in 1908 with an area of about 10 hectares and a few humble pavilions to house the animals. At that time only several dozens of species were shown, such as lions, tigers, leopards and monkeys. Now Beijing Zoo covers an area of 90 hectares (222.4 acres). The animal houses and enclosures, with a total floor space of 40,000 square metres, include those for pandas, elephants, brown and polar bears, tigers, hippopotami, rhinoceros, antelopes, giraffes and reptiles. The zoo currently houses more than 5,500 animals from over 650 species. Among them are giant pandas, golden monkeys, addaxes, tigers from Northeast China, elks, yaks, precious birds and gold fish. Also on show are rare animals from various continents, such as hippopotami, zebras, giraffes, chimpanzees, lions and antelopes from Africa, parrots from South America, birds and kangaroos from Australia, polar bears from the Arctic, bisons from Europe and Asian apes.

Beijing Zoo is China's largest treasure house of animals and birds and has become one of the ten biggest zoos in the world.

Giant Panda 大熊猫

One of the most famous mammals in the world, the giant panda is meek and looks like a bear. With the exception of its shoulders, its limbs and the rims of its ears and eyes, which are black, this lovable animal is white

315

all over. Statistics show that China now has only approximately 1, 000 giant pandas living in the wild, in some remote mountain areas of Sichuan, Gansu and Shaanxi provinces.

The animal has long been a symbol of the world's wildlife protection effort. According to a plan developed by China's Ministry of Forestry, 28 giant panda reserves will be established in China by 2010.

Zoological research has proved that giant panda came into existence 600, 000 to 700, 000 years ago. Subsequent drastic changes in the climate resulted in deforestation, which threatened its existence. The panda used to be a ferocious carnivore, but with environmental changes, it gradually became accustomed to a diet of mainly bamboo. As its natural habitation shrank, its numbers decreased, and the panda itself became docile.

To protect this rare animal, the Chinese Government has devoted major efforts to protecting giant pandas, building 25 nature reserves for them scattered across more than 30 counties in China's Sichuan, Gansu and Shaanxi provinces.

In 1955, giant pandas were exhibited in Beijing Zoo. In 1978, by artificial insemination, the female giant panda Juanjuan gave birth to twins, one of which survived. Chinese pandas now symbolize the friendship between the Chinese people and the people of other countries. They have been sent to the Democratic People's Republic of Korea, Japan, the United States, France, Britain, Germany, Spain, Mexico and other countries.

Giant pandas live in humid and dense bamboo groves in mountainous areas at altitudes ranging from 2, 000 to 4, 000 metres. They are afraid of living in extreme weather conditions and make their lairs in tree holes or mountain caves. They seldom live in groups and eat bamboo leaves, sprouts and shoots. They mostly mate in April and May and give birth in autumn, with one or two cubs in each litter and occasionally three.

China has established 33 giant panda protection zones, encompassing 17, 000 square kilometres (6, 562 square miles). Currently, China has more than 1, 100 nature reserves, representing 12. 4 per cent of its total land area. According to government plans, China should be able to boast 1, 800 nature reserves by 2010, covering 155 million hectares (383 million acres) in area, or 16. 14 per cent of China's total land area.

Volkswagon Supports Panda Research Centre

An advanced Panda Research Centre, a centre devoted to the conservation of giant pandas through scientific research and breeding was established at Beijing Zoo backed with funding from Volkswagon AG. On October 4, 1999, Ursula Piech, on behalf of her husband Dr Ferdinand Piech, chairman of the Management Board of Volkswagon AG, handed over a check worth US$492, 000 to Zong Ying, director of Beijing Zoo. Ursula Piech said that the panda is recognized globally as the mascot of China. However, the total number of pandas, which are threatened to the verge of extinction is about 1, 000 across the world. The funds from Volkswagon are used to construct research buildings and purchase much-needed research equipment. Volkswagon provided the Panda Research Centre with great support. At present, research conditions and equipment are upgraded substantially to conduct more research.

There are about 20 research staff members in the centre, most of them are zoologists and behaviourists. These full-time research fellows are devoted to basic science and applied basic science in panda research. In 1999, there were 17 pandas at Beijing Zoo, which made research more viable for the Panda Research Centre. The first research centre specializing in panda study was established in Chengdu, capital of Sichuan Province in 1987. In Beijing, a group of researchers of National Animal Research Centre (NARC) have been researching pandas since the centre was set up in 1985. The centre has achieved outstanding results in its previous panda research, especially in propagation, production of nutrient feed and breeding. In 1992, the centre succeeded in a trial to produce a full artificially bred panda. The newborn panda was raised by raisers and researchers. China heads panda research in the world. For instance, artificial insemination and propagation were successfully conducted by Chinese scientists in 1978. A breakthrough was made in the field of cloning technology in 1997. However, China's panda research faces many difficulties nowadays. It especially suffers from shortage of funds, outdated techniques and a drain on researchers. We try our best to gain financial and technological support from foreign countries.

United Parcel Service (UPS) offers help in panda delivery

317

The specially-equipped aircraft "UPS Panda Express" from the United Parcel Service (UPS) airlifted a pair of giant pandas — "Jiu Jiu" and "Hua Hua" from Beijing to Atlanta, Georgia in the United States on November 5, 1999. This is the first time since 1996 that giant pandas have arrived in the United States. With its speedy, reliable services and global reach network, UPS has established a solid, international reputation as a top parcel service company.

UPS will also donate US$ 625, 000 to Zoo Atlanta over the next five years for the scientific research of panda breeding, which will greatly contribute to the plight of the rare species.

To assist its panda delivery, UPS also launched a panda-packed web site at www. pandaexpress. ups. com. Visitors to the site will find background information of the pandas, the most recent news of the shipment as well as a number of photos and pictures.

Giant Pandas

To save the precious animals, the Ministry of Forestry is pushing for the construction of 17 "biological corridors" connecting existing habitats and reserves, as part of the Giant Panda and its habitat Conservation Project. Only about 1, 000 giant pandas remain scattered in the wild across vast areas of Shaanxi, Gansu and Sichuan provinces. They are separated in reserves or isolated groups which accommodate anywhere from just a few up to 100 pandas. The biological corridors, which will be forest runs about 2 kilometres wide between two areas of natural habitat or between a habitat and a reserve, will conceal the pandas from roads and villages and enable different groups of pandas to meet. According to the overall protection plan for giant pandas, ratified in 1993, the ministry has improved the 13 existing reserves and set up another 14. It took a total of more than 200 million yuan (US$24. 1 million) to complete the whole project from 1993 to 2002, 40 per cent of which were supplied by the State and the rest by domestic and international organizations. In a long-term Sino-US co-operation program, China will use the annual US$ 1. 2 million fund provided by a group of US zoos to construct more panda reserves and the biological corridors. In return, the US San Diego Zoo will conduct reproduction research on two Chinese pandas. Experts said that international co-operation in research on the breeding of endangered species including the giant panda is of great significance. A giant-panda breeding centre in the Wolong Reserve, Sichuan Province, currently has 20 wild pandas taken from different areas inhabited by the giant pandas. These pandas cannot be returned to the wild after being rescued and artificially fed. But they should enable the centre to breed "genetically perfect" pandas. They have been sporadic recent reports of baby pandas being seen in the wild. This suggests that reproduction is taking shape after the catastrophe in the 1980s when arrow bamboo, pandas' staple food, blossomed and thus became inedible. The estimate of 1, 000 pandas in the wild shows that the animals have made their first step out of the shadow of extinction.

Zoo Aquarium. A million-dollar plate of glass made in the United States was delivered to Beijing Zoo in early April 1997, to be installed in the Beijing Aquarium as the second largest aquarium panel in the world. The 10-metre-long, 6-metre-high, and 23-ton-weight glass wall is second in size only to one installed in an aquarium in San Francisco, in the United

States. The 16-metre-long and 5.5-metre-high window was designed for the shark pool. Made of acrylic, the windows are superior to glass in transparency and solidity. Although the glass is 22 centimetres thick, its transparency is 99 per cent. The aquarium, occupying an area of 35,000 square metres in the Beijing Zoo, cost US$ 56 million. The project was co-sponsored by the Beijing Zoo and Pexlanda International Ltd of Hong Kong. It went into operation in early 1998.

Pandas Arrive at New US Home

Two giant panda cubs, Mei Xiang and Tian Tian, from Southwest China's Sichuan Province, arrived safely in the US capital of Washington on December 6, 2000 on route to their new home at the Washington National Zoo. The newly arrivals are Tian Tian, a three-and-a-half-year-old male whose name means more and more, weighing in at 80 kilograms. The other is Mei Xiang, a two-and-a-half-year-old female whose name means beautiful fragrance. She weighs 50 kilograms. The duo arrived at what will be their new home for the next 10 years in excellent health.

US delivery company FedEx sent a MD-11 jet named "Panda One" to Chengdu, capital of Sichuan Province, to collect the animals. After arriving at Washington airport, the two pandas were then delivered by vehicle to the zoo. Visitors will be able to see them from January 2001. The zoo has spent US$ 8 million on building the pandas' house and a 10-person team is responsible for their daily welfare. The two pandas join five others of their species in the United States, three of which are at the San Diego Zoo and two at the Atlanta Zoo. The pandas, both born at the Wolong Giant Panda Reserve, are on loan to the Washington National Zoo for scientific research following an agreement between the China Wildlife Conservation Association and the US Zoo.

Chinese and American scientists are working together to develop an international breeding programme to protect the endangered species.

Blood Atlas was completed

China's first panda blood atlas was completed recently in Beijing. Experts say the atlas will be of great help in the study and protection of pandas. With the help of a microscopic analyzer that can magnify things 20,000 times their actual size, two cytologists from Chinese medical Sciences University created the atlas after conducting a long-term study of the blood cells and monocytes of healthy pandas at Beijing Zoo. People can now quickly find out whether a panda is ill or what diseases it is suffering from, by comparing it with the atlas in terms of shape, number and colour of cells in a tiny drop of blood, according to the experts. In addition to pandas, they have so far created blood atlases for more than 40 of the endangered wild animals including Siberian tigers and golden-hair monkeys.

Leaving Giant Panda on Its Own

China's endangered animal, the giant panda has a better chance of survival if left to breed on its own in the wild, without intervention from high-tech science. Pan Wenshi, China's most famous giant panda specialist and a professor from Peking University said that the giant panda possesses normal reproductive capabilities and does not need cloning. There are about 1, 000 pandas living in the wild, most of which live on the mountains in West and Southwest China. Most animal experts believe that the species faces extinction because of the animals' poor reproductive capabilities. However, Pan Wenshi, who has led research teams to track down giant pandas in the Qinling Ranges in West China for 13 years, said that the animals could increase their population without any help from mankind. The shrinking distribution of the giant panda and a drop in the number of the endangered animals that has occurred since the mid-20th century are just a short-term evolution of giant pandas. According to Professor Pan, over the past 10 years, the population of the giant pandas has been increased at an annual rate of 4. 1 per cent—even higher than that of human beings! Pan Wenshi's team has also discovered that DNA diversity of the giant pandas in the Qinling Ranges has not been degraded due to inbreeding, which is common among the species. Professor Pan Wenshi, has been engaged in scientific research and field inspections into wildlife including giant panda and white-headed leaf monkey, and has won numerous awards and recognition for his work in wildlife protection. He is a recipient of the Paul Getty Prize, the highest prize given by the World Wildlife Fund. Professor Pan and other researchers of his team have put radio collars on giant pandas to help gather information about their habitats, frequency of activities, seasonal migration, mating and food gathering habits. They have also conducted ground investigations and studied behavior patterns with the help of satellite remote sensing. Pan Wenshi attributed the shrinking population to increased human activities. Professor Pan's theory about the long-term survival of giant pandas is echoed by Zhang Hemin, head of the China Giant Pandas Protection Centre at Wolong, Sichuan Province, and Zhang Guiquan, another giant panda researcher with the same centre. Both Zhangs have said the impact of human beings on nature is the main cause of the decline of the giant panda.

320

Beijing Aquarium 北京海洋馆

On October 17, 1993, the Beijing Zoo and Hong Kong Pexlanda International Ltd. signed a contract to build a modern aquarium in the capital.

Covering an area of 35, 000 square metres, with a floor space of 42, 000 square metres, the Beijing Aquarium is the largest underwater world of its kind in an inland city in China. More than 50, 000 fish of 1, 300 varieties are displayed. The aquarium also houses sea lions, dolphins and whales. Located in the zoo, the aquarium includes an invertebrate aquarium, a shark aquarium and a tank to display marine life from the South China Sea and Pacific Ocean. In the ocean theatre, the visitor can see sea animals perform. The complex also includes an audio-visual room, information room, reading room and workshop where seawater will be produced. The aim of investing in the aquarium is to let more people, especially youngsters and children, benefit from it, and offer a place for research and surveying sea animals.

The total investment was nearly US$ 100 million. The Hong Kong company helped to build the aquarium within four years from 1996 to 1999 and was officially opened to the public on September 28, 1999.

Beihai Park
北 海 公 园

Beihai(North Sea) Park is one of the most popular parks in the city of Beijing. It encompasses over 68 hectares (168 acres), more than half of it is taken up by the lake (area of the surface of the water is 380, 100 square metres). Early in the 10th century, the Liao Dynasty built a secondary imperial residence here, called Yaoyu or Jade Islet. When the Jin took over, they renamed the capital Zhongdu, meaning Central Capital, and built an imperial palace. Qionghua (Jade Flowery) Islet was built of earth dug out from the lake, and the rocks used for piling on the hill were brought from Kaifeng, Henan Province.

During the Yuan Dynasty, the place was rebuilt three times, and Guanghandian or the Palace in the Moon where Kublai Khan used to live and many other palace buildings were built on top of the hill. It was in this palace that Kublai Khan received Marco Polo. Unfortunately it was destroyed. The Islet became the center of Dadu (Great Capital) and is still situated in the heart of modern Beijing. The Ming Dynasty saw more construction and renovation: the Five-Dragon Pavilions and the Nine-Dragon Screen on the north bank of the lake and many pavilions and galleries were erected during that period. From the White Dagoba, visitors can have an excellent view of the Five-Dragon Pavilions standing on the opposite bank of the lake, with colourful ferry boats travelling back and forth between the

321

shores. During the reign of Emperor Qianlong, construction lasted for 30 years. The project included many other pavilions, halls and terraces which made the park even more harmonious in design.

The layout of the park is based on an ancient Chinese legend. According to the legend, there were supposed to be three islands to the east of Bohai Bay where the gods lived. One of them was called Penglai Island where a kind of herbal medicine grew, that was supposed to prolong life. The first emperor of the Qin Dynasty wanted to live forever. He sent people to the islands to look for the longevity medicine, but failed. Emperor Wudi of the Han Dynasty also wanted to live an eternal life. He ordered that a big pool

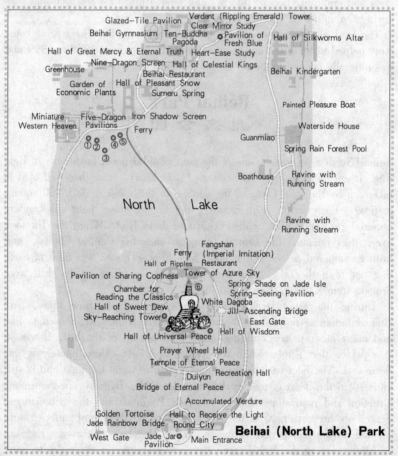

322

Glazed-Tile Pavilion   Verdant (Rippling Emerald) Tower
                       Clear Mirror Study
Beihai Gymnasium Ten-Buddha   Pavilion of
                  Pagoda   Fresh Blue   Hall of Silkworms Altar
Hall of Great Mercy & Eternal Truth Heart-Ease Study
          Nine-Dragon Screen Hall of Celestial Kings
Greenhouse   Beihai Kindergarten
              Beihai Restaurant
Garden of   Hall of Pleasant Snow
Economic Plants   Sumeru Spring
                                              Painted Pleasure Boat
Miniature   Five-Dragon Iron Shadow Screen
Western Heaven Pavilions   Waterside House
                      Ferry
                ① ② ⑤   Guanmiao   Spring Rain Forest Pool
                ③ ④
                ③   Boathouse   Ravine with
                                               Running Stream

North   Lake   Ravine with
                                   Running Stream

                    Fangshan
              Ferry (Imperial Imitation)
          Hall of Ripples Restaurant
Pavilion of Sharing Coolness Tower of Azure Sky
       Chamber for   ⑥   Spring Shade on Jade Isle
Reading the Classics   White Dagoba Spring-Seeing Pavilion
  Hall of Sweet Dew   Jill-Ascending Bridge
Sky-Reaching Tower   East Gate
              Hall of Universal Peace Hall of Wisdom
           Prayer Wheel Hall
         Temple of Eternal Peace
              Duiyun Recreation Hall
       Bridge of Eternal Peace
                   Accumulated Verdure
       Golden Tortoise   Hall to Receive the Light
  Jade Rainbow Bridge   Round City
    West Gate   Jade Jar   Main Entrance
               Pavilion

Beihai (North Lake) Park

①Floating Emerald Pavilion ②Surging Good Fortune Pavilion ③Pavilion of Dragons' Benevolence
④Auspicious Clarity Pavilion ⑤Fragrance Pavilion ⑥Hall of Historic Site

be dug at the back of his palace, complete with three artificial hills to represent Panglai and the other islands. So these legendary hills were built in the eastern capital of Luoyang during the Sui Dynasty and also in the Tang Dynasty capital of Chang'an (today's Xi'an). Such a traditional style of gardening was followed during the succeeding dynasties and Beihai Park was built after this traditional style.

In summer, Beihai Park is an ideal place to go to escape from the blazing summer heat. Tourists can paddle around in a bizarre assortment of boats. There are odd, duck-shaped paddle boats, and two types of motor boats: three-seated regular and one-person UFOs (you have to see it to understand). In winter, the lake freezes over and Beihai Park turns into a huge skating rink.

White Dagoba 白塔

Towering at the top of Qionghua Islet, the White Dagoba was built in 1651 on the former site of the Palace in the Moon. At the suggestion of a famous Tibetan lama priest named Momhan, Emperor Shunzhi, first emperor of the Qing Dynasty agreed to the suggestion as a gesture of devotion to the Buddhist belief and a desire for unification among China's various nationalities. The dagoba was damaged in an earthquake and reconstructed on two occasions. It stands 35.9 metres high, resting on a square base built of huge stone slabs, and is topped by two bronze parasols, with 14 bronze bells hanging around them. It resembles a huge umbrella resting on a densely-wooded island. Since it was the highest point in old Beijing, it served as a vantage point of military significance.

The Bridge of Eternal Peace was built in the 13th century in the early part of the Yuan Dynasty.

Beihai (North Sea) 北海

323

The lake is called Beihai in Chinese, meaning "north sea." J It is 68 hectares in area, with an average depth of 2 metres. The water comes from the Jade Spring Hill and Yongding River, northwest of the city. Boating and fishing are popular here in spring, summer and autumn, and people come here to skate in winter.

Jade Islet Spring Shade 琼岛春阴

On the eastern side of the Islet stands a tablet known as the Jade Islet Spring Shade, one of the eight beautiful scenes in ancient Beijing. The others are Yuquan Baotu 玉泉趵突 (Leopard Leaping Fountain of Yuquan), Taiye Qiufeng 太液秋风 (Autumn Wind of Taiye), Jimen

Yanshu 蓟门烟树 (Fog Tree of Jimen), Xishan Qingxue 西山晴雪 (Sunny or Snowy Days of Western Hills), Lugou Xiaoyue 卢沟晓月 (Morning Moon over Lugou Bridge), Jintai Xizhao 金台夕照 (Sunset of Jintai) and Juyong Diecui 居庸叠翠 (Layers of Green Mounts Near Juyong Pass).

Qing Emperor Qianlong was so fascinated by the beautiful scene here that he wrote a poem and an inscription that reads Jade Islet Spring Shade. The inscription was later carved on the facade of the tablet and the poem on the back. The tablet is enclosed by marble balustrades. Close by the tablet a path leads to the top of the hill.

Fangshan Restaurant 仿膳餐厅

Enter Beihai Park by the east gate, cross the bridge, turn right and walk along the lakeside for 5 minutes, you will get to Yilantang (Hall of Gentle Ripple) on the Qionghua Islet where Fangshan Restaurant is located. With a hill behind and a lake in front, the restaurant offers a picturesque view. There are 11 halls, large and small, which can accommodate a total of 250 people. The dishes and desserts are imitations of imperial cuisine.

Haopujian (As Between the Hao & Pu Streams) 濠濮涧

It was first built in 1757. The place is surrounded by rocky formations, covered with trees, decorated with winding stone bridges and spacious halls in an environment of quiet seclusion. Sometimes Empress Dowager Cixi came here to spend her summer days and listen to traditional storytelling.

Huafangzhai (Studio of Colourfully-Painted Pleasure Boat) 画舫斋

It lies on the east shore of the lake. It consists of several water surface buildings. In the centre is a pond surrounded by winding galleries. On the left is Guketing (Courtyards with Old Trees), in front of which is an old ash-tree planted in the Tang Dynasty (618-907). Nowadays, the Studio is often used for exhibitions of calligraphy, paintings and photographs.

324

White Marble Pillar 汉白玉柱子

The White Marble Pillar with the design of coiling dragons, located to the northwest of the Dagoba, stands midway along the hillside.

On its top is the bronze statue of an immortal holding a plate, which is named Chenglupan (Receptacle of Dew). Legend has it that Emperor Wudi of the Han Dynasty (206 BC-220 AD) once used this method to gather dew-drops to mix the medicine he took for longevity. It is on this basis of the legend that Emperor Qianlong of the Qing Dynasty had this structure built.

Qingxiaolou (Hall for Night Parties) 庆霄楼

The Hall for Night Parties lies on the western part of the Islet. In the imperial days, on the Lantern Festival (the 15th day of the 1st month of the Chinese lunar calendar), Empress Dowager Cixi would come to enjoy the skating games here.

Yuegulou (Chamber for Reading the Classics) 阅古楼

The Chamber is located on the western side of the Jade Islet. During the reign of Emperor Qianlong (1736-1795), a collection of famous calligraphic works up to the Wei and Jin dynasties (220-420), possessed by the imperial court, were on stone tablets, rubbings, which constitute the "Sanxitang (Hall of Three Rarities) Model Calligraphy." The total comes to 495 pieces, forming a collection of China's treasures in the art of calligraphy.

Five-Dragon Pavilions 五龙亭

The Five-Dragon Pavilions were built in 1602 and renovated several times under the Qing.

The Qing emperors went fishing, enjoyed campfires or moonlit nights. Since the pavilions were built over the water, they were called dragon-pavilions.

Double-Side Nine-Dragon Screen 九龙壁

The Double-Side Nine-Dragon Screen (the only one in China) was built of 424 pieces of coloured glazed tiles in 1602 in the Ming Dynasty (1368 – 1644). The screen is 6. 65 metres high, 25. 86 metres long and 1. 42 metres thick. It shows nine dragons playing in the waves. The Nine-Dragon Screen in Beihai Park is one of the indispensable sights for foreign tourists to Beijing to take in if they wish to follow the traces of China's dragons. In nine different postures the nine dragons equally portray fierceness and vigour. Tourists marvel at the great artistic merit and the beautiful modelling of this ancient art object. On this Nine-Dragon Screen there are altogether 635 dragons, big or small.

There are four nine-dragon screens in China: the largest one is in Nanning, Guangxi Zhuang Autonomous Region, one in Datong, Shanxi Province; the best one is in Beihai Park and the fourth one is in the Forbidden City.

325

Tower of Ten Thousand Buddhas 万佛楼

Located at the northwestern corner of the compound, the Tower of Ten

Thousand Buddhas was built in 1771 in honour of the 80th birthday of Emperor Qianlong's mother. The tower contained 10, 000 niches, each holding a gilded Amitayus Buddha. It's a pity they were looted when the Allied Forces of the Eight Powers invaded Beijing in 1900.

Miaoxiangting (Pavilion of Buddhist Apprehension)
妙香亭

The pavilion is octagonal in shape. Emperor Qianlong of the Qing Dynasty had Wanfolou (House of Ten Thousand Buddhist Deities) built in celebration of his mother's eightieth birthday. The pavilion is part of the construction. In the pavilion there is a stone pagoda, on which are carved sixteen Buddhist figures. Each one of them is full of life and marvelous in form.

Iron Shadow Screen 铁影壁

This is a cultural relic from the Yuan Dynasty. It stands 3. 56 metres long and 1. 89 metres high. There are some simple but lively animal carvings on both sides. The colour of the screen looks like iron, actually it is carved out of neutral igneous rock, hence the name.

Jingxinzhai 静心斋

Jingxinzhai (Heart-Ease Study) is a fascinating garden located on the northern shores of Beihai. The whole garden is surrounded by a gilded and painted zigzag corridor that follows the shape of the hills. The garden was first named Jingqingzhai (Clear Mirror Study) built with fine workmanship in 1758 and was known as the "miniature garden of Qianlong." The Qing emperors and empresses used to come here to relax after worshipping Gods at Xiaoxitian (Little Western Sky) in Beihai. Empress Dowager Cixi made it her favourite resort because of its quietness and seclusion and a special narrow-gauge railway line was built from her residence at Zhongnanhai right down to the entrance of the garden. In 1913, this place was renovated and renamed Jingxinzhai.

The garden combines the special feature of gardening in areas both north and south of the Yangtze River. It is ingeniously designed, novel in style, made up of three courtyards and consists chiefly of rockeries.

Behind the elegant north gate of the garden is a pond that takes up one whole courtyard and has water lilies in its clear water. In the pond stands an exquisite piece of rock from Lake Taihu and the spacious Jingxinzhai stands right behind the pond.

East of Jingxinzhai is a small courtyard. The main building facing south is Baoshu Study, said to be the study of the crown princes of the Qing Dy-

326

nasty. The east wing, called Yunqinzhai (Zither Room), faces a small lotus pond fed by water from the lake, which gives a jingle-jangling sound like jade falling to the ground. In the south is a wall with different shapes of cut-outs through which one can enjoy a panoramic view of Beihai. No wonder there is a couplet in the Zither Room, which reads: "A unique place to enjoy oneself; a combination of sound and view."

Behind the study is a rock garden where bubbling spring-water flows through crevices into the lotus pond. Right in the middle of the pond stands Qinquanlang (Refreshing Spring Corridor) decorated with vermilion beams and painted columns.

It is a wonderful place for relaxation on mid-summer days. Qinquanlang is connected with the southern shores by a zigzag bridge in the east and a marble bridge in the west. This marble bridge looks like a jade belt, which is supported at each end by two life-like unicorns bending their backs and looking straight ahead. Peichawu(Tea Baking Place) is located to the southeast of the bridge. It faces Yanhuaxuan (Room for Keeping Paintings), which is diagonally opposite Huafengshi (Room for Painting Peaks) in the southwest of the garden. It is so well designed that it enables visitors to enjoy views from the room from two different angles.

The different shaped rockeries were said to be modelled after the works of famous landscape painters. There are narrow paths between the rockeries. In the west of the garden is a group of rockeries made of Taihu rocks which look like a lotus flower in full bloom. Zhenluanting, an exquisite pavilion right in its centre, provides a bird's eye view of the garden. The place was named Lianduozhugong (Lotus and Pearl Palace) by Emperor Qianlong for its unique beauty.

The Small Sukhavati Garden 西天梵境

Located in the northwestern part of Beihai Park, the Small Sukhavati (Pure Land) Garden was built in 1770 by Qing Emperor Qianlong to celebrate his mother's birthday. The main hall in the garden is the largest square pavilion in Asia. It is surrounded with water but easy of access by bridges. It is accompanied by four glazed gateways extending in four directions with one small pavilion at each corner. Inside the hall there is a moulded Buddhist Sumeru mountain with a seated Sakyamuni, with Ananda and Mahakasyapa standing by each side and Bodhisttvas and Arhats of various symbolic gestures arranged around. The mountain is embellished with ancient towers and temples, exotic flowers and rare trees, and curling mists and clouds, making it look like the legendary "Western Paradise" (Sukhavati). Emperor Qianlong once inscribed the words "Pure Land" in mandarin Chinese on a board, which is still hung high in the hall. These features make the building a precious Buddhist architectural work. The garden was closed for reason of damages and safety since 1952. The departments concerned have made efforts to restore and conserve the garden especially during the period from 1987 to 1993. The Sukhavati Garden was finally reopened to domestic and foreign tourists in early 1994.

Within the resorted Sukhavati Garden tourists will acquire a vivid experience of the mountain itself and will find sculptures of the Buddhist Mi School in the cave.

Yong'an (Eternal Peace) Temple 永安寺

Yong'an Temple on the Qionghuadao Islet in the centre of Beihai Park reopened to public after intensive renovation in 1993. The temple is hardly new. It was first built in 1651, though the history of the park dates a few centuries earlier, when the Dagoba, symbol of the park, was constructed on the top of the hill.

But Yong'an Temple has long been in disrepair. Part of it had toppled with the passage of time, until it was restored earlier 1993. The temple has now taken on an entirely new face with its freshly-painted walls and roofs, dazzling-array of Buddha statues and cultural relics. And, for the first time in the park's history.

The components of the temple—three main halls and several auxiliary ones—are arranged along the slope on six terraces, with the White Dagoba atop the tiny island. The first statues are the four guardians of Dharmer. Heavenly Kings, as they are dubbed. They look ferocious and each has something in hand: please read Yonghegong Lamasery page 433. Sakyamuni, founder of Buddhism, and his main disciples, eight Bodhisattva and 18 Arhats, are enshrined in the Falun Hall—a common sight in a temple of this kind. The falun, or prayer wheel cylinder, is a bell-like instrument used in religious rituals. There are two falun sets in front of the hall.

Pu'an (Universal Peace) Hall houses another group of Buddhist statues, totally different from the first ones. Facing outwards, Tsong Kha-pa, founder of Tibetan Buddhism's Gelugpa (Yellow) Sect, sits on an Altar and his two beloved disciples, the First Dalai (the famous Songstang Kampo) and the First Bainqen are at his sides. This sect of the Tibetan Buddhism is represented by their yellow caps, colour that actually dominates the entire hall.

In other auxiliary halls are religious implements, including silver bowls, bugles and prayer wheels, which are used for rituals like Monlam, or the

Grand Summoning Ceremony. Silk-woven or embroidered tangkas—scroll paintings with Buddhist images—are in traditional Tibetan style, a collage of colours against a deep blue backdrop. Green bamboo grows luxuriantly in the yard behind Falun Hall, and its sweet smell lures visitors to linger just a little longer. It is possible to have a rest in one of the two exquisitely designed pavilions half-way to the Dagoba. Two steles erected in one of the yards tell the origins of the temple and the Dagoba. They are inscribed in Chinese, Manchu, Mongolian and Tibetan.

A steep stone stairway leads to the top, which provides a mesmerizing view. To the south is Zhongnanhai (Central and South Sea), where the headquarters of the Communist Party of China is located. The Forbidden City nearby is a stretch of green and yellow glazed-tile roofs. Toward Beihai Park, the lotuses have withered in the early autumn chill but the trees are still green. Swan-shaped pedal boats creak their way across the pond and pedestrians roam on the cobblestone paths in the imperial garden, believed to be the earliest ever built.

The White Dagoba, together with a painting depicting Emperor Shunzhi (the first emperor of the Qing Dynasty) meeting with the Fifth Dalai are witnesses of the Central Government Tibet alliance. The 36-metre high Tibetan style building (the White Dagoba) the most famed landmark at Beihai Park, was built in honour of a visiting Dalai Lama and later to house Buddhist relics. The Dagoba was whitewashed under the renovation project in 1993. Its top is a gilded copper lid decorated with dozens of copper bells. Their jingle carries far in the wind, reminding the tourist a dreamland.

Round City
团 城

The Round City, 4,500 square metres in area, stands at the south gate of Beihai Park. It is surrounded by a 5-metre-high circular wall and has a distinctive courtyard with halls, pavilions and ancient trees. It was originally an islet formed from the lake excavations and served as an imperial garden.

The major building in the Round City is Chengguangdian (the Hall to Receive the Light) built during the Yuan Dynasty and renovated twice in the Ming and Qing dynasties. In the middle of the Round City is Yuwengting (Jade Jar Pavilion) with a blue roof and white columns. The Round City is of great artistic value in the history of ancient gardening in China.

Lacebark Pine (Pinus Bungeana) 白皮松（白果松）

When you go up the terrace, you can see an ancient pinus bungeana (lacebark pine) on your right about 20 metres tall. The pine was planted in the Jin Dynasty, one of the oldest in Beijing. The cypress trees in front of the Hall to Receive the Light are all several hundred years old. Empreor Qianlong is said to have granted titles to these ancient trees: for example, the General in White Robe 白袍将军，for the lacebark pine. East of the Hall to Receive the Light there is an 800 year-old tree. It is 10. 46 metres high, 94. 6 centimeters in diameter, shades the sun from 107. 6 square metres. The pine was named the Sunshade Marquess 遮荫侯 by Emperor Qianlong of the Qing Dynasty as he once sheltered under it on a hot summer day. A lightning rod has been placed on top of the tree, and it is still growing healthily although one of its branches was broken by heavy snow in 1960.

In Beijing detailed records of 4, 200 pine trees, which are more than 300 years old, have been compiled. Similar work is also being carried out on some another 20,000 trees, aged between 100 and 300 years.

Since 1983, detailed records have been built up listing each tree's age, height, diameter, shade area, and environment and including photographs and any legendary story attached to the tree. The information is fed into a computer and is used for research work aiming at better protecting these aged trees.

Local groups set up to compile records in parks, at historical sites and scenic spots are also now caring for the old trees by providing manure, irrigation and insecticides.

Jade Jar 玉瓮

330

The Jade Jar, which is 0. 70 metre high, 1. 82 metres long, 1. 35 metres wide, 4. 93 metres in perimeter and its depth being 0. 55 metre, weighing 3. 5 tons, was used as a wine vessel by Kublai Khan (1215-1294; reigned 1260-1294) during the Yuan Dynasty (1279-1368). It was originally kept in the Palace in the Moon. It was carved out of a single piece of black jade in 1265 during the Yuan Dynasty. On its outer surface are designs of sea dragons and other marine beasts amidst rolling waves, and inside is inscribed a poem by Emperor Qianlong about the jar. After the Palace in the Moon collapsed in the Ming Dynasty, the Jade Jar was taken to True Martial Temple 真武庙, where it was used by Taoist priests as a pickle jar. It was recovered in 1749. A pavilion was built especially to house it on the order of Emperor Qianlong (1736-1795).

Hall to Receive the Light 承光殿

The Hall to Receive the Light was built in 1746 after the style of the watchtower in the Palace Museum. It has two verandahs, one on the east side and the other on the west. To the west in the rear are the Pavilion of Penetrating Fragrance and the Pavilion of Clear Ripples 镜澜亭 . To the east are the Ancient Musical Pipe Pavilion 古籁堂 and the Pavilion of Scattered Clouds.

Jade Buddha 白玉坐像佛

In the hall is a statue of Buddha, 1. 6 metres high, carved out of a very fine piece of white jade. The head and clothes are inlaid with red and green precious stones. The statue is said to have come from Burma during the reign of Qing Emperor Guangxu (1875-1908). The knife scar on its left arm was cut by the Allied Forces of the Eight Powers in 1900.

Ancient Qing Dynasty Fortress
团 城 演 武 厅

Located in the western suburbs of Beijing, the Qing Dynasty military base was built in 1748 by Emperor Qianlong. There used to be many structures, but now only a twin-tower compound, two pavilions and a stone fortress are still standing. For many years the military base and the buildings were shrouded in mystery.

The twin-tower compound is still magnificent despite the ravages of time. The site is called the Round City because two big-roofed towers were built on the top of a thick fortified wall that encircled an opening, like a city wall. Unlike its two namesakes, one in Beihai Park and the other at the Summer Palace, this compound was not for imperial recreation, but for the emperors to view battle exercises by the elite Manchu troops.

Entering the vaulted gate, you will find yourself in an arena-like opening about 40 metres in diameter. Flagstones form the floor of the arena, which is flanked by two inner houses. It is not known for what they were used. There are two stairways leading to the top of the wall. The wall is damaged in places by tree roots that grew between the bricks and the stone slabs. The compound was used as a pigeon farm for many years before 1981. In fact, the whole Qing Dynasty military base was developed as a farm and between 1949 and 1981 was used to raise chickens, pigs, rabbits and pigeons. The damage to the site was enormous, but visitors still can envisage

331

its heyday through the inscriptions on two stone monuments. One is in the compound, the other in the pavilion. Written in the Manchurian, Chinese, Mongolian and Tibetan languages, the inscriptions tell why and how Manchu troops exercised here. One inscription says: "In preparation for Jinchuan campaign, stone fortresses were built at the foot of the Western Hills. Elite Manchu soldiers were selected to practice their scaling skills." The fortresses were modeled after those used by rebels in mountainous Sichuan. In no more than a month, 2,000 soldiers mastered the assault skill, says the inscription. But the geographic barriers made the rebels unconquerable. To save the face of Manchu troops, the enemies were cajoled into surrender. Nevertheless Emperor Qianlong erected the monument to extol the triumph of the Manchu soldiers. He even renamed a temple there as the Temple of Triumph, which was later destroyed. During the reign of Qianlong (1736-1795), the Qing Dynasty knew its greatest prosperity and saw its fastest expansion. It incorporated Chinese Turkistan into its territory and renamed it Xinjiang. The monument inside the twin-tower compound records the military exploits of the Qing army in suppressing rebels in Xinjiang and conquering Ili and Kashi, areas bordering Russia. Qing Emperor Qianlong was a vainglorious ruler. He liked to boast about his 10 major victories.

Even though some were won at a heavy price. Nowadays, many buildings at the base have vanished. There used to be nine fortresses but only one survived.

West of the ruined Temple of Triumph is a place called the Little Garrison where prisoners captured from Sichuan were held. After more than 200 years, their descendants have been absorbed in the local population. The big field in front of the twin-tower compound used to be the main drilling ground. It is now an orchard.

In 1981, the Beijing Cultural Relics Protection Bureau acquired the area as a new site for protection, and had invested an initial 500,000 yuan (US$91,743) in its restoration.

Coal Hill Park
景 山 公 园

(the hill is 44.6 metres high and its elevation being 88.7 metres)

The Coal Hill Park lies right to the north of the Palace Museum. It used to be a private garden of the imperial family. When the Imperial Palace was built in the early Ming Dynasty, the earth excavated to make the moat was piled up, and five peaks took shape. Coal was once heaped around the foot of the hill, it is therefore also known as Coal Hill. In Qianlong's time, fruit trees grew and birds were raised in the grounds, the place was then called the Hundred Fruits Garden. Feudal emperors came here to climb the hill, attend the banquets, shoot arrows and enjoy flowers as well. The hill is just behind the Forbidden City. It used to be a natural screen. In the Ming and Qing dynasties, it was regarded as "Dominating Hill", a symbol of stability of the feudal rulers. Five pavilions were later built on the ridges, From east to west they are: Wonderful View Pavilion 观妙亭, Surrounding View Pavilion 周赏亭, Everlasting Spring Pavilion 万春亭, Panoramic View Pavilion 富览亭 and Harmonious Fragrance Pavilion 辑芳亭. From the hilltop, visitors can have a bird's-eye view of the city. There used to be a bronze statue of a god in each of the pavilions. Unfortunately four of them were stolen by the Allied Forces of the Eight Powers in 1900, and the one on the uppermost pavilion was totally damaged.

Entering the front gate, you come to Chamber of Beautiful Expectation 绮望楼 which stands with its back to the hill over 44 metres high. In the old days there was a Confucius' shrine in the building, where the Qing officials and scholars paid their respects to him. It is now a gift shop.

Coal Hill (Jingshan) Park

Hall of Imperial Longevity
Greenhouse
Ginkgo Orchard
Chinese Flowering Crabapple Orchard
Beijing Children's Palace
Sports Field of Children's Palace
Children's Sports Ground
Hall of View of Virtue
Yangtao (Actinidia chinensis) Orchard
Chinese Herbaceous Peony Garden
Vineyard
Peony Garden
West Gate
East Gate
Persimmon Orchard
Everlasting Spring Pavilion
Surrounding View Pavilion
Panoramic View Pavilion
Wonderful View Pavilion
Harmonious Fragrant Pavilion
Chamber of Beautiful Expectation
The site where Emperor Chongzhen of the Ming Dynasty hanged himself
Apple Orchard
South Gate
Peach Orchard
Jingshan Qianjie

On your way up the hill from the eastern slope, you will come across a locust tree right below the Wonderful View Pavilion. There was formerly an old locust tree from which the last Ming Emperor Chongzhen hanged himself when a peasant army led by Li Zicheng broke into Beijing in 1644. A new tree has been planted to mark the site.

In the Ming and Qing dynasties there were a lot of trees, cranes and deer, and fruit trees within this compound. It was then named the Hundred Fruits Garden 百果园. Feudal emperors came here to climb the hill, attend the banquets, shoot arrows, and enjoy flowers as well. The Coal Hill is just behind the Forbidden City, and it used to be a natural screen. In the Ming and Qing dynasties, it was regarded as "Overlooking Hill 镇山," a symbol of stability of the feudal rulers.

On top of the hill, you will find the park located on the meridian line. It starts from Yongdingmen Gate at the southernmost city limit and runs northward through the Front Gate, Tian'anmen, the Forbidden City to the Everlasting Spring Pavilion and leads on to the Drum Tower and Bell Tower to the north. Looking southward on a bright sunny day, the yellow glazed-tile roofs of the Forbidden City glitter like thousands of gilded fish scales under the sun. To the southwest lies the North Sea, Middle Sea and the South Sea. Further to the west is the White Dagoba which emerges on the island in Beihai Park like a maiden in her white sari, pretty, elegant and graceful. At night, the scene is unusually striking.

Behind the hill is Shouhuangdian (Hall of Imperial Longevity) where the portraits of the ancestors of Qing court were housed. To its east is Guandedian (Hall of View of Virtue) used as a temporary resting place for deceased emperors before burial.

The Coal Hill Park was opened to the public in 1928. After 1949, the buildings were renovated and flowers and fruit trees were planted. The Hall of Imperial Longevity was turned into a Children's Palace. Now the Coal Hill Park has become one of the popular holiday resorts for the people of Beijing.

The Coal Hill Park was listed as a national key relic under special preservation in 2001.

Coal Hill Park—Giant Buddha 景山公园——一尊大佛

The Beijing Evening News reported on June 22, 1987 that viewed from the air, the Coal Hill Park is just like a smiling giant Buddha. This was a new discovery in testing remote sensing colorful images by the remote sensing technical experts of the Ministry of Geology and Mineral Resources. The surrounding wall of the Coal Hill Park is like a big scenery frame. The delightful scenery in the park forms a huge Buddha sitting in the centre. The experts said that perhaps it was designed by the ancient builders or it was an accidental coincidence. It remains to be studied and verified in the days to come.

New Theory About Old Beijing 老北京新理论

According to the Remote Sensing Centre of the Ministry of Geology and Mineral Resources, Guo Jibin discovered from a remote sensing photo of Beijing that the layout of the old city with the Forbidden City, the Coal Hill Park, the Drum Tower and the Bell Tower, form the shape of a dragon, while the man dug imperial lake gardens form another dragon.

According to Guo, the dragon formed by the Imperial City is about 4.5 kilometres long, from the Golden Water River in the south straight to the Bell Tower in the north. Tian'anmen (Gate of Heavenly Peace), together with the Golden Water River and the white marble bridge over the river, form the mouth of the dragon, and West and East Chang'an (Eternal Peace) boulevards are its tentacles. The symmetrically situated and equal sized Altar of Land and Grain (today's Zhongshan "Dr Sun Yat-sen" Park) and the Imperial Ancestral Temple (today's Working People's Cultural Palace) are the two eyes of the dragon. The wide paved path from Wumen (Meridian Gate) to the Gate of Heavenly Peace is the bridge of the dragon's nose. The Forbidden City, together with the Coal Hill Park and a straight road leading north to the Drum Tower and the Bell Tower, give the dragon its body and tail. Standing on the top of Coal Hill and looking southward, the golden glazed tiles of the imperial palaces appear just like the scales of the dragon shining in the sun, while further south, the semi-circular-shaped watchtower and Zhengyangmen (South-Facing Gate), seen from the sky above, appear just like a pearl the dragon is playing with. The specially-structured corner towers of the Forbidden City are the four powerful claws of the dragon.

To the west of the "building-formed dragon" lies a "water dragon" formed by the imperial lake gardens. Running from south to north, they are Nanhai (South Lake), the head of the dragon; Zhonghai (Central Lake) and Beihai (North Lake) the dragon's body; and Housanhai (The Three Rear Lakes), which give the dragon its tail.

The layout of the Imperial City shows a strong tint of imperial authority and divine authority. Apart from some traditional regularities in ancient building planning, the Eight Diagrams and other forms of divination were also used in planning these two dragons. The shapes of these two dragons are not very much like the figure of today's dragon, but compared with the dragon carvings and ornamental patterns on some cultural relics of several thousand years ago, the similarities are obvious.

The new discovery is regarded as far-fetched by some experts, owing to the lack of evidence from historical records. But other experts think it is quite reasonable, and the difference of opinion has caused a lot of discussions in ancient building research circles.

From the air, visitors can get a sense of the symmetrical beauty of Beijing. There are three rectangles inside one another. The length of the two smaller rectangles run north to south, while the length of the largest runs east-west. The south side of the largest rectangle is connected to a fourth rectangle that is slightly longer and narrower.

The innermost rectangle forms the Forbidden City—once the residence of Ming and Qing emperors, now the Palace Museum.

The second rectangle outlines the previous boundaries of the Imperial City. Of the vermilion brick walls that once surrounded the old city, only the south wall on Chang'an Boulevard is still standing. Within the Imperial City, Beihai and Coal Hill parks are towards the north; Zhongshan Park and the Beijing Working People's Cultural Palace in the south. Once part of the Imperial City and just west of the Forbidden City is a large compound called Zhongnanhai. The Chinese central government is based there today. Early in the 13th century, when Kublai Khan, founder of the Yuan Dynasty (1279-1368), set out to build a new capital, he shifted the centre of the city to what is today's Beihai Park. He constructed imposing palaces and boulevards. The new city was named Dadu (Great Capital) and made a strong impression on Marco Polo (1254-1324). Marco Polo was the first European to cross Asia to China and leave a record of what he found. Even though the city of Dadu was demolished in wars, traces of it gave ideas to its future architects. This grand construction project stared in the 15th century lay a solid foundation. Zhu Yuanzhang of the Ming Dynasty (1368-1644), founded his imperial capital in Nanjing. Rising from the gutter to become the ruler of the 14th century China, Zhu Yuanzhang liked to do things on a grand scale. The imperial capital was encircled by a 48-kilometre-long wall. Today the massive brick structure is still there, making Nanjing the largest walled city in the world. In the grand capital, Zhu Yuanzhang realized his desire to centralize power and impose strict discipline and solidarity on the bureaucracy and the population. He enforced his desire with a reign of terror. When the dynastic founder died in 1398, the throne in Nanjing, following the principle of primogeniture, went to Zhu Yunwen, the surviving grandson of the elder Zhu's first son. Within a year Zhu Di, the fourth son of Zhu Yuanzhang, rebelled. The fighting went on for three years, and in 1402 Zhu Di finally won. In 1406, dynastic rulers made plans to construct palaces in Beijing the following year. Officials were assigned to Sichuan, Hubei, Guangxi and Zhejiang to prepare raw materials, while thousands of artisans and workers were recruited from throughout the country to report to Beijing for construction. All the imperial temples, palaces and gates were built just like Nanjing's imperial layout, only bigger and fancier, according to Zhu Di's orders. In doing this reconstruction, the third emperor of the Ming Dynasty intended to change the imperial scheme of the first emperor. In 1415, construction of the outer city of Beijing began. The project took 14 years. It engaged 100,000 artisans and a million workmen. The city wall was 12.5 metres high and 22 kilometres long. If you make the flight, better start from southernmost site of the Yongdingmen Gate, now torn down for a road between the Temple of Heaven and Xiannongtan Altar. A north-south axis, 8 kilometres long, runs through the centre of Beijing. It begins at the Bell and Drum towers (now on the Second Ring Road) to the north, crosses straight over Coal Hill, enters the Forbidden City through the Shenwumen Gate, exits through the Wumen Gate and Tian'anmen Gate, continues through Zhengyangmen Gate in the old southern wall of the Inner City and ends at Yongdingmen Gate, the southern entrance to the Outer City. The Forbidden City was positioned at dead center of this axis to symbolize the central authority of dynastic rule, while Coal Hill was built upon the debris of the Yuan capital Dadu to demonstrate the overwhelming strength of the dynasty.

The rest of Beijing hinges on the north-south axis. East and west of the main axis is perfect symmetry, park for park, market for market. Most of the city's larger avenues run north-south, parallel to the main axis, while smaller streets and alleys (_hutong_) run horizontally. The entire arrangement, initiated by Zhu Di and enhanced during later reigns and with major reconstruction by the succeeding Qing Dynasty, is the largest exhibit of ancient Chinese urban planning. In 1421, Emperor Yongle, Zhu Di's title, made Beijing the national capital. Nanjing was demoted to "rear echelon capital." Beijing today retains many facets of its centuries-old planning, but it has subjected them to intensive modern development.

337

Zhongshan (Dr Sun Yat-sen) Park
中 山 公 园

Covering an area of 24 hectares (59.3 acres), the Zhongshan Park lies west of Tian'anmen Gate. About a thousand years ago, this park used to be the site of Xingguosi (Temple of National Revival) in the northeastern part of the city of Yanjing (Yan Capital, the old name of Beijing) during the Liao and Jin dynasties(916-1234). The original buildings vanished long ago, but some of the ancient cypresses still survive. During the reign of Emperor Yongle (1403-1424) of the Ming Dynasty, when Beijing was made the capital in 1420, the Taimiao (Imperial Ancetral Temple) and the Shejitan (Altar of Land and Grain) were built. The altar was erected in 1421. In 1914, it was converted into the Central Park, and in 1928 it got its present name: Zhongshan Park, in memory of Dr Sun Yat-sen. Since 1949, it has greatly improved both in natural beauty and in recreational facilities.

The whole park is permeated by a peaceful atmosphere. Behind the colourful flower "vase" stands a memorial arch of white marble with the inscription "Defend Peace."

This is a huge, artful and intricate rock lying behind the marble archway at the end of a pine-shaded path. It was transferred from the ruins of Yuanmingyuan (Park of Perfection and Brightness). From here to the north of an area of flower-beds, a grove of ancient cypresses provides an extraordinary view. Seven of these trees are particularly large; each would need four persons to encircle with their arms outstretched full length. They are believed to be about a thousand years old. Behind the grove and before entering into Shejitan, a pair of statues of sitting lions, carved in stone, lie a heroic manner. They were discovered in1918 in the ruins of an ancient temple in Taming County, Hebei Province. Entering the altar by its south gate, the perspective immediately becomes different and enchanting. To the east is the Music Hall, now rebuilt into an amphitheatre with round pillars. Here many well-known and popular dramas are often presented and concerts are frequently held. Shrubs, peony beds and well-kept lawns are everywhere. During late spring and early summer, the peonies are in full blossom: many of them are rare and valuable species. From the garden, a straight path leads to the altar, which was once used by the emperors of the Ming and Qing dynasties for offering sacrifices to the gods of land and grains. The altar is a square terrace of white marble with three tiers. The top tier is sectioned and filled with earth in five different colours (red, black, blue, white, and yellow) to symbolize the feudal dictum: "All land under heaven belongs to the emperor." North of the altar is the Baidian (Hall of Worship). Built in 1425 in the Ming Dynasty, it is now the best-preserved Ming Dynasty temple of wooden structure in Beijing. There is no ceiling under the roof, so the beams and posts are exposed. In

1928, it was renamed the Dr Sun Yat-sen Memorial Hall. Since 1949, the building has been thoroughly repaired and redecorated.

The building behind this was formerly the front gateway of the altar, inside which 72 iron halberds were kept. They were looted away when the combined forces of the eight imperialist powers invaded Beijing in 1900. Further back are the Cypress Yard and Houhu (Rear Moat). In the courtyard tourists may find tables built with Han Dynasty bricks in quaint patterns. East of the altar is a very quiet section containing pavilions, rockeries, unique rocks, a teahouse and a restaurant.

Going westward along a covered corridor from the south gate of the park, tourists can reach the goldfish breeding ground, where many rare species of the fish are kept. Further on is the quietest spot in the park area, where a rich variety of pavilions, bridges, rocky hills, flowers, and trees are artfully laid out, centering around a lotus pond. The Water Pavilion, built over water on three sides, is now used for exhibitions of various kinds. Proceeding northward from here tourists come to Lantingbeiting (Pavilion of the Orchard Pavilion Steles). To the east is the Tanghuawu (Tang Flower Village), a hot house where many rare flowers and plants such as the Canaan lily, orchid, and lemon trees are displayed all the year round. Further east lies the Xiliting (Pavilion for Rehearsing Rites). This was formerly the Honglusi (Office of Rites) in the Ming and Qing dynasties, which moved from Pingpu Street to the present location. Here, officials who were for the first time received by the emperor rehearsed the rites before their audience took place.

The western section of the park is the busiest. Here, in the midst of the cypress grove, are many pavilions and artificial rockeries, as well as a hall of entertainment and a ground for riding on an electric horse. In the cypress grove itself, colourful lights are hung, under which tourists may drink tea, listen to music, play chess or simply chat on summer evenings.

The park is also well-known for its great variety of flowers and goldfish, ancient halls and cypresses, the charming pavilions, summer houses and grotesque rock gardens. The park attracts millions of visitors each year.

Giant Pipe Organ Set Up

The largest organ in China was installed on December 8, 1999 at Beijing's Zhongshan Concert Hall. Made of more than 3, 000 pipes, the organ is 12 metres high and weighs 20 tons. It was produced by the Austin, a US company that is a major producer of organs in the world.

Celebration of the installation of the organ was held on December 8, 1999. Under the baton of Tan Lihua, the Beijing Symphony Orchestra performed dames Chinese composer Zhao Jiping's "Symphony 2000. "

Carol Williams was the first organist to give concerts at the Concert Hall of Zhongshan Park in Beijing. The British organist spent five years at the Royal Academy of Music, where she specialized in playing the organ as a student of David Sanger after a brief period with the late Douglas Hawkridge. Williams lied in Paris to study with Daniel Roth, the organist at the Church of St Surplice. She was at one time the deputy organist at St Columbia's Church of Scotland in London's Knightsbridge. In 1999, Williams released a CD titled "Music from Blenheim Palace," in which she recorded Edouard Silass "Fantasia," Arthur Sullivan's "Lost Chord" and Mendelssohn's "Ode for the Wings of a Dove." Williams gave two concerts in Beijing on April 28 and 30, 2000. The first concert was titled "From Bach to Saint-Sarns." Together with the Beijing Symphony Orchestra and conductor Tan Lihua, Williams played classical pieces, traditional tunes and ragtime works. The program included Bach's "Aria from Suite in D," Scott Joplin's "The Entertainer," "Green Sleeves" and Saint-Saen's Symphony 111 in C minor, opus 78. "The second concert was a solo organ recital. Williams played John Philip Sousa's "The Washington Post March," "Scott Joplin's Maple Leaf Rag" and the theme from the film, "Titanic."

Taoranting (Joyous Pavilion) Park
陶 然 亭 公 园

The Joyous Pavilion Park lies in the south of the Outer City, near the Altar of the God of Agriculture. It has earned its nation-wide reputation since the end of the Qing Dynasty (1644-1911). However, the place was by no means a scenic spot. It owed its fame to the fact that earlier, the best scenic areas and hill pavilions were largely inaccessible to the public, and men of letters gathered here for relaxation because it was virtually the only available spot of that kind. In the Qing Dynasty, when autumn came, many scholars would come to this elevated ground to drink wine and write poems. For common people, such an elevated place to view the city from was almost unattainable elsewhere. In the first place, their buildings were not allowed to be built higher than the palace edifices; secondly, most of the natural elevations of the city were possessed by the imperial family. Within the compound of the park, the high spot where the Cibei'an (Temple of Mercy) built in the Yuan Dynasty (1279-1368) was situated. It was therefore much sought after. It was surrounded by water on three sides, and that was considered to be enough to make a lovely landscape.

The beauty of the place was greatly exaggerated by the cultivated pens of the scholars who were in Beijing for civil examinations, and by other men of letters bringing it an undeserved reputation.

As far back as in the Warring States Period (475 BC-221 BC), the area was inhabited by working people. Many relics of that period were dug out in 1953 while the pond was dredged and deepened. About 900 years ago in the Liao Dynasty, this spot was the eastern suburb. It was criss-crossed by ditches and streams, a common pattern in southern China. On the southwest tip of the land that pushes out into the centre of a reed-filled pond is a hill, the site of the Temple of Mercy built in the Yuan Dynasty (1279-1368). Two stone pillars still stand, one erected in the Liao Dynasty, and the other in the Jin Dynasty (1115-1234). In the Ming and Qing dynasties, kilns for making bricks and tiles were built here, and the present Yaotai (Kiln Terrace) was the site of these kilns. In 1695, Jiangzao, secretary of the Board of Works of the Qing court, built a 3-room wing west of this old temple, and named it the Taoranting (Joyous Pavilion), after the poem by Bai Juyi, a famous poet of the Tang Dynasty: When chrysanthemums are in bloom and our homebrew is ready, let's enjoy them together. In later ages, the people adopted this name for the entire area. The place was so neglected, however, that before in 1949 it was no more than a dirty muddy hole choked with reeds. Many tourists were under the impression that there had been a gorgeous pavilion, but this was not the case, for in former times, the word ting had various other meanings besides "pavilion." At one time in Chinese history, there was an order calling for construction of a small house every five kilometres to provide travellers with a place to rest. The structures so erected were called ting, word denoting practically any small-sized building used for resting purposes. This 3-room building in the park has been repaired many times. It is now a teahouse. The slab which bears Jiangzao's handwriting is still set in the wall of one of the rooms, and another tablet also made from his handwriting, bearing the characters "Taoran," is placed on top of the gate to the temple.

In 1952, the People's Government had this muddy pond dredged and made into a lake of about 19 hectares in area, in which fish are bred to supply the market. The earth that was dug from the lake was used to make seven hillocks, on which small look-out pavilions were erected. Thousands of square metres of turf have been laid in the compound and flowers now vie with trees and shrubs to offer tourists the charm of the park.

The Joyous Pavilion Park was at one time a centre of revolutionary activities, for Li Dazhao rented one of the three side rooms of the Temple of

Mercy while he was in Beijing working to further the revolution and many meetings were held here. Nowadays, the park has become a true scenic spot.

At Taoranting Park, 20 pavilions were erected from 1989 to 1993. The park is now home to 36 pavilions, including miniature models of famous structures from other parks of the country. Eventually the park hopes to house 100 pavilions.

Grand View Garden
大 观 园

Located in Xuanwu District southwest of Beijing, the present Grand View Garden is replica of Daguanyuan, the magnificent garden of an imperial family described in the well-known Chinese novel *A Dream of Red Mansions* by a Qing Dynasty writer Cao Xueqin (?-1763). The site used to be a park dotted with willows and pines. In 1984, the China Television Film Production Centre decided to use it as the setting to shoot garden scenes for the TV series A Dream of Red Mansions. The Xuanwu District Government then suggested that the temporary garden be turned into a permanent scenic spot. Thus the plan to build the Grand View Garden faithful to the writer's description has come into being.

The project started in June 1984 and was completed in 1988. The Grand View Garden covers a total area of 12.5 hectares (31.25 acres) and includes more than 40 scenic spots illustrating the main plots in the garden. The stonework covers an area of more than 8,000 square metres and the lakes and canals 2.4 hectares (24,000 square metres). The construction work is divided into three stages, of which the first stage in the southern part of the garden cost about 4 million yuan (US$1.4 million) and was opened to the public in early 1985. It includes a front gate, four courtyards, Qinfang Bridge, Dicui Pavilion, winding paths and other scenic sites. Every effort has been made to be accurate in reproduction of Daguangyuan. Horticulturists, architects, archaeologists and experts on the history of the famous novel were asked to pay much attention to the layout of the whole garden, the location of trees, the arrangement of the rockeries, and the decoration of the main characters' homes.

Yihongyuan (Happy Red Court), located west of Qinfang Bridge, used to be the residence of Jia Baoyu, hero of the novel.

Xiaoxiangguan (Bamboo Lodge), a small and simple courtyard decorated in light green with slim bamboo's grown in the courtyard, housed the weak and unlucky Lin Daiyu, heroine of the novel. Jia Baoyu's sister-in-law, widow Li Wan lived in an eastern courtyard called Daoxiangcun (Paddy-Sweet Cottage).

Two stone lions, carved by the veteran artisans from Quyang County in Hebei Province, stand as guards at the front and the gate is flanked by sloping walls. Inside the garden more than 2,000 flowers and trees have been planted, 500 square metres of lawn laid out and hundreds of potted plants arranged.

The famous Lake Tai stones have been used here to pile the rockeries in different artistic postures.

The Altar of Earth Park
地 坛 公 园

Built in 1530, the Altar of Earth is located in the northern part of Beijing, a little way off Andingmenwai Street. Extending over an area of 37 hectares (91.43 acres), it was surrounded by a double square enclosure. The outer enclosure no longer stands but its west gate remains.

For more than four centuries, the Altar of Earth was the sacred place where the emperors of the Ming and Qing dynasties worshipped the God of Earth. The place, formally reopened in 1984, has been converted into a park mainly serving the aged.

A centre for the aged opened there in 1984. At the centre, the public can play chess, billiards, and table tennis, or listen to lectures on flower-growing, learn *taijiquan* (a kind of traditional Chinese shadow boxing) or *qigong* (a system of deep breathing exercises).

In 1420, the third Ming Emperor Yongle had the Temple of Heaven and Earth built in the southern part of Beijing. There he offered sacrifices to Heaven at the annual Winter Solstice and to Earth at the Summer Solstice. Having received a suggestion to worship Heaven and Earth separately, in 1530 Emperor Jiajing (1522-1566) ordered that the Circular Mound Altar be constructed for the worship of Heaven in Tiantan (now called the Temple of Heaven) and that Fangzetan (Square Stream Altar) be constructed for the worship of Earth in the Northern City. Fangzetan was renamed Ditan in 1534.

The largest structure in the Altar of Earth is the altar known as Fangzetan—so called because a moat surrounds it. A sculpted stone dragonhead is fixed on the west side of the southern corner of the moat wall; water was brought from a well through the dragon head. Fangzetan was built on a

343

north-south axis, and it is surrounded by two square enclosures, both painted red and surmounted with yellow glazed-tiles. Both inner and outer enclosures have triple white marble gates to the north and one gate to the east, south and west.

The altar is a two-tiered square terrace surfaced with flagstones; its facades are yellow glazed bricks. Each terrace is one metre high and has a flight of eight steps leading up to it. The upper terrace is 20 metres wide and the lower one 35 metres. The even numbers six and eight, symbols of the earth, and multiples of six and eight recur several times in the arrangement of the square flagstones.

On the west and east sides of the lower terrace lie four groups of stone sculptûres, 23 in all. They symbolize 15 mountains, including Mount Taishan and Mount Huashan; four rivers, including the Changjiang (Yangtze) River and Yellow River, and four seas (ancient Chinese believed that China was surrounded by four seas). There are more than 20 holes in the two terraces. They held flagstaffs and poles for banners and tents used during ceremonies.

The ceremonies for worshipping the Earth took place once a year, at the Summer Solstice.

On important occasions such as an emperor's coronation, birthday, marriage or funeral, a representative of the emperor would come to "report" to the God of Earth.

The Altar of Earth was no longer used after the overthrow of the Qing Dynasty in1911; it became a public park in 1925. It was once badly plundered and, because of years of neglect, became a wilderness choked with head-high weeds.

The people's government gave the Altar of Earth a new look in 1957, when it was once more turned into a park. The buildings were repaired and an orchard built as well as a large number of trees and flowers were planted.

An overall renovation of the park started in 1981. The people's government allocated a large sum of money for the renovation. Most of the buildings already have taken on a new look. A *pailou* or archway and a Bell Tower, neither of which had existed before, have been built on the spots.

Built in the same year with the Altar of Earth were the Altar of the Sun in the eastern city, the Altar of the Moon in the western city and the Altar of the God of Agriculture in the southern city. The emperor worshipped the God of the Sun at the Altar of the Sun at the Spring Equinox and the God of the Moon at the Autumn Equinox. Both the Altar of the Sun and the Altar of the Moon, more or less like the Altar of Earth but smaller, are now public parks. The emperor used to make annual sacrifices to the Altar of the God of Agriculture and perform the rite of ploughing the first furrow there at the beginning of spring each year. It is now the site of a stadium that accommodates 30, 000 people.

Fragrant Hills Park
香 山 公 园

Fragrant Hills Park, about 30 kilometres northwest of Beijing, is one of the most favourite resorts on the city's outskirts. It covers an area of 160 hectares (395. 36 acres).

In 1186, in the Jin Dynasty, the Fragrant Hills Temple was built and terraces, pavilions and pagodas were added by the subsequent dynasties. The area was later converted into a park and was named the Park of Tranquility and Pleasure.

Along with Yuanmingyuan (the Old Summer Palace) and the Summer Palace, the park was twice destroyed in 1860 and in 1900. The destruction was so serious that the reconstruction efforts made in the later years were never able to restore its original scale and splendour. After 1949, large-scale restoration took place and now the Fragrant Hills Park is a pop-

Fragrant Hills Park

North Gate
Lower Station
Spectacles Lake
Middle Station
Unbosoming Chamber
Cable Car
Temple of Brilliance
Fragrant Hills Villa
Glazed-Tile Pagoda
Tiered-Cloud Villa
Pine-Forest Restaurant
Upper Station
Western Hills Shimmering in Show
Fourth Courtyard of Jade Flower
Peak-Viewing Pavilion
East Gate
Third Courtyard of Jade Flower
Flat Terrace
Pavilion of Scattered Clouds
Pavilion of Varied Scenery
Jade Flower Villa
Xiangshan (Fragrant Hills) Hotel
Moonlight Villa
Incense Burner Peak
Eighteen-Windings Road
Lofty Wind Pavilion
Calm & Emerald Lake
Sun-Facing Cave
Jade Scepter Cliff
Temple of Red Glow
Half-Way-Up-the-Mountain Pavilion
Jade Fragrant Hall
Red Leaf Grove
White-Pine Pavilion
Site of Xiangshan Temple
Twin Lakes Villa
Viewing Cloud-Rising

ular tourist destination in late autumn for holidaymakers when the smoke tree leaves redden. The brilliant foliage is the main attraction for visitors. No one is sure where the smoke trees originated. Legend has it that a south wind carried the seeds of the red-leaf trees to Beijing. Then the seeds survived, and as years passed they grew into a lovely forest. Another story goes that the smoke trees were transplanted to the area by Emperor Qianlong (1736-1795) in the Qing Dynasty. In every November, the frosted leaves of these trees, along with the persimmons and maples, spread over the Fragrant Hills like a thick red blanket. For two centuries, it has been a resort for the residents in Beijing.

In 1997, an invasion of Mushi, a mosquito-like insect with an appetite for smoke tree leaves, left the frost withered, its beauty gone. Mushi suck the sap from the leaves, shriveling them and leaving ugly spots instead of rich greens and reds. To save the trees, the Beijing Garden Administration and Fragrant Hills Park launched a campaign against the seasonal pests. They built two roads through the smoke trees to allow workers to reach the trees and spray them with insecticide. Timely information combined with smoke from smudge pots completely eliminated Mushi there. Putting of nutritional supplement bars at the roots of 450 comparatively weak smoke trees not only saved them but also ensured their healthy growth. Another piece of good news is that more than 90 per cent of 1998's seedlings were alive and the newly introduced American Smoke Trees settled well there. This is due in large part to a recently built 2, 000-metre-long water pipeline through the forest, which keeps more than 6, 000 smoke trees from drought. Each year the gardeners regularly trim off twigs to increase the sunshine among the smoke trees. This is much more trouble for the gardeners, but it will greatly reduce the number of rotten leaves. The 79 hectares (197. 5 acres) of smoke trees make a green scarf for the Fragrant Hills, shining in the bright early autumn sunshine and their shimmering leaves are intact and thick. It attracts domestic and overseas visitors each late autumn with its charming blazing red leaves on the smoke trees

Major places of interest in the park include:

Spectacles Lake 眼镜湖

Built in 1745, the Spectacles Lake actually consists of two ponds separated and spanned by a stone bridge. When the water reflects the sunlight, the twin lakes resemble a pair of spectacles, hence the name. On the shore is a small stone cave with a spring above it. The water drips down over the entrance of the cave, forming a water screen that freezes into icicles in winter.

Studio of Tranquil Heart 见心斋

It was first built in mid-16th century under the Ming and was reconstructed in the Qing period. In the enclosure there is a large semi-circular pool in the shape of a heart. The studio was burned down in 1860 and was renovated after 1949.

Bright Temple 昭庙

Lying to the south of the Studio of Tranquil Heart, the Bright Temple was built in 1780 as a residence for the Sixth Bainqen Erdeni (1739-1781) when he visited Beijing. The compound has a 10-metre-high red terrace in Tibetan style. It was destroyed by the Anglo-French troops in 1860.

Glazed-Tile Pagoda 琉璃瓦塔

It is a 7-storey-octagonal pagoda of yellow and green glazed-tiles built on a stone base. Bronze bells hang from the eaves of each storey and when they ring in breeze, the pleasing tinkles break the stillness of the hills.

Yuhua Villa 玉华山庄

The Yuhua Villa was one of the 28 sights in the park. It is now a courtyard where visitors can take a rest and have a cup of tea. It is a good spot for viewing red leaves in late autumn. North of the Villa is the Hibiscus Hall, an elegant courtyard full of flowers and shrubs.

Baisongting (The Lacebark Pine Pavilion) 白松亭

The Lacebark Pine Pavilion is situated to the west of the Xiangshan Temple. It is a round 6-pillar pavilion nestling amid the white-bark pine trees which stand tall and erect. It is a quiet and peaceful place.

347

Ruins of the Xiangshan (Fragrant Hills) Temple
香山寺遗址

Not far from the entrance stands a stone arch. It is the site of the ancient Xiangshan Temple built into the landscape in 1186. There were originally five successive halls and side chambers. In 1860 the temple was burned down by the Anglo-French troops. Now only the terraces and the foundations of the buildings are left.

Banshanting (The Mid-Hill Pavilion) & Langfengting (Lofty Wind Pavilion) 半山亭和阆风亭

Behind the Xiangshan Temple there is a walk which runs across a section of forest. Climbing the hills along the winding path, visitors will come to a splendid scene. There stand half way up the hill two thatched pavilions, Banshanting and Langfengting.

Shuangqing Villa 双清别墅

In the southeast corner of the park is a small pool fed by two springs named Shuangqing or "Two Streams." The water from these springs is not only clear but also rare in north China. It contains no alkali in it.

In March, 1949 when the Central Committee of the Chinese Communist Party was moved to Beijing, the Fragrant Hills Park became its seat. Here the late Chairman Mao Zedong and other Chinese leaders did a lot of work for the liberation of whole China and the founding of the People's Republic of China. In November of the same year, the seat was moved to Zhongnanhai near Tian'anmen Square.

Xianglufeng (The Incense Burner Peak) 香炉峰

The Incense Burner Peak is the summit of the Fragrant Hills. To its west is a precipice nicknamed the Devil Frowning Peak, which is very difficult to climb. On top of the hill is a huge piece of rock, which looks like an incense burner at a distance, so it is also named the Incense Burner Peak. It is 557 metres above sea level, the highest peak among the nearby hills. Up there, visitors can have a magnificent view of the surrounding area.

Xiangshan (Fragrant Hills) Hotel ★★★★ 香山饭店

Xiangshan Hotel is situated at the foot of the Fragrant Hills in the western suburbs of Beijing. With 322 guest rooms, the hotel was designed by the world-famous Chinese-American architect Ieoh Ming Pei. It was opened in early 1983. The central atrium and the main artificial garden are the most successful parts of the hotel. In the garden is a man-made lake of 1,400 square metres.

On the terrace above the lake stands a miniature "stone forest," with weirdly shaped rocks shipped here all the way from the Stone Forest near Kunming, Southwest China.

Smoke Trees 黄栌

Autumn is the busiest period for the Fragrant Hills when the red leaves there always attract millions of people from China and abroad.

The Fragrant Hills have more than 99,000 smoke trees, of which approximately 100 trees have a history of 300 years. When the frosty season comes, the mountain looks like a flaming cloud stretching to the sky. Legend has it that in the Qing Dynasty, Emperor Qianlong (1736-1795) had the Tranquility Garden constructed there. He visited it after the garden was completed. The emperor felt that the garden had everything except a trace of autumn. Therefore, he ordered Liu Yong, an official in charge of gardening, to come and bring autumn with him in three days or his whole family would be beheaded.

Liu Yong felt hopeless but suddenly he got an inspiration. He handed a message boldly to the emperor. The message read the autumn was in the emperor Majesty's command, please authorize him and tell him how to make the autumn scene there more beautiful. The emperor was very happy and wrote three Chinese characters meaning "Forest of Splendid Autumn" in brush and a note beside the writing showed a forest of smoke trees. Liu Yong took the hint and planted a hundred smoke trees. From that time on, the northwest wind has brought the seeds to the south slope and formed the magnificent scenery of today.

The Ruins of Yuanmingyuan
圆 明 园 遗 址

Yuanmingyuan or the Garden of Perfection and Brightness, located on the northwestern outskirts of Beijing, is one of the five famous gardens built during the Qing Dynasty. With its charming landscape and numerous springs, the area has always been the site of gardens and parks. In 1723 when Qing Emperor Yongzheng succeeded the throne, he ordered Yuanmingyuan be built and its construction lasted over a period of 150 years.

Yuanmingyuan actually included three separate gardens. The one dating back to the Yongzheng period (1723-1735) was called Yuanmingyuan and the other two gardens added in its vicinity under the Qianlong's reign (1736-1795) were called Changchunyuan (Garden of Everlasting Spring) and Wanchunyuan (Garden of Eternal Spring). The three put together, Yuanmingyuan encompassed 347 hectares (867. 5 acres) of land with constructions totalling 160, 000 square metres of floor space. Its major part was constructed as the model of classical Chinese garden designed at its peak and a paragon of Eastern art. Meanwhile, Giuseppe Castiglione (1688-1766), or Lang Shining as known in China, the imperial court artist from Italy, and other Western Missionaries working with the Qing court contributed their creativity to the building of a significant part of the palace. The pavilions took on designs that integrated Western and Eastern aesthetics. and in the southern part of the garden were built three rows of palaces, with the Hall of Uprightness and Brilliance standing at its centre.

The garden was later expanded. Lakes and canals were excavated, hills made and trees planted. More palaces and pavilions were built to add beauty to the landscape. Five Qing emperors—Yongzheng, Qianlong, Jiaqing, Daoguang, and Xianfeng—spent most of their time in Yuanmingyuan, holding audiences and attending to state affairs.

The landscaping of Yuanmingyuan was based on the famous gardens in South China, which embodied the fine tradition of Chinese gardening and the refined skills of Chinese art and architecture. Halls and pavilions were built into the landscape, halfway up the hills, in the valleys or in mid-lakes. The interiors used partitions, screens and decorative windows to give a sense of close proximity to the outside world.

Yuanmingyuan, in its furnishings and decor, collected the best of the Eastern art pieces—paintings, ceramics and porcelain and glasswares—which should match the collections and buildings in France's Versailles. The bronze ox, tiger and monkey along with nine other bronze animal heads, once stood atop the shoulders of human statues. Placed on two sides of an exquisite fountain in front of the huge Haiyantang Hall, they represent the 12 animals in the Chinese zodiac as well as each of the 12 two-hour periods a day. Water would spout forth from the mouth of the heads during each of the two-hour periods. At 12 pm, water would spurt from all 12 statues at the same time to create spectacles. Artistically, the bronze heads took on different designs. Each offering his vivid expression, the bronze statues were made using top workmanship in the imperial dynasty. The relics experts attending the preview expressed the most favour for the monkey. The design of the monkey incorporated the face and nose of the Chinese Monkey King. And the horns on the ox head are definitely of Western style. While the head of the tiger, king of the animals, looks plain, he bears on his forehead the hallmark wrinkles resembling the Chinese character wang, or the king. The bronze heads provide valuable materials for studies on the art exchanges between the East and West in the 17th and 18th centuries, especially in the field of sculpture. In 1860, the British and French invaders entered Yuanmingyuan's gardens to plunder and burn during the Second Opium War (1856-1860). In 1900, Yuanmingyuan was again plundered by the Allied Forces of the Eight Powers. Warlords and bandits stole or destroyed what was left. As a correspondent for the British newspaper, the Times, described in his dispatch on November 7 that year, every soldier on the spot tried to grab as many spoils as possible. Fires raged for three days and nights. Of the hundreds of pavilions, shrines, halls and other building complexes, only 29 in remote northern corner and in the lakes were unscathed. The Haiyantang Hall was left with only a few pillars, beams and its arch. The 12 bronze animals of the zodiac were looted and taken out of the country with countless other precious objects from the palace. Lu Yanzhen, senior researcher in imperial court history with the Forbidden City said there must be a lot of time-pieces—possibly the best of the period, but none are left. During their travels abroad after China opened to the outside world in 1979, leading Chinese historians, archaeologists and relics connoisseurs have had chances to view some of the looted relics in leading museums and libraries in Europe and North America.

With the exception of the three heads, only four others of the 12 animal heads have surfaced and have known owners after they were smuggled abroad. the horse, now kept by a collector in Taiwan, was returned to Beijing for temporary viewing at an exhibition in 1995. While the pig is stored in a museum in New York, the rat and rabbit are preserved in private collections in France. The whereabouts of the remaining five remain unknown.

The return of the three bronze heads—the looted relics—to Beijing（被掠夺的文物回到北京）has sparked another round of discussion about what to do to preserve Yuanmingyuan. Following the steps of the British and French soldiers, soldiers of the Eight Allied Powers, during their invasion of Beijing, swept away the valuables, destroyed the remaining buildings, and even cut down all the trees. the locals began to move in and took away the old bricks and stone pieces in 1917, when the government had decided to stop further maintenance. Some farming also started at the ruins.

When New China was founded in 1949, the part of Yuanmingyuan which included the ruins granite pillars of the former Haiyantang Hall, the brick labyrinth and some of the water ways were bordered up and opened as a public park. But today, leading historians, archaeologists, architects and many people are increasingly dissatisfied with the status quo of Yuanmingyuan. In an effort to attract more tourists, a succession of the park management during the past two decades have added scenes that were not in the palace. For many years, a part of the original palace was reduced to garbage dumps and a slum where migrants lived while a number of factories operated in another part of the original Yuanmingyuan.

After years of public outcry as well as urging from leading experts, the Haidian District Government has been working during the past three years to clear the area adjacent to the current park proper. Factories have since been moved. About 600 families have been relocated from inside to apartments outside the palace ground.

Having complied an anthology of all major original scenery within the Old Summer Palace, He Zhongyi and a number of people have expressed their beliefs that work should be done to restore a few of the traditional Chinese buildings and pavilions. However, others suggest that the ruins be left alone. they believe efforts should only be made to preserve what remains. Lu Jimin said that the ruins will remind the posterity of the humiliation we Chinese suffered in the past.

With the return of the three bronze heads and the hexagonal porcelain vase, attention had also been turned to the treasures that still wander adrift abroad.

The rare relics are exhibited at Poly Art Museum with more than 100 bronze artifacts collected by Poly from overseas in the past few years. The hexagonal porcelain vase, the fourth piece of looted relics auction in Hong Kong is exhibited at the Capital Museum in Beijing.

The pieces that escaped destruction include the marble columns standing on the Peking University campus and the Beijing Library courtyard. The stone screens with carvings of banners and armor, which were moved to other places, have been returned to Yuanmingyuan.

Soon after the founding of New China, the late Premier Zhou Enlai gave an instruction that Yuanmingyuan should be preserved. Now, outlines of the imperial garden can still be traced, and much of the area has been planted with trees. Paths and bridges have been renovated.

A museum has been set up showing the history of Yuanmingyuan and plans for its future restoration.

A 1,997-kilogram, 2.22-metre-high bronze vessel presented by Hong Kong youths to the motherland 10 days before Hong Kong's return was officially unveiled on June 21, 1997 at Yuanmingyuan (Old Summer Palace) in Beijing. Modelled after "*Simuwu*" an ancient square cooking vessel with two looped handles and four legs, the vessel expressed the youths best wishes to the nation.

Statue Stands for Rejuvenation

A giant four-legged bronze statue, symbolizing power and sovereignty according to Chinese tradition, was unveiled on January 28, 2000 at the Yuanmingyuan Park. The statue, named the "Centennial *Ding**" of Chinese Rejuvenation," stands 5.6 metres high and 2.5 metres wide at the square in front of the park gate. On the statue's body are figures of a dragon, tiger, phoenix and other legendary animals, which stand for heaven,

---

* *Ding*, an ancient type of cooking vessel that has come to symbolize power, was placed at the Yuanmingyuan Park on January 28, 2000.

earth, and the four directions. Combining designs from the Xia and Shang dynasties 5,000 years ago and as late as the last feudal dynasty, Qing, the new one symbolizes the people's hope to rejuvenate the nation with prosperity, power, and solidarity.

Fuhai (the Lake of Blessings) 福海

Reconstruction of the Lake of Blessings, which was destroyed in 1860, was begun in December, 1984 as the State Council approved joint venture and completed in October, 1985. Half a million cubic meters of clean water from the Miyun Reservoir poured into the 28-hectare (69.2 acres) lake, which is similar in size to the Beihai Lake in downtown Beijing. The Lake of Blessings has three neatly mounted islets in the centre, a hexagonal pavilion on the east islet, and six stone arch bridges. The project cost 3.5 million yuan (US$423,000). Two hundred boats, including five motorboats are now available for use by tourists.

Reconstruction of Yuanmingyuan

Yuanmingyuan, once a showpiece of ancient Chinese architecture and gardens also known as the Old Summer Palace, will be rebuilt after years of debate. After its construction, the park will be divided into six areas: Western-style buildings, a cultural relics exhibition, out-door relics, a leisure and entertainment area and a service and administration area. These features are in plans made by the Beijing Urban Planning and Designing Institution. Yuanmingyuan, an imperial garden larger than the present Summer Palace west of it, was built during the Qing Dynasty (1644-1911). French and British troops looted and burned it in 1860. Today visitors may tour the broken walls and posts and reconstruct the park in their minds. The exhibition hall will show cultural relics from the park and its history. Architects first raised the idea of reconstruction in 1983, but it evoked fierce debate about whether the park should be rebuilt or not. Some experts suggested that the park be restored completely according to its original design to exhibit the imperial culture. Those opposed, including architects and National People's Congress members, said that the park could never be exquisite again after the 1860 war. They said the park's main value is that the remains serve to teach about the country's humiliating past. New construction will make up less than 10 per cent of the total showpieces. Most of it are functional construction such as bridges and pavilions. After the project is done, shops inside the park that are not in keeping with the park's style will be closed. And more than 600 families living in the park, plus 10 institutions that called it home, moved out by December 2000. But the park

353

won't be closed during the renovation. Visitors will see the construction as well as the imperial remains. The park was first built in 1709 and underwent 150 years of construction under five emperors of the Qing Dynasty. After Yuanmingyuan was looted and burned, many of the relics were removed in the following decades.

The reconstruction of an 11-kilometre wall bordering the ruins of Yuanmingyuan, which was also called garden of the gardens were completed by the end of 2001. The walls strictly follow the garden's original design. With a total investment of 11 million yuan (US$1.3 million), the project reconstructed 2 kilometres and repaired 1 kilometre of wall in 2001 alone. The whole project, which started in 1985, saw 3 kilometres of wall finished in the 1980s and 6 kilometres in 1994, using municipal government grants and donations from individuals. A total of 615 families have already moved out of the garden at a cost of 280 million yuan (US$34 million). Regulations about protecting the garden had been drafted before the end of May 2001 by the administrative department of the park.

Central and South Seas (Zhongnanhai)
中　南　海

Now we come to the Central and South Seas or Zhongnanhai in Chinese. It is located on the west of the Forbidden City. The area used to be called "three seas," Western Lake or Pool of Great Secretion 太液池. It covers an area of 100 hectares (247 acres), of which the Seas occupies 47 hectares (116 acres). It was first built in Liao (907-1125) and rebuilt in Jin (1115-1234), Yuan (1279-1368), Ming (1368-1644), and Qing (1644-1911) dynasties. The area between New China Gate 新华门 on Chang'an Boulevard in the south and Yingtai 瀛台 (Sea Terrace Island) in the north is called the South Lake. The area north of the Hall of Diligent Government 勤政殿 and south of the Temple of Endless Blessings 万善堂 is called the Central Lake, which is connected to the South Lake by a lock located near the old eastern gate of the area; and the area north of the Hall of Received Brilliance 承光殿 and south of the Five-Dragon Pavilions 五龙亭 is known as the North Lake or Beihai. A long white marble bridge — the Golden Tortoise Jade Rainbow Bridge 金鳌玉蛛桥 (formerly Golden Sea Bridge or Imperial River Bridge 原名金海桥或御河桥)—divides the Central Lake from the North Lake. The water supply for the lakes comes from the Jade Spring Hill 玉泉山 to the west of Beijing and enters the city at the Gate of Moral Victory 德胜门 in the northwest corner of the old city limits. The beautiful natural hills and ponds in this area inspired the emperors of the Liao Dynasty (907-1125) to choose this area as their pleasure park and called the North Lake the Jade Islet. During the Jin Dynasty (1115-1234), the North Lake became the site of the emperors' winter palace. In the Yuan Dynasty (1279-1368), the lakes were enclosed to become part of the Imperial Palace in the Mongol capital of Dadu (Great Capital), and the lakes were granted a new name — the Pool of Great Secretion 太液池. At that time, the lakes were widened and deepened, and the mud dredged from them was heaped up to the north of the Forbidden City to form Coal Hill (Prospect) Park. The lakes attained their present dimensions of two kilometres from south to north and, at their widest point, 200 metres from east to west. When Emperor Yongle (1403-1424) of the Ming Dynasty (1368-1644) rebuilt the Imperial Palace in 1417, he extended the palace walls to enclose both the former Yuan palace and the gardens to the west. Hence the Ming and Qing dynasties, the area became known as the Western Gardens 西苑 and continued to serve palace residents as a place of leisure. During the Qing Dynasty (1644-1911), refurbishment of the area continued on a grand scale, and the majority of the structures and relics, which remain today date from that period. After the overthrown of the Qing Dynasty in 1911, the Central and South lakes were turned into a park for a short period of time and served as the headquarters of the government of Yuan Shikai (1859-1916). Since the founding of the People's Republic of China, it has been the headquarters of the Central Committee of the Chinese Communist Party and the State Council of the People's Republic of China. It is now not only the supreme leading centre for the whole nation, but also one of the important places for both the Chinese people and international friendly intercourse. The late Chairman Mao Zedong(1893-1976) and the late Premier Zhou Enlai (1898-1976) used to live in it.

355

The World Park in Beijing
北京世界公园

Located in the Fengtai District of Beijing 16 kilometres from the city proper, the World Park in Beijing features 106 of the most famous sites from 14 countries and regions the world over.

The park, encompassing 46.7 hectares (115.4 acres), consists of two parts:

The scenic area in miniature displayed according to the position of its country on the map, and a shopping, dining and entertainment area. The entertainment area is situated in an international folkloric village characterized by buildings in the American and European styles. Tourists can take an electric train and a motorboat through the park to simulate a trip around the world.

The park includes most of the recognized spots of interest on the globe. Among these are the Wooden Pagoda in China's Ying County, the world's oldest and best preserved wooden pagoda, the Leaning Tower of Pisa, the Pharoas of Alexandria and Eiffet Tower in Paris. China's Qingyingjing Park, Japan's Katzura Imperial Villa, and an old style garden of the US are grouped together to represent the splendour of the world's different gardening styles and in recognition of the many distinctive forms which landscape gardening has taken in China.

Great efforts were made to build the structures out of the same materials as the real ones, and marble and granite surfaces, together with copper and gilded sculptures help produce a realistic effect. For instance, the Pyramid is made of 200,000 white marble bricks, each as large as a bar of soap. Red Square is paved with over 5 million red bricks smaller than mahjong tiles. Lawns in the park are dotted with 100 well-known sculptures, among them the Statue of Liberty, the Little Mermaid from Copenhagan, Michelangelo's David and the Venus de Milo.

The park also has a fountain operated by laser beams, a plant maze and a fairyland in which children and adults alike can enjoy themselves. Regular international parades of folklore are planned to provide tourists with a chance to view folk customs from different countries.

China Ethnic Culture Park
中 华 民 族 园

China Ethnic Culture Park is located near the Olympic Sports Centre in the northern part of the city of Beijing. The park is a large cultural venue featuring traditional architecture of various ethnic groups, folklore, singing and dancing performances, handicraft works and national food. The park, encompassing 45 hectares(111. 2 acres), is composed of 37 ethnic group villages and some 40 ethnic group scenic spots. These ethnic groups include the Bai, Tibetan, Naxi, Mosu, Dulong and Nu minorities. The China Ethnic Culture Park boasts some large minority-style architectures including the Museum of the Chinese nationalities with an exhibition area of 1, 000 square metres, the Chinese nationalities Song and Dance Theatre with 800 seats, the Big Fall Square large enough to hold 4, 000 people, and the Three-Pagoda Nationalities Get-Together Square large enough to accommodate 6, 000 people. In the past few years, the China Ethnic Culture Park has played host to the closing ceremony of the Far-East and South Pacific Games for the disabled, the Evening Party of the World Conference of Archives, the closing ceremony of the World Conference of Military Medical Science, the Evening Party of the World Conference of Geology, and some other domestic and international conferences and activities. The Closing Ceremony of the XX UIA Conference was also held here.

China is home to 55 ethnic groups (minority nationalities), and each with a diverse cultural heritage, different customs and costumes, and unique arts and crafts.

China Millennium Monument
中 华 世 纪 坛

Located to the west of Chang'an (Eternal Peace) Boulevard, and the Military Museum on the north side of Fuxing Road, the 4. 5-hectare (11. 12 acres) area incorporates an elegant dome-shaped structure which is approached along a bronze-clad walk-way through a landscaped square. Within the building structure is a major meeting hall and the memorial site is dotted with special statues and sculptures. Construction of China Millennium Monument began on March 2, 1999, and the end of 1999 completed it. The monument is an embodiment of China's splendid national culture and its ancient civilization. It is a centre of patriotic education and international cultural exchange. The monument is also a symbol of the unification of the nation to celebrate the return of Macao. And it is also China's symbolic memorial building to commemorate the 50th anniversary of the founding of the People's Republic of China and greet the new millennium.

Encompassing 30, 000 square metres, the monument is made up of nine parts, including the symbolic principal structure, a bronze-paved path leading to the main structure, and an exhibition hall for works of art. Hundreds of architects and artists participated in the design of the project, which was built using modern technology and is quite different from China's traditional commemorative structures. The exhibition hall, built using the most advanced technology and equipment, provides a fine space for art works from the 20th century and other parts of the world.

The monument is a structure combining the spirit of traditional Chinese culture with modern architectural art, and integrating sculpture, mural painting, and other art forms. It represents not only an eternal memory of the turn of the 20th century, but also a centre for cultural, artistic, and scientific exhibitions from home and abroad and, most importantly, an inspiration to patriotism.

Building the monument's foundation, which requires an investment of 200 million yuan (US$24 million), was completed by the turn of the 20th century. The government has announced that the monument is a public welfare project which welcomes donations from overseas Chinese and foreign countries. The committee established a special fund for the public to donate money or materials for the project.

In May 1999, Mr He Hongshen, deputy director of the Preparatory Committee for the Macao Special Administrative Region donated US$3 million at the ceremony in honour of the first donation for the project.

President Jiang Zemin inscribed the name of China's newly completed 21st Century Altar.

In December, 1999, a 262-metre-long raised pathway paved with bronze plates will highlight the China Century Monument., an altar being constructed in the capital city to commemorate the new millennium. The plate is inscribed with the text of 5,000 years of Chinese history. Of the 262 plates to be placed on the pathway at Yuyuantan Park, the first was installed at 10 am on November 12, 1999. The south end of the path is near Holy Fire Square and ends at the century monument's main structure of the altar. The 180,000-character record covers important events in China's history. The last bronze plate placed in the path will remain blank, pending future historical moments. A unique aspect of the path will be a 5-millimetre-thick stream of water, which will cover the plates year round. Visitors to the monument can walk along the pathway and tread atop the inscriptions covered by a thin shield of water to reach the altar. Visitors can see their shadows in the water, feeling absorbed in the history of our nation. The flowing water and the steps from visitors will not damage the inscriptions, thanks to the special way the plates were designed. The expected life of the inscription is 3,300 years.

Needle points way to millennium

Workers hoisted up the Spatio-Temporal Needle, a 27-metre-high metal column weighing 17 tons, in Beijing on November 20, 1999. The column, which took four hours to install, stands right in the middle of the China Millennium Monument, which was built for a celebration on December 31, 1999.

Millennium Bell

Workers hanged a newly made copper bell named the Millennium Bell at

Beijing China Millennium Monument on December 22, 1999. The 3.4-metre-wide, 6.8-metre-high bell weighs 50 tons and was rung to celebrate the new millennium.

Drum Tower
鼓 楼

Located in the centre of "Dadu" (the Yuan name for the capital city), the Drum Tower was first built in 1272. At first the tower was named Qi Zheng Lou (or Orderly Administration Tower). After only a few years the tower was burned down in a big fire and then rebuilt on the same site in 1297. In the Ming Dynasty (1368-1644) Emperor Yongle ordered that the Drum Tower be rebuilt. This time the tower was placed exactly on the central axis from south to north. In 1950, a stone tablet was unearthed from under the Houman Bridge right in front of the Drum Tower. On the tablet were carved a mouse and the two Chinese characters for Beijing. The mouse symbolizes the centre among the 12 animals that represent the 12 Earthly Branches. Therefore, this carved inscription hints that the bridge is right on the central axis, which starts from the Zhengyangmen Gate in the south, crosses through the Forbidden City, passes the Coal Hill, and then stretches to the Bell Tower on the north. On a terrace four metres high, 55.6 metres wide and 30 metres long, the five wooden framed halls of the tower are roofed with yellow glazed tiles. While in the Qing Dynasty (1644-1911), the Drum Tower was renovated twice, once in 1800 and the second time in 1894. In 1924, the Drum Tower was given another name, Ming Chi Lou meaning Remembering Humiliations Tower, in order to arouse the people's patriotic enthusiasm to save China from imperialist powers. A popular educational hall was then opened inside the tower, which displayed ancient weapons and armor, cultural relics, and photographs of recent popular scientific inventions. During the wartime period after the September 18th Incident (the seizure of Shenyang in 1931 by the Japanese invaders as a move towards their occupation of the entire Northeast), an exhibition on the second floor of the Drum Tower showed a large map of China with a Japanese flag and rifle bayonet pointing to the Northeast. When the Drum Tower was set up, it was equipped with 24 drums, only one of which has survived. The other 23 were destroyed by the Allied Forces of Eight Imperialist Powers in 1900.

Since the establishment of the People's Republic of China in 1949, the Drum Tower has been used as a cultural centre. In 1984, the Drum Tower was thoroughly renovated once again, with the financial help from the State Cultural Relics Bureau and the Beijing Municipal People's Government.

Bell Tower
钟　　楼

To the north of the Drum Tower stands the Bell Tower, which was first built in 1272. Later it was burnt down. In 1420 it was rebuilt, then burnt down again.

In 1745, Qing Emperor Qianlong ordered the Bell Tower to be rebuilt. For fire prevention, the tower was built with bricks and stones this time. A stone tablet with an inscription by Emperor Qianlong was erected in front of the tower.

The Bell Tower stands 47.9 metres in height and covers an area of more than 6,000 square metres. It is double eaved with black glazed tiles. A 25-ton iron bell was originally hung in the tower but it was later replaced by a much louder giant bronze bell, weighing 42 tons. The bronze bell, 5.4 metres in height, 3.4 metres in diameter and 0.27 metre in thickness, was cast in a foundry west of the Old Drum Tower Street during the period from 1403 to 1424. Made of "sound bronze," the sound of its tolling reaches dozens of kilometres away. Together in regular harmony, the drum and bell were "beaten" every morning at five o'clock to mark the day's beginning and beaten once again at seven o'clock every evening to mark the night watch time. High ranking civil officials and military officers in the imperial court, soldiers in the militia and the common people worked and rested in accordance with the chronometry of the drum and bell system. Famous for its resounding tone, the bell also had a legend surrounding it. When the bronze bell was being cast in the foundry, the workers spent more than a year on the work, but all in vain. The emperor had set a date after which all the workers would be put to death. To help her poor father finish the work, the young daughter of old supervisor Deng attempted to "move heaven" by sacrificing herself and jumped into the molten bronze. Her father tried to stop her but was able to save only one of his daughter's embroidered shoes. The dead girl was honored by the emperor as the Female Deity of the Gold Furnace, and a temple was set up in her honor before the furnace. After the bronze bell was cast and hung, its melodious sound could be heard far and wide on fine days, but on rainy and windy days, its tone would turn sad. Then mothers would tell their children that the plaintive sound was the voice of the Goddess of the Gold

Bell asking for her missing shoe.

For more than seven hundred years, the Drum and Bell towers have experienced many vicissitudes, the ups and downs of life's fortunes. The surface of the bronze bell in the Bell Tower shows a "scar" left by the bayonets of foreign invaders.

The Ancient Beijing Observatory
北京古观象台

Located off the Chang'an (Eternal Peace) Boulevard near the Beijing Railway Station, the Ancient Beijing Observatory was first built in 1442 during the Ming Dynasty (1368-1644). It is one of the oldest observatories in the world. The observatory was renovated in the early 1980s and reopened to the public in April 1983. After renovation it is very much as it was when it served the imperial court. In 1227, when the Northern Song Dynasty (960-1127) was overthrown, the astronomical instruments in the capital at Bianliang (today's Kaifeng, Henan Province) were moved to Beijing (then called Zhongdu, meaning Central Capital) by the Jin rulers and installed in the Jin Chief Astronomer's Observatory. When the Yuan Dynasty (1279-1368) succeeded the Jin Dynasty (1115-1234) and established its capital in Beijing, it built a new observatory just north of the site of the present-day structure in 1279. The instruments designed by Wang Xun and Guo Shoujin and built by Nepalese craftsman Arniko served virtually unchanged as the basis of astronomical work for the last 500 years.

In 1368 when the first Ming Emperor Zhu Yuanzhang moved the capital to Nanjing, these astronomical instruments were brought to the city. The third Emperor Yongle of the Ming Dynasty took power in 1403 and moved the capital from Nanjing to Beijing in 1420. He did not dare to move these instruments because the tomb of the first Ming Emperor was in Nanjing. Instead he sent some artisans to the city in 1437 to make wooden copies of the Song armillary sphere and the Yuan guibiao (a type of sundial) and abridged armilla (a simplified form of the armillary sphere). A new set of bronze instruments was then cast in Beijing modelled after these wooden copies.

At the same time, a new observatory was constructed on the site of the water tower to the southeast of the old capital. It was during that period that the Ancient Beijing Observatory took on its present scale and layout and was equipped with such traditional instruments as the armillary sphere, the abridged armilla, and the celestial globe on the observatory

361

platform, as well as the guibiao and the water clock below the platform.

During the period from 1662 to 1722, Ferdinand Verbient, a Belgian missionary, was put in charge of introducing European astronomical measurements and instrumentation in the Imperial Astronomical Bureau. Between 1669 and 1673, he supervised the construction of a celestial globe, an equatorial theodolite, a zodiac theodolite, an altazimuth, a quadrant, and an ancient sextant. Later another altazimuth and an armilla were built in 1715 and 1744 respectively.

In 1900, when the Allied Forces of Eight Powers invaded Beijing, everything was looted at the observatory. The French troops shipped the equatorial armilla, the ecliptic armilla, the azimuth theodolite, the quadrant and the abridged armilla to the French Embassy to China in Beijing. Two years later in 1902, under the pressure of public opinion, these astronomical instruments were returned to China. The Ming made armillary sphere, and Qing made armillary sphere, and Qing made celestial globe, armilla, azimuth theodolite, and the sextant were taken away by the Germans to Berlin. It was not until 1921 that these instruments were sent back to Beijing after World War I in compliance with the Versailles Peace Treaty.

After September 18, 1931 when the Japanese militarists launched a large-scale invasion to North China Plain, Chinese scientists shipped some of the instruments to Nanjing in 1932 for the sake of the cultural relics. Today they are displayed at Purple Hills Observatory and Nanjing Museum respectively.

Nowadays, on the platform of the Ancient Beijing Observatory as the visitor climbs it from right to left are displayed an armilla, a quadrant, a celestial globe, an ecliptic armilla, an altazimuth, an azimuth theodolite, a sextant and an equatorial armilla.

The brick terraced observatory consists of a 17-metre high platform. The top of the platform is 23. 9 metres from west to east and 20. 4 metres from north to south.

Chaoyang Park
朝 阳 公 园

Of all the 135 parks in Beijing, Chaoyang Park, the largest park ever built in Beijing, is seeking overseas co-operation in an effort to construct new recreation facilities. The park has built five major projects on an area of 60, 000 square metres at a cost of US$ 100 million. The projects include a water park, a movie theatre complex, an amusement park and a beach resort. Chaoyang Park, which covers 320 hectares (790. 72 acres), including 67 hectares (165. 6 acres) of water space, near the embassy quarters area in eastern Beijing, opened on September 29, 1999, as one of 67 key projects marking the 50th anniversary of the People's Republic of China. The park's size is approximately 20 hectares (49. 42 acres) larger than the world-famous Summer Palace, the imperial garden built on the western outskirts of Beijing during the Qing Dynasty.

Prince Gong's Mansion (Residence of the Last Qing Emperor's Father)
恭 王 府

Prince Gong's Mansion was first built in front of Lion Alley in the eastern sector of Di'anmen (Gate of Earthly Peace) Dongjie (east street). But the present Prince Gong's Mansion is located at 17 Qianhai Xijie on the east bank of Shicha Lake. The mansion is the most exquisitely decorated and best preserved of the princes' mansions in the capital. Besides the residence there is also a large garden.

Prince Gong (1832-1898), or Yixin, was the most prominent figure in Empress Dowager Cixi's (1835-1908) times. His palace is among the best-preserved Qing Dynasty (1644-1911) architecture in Beijing. A large garden covers the north half of the 5. 7 square kilometres of grounds, and the front gate combines Chinese and Western designs. Although Qing Dynasty rulers were known for strict observance to ancient customs, they could not escape the influence of Western civilization. The gate tells the story of how different civilizations can co-exist in harmony. Inside the gate stands a 5-metre-high stone. Like the other stones in the garden, it came from Lake Tai in Wuxi, Jiangsu Province. The stone attracts visitors' attention and thereby prevents the intricacies of the garden from being taken in at one glance. Named "Peak of Self-Enjoyment," the stone typifies ancient Chinese scholars' pride in keeping apart from worldly ways. As an educated man, Prince Gong shared this view, but he also was an important official. In 1861, when Emperor Xianfeng (ruled 1851-1861) fell seriously ill, Cixi's 6-year-old son Zaichun was the only eligible successor. But Xianfeng sensed her ambition and named eight ministers to aid the new Emperor Tongzhi (ruled 1862-1874) . That winter, Cixi sought Prince Gong's help and captured the eight ministers, three of whom she promptly ordered suffocated. From then on, Cixi attended to the state affairs, with a veil to separate her and the obedient court. Prince Gong's crucial role in building Cixi's power nevertheless did not endear him to her. Cixi never ceased suspecting him. In the ensuing 40 years, she dismissed him twice and kept a firm grip on power. Therefore, it is not surprising that Prince Gong had the "Peak of Self-Enjoyment" set to comfort himself and appease the distrustful Empress Dowager. A few steps north of the peak, Flowing Cup Pavilion nestles in a pile of stones. A tiny tunnel linked with the garden stream snakes through the stone floor. Merry-makers would play a drinking game by floating wine cups through the tunnel. When a cup became lodged in it, the person closest to the cup would have to drink from it. The tradition came from Eastern Jin Dynasty (AD 317-AD 420) practice. In those days, people celebrated the third day of the third lunar month by bathing in the garden's streams in hopes of gaining good luck and health. In the Qing Dynasty, the Manchurian rulers eagerly indulged in the practice at Flowing-Cup Pavilion. Furthermore, the water on which the wine cups floated came from the Jade Spring Hill on the western outskirts of Beijing. Prince Gong's Mansion was the only place outside the Forbidden City that could use the sacred water.

Through several moon-shaped gates and covered corridors north of the pavilion, an elegant building nestles among bamboo and Chinese parasols. Its roofs point upward like the wings of a flying bird, and the pillars are all painted like bamboo. This is the "Hermit Cottage amid Green Bamboo." Legend has it that Shun (c. 2250 BC), one of the three prehistoric kings in Chinese civilization, died on a southern inspection tour. His two wives wept so bitterly their tears spotted every nearby bamboo tree. In his great work *A Dream of Red Mansions*, Cao Xueqin (?-1763) designed a similar bamboo house for the sentimental character Lin Daiyu. A few steps away from the hermit Cottage is the highest spot in the garden, the Terrace of Inviting the Moon. In the *A Dream of Red Mansions*, the once-prosperous Jia family celebrated a Mid-Autumn Festival such a terrace in their Grand View Garden. East and west of the terrace two covered corridors tilting down the hill. Downhill from the terrace is the Cave of Mystic Clouds. Stretching east and west, the cave is shaped like a flying bat, "fu," (meaning happiness in Chinese). At the cave centre, which also falls on the main axis of the garden, there stands a stele inscribed in Emperor Kangxi's handwriting "fu." No one knows for sure how it had got it, because nobody was allowed to move or imitate the Emperor's handwriting in the Qing Dynasty. One theory is that Emperor Qianlong (ruled 1736-1795) gave it to his favourite minister He Shen 和珅 (1750-1799).

Most researchers agree that He Shen lived there before Prince Gong. As the father of the emperor's son-in-law, He Shen enjoyed unrivaled power and prestige. In the last two decades of Qianlong's rule, He Shen amassed 800 million taels of silver and enlarged his palace several times. When Emperor Qianlong died, Emperor Jiaqing (ruled 1796-1820) immediately arrested He Shen and gave him a rope to hang himself. Among the 20 charges against He Shen, Emperor Jiaqing said the setting of his garden was too similar to that of the imperial garden, Yuanmingyuan (the Old Summer Palace), a crime that could lead to the execution of He Shen's entire family. In front of the terrace and the cave is the Hall of Tranquility and Goodness. Here Prince Gong met with many foreign guests.

In early 1861, before fleeing English and French troops, Emperor Xianfeng asked his younger brother, Prince Gong, to chair an office that could deal with the foreigners. Thus came the famous "Zongliyamen" (Government Office of Dealing with Foreign Affairs). Under Prince Gong's leadership, this quasi-foreign ministry borrowed astounding sums from Western allies to establish the first Chinese navy, and more importantly, to quash the unceasing peasant uprisings, the biggest one being the "Taiping Heavenly Kingdom Revolution (1851-1864), and the "Boxer Uprising" (1900). It is very likely that in the Hall of Tranquillity and Goodness, the Qing rulers and their Western allies made several secret deals. To the west of the hall is a 400-square metre pond. South of the pond is the cherry-shaped Fragrance Pavilion and a 20-metre mini city wall. The lintel of the city gate bears the carving: "Yu Pass, " the original name of the Shanhaiguan (Mountain and Sea) Pass in northern Hebei Province. Built in 1381, the Shanhaiguan Pass, is between the Bohai Sea to the south and the Jiaoshan Mountain to the north. It is the eastern starting point of the Great Wall and the only pass between the northeast and central China. Before conquering the rest of China and naming Beijing the Qing Dynasty capital in 1644, the nomadic ancestors of Manchu rulers lived in the northeast for thousands of years. With a miniature Shanhaiguan Pass, Prince Gong not only provided a unique wall for his garden, but also expressed his faithfulness to his Manchurian origins. As the years passed, neither the Shanhaiguan Pass nor Prince Gong's faithfulness maintained the Manchu reign.

The princes' mansions and large-scale private houses in Beijing were often built with walled flower gardens laid out either behind or to the sides of the main buildings. Nowadays, a few such mansions dating from the Qing Dynasty are still standing. These gardens are ingeniously constructed with complementary buildings and terraces, well-spaced vegetation and hill paths that wind their way around cool and tranquil grottos. They are an exquisite combination of classical Chinese architecture and tasteful landscape.

Beginning from as early as AD 1421, a lot of princes' mansions were built in this city. As time went by, few such mansions have been left so far.

In 1911, 14 years after Prince Gong's death, the three-century Qing Dynasty finally collapsed amid internal revolutions and foreign invasions, leaving places like Prince Gong's Mansion to stand proof of that turbulent period of history.

The Old Beijing Mini Landscape Park
老北京微缩景园
(about 40 kilometres from the city)

Located at Nankou some 40 kilometres away from the city, the Old Beijing Mini Landscape Park is a joint venture of the America Shi Tai Group Stock Co. Ltd., Changping Foreign Economic Relations and Trade Corporation and Changping Nankou Town Industrial Enterprises Corporation. Construction of the park, lasting only 16 months, first began on April 18, 1993 and was finished and opened to the public on August 18, 1994. The total cost for building the park was US\$ 2. 4 million.

Covering an area of 132. 5 acres of land, the Old Beijing Mini Landscape Park includes old Beijing scenes, its traditions and folk life, and a reception and administrative quarter. On a scale of 1: 15, the park brings to the public the Beijing of the Ming and Qing dynasties—its rigorous arrangements, grand styles, strewn skyline and natural adornment.

Apart from more than 100 fine and vivid miniaturized spots the park offers eight performance areas for imperial and folk arts and Beijing style services. The park also provides photographic and video service. It supplies wheelchairs and carriages for disabled children. There are many choices open to tourists who are looking for a suitable vehicle to ride around the park: super dragon wagon, dragon wagon, old fashioned car, Western carriage, tricycle, mule carriage and rickshaw. The park also provides dwarfhorses, camels, imperial carriages and sedans carried by two, four and eight people. The park in addition provides VIP and exhibition rooms that display Beijing's historical development.

The aim of miniaturizing ancient Beijing is to bring back the city as it had been in the past. Publicizing the cultures and traditions over the past thousands of years will surely give both Chinese and overseas visitors the opportunity to see what Beijing once looked like and how people lived during the times of the ancient dynasties.

More than 40 construction companies were involved in building this park, using more than 30 million bricks in all. Many vividly recreated scenes from ancient life are featured in the park. For example, cricket fighting is arranged for visitors. Cricket fighting was once popular in the imperial palace as well as on Beijing streets. Ancient Beijing had special cricket fighting places for the upper, middle and lower classes, and what a fascinating scene it is!

The park also has a bird market, a children's paradise as in the old days, an open-air teahouse and puppet shows. Film shows about life in old Beijing will surely cultivate tourists' tour of the park.

Cherry Ditch Garden
櫻 桃 沟

On the west side of the Shou'an Hill in the western suburbs of Beijing lies the quiet Cherry Ditch Garden, rarely patronized by tourists. Starting from the rear of the Temple of the Reclining Buddha, westward along the foot of the Shou'an Hill, a ditch lying between two hills can be found. It is wide at its mouth but narrow in its interior course. The place is called Tuigu (Retreat Valley). A stream called the Water-End or Water-Head flows through it, and since it runs all the way to the Temple of the Reclining Buddha, tourists may also find their way to the Cherry Ditch by following its banks from the temple. Along the entire course tourists will find grotesque rocks. As the name implies, the place was once filled with cherry trees, but now they grow only at the south of the ditch. Going east along the stream, at the end of the path, a stone bridge connects the two hills. West of the bridge, the gate of the Luyanjingshe (Fine Villa on Deer Cliff) invites tourists, and behind it is the picturesque Cherry Ditch Garden. The entire compound was originally a private villa built on the slope of the hill. Near the entrance are groves of verdurous bamboo; along the path leading into the garden the ground is shaded by full grown trees. In spring and summer, the hues and aroma of wild, seasonal flowers add much to the charm. The numerous natural rocky cliffs alongside the path offer even more scenic beauty.

At the end of the stream a spring rises from a huge rock. Beside it is the Bailuyan (White Deer Cave), inside of which lies a stone bed. Legend

367

has it that a holy man, roaming through the country on a white deer, saw the beautiful scenery of this place and decided to make it his home. Tourists may doubt the story, but the beauty of the place is undeniable.

It is said that cherry trees grew around the Guanghui Buddhist Convent, hence the name Yingtaogou. The cherry trees disappeared long ago, but the name continues to be used.

The Eight Great Temples of the Western Hills
西 山 八 大 处

The Eight Great Temples is the traditional name given to eight Buddhist temples nestled among the clouds on Cuiwei Hill and Lushi Hill in the Western Hills district of Beijing.

The Temple of Eternal Peace 长安寺

The Temple of Eternal Peace is the first temple of the Eight Great Temples of the Western Hills. It is situated on the plain at the foot of Cuiwei Hill. Built in 1504 during the Ming Dynasty and revamped in 1671 during the Qing Dynasty, the temple is comprised of two courtyards, the first containing the Hall of Sakyamuni, the founder of Buddhism and the second the Niangniang (a female deity) Hall. The Hall of Sakyamuni Buddha contains a bronze statue of Guan Yu, a hero of the Three Kingdoms Period (AD 220-AD 280) who was later worshipped as the God of War. Chinese Buddhists worshiped Guan Yu or Lord Guan (AD 160-AD 219) as a temple guardian. In the south corner of the covered corridor in the rear part of the hall is a bronze bell cast in 1600 by imperial command. It is wonderfully preserved after more than 400 years. In front of the Sakyamuni Hall there is an urn-shaped bell struck as part of Buddhist rituals, which also dates from the Ming Dynasty. In the rear courtyard, there are two lacebark pines 两棵白皮龙爪松 reputed to date from the Yuan Dynasty.

368

The Temple of Divine Light 灵光寺

The Temple of Divine Light is the second temple of the Eight Great Temples of the Western Hills. Approximately 500 metres up Cuiwei Hill, tourists come to the Temple of Divine Light. It was first built during the period 766 to 779 in the Tang Dynasty (618-907). Originally called the Dragon Spring Temple 龙泉寺, its name was changed to the Mountain of Awakening Temple 觉山寺 in 1162. In 1428, during the Ming Dynasty, it was restored and resumed its old name, and in 1478, it was finally given its present name. The only extant component of the original temple is the fish pond located behind the halls at the foot of a small cliff. The pond is filled with large and colorful goldfish, some more than half a metre long. Legend has it that fish were placed in the pond before 1851.

The temple originally contained a number of fine old buildings, carvings and statues, but unfortunately the Eight Power Allied Forces destroyed all these when they occupied Beijing in 1900. One notable structure was a large octagonal Liao Dynasty (916-1125) pagoda built of carved bricks in 1071. Originally situated to the east of the goldfish pond, it was called the Pagoda for Entertaining Immortals 招仙塔 . All that remains now is its foundation. The pagoda is important in the history of Buddhism in China since, according to the record, when Buddha was cremated all that remained in his ashes were four teeth, one of which was brought to China in the 11th century and placed here. The Liao Dynasty history records that Emperor Daozong (ruled 1055-1100) placed the tooth in a pagoda here. After the destruction of the pagoda in 1900, monks searching through the rubble found a stone chest containing a wooden box in which they discovered the Buddha's tooth. The tooth remained in the temple until 1955 when it was removed to the Guangji (Great Charity) Temple by the Chinese Buddhist Association and placed in the Hall of Buddhist Relics. During the period 1958 to the spring of 1964, the People's Government built a new 51-metre-high, 13-storey pagoda on the site of the Liao foundation and named it the "Pagoda of the Buddha's Tooth." A row of old monastery buildings to the north of the pond has been restored.

Three Hills Convent 三山庵

Three Hills Convent is the third temple of the Eight Great Temples of the Western Hills. It is situated among the Cuiwei Hill 翠微山, Pingpo Hill 平坡山 and Lushi Hill 卢师山, hence the name. The year of building the convent is unknown, but it was renovated during Emperor Qianlong's reign (1736-1795). The convent is not large and consists of only one courtyard, it is of rather exquisite construction. At the doorway of the main hall there is a rectangular "Cloud and Water Stone," carved with images of scenery, human figures and animals. To the east of the main hall is a small kiosk with an inscribed plaque, which reads: "Cuiwei Hill is part of a painting." Looking out from here, tourists can see many peaks covered with pines and cypresses. The temple is set in the midst of a dense forest that provides a cool and pleasant place for a stroll. During the hottest days, tourists will find an ideal place to flee the heat.

The Temple of Great Compassion 大悲寺

The Temple of Great Compassion is the fourth temple of the Eight Great Temples of the Western Hills. Climbing up the Three Hills Convent, tourists pass a lot of strange rock formations before reaching the fourth of the Eight Great Temples, the Temple of Great Compassion situated on the half slope of the Pingpo Hill. The temple was first built in the Yuan Dynasty (1279-1368). It got its present name in 1712 and restored in 1975. The three main halls in the temple compound date from different eras of the Ming Dynasty (1368-1644), the most recently built being the rearmost Hall of Great Compassion. On the front hall hangs a plaque inscribed with the words "Sea of Compassion," and the courtyard before it is thickly planted with a rare species of bamboo, which remains green throughout the winter. The courtyards also contain potted landscapes, fragrant plants and decorative rockeries. Also of interest to tourists are the two huge ginkgo trees in the rear courtyard, reputed to be more than 800 years old. The carved statues of the eighteen Arhats (Immortals) in the front hall of the temple are some of the finest in all of the Eight Great Temples. Legend has it that the renowned Yuan Dynasty sculptor Liu Yuan made them.

The Dragon King Temple 龙王堂

Located to the northwest of the Temple of Great Compassion, the Dragon King Temple is the fifth of the Eight Great Temples, and is also known as Dragon Spring Convent 龙泉庵 . It was built in 1672. Entering the temple, tourists first notice the sound of a bubbling spring breaking the stillness. The spring bubbles up from beneath a cliff behind the second courtyard and flows through the first courtyard and out of a carved stone spigot in the shape of a dragon's head 石螭吻(石雕龙头)into a pond. The water of this eternally flowing spring is clear and sweet and never freezes in winter. A Pavilion for Listening to the spring stands nearby. Behind the pond is the Hall of the Dragon King. Legend has it that the hall is the residence of the Dragon King. The hall is surrounded by luxuriant green bamboo. The Pavilion of Reclining Leisure and the Pavilion for Listening to the Spring, both of which are built up against the side of the mountain, are wonderful spots for viewing the distant hills.

The Temple of Fragrant World 香界寺

The Temple of Fragrant World is the sixth of the Eight Great Temples. Also known as the Pingpo Temple 平坡寺, the Temple of the Fragrant World is the largest temple complex in the entire area. Some people say that it was first built in the Yuan Dynasty (1279-1368), while others say the temple was constructed in the Tang Dynasty (618-907). It was rebuilt in 1425 in the Ming Dynasty (1368-1644). It was reconstructed in 1678 and revamped in 1748. In the past, it served as the summer villa of Chinese emperors and the Travelling Palace 行宫 and Scripture Repository 藏经楼 erected by Emperor Qianlong can still be seen. The temple boasts five courtyards and also contains many historical relics as well as paintings and calligraphy by celebrities.

The Precious Pearl Cavern 宝珠洞

The Precious Pearl Cavern is the seventh of the Eight Great Temples. The cavern is built on the top of the Pingpo Hill. There is a main hall and two annex buildings. The hall built behind the memorial archway is the noted Precious Pearl Temple. It is the highest point in all the Eight Great Temples, and thus the open gazebo in front of the temple is named "The Pavilion for Distant Viewing." On fine days, tourists can see the entire Beijing, with Kunming Lake to the east, the Yongding River to the southwest, the plains to the south and the city skyline in the centre. Immediately below are the other seven temples. The temple's name derives from the cavern behind the main hall and a stone near its mouth, which resembles a large pearl. Though the floor area of the cave is no more than 25 square metres, a Qing monk named Hai Xiu lived there for 40 years. A statue of this long-term resident standing inside the cavern is popularly known as the "King-of-the-Ghost Bodhisattva."

The Mysterious Demon Cliff 秘魔岩

Located on the top of the Lushi Hill, the Mysterious Demon Cliff is the eighth of the Eight Great Temples. It was first built in the Sui Dynasty (581-618). It was given its present name in the period 1457 to 1464 in the Ming Dynasty. Climbing up the Lushi Hill, tourists pass through a dense grove of trees before coming to an old temple known as the Temple of Buddhahood 证果寺 or the Temple of Pacifying the Nation (Zhengguosi—the two Chinese names are nearly homonymic). Inside the temple courtyard there are exquisitely wrought rockery hills. Directly in front of the main hall is a stone tablet testifying to the Buddha's mercy, and behind it a two-metre-high bronze bell, both dating from the Ming Dynasty. Following the winding path from the western gate of the temple past another pavilion, tourists come to the last of the Eight Great Temples, the Mysterious Demon Cliff. The main feature of the cliff is a large overhanging rock which, when seen from afar, suggests the image of a roaring lion.

On the stone are carved the words, "Natural Secluded Valley" and a number of inscriptions of visitors from all over the world. A stone house built into the cliff is reputed to have been the home of the monk Lu Shi, who in the 7th century travelled from southern China to the outskirts of the capital in a rowboat. Legend has it that a pair of dragons he had accepted as his disciples came to the aid of the local people by ending a terrible drought, whereupon the hill was dubbed Lushi Hill and the Mysterious Demon Cliff renamed Lushi Cave. Down through the ages, the two dragon-disciples have been the subject of numerous folktales and the object of respect and worship for their good deeds. The Temple of Buddhahood, one of the older and larger temples in the area, was first built in the Sui and Tang dynasties more than 1,400 years ago. The name was changed several times during the ages, yet each of these changes reflected the temple's close association with Lu Shi and his auspicious dragons. The present name of the temple was fixed in 1460 during the Ming Dynasty, and many of the buildings that remain show evidence of the Ming architectural style.

Lugouqiao (Marco Polo) Bridge
卢 沟 桥

Lugouqiao (literally the Bridge Over the Reed Ditch) has been made famous by at least three historic events: Marco Polo's description, Emperor Qianlong's inscription and the outbreak of the War Against the Japanese Aggressors. Officially the bridge was called the "Lugou Stone Bridge," and it was completely built of white stone and looked majestic with a total of 485 stone lions lined on the balustrades of both sides. Apart from minor maintenance repairs made during subsequent dynasties, historical records show that it underwent a major restoration in 1689 after two arches were washed away by floods. It was on that occasion that the river was renamed Yongding (Eternal Stability), but the name of the bridge remained Lugou.

Located 15 kilometres away in southwestern part of Beijing from Tian'anmen, Marco Polo Bridge is the only existing multi-arch stone bridge spanning on the Yongding (Eternal Stability) River. The bridge is 260 metres in length, 9.3 metres in width, 10 piers and 11 arches. In 1961, the bridge was listed as one of the important monuments under special preservation by the State Council. The bridge was "retired" (no vehicle was allowed to pass through on it) in 1968. The lions, big or small on the bridge, got chemical treatment in 1992 and 1999 respectively and the result was satisfactory.

Marco Polo, the great Italian traveller, saw it towards the end of the year 1276 during his tours in China under the Yuan Dynasty. In the book of travelogues bearing his name, which came out years later, Marco Polo gave a detailed description of it " —a very great stone bridge—For you may know that there are few of them in the world so beautiful, nor its equal—It is made like this. I tell you that it is quite three hundred paces long and quite eight paces wide, for ten horsemen can well go there one beside the other—It is all of grey marble very well worked and well founded. There is above each side of the bridge a beautiful curtain or wall of flags of marble and pillars made so, as I shall tell you—And there is fixed at the head of the bridge a marble pillar, and below the pillar a marble lion—very beautiful and large and well made." This description earned the bridge its name, Marco Polo, in the Western World. However, Marco Polo may have suffered a slip of memory when he gave the number of arches of the bridge as 24 instead of the 11 that it has always had. Incidentally it may be interesting to note that Marco Polo called the bridge "Pulisangin." This is because, as some scholars point out, the upper course of the river Lugou or Yongding is the River Sanggan, and the river itself may have been known at the time as Sanggan or Sangin. As for "puli," it came from Persian word "puli," which means bridge. Therefore, Pulisangin was an international coinage for the "bridge on the Sanggan River"—a name highly indicative of the amount of intercourse between China at the time and countries to her west.

Almost from its very inception, namely in the Mingchang period (1190-1208) of the Jin Dynasty, the bridge was listed by travellers and men of letters as one of the "Eight Scenic Spots of Yanjing (Beijing)" under the descriptive title "Lugou Xiaoyue" or Moon Over Lugou at Daybreak (The Morning Moon Over Lugou Bridge). Substitutions and rewordings were made in the listing of the eight subsequent periods under the Yuan, Ming, and Qing dynasties; but "Lugou Xiaoyue" has remained throughout. In 1751 Emperor Qianlong of the Qing Dynasty (1644-1911) personally edited the poetic titles for the eight views of Beijing, and wrote in his elegant hand the inscriptions for the steles marking the respective beauty spots, including the "Lugou Xiaoyue" tablet which still stands on guard by the bridge.

Less than two hundred years after the erection of the stele, the bridge witnessed, in July 1937, the Japanese aggressors provoking Chinese troops into a protracted war of resistance ending only in 1945; but the bridge itself had been largely spared the ravages of war. For this and other reasons, the Marco Polo Bridge has been a favourite subject for Chinese poets and painters. And ancient pictures of the bridge are of particular interest to scholars and historians.

Facelift of Old Defence

Workers renovated the ancient city of Wanping 宛平城, located in the southwestern outskirts of Beijing. The Beijing Municipal Government allocated 330 million yuan (US$39.9 million) to the renovation project, which kicked off on November 2, 2001 and was completed by June 2002. Built in 1640, the ancient city gained prominence after the Marco Polo Bridge Incident on July 7, 1937, which marked the beginning of China's War of Resistance Against Japan.

The city wall was 640 metres from east to west, 320 metres from north to south, 7.18 metres high, and its perimeter being 1920 metres. There were totally more than 200,000 square metres within the city. Though its layout was quite small, it looked just like an impregnable pass. In March 1961, the city together with the Marco Polo Bridge was listed for special preservation by the Chinese Government.

The revamping project included 640-metre-long wall with 7.18 metres in height, the outer surface of the southern city wall encompassing 4,595.2 square metres, rebuilt 4 turrets, 2 central towers and 4 subsidiary rooms. In the process of renovation, the bullet holes and the vestiges of the Japanese aggression will retain according to the original state.

Marco Polo(1245-1324)马可·波罗

Marco Polo was born in 1254, the son of Niccolo Polo, a Venetian merchant. His father and uncle had already visited China once in 1260 when Marco Polo joined them for the second journey in 1271. They spent the next twenty years travelling in the service of Kublai Khan. There is evidence that Marco Polo travelled extensively in the Mongol empire, and although the course of his later travels is open to debate, it is fairly certain that he visited India and made at least one journey for Peking southwest as far as Burma (Myanmar). The Polos returned home to Venice by a long route in 1292, and in 1298/9 Marco Polo was a prisoner of war at Genoa. It was probably in prison they wrote *The Travels*; a product of an observant merchant and a professional romancer. Marco Polo died in 1324 and left the bulk of his possessions accrued on his *travels* to be divided between his three daughters.

The world known Italian traveller Marco Polo was born in 1254 in a Venetian family. In 1260, Marco's father Nicolo Polo and his uncle Maffeo came on a trading journey to Asia.

Kublai Khan was pleased with the detailed answers by the Polo brothers to his questions about Western countries. An envoy, Kejiada, was sent to go to Rome with the Polos.

As the pope had died, the Polo brothers decided to start eastward again with the promising young boy Marco Polo who longed to come to China.

The Polos travelled for three and a half years before reaching China. They passed the Iranian Plateau and the desert of Central Asia, and finally reached Shangdu in Inner Mongolia in 1275. They were warmly welcomed by Kublai Khan, and Marco Polo was included in the list of his honorary guests. Kublai Khan was pleased with Marco's brightness and conscientiousness and sent him as an imperial commissioner to many cities in China. For three years, Marco Polo was governor of Yangzhou near Shanghai. A couple of years later, he acted as an imperial envoy and a deputy privy councilor. He was also dispatched by Kublai Khan on distant missions to Burma (presently Myanmar), Viet Nam, the Philippines, India and some other countries.

As the three Polos stayed at the Yuan court for 17 years, they yearned for home. Kublai Khan did all he could to keep them. Finally, in 1295, after escorting the Mongolian princess Cocacin to Persia for marriage, they returned to Venice.

After returning home, Marco Polo kept telling people about his experiences in China. In 1298, in a naval battle between Venice and Genoa, Marco Polo was wounded and captured. In the prison he met Rusticiano, also a captive, who took down Marco's experience at his dictation to create the world-renowned *Travels of Marco Polo*, a systematic record of Marco Polo's years in China and in countries in central, western and southeastern Asia.

The part on China was a vivid portrayal and a valuable first-hand account. The book also described the use of coal, silkworm breeding, coinage, bridge and palace architecture, city planning, municipal administration, social welfare undertakings and afforestation in China.

Marco Polo also brought with him the Chinese cookery to Italy. Dumpling (ravioli) and noodles (spaghetti) are on the list of Chinese cuisine.

In the 13th century, China's economy, culture, science and technology were among the most advanced in the world. Many of his claims were doubted in the West.

It is said that at his deathbed in 1324 people tried to persuade him to deny what he had said. But Marco Polo declared that his only regret was telling only half of what he had seen. His book has played an important

375

role in promoting the interflow of communication, economy, culture, science and technology between the East and the West.

In the book Kublai Khan was held in high esteem. His name is linked with fancy, travel and adventure, longing to know new things and understand the world.

In 1981, a film about Marco Polo was shot that cost US$20 million.

Stone Flower Cave
石　花　洞

Located in Fangshan District, about 55 kilometres southwest of Beijing, and discovered more than 550 years ago, the Stone Flower Cave is a new sightseeing spot in the Capital City.

The cave is on seven levels with an asphalt road straight to the entrance. It is one of the biggest caves in China, and contains a superb collection of beautiful sights. At present, only three levels (from level one to level three) are open to the public with a total length of 1,900 metres.

The first level is more than 300 metres long, and contains a corridor, a pool like a lotus flower, three big halls, and a cave with an inner cave. All these caves are 10 to 20 metres high and 4 to 30 metres wide.

The corridor is 2 to 3 metres high and 2 to 5 metres wide. The second level is 30 metres below the first level. Its total length is nearly 1,000 metres, and there are lots of branches connected with the cave and stone or iron stairs for visitors. Visitors can enjoy stalactites, cobbles, stone curtains, stone pillars, and stone flowers everywhere inside the cave—an eye-opening experience.

The Stone Flower Cave was opened to public in September 1987. Approximately 400,000 tourists visit the cave each year.

Silver Fox Cave
银　狐　洞

Located in a remote village in Fangshan District, southwest of Beijing, Silver Fox Cave was discovered by chance in July 1991. It is on the site of a small village-run coal pit that is still operating today. Local miners used to put debris such as rocks and earth into a hole they had dug there. To their surprise, the hole never seemed to fill up. Therefore, a miner scooted down the hole and discovered the cave.

The cave is believed to be about 6, 000 metres long and is the largest of its kind in North China. Only half has been explored and opened to tourists. Walking down 120 metres of stairs, visitors reach a coalmine corridor. Leading deep into the cave, the corridor is about 650 metres long, but less than two metres high.

The facilities in the cave, such as lighting, railings and walkways, are not very good because of a shortage of funds. But that makes it even more challenging for visitors who enjoy exploring. However, the most marvelous likeness in the cave is the silver fox, which gives the cave its name. The fox hides in a small hole in the side of the cave. It is a two-metre-long crystal covered with "thorns" that makes it look just like a furry silver fox hanging upside down from the cave wall. The fox's head is hidden in the rock and its bare tail swings in the air.

Another wonder is called e'guan (goose's neck) or soda straws. They are long, hollow tubes that look so brittle that visitors think a gentle breeze would shatter them. Some experts say, they grow only one centimetre a century. There is one soda straw alone that measures two metres long.

A subterranean river also runs through the cave. A 350-metre section is wide enough for a boat and visitors can take a fantasy boat ride on the river. As they float along the imaginative underground landscape, they will notice how clear and transparent the spring fed water of the river is, and will long remember their unusual experience.

Ten Ferries (*Shidu*)
十　　渡

The scenery of the Ten Ferries can compare with that of Guilin. It is situated 90 kilometres of southwest of Beijing, along the Juma River. The River originates in Taihang Mountain in Shanxi Province and flows into the sea in Hebei Province. On its way the River zigzags 10 times through the mountains ranges in Fangshan District, forming ten docking berths for ferries, hence the name Shidu, meaning the Ten Ferries.

With fantastic mountain peaks and ranges reflected in the water, this area resembles the Li River landscape in Guilin, Guangxi Zhuang Autonomous Region. A gigantic rock about 10 metres high named Terrace of Viewing Buddha stands by the ninth ferry. Looking from a small pavilion built on the rock, which resembles a stone Buddha. At the eighth ferry, tourists can enjoy the exciting sport imported from New Zealand: Bungy Jumping.

Scheduled buses depart from Lianhuachi Long-Distance Bus Station, or take an early morning train from Yongdingmen Railway Station.

Jinhai Lake
金 海 湖

Jinhai Lake, 15 kilometres east of Pinggu District seat, and some 88 kilometres away from the Beijing city proper, was awarded the Best Scenic Spot Prize among the 40 scenic spots in Beijing. The lake features undulating hills covered with lush vegetation and a vast expanse of misty water and dotted with kiosks, pavilions, cliffs, and strange rocks and exquisite caves as well as many historic sites. Visitors can see a unity of classic elegance of integrated countryside and splendidness of ornamented buildings. Visitors can also ascend the hills, visit the historic sites, explore the secluded places, go boating or angling and taste delicacies, feeling relaxed and happy.

Construction of the reservoir started on October 18, 1959 and was completed in late 1960 lasting one year. More than 15,000 people were involved in the project. At that time the total capacity of the reservoir was only 18.50 million cubic metres. In 1969 the reservoir was expanded, with a capacity of 53.60 million cubic metres. While in 1973 the reservoir was further expanded. The height of the dam is 118.5 metres and the length 1,500 metres. The total storage capacity of the reservoir reached 121 million cubic metres more than a double than the original storage of capacity. The network for irrigation of the reservoir totals more than 160 kilometres and 124,000 mu (8,267 hectares) of land has been brought under irrigation. In 1985, The reservoir was developed into a tourist scenic spot and was named Jinhai Lake. In 1990, two of the aquatic sports events of the 11th Asian Games were held here. The scenery of the Jinhai Lake is well-known both at home and abroad.

Jinhai Hotel, a garden-style hotel, lies on the west embankment of the Jinhai Lake. The hotel is a good combination of both Chinese and Western architectural styles, featuring winding paths and brilliant buildings. The hotel offers quality food and lodging for both Chinese and foreign visitors, and overseas Chinese, and compatriots for Hong Kong, Macao and Taiwan as well who come for sightseeing, to attend meetings or to recuperate. There are standard double rooms, and suites furnished with independent air conditioner, central acoustics call system, TV set, telephone and high grade sanitary facilities. The three restaurants serve tourists with

Sichuan-and Shandong-style food and Western food, and also they undertake banquets of various kinds. The famous "whole fish feast" is made of fresh fish from the lake.

More Water Resources Found on the Outlying Area of Beijing

Plenty of underground water resources have been found in northeastern Beijing, which may ease the city's water shortages. The survey group sank a well in Zhongqiao Village, Pinggu District in April 2001 and found plenty of high quality groundwater. The groundwater in Pinggu District is expected to be able to provide the city's urban areas with more than 100 million cubic metres of water a year. The average groundwater supply in Pinggu District is more than 200 million cubic metres per year. Since the district's yearly water consumption is only 100 million cubic metres, the extra groundwater supply flows to nearby Hebei Province through an underground percolation system and underground rivers. The survey group plans to drill 20 wells in the district to help establish a new groundwater base for urban areas of Beijing. The plan will be submitted to the local government for approval. After years of investigation, the survey group has drawn a map of water resources in Beijing and has discovered that abundant groundwater resources are held in store in certain areas including Pinggu District and Fangshan District in southwestern Beijing. The city relies heavily on its groundwater supply, which accounts for 80 per cent of the city's total water supply each year. The remaining 20 per cent of the water supply comes from the Miyun and Guanting reservoirs. The city consumes 4 billion cubic metres of water per year. The city has suffered from serious drought over the past two years. The concept of saving water has been introduced in the city along with the wide use of water-saving taps and the implementation of a wastewater discharge fee. Chinese cities have been calculated to suffer total annual water shortages of 6 billion cubic metres. And China's per capita water resources are less than one-fourth of the world's average.

Nanhaizi *Milu* (Deer) Park
南海子麋鹿公园

The Nanhaizi *Milu* Park, located in the Daxing District about 20 kilometres south of Beijing, covers an area of 67 hectares (165.56 acres). The park is encircled by a wall, which is 3,700 metres long and 2.5 metres high. About 7 hectares (17.3 acres) of grass—the *milu's* food—has been planted and the shelters for the *milu* have been set up.

The *milu*, known as Pere David Deer in the West, is a rare species on the verge of extinction. According to an agreement for reintroduction between the British Marquis and the Chinese Government signed in July 1985, the deer were raised under semi-wild conditions in Beijing's Nanhaizi, site of an imperial hunting ground where the animals were last seen in China in 1900. The 22 deer returned to their native habitat of Beijing in August 1985 as gifts from the Marquis of Tavistock at Woburn Abbey, England.

The *milu* originated in China but were extinct in the country for more than 80 years because of the upheavals of the late 19th century, particularly the chaos created by invading forces. The 11th Duke of Bedford, the great grandfather of the present Marquis of Tavistock, bought all the 18 *milu* in Europe in the early 20th century and kept them in a semi-wild condition on his estate.

All the deer now alive are descendants of the original 18 at Woburn Abbey, which had 400 in 1985. The deer have been extinct in the wild for more than 1,600 years and in China for nearly a century. By June 2000, there were more than 500 deer in the Nanhaizi *Milu* Park in Bejing as against 38 in 1985.

Longqing Gorge (Ancient City Reservoir)
龙庆峡(古城水库)

Located 80 kilometres to the north of Beijing, Longqing Gorge is known for its ice lantern festival held annually for more than 10 years during every spring festival. But tourists might not know that the gorge used to be a popular pilgrimage site for devotees to Buddha during the Ming Dynasty (1368-1644). The Court of Immortal (Shenxianyuan), located on the cliff 200 metres above the water, has now been renovated for tourists to view the gorge's religious evolution. A temple built in 1639, the Court of Immortal used to draw thousands of men and women to attend its temple fair held on March 3 in the Chinese lunar calendar.

Originally a reservoir nestled among the Jundu Mountains in Yanqing County, the gorge opened to tourists in 1984. It was listed in 1986 as one of the New Sixteen Scenic Spots and Historical Sites in Beijing. With huge investment injected in 1998 after its restructuring under a shareholding company, the gorge had been able to develop more sightseeing sites to draw more tourists from home and abroad.

Ancient Cliff and Wood Fossils
古崖居和木化石

At the foot of Haituo Hill 15 kilometres northwest of Yanqing County, Beijing, lies a valley lined with steep cliffs. Scattered throughout the cliffs are pavilion-shaped caves, remnants of an ancient stone cave village. In 1990, the Beijing Municipal Cultural Relics Bureau designated it Guyaju—the Ancient Cliff Compound. Even today, its origin remains a mystery. When, why and by whom was this compound built? While some people say they were shelters for troops, others believe they were bandits' fortresses. Still others argued that they were constructed by the Shanrong tribe of the Spring and Autumn Periods (770 BC-476 BC). So far, no unanimous conclusion has solved this mystery.

The Ancient Cliff Compound's 117 caves are divided into two sections: ninety-one in front and twenty-six in the rear. Varying from singles to two- and three-room suites, many caves are interconnected. Some caves contain well-preserved doors, windows, and stovepipes. In the middle of the ridge is a palace-like-cave called Guantangzi (Official Hall). This spacious hall's roof is propped up by four elaborately-sculpted stone pillars over a large stone desk in the centre. To make the compound more accessible to tourists, highways were paved to the site in 1990. Since then, antique collectors and explorers have been flocking here all the year round.

About 50 kilometres east of the compound is Xiadelongwan Village. East of the village on the north bank of the Baihe River is a hill, which offers a bird's-eye view of a 400-metre-wide band of wooden fossils. Formed in the late Jurassic Period 侏罗纪 (135 million years ago) and up to 2.5 metres in diametre, the wood fossils are yellowish-brown, one is the Shituo—a huge fossil trunk over four metres long—which spans a stream with each end thrust into a mountain.

381

Songshan Park
松 山 公 园

Under the national protection by the State Council since 1986, Songshan Primeval Forest Park consists of more than 200 hectares (494.2 acres) of natural Chinese pines and 1,040 hectares (2,570 acres) of artificial Chinese pines. It encompasses 36, 000 hectares (88, 956 acres). Bubbling in the dense forest are the hot springs of the Tangquan Taoist Temple, with waters rich in minerals reaching temperatures over 40 degrees Celsius. The perfect spot for bathing, it was discovered as early as the Beiwei Period (AD 386-AD 534) to create a place for convalescing among secluded beauty. Built in memory of renowned Qin Dynasty calligrapher Wang Cizhong from Yanqing County, Cizhong Temple is another temple standing among the springs. The famous writer Li Daoyuan referred to Cizhong Temple as a place for rejuvenation in his Note of Water Classics, "In Cizhong Temple, the hot springs can cure hundreds of diseases. "

In addition to hot springs, Songshan Park boasts gorgeous scenery. Running through nearby hills atop a rugged cliff is the Eight Immortals Cave, which offers a bird's eye view of the deep valley and clear mountain streams; numerous sights dot the landscape, including the Mandarin Duck Rock, the Pond of Pine Trees and the Moon, the Wall of Flying Dragons, the heaven Tortoise, the Pond for Enjoying Music, Echoing Cliff, the Lions Drinking Water, and the Golden Toad Seeing the Moon. The hectares of pine trees—the oldest ones being over 600 years old—are home to various wild animals from small birds to tigers and leopards. The Songshan Specimen Show Room houses wildlife samples from the forest. In Songshan Park, tourists can enjoy modern facilities including hotels, restaurants, conference halls, and—most importantly—bathing rooms in the hot springs.

PROFILE OF THE
PRIME SIGHTS (2)

第三部分　主要名胜介绍 (2)

The Museum of Chinese History
中国历史博物馆

With a floor space of 8, 000 square metres, the Museum of Chinese History has permanent exhibitions covering important occasions in Chinese history, a period from 1. 7 million years ago in the primitive period down to 1919—the May 4th Movement. Among the 300, 000 precious treasures, the stoneware, bronze works and ancient currencies are the most famous. Many of the 230, 000 volumes of books stored here are the only copies in the world.

The building was constructed in 1958 and completed in 1959, with a total floor space of 65, 000 square metres. It falls into four parts, and we are going to show you the major exhibits.

The Primitive Society (2. 5 million to 4, 000 years ago)
原始社会

1. These two tooth fossils of Yuanmou Man date back to 2. 5 million years ago. Yuanmou Man is a representative of the earliest stage of human beings ever discovered in China.
2. This is a skull fossil of the famous Peking Man discovered at Zhoukoudian 48 kilometres southwest of Beijing. About 40 body fossils were exhumed there. The Peking Man lived 690, 000 years ago.
3. These are the implements made and used by Peking Man. The ashes and charred bones are evidence of use of fire by Peking Man.
4. These are animals living in the same period of time as Peking Man who lived on hunting and collecting wild plants. This showcase describes how Peking Man lived at the time.
5. This is the horn fossil of a wild ox with a history of 100, 000 years. During the period from 400, 000 to 10, 000 years ago, the primitive men continued to live on hunting and collecting wild plants. Some of them were discovered at Zhoukoudian. Their physical features are basically similar to those of modern men.
6. These are bone needles made by Upper Cave Man who lived 10, 000 years ago. They invented the technique of perforating and polishing the animals' teeth, which they wore around the necks. This is what we call necklace now. The primitive women had already developed a sense of beauty.
7. This showcase describes the primitive men who lived during the period

of matriarchal clan commune about 10, 000 years ago. Archaeologists now believe people may have lived in Beijing as long as 27, 000 years ago, nearly 16, 000 years earlier than previously thought. This was the 1992 finding of a group of Chinese and British researchers using an accelerated mass spectrometre radiocarbon dating device. The researchers from Oxford University in England dated 12 fossil bone samples which had been unearthed in an upper cave site at Zhoukoudian in the western suburbs of Beijing where fossil bones at least 10 individuals have been found. The results have pushed the age for the cultural phase further back to between 24, 000 and 29, 000 years ago. All this indicated that the ancestors of modern Chinese began wearing clothes, earrings and burying the dead as early as 25, 000 years ago.

8. Here on show is millet dating back to over 6, 000 years ago. It was discovered in Banpo Village, Xi'an. Primitive farm production appeared at that time.

9. These pottery pieces were made in Shaanxi area 6, 000 to 7, 000 years ago. Besides making pottery pieces, the primitive men also learned weaving and spinning.

10. This is the tomb of a 17-year-old girl, unearthed in Shaanxi. These are the funerary objects, which show that women were held in respect during the period of matriarchal clan commune.

11. These symbols on the pots are supposed to be the earliest forms of Chinese characters.

12. A village of the primitive society, dating back to 6, 000 to 7, 000 years ago, was discovered in Yuyao, Zhejiang Province. These are farm tools, paddy rice and a mat.

13. You see here the remains of a house found in Baoji, Shaanxi Province, which were moved here later from the site. It is half-hidden under the ground with entrance in the middle. The pottery jar was used for keeping tinder. A primitive village with over 20 houses was discovered in the same place.

14. Men played a major role during the period of patriarchal clan commune, about 4, 000 to 5, 000 years ago. Sickles and ploughs were used for farming. This led to the development of agriculture.

15. The use of wheel in pottery making was introduced. Special handicrafts production was developed.

16. These are jade pieces found in Shandong, Jiangsu and Henan provinces. Barter took place with the development of farm production.

17. Funerary objects in a tomb where a man, a woman and a child were buried together show the emergence of private property, patriarchy and

polarization between the rich and the poor. In some of the tombs found in Shandong Province, funerary objects were rich and plenty, while in others simple and few.

18. These are primitive Chinese ideographs on pottery. The lower part represents a ridged mountain, while the upper part stands for the rising sun. This character shows the dawn of a day.

The Slave Society (21st century BC to 476 BC) 奴隶社会

19. This painting describes an ancient Chinese legend in which Yu the Great led the people to control the Yellow River floods. A son of Yu the Great established China's first imperial hereditary dynasty the Xia Dynasty (2070 BC-1600 BC).

20. These are the weapons made in the Shang Dynasty (1600 BC-1046 BC). The remains of the palace and the city walls were unearthed in Henan. The state apparatus of the slave owning system was quite complete. At that time the city was the centre of the ruling slave owners.

21. According to historical records, the main crops in the Shang Dynasty were rice and wheat. Due to the development of agriculture, breweries were set up.

22. These are the earliest porcelain pieces uncovered in Henan. With the development of handicrafts production, primitive porcelain appeared.

23. This indicates the process of bronze smelting and casting. These are malachite and charcoal, used for bronze smelting.

24. This is a bronze wine vessel of the early Shang period. It was uncovered in a tomb in 1976. The owner of the tomb was a woman general. This special shape vessel is the only one ever found in China and the world.

25. This is a bronze vessel of the Shang Dynasty, known as *simuwuding*. It weighs 875 kilos, the heaviest ever discovered in China. It was a sacrificial vessel offered by King Wenting to his mother, which was unearthed at Anyang, Henan Province.

26. This is a wine vessel with four ramheads, called *zun* in Chinese.

27. These are jade pieces discovered in the tomb of a woman general. The carvings on them are elegant.

28. The whole set of musical instruments was made of stone, with tiger designs on them. They were produced in the Shang Dynasty.

29. These are cowry shells used as currency during that period.

30. The use of characters was quite common in the Shang Dynasty. People engraved characters on oracle bones, called the oracle bone inscriptions, which consisted of more than 5,000 pictographic characters. At

387

present, we can only recognize one third of them.

31. This is the model of a tomb unearthed at Anyang, Henan Province in 1950, where 79 slaves were found buried as human sacrifices along with the slave owner. On the two terraces were discovered 45 individuals, while at the base 34 skulls and 6 chariots. Around the tomb are 7 large pits for sacrificial service where over 300 skeletons of slaves were uncovered. When the slaveowner died, the slaves were killed and served as human sacrifices. Some were found buried alive with their arms tied up while others, as shown by their posture, died after a painful struggle.

32. This is a bronze tripod of the Western Zhou Dynasty (1046 BC-771 BC) with inscription recording the bestowal of 1, 709 slaves by King Kang upon a nobleman named Yu. It is known as *Dayuding* in China.

33. This is the model of a chariot used by the nobility. The chariot was drawn by two horses.

34. This bronze object, known as *Guojizibai* vessel, was unearthed in the Qing Dynasty, with 110 characters inside. It was recorded that a nobleman fought bravely in the battle. He was rewarded the vessel by King Xuan for his bravery.

35. These are the iron wares of the Spring and Autumn Period, discovered in Hunan Province. The technique of mining and iron making was developed in China at that time.

36. During the Spring and Autumn Period, iron ware was made. The currency used then was cast in the shape of farm implements, such as spades.

37. This part describes the armed revolt by the slaves who pounded the rule of the slave owner in the late period of the Slave-owning Society.

38. This is a portrait of Confucius (551 BC-479 BC), a famous educationist and a great thinker in the Chinese history. These are the works by Confucius. In his later years he was engaged in teaching and compiling books. He exerted an important influence on the development of Chinese culture and education. He was the founder of the Confucian school.

39. This is a portrait of Sun Zi, a strategist of the Spring and Autumn Period. "Know the enemy and know yourself, and you will win all battles. " This quotation from his famous work Military Strategy and Tactics still holds good in modern military tactics. The bamboo strips with the quotation were uncovered in Shandong Province in 1972.

The Feudal Society (457 BC to AD 1840) 封建社会

40. The early stage of the feudal society was in a rival state, which had seven kingdoms (ducal states). This picture shows that the newly rising landlord class carried out political reforms and consolidated their rule.

41. These were passes issued by the King of the State of Chu in Hubei area, one was used for land traffic and the other for sea travel, like your passports today. They showed the strengthening of the imperial power.

42. These funerary objects, totaling more than 800 pieces, were uncovered in the tomb of a landlord in Henan Province. The technique of making lacquerwares and containers was quite developed. They indicated the strengthening of political and economic power of the landlord class in the early period of the feudal society.

43. This was uncovered in the tomb of a peasant in Shijiazhuang, Hebei Province. Small peasant economy emerged and iron implements were employed widely. Water conservation projects were built. The famous *Dujiangyan* irrigation project was designed by Li Bing over 2,000 years ago. It still plays an effective role in farming in Sichuan Province.

44. As currencies in China were not standardized at that time, different shapes of currency were made in various places. Some are in the shape of knives, others look like spades, and still others are round in shape. Some of them are made of gold. Gold is mined in more than 20 places in China now. China turned out 181.83 tons of gold in 2001.

45. This section deals with the achievements in the fields of ideology and culture during the early period of the feudal society. These were famous philosophical thinkers of the time. Meng Ke (c. BC 372-c. 278 BC) was a faithful follower of Confucius. Bian Que was a folk physician who used the method of feeling pulse to diagnose the illness of patients, thus laying the foundation for treating diseases with Chinese medicine. Qu Yuan (c. 340 BC-c. 278 BC) was a famous poet who wrote a lot of poems eulogizing the motherland and the people.

46. This is the portrait of Qinshihuang, the first Emperor of the Qin Dynasty, who established the first centralized feudal state in the Chinese history.

47. This is a tiger tally used by Qinshihuang (259 BC-210 BC; reigned: 246-210) for deploying the army. It looks like a small tiger. Half of it was in the hand of the emperor, and the other half was held by the general in command. The two halves must match when troops were to be deployed. In other words, without the order of the emperor, nobody

was allowed to dispatch the troops. The troops were under the strict control of the emperor.

48. This part tells us how Qinshihuang standardized the scripts, currency, and weights and measures after he unified China. He connected the various sections of the walls built by the different kingdoms and had the world-famous 6,700-kilometre-long Great Wall constructed.

49. These are terra cotta-warriors and horses discovered in Lintong near Xi'an in 1974. Altogether more than 6,000 figures were uncovered. They were arranged in military formation. It reflects the political and military development and high artistic talent of the labouring people in the Qin Dynasty. The Terra-Cotta Warrior and Horses Museum of Qin-shihuang Mausoleum was established in 1979.

50. This is a picture of Qinshihuang Mausoleum. According to historical records, 700,000 people were involved in building the tomb.

51. The cruel exploitation of the Qin rulers gave rise to revolt on the part of the people. The first peasant uprising in China broke out in 209 BC in Anhui Province. This picture depicts the scene of the uprising at the early stage. The uprising was led by Chen Sheng and Wu Guang.

52. The peasant uprising overthrew the Qin Dynasty which lasted for 15 years. In 206 BC, Liu Bang established the Western Han Dynasty.

53. These are part of the over 2,500 pottery figures of infantry and cavalry unearthed in 1965 in Shaanxi Province. These pottery soldiers represented the standing army established in the Western Han Dynasty and the powerful military strength of the time.

54. It is a 2,000 year old mural discovered in the remains of an iron foundry in Hunan Province. It shows that coal was used as fuel for iron smelting.

390

55. This is a piece of silk fabrics unearthed at Mawangdui in Changsha, Hunan Province. This long gown was worn by the mummy. It weighs only 49 grams. The lacquerwares discovered in Mawangdui show that handicrafts technique made much headway at the time.

56. This is a waterwheel made in AD 31. It was used to push the bellows for iron smelting. In Europe hydraulic bellows were not used until 12th century AD.

57. This is the model of a castle owned by a landlord, which was excavated from a tomb. The landlords maintained private armed forces to protect their manorial estates. This is also an embodiment of the strength of the landlord class.

58. Zhang Heng (AD 78-AD 139) was an outstanding scientist of the Eastern Han Dynasty. He invented the world's first seismograph consisting

of a bronze urn 1. 9 metres in diameter and with a central pendulum. An earth tremor would cause the pendulum to activate a set of levers which release a bronze ball held in the mouth of one of the eight dragons on the surface of the urn. Thus it could indicate when and in what direction the earthquake was taking place.

59. This is a piece of primitive paper dating back to the Western Han Dynasty, discovered in Shaanxi Province. It was made of plant fibre. Paper was invented in the Western Han Dynasty, and was improved and popularized in the Eastern Han Dynasty. Hua Tuo (?- AD 208), a famous Han Dynasty physician, was the first to use anaesthesia for operation. Han Dynasty saw high attainments in science and culture.

60. This is the portrait of a famous Chinese historian Sima Qian (c. 145 BC-135 BC) who wrote the *Historical Records*.

61. This is the pottery figure of a story-teller unearthed in Sichuan Province. He is so confident and expressive. The figure shows the vividness of sculptural art at the time.

62. In the Western Han Dynasty, a road was built from China's Central Plain area to West Asia and the road was later known as the Silk Road.

63. These are the silk fabrics and bronze mirrors found along the Silk Road.

64. This section is devoted to the period in which China was reduced to feudal separatist rule. It was called the period of the Three Kingdoms. Cao Cao (AD 155-AD 220) was a famous statesman and strategist who unified northern China for a time. Zhuge Liang (AD 181-AD 234) was also a famous strategist and statesman. He adopted a friendly policy towards the minority people in southwest China. Also he paid much attention to the development of agriculture in that area.

65. This is a water mill driven by hydraulic power for processing grain. It is still in use in South China.

66. This is the model of a point to the south chariot which had a mechanism that enabled a pointer to indicate the south, no matter which way the cart turned.

67. This is an odometre. A set of gears engaged with the hub caused the figurine to beat the drum once every 500 metres.

68. Zu Chongzhi (429-500) was the first in the world to work out the *pi* to be between 3. 1415926 and 3. 1415927. He also made notable contributions to astronomy, the calendar system and mechanical design.

69. These are the carved stone Buddhas from Yungang, Shanxi Province, during the Wei and Tang dynasties. Buddhism was introduced to China in the 1st century BC, in the Western Han Dynasty. It originated

in ancient India in the 6th century BC. The founder of Buddhism was Sakyamuni.

70. This section is devoted to the Sui Dynasty, which lasted from AD 581 to AD 618. The founding of the Sui Dynasty marked the end of the feudal separatist rule and China was reunified again. The Grand Canal from Hangzhou, Zhejiang Province to the vicinity of Beijing was built during that period, from 605 to 610. Its total length is 1,794 kilometres. It played an important role in developing the economy in the north and the south. Part of it is now open to visitors in the South.

71. This is the tomb of a nine-year-old girl unearthed in Shaanxi Province. In the tomb more than one hundred artifacts were discovered. The little girl was one of the royal family members. The relics show that the aristocrats led a life of extravagance.

72. Zhaozhou Bridge, designed and built by Li Chun from 605 to 617, has stood the tests of earthquakes, floods and traffic for over 1,300 years. It is the world's oldest single arch stone bridge still in use today. To protect this monument, a parallel bridge was built in 1980s. The main arch of the old bridge has a span of 37 metres and the total length of the bridge is 54 metres. The two minor arches at each end are known as open spandrelled arches.

73. Thirty years later, the Sui Dynasty was overthrown and was succeeded by the Tang Dynasty. Wu Zetian (624-705) was an outstanding stateswoman who was in power for 50 years. She was the only female emperor in the history of feudal China. She made some contributions to the development of economy, politics and culture at the time.

74. These are the farm implements used in the Tang Dynasty. People then knew how to use ploughs. This kind of plough can still be seen in the rural areas in China.

75. A Tang Dynasty granary was uncovered. These are the grains dating back to over one thousand years ago. At that time there were a lot of grains in Luoyang. Agriculture was developed to a certain extent.

76. These are the mirrors, metal articles and tri colour Tang horses. Such beautiful colours were made from raw materials, such as copper dioxide and other things.

77. Chang'an (presently Xi'an) was the capital of the Tang Dynasty. According to written history, the city of Chang'an covered an area of 35 square kilometres with a population of one million. It was China's political, economic and cultural centre in the Tang Dynasty.

78. These are the remains of the palaces. The picture is a representation of the palaces which resemble the three palaces in the front part of the

Forbidden City.

79. This is a picture showing the remains of the city gates in Chang'an (today's Xi'an). In the picture as you can see, there were five gates of Chang'an City at the time.

80. The marriage of the Tang Princess Wencheng (?-680) to Tibetan Prince Songtsen Gampo (617-650) promoted the economic and cultural exchanges between the two nationalities.

81. These are the dumplings, cakes unearthed from Xinjiang, which show that the living habits of the people there were the same as those in the hinterland.

82. In Xinjiang, cotton and cotton seeds were found. As early as the Tang Dynasty the people there began to cultivate cotton.

83. Monk Jianzhen (688-763) went to Japan in AD 753 to preach Buddhist teachings which helped promote the cultural exchanges between China and Japan.

84. The famous monk Xuanzang (602-664) started his journey from Chang'an to study in India and other countries. He spent 17 years in the journeys to the western regions, and brought back with him over 600 books of Buddhist scriptures. He also wrote a book entitled *Pilgrimage to the West* in the Tang Dynasty. The book recorded what he saw and heard on the way. On the basis of this book a Ming Dynasty literati wrote the novel *Pilgrimage to the West*.

85. This is a stele which recorded the introduction of Christianity into China in the early Tang Dynasty.

86. This is the earliest wood block printing in the world, dating back to AD 868. Wood block printing was invented in the Sui Dynasty and raised to a higher stage in the Tang Dynasty. Literature and art flourished at the time.

87. They were well-known poets of the Tang Dynasty, the greatest ones being Li Bai (701-762) and Du Fu (712-770).

88. This is the model of a wooden structure still in existence in Shanxi Province. The building is located in Wutai, Shanxi. It is one of the two Tang Dynasty wooden structures still standing.

89. This is a bust of Huang Cao, leader of the peasant uprising at the end of the Tang Dynasty. Led by him the peasant troops broke into Chang'an, the capital of the Tang Dynasty in 880. Two decades later the Tang Dynasty was overthrown.

90. This section is devoted to the period in which Liao, Song, Western Xia and Jin dynasties co-existed from 916 to 1280.

    This ancient marble sculpture looted from a tomb of a governor in the

Five Dynasties (907-960) finally made it home on May 26, 2001. The bas-relief carving was one of 10 looted from the tomb of Wang Chuzhi seven years ago and since then it has been moved from place to place in China and then abroad for one and a half years. On May 28, 2001, it was displayed for the first time to audience in its motherland at the Museum of Chinese History in Beijing. The US Customs Service at a ceremony in New York returned the painted 10th-century relief sculpture, looted from Wang's tomb in Xiyanchuan Village of Quyang County, Hebei Province, to China after being seized at a Christie's auction house. The sculpture is listed in the "most valuable category" in China's classification of cultural relics. Despite its age, the guardian sculpture is still in fairly good condition. The guardian is depicted with red robe, golden helmet and green armor. He holds a long sword and stands on the back of a bull. A phoenix dances behind the warrior, adding a touch of mystery to the overall effect. The 144-centimetre long, 58-centimetre wide sculpture is a rare, well-preserved artifact that forms a link between the art styles of two dynasties. Historical records suggest that Wang was a high official that died in AD 923, having served rulers of both the Tang Dynasty (AD 618-AD 907) and Later Liang (AD 907-AD 923), of the Five Dynasties. The decoration in Wang's tomb followed the imperial Tang Dynasty model, with lively painted wall mural's lining passageways and tomb chambers. Tang painting was mostly figurative. But the design of Wang's tomb, though essentially in a Tang style, anticipated future artistic developments. There were 18 painted marble relief sculptures in Wang's tomb, which was a complex of rooms arranged on a north-south axis, accessed via a ramp from the south. Archaeologists said there should be two guardian sculptures at the gateway of the tomb, two official sculptures in the room in front of the coffin chamber, 12 sculptures of the 12 symbolic animals of the Earthly Branches on the wall of the coffin chamber, and two sculptures featuring female musicians on the wall of the room behind the coffin chamber. But much of Wang's tomb had been looted prior to excavation in 1995. Only eight painted marble relief sculptures survived, including six of the 12 symbolic animals and two female musician sculptures.

Return of Treasure Looking at the catalogue of a Christie's auction house in New York in February 2000, a visiting scholar from Beijing found a sculpture he suspected to be the one looted from Wang's tomb. He immediately informed both the State and Hebei Province Administrations of Cultural Heritage. They sought help from the US authorities and the International Criminal Police Organization. The Chinese officials filed papers and provided evidence to show the sculpture had been stolen from Wang's tomb. Federal authorities then blocked the sale and filed papers in the Southern District Court of New York to try to formally recover the sculpture. Attorney Mary Jo White said in court papers she was seeking the return of the sculpture to China because it was a cultural property taken from a relic site under State protection and removed from China illegally. Its value was estimated at between US$ 400,000-500,000, the court papers said. The court action "serves notice to traffickers in looted antiquities that these national treasures will be seized and returned to their rightful owners." The US court paper said the marble figure sculpture was transported into the United States by a Korean Air 312 airline on July 25, 1999, with a declared value of US$140,000. The court paper said that in December 1999, a Hong Kong gallery consigned the sculpture to Christie's for a March 2000 auction. Pictures in the auction house catalogue helped cultural experts identify the piece as one of the stolen sculptures. In the catalogue, the sculpture was described as appearing "to be painted and carved marble wall panels from the Five Dynasties tomb of Wang Chuzhi." Joe Gunderson, a spokesman fro Christie's, said the auction house withdrew the object from its Asian art sale when it learned it might be a stolen relic. The seizure of the sculpture marks a rare triumph over international art smugglers who are systematically robbing imperial Chinese tombs, sometimes destroying them in the process by using explosives. After negotiation with the United States, Chinese officials finally saw the return of the sculpture. Chinese and US authorities were working together to track down the smugglers who brought the sculpture to an art gallery in Hong Kong, a common route to Western markets for objects stolen from ancient tombs in China. Most Chinese grave robbers' loot usually ends up in expensively decorated living rooms on New York's "Upper East Side." A US collector who found that one of his artifacts was a sculpture stolen from Wang's tomb returned another guardian sculpture in Wang's tomb to China in June 2000. Now the two sculptures are displayed together at the Museum of Chinese History. The whereabouts of the other eight sculptures looted from Wang's tomb are still unknown. Officials with the Ministry of Public Security said they would continue to investigate.

Anti-Smuggling Effort Grave robbing has increased sharply in the past 10 years alongside the expanding market economy, as more people look to business to create personal wealth. Education, especially art education, is lagging far behind, and this means people are less aware of the need for cultural relics protection. According to the State Administration of Cultural Heritage, more than 40,000 tombs were reported robbed between 1979 and 1990. Chinese Customs officials said that between 1981 and 1989 they investigated 3,081 cases of artifacts smuggling, and confiscated 70,226 items. From 1991 to 1994, Chinese customs confiscated 46,000 items. In 1997, Chinese Customs investigated more than 600 artifacts smuggling cases and confiscated 11,200 items. China has imposed restrictions on the export of cultural relics. Since the 1950s, it has signed three international covenants on the prevention of the outlaw of cultural items. Chinese authorities typically mete out severe punishments to any smugglers they catch. Earlier in 2000, three men were executed for stealing 15 Tang Dynasty murals, but important antiquities continue to flow through China's porous boundaries.

Millions of Chinese relics can be found in more than 200 museums in 47 foreign countries. Most of them were stolen at a time when foreign countries occupied parts of China, mainly after the Opium War in 1840. The New York Metropolitan Museum of Art reportedly has the lion's share of Chinese paintings removed from China, but the British Museum is said to have the best collection of Chinese paintings, including some rare and high-quality ancient collections. The French Guimet Museum reportedly has the finest collection of Chinese ceramics and pottery, some of the cream of the all the dynasties' relics. Over the past few years, central government and non-governmental organizations have stepped up attempts to track down relics, which have been smuggled out the country. In 1999, China successfully brought more than 3,000 Chinese relics from the United Kingdom in line with international covenants. In April 2001, the Canadian National Museum returned a bas-relief statue to China, which was stolen decades ago from the Longmen Grottoes in Luoyang, Henan Province.

91. Here is the portrait of Zhao Kuangyin (927-976; reigned: 960-976) who established the Song Dynasty in 960. This is a sketch map showing the capital city of Kaifeng.

92. This picture shows the well-known Marco Polo Bridge built in 1192, in the Jin Dynasty, which made Beijing its capital for the first time in the history of China.

93. These are the porcelain vases and wares produced in Henan, Zhejiang and Hebei provinces. There were five famous kilns such as Guan 官, Ge 哥(Zhejiang), Ru 汝, Jun 钧(Henan) and Ding 定 (Hebei), each of

these kilns turned out porcelain wares in different designs and colours.

94. This is a Song Dynasty painting Riverside Scene at Qingming Festival. It depicts the economic prosperity in Kaifeng, Henan Province. It is 5 metres in length with more than 500 figures in it.

95. Here you can see the display of gunpowder. According to historical records, people began to use gun powder in the Tang Dynasty for cultural entertainment and cutting into mountains. Towards the end of the Tang Dynasty, gun powder was used in battles. This is the world's first bronze cannon.

96. In the Yuan Dynasty, rockets were invented and they were able to fly some distance with the help of gun powder.

97. Bi Sheng (?-1051) invented the movable type printing technique which was an improvement on that of the wood block printing. The modern printing technique is developed on that basis.

98. More than 2,000 years ago, China began to use magnet to show direction. The magnetic needle was made in the Song Dynasty and the mariner's compass was invented and employed in navigation. There were four famous inventions in China: paper making, gun powder, compass and movable type printing.

99. Now we come to a Song Dynasty acupuncture manikin used in teaching. It is hollow inside with many holes indicating the acupuncture points. It was filled with water and the points were covered with wax. If one succeeded in getting at the right points, water would come out through the holes.

100. This is a wooden pagoda, 66.6 metres high, built in 1056, with a history of over 900 years. Not a single nail was used for the construction. It is the highest wooden structure in China still standing in Yingxian County, Shanxi Province. During its renovation in 1977, some Buddhist images and sutras were found in the pagoda.

101. This is a portrait of Kublai Khan (1215-1294), leader of the Mongolian nationality, who unified China in 1279. Beijing was then named *Dadu*, the capital of the Yuan Dynasty.

102. This is a map of Beijing at the time. The south city wall ran along the present day Chang'an Boulevard. These were building materials.

103. This picture depicts the shipment of timber under Lugouqiao (Marco Polo) Bridge. The bridge was destroyed by a big flood and rebuilt in 1698.

104. In the Yuan Dynasty, the Venetian traveller Marco Polo(1245-1324) came to Beijing in 1275. He lived in China for 17 years. After he went back to Italy he had the book *Travels of Marco Polo* written.

105. This is a picture of Guo Shoujing (1231-1316) who devised a calendar which determined 365. 2425 days to be a year, with an error of only 26 second. Guo Shoujing played an important role in discovering the water source for *Dadu*, an old name for Beijing. This eminent scientist also invented many astronomical instruments which were among the most advanced in the world at the time.

106. This is a water clock (clepsydra) which has 4 containers and time is measured by constant flow of water.

107. Cruel exploitation and oppression by Mongolian and Han landlords provoked sustained resistance from people of various nationalities. The flames of revolt swept the country, bringing to an end the rule of the Yuan Dynasty. Finally, Zhu Yuanzhang (1328-1398; reigned 1368-1398) set up the Ming Dynasty and made Nanjing its capital in 1368. In 1420 when the Forbidden City was completed, Yongle, the third emperor of the Ming Dynasty, moved the capital back from Nanjing to Beijing in 1421.

108. This painting shows Beijing 300 years ago. It describes the economic prosperity of the city in the Ming Dynasty.

109. According to historical records, paintings and abacus appeared in China in the Song Dynasty. The abacus made in the Ming Dynasty became adequate.

110. At the beginning of the 15th century Zheng He (1371-1435) led his fleet to make 7 long voyages. He had been to over 30 countries and regions, as far as the Red Sea and the east coast of Africa. His voyages promoted China's trade relations with Asian and African countries.

111. This painting depicts China's earliest struggle waged by the city workers. The contingent of handicraftsmen became stronger as a result of the growth of capitalist rudiments. They rose in arms against the feudal rulers.

112. The gold crown, weighing 800 grams, and "phoenix" headdress, 2. 9 kilos, were found in Dingling in 1958. The "phoenix" headdress was decorated with kingfisher's feathers. Eight million taels of silver were spent on construction of Dingling.

113. The book describes how the people in Henan suffered from floods. They had to eat tree barks and grass roots and fled from famine when the emperor spent a fabulous amount of money on his tomb.

114. In 1644 when the peasant leader Li Zicheng (1606-1645) and his insurgent army broke into Beijing, the last Ming Emperor Chongzhen (1628-1644) hanged himself on a locust tree in Coal Hill Park right

behind the Forbidden City. The Ming Dynasty collapsed.

115. The Qing Dynasty, established by the Manchus, was the last feudal dynasty in the history of China. Kangxi (1654-1722; reigned: 1662-1722) was an outstanding statesman of the Qing Dynasty. He ruled China for 61 years and played a very important role in unifying and consolidating China.

116. Here is the seal used by the emperor. These are the seals for the Manchu army.

117. The year of 1624 saw the Dutch colonialists' aggression of Taiwan. In 1661 the national hero Zheng Chenggong (1624-1662) led 25, 000 soldiers to recover Taiwan from the Dutch colonialists.

118. This is a cannon used by him. This was a Dutch colonialists' surrender. It is a painting of Zheng Chenggong presented to the Chinese Government by his 9th generation grandson.

119. In mid-7th century, tzarist Russia, pursuing an expansionist policy along the Heilongjiang River and Wusuli River, occupied large stretch of China's territory and forced the Qing Government to sign the Nipchu Treaty.

120. These are the imperial writings inscribed on gold panels granted to Dalai Lama by the Qing Court. It reflected the strengthening of the relations between the central government and Tibet during the Qing Dynasty.

121. China had 50 minority nationalities in the Qing Dynasty. The history of China has been jointly created by various nationalities. These are the costumes of different minority nationalities. They are much more colourful than those of the Han nationality.

122. These are silk fabrics and porcelain pieces produced during the Qing period. Handicrafts made new progress and the seeds of capitalism grew fast.

123. This painting shows the street west of the Front Gate, Beijing, during the Qing period. It depicts the scene of Emperor Qianlong's outing. The law stipulated that all the windows and gates along the route had to be tightly shut.

124. These are enamel wares made in the Qing Dynasty. We can see Western designs on some of the enamel wares. This shows the introduction of Western culture into China.

125. In the Qing Dynasty, the main products for export were porcelain, raw silk, silk fabrics and tea. The port of China for export was Amoy (today's Xiamen).

126. These are tobacco, sunflower, potato, tomato, and others introduced

into China from America and Latin America.

127. These are the European commodities: the clock from France, the woolen materials from England and the telescope from Germany.

128. This is Cao Xueqin (?-1763) who wrote *A Dream of Red Mansions.*

The Semi Colonial & Semi Feudal Society (1840 to 1919)
半殖民地半封建社会

129. This section is devoted to the Opium War in 1840. Due to the constant infiltration of imperialism, China was gradually reduced to a semi feudal society. In 1839, the army and civilians of Guangzhou, led by Lin Zexu (1785-1850) resist smuggling of opium into China by the British. In 1840, the Opium War broke out. The people of Sanyuanli rose against the enemy. These are the weapons captured by the people of Sanyuanli in Guangzhou.

130. This part displays how Hong Xiuquan (1814-1864) led the Taiping Heavenly Kingdom Revolution, China's largest peasant uprising to fight against the Qing Dynasty. Hong Xiuquan proclaimed the uprising in 1851 at Jintian Village. Guangxi and made Nanjing its capital in 1853. The movement lasted for 14 years and 1864 saw the failure of the Taiping Heavenly Kingdom Revolution which was suppressed by both domestic and foreign enemies.

131. This section deals with the Sino-French War in 1884 and Sino-Japanese War in 1894.

132. This part shows how the national industry developed in the 70s of the 19th century along with the emergence of the bourgeoisie. Before that the Chinese workers employed in foreign factories were already part of the Chinese working class of the early period.

133. Actuated by the grave national crisis China was facing at the time, bourgeois reformists represented by Kang Youwei (1858-1927) and Liang Qichao (1873-1927) demanded that the Qing Government resist foreign enemies, reform outdated laws, learn from the West and develop capitalism. In modern Chinese history, this is known as the Reform Movement of 1898. Feudal die-hards with Empress Dowager Cixi as the ringleader considered the movement worse than a catastrophe. They flagrantly declared that they "would rather lose the country than carry out the reform" and brutally put down the movement. During the movement, Jingshi University (today's Peking University) was founded. This was the first university in China that offered courses of Western culture to Chinese students.

134. The caricature map was drawn by a patriot showing China's critical

situation of the time. In the map, *the bear* stands for tzarist Russia with its sphere of influence in northeast China; *the tiger* for Britain with its sphere of influence in central China; *the frog* for France in Guangdong, Guangxi, Yunnan and Sichuan provinces; *the sun* for Japan in Fujian Province and Taiwan Island; *the sausage* for Germany with its sphere of influence in Shangdong Province; *the eagle* for the United States which was a late-comer because it was then busily engaged in the war over the Philippine Islands. The U. S. put forward a so-called "Open Door" policy. China was then facing the danger of being carved up by imperialist powers, while the Qing rulers still indulged themselves in enjoyment.

135. Yihetuan Movement or the Boxers Rebellion broke out in 1900. The Allied Forces of the Eight Powers (aggressive forces sent by Britain, the United States, Germany, France, tsarist Russia, Japan, Italy and Austria in 1900, to suppress the anti-imperialist Yiheduan Movement of the Chinese people, known as the West as the Boxer Rebellion) helped the Qing Dynasty to put down the boxers. Though ended in failure, the movement gave an impetus to the rising of the bourgeois democratic revolution.

136. This picture shows a group of boxers being paraded to the execution ground, dauntless before the enemy in the face of death.

137. Wuchang Uprising broke out in 1911. The bourgeois democratic revolution led by Dr Sun Yat-sen (1866-1925) brought to an end the 2, 000-year-old feudal system. By the end of 1911, Dr Sun Yat-sen came back to China from abroad, and became the Provisional President of the Republic of China.

138. The fruits of this revolution were usurped by the imperialist-backed feudal warlord Yuan Shikai (1859-1916). The Chinese people were still under imperialist and feudal oppression.

401

139. This is an iron blood flag. The dark colour represents iron and the red, blood. The 18 yellow spots stand for 18 provinces which took part in the uprising. The five colours were symbols of the Han, Mongolian, Manchu, Hui and Tibetan nationalities.

140. Influenced by the October Revolution, the May 4th Movement, a patriotic anti-imperialist and anti feudal movement, broke out in Beijing in 1919. A month later, the Chinese working class went on strike and entered the political arena as an independent force. This ushered in an entirely new historical period in the Chinese revolution.

141. The Yangtze River, the Yellow River, the Great Wall and the Himalayas—China is a land of enchanting beauty.

The Great Hall of the People
人 民 大 会 堂

(workers put the new national emblem on the Great Hall of the People on August 3, 2001. The gilded bronze emblem, 5. 2 metres wide, 5. 6 metres tall and weighing 1. 75 tons, replaced the wooden one which had been used for the past five decades)

Construction of the Great Hall of the People started in October 1958 and was completed by the end of August 1959, taking ten months altogether.

It has a total floor space of 171, 800 square metres, 20, 000 square metres more than that of the Palace Museum (known as the Forbidden City in the West) in the neighbourhood. It is 206 metres long and 336 metres wide. Its highest point is 46. 5 metres from the ground. The entire building is propped up using 134 giant columns, is magnificent in architectural style and carries rich national tints.

It consists of three major sections: in the north is the Banquet Hall that accommodates 5, 000 people; in the centre is the Grand Auditorium with a seating capacity of 10, 000; offices of the Standing Committee of the National People's Congress are in the south. The Great Hall of the People boasts more than 300 multi-functional feast halls, meeting rooms and offices. They include over 30 meeting rooms named after various provinces, autonomous regions, municipalities and special administrative regions; they reflect the features of these areas and Chinese national style.

Its local features distinguish each of the rooms. Today, we'll visit some of them. They are the reception rooms of Taiwan Province, Sichuan Province, Hunan Province, Liaoning Province, Guangdong Province, Shanghai Municipality and Beijing Municipality.

402

We are now in the central foyer. It's for the people attending meetings to take a rest during intervals. The floor is paved with natural marble and the 20 pillars are made of white marble. Each crystal glass chandelier weighs 1. 2 tons.

The Great Hall of the People has become an important venue for China's most important political, economic, cultural and diplomatic activities.

Taiwan Reception Room 台湾厅

These are carvings of bamboo roots and soft stones and those are Fujian lacquerwares.

The painting on the screen depicts a warm welcome given by the people on Taiwan Island to Zheng Chenggong, a national hero who recovered the island from the Dutch in 1661.

On the wall are landscape oil paintings of Ali Mountain, the Jade Mountain, the Sun and Moon Lake and Shuhua Highway.

This screen bears a passage quoted from Chinese classics stating that Taiwan has been an inseparable part of China since ancient times. The calligraphy is done by Yu Liqun, widow of Guo Moruo.

When the People's Congress is in session, the provincial reception rooms are used for group discussions by deputies representing the respective regions. They are also used for receiving foreign guests, holding official talks and small banquets.

Sichuan Reception Room 四川厅

Sichuan embroidery is one of the four major embroideries in China. This piece is double size raised with a beautiful name of Hibiscus Carp. The giant panda and golden-hair monkey, among the rarest animals in the world, are from Sichuan Province. These thin, translucent curtains are made of bamboo filaments.

The four filigree plaques on the wall are made of silver. These are objects of glass carving. This is carved screen made of wood and bamboo.

Recently sent from Sichuan Province are four pieces carved out of tree roots, ranging from 430, 420, 640 to 730 years old.

This piece of embroidery shows the Red Army forcing their way across the iron suspension bridge on the Dadu River, a famous episode during the Long March.

The 10,000-Seat Auditorium 万人礼堂

The auditorium is used for important occasions such as sessions of the National People's Congress, the Party Congress and mass political rallies to support the just struggle of the people of other countries. The massive hall is 76 metres in width, 60 metres in length and 32 metres in height, with a balcony and a gallery. There are 3,600 seats on the ground floor, 3,500 on the balcony and 2,500 on the gallery. The stage can hold a presidium of 300 to 500 people. The total seating capacity is ten thousand. It is also used for festive celebrations and grand stage shows. The proscenium can be converted into an orchestra pit by removing the floor boards.

The seats on the ground floor are equipped with earphones, through which one can hear a simultaneous translation of a speech in any one of 12 different languages. Every two seats share a loudspeaker and every four seats a microphone for extemporaneous speeches. On the ceiling are 500

403

star lights with an enormous red star in the centre. Seventy light beams radiate in all directions enclosed by a ring of 40 sunflower petals, which in turn is skirted by three layers of hidden lights in the form of expanding waves. This beautiful pattern symbolizes the close unity of the people of the whole country around the Party in their forward march from victory to victory. The ones that have no light are ventilation holes.

The auditorium has three main features: people can evacuate rapidly through its 32 doors; the fan shape hall provides a good view of the presidium from any angle; the acoustics is very good.

Built in lighting equipment for filming documentaries is set in a crescent shape facing the stage.

Hunan Reception Room 湖南厅

Hunan is famous for its embroidery and Liling porcelain. Hunan embroidery is one of the four major embroideries in China: Sichuan, Hunan, Suzhou and Guangdong embroideries. This is a piece of embroidery showing a view of Shaoshan Village where Chairman Mao was born. This piece shows the peacock in full plumage.

The four plates on the wall show the four seasons of the year, Spring, Summer, Autumn and Winter, from right to left.

These are gilded porcelain vases with nine dragon designs.

Chrysanthemum stone is a specialty from the Liuyang River bed. It comes in various shades of grey and black, with vivid, natural floral patterns, like chrysanthemum in full bloom or in bud.

This traditional Chinese painting shows the surge of Dongting Lake and that one shows the beautiful cliff of Nantian.

This wine container with a four ram head design is made of smoky quartz.

Liaoning Reception Room 辽宁厅

Liaoning Province is known for its heavy industry. This oil painting shows the night scene of Anshan Iron and Steel Company.

These are glass vases. The chandelier and the screen are made of crystal glass. The screen with a stainless steel frame weighs 2.2 tons. This picture is a mosaic of sea shells.

Some more pictures on the wall: a mosaic of bird feather and a mosaic of sorghum straw. This oil painting shows the Bangchui Island in Dalian.

Balcony 楼座

The balcony is for non-voting deputies and foreign envoys. A loudspeaker is installed at the back of each seat on the balcony and the gallery. Simultaneous translation in different languages is provided for by block allocation of seats. The volume control is installed on the left arm of the seat.

Guangdong Reception Room 广东厅

The furniture in this room is made of black wood. It is hard and smooth, and in natural colour. To black wood furniture, no paint is ever applied.

This is a piece of ivory carving of 50 centrifugal turning balls one over the other.

A piece of ivory carving, 1. 5 metres long, showing the Guangzhou Uprising in 1927. A piece of ivory carving, 1. 2 metres long, showing the Pearl River embankment.

This screen is also made of black wood. The carving shows the National Peasant Movement Institute, initiated and run by Chairman Mao in the years of 1924 and 1925.

These are pieces of gold plated open work of box wood.

The porcelain basket is made by Shiwan Pottery and Porcelain Factory in Guangzhou.

Shanghai Reception Room 上海厅

A piece of wood carving, gilded, showing the Palace in the Moon. Pieces of box wood carving depicting agriculture, forestry, animal husbandry, sideline occupations and fishery.

Banquet Hall 宴会厅

It is 76 metres in length, 102 metres in width and 15 metres high, with a floor space of over 7, 000 square metres, almost the size of a football field.

It can seat 5, 000 people for a banquet and hold 10, 000 for a reception. This is a platform where toasts are proposed at a banquet and short performances are staged. The two back doors lead to the kitchens. At the further end of the hall is a gallery for the band and the side galleries are for the press. There are 28 gilded gallery pillars, one metre in diameter. The chandelier on the ceiling with a sunflower design is made of crystal glass.

Beijing Reception Room 北京厅

Cloisonné and ivory carving are among Beijing' s four famous arts and crafts. These two pieces of ivory carving are 2. 04 metres long each. One shows old Beijing and the other new Beijing. This piece of lacquerware shows the Summer Palace. The traditional Chinese paintings are done by artists in Beijing. The potted plants are made of plastic. (in the small hall) This piece of ivory carving shows the Zunyi Conference. This piece is made of malachite. The flowers are made of agate.

Greeting Hall 迎宾厅

This is where official guests are greeted. Souvenir pictures of the party are usually taken here against the background of this traditional Chinese painting, which is 9 metres long and 6 metres wide.

The theme of the painting is based on a poem by Chairman Mao entitled *Snow*. It brings out well the beauty of our motherland, as the caption says *Our Land So Fair* 江山如此多娇.

The floor is covered with an enormous Tianjin made carpet, the biggest one in this building. It weighs three tons, 23 metres wide and 16 metres long. A pair of big bodiless lacquer vases stands on two sides. They were made on wooden frames and the frames were removed after the vases were completed. They are products of Fujian Province.

The staircase, totaling 63 steps, is made of white marble. The marble used for building the Great Hall of the People came from Yunnan, Shandong and Hebei provinces.

(the Great Hall of the People was designed by the Beijing Designing Institute. Designers from various provinces and municipalities also took part in designing during the period of construction in 1958, about 14,000 people worked round the clock on the site)

The Hall of Hong Kong 香港厅

Located in the southwest part of the Great Hall of the People, the Hall of Hong Kong covers an area of 1,728 square metres and is the largest of all the 32 halls representing China's provinces, autonomous regions or municipalities there.

The Hall of Hong Kong has two parts: a main reception room and a multi-functional room. An 818-square-metre garden is on the roof. The design of two entrances and two rooms of the Hall of Hong Kong is unique in the Great Hall of the People and the significance of the return of Hong Kong is reflected in the architectural details. An embroidered tapestry is placed on the wall of the reception room, depicting Victoria Harbour at night. In the corridor outside the multi-functional room is a group of sculptures of white dolphins, symbols of the celebration of the return of Hong Kong. The copper mural in the multi-functional room reflects the 100-year changes since the Opium War in mid-19th century.

The inscription of "carry out the principle of one country, two systems and maintain the prosperity and stability of Hong Kong" was written by President Jiang Zemin in June 1997 to mark the completion of the Hall of Hong Kong of the Great Hall of the People.

The proposal to establish the Hall of Hong Kong was first made in 1985 by Fei Yimin, a Hong Kong deputy to the National People's Congress.

The Great Hall of the People is the site of China's important political and diplomatic activities. Late Premier Zhou Enlai said that each administrative region of China will have a hall in it.

Peng Zhen, Wan Li and Qiao Shi, chairmen of various terms of the National People's Congress Standing Committee, all emphasized the importance of the establishment of the Hall of Hong Kong in the Great Hall of the People.

Valuable Dragon to Welcome Hong Kong Return

To celebrate the return of Hong Kong to the motherland, a priceless art treasure, "Giant Dragon Greeting the Pearl" (巨龙迎珠)was presented to the public in June 1997 Beijing.

Beijing Heguang International Jewellry Co., Ltd. made the large national treasure, which was designed by Ji Shuguo and made mainly by Zhuang Qing and Li Liansuo. The three are great masters of art.

The art work shows a giant dragon standing on the water and clouds while joyfully holding a bright pearl in its front claw. The dragon is the emblem of the Chinese nation while Hong Kong is looked on as "the Pearl of the East." The work is 1, 800 millimetres high and 1, 997. 71 millimetres long. It is made of all kinds of expensive materials including gold, silver, pearl, gems and jade. The main body of the dragon is made in accordance with gold inlaid work. The eyes of the dragon are inlaid with two gems, each with a diameter of 24 millimetres. The horns of the dragon are set with first-class jade, which is carved according to Chinese traditional work of inlaying gold with jade. On the two sides of the dragon's back, there are 56 precious and cheerful gems, each 18 millimetres in diameter, which means China's 56 nationalities greet the return of Hong Kong cheerily.

407

Imperial Archives (Huangshicheng)
皇 史 宬

Located on the eastern side of the Forbidden City, Huangshicheng, the imperial archives in the Ming (1368-1644) and Qing (1644-1911) dynasties collected the emperors' record, imperial edicts and imperial genealogies. It is China's oldest imperial archives built in 1534 that have survived more than 400 years to become a model for record keeping. Important documents, such as copies of the Yongle Encyclopedia, China's first encyclopedia, the Compendia of Qing Law, and the collection of the imperial general's seals were also held in the archives.

As opposed to the halls of the Forbidden City, which are constructed of wood, Huangshicheng was made completely of stone with more than 2,000 square meters. No beams or pillars support its arched roof. Archivists say that the design and craftsmanship of the archives helped to prevent the files from fire, damp, worms and rot.

Since 1949, the Imperial Archives have been renovated according to its original design.

Earliest Paper

An irregularly shaped-piece of linen paper has been claimed by Chinese experts as the earliest example of paper yet found in the world. Their finding indicates that China's paper-making history may have begun 200 years earlier than is generally accepted. The piece of paper, about the size of the palm of a hand, was exhibited during the 13th International Congress on Archives in Beijing in September 1996. It was unearthed from the ruins of an ancient staging post in Dunhuang in Northwest China's Gansu Province. It is just example of paper extant from China's Western Han Dynasty (206 BC-AD 23). Along with several piles of blank paper, a piece of paper with 30 Chinese characters written in an ancient style of calligraphy characteristic of the Western Han Dynasty was also discovered.

Imperial College (Guozijian)
国 子 监

The Imperial College is located just to the west of the Confucian Temple. It used to be the highest institution of learning in the Yuan, Ming and Qing dynasties (1279-1911). Built in 1784, the Biyong Hall(辟雍殿), the main structure in the Guozijian complex, was opened to the public in spring 1998 for the first time. The hall is the place where the emperors gave lectures on the classics. When an emperor was enthroned, he would first pay homage to the Confucian Temple, then go to the Imperial College to give a short speech on Confucianism or other Chinese classics on traditional Chinese thought. According to *The Book of Poetry* (*Shijing*), "Biyong" was a place for beating drums and bells or performing ritual and ceremonial music. In the Zhou Dynasty (1046 BC - 221 BC), "Biyong" was described as a place encircled by water.

In the Qing Dynasty (1644-1911), starting with Emperor Kangxi (1662-1722), every new emperor had to give a lecture in the Imperial College after he assumed the throne. This tradition was called "Lin Yong," literally to give lecture in the Imperial College. Ruling at the height of the Qing Dynasty and renowned for both his history sophistication and his martial art skills, Emperor Qianlong (1736-1795) was regarded as a wise ruler. The idea of building the "Biyong" dates back to the third year (1738) of Qianlong's reign, when he paid a visit to the Imperial College for the first time. He complained that the imperial lectures in Yilun Hall were little more than a gesture and he never forgot his dissatisfaction. In 1783, Emperor Qianlong gave an order: "The Imperial College is a place for the gathering of the talents. It should be grand in size. The regulations for rituals in Biyong have been inadequate since its establishment in the Yuan Dynasty (1279-1368) and must now be perfected." Emperor Qianlong was determined to see Biyong completed in his lifetime as a symbol of his remarkable achievements. Therefore, he attached great importance to the project. The hall was built in 1784. Covering a total area of 310 square metres, Biyong consists of one main hall, which is divided into 9 small rooms. The hall is a unique building: round outside, square inside, with a moat crossed by four stone bridges leading to the four outer gates, symbolizing that the imperial lectures would be disseminated in all directions. The hall is square in shape, 17. 6 metres in length and width, 20 metres in height. The roof has four sloping sides and four ridgepoles with upturned double-eaves, covered with yellow glazed tiles. Under the front eaves there is a tablet with the Chinese characters "Biyong," written by Emperor Qianlong. On the left and right of the entrance hang inscriptions written by Emperor Qianlong and Emperor Daoguang, encouraging students to study hard and hold knowledge in high esteem. In the hall, the vaulted roof is rich in architectural decoration. The hall has no supporting pillars. It was designed to create an aura of solemnity. The original drawing of Biyong Hall had four supporting pillars. He Shen, the then minister of the Office of Official Personnel Affairs during Emperor Qianlong's reign suggested that four crossbeams be used instead of using supporting pillars. His suggestion saved 4, 400 taels of silver. This was the only meritorious action of this very corrupt official. In the centre of the hall is the throne with a screen behind it. these two objects symbolized imperial power. The screen was inscribed with four poems written by Emperor Qianlong. Before the throne sits a sandalwood table carved with dragons in clouds. On both sides of the throne stand enameled mythical deer-like animals. The style of the architecture reflects the spirit of education in feudal China. In the early spring of 1784 after its completion, Emperor Qianlong made a personal visit to Biyong and a grand ceremony was held. According to "the Official History of the Imperial College, " the emperor delivered a speech to an audience of more than 4, 000 people including the students of noble families and ministers and other officials who all knelt down and listened with full attention. It happened to rain at that time and the listeners were drenched and bedraggled, but none of them dared to speak or move. Unique in structure and historically and artistically of great value, Biyong Hall is classed as one of the "Six Great Halls" of China.

New Capital Library

Located at southeastern Beijing's Huawei Overpass, the new Capital Library occupies an area of 37, 000 square metres, three times the size of the old one. It opened to the public on May 1, 2000. The new library allows visitors to access resources both at the library and at home. Readers no longer have to go to the library to look up reference material or borrow a book. Instead, all they need to do would only be to click the mouse. If the books or materials are already on loan to another library user, the visitor can reserve them and the library will notify the visitor as soon as the materials are in. The library will ultimately serve as a hub of information in the future, not only serving as a rich depot of information itself, but also a channel connecting readers to information resources around the world. In addition to the library's own resources, users will have access to the huge amount of information collected by various domestic and foreign institutions, organizations and even governments. If a reader can not find what he needs, he can ask the library to look it up for him. While it was extremely difficult for outsiders to get what they wanted from an enormous sea of information, in many cases professionals like those on the library's staff will find the search process a piece of cake.

Centre for Ancient Coins
古 钱 币 中 心

On October 27, 1993, an exhibition hall for ancient coins opened in Beijing. Situated at Deshengmen (Gate of Virtuous Triumph) Gate in Xicheng District, the 300-square-metre hall contains more than 1, 000 coins, including 100 rare ones. The Hall is one of the major exhibition centres for ancient coins in China. Coins now on display include horse shoe gold coins of the Han Dynasty (206 BC-AD 220), copper plated coins of the Southern Song Dynasty (1127-1279), silver coins of the Ming Dynasty (1368-1644) and gold coins of the Qing Dynasty (1644-1911). The earliest Chinese coins were made of shell and used in the Shang and Zhou dynasties (1046 BC-256 BC). Later coins were made of bone, jade, and stone before the popular use of metal coins. When the first emperor of the Qin Dynasty unified China in 221 BC, standard coins were circulated in the country.

Sponsored by the Beijing Antique and Ancient Coins Company, the exhibition hall is also a place for research and sales of ancient coins. To help collectors identify true and false ancient coins, the exhibition hall displays some false coins for reference.

Crock and Tile Market Church (Gangwashi Jiaotang)
缸 瓦 市 教 堂

Located at 57 South Xisi Street, Crock and Tile Market Church can accommodate 500 worshippers, and contains an office, chapel and baptismal font. The church was first built at the beginning of the 20th century to house the London Missionary Society. Since the merger of 1958, the church has been part of the Chinese Christian Council, and its formal name is now the Gangwashi Protestant Church of Beijing. It was closed during the "cultural revolution." After undergoing repairs it was reopened on July 13, 1980.

Worship services are held every Sunday. There are also Bible classes on Tuesday evenings and prayer-meetings on Thursday mornings. The congregation consists of both Chinese and foreign Christians.

411

The Neighbourhood Committee of the West Chang'an Boulevard
西长安街街道委员会

The West Chang'an Boulevard Neighbourhood is located to the west of Tian'anmen Gate. It covers an area of 4.5 square kilometres.

The neighbourhood has a total of 22,000 families with 82,000 people and is under the leadership of the West City District Government. Under the neighbourhood are 34 residents' committees and 5 kindergartens. The Lianzi Residents' Committee covers 3 lanes, with 2, 400 people in 690 households. It is a mass organization and has 15 members, who are elected by the residents.

The function of the residents' committee is to organize the residents to study politics and pay attention to state affairs. They are organized into small groups in which they study twice a week. To organize women to take part in work is also the responsibility of the residents' committee. They are divided into painting group, sewing or embroidery group according to their skill. They do processing work for big factories. Most of them are older women and they get pay. To help prevent disease and do health work, the residents' committee runs a clinic in which five health workers are working. They were chosen and sent to big hospitals for three month training. The residents call them bare foot doctors. Their job is to put prevention first. They go to the mountain areas and the suburbs to collect herbal medicine in different seasons. They treat minor cases and give inoculations to the children in the area free of charge. They do a lot of work on family planning. The community has also established an after school activity center to educate the youngsters so that the parents need not worry about their children at home. The youngsters are also organized to take part in various kinds of sports after school.

Clinic 卫生站

The clinic is set up for prevention and treatment of diseases.

It treats minor cases and helps do health work especially for women and children, with emphasis on prevention. The health workers make home call when a baby is born, instruct the mother to pay attention to dietetic hygiene, B. C. G. inoculation given to the baby. Smallpox vaccination is given to the baby when he is one-year-old and inoculations against diphtheria, whooping cough and tetanus are given every year. After home call, the health workers keep a health card for each baby. When the child goes to school, the health card is passed on to the school. The health workers take on the responsibility of checking women for breast cancer and uterus cancer so that they are discovered at an early stage and could be treated in time. The clinic also takes care of family planning. The health workers emphasize among women of child-bearing age the importance of family planning and tell them how to use contraceptives. They publicize the benefits of planned parenthood. Contraceptives and devices are provided free of charge. In medical care, they combine traditional Chinese medicine with Western medicine. They take blood pressure of the patients and treat them with massage, acupuncture, cupping, plum blossom needles and so on. Home delivery of medicine is offered to bed ridden people.

Usually there are seven different groups under any given neighbourhood committee, including public security, mediation, social welfare, public health, women's affairs, family planning and juvenile education. According to the Neighbourhood Committee Organization Law, neighbourhood committees are grassroots self-government and administrative organs responsible for community activities. The standard urban management system is designed to enable urban residents to manage, educate and help themselves, and grants the right to self businesses-management of community affairs. To meet the need of a market-oriented economy, many of Beijing's neighbourhood committees have developed neighbourhood, especially in the service industry. In the past neighbourhood-run businesses stuck to foodstuffs, textiles, printing and garment making. But nowadays they have expanded their scope to include telecommunications, advertising, decoration, leasing of automobiles, culture and arts.

More Wives Divorce Husbands in China

Since the early 1990s, China has witnessed a steady rise in the number of divorce cases. In 1990, about 800, 000 couples ended their marriages, a figure that has zoomed to a record of 1. 21 million in 2000. Legal actions on divorces are also on the rise. Chinese courts at all levels dealt with 1. 2 million divorce cases in 1999, a sharp growth from just 272, 000 cases in 1980. This amounts to an annual growth rate of 8. 1 per cent. Despite the continuous surge in divorces, Chinese divorce rates remains low compared with other countries, especially with its developed peers. China's divorce rate ranks only in 55th of the 72 countries in an early 2001 United Nations statistics, and the rate is lower than in the US, Japan and many developing countries. One reason for the rise of cases in China is that women have become bolder about demanding divorces and using the legal system. In major cities like Beijing and Shanghai, about 70 per cent of divorces are filed by women. Chinese women, especially in big cities, have jobs and personal careers. They are more economically independent, which helps reduce their reliance on husbands. This gives them the ability to protect themselves from bad marriages or domestic violence. Meanwhile, an increasing mobility of the Chinese population prompts people to expand their social lives, enabling them to find better lovers. Unlike 20 years ago when Chinese people were bound in State-owned firms, which offered cradle-to-grave welfare, Chinese people now can be free to choose jobs, locations for careers and dating partners. Public opinion about divorce is also becoming more liberal. Once a taboo topic is Chinese tradition that embarrassed the divorcees and offended the community, times have now changed. People are more open to the topic, and they know that it is a normal issue, like marriages and health cares. This has created a good climate for couples to end their bitterness and walk out of the shadow of broken ties.

Hutong (Lanes) of Beijing
北 京 的 胡 同

The word "*hutong*," which is what the small back streets or lanes of Beijing are called, is an unusual term used only in Beijing and a few northern cities in China. In fact, it was originally a Han language term, but came from Mongolian roots. In the northern grasslands communities tended to form around wells, so "hot," or "well" in Mongolian, came also to mean a town, and a Hudu or Hudun, variants of it, a camp or village.

Later it was applied to a small street. The sound gradually changed to *hutong*.

Small streets in Beijing began to be called *hutong* after the Nüzhen people from the northeast, who founded the Jin Dynasty, captured the city in 1127 and made it their capital. (their language has similarities to Mongolian)

The custom became more widespread when the city was the capital of the Yuan Dynasty after the Mongol conquest.

Beijing's history is preserved in the names of its *hutong*. Some retain the names of some famous persons who once lived there, such as Yongkang Hou *Hutong* for Prince Yongkang and Wu Liang Daren for his Excellency Wu Liang. Others are named for well-known craftsmen or shops, such as Doufu Chen *Hutong* for a beancurd seller named Chen, and Fenfang Liu Jia for the home of a maker of bean vermicelli Liu. There are also lanes with names like Jinyu (Goldfish), Dengcao (Lighting Rush), and Shoupa (Handkerchief).

Generally speaking, when one of the winding *hutong* makes a major turn, it takes on a new name. In the Qing Dynasty (1644-1911), there were totally 2, 077 *hutong;* In 1944 there were 3, 200 *hutong;* while in 1970s, there were 1, 316 *hutong;* in 2001, 800 *hutong* remained in Beijing. In the wider ones two buses can pass. The narrowest spot is the southern end of Gaoxiao *Hutong*, through which only one person can walk

414

at a time. The longest, Rongxian (Embroidery Floss) *Hutong*, is two kilometres long. The shortest is Yichi Dajie (One-foot Street), which is actually twenty metres long.

With the development of the city, many *hutongs* have been demolished to make way for building high rises. Without these *hutongs*, the memory of the traditional life and culture in Beijing will disappear. Therefore, the city has set aside designated parts of downtown Beijing as off-limits to urban renovation. These areas include the neighbourhoods around the Forbidden City, Beihai Park and the Lama Temple. Experts worry that urban renovation is likely to break the traditional fabric of the city, making it difficult for the younger generations to fathom the life of old Beijing.

Ju'er *Hutong* 菊儿胡同

The compound at Ju'er *Hutong* in the centre of Beijing was completed in 1993. It is one of the successful projects in the renovation of old residences. It is built on the site of a former classic Beijing quadrangle inhabited by a dozen families and now accommodates more than 40 households.

The compound, constructed in the style of a typical Beijing quadrangle with gray tiles and bricks, is in harmony with the surrounding old buildings. In an effort to make the residents more comfortable, the architects built the new compound with two to three storeys inside a construction area totaling 14, 800 square metres. They improved the light and water supply in all apartments. Wu Lingyong, a professor at Qinghua University, was in charge of designing the project.

Dongjiaominxiang
(Former Legation Quarters)
东 交 民 巷

415

This area used to be the legation quarter, established after the Boxer Rebellion of 1900. Dongjiaominxiang is the main street stretching from west to east across the quarters. The old legation quarter used the southern city wall (today's Second Inner Ring Road) as the southern side of its boundary. It had its own wall and gates at the west, north, and east sides, which are now Tian'anmen (Gate of Heavenly Peace) Square, East Chang'an (Eternal Peace) Boulevard, and Chongwenmennei Street. In the past, there were various kinds of buildings in the legation quarter, including barracks, hospital, hotel, church, club, banks, and post office.

The architectural styles employed in the legation quarter reflected a variety of foreign influences. During the time of construction, there were two main styles of world architecture. One emphasized the revival of the architectural style of the past. The other was modern, aiming at the 20th century. The architecture of the past was very popular in Europe and North America. It can be labeled a kind of "eclecticism, between the classical revival and romanticism." The buildings in the legation quarter are in this category, although they differ in form and style. There were only two exceptions among these legation houses. One was the British legation, part of which was the former residence of a Qing Dynasty prince, and the other was the Spanish legation house, which was a local citizen's residence. Some of these old legation buildings remain in splendid style and are still in use, but many others were destroyed.

The first group of buildings to the northern side of Dongjiaominxiang Alley's western end was the former French hospital. Across the street were the sites of former barracks and legation of the United States. Next to the US legation was the site of the Dutch legation. The Dutch legation's former entrance was a brick structure with a pillar on each side. It can still be recognized, although the gateway has been blocked up by bricks. To the east of the Dutch legation was the National City Bank of New York. It is distinctive due to its well preserved four tall, thick, decorative columns. It is now the office of the Beijing Fire Control Bureau. To its north across the street was the site of the former Russian legation and barracks, now the site of the Supreme People's Court. Most of the old buildings have disappeared and a big new court building has been erected. Still in existence is the Russian Legation Lane, renamed USSR Legation Lane in 1917; the sign board still exists. It is between the former Russian legation and barracks. To the north of the Russian legation was the British legation and barracks, which covered the largest area. Some of its buildings and its former entrance gate are in good condition. The Chinese-style roofs of these buildings can easily be seen from the street.

To the east of the British and Russian legations there was once a canal running from north to south. The water came from the Jade Spring, west of the Summer Palace, through the Imperial City, flowing southward and out of the old city wall through the Water Gate. The canal was covered in 1925 and has become a street, now called Zhengyilu Street. Across the former canal, opposite the British legation, was the Japanese legation and barracks. The main structure of its entrance is quite well kept, but its decorations have been removed. It is now the seat of the municipal government. South of the Japanese barracks at Zhengyilu Street and Dongjiaominxiang Alley stands a well-preserved two-storey building. It has a dome above its entrance and is handsomely decorated. Inside the building, the ceilings and walls have been renovated according to their original designs.

The marble wainscoting and fireplaces are still in good condition, although the fireplaces are not used in the wintertime. The building is a mixture of Gothic Revival and Neoclassic. It used to be the former office of the Japanese Yokohama Species Bank and is now the office of China Huacheng Finance Corporation. East of the Japanese area is now a post office. Its old tiled floor is still in fine condition. Further eastward was the site of the former French legation. It has a very imposing entrance gate, which may remind people of the Gate of Triumph and the watch tower of the old Chinese city wall.

Across Dongjiaominxiang Alley and opposite the French legation and Yokohama Species Bank were the sites of the former German legation, the Banque Franco Chinoise and Wagon Lits Hotel which were wrecked in fires in the past. A modern hotel (the Capital Hotel) and Hongdu Fashion Company are now situated there.

North of the Japanese and French legations was the Italian legation and barracks. The Chinese People's Association for Friendship with Foreign Countries is now based there. Its gatehouses and part of the buildings in the courtyard still exist. East of the Italian, French and German legations runs another street paralleled to Zhengyilu Street. It is Taijichang Street (originally called Marco Polo Street).

On the eastern side of Taijichang Street from north to the south were the sites of the former Austrian legation, Peking Club, French barracks, a Catholic church, and the Belgian legation. The entrance of the Belgian legation no longer exists but the decorative brickwork above the building's roofs can still be observed clearly from the outside. Several villas like two-storey buildings are well kept and have been renovated. The former Belgian legation is now the Zijin Guest House.

Across Dongjiaominxiang Alley and opposite the Belgian legation is a Catholic church, which was renovated recently. The main building of the former Peking Club is in its original form but has been repainted. It now houses the Standing Committee of the Beijing People's Congress.

Walking eastward from the Catholic Church along Dongjiaominxiang Alley, vacationers can see the former office building of the Deutsche Asiatische Bank. The distinguishing shape of its tower roof looks much like the bell tower roof of the famous Aschaffenburg built in the 16th century. Its decorative iron window grills are still in place. It has become, together with the former German hospital to its north, part of the Beijing Hospital.

A walk along this old legation quarter is highly recommended, because

417

you may experience a kind of nostalgia, a feeling that you are walking along the streets of Europe in old China.

The legation quarter architectural complex of Dongjiaominxiang was listed as a national key relic under special preservation in 2001.

Siheyuan (Dwelling Compounds) in Beijing
北京的四合院

Dwelling compounds or quadrangles (*Siheyuan*) in Beijing are one important aspect of the city's architectural heritage.

Beijing's dwelling compounds are generally rectangular, with the four sides squarely facing the cardinal points. Almost every dwelling compound is surrounded by high walls, with an open courtyard in the centre. The buildings on four sides are usually one storey high.

Stepping over the high wooden base of the front gate of a large compound, you will find a brick screen located a few feet inside. In front of the screen is the outer courtyard, which is flanked by structures to the east and west. In former days, these were the kitchen and servants' living quarters. A red-painted gate leads through the north wall of the outer court into the inner courtyard. The main building faces south to get the maximum possible sunshine in winter, and the eaves provide a pleasant shade in summer when the sun is high. The building is divided into three or five rooms: living or community rooms in the center with smaller bedroom or studies at each end. The buildings facing east and west on each side of the court were constructed to accommodate married children and their families. Some dwelling compounds consist of several courtyards. With no steel or concrete, the entire dwelling was built of bricks and wood. The compounds are quiet, beautiful and compact. Beijing residents like to live in them and even foreigners find them attractive.

Nowadays, these peaceful quadrangles are hard to find in Beijing. The reasons are as follows:

Since New China was founded, a large-scale construction programme has been carried out in the city, causing the demolition of some dwelling compounds.

In the short period after 1949, government offices occupied some quadrangles. Later they were demolished to build office buildings.

During the "cultural revolution" (1966-1976), air-raid shelters were dug everywhere in Beijing, resulting in the destruction of some dwelling compounds.

418

In recent years many residential buildings have been constructed to ease the housing shortage and provide better accommodation for the people. Some were built on the sites of demolished dwelling compounds. Outer compounds have been changed or distorted beyond recognition because the residents have added kitchens in the courtyards.

Today, Beijing still has about 400,000 residential quadrangles, mainly distributed over the East, West, Xuanwu and Chongwen districts of the city. Those in the East and West districts are in the best shape. The departments concerned with the preservation of cultural relics in Beijing have earmarked a number of good quality dwelling compounds for protection. In addition, the urban construction departments have worked out a plan to limit high buildings in the city proper to protect the dwelling compounds.

Shichahai Quarter and Prince Gong Palace are located north of Beihai Park. This area is surrounded by several once imperial gardens, dozens of winding *hutongs* (alleys) and thousands of common *siheyuan* (quadrangle courtyards). No other scenic spots in this sprawling capital offers up its past in such an effervescent, amicable manner. Biking is the best way to tour this quarter, which is a perfect combination of imperial residences, lakes, *hutongs* and modern, everyday life.

The best-kept courtyard house in this region is the Prince Gong Palace. Located on the northern shore of Shichahai Lake, the palace consists of three lines of buildings. A garden lies at the back of the residence. Altogether, the complex has more than 20 separate areas, each different in layout and style.

"Spirit wall" was erected inside the main gate of walled compounds to keep out evil spirits (which travelled exclusively in straight lines) as well as more innocent curiosity seekers.

Quadrangle Terms 四合院术语

- A quadrangle is a compound with rows of rooms built in the four directions so that a square inner courtyard is formed at the centre.
- Old Beijing residents use to call it *Si He Fang* (*Si He* means surrounding from four directions).
- Principal Room 正房—are those on the north side facing the south.
- Wing Rooms 厢房—On the east and west sides of the inner courtyard, there are 3 rooms respectably with doors open facing the courtyard. These are called wing rooms.
- Side Rooms 耳房—Smaller and lower rooms may be attached to either side of the principal rooms, looking just like ears on either side of a face, thus they are called Ear Rooms, literally side rooms.

- Reversibly-Set Room 倒座房
- Inner Quarters 内宅
- Outer Quarters 外宅
- Drooping Flowers Gate; Ping Men (Screen Door) 垂花门
- Drooping Flowers Gate with a single rolling facet 单卷棚式垂花门
- Drooping Flowers Gate's Rim of the Eaves 垂花门的檐口
- Lintels 门楣
- Windows of various forms 什锦窗
- Drooping Lotus Columns 垂莲柱
- Pavilion with Cup-flowing Throughs 流杯亭
- The End of the Drooping Column with Decorations of Carved Lotus Flowers 雕饰仰覆莲花的垂花柱头
- The End of the Drooping Column with Carved Pattern of Willow Swaying in the Breeze 雕饰风摆柳图案的垂柱头
- The Square End of the Drooping Column with Carved Patterns of Flowers and Grasses 雕饰花草图案的方形垂柱头
- Drooping Flowers Gate's Flowery Shielding 垂花门的花罩
- the Front View of the Drooping Flowers Gate 垂花门的正面观
- Drum Stone 抱鼓石
- Brick-carving Couplets 砖雕楹联
- Corridor 游廊
- The Climbing Corridor Which Rises along the Slope. 沿山势斜坡而上的爬山廊
- Painted with Suzhou-style Colored Paintings 苏式彩画
- Gray Tube-shaped Tiles 青筒瓦
- Drooping Flowers Gate in Beijing quadrangles fall into two categories 北京四合院的垂花门分两类:
  ① Those with a facet composed by a a pointed-topped facet and a coiling facet looking both vivid and dignified, and presenting a sense of rhythm(富于韵律感)by the undulating top. 一殿一卷式垂花门
  ② Those with only a single facet looking elegant though somewhat lacking in vividness 不失高雅, and they are widely adopted in a considerable number of quadrangles. 单卷棚垂花门
- All Drooping Flowers Gates have two following functions 所有的垂花门有两种作用:
  ① The function of defending; 防卫功能
  ② The function of screening, which is the major one. 起屏障作用
- Large-scaled Quadrangle 大型四合院
- Drooping Lotus 垂莲
- "Endless Coming Generations" 子孙万代

- "Three Mates in Bitterly Cold Days" 岁寒三友
- Fortune, Emolument, Longevity, and Happiness 福、禄、寿、喜
- Gate of a residence 宅门
- Inner Quarter 内宅
- Second Gate or Inner Gate 二门,又称内门
  In China's feudal society, maidens were not allowed to go out of the main entrance or step on the threshold of Er Men (Drooping Flowers Gate). 在中国封建社会,未出嫁的香闺小姐大门不出,二门不迈。
- Screen wall 影壁
- There are three kinds of frequently-seen screen walls. 常见的影壁有三种
  ① *Yi Zi* Screen Wall 一字影壁
  ② *Yan Chi* (Wild-goose-wing-shaped) Screen Wall 雁翅影壁
  ③ *Fan Ba Zi* Screen Wall or Pie Shan Screen Wall 反八字影壁或撇山影壁
- Peonies—Detailed Corner Pattern Carvings on a Screen Wall 影壁细部岔角花雕刻——牡丹花
- to present a sense of vitality 生机昂然
- Screen Door 屏门
- 5-bay across with 3 pairs of doors at the center 面宽五开间,中间三间开门
- It is of the superlative form of gates of residents for princes according to regulations. 他是王府大门中型制最高的
- In the feudal society, a strict hierarchy wad formed, thus residences and their gate were the direct representatives of the owners' ranks and social statues. 在等级森严的封建社会,住宅及其大门直接代表主人的品第等级和社会地位。
- Hence the sayings "of the same family status" and "being well-matched in social and economic status" 所谓"门第相当"和"门当户对",就是这个意思。
- Classified by their forms, gates of quadrangle residences in Beijing fall into two categories: 北京四合院住宅的大门,从建筑形式上可分为两类
  ① House-typed Gate(composed by one or more rooms) 屋宇式大门
  ② Wall-typed Gate(open on the spot where two sections of walls meet) 墙垣式门
- Shielding Room 罩房
- Shielding Building 罩楼
- Posterior Shielding Rooms 后罩房
- Western Wing Room 西厢房

- Posterior Shielding Storeyed Building 后罩楼
- Short-cut Corridor 抄手游廊
- Bobbin Gate of Corridor 廊门筒子
- Central Room 堂屋
- Inner Room 套间
- Small Yard 小天井
- Side Courtyard 跨院
- Moon-shaped Opening 月洞门
- The Framed Scene 框景
- Corner Door 角门
- Hard Gable Style 硬山式
- Cymbal-shaped knockers—decorations of the door 门钹——大门饰件
- Clasps 门簪
- Couplets—对联 expressing the ideals, pursuance, wishes or believes of the owners 表达出主人的理想、追求、愿望或信念
- Five Bats Presenting Longevity 五福捧寿
- Lions and Silk Ball 狮子绣球
- Peonies of Wealth and Rank 富贵牡丹
- All things will go on as people wish. 万事如意
- Brick Carving 砖雕
- Western-style Gate—another variety of wall-typed gate 西洋式门
- The construction of a quadrangle look gorgeous: greenish bricks, gray tiles, milky steps and red columns.
- Looking down at a quadrangle from the air 俯瞰四合院
- A panoramic night view of a quadrangle 俯瞰四合院夜景
- The basic setups and architectural features of quadrangles
- Groups of neighboring quadrangles
- The quadrangle implies profound cultural connotations and is the carrier of traditional Chinese culture.
- The pattern composed by bats and the character "*shou* 寿" (longevity) express the wish of attaining both happiness and a long, long life.
- A pattern with Chinese roses in a vase means "Safe in All Seasons."
- Inlaid auspicious calligraphy on walls in rooms are collected admonitions from ancient worthies and famous sayings from all ages.
- Eulogize the beautiful landscapes, or bear the ways of acting in society, or praise high aspirations
- To stay in a such decorated courtyard in really like lingering in a hall of traditional Chinese culture.
- Beijing's quadrangles have existed for several hundred years because they possess strong points incomparable for other types of residents.

- It is a special kind of feeling.
- In traditional Chinese buildings, fittings include the doors, windows, shielding and partitions. 中国古代建筑中，将门、窗、户、牗（音"又"）、花罩、隔断等通称为装修。
- Partition Doors of Rooms 隔扇门
- Curtain Shelves and Ventilating Doors 帘架风门
- Windows which can be propped up and down 支摘窗
- Inner fittings include the bed-like compartment covered with gauze, flowery shielding, shielding of the Kangs, shelves with diversified holding spaces, octagonal shielding, wall boards (wooden partitions), caisson ceilings etc. 室内装修有碧纱厨、花罩、几腿罩、炕罩、栏杆罩、圆光罩、多宝格、八角罩、板壁、天花板等等。
- To be fit on or taken down 可拆可装
- Palace Lantern 官灯
- An Elliptic "Beauty Mirror" 椭圆形丽人镜
- Flowery Shielding Reaching the Ground 落地花罩
- Chinese Catalpa 楸木
- *Nanmu* (a kind of cider; This kind of *nanmu* can give off an unusual scent reputed to repel mosquitoes in summer) 楠木
- Camphorwood 樟木
- Red Sandalwood 紫檀
- Padauk 红木
- Rose Wood 花梨
- Korean Pine 红松
- Do not lose shape 不易走形
- An old-fashioned wooden armchair 太师椅
- The Long Narrow Table 条几案
- "8-Immortal" Table 八仙桌
- Flower Stand 花架
- Mirror Stand 镜架
- Duster Holding Vase 掸瓶
- Carved Decorations 雕饰
- Colored Paintings 彩绘
- Magpie on the Branch 喜鹊登梅
- To kill three birds with one stone 一举三得
- The theory of geomancy 风水理论
- Geomancer 风水先生
- To stay clear of calamities and to tend toward propitiousness 趋吉避凶
- The fit-ups 装修
- Carved decorations 雕刻装饰

- Colored-paintings 彩画
- Embody folk customs, social practices and traditional culture
- Express people's pursuance for happiness, fineness, prosperity and aus-
piciousness
- Large quadrangle with a garden 带花园的四合院
- Panoramic view of a medium-sized quadrangle 中型四合院乌瞰
- To provide unique appeal and enjoyment 别有一番情趣和享受

Be Well-Matched in Social and Economic Status
门 当 户 对

On the lintel of the door of an ancient building, there are usually two or four spherical pillars protruding 40 centimeters, commonly known as *mendang* (门档) in Chinese.

Outside the door frame stand two flat-shaped blocks of stone, called *mendun* (门墩) in Chinese, leaning against the threshold, one on each side with stones, about one metre high known as *hudan* (户旦).

In ancient times in China, when wealthy families had celebrations or marriage ceremonies, colorful lanterns were hung from the lintels as a sign of congratulation. The stones by the side of the door showed the wealth and power of the family. Also they were used as stepping stones for people to mount horses. Therefore, *hudan* (户旦) are also called horse-mounting stones.

Ancient lintels were required to have *hudan*. Otherwise, the one meter-high threshold would block the doorway. The person who created Hu-dan was a true craftsman.

Usually seen on both sides of the front and central gates, *mendun* stones in various shapes, are used to fix the gate frame and the door axle. Though the course of history, the outer *mendun* have grown into diverse statues symbolizing the social status of the family in the *siheyuan*. With a love of handicrafts and curiosity about the Chinese society, Iwanmoto and his wife left their home in Osaka, Japan, for Beijing, in 1995 to study Chinese and painting after retirement. But an accidental discovery six months into his study changed his course completely. Iwanmoto believed that his greatest accomplishment in the past three years is the guide of *mendun* in the four old districts. Among the 6, 203 *mendun* he noted by the end of October 1998, about 900 are worth protecting. he believed that this is the ancestor of the more elaborated mendun which appeared in the late Ming and Qing dynasties between the 14th and the 20th centuries. With detailed sketches and pictures, Iwanmoto explained how the box-shaped form grew into drums carved with a lotus on each side. Auspicious designs with animals, plants and people changed into a lion, a vase, or polyhedrons. He guessed that *mendun* with lions were the privilege of royalty. He found only 37 single examples. The most popular *mendun* in Beijing are shaped like boxes, there are 4, 339 of them. Such *mendun* might have indicated that an official resided inside. The drum-shaped *mendun* number 1, 823. Their owners could have been generals or officers. In contrast, he found only two pairs of vase-shaped *mendun* and two pairs of polyhedrons, whose owners must have been very special.

The Temple of Confucius (551 BC-479 BC)
孔　　庙

The Temple of Confucius, the present site of the Capital Museum is located in Guozijian Street. It is here that Confucius was worshipped during the Yuan, Ming and Qing dynasties (1279-1911). The temple was first built by in 1302 in the Yuan Dynasty, and was restored and rebuilt on several occasions during the Ming and Qing dynasties. In 1737, during the reign of Qing Emperor Qianlong, the major hall was renovated and was recovered with magnificent yellow glazed roof tiles. In 1906, when the worship of Confucius was further emphasized by the Qing Government, the temple underwent extensive restoration which lasted until 1916.

Covering a total area of 22, 000 square metres, the temple makes up four courtyards. The principal structures include Xianshimen 先师门 (Gate of Ancient Teacher), Dachengmen 大成门 (Gate of Great Accomplishment), Dachengdian 大成殿 (Hall of Great Accomplishment), Chongshengci 崇圣祠 (Worship Hall), the eastern part of the front courtyard is taken up by the Pavilions for Stone Tablets, the Holy Kitchen, the Pavilion for Sacrificial Animals and the Well Pavilion; in the west, there are more pavilions for Stone Tablets, the hall of Vegetarian Diet and the Gate of Reverence which opens onto Guozijian (Imperial Academy). On either side of the courtyard, are arranged 198 stone tablets bearing 51, 624 names of Advanced Scholars of the Yuan, Ming and Qing dynasties who passed the triennial imperial examinations. Inside the Gate of Great Accomplishment are placed ten stone drums which were made on ancient models 1736 to 1795 of the Qing Dynasty and erected two tablets associated with the event.

425

It was the Hall of Great Accomplishment where Confucius was worshipped. The stately, grand hall with its double eaves is flanked by the east and west wings. The east wing now houses an exhibition of the history of Beijing.

In the compound of the temple, there are fourteen other pavilions for Stone Tablets of the Ming and Qing dynasties where inscriptions of great historical value are carved.

The Following Order of Arrangement of the Six Classics Is as Follows 六艺依次如下：

1. *Shi* 诗 or The Book of Poetry (Songs)
2. *Shu* 书 or The Book of History
3. *Li* 礼 or The Book of Rites
4. *Yue* 乐 or The Book of Music
5. *Yi* 易 or The Book of Changes
6. *Chunqiu* 春秋 or The Spring and Autumn Annals

Modern scholars regard Confucius as the author of some of the classics and the compiler or organizer of the others. He is supposed to have arranged his own works in a sort of psychological order, from simple to complex, as a great teacher would do, *Shi*, *Shu*, *Li* and *Yue* constitute the general course of study, while *Yi* and *Chunqiu* are more of a technical nature and represent ancient concepts brought forward and captured in Confucius time, and constitute a higher course of study. *Shi* and *Shu* are used for reading or symbolic education; *Li* and *Yue* are for practice or moral education; *Yi* and *Chunqiu* represent the philosophy of Confucius. They contain his social and political theories and cannot be understood by ordinary students. They are the technical learning and belong to a higher form of education. That is why they are put at the end of the whole course of study. The *Yi* or The Book of Change has origins from ancient times rooted in the *Yin Yang* and Five Agencies theory.

Confucius was primarily a moral teacher. Lover (*Ren*), the rules of proper conduct (*Li*) filial piety, and the doctrine of the Mean (*Zhongyong*) are the four main topics of the moral teaching of Confucius.

In his teaching on love (*Ren*), he emphasized the sanctity of and value of the individual, and the importance of his motive and will in moral conduct; yet at the same time he did not neglect the social aspect of love. The motive of love only, without the act of love toward others, is not true love. A hallmark of Confucius thought throughout is his emphasis on just this balance of inner and outer virtue, where inner refinement and purity naturally expresses outward.

In his teaching of *Li* he emphasized the value of the cultural heritage of

426

society and the accepted rules of proper conduct. But he was aware of the evils that might result from the over emphasis on *Li;* formalism, hypocrisy, or arbitrariness. Morality would become an external thing; to abide by customary regulations or accepted rules only would be regarded as moral, and the beach of them would be regarded as sinful. In order to safeguard one against such dangers, on the one hand, Confucius emphasized the value of love *(Ren),* and on the other hand, gave new interpretations on Li by putting the individual motive, especially sincerity and reverence, as the foundation of *Li.*

In his teaching on filial piety, he emphasized the extension of the emotional power that derives from the love of one's parents to the wider moral and social applications. Filial piety was, to Confucius, a strong moving force, very similar to that of the religious passion, which drives and attracts the individual to establish himself and walk according to the Way *(Tao),* so that the names of his parents might be glorified.

In his teaching on the doctrine of the Mean, Confucius emphasized a sort of balanced life, or a state of complacency in thought and in the shifting emphasis between social heritage and freedom. The Confucian Doctrine of the Mean can be regarded as the doctrine synthesis between any two extremes in these life arts.

The substance of the teaching of Confucius can be grouped under three headings, namely; moral, intellectual, and religious. Confucius was mainly interested in the moral life of men. The intellectual aim of his teaching was in general subordinate to his moral aim, and his religious teaching was chiefly reflective of the traditional beliefs. He had very few comments.

Both intellectual knowledge and religious beliefs were, according to him, useless and not worth teaching if they could not contribute towards the betterment of the practical moral life of the individual. Again, we can recognize in this a balance of inner and outer refinement, with the outer values showing themselves in social expressions yet always motivated by inner human spiritual development (and reflective of a person's true inner state).

The moral teachings of Confucius can be said to have been centred around the four main topics— *Ren, Li, Xiao, and Zhongyong.*

The ancestors of Confucius were of the royal family of Song, but his great grandfather had moved to Lu State, where the family became impoverished. Confucius did not receive much formal education and had no regular teacher.

At fifteen he had his mind bent on learning. From that time on he studied very hard, generally by himself, sometimes in consultation with more elderly and experienced scholars. At thirty, he stood firm. At forty, he had no doubts. At fifty, he knew the decrees of Heaven. At sixty, his ear was obedient organ. At seventy, he could follow what his heart desired without transgressing what was right. He studied extensively and was familiar with the traditional literature of all times. and was an inspiring teacher who taught tirelessly.

The aim of the teaching of Confucius was to bring about social reforms through education, the individuals of society; to put forth an ideal social order through cultivating ideal ways of life and a full development of the personality of the individual. Confucius put the importance of education on the same level as that of population and wealth, and regarded these as the three essentials of any nation.

Confucius was fully aware of the importance of social institutions to ensure the stability and safety of individuals. Society must adjust itself to the individual in order to escape stagnation, and the individual must also adjust himself to society in order to become human, no one can live or develop as a human without the help of society. Therefore, Confucius did not teach people, as the pessimists of his time did, to flee from the world and to become irresponsible hermits or political nihilists. Confucius thought what was needed was work in society to bring about social reforms through education.

The two favourite subjects in the teaching of Confucius, as recorded in The Analects, are love (Ren), and the rules of proper conduct (Li). Li may mean propriety or ceremony or rite in its narrower sense; In its broader sense it may mean the rules of proper conduct in general. Such rules of proper conduct (Li) are really knowable in a deeply internal matter and represent a sort of unwritten law, outwardly expressed as norms and regulations deeply recognized by a society. They are the most important social product to ensure the solidarity of society according to universal human principles. Love (Ren) is another favorite theme of the teaching of Confucius. It presupposes and ensures the importance and uniqueness of every individual. The full development of the personality of the individual is very much emphasized in the teaching of Confucius, and Ren/Love is closely to the notice of humanness, compassion and compassionate service in a social setting as an expression of full human potential.

An international conference on Confucianism earlier in October 1999 broadened scholars' understanding of the ancient Chinese theorist who has deeply affected Asia and may offer insights for the rest of the world as well. The forum was called the Commemoration Conference for the 2550th birthday of Confucius. Professor Rosita Delios (female) from Australia's

428

Bond University maintained that the Confucian ideal of the "*Datong* (all under Heaven are one, or great unity)" could help guide a multi-ethnic world. The most important aspect of "*Datong*" is that many different thoughts and cultures can coexist as manifestations of one advancing principle. This principle today is the trend of globalization. Confucius said: "To develop yourself, you must make others develop first, and to make yourself prosper, you must make others prosper first. "

Bryan W. Van Norden, PhD. was an Assistant Professor at the Philosophy Department of Vassar College in the state of New York said that Confucius was of the four most influential individuals in world history, along with Jesus Christ, the Buddha, and Mohammed.

Confucius has had a deep, long-lasting and largely positive effect on all the East Asian civilizations, as well as on Viet Nam and Singapore. Confucius was much admired by many figures of the Western Enlightenment, who regarded his idea as a rational alternative to traditional European religious views. Confucianism emphasizes five things: living in and for this world, the family, education, and tradition and ritual.

First and foremost, Confucius emphasized acting in and for this world, as opposed to being concerned with any supernatural realm or afterlife. When one of Confucius' disciples asked about how to serve the ghosts and spirits, Confucius responded: "You are not yet able to serve people—how can you serve the ghosts and spirits? When the disciple went on to ask about death, Confucius simply told him: "You do not yet understand life—how could you possibly understand death?"

Living in this world, the most important thing is the family. But this does not mean that one should ignore the well-being of strangers. As one of Confucius' disciples said: "Within the four seas, all men are brothers. " Confucians believe that it is only by learning to love and respect people in one's own family that one learns to love and respect those outside the family.

In the West, education is often seen as ethically neutral. For Confucians, education should help build good character. All Confucians are educated in literature and ritual. Some Confucians have become experts in medicine, applied mathematics and water conservancy in order to use that knowledge to help others.

Confucians revere traditional literature and rituals. Although they are frequently original poets and novelists, Confucians believe that traditional literature is important for the beauty of its styles of expression and helps one internalize values such as loyalty and concern for others. Similarly, learning and practicing rituals help build character by making it clear and how others should treat you.

Ritual also provides a channel for the expression of individual feelings, especially strong emotions such as grief over death or love. Western psychologists now recognize the importance of "having boundaries" in interpersonal relationships, and this is much like the role performed by Confucian ritual. It seems that Western scholars are now rediscovering what Confucians have long known. Although only a few US colleges and universities offer courses on Chinese philosophy, these are usually among the most popular classes on campus. Unfortunately, many people in the United States do not get a chance to study the teachings of Confucius, and have only a distorted understanding of him.

Bugs Fight to Preserve Ancient Trees at Temple

Strange multi-legged creatures were brought to this Confucius Temple in mid-April 2000 to undertake the important task of protecting ancient trees around the temple forever. Ladybugs, the natural enemy of the aphid (worm), are being used by the Chinese Academy of Agricultural Sciences to prevent the pests from damaging the temple. No pesticides are needed because ladybugs can do the job, plus they will not create pollution or damage the cultural relics. And it is really cheap. The Confucius Temple, built in the Yuan Dynasty (1279-1368), is surrounded by 108 ancient cypress and Chinese scholar trees, some of which are 700 years old. The Acedemy used to spray pesticide on the ancient trees eight times a year. Insect pests have disappeared, but some parts of the buildings and stone tablets have been stained.

Confucius on TV

The first TV series on Confucianism, entitled "Cultural Giant: Confucius," was completed in early 2001 and has been shown at home and abroad. Confucius, respected for centuries as China's "great perfection, ultimate sage, and foremost teacher," developed his philosophical theories stressing benevolence and traditional rites, called Confucianism in the West, during China's Spring and Autumn Period (770 BC-476 BC). The 30-part series, made at a cost of 18 million yuan (US$2.16 million) and bringing together a great quantity of precious documents and data gathered nationwide, captures the essence of Confucianism, according to general producer Kong Xiangjin, a 75th-generation grandson of Confucius. The series has been highly praised by academicians at home and abroad, Professor Du Weiming, a world-famous Harvard University authority on Chinese culture, says the series is unprecedented in scope and undoubtedly a great contribution to Chinese culture and to culture throughout the world.

Educational Viewpoints of Confucius 孔子的教育观

1. The characteristics of learning process; 学习过程的特点
   Personal practice 亲身实践, read books written by forefathers 读前人书, hearing and seeing are inseparable. 闻、见也是不可少的。
2. No matter who he is should enjoy education 有教无类—educational guiding policy. 教学方针
3. Teach students in accordance with their aptitude. 因材施教—teaching principle. 教学原则
4. Elicitation method 启发式—teaching principle 教学原则
5. Teaching and learning are the relationship of dialectical unity. 教学是辩证统一的关系。

White Cloud Taoist Temple (Baiyunguan)
白 云 观

Situated in the West City District, the White Cloud Taoist Temple formally reopened in 1984 for the first time since 1949. It is the largest and the only one of its kind open to the public.

Taoism, a religion native to China, has a history of 1, 800 years. It originated from shamanism and the various practices intended to ensure immortality in the Qin (221 BC-206 BC) and Western Han (206 BC-AD 23) dynasties. Zhang Daoling is credited with founding the religion of Taoism on Heming Mountain (in Dayi County, Sichuan Province) during the reign of Emperor Shundi (AD 126-AD 144).

Laozi, the ancient Chinese philosopher, is the chief deity of Taoism and is honored as Taishanglaojun (Lord the Most High). Taoists believe that Tao (the Way), Laozi's school of thought, is all-embracing and external, conceiving and governing everything, including the sky and the earth. They also believe they can attain longevity and become one with the Tao through special practices of meditation.

The White Cloud Taoist Temple is the chief temple of the Quanzhen Taoist sect and the centre of the Longmen sub-sect. According to historical records, Emperor Xuanzong (712-756) of the Tang Dynasty built a temple called Tianchangguan to enshrine a stone statue of Laozi. The Tianchangguan was burned down in 1202, but was rebuilt from 1203 to 1216 and renamed Taiji Palace. It was later damaged during war.

Emperor Genghis Khan (1206-1227) of the Yuan Dynasty ordered the

431

temple rebuilt and invited Qiu Changchun, founder of the Longmen sub-sect under the Quanzhen sect, to live there in 1224. Qiu died in 1227 and the Emperor renamed the temple Changchun Palace in his memory.

The temple got its present name in the Ming Dynasty (1368-1644) and was damaged twice by war and fire, and rebuilt and repaired several times. Today it is more or less the same as it was after renovation in 1706.

Before 1949, a large fair was held in the temple during the first 20 days of the first lunar month. People came from far away to venerate the enshrined statues, do business and enjoy themselves.

Since 1949, the Chinese Government has had a policy of freedom of religion, and it has protected cultural relics and historical sites. Twice, in 1956 and 1981, the government allocated large sums of money to renovate the temple. During the "cultural revolution" it was preserved intact, thanks to an army unit stationed here.

The temple is fronted by a magnificent archway. Its buildings are laid out around three parallel axes in several courtyards.

On the central axis, from south to north, are the shrine halls of Lingguan (the door guard), the Jade Emperor, Qiu Changchun, Siyu (four major deities) and Laolu (the old way).

Qiu Changchun Hall is on the site where Qiu died in 1227. Inside the hall, Qiu's statue is enshrined. In front of the statue is a valuable relic— a huge bowl made of the knotted root of tree. It was given in offering by Emperor Qianlong (1736-1795). Qiu's remains are buried beneath the bowl, into which the faithful still offer money.

In Laolu Hall are seven statues of Taoist saints, including Qiu Changchun. On the right is a drum dating from the Ming Dynasty with a dragon painted on the leather drumhead.

Along the west axis stand shrine halls of Yuanjun (major female deities), Yuanhen (60-year-old deities), Baxian (the eight immortals), Luzu (or Lu Dongbin), and the Citang (the ancestral worship hall).

Yuanchen Hall dates from 1190 when it was built by Emperor Zhangzong (1190-1208) of the Jin Dynasty to worship the deity of the year in which his mother was born. On the side walls are portraits of each of the deities for the 60-year cycle of the Chinese lunar calendar. Some visitors like to find the deity of the year in which they were born. This hall has been the most frequently visited by worshippers over the centuries.

In the temple are about 30 Taoist priests, who came from Hebei, Henan, Hubei Jiangxi, Zhejiang and other provinces. They are in robes and wear their hair long and tied into a knot that is kept in place with a silver or jade pin. Some also wear a head-band.

The temple was listed by the Chinese Government as a national key relic under special preservation in 2001.

Yonghegong Lamasery and Buddhist Glossary
雍和宫及佛教术语

Yonghegong (The Lama Temple) is a famous lamasery located in the northeastern part of the old city of Beijing. It was a palatial residence built in 1694 by Qing Emperor Kangxi for his fourth son, Prince Yongzheng who later succeeded to the throne. This magnificent temple consists of five main buildings lying on the north-south axis, with annex halls standing on both sides. The temple is listed by the Chinese Government as one of the important historical monuments under special preservation. After the death of his father, Emperor Yongzheng moved to the Forbidden City. The compound was closed to ordinary people and was renamed Yonghegong (the Palace of Harmony). Green roof tiles were replaced by yellow ones to suit a monarch's home. In 1744 his successor Emperor Qianlong converted the palace into a lamasery.

Several renovations have been carried out since 1949. The temple has taken on a new look and was reopened to the public in 1981. It is now not only a functional lama temple, but also a tourist attraction.

Of interest to visitors in the Lama Temple are the 18-metre-high Maitreya statue engraved from a 26-metre-long white sandalwood log, "the Five Hundred Arhats Hill" made of gold, silver, copper, iron and tin, and the niche carved out of *nanmu* (this kind of Phoebe *nanmu* can give off an unusual scent reputed to repel mosquitoes in summer). These three objects are accredited as the three matchless masterpieces 三绝 in the Lama Temple. 五百罗汉山、26 米高的白檀木巨佛和照佛及佛龛称为雍和宫的"三绝"。

Yonghemen (The Gate of Harmony) 雍和门

It is actually a hall rather than a gate. Following the Buddhist tradition, the first hall in a lamasery is usually called the Maitreya's shrine or the Hall of Heavenly Kings. In this hall *Mile* or Maitreya in Sanskrit, the Laughing Buddha always greets people with a smiling face. A Bodhisattva is often worshipped in China as a fat, laughing man. He is known in China as the Big-Belly Buddha. Legend has it that he was born mere than

Lama Temple

Hall of Infinite Happiness
Perpetual Tranquility Pavilion
Eternal Health Pavilion
Tower of the Shining Buddha
Hall of the Dharmacackra (Wheel of the Dharma)
Ordination Terrace
Panchan Hall
West Auxiliary Hall
East Auxiliary Hall
Hall of Eternal Blessing
Mathematics Hall
Hall of Harmony & Peace
Medicine Hall (Bhaisajyagure Hall)
Imperial Hand-Writing Pavilion (Pavilion of Four Languages)
Exoteric Hall
Esoteric Hall
Gate of Harmony & Peace
West Pavilion (housing a stone tablet)
East Pavilion (housing a stone tablet)
Drum Tower
Bell Tower
Gate of Luminant Peace
Arts & Crafts Shop
Imperial Carriage Pathway
Arts & Crafts Shop
Memorial Archway
Entrance Decorated Archway
Decorated Archway
Screen Wall

1,000 years ago and became a monk in Yuelin Temple in Fenghua County, Zhejiang Province. He often went spreading Buddhism with a bag in his hand begging for food, so people usually called him the Bag Buddha. He is also known as the Laughing Buddha because he always smiles. It is said that before his death he was sitting on a piece of stone slab, telling people that he was the reincarnation of the Future Buddha Maitreya. According to what he said people called him Buddha Maitreya after his death.

On each side of Buddha Maitreya, there is a sandalwood pagoda. On the pagoda stand many small Buddhist images, which were symbols of longevity. Hence, the Longevity Pagoda.

On both sides of Maitreya's shrine are seated four fearsome looking Heavenly Kings or Celestial Guardians, two on each side.

The Buddhist theory goes that the earth is divided into four worlds: northern, southern, eastern and western. Each of the four worlds is guarded by one of the Four Heavenly Kings.

The one with a sword is the Southern World Heavenly King named *Zengzhang* 增长. When ghosts and monsters dare to step in, he chants an incantation and throws his magic sword up into the sky. In a flash the sword flies down like lightning, hitting, sometimes even killing the intruder.

Next to him sits *Chiguo* 持国, the Eastern World Heavenly King, who plays a pipa, a 4-stringed Chinese lute. On the battlefield, he plucks the musical instrument and gives his enemy a headache. So he wins the battle.

Opposite to him is *Duowen* 多闻, the Northern World Heavenly King, who carries a huge umbrella. Whenever he puts up his umbrella, the sky over the battlefield turns dark and a cyclonic storm howls, sending sand and rocks whirling about. The eyesight of his rivals is sure to be impaired. Hardly has he shut up the umbrella when the rivals are drawn into it and arrested.

The one with a water snake is the Western World Heavenly King *Guangmu* 广目. Once released, the snake mounts the clouds and rides the mists. All of a sudden, this animal spurts out water and disperses his enemy.

Weituo (Skanda) 韦驮 (塞建陀)

Behind the shrine of Maitreya stands the statue of Weituo facing backwards to a large courtyard. Because he made great contributions towards guarding the graveyard of Sakyamuni, he was appointed protector of Buddhism and ranked first among the 32 guardian generals. He holds in his hand a Monster-surrender Stick, named Vajra (a symbol of might), used for defeating and conquering evil spirits or devils.

At first, Weituo, together with the two generals *Heng* and *Ha*, and the Four Heavenly Kings, were all supernatural generals who protected Buddhist doctrines. All of them took on the responsibility of guarding the Buddhist temples. However, each had his work to do. Weituo, also known as Weituo Tian, or Weituo Buddhisattava, is one of the eight generals under the leadership of the "Southern World Heavenly King" named *Zengzhang*. Each of the Four Heavenly Kings had eight generals totaling 32 generals in all and Weituo ranked first among all the guarding generals. According to Buddhism, Buddha issued decrees that Weituo be responsible to protect those people who became monks and nuns and to shield and sustain Buddhist doctrines.

Weituo was regarded as *Shen Xing Tai Bao* and was good at flying over the ground. Buddhism says that after Tathagata (Buddha) was cremated, suddenly a fast moving ghost stole Buddha's two teeth and escaped with them. After Weituo discovered this he was enraged and ran through the air after it. Although the ghost was moving fast and was very agile, he was no match for the fleet-footed Weituo and finally it was caught. Weituo took back the Buddha's teeth and thereafter, he was assigned the special job of guarding the graveyard of Sakyamuni, founder of Buddhism.

After Buddhism was introduced to China about 2,000 years ago, Weituo with an Indian origin thoroughly changed his appearance and became an ancient Chinese military general. His statue is armed with a golden suit of armor. The statue shows him to be young, majestically-looking with martial bearing.

Bronze Incense Burner 铜薰炉

This incense burner was cast in 1748. It stands 4.2 metres high with six openings to let out flames. Above each opening two dragons playing with a pearl are cast in bas-relief, while on the pedestal a design with three lions contesting for a ball is portrayed. As one of the two bronze tripods of its kind ever found in China, this is really a treasure trove. The other one stands in the Imperial Garden in the Palace Museum.

Imperial Handwriting Pavilion 御碑亭 (四体文碑亭)

In the pavilion there is a stone stele erected in 1792. On the stele are inscriptions in four languages: Manchu on the front side; Mongolian on the eastern side; Tibetan on the western side and on its back Han language written by Emperor Qianlong. It records the origin of Lamaism and the Emperor's attitude towards it. That's why the pavilion is called Imperial Handwriting Pavilion. The inscriptions are in four languages, so it is also known as the Pavilion of Four Languages.

Lamaism was quite popular in the Qing Dynasty. Lama means "teacher" or "superior being." At the very beginning only the monks on the top ranks were called lamas. Later it became an honourable title for all the monks.

Mount Sumeru* (Mount Xumi) 须弥山

Mount Sumeru, a Ming bronze sculpture, is a representation of the Buddhist world outlook. According to Buddhist tradition, Mount Sumeru is supposed to be the centre of the world. On the top of it lies the legendary paradise where Sakyamuni and men of moral integrity live after death. The

436

---

*Sumeru, which iterally means "mountain of marvellous height."

position of the stars near the peak roughly corresponds to the findings of modern astronomy. On the slopes are the dwellings for mankind and the Heavenly Kings. At the bottom, the floral design stands for sea waves. Below the seas evil spirits, devils or criminals abide in Hell.

Four Study Halls 四学殿

On either side of the courtyard are four subsidiary halls devoted to the lamas' studies of specialized subjects: medicine in the Medicine Hall; mathematics in the Mathematics Hall; esoteric in the Esoteric Hall; Buddhist philosophy in the Esoteric Hall. The courses for students are: Tibetan language, the religious discipline of the Yellow Sect, the traditional sutras and religious rituals. Half of their time is spent in classroom studies and the rest in services in the compound. They follow monastic discipline and are expected to become successors to the elder lamas staffing the temple at present.

Yonghegong (The Hall of Harmony) 雍和宫

The second main hall is the Hall of Harmony, formerly a meeting place for Emperor Yongzheng. Buddhism has it that the second main hall is usually called Mahavira Hall, or Daxiongbaodian (the Great Temple of Powerful Treasure) in Chinese, Mahavira is an honorable title for Sakyamuni. On the central altar are placed Buddhas of the Three Ages: Sakyamuni, Buddha of the Present in the middle, who created Buddhism about 2,500 years ago; Buddha of the Past Yeja, on the left; Buddha of the Future Maitreya on the right. In front of Sakyamuni are his two disciples, Ananda on the left, Mahakasyapa on the right. In the hands of some of the Buddhas are ribbons known as *hada*, a most precious gift to the Honourable.

Placed on the altar in front of the Buddhas of the Three Ages are the seven treasures: gold, silver, jade, pearl, sea shell, diamond, jadeite; and the eight magic weapons: the wheel of the law, the conch shell, the state umbrella, the canopy, the lotus flower, the covered vase, the pair of fish and the endless knot.

The top lamas are divided into three ranks; Buddha, Bodhisattva and Arhat.

On both sides of the hall stand eighteen Arhats. It is said that they were disciples of Sakyamuni and instructed by Sakyamuni to stay on earth to diffuse Buddhism if they wished to attain Buddhahood.

Here is a painting of Thousand-hand-and-eye Bodhisattva. It is said that he could see all the human bitterness and difficulties and help people to overcome them. That's why he has a thousand hands and eyes.

437

Yongyoudian (Hall of Eternal Blessing) 永佑殿

The third main hall in the temple is Yongyoudian (Hall of Eternal Blessing.) It used to be the bedroom for Emperor Yongzheng when he was still a prince, and the place where his coffin was kept before it was moved to the Western Qing Tombs.

The present name of the building was given by Emperor Qianlong, his son, to show his eternal blessing. Emperor Qianlong came here frequently to offer sacrifices to his deceased father. Lamas came here to do Buddhist service.

In this building are three big Buddhas carved out of wood. On the left is the Buddha of Pharmacy who is the patron of medicine and cures diseases of all kinds.

On the right is the Lion-Roaring Buddha who preaches Buddhism and threatens devils and evil spirits with a loud voice that sounds like a lion roaring. In the middle is Buddha Amitayus or the Longevity Buddha, the founder of the legendary paradise. Buddhists believe that if they follow the method used by Amitayus to practice Buddhism they could enjoy long life and peace, and could be permitted to go to the legendary paradise after death. That's why they always say "Amitayus."

White Para and Green Para 白度母和绿度母

There are two paintings on the walls, one on each side. The one in white color is a painting of White Para; the other is Green Para, which is not a painting, but a piece of embroidery made by Emperor Qianlong's mother. According to the Buddhist theory, there are 21 Paras altogether. Paras are supposed to be the incarnations of Guanyin Bodhisattva who helps Sakyamuni save the suffering people on earth.

438

Falundian (Hall of the Wheel of the Law*) 法轮殿

The fourth main hall in the temple is Falundian, the Hall of the Wheel of the Law, where the lamas assemble to say morning prayers, do services and carry out other religious activities. On display are some musical instruments.

1. Tsong Kha-pa (1357-1419) 宗喀巴

In the centre of the hall is a huge gilded bronze statue of Tsong Kha-pa, founder of the Yellow Sect. He was born in Qinghai Province over 600

* The Wheel of the Law　an emblem of the power of the Buddhist doctrine, which crushes all delusions and superstitions just as a wheel crushes anything it passes over

years ago and became a lama in Tibet when he was only 14 years old. Lamaism was divided into five sects: Red, Flowery, Black, White and Yellow. When Tsong Kha-pa was young, the Red Sect was popular, and the lama's hat was red outside and yellow inside. The Red Sect of Lamaism stipulated that the head lamas were allowed to get married and their posts hereditary. Seeing the defects of such a practice, he reformed it by turning the hat inside out, that is yellow outside and red inside, which was the symbol of the Yellow Sect. He put onward 253 commandments, including the prohibition of marriage and the hereditary system. Due to these strict commandments and prohibitions, not only did he win popular support from the lamas, but from the Ming rulers as well. He soon gained both the power of administration and religion in Tibet. With a shorter history, the Yellow Sect developed and became popular rapidly. Each sect has a head lama known as the Living Buddha to control its own sect. For the Yellow Sect, the two Living Buddhas are Dalai and Bainqen Erdeni.

The statue of Great master Tsong Kpa-pa is a six-metre-high bronze Buddha sitting on a lotus stand. With a sword in his right hand and scriptures in his left-hand, the statue symbolizes wisdom and power. It cost 200,000 silver dollars to cast the statue in 1924. More than six decades later, a patina replaced its once bright shine.

In 1982, the statue was gilded. But very few people realize the goldleaf came from the trashcan—rubbish tossed out from the room of an old lama who died in the spring of that year. He Nima, a sharp-eyed lama aged 70, spotted a small pillow of the deceased in the trash early one morning, and although it was dirty and seemed of no value, he took it back to his room to save it. Several days later, the lama's niece was visiting him and spied the dirty pillow on his bed. "Why do you keep this pillow?" she said. "I could buy you a new one." The lama said that wasn't necessary. He had money. "I just felt it's a pity to throw it away. It's still useful." The niece said in that case she'd take it home and clean it for him. When she emptied the pillow, a golden necklace and two pairs of golden bracelets tumbled out. Dumbfounded, she returned to tell her uncle what she had found. He offered them to the temple to restore the statue of Tsong Kpa-pa. The temple's committee of religious affairs exchanged the jewelry for goldleaf. That August, lamas and monks from across the country attended a ceremony at the temple where the statue was unveiled, adorned in its bright new skin of gold.

2. Dalai Lama and Panchen Erdeni 达赖喇嘛和班禅额尔德尼

When Tsong Kha-pa was alive, he had two famous disciples named Dalai

439

and Panchen, who were later deemed the reincarnations of Tsong Kha-pa and succeeded to the throne of the Living Buddhas after Tsong Kha-pa's death with the titles of the First Dalai Lama and the First Panchen Erdeni. After that, the succeeding Living Buddhas inherited the titles. Up till now already the Fourteenth Dalai Lama and the Eleventh Panchen Erdeni exist. On either side of the statue of Tsong Kha-pa is a throne, the one on the left is for Dalai Lama when he came to preach; the one on the right for Panchen Erdeni. In 1954 Panchen Erdeni held Buddhist ceremonies here. "Dalai" means vast sea in Mongolian, and "Lama" means teacher in Tibetan.

3. The Reincarnation System 转世制度

The Fifth Dalai Lama 达赖五世 (1617-1682) declared that in the future when a Dalai Lama died his spirit would pass out of the corpse into an infant boy who had been born right at the moment of the Dalai Lama's death. The problem was to find the right child. In some cases the dying Dalai Lama would predict where his incarnation could be found. Quite often there were many babies born at the same moment and the investigation had to last for years. The child's body must confirm to the ideal shape, notably a large head and generous ears, which were considered indicative of wisdom. Objects belonging to the Dalai Lama were identified, which would help establish whether the child was the living incarnation of the Dalai Lama.

When the child was two to six years old, he was taken away from home by his Regents for training. The parents of the chosen child, usually of humble origin, were also brought to Lhasa and given noble status. The Regents exercised full power until the Buddha incarnate reached the age of eighteen.

As the old reincarnation system had many disadvantages, Emperor Qianlong introduced in 1792 a new method of "drawing lots from the gold urn." The new system stipulated that many children were to be selected from various places after the death of a Living Buddha, and each child had a lot with his name inscribed on it. All the lots were to be put into a gold urn; lamas were to recite Buddhist scriptures. Buddhists believed that recitation of Buddhist scriptures was a process to reincarnate the dead. While people were watching, the high commissioners sent by the emperor would pick up the lot dropped out of the shaking urn and show it to the people. So the child with his name on it would be considered the reincarnation of the Living Buddha.

4. Frescoes 壁画

The frescoes on the side walls tell us about the life of Sakyamuni, showing how he was born from the armpit of his mother, and how he finally created and preached Buddhism. They were retouched in 1953 according to the o-riginal design.

5. Scripture-Turning Wheel 经典转轮

The wheel is called the Scripture-Turning Wheel. It is said that each wheel, big or small, is stuffed with Buddhist scripture. If you turn it one revolution, it means you have already read all the Buddhist scripture once.

6. Buddhist Scriptures 佛经

Along the walls on both sides of the hall stand bookcases holding 108 vol-umes of the Buddhist Sutras in Tibetan language translated from ancient Indian language. It is titled The Great Tibetan Buddhist Sutra, with 207 volumes of the sequel of the Sutras. Now very few such Buddhist scriptures are preserved in perfect condition.

7. Mountain of Five Hundred Arhats 五百罗汉山

The mountain is carved out of black wood and the arhats modelled out of gold, silver, bronze, iron and tin. Five hundred arhats are worshipped in some Buddhist temples. When Sakyamuni preached, there was no written scripture. Later his 500 disciples wrote down the Great Tibetan Buddhist Sutra according to what he preached. For their contributions, they were upgraded from lamas to arhats. Here a vivid picture shows they were on the road to Buddhahood.

8. Fish-and-Dragon Evolving Basin 鱼龙变化盆（三洗盆）

This Fish-and-Dragon Evolving Basin is carved out of ebony wood. Bud-dhism has it that human beings evolved from fish, and those who have both ability and political integrity could continuously evolve to dragons. Emper-or Qianlong had a bath in the basin when he was three days old. His mother hoped that her son would evolve to a dragon. So the basin is also called Three-day-old Emperor Washing Basin.

Wanfuge (Ten-Thousand-Happiness Pavilion) 万福阁

This pavilion is also named the Tower of the Great Buddha. In the centre of the building is a huge statue of Maitreya, Buddha of the Future, carved out of a single trunk of white sandalwood with a total cost of 80,000 taels of silver (2,500 kilos of silver) an entry in the Guinness Book of World Records in 1990. It is 26 metres high, 18 metres above the ground and 8 metres under the ground, and 8 metres in diameter. More than 1,000 me-tres of satin was used to make a yellow robe for the huge Buddha.

The temple was converted into a lamasery in 1744, but this part was not completed until 1750. Emperor Qianlong felt that the area at the rear of the lamasery was too bare and planned to build a high tower as a protective

441

screen, but it was very difficult to find a sandalwood tree of such size. The Tibetan envoy heard this in Beijing and told the Seventh Dalai Lama about it. Shortly afterwards, a white sandalwood tree was brought to Nepal from India by the king of Nepal. The Seventh Dalai Lama bartered this huge sandalwood tree with a huge precious gems from Nepal, and sent it here as a gift to the emperor to express his thanks because Emperor Qianlong had sent troops to Tibet to put down a rebellion and turned back the power to the Seventh Dalai Lama. It took three years to ship this huge tree from the banks of the Yangtze River, through the Grand Canal and up to Beijing and another three years for carving and erection. The hall was built later. In 1750 it was entirely completed. Behind the Great Buddha, there are ten thousand small Buddhas on three stories. Hence the name, Ten-Thousand-Happiness Pavilion.

First refurbished in 1953, the temple was again restored in 1978, and opened to public in 1981. The latest effort, which started in 1992, focused on the renewal of the Giant Buddha Maitreya and was completed in October 1993. The two-year facelift cost more than 500,000 yuan (US $87,719) State funds most of which was spent on coating the statue with 2.5 kilos of gold foil. According to the Guinness Book of World Records, the Maitreya is the tallest and biggest in the world today.

Zhaofolou (Tower of the Shining Buddha) 照佛楼

The building was built in 1694. Qianlong's mother used to pray here.

Buddhist Glossary 佛教术语

1. Sakyamuni 释迦牟尼

Founder of Buddhism, also known as Gautama, Sakyamuni. Born in 565 BC, he was a son of the Gautama family in the Sakya clan, India. His father was King of Suddhodhana of Kapilavastu and his mother's name was Maya. He grew up amidst palatial luxuries, and his father prevented him from being exposed to the miseries of life. Deeply disturbed by the reality of old age, sickness and death, Sakyamuni tried to seek the answer to the misery of existence and a way of release from the intolerable cycle of endless rebirths to which all living things are subject. One day at Bodhagaya he was seated under a pipal tree (an Indian fig tree or bodhi tree) and it is believed that he was enlightened. He then propagated Buddhist doctrines for 45 years in central India and was highly esteemed to be the Buddha (the Awakened). He died at the age of 80 under a pipal tree.

2. Maitreya 弥勒佛

Maitreya was one of the Bodhisattvas or potential Buddha of Mahayana Buddhism, which was much favored in China. He had achieved perfect enlightenment and could gain Nirvana directly, but he renounced it because he wanted to bring salvation first to all suffering mankind. Unlike the Buddha who is always a simple figure without adornment, the Bodhisattvas are crowned and loaded with jewels. The best-known ones are Avalokitesvara, Manjusri, Samantabhadra and Ksitigarbha. By the Sui and Tang dynasties, Buddhism in China had become simplified and turned into a Chinese style. For instance, some Bodhisattvas were converted into those of Chinese origin. Maitreya, regarded as a deity, is one of them.

3. Ananda 安纳, 韦驮

Ananda is Sakyamuni's cousin and one of his chief disciples. As the master of hearing and memory, he kept following Sakyamuni closely for 25 years. He is said to have compiled the sutras and reckoned to be the second patriarch. Dressed as a monk, he often appears together with Mahakasyapa in support of Sakyamuni.

4. Kasyapa-matanga 迦叶

In Chinese Buddhism, Kasyapa-matanga is accepted as the chief disciple of Sakyamuni and the first patriarch after his death. He is shown as an elderly monk and often appears with Ananda in support of the Buddha, sometimes with two other Bodhisattvas as well.

5. Avalokitesvara 观音—**the Hermaphroditic Guanyin**

Avalokitesvara or Guanyin is the left attendant of Amitabha Buddha. He appears as one of the Three Western Sages headed by Amitabha Buddha. Guanyin is described as a Bodhisattva of Great Mercy, who helps the needy and relieves the distressed, cures the disabled and saves a sinking vessel whenever they call his title Bodhisattva Guanyin.

Avalokitesvara, usually standing or sitting on a lotus flower with a treasure vase full of dew held in her right hand, was introduced into China with Mahayana Buddhism and was first known as "Guanshiyin." In the Tang Dynasty the Chinese character "shi" was left out because it happened to be part of the name of the reigning emperor. Thus Guanyin became the usual name.

Buddhism has it that Guanyin has 33 different images with 32 incarnations. Many of the images are female ones. As early as the Northern and Southern dynasties, the female image of Guanyin appeared, and became quite popular in the Tang Dynasty.

Guanyin has many names: the White-Robed Guanyin, Dragon-Head Guanyin, Fish-Basket Guanyin, Water and Moon Guanyin, Medicine-Bestowing Guanyin, etc. Sometimes Guanyin stands on a lotus flower.

Bodhisattva Guanyin gained enlightenment on Mount Putuo, one of China's four famous Buddhist mountains located on Zhoushan Islands, Zhejiang Province, East China.

Guanyin in female image is often depicted holding a tiny chinaware flask in her hand. In the Hall of Guanyin, these goddess images sometimes sit amidst burning red candles. On her three birthdays, lots of aged pilgrims came in and kowtowed before them with offerings of incense. Her birthdays fall on the 19th day of the 2nd, the 6th and 9th lunar months, said to be the time for the Bodhisattva to achieve Nirvana or ascend to the Buddhist Western Happy Region.

6. Bhaisajya-guru 药师佛

Bhaisajya-guru or The Buddha of Pharmacy, founder of the so-called "Eastern Pure Glazed World," is said to be able to protect people from disaster and lengthen their lives. Sick people sometimes go to the Buddha, burn incense and candles and kowtow and wish that they would be given help their diseases cured and that they would enjoy good health.

7. The Three Eastern Sages 东方三圣

Buddha of Pharmacy; Sun-illuminating Bodhisattva (left attendant); Moon-illuminating Bodhisattva (right attendant).

8. The Three Western Sages 西方三圣

Bodhisattva of Great Mercy (left attendant); Mahasthamaprapta (right attendant); Amitabha, the Buddha of Boundless Splendour, founder of the Western Paradise.

9. Manjusri 文殊

Manjusri or The Bodhisattva of Wisdom, or Wenshu in Chinese, is the left attendant of Sakyamuni. His birthplace is said to be on Mount Wutai, North China. As the left attendant of Sakyamuni, he is in charge of wisdom, usually shown riding a lion.

10. Samantabhadra 普贤

444

Standing side by side with Wenshu, Puxian or the Bodhisattva of Universal Benevolence is the right attendant of Sakyamuni. Mount Emei in Sichuan Province, Southwest China, has been known as the place where he gained enlightenment. He is often shown riding an elephant.

11. Mahayana 大乘佛教

Buddhism has two principal groups, Mahayana (Great Vehicle) and Hinayana (Small Vehicle). Mahayana, the Buddhist school formed in the first century AD, asserts the existence of a series of Buddhas and Bodhisattvas and that salvation may be gained by invocations to them.

Mahayanists hold that Buddhism should show mercy on all creatures and ferry them across the so-called life-and-death bridge to get to the other bank, where they are able to be conscious of the truth of Buddhism and become Bodhisattvas. Mahayana was popular in China and Korea.

12. Hinayana 小乘佛教

All the Buddhist groups that existed before Mahayana are known as Hinayana. Its doctrine is much nearer to the original teaching of the Buddha than Mahayana. Hinayana regards Sakyamuni, founder of Buddhism, as the only Buddha. What it seeks is to free oneself. Mahayanists hold that Hinayanists seek personal arhatship, and the destruction of body and mind and extinction in Nirvana. Hinayana spreads in Asian and southeast Asian countries such as Sri Lanka, Thailand, Cambodia and Myanmar.

13. Arhat 罗汉

The highest attainment for Hinayana, arhat has three characteristics.

1) Nothing can bring vexation on them.
2) They are supported by celestial devotees.
3) They will never suffer from transmigration of the soul while in the state of Nirvana.

Ranking next to Buddha, Bodhisattvas are said to command even more supernatural power in addition to the three characteristics the arhats enjoy. That's why common people would rather have faith in Mahayana so as to become Bodhisattvas.

Sometimes 16 arhats instead of 18 are found in Buddhist temples. Why?

In a famous Buddhist classic written by Nandimitra of Sri Lanka, 16 arhats were recorded in detail. The classic was translated into Chinese by noted Tang Dynasty monk Xuanzang (AD 602-AD 664). The 17th Arhat is Nandimitra. The 18th Arhat repeats the arhat of No. One.

The eighteen Arhats are as follows:

(1) Pindolabhadradvaja　　　宾度罗跋啰迦惰阇
(2) Kanakavtsa　　　迦诺迦伐蹉
(3) Kanakabharadvaja　　　迦诺迦跋厘惰阇
(4) Supinda　　　苏频陀
(5) Nakula　　　诺讵罗
(6) Bhadra　　　跋陀罗
(7) Korika　　　迦哩迦
(8) Vajraputra　　　伐阇罗弗多罗
(9) Supaka　　　戌博迦
(10) Panthaka　　　半托迦
(11) Rahula　　　罗睺罗
(12) Nagasena　　　那伽犀那
(13) Ingata　　　因揭陀
(14) Vanavasin　　　伐那娑斯
(15) Ajita　　　阿氏多

(16) Cudapanthaka or Suddhipanthaka　注茶半托迦
(17) Nandimitra　庆友尊者
(18) Pindolabhadradvaja　宾度罗跋啰迦惰阇

14. Wooden Fish(*Muyu**) 木鱼

Wooden fish or *muyu* are often found in Buddhist temples. There are two kinds of wooden fish. One is shaped like a fish and hangs in front of the Abstinence Hall in the temple. It is a clapper beaten to announce mealtime in the morning and at noon. Another is round, made of a hollow wooden block, used by monks to beat rhythm when chanting sutras. It is said that when the sutras were brought to China from India, they were dropped into the sea and eaten by a fish. The monks beat the fish, forcing it to throw out the sutras from its mouth.

So in Buddhist temples in China, monks are sometimes seen beating a wooden fish when they chant sutras.

15. Ksitigarbha 地藏

Ksitigarbha or *Dizang* is one of the Mahayana Bodhisattvas of Buddhism. Buddhism has it that after the death of Sakyamuni and before the emergence of Maitreya, *Dizang* was the Bodhisattva that saved all the living creatures in Heaven and in Hell.

Like the earth, he was believed to have possessed an unlimited amount of the best strains of seeds.

16. The Seven Treasures 七珍 are seven kinds of offerings put in front of Buddhist figures. They are as follows: 主要供在喇嘛寺里,七珍如下:

(1) The Precious Wheel 轮宝: It means that people can be reincarnated in all ages. 表示佛教如全轮常转。

(2) The Precious Mani 摩尼宝: It represents abundant treasures. Its meaning is wisdom and brightness which symbolizes in Buddhist law, and doctrine reached perfection. 表示佛教圆明光莹

(3) Deified Girl 女宝: It symbolizes wonderfulness, quietness, and mercy. 表示佛教妙静和平

(4) Royal Minister 臣宝: The royal minister stands for the Patron Saint 守护神 . The meaning is loyal. 表示持守戒律。

(5) The Elephant 象宝: It symbolizes the grand power. 表示佛教力大无比。

(6) The Horse 马宝: It is a symbol of going far away. It means that the strength of Buddhist influence can be spread far and wide. 表示佛教

---

* *Muyu*　a percussion instrument made of a hollow wooden block, originally used by Buddhist priests to beat rhythm when chanting scriptures

佛播广远。

(7) Royal General 将军宝: The royal general symbolizes recapture. It means that Buddhism can defeat all evil forces in the world. 表示佛教能克服各种困难,战胜各种强敌。

17. The Eight Treasures are implements used by Buddha, also called the eight auspicious emblems symbolizing good luck. 八宝是佛教中常用的器物,常以其象征吉祥,故又称八吉祥。它们是:

(1) The Conch of Law (Conch) 法螺: It stands for the Buddhist sound of luck, and happiness. 表示佛音远播。

(2) The Wheel of Law (Wheel) 法轮: It symbolizes the law of Karma and rebirth that Buddhism can be reincarnated endlessly. 表示法轮常转。

(3) The Umbrella 宝伞: It is symbolic of Buddhism that is just an umbrella, which can protect the people. 表示庇护万法。

(4) Canopy (The White Canopy/Lid) 白盖: It stands for the endless power of Buddhism and it can cover the universe. 表示佛法和力量。

(5) Lotus Flower 莲花: It symbolizes the purity of the Buddha that cannot be tainted with the dust of common customs, and it also represents awakening or enlightenment. In its closed position it is a potential only. Fully opened means fully awakened. 表示佛教清静不染尘俗。

(6) The Precious Vase (Water Bottle or Jar) 宝瓶: It represents the Buddhist perfection, and boundless benevolence. 表示功德圆满。

(7) Goldfish (The Double Fish) 金鱼 / 双鱼: It is a symbol of Buddhist freedom, and extrication. 表示自由和解脱。

(8) Knotted Cord (The Intestine) 盘长: It symbolizes the circle round the Buddhist doctrine, which links up the beginning, and the end. 表示佛教教义贯穿始终。

Religion in China 中国的宗教

Freedom of religious belief in China is guaranteed by law. Normal activities of different religions can be carried out in China according to their rights prescribed by the Constitution and law. Buddhism and Taoism are comparatively widespread in China, but there is no correct estimate of the number of their devotees.

There are more than 100 million religious followers in China, more than 85,000 places of worship, and 3,000 religious communities with 30,000 clergy to serve the spiritual needs of their followers.

Of the top five religions, Buddhism, the most influential, has a history of more than 2,000 years in China. There are now over 9,500 Buddhist temples and monasteries with 200,000 monks and nuns registered at temples throughout China. Taoism, native to the country, has a history of more than 1, 700 years. There are over 6, 000 Taoist priests and nuns who live in the temples, with more than 600 temples and monasteries open to the public. Islam was introduced to China in the seventh century. There are about 20 million Muslims and more than 35, 000 mosques. Catholicism and Protestantism boomed in China with the Opium War in the 1840s. There are about 4 million Catholics, including 2, 700 clergymen, and 4, 000 Catholic churches, over 10 million Christians or Protestants, including 18, 000 missionaries, 8, 000 churches and 20, 000 simply equipped meeting places in China. China now has 2, 000 religious social organizations and 48 religious schools and colleges. All religious organizations operate their own affairs independently, run seminaries to suit their own needs, publish their classical works and other publications and have service organs to serve public interest. Religious scriptures, books and magazines are published by various religions. China's Constitution stipulates that the state protects normal religious activities. No one may make use of religion to engage in activities that disrupt public order, impair the health of citizens or interfere with the educational system of the state. In order to ensure that Chinese citizens really enjoy the freedom of religious belief, religious bodies and religious affairs are not subject to any foreign domination.

President Jiang Zemin said at a three-day national work conference on the subject, which ended on December 12, 2001. China will effectively implement the policy of "freedom for religious belief" and conduct religious work according to law. Religious work enjoys an important status in the country's affairs. Under the new situation, the Party's leadership over religion should be strengthened. The work on religion is closely linked with the commitment between different ethnic groups, social stability, national security and reunification, as well as China's relations with foreign countries. The influence of religion on political and social lives in today's world should never be underestimated. Communist Party members do not believe in any religion but treat religion with a scientific point of view. Freedom for religious belief is a basic right enjoyed by all citizens according to the Constitution, and to respect and protect such a right embodies the Party's commitment to protect human rights. On the one hand, each person enjoys the freedom of believing or not believing in religion. While on the other hand, religious work should be conducted within the scope of constitution and laws. Religious works should not obstruct social work, working order and living order. Any religion is not allowed to interfere in the country's administrative, judicial and educational works. Religion should never be allowed to be used for opposing the Party leadership and socialist system, destroying national reunification and ethnic unity, as well as harming national interests. Religious people should love their country, support the socialist system and Party leadership, and obey the country's laws. China adopts the principle of separating politics from religions, stressing no religion has the right to override the Constitution and laws. The principle of independence must be followed and foreign interference in China's religious work should be absolutely prohibited.

The Rules on the Religious Activities of Foreigners in China

中华人民共和国境内外国人宗教活动管理规定实施细则

The Rules for the Implementation of the Provisions on the Administration of Religious Activities of Aliens Within the Territory of the People's Republic of China.

Article 1　These Rules are formulated in accordance with the Provisions on the Administration of Religious Activities of Aliens Within the Territory of the People's Republic of China.

Article 2　Aliens within the territory of the People's Republic of China are referred to as those who are within Chinese territory without Chinese nationalities pursuant to the Nationality Law of the People's Republic of China, including long-term residing China personnel and short-term visiting China personnel.

Article 3　Religious activities of aliens within Chinese territory are referred to as the religious ceremonies that aliens conduct or participate in according to their own religious belief customs, the contacts with Chinese religious bodies, sites for religious activities and religious personnel in respect of religion, and other relevant activities.

Article 4　The People's Republic of China respects the freedom of religious belief of aliens within Chinese territory, and protects and administrates the religious activities of aliens within Chinese territory in accordance with law. The People's Republic of China protects friendly contacts and cultural and academic exchanges of aliens within Chinese territory with Chinese religious circles in respect of religion in accordance with law.

Article 5　Aliens may participate in religious activities at Buddhist monasteries, Taoist temples, mosques, churches lawfully registered within Chinese territory according to their own religious belief.

Article 6　At the invitation of Chinese religious bodies at or above the level of province, autonomous region or municipality directly under the central government, aliens visiting China as religious personnel may preach and expound the scripture at lawfully registered sites for religious activities. At the invitation of Chinese religious bodies at or above the level of province, autonomous region or municipality directly under the central government, and after approved by the department of religious affairs of the people's governments at or above the provincial level, aliens entering China as other status may preach and expound the scripture at lawfully registered sites for religious activities. Foreign religious personnel who are invited to preach and expound the scripture at the lawfully registered sites for religious activities shall abide by the administrative rules of these sites and respect the belief customs of the personnel of these sites.

Article 7　The collective religious activities of aliens within Chinese territory shall be conducted at the Buddhist monasteries, Taoist temples, mosques, churches recognized by the departments of religious affairs of the people's government at or above the county level, or at the temporary sites appointed by the departments of religious affairs of the people's governments of province, autonomous region or municipality directly under the central government. Where aliens within Chinese territory collectively conduct religious activities at temporary sites, they shall be administrated by the departments of religious affairs of the people's governments at or above the county level.

Article 8   The friendly contacts and cultural and academic exchanges of aliens with Chinese religious circles shall be conducted via Chinese religious bodies at or above the level of province, autonomous region or municipality directly under the central government.

Article 9   Foreign religious organizations that have no corresponding legitimate Chinese religious organizations within Chines territory and their members must get consent from the departments of religious affairs of the people's governments at provincial level and approval from the State Administration for Religious Affairs before conducting contacts in the name of these organizations or as religious personnel with relevant departments of Chinese government or Chinese religious circles.

Article 10   Following consent by Chinese religious bodies, aliens within Chinese territory may invite Chinese religious personnel to conduct such religious ceremonies as baptism, weddings, funerals, Taoist or Buddhist rites according to each religious customs. Among these ceremonies, the aliens conducting weddings must be males and females who have already set up a marriage relationship in accordance with law. The Chinese religious personnel are referred to those who have been recognized and recorded by lawfully registered religious bodies.

Article 11   Following consent by national religious bodies or relevant religious bodies at the level of province, autonomous region or municipality directly under the central government, and approved by the departments of religious affairs of the local people's governments at or above the provincial level, aliens entering Chinese territory may carry religious articles used in religious cultural and academic exchanges in accordance with academic exchanges. Where the religious articles conform to the stipulations of the previous paragraph and the relevant provisions of the Chinese customs. They shall be passed by the customs based on the certificates issued by the departments of religious affairs of the people's governments of province, autonomous region and municipality directly under the central government or the State Administration for Religious Affairs.

Article 12   It is prohibited to bring the following religious printed matters, religious audio-visual products and other articles into Chinese territory.

* If the amount exceeds that for personal rational use, and they do not belong to the category stipulated in Article 11;
* If the contents of these articles are detrimental to Chinese national security and public interests of Chinese society. Where the religious printed matter, religious audio-visual products and other religious articles are found to be those mentioned in previous paragraph, the case shall be dealt with by the customs in accordance with law. Where the religious printed matters, religious audio-visual products and other religious articles, which violate the stipulations of the first paragraph have been brought into Chinese territory or transported into Chinese territory by other means, once being found, they shall be dealt with the departments of religious affairs or other related departments of the people's governments at or above the county level in accordance with law.

Article 13   The enrollment to study abroad or capital provided to China by foreign organizations or individuals for the purpose of training religious personnel shall be accepted by Chinese national religious bodies on the basis of need, and the study abroad personnel shall be selected and dispatched by Chinese national religious bodies as a whole plan. Foreign organizations or individuals may not recruit students within Chinese territory for their study and training abroad as religious personnel without permission.

Article 14   Aliens who intend to come to China to studying at Chinese religious institutions must conform to the stipulations set by the Provisions on the Administration of Accepting Foreign Students by Chinese Institutions of Higher Learning, get approval from Chinese national religious bodies, and keep records at the State Administration for Religious Affairs.

Article 15   Aliens who intend to come to China to teach at Chinese religious institutions must be subject to the Methods of Engaging Foreign Professionals by Religious Institutions.

Article 16   Aliens who conduct religious activities within Chinese territory shall abide by Chinese laws and regulations. Aliens may not intervene in the establishment and change of Chinese religious bodies or sites for religious activities, the selecting, appointing and changing of religious personnel by Chinese religious bodies, nor may they intervene in or manipulate other internal affairs of Chinese religious bodies. Within Chinese territory, aliens may not establish religious organizations, institute religious offices, set up sites for religious activities, run religious institutions or hold religious classes in any names or forms.

Article 17   Aliens may not engage in the following missionary activities within Chinese territory:

- Appointing religious personnel among Chinese citizens;
- Developing religious followers among Chinese citizens;
- Preaching and expounding the scripture at the sites for religious activities without permission;
- Preaching and expounding the scripture or conducting religious gathering activities at the places outside the lawfully registered sites for religious activities;
- Conducting religious activities with Chinese citizens at temporary sites for religious activities, except that of Chinese citizens who are Chinese religious personnel who are invited to preside over religious activities;
- Producing or selling religious books and journeys, religious audio-visual products, religious electronic goods, or other religious articles;
- Distributing religious propaganda materials;
- Other missionary activities.

Article 18   Where the international religious organizations, offices and their members intend to contact or conduct other related activities with Chinese religious bodies, sites for religious affairs and religious personnel, they shall make applications to the departments of religious affairs of the people's governments at or above the provincial level in advance. The contact or other related activities may be conducted only after approval by the departments of religious affairs of the people's governments at or above the provincial level.

Article 19   Where aliens within Chinese territory conduct religious activities that violate these Rules, the departments of religious affairs and other related departments of the people's governments at or above the county level shall stop them in accordance with law. Where religious activities conducted by aliens within Chinese territory violate these Rules as well as the Law of the Control on the Entry and Exit of Aliens of the People's

Republic of China and the Regulations on Administrative Penalties for Public Security, the aliens shall be dealt with by the public organs in accordance with law; where a crime is constituted, the aliens shall be investigated for their criminal liability by the judicial organs in accordance with law.

Article 20   These Rules are applicable to religious activities conducted by foreign organizations within Chinese territory.

Article 21   The State Administration for Religious Affairs shall be responsible for the interpretation of these Rules.

Article 22   These Rules shall enter into force as of the date of promulgation.

(SOURCE: China Daily)

Dongsi Mosque
东 四 清 真 寺

Located at 13 South Dongsi Street, the Dongsi Mosque was first constructed in the Ming Dynasty (1368-1644). It has been restored and renovated many times. In 1952 and in 1974, funds were provided by the government to restore the mosque as a centre for both Chinese and foreign Muslims in Beijing. It is now the headquarters of the Beijing branch of the Chinese Islamic Association.

The Mosque is formed around three Chinese-style courtyards, with ablution rooms, a library and a prayer hall at the rear. The Prayer Hall is the only survival from the Ming Dynasty and has now been restored to its original splendor after many years of neglect. In front is a paved courtyard planted with gingko trees and flowering shrubs. At one end of the hall verandah is a bell which used to top the minaret (no longer in existence); at the other end of the verandah is a stele with an inscription from the Wanli period (1573-1620) of the Ming Dynasty. The vestibule of the hall is wooden structure in Chinese style. At the rear of the hall are three brick chambers with vaulted ceilings without supporting pillars in Arabic styles; the floor is painted red and carpeted. The mithrab, which should be in the central chamber, is missing. The inner hall is large and grand; the pillars are gilded with a lotus and arabesque design and the beams are painted. In the centre of the hall hangs a horizontal board with saying from the Qur'an inscribed in Arabic. The polished wooden floor is covered with rows of prayers mats, which can accommodate 500 people on important occasions such as Id al-Fitr (the breaking of Ramadan) and Id al-Adzha (also known as Qurban or Corban). Marriage and funeral services are also held here, and Chinese and foreign Muslims in Beijing may come for daily or weekly services. There is a separate area in the main hall for women.

The library houses valuable manuscripts of the Qur'an, the Hadith, a collection of short narratives expounding the sunna (tradition) of the prophet, and Islamic law, transcribed by imams in different periods in Chinese history, works of Islamic philosophy, history and literature, and Islamic classics and other works published in Egypt, India, Turkey and Pakistan. Most of the manuscripts are approximately two or three hundred years old; one particularly valuable manuscript of the Qur'an is about 700 years old.

Niujie (Ox Street) Mosque
牛 街 清 真 寺

The *Niujie* (Ox Street) Mosque in Beijing's Xuanwu District, the spiritual centre for the 10,000 Muslims living in the vicinity, is the biggest and oldest in Beijing.

The mosque is a mixture of Islamic and Chinese cultures. The outside shows the Chinese influence while the inside decoration is rich in Islamic flavor.

Founded in 996 during the Song Dynasty (960-1279), the mosque was rebuilt in 1442 in the Ming Dynasty and expanded in 1696 under the Qing Dynasty. It consists of an observation tower, prayer hall, and minaret with a pavilion on each side.

The observation tower is just behind the entrance. It was built and originally used for astronomical observations needed for drawing up the Islamic calendar.

The hexagonal wooden structure is also Chinese outside but Islamic inside, with Arabic designs on the ceiling and the beams.

The prayer hall, with its courtyard to the east, consists of five major areas. The three central areas, running lengthwise, are divided into five bays, some narrow with coffered ceilings, and some wide with high-beam ceilings. The two side wings have plain ceilings with beams laid lengthwise. At the entrance of the hall, the ceiling bears the Arabic names of noted imams around the world. Farther in, Chinese flower and cloud paintings mingle with Arabic inscriptions and patterns on the coffered ceilings, and the chandeliers are slightly reminiscent of Venetian glass. There is an arch between each pair of pillars, gleaming with gold patterns.

The minaret (calling tower), a two-storey obelisk in the centre of the

453

courtyard, was originally built as a script depository. Later imams used it as a calling tower. When prayer time came, they ascended the tower and recited the Koran, and Muslims living in the vicinity came to listen. On the ground floor is a large copper cauldron, which was used to prepare communal meals.

To the southeast of the tower lie the tombs of two Muslims who came from the Middle East and preached in the Mosque. The tomb for Ahmad Burdani was built in 1320, and the one for Ali in 1283. Both came from ancient Persia. The tombstones bear Arabic inscriptions and have been set into a nearby wall.

In the imam's library, there are Koran manuscripts and old wooden printing blocks. The mosque used to be a printing house as well.

At the south of the courtyard are the men's and women's prayer preparation bathrooms.

There are long-beaked kettles for the devout to use to wash their nostrils, ears, and mouths. It is considered sacrilegious to enter the mosque without cleaning oneself.

Muslims must wash their whole bodies on Friday, the major prayer day. They only need to wash their heads, hands and feet on other days.

Muslims are supposed to pray five times a day at dawn, at mid-day, in the afternoon, at dusk, and in the evening. Adults who have no time to pray during their working hours come in the early morning before work and in the evening after work.

Non-Muslim visitors are also welcome, but they have to make arrangements in advance. They may have a look around and hear explanations from the imams or staff of the Islamic Society. But when prayer is going on, they are not permitted to enter the prayer hall.

Rebuilding *Niujie* (Ox Street) The Beijing Municipal Government has started rebuilding a residential area mainly inhabited by Muslims. The work on the 35.9-hectare area around Niujie Street will involve moving 7,500 families, 58 per cent of whom are Muslims. The project will turn Niujie Street into a Muslim-style commercial street. The area will be home to multi-storey buildings, schools, kindergartens and public facilities. Niujie is presently a narrow street where most people live in old houses with a per capita floor space of 5.1 square metres. In recent years, the Beijing government has completed a number of infrastructure projects to improve water, electricity, heat and gas supplies there.

The Temple of Universal Awakening or the Temple of the Reclining Buddha
十方普觉寺或卧佛寺

Commonly known as the Temple of the Reclining Buddha which is situated at the foot of the Western Hills about 30 kilometers west of Beijing. It was first built in the 7th century at a cost of 5 million taels of silver. When it was renovated and expanded in the Yuan Dynasty, a huge statue of recumbent Buddha was cast. It was renamed the Temple of Eternal Peace during the Ming period. When it was restored under the Qing, it was given another name: the Temple of Universal Awakening. It is generally referred to as the Temple of the Reclining Buddha.

The way leading to the temple is lined by towering ancient cypresses, with a glazed archway standing right in front of the temple.

The archway is made of marble, crowned with glazed tiles of various shapes and colors. In the centre of the first courtyard is a little pond with a stone bridge spanning it. The Bell Tower and the Drum Tower stand respectively on each side of the courtyard.

The buildings are symmetrically laid out. Five main halls stand one after another, all with side halls on both sides. The third hall is the Hall of the Reclining Buddha, containing a copper statue 5.2 metres in length in recumbent position with one arm straightened and the other turned to support the head. It was claimed that

Temple of Reclining Buddha

Hall of Dragon King
Pavilion of Longevity Hill
Ten—Thousand—Pine Pavilion
Depository of Buddhist Texts
Reclining Buddha Temple Villa
Hall of Reclining Buddha
Travelling Palace Restaurant
Hall of the Buddhas of the Three Ages
Travelling Palace Courtyard
Hall of Heavenly King
Front Gate
Bell Tower   Drum Tower
Water Fountain Courtyard
Glazed—Tiles Archway
Lily Magnolia Garden
Perennial Root Flower & Plants Garden

455

54 tons of copper was used to cast the enormous statue at a cost of 50 million silver taels. The statue was completed in 1321. Around the Reclining Buddha are twelve smaller statues. It is said that the posture of the group represents a scene in which Sakyamuni was giving instructions to his disciples under the bodhi tree while he was ill. To make the setting conform to the story, several bodhi trees were planted in the temple. They are believed to have come from India. The bodhi tree has long, narrow, dark-green leaves, and its white flowers blossom in late spring and early summer, resembling myriad of little white jade pagodas hanging upside down amidst the dark leaves. The buildings were renovated and redecorated after 1949.

Beijing set up a large greenhouse within the Beijing Botanical Garden in the western suburbs in 1999. The greenhouse covers an area of 8, 000 square metres, which is the largest one in China. The greenhouse is composed of four parts to exhibit tropical, desert, special and ordinary plants.

The temple was listed by the Chinese Government as a national key relic under special preservation in 2001.

The Temple of Azure Clouds
碧 云 寺

The Temple of Azure Clouds lies at the foot of the Western Hills. Its landmark the Diamond Throne Pagoda can be seen towering amidst green trees from a far distance.

The Temple was first built in 1366 before the collapse of the Yuan Dynasty. Under the Ming two powerful eunuchs, Yu Jing and Wei Zhongxian(1568-1627), had it expanded at various periods, trying to make it their burial ground, but they didn't succeed.

In 1748 during the Qing Dynasty, large-scale construction work was done. The Hall of Arhats designed after the Jingci Monastery in Hangzhou and the

456

Diamond Throne Pagoda at the rear of the temple were built in that period. Before 1949, the buildings in the temple were quite run down. Since 1954, they have been renovated and painted anew, and Sun Yat-sen Memorial Hall was rebuilt to pay tribute to this great pioneer of the Chinese revolution.

Entering the gate you can see the Bell Tower and the Drum Tower, one on each side.

Wei Zhongxian cleverly rose to power by obtaining a position as purveyor of food to the concubine of Emperor Wanli's son, and later, in the 1620s, dominated the court life of Wanli's grandson. At the peak of his influence, Wei Zhongxian was able to publish historical works bilittling his bureaucratic enemies, and to order that temples in his honor be erected all across China.

The temple was listed as a national key relic by the Chinese Government under special preservation in 2001.

Temple Gate 山门

Inside the gate there used to be two statues of gate guardians known to the Chinese as the two Generals, *"Heng and Ha."*

Hall of Heavenly Kings 天王殿

The Hall now contains a bronze statue of Maitreya Buddha, a piece of Ming Dynasty work. In the hall, there used to be four statues of the Heavenly Kings. They were destroyed in the 1920s by the warlords. But in the gateway leading to the Hall of Arhats, visitors can still see another four statues of the Heavenly Kings.

The courtyard has an ancient bodhi tree, pines and gingkoes and two stone pillars with Buddhist inscriptions. Inside the hall are brightly painted clay figures, which tell the story of Xuanzang(Tripitaka)(602-664), a famous Tang Dynasty monk, on a pilgrimage to the West in search of Buddhist sutras.

Heavenly Kings 天王

The four Heavenly Kings are the protectors of the temple, and the four quarters of the universe and the four seasons of the year are also supposedly under their control.

The blue one with a lute is the God of Summer who watches the East.

The black one with a snake and a *pipa* (a plucked string instrument with a fretted fingerboard) is the God of Autumn who watches the North.

The red one with an umbrella is the God of Spring who watches the

457

South.

The white one with a sword is the God of Winter who watches the West.

Hall of Arhats 罗汉堂

In the hall there are altogether 508 statues representing the disciples of the Buddha, each in a different pose and with a different facial expression. Eight of them are the personal disciples of Sakyamuni, and the other 500 are the saints. Each one is marked with a number. No. 444 Arhat is said to be the reincarnation of Qing Emperor Qianlong. Legend has it that Emperor Qianlong wanted to be an arhat. The pose of No. 444 Arhat is similar to that of the arhat he disguised. Years later, this "false arhat" joined the rank of arhats. All of them were redecorated recently. Not far from the north gate of the hall, there is a small figure named Jigong (a legendary figure in ancient China, is well-known for his readiness to help good people in trouble and to punish bad people and corrupt officials—hence his reputation as a "Living Buddha"), squatting on a roof beam. It is said that he was a latecomer, and because of his junior rank he could not find a seat and had to perch up in the roof. North of the Hall of Arhats lies the Spring Garden, where a spring flows from the crevices. The Three Immortals Cave is another feature of interest in the garden.

Near Sun Yat-sen Memorial Hall there are three arches each built of a different material: one of wood, one of stone and the third of brick. A pair of circular pavilions is also found here.

Dr Sun Yat-sen Memorial Hall 孙中山先生纪念堂

Before 1949, the hall was dilapidated. Except for a portait of Dr Sun Yat-sen and a few old wreaths, it was practically empty. In 1954 the Chinese Government refurbished the temple and Sun Yat-sen Memorial Hall was reconstructed. There is a bust of Sun Yat-sen in the hall. On the right is a glass coffin with a steel lid, a gift from the Soviet Government. It arrived in China in 1925, two weeks after Sun Yat-sen's body had been encoffined. There are two exhibition rooms, one on each side of the Memorial Hall. In the north room are pictures of Dr Sun's early revolutionary activities. In the south room are pictures showing how he led the Chinese people in the democratic revolution. Behind the hall on the hillside stands the Diamond Throne Pagoda. After Sun Yat-sen's death in March, 1925 his coffin was entombed in its base. In May it was moved to Nanjing. His hat and clothes were then buried in the base instead, and the Diamond Throne Pagoda has also been known as the Hat-and-Clothes Tomb of Dr Sun Yat-sen.

458

Dr Sun Yat-sen (1866-1925) 孙中山先生生平

Dr Sun Yat-sen, a great pioneer of the Chinese bourgeois revolution, was born in 1866. He graduated from a medical college in Hongkong in 1892 and, under the cover of practicing medicine. He began to engage in political activities for national salvation. In 1894 he set up Revive China Society, China's first bourgeois revolutionary organization. He organized Revolutionary League in 1905 and for the first time publicly advocated Nationalism, Democracy and the People's Livelihood. The 1911 Revolution led by him overthrew China's feudal system that lasted for over 2,000 years. On January 1, 1912, Sun Yat-sen took the oath of office for presidency and proclaimed the founding of the Republic of China. Soon afterwards Dr Sun Yat-sen resigned and the political power was usurped by the notorious warlord Yuan Shikai. In 1924 Dr Sun Yat-sen implemented the three policies of alliance with Soviet Russia, alliance with the Communist Party, and support for the workers, and peasants' movements. He passed away in Beijing on March 12, 1925 at the age of 59.

The main streets of some of China's major cities are named after him and memorial meetings are held each year to commemorate his contributions to the Chinese Democratic Revolution.

Diamond Throne Pagoda 金刚宝座塔

Standing at the rear of the temple, it was designed after the Diamond Throne Temple in Central India but built and decorated in the Chinese style. On the 34-metre-high platform built entirely of white marble stand two small-sized dagobas and five 13-layer close-eave stupas. The stupas used to be the graves of monks in China and the Buddha's tooth relic is said to be kept inside. The foundation is triple-tiered: the first two storeys have stairs and on the third there are a number of niches containing fine Buddhist images in relief. An internal stairway leads from the bottom up to the platform of the foundation, from where visitors can have a panoramic view of the surrounding area.

459

The Pool and Cudrania Temple
潭　柘　寺
(about 45 kilometres from the city)

In between the Mahavira Hall and Vairochana Pavilion the Pool and Cudrania Temple is situated 45 kilometres west of the city. For centuries, there has been a saying: "First there was the Pool and Cudrania Temple, then came Beijing." It dates back 1,600 years to the Jin Dynasty, when it was known as the Temple of Auspicious Fortune. In the Tang Dynasty, it was expanded and renamed the Dragon Spring Temple. It has been popularly known as the Pool and Cudrania Temple because of the Dragon Pool and cudrania trees on the hill behind the temple. The buildings were mostly rebuilt in the Ming and Qing dynasties.

The temple was built into the landscape and laid out in a beautiful setting. In front of the gate are ancient pines believed to be several hundred years old.

Several groups of buildings stand on the terraces one higher than the other. Their distribution is symmetrical, typical of Ming temple architecture.

The buildings spacious and imposing, are arranged in three main north-south axes. Along the central axis are the Archway, the Front Gate, Deveraja Hall, Mahavira Hall and Vairochana Pavilion.

The temple was listed by the Chinese Government as a national key relic under special preservation in 2001.

Hall of Heavenly Kings 天王殿 (please read Yonghegong Lamasery)

Chiwen 鸱吻 *Chiwen* refers to the glazed-tiled figures and animals on the ridge of the roof. The roofs of the ancient Chinese buildings were constructed with decorations in a unique style and in various forms. On the ridge of the roof are *Chiwen*, one at each end. Legend has it that *Chiwen* can be used as fountain to make rain to prevent fire.

Chiwen decorations first appeared in the first century BC during the Western Han Dynasty (206 BC-AD 23). It has a fan-shaped sword on its back and is supposedly fixed on the roof, so that it can not run away. The pair of *Chiwen* here, bright and vivid, date back to the Yuan Dynasty and are rarely seen in the Beijing area.

Mahavira Hall (*Daxiongbaodian**) 大雄宝殿

Daxiong means a powerful warrior with dauntless courage, an honorable title for Sakyamuni. In the hall there is a statue of Sakyamuni, funder of Buddhism. He preached Buddhism for 45 years and died at the age of 80.

460

---

* *Daxiongbaodian* the Precious Hall of the Great Hero (the main hall of a Buddhist temple, in which Sakyamuni is the central figure of a triad enthroned upon lotus pedestals, the two others being usually Ananda and Kasyapa, his two favourite disciples)

On the right is a statue of Mahakasyapa, one of the ten disciples of Sakyamuni. It is said that he was of eminent virtue and was reckoned to be the first patriarch. After Sakyamuni died he continued his career.

On the left is a statue of Ananda. Also one of the ten disciples of Sakyamuni, Ananda was the master of hearing and memory and was reckoned to be the second patriarch. He followed Sakyamuni for more than 20 years and is said to have compiled the Buddhist sutras. Dressed as a monk, he often appears together with Mahakasyapa in front of Sakyamuni.

"Emperor of Trees" "帝王树"

In between the Mahavira Hall and Vairochana Pavilion grows an ancient gingko tree, known as the "Emperor of Trees." The name was given by Qing Emperor Qianlong. The gingko tree is said to have been planted in the Liao Dynasty with a history of over one thousand years and is still a mass of branches and leaves. It is about 40 metres high and takes six people with their arms outstretched to encircle it. Across to the west is another gingko, planted later. Male gingko tree is fruitless while female gingko bears fruit either for eating or for use as medicine.

Vairochana Pavilion 毗卢阁

The Vairochana Pavilion is the highest building on the central axis. It offers an excellent view of the temple grounds and the surrounding hills. The Pavilion is a 2-storey structure.

On the first floor, there are five statues. From left to right:

The first one is Maitreya, standing for wisdom 智慧.

The second one signifies undertaking 事业.

The third shows the Buddha of the Future 大日如来之意.

The fourth represents awakening 觉性.

The fifth symbolizes happiness and virtue 福德.

Ordination Altar 戒坛

The Ordination Altar is the place for the ordination of novices into the Buddhist priesthood.

Guanyin (Bodhisattva of Great Mercy) Hall 观音庙

In the Guanyin Hall there used to be a "prayer brick" used by Yuan Princess Miaoyan, daughter of Kublai Khan. She lived as a nun in the temple and came here to pray everyday. Years later, her footprints were deeply marked on the brick where she stood. Hence the name: the "prayer brick."

461

Stone Fish 石鱼

West of Guanyin Hall stands the Hall of the Dragon King, which is located in the northwest extremity of the temple. In the aisle of the hall is a stonefish, 1.5 metres long, weighing 75 kilograms. When struck, it produces clear and pleasing sound. It was made in Emperor Kangxi's time. Legend has it that Dragon King presented the stonefish, a treasure of the Dragon Palace in the South Sea, to the Jade Emperor (the Supreme Deity of Taoism). When there was a serious drought and when epidemics ran amuck, the Jade Emperor bestowed the stonefish on the Pool and Cudrania Temple to help people dispel calamities. One night, the stonefish descended from the sky and landed on the courtyard. The scaly body of the fish was divided into 13 parts, representing 13 provinces. Whenever the part for the province was struck, there would be rain for that province. The stonefish is a reproduction.

Floating Cups Pavilion 流杯亭

To the east of the central axis is a group of buildings in traditional Chinese courtyard style: abbot's rooms and two palaces for the Qing emperors when they visited the temple. In the courtyard stands the Floating Cups Pavilion. On the marble floor of the pavilion is a shallow channel shaped like a coiled dragon through which the spring water flows. In the old days people used to float wine cups on the spring water. The cups were carried along the channel to other spots where other people would pick them up and drink the wine. This place has got a beautiful name: Floating Wine Cups in the Winding Stream.

Bronze Cauldron 铜锅

East of the Hall of Heavenly Kings is a kitchen used by the monks in the past. In the kitchen is a bronze cauldron, 1.1 metres high and 1.85 metres in diameter. This cauldron was used by the monks for cooking vegetables.

Pagodas 塔林

In front of the temple stands the Hall of Ease and Joy, formerly the quarters for the monks after retirement. Further down is the pagoda courtyard, which contains a total of 72 pagodas dating from the Jin, Yuan, Ming and Qing dynasties. Built during different periods and in different styles, the pagodas make valuable material in the study of pagoda architecture. These pagodas are listed as historical relics under special preservation.

Dragon Pool 龙潭

The Dragon Pool is located on the hill behind the temple. In the old days, the spring water was very clear and flowed down in a constant stream. Unfortunately, the pool has dried up.

More than one thousand years ago, China began to use cudrania for silk-worm raising. Cudrania blooms in summer. Its fruit is edible, and its roots, bark and stem can be used as medicine.

Jietaisi (Ordination Terrace Temple)
戒 台 寺
(about 35 kilometres from the city)

The temple is located at Ma'anshan (Saddle Hill) in the Western Hills, 35 kilometres west of Beijing. It was built in 622 in the Tang Dynasty, and was known as the Wisdom Accumulation Temple. In the Liao Dynasty, a monk named Fajun had an altar built here for the ordination of novices into the Buddhist priesthood. It was renovated and renamed the Longevity Temple under the Ming. The temple is commonly known as Jietaisi, Ordination Terrace Temple or "the place for selecting Buddhas." Most of the present buildings were reconstructed in the Qing Dynasty.

The Mahavira Hall, the main hall in the Temple, originally contained ten carved sandalwood chairs made in the Ming Dynasty. Three of them were placed high above, for the abbot and two elders, and another three to the left and four to the right, for the witnesses to the ordination ceremony. Outside the hall there are two steles, one erected in the Jin Dynasty and the other in the Liao. In the northeast compound is the Ordination Altar made of white marble. It is a three level altar over three metres high. The base is carved with figures of several hundred deities. Twenty-four of them are one metre high. They wear helmets and armour and look like warriors. The rest are about one-third their size. South of the altar is the Upali Hall, which contains the image of the Arhat Upali, one of the disciples of the Buddha.

South of the altar is the pagoda courtyard, in which stand two pagodas built in the Liao and Yuan dynasties. Not far from the courtyard is the Hall of the Brilliant Kings with a stone balustrade in front enclosing three stone pillars. They are inscribed with Buddhist sutras and images. Two of them were erected in the Liao Dynasty and the other dates from the Yuan, all in good condition. The temple is famous for its ancient pine trees: the

463

Reclining-Dragon Pine, the Unrestrained Pine, the Nine-Dragon Pine, the Embracing-Pagoda Pine and the Sensitive Pine. It is said that if you sway one of the branches of the Sensitive Pine, the whole tree will shake.

Just as the Pool and Cudrania Temple is famous for its spring water, the Ordination Terrace Temple is noted for its ancient pine trees, which date from the Liao and Jin dynasties and are still growing luxuriantly.

Yunju (Heavenly Living) Temple
云 居 寺
(about 70 kilometres from the city)

On April 28, 1987, Zhao Puchu 赵朴初 (1909-2000), then the head of China's Buddhist Association announced the discovery of two fragments of the bone relics of Sakyamuni, founder of Buddhism. Known as sartra in Sanskrit, the bones were found in 1981 inside two gold bone bowls, which were contained inside five progressively smaller boxes in a cave at the Yunju (Heavenly Living) Temple some 75 kilometres southwest of the city of Beijing. Zhao told reporters at a news conference that the bones, about the size of a sand grain, fitted closely descriptions in records from the Ming Dynasty (1368-1644).

The relics are one of the important discoveries in Chinese history and Buddhism. It was only made public at the time when the restoration of the temple was nearly finished. The bone bowls are displayed there.

Records said that there were originally three bone bowls, although it was not known how they arrived at the temple. The Buddhist bones were discovered and removed for three days by a Ming Dynasty empress in the 15th century and one bowl was lost. Alongside the remaining bowls were found two pearls and curses carved into the lid of the smallest box.

Nestling in the mountains, the Yunju Temple is also famed for its 14, 278 stone slabs (tablets) inscribed with Buddhist scriptures in 17 million characters.

In a tower and nine grottoes were engraved by 13 generations of monk starting in the Sui Dynasty (581-618) to the Ming Dynasty (1368-1644). The temple has been ranked with the Dunhuang Grottoes, a well-known store of Buddhist literature in Northwest China. The stone slabs were mostly excavated during the 1950s. The largest slabs are 2. 5 metres long and 60 centimetres wide while the smallest is 76 centimetres long and 40 centimetres wide. If they are placed in a row, they would extend for 20 kilometres.

In 1956, when archaeologists were searching unsuccessfully for the caves, they found a slab in the house of a local farmer. It indicated the location of the relics. Since large-scale restoration of the temple started in 1984, the government has funded the project, while Buddhists in China, Japan, Hong Kong and Southeast Asian countries have donated more than one million yuan (US\$183, 486). At present, a four-storey hall, which covers 3, 000 square metres has been completed.

Some 80, 000 trees have been planted in and around the temple and a 12-kilometre-long road has been built linking the temple with the high-ways. Two more halls, including one to enshrine Sakyamuni, the founder of Buddhism, was built in 1990 and a 2, 000-square-metre storeroom was erected to house 77, 000 wooden blocks engraved with tripitaka in the Qing Dynasty (1644-1911). About 7, 000 such wooden blocks have already been shipped to the temple, adding that China has only about eight sets of tripitaka rubbings, which are now kept in Peking University, the Adminis-tration of Museums and Archaeological Materials and Jilin University. When all the 77, 000 blocks arrive, the Yunju Temple will become China's largest museum of Buddhist scriptures.

The temple was destroyed in 1942 by Japanese artillery, but the stone slabs remained intact in underground caves. Renovation began in 1984 and was completed in 1991. Now monks have been invited back to the temple and two fragments of the bone ashes of Sakyamuni, which came to the temple in late Sui Dynasty more than 1, 400 years ago, are displayed here again.

A total of 10, 082 tablets inscribed in the Liao (907-1125) and Jin (1115-1234) dynasties were put into underground storage vaults filled with nitrogen near Yunju Temple, where they were unearthed in 1957, by September 9, 1999. The measure, the first of its kind in China, aimed to protect the priceless tablets, some of which had already been damaged by air pollution and inadequate protection methods. The tablets' incorruptions were first made by a senior monk at Yunju Temple in AD 605, and for the next thousand years monks at the temple continued the work, ultimately transferring 1, 122 books of scripture onto 14, 278 stone tablets, enough to stretch 12. 5 kilometres if they were put end to end. The tablets were buried by the monks in nine caves near the temple, until they were exca-vated in 1957. Scholars say that the tablets have great historical, politi-cal, economic, and cultural significance, and are valuable for the study of the development of calligraphy and carving. They are also an important reference source for collating Buddhist scriptures. The tablets stored in the underground safe are well protected. But the cost of such storage is high, with nitrogen in the safe costing more than 200, 000 yuan (US$24, 000) a year. It costs nearly 20 million yuan (US$2. 4 million) to store the items underground, which mainly comes from the government and donations.

But the other 4, 196 inscribed tablets during Sui (581-618) and Tang (618-907) dynasties have been left in nine caves which are threatened by air exposure, pollution and underground water. Copies of all the tablets have been taken. Some sayings from the Liao and Jin dynasties have been published.

More than 2, 000 of the tablets are put on display at the temple and the rest are buried under proper temperature, ventilation, and moisture controls thanks to new technology in the underground storage vaults.

Experts suggest that the talbets at the Yunju Temple be registered on the United Nations' World Heritage List to help protect them.

Tangshang Village, Xiayunling Township, Fangshan District—the Birthplace of One of the Most Popular Songs in China
房山区霞云岭乡堂上村

President and General Secretary of the Communist Party of China Jiang Zemin wrote an inscription on June 6, 2001 for a local village, which was the birthplace of one of the most popular songs in China, "Without the Communist Party, there would be no New China 没有共产党就没有新中国." His inscription is a rendering of the title of the song using the traditional Chinese writing brush.

In October 1943, Cao Huoxing 词曲作者曹火星, a member of an anti-Japanese publicity squad, came to the village of Tangshang, and using an old folk melody wrote the words to the song, which was then titled "Without the Communist Party, there would be no China 没有共产党就没有中国."

The Fahai Temple
法 海 寺

Located at the southern foot of Cuiwei Mountain in the Shijingshan District of the western suburbs of Beijing, construction on the Fahai (Sea of Dharma) Temple was begun in 1439 by the Board of Works in the Ming Dy-

466

nasty (1368-1644). Funds were raised by Li Tong 李童, a favourite official eunuch of the Ming Emperor. The temple was completed in 1443 and named by Emperor Yingzong more than 500 years ago.

The temple used to consist of a main hall (Mahavira Hall), four subsidiary halls, a bell tower, a drum tower, and several supplementary rooms. All the buildings were decorated with remarkable murals. But unfortunately, only the main hall and several side rooms survived, making the remaining murals even more precious.

According to historical records, the paintings were executed by famous artisans recruited from all over China, under the supervision of renowned court painters.

Covering 236. 7 square metres in the Mahavira Hall, the existing murals are distributed on the fan-shaped eastern, western and rear walls, and are considered to be the best-preserved Ming Dynasty murals in China. Experts think it is a wonder that after more than 500 years the murals are still intact and look almost as bright and clear as they were when freshly finished, with an imposing atmosphere of grandeur, thanks to the mineral pigments used for staining the paintings. The 77 figures in the murals show a splendid and dignified grand gathering of Bodhisattvas, male and female, young and old, handsome and ugly, the lifelike celestial beings and entirely different from each other. But their spirits are linked with a unified belief and morale, presenting a pious atmosphere characteristic to such religious occasions. Executed in precious perspective and with a very refined style and meticulous brushwork, the females in the paintings look gentle and the males robust. Women's ornaments and men's armors and weapons are in bold relief, all made from gold thread, employing a unique technique in decoration.

All the figures have distinctively individual characteristics but the portraits of the three principal Bodhisattvas are especially well done. And of the three, the 1. 6 metre-high Guanyin (Avolokitesvara) is the most magnificent, looking spirited, affable, pure and far from the mortal world. She is bare-chested and graceful, with a transparent gauze kerchief draped casually over her shoulders.

Decorated with flowers embroidered with hair thin gold threads, her almost invisible kerchief seems buoyant, allowing the visitor to feel the benevolent goddess breath. Clouds separate the celestial beings from the world of the mortals, manifested by rocks, streams, and such plants as bodhitrees, peonies, lilies, lotuses and bananas.

Many Buddhas have small animals around them, which are equally true to life. A white six ranked elephant, moved by Buddha's preaching,

467

sheds tears. The tears just gather and seem to be about to stream down its face at the next blink. A fox looks back at its master, the fine hair and thin veins on its pricked ears clearly seen. It is said that these works represent the highest artistic standard of decorative art from the Ming Dynasty. The exquisite creations adhere to traditional designs that prevailed in the Tang (618-907) and Song (960-1279) dynasties but with the artisans' individual styles or temperament typical of the Ming Dynasty. The Fahai Temple thus provides a good example of the integration of traditional modes with styles of the period in ancient Chinese paintings. Therefore, some celebrated experts from Beijing's cultural relics and fine art circles treasure the murals of that period in the Fahai Temple. The murals not only enrich the profuse collections of cultural relics in Beijing but also rival Western masterpieces. The murals in the temple are outstanding among the wall paintings of the same period in the world. Compared to the wall paintings of Dunhuang and Yongle Palace, it is unique in its own right with its own salient features. As such these murals truly do rival Western masterpieces of the Renaissance Period(14 – 16 century), and merit a visit by every serious traveler interested in the unique history of China.

The drawing technology is superb. It has been preserved for over 500 years without peeling and is still in perfect condition. Even the colours have not faded with the leakage of water. Experts believe that certain elements were mixed into the construction materials as well as into the paint. To find the answer to the riddle is expected to be an important part of the mural studies.

The local government has been paying great attention to the preservation of the temple and especially its murals by investing a large sum of money in restoring the temple.

Beijing's Bureau of Cultural Relics invested 10 million yuan (US$1.2 million) in restoring the Doctor Hall and the Hall of Buddhist Scriptures in the temple, which were destroyed by a fire at the end of the 20th century. The relics authority will preserve all of the original murals. The rebuilding of the halls is just small part of Beijing's plans for relic protection.

White Dagoba (Stupa) Temple
白　塔　寺

The White Dagoba Temple is situated in the western section of the city. The White Dagoba in the temple is the twin of the one on Qionghua Islet in Beihai Park.

It was built in 1271, when the stone balustrades were added. The temple Shengshouwan's ansi (Temple of the Emperor's Longevity and Safety) was erected on the site in 1279 but was burned down by a fire in 1291. In 1457, the temple was replaced by a new name Miaoyinsi (Temple of Divine Retribution), which is the White Dagoba Temple of today.

The dagoba stands in the back of the temple, and has a base more than 30 metres in circumference. The upper part of the structure is like the tip of an auger with 13 rings, topped by a round, engraved copper plate, the edge of which is hung with iron bells. A small bronze pagoda is placed on the copper plate. During renovation in 1978, several Buddhist precious cultural relics of the Qing Dynasty (1644-1911) were found inside the top of the dagoba.

The temple had been partly damaged and blocked from view since 1969 by houses built by residents nearby. Renovation of the 13-storey, 50. 9-metre-high White Dagoba started in June 1997 and was completed its first phase in October 1998 with a budget of over 40 million yuan (US\$ 4. 8 million). As one of the most significant symbols of old Beijing, the White Pagoda Temple has been restored to its former appearance, and was reopened to the public on October 25, 1998. The dagoba was designed by a Nepalese engineer. He was then holding office in the Yuan government as a holy place for Buddhist rituals. Its building was one of the most important projects in the construction plan of Dadu (an old name for Beijing), which was drawn as the Capital by Kublai Khan (1215-1294), the first Emperor of the Yuan Dynasty (1279-1368). The White Dagoba inside is the biggest and earliest remaining pagoda in the Tibetan lamaist-style in China.

The temple, one of the first 18 places of historical value in Beijing, which was placed under State protection in 1961, was constructed between 1271 and 1279 with imperial edict from Kublai Khan, the founder of the Yuan Dynasty.

469

The second stage of the restoration of the White Dagoba Temple started in 2002. It is a landmark structure from the Yuan Dynasty (1279-1368) and was an important political and cultural centre of the dynasty. The relics are the only ones from the Yuan Dynasty that have been kept intact, free of any destruction.

The Temple of Enlightenment (*Dajuesi*)
大　觉　寺

The Temple of Enlightenment lies at the foot of Yangtai Hill in northern

Haidian District in Beijing. The rolling hills here are said to resemble a sleeping lion. The vista of two flanking temples — the Lotus (Lianhuasi) and the Universal Grace (Puzhaosi) — sitting atop hilltops to the west and east of the Temple of Enlightenment is popularly described as "A Lion Rolling Two Embroidered Balls " or "A Buddha and Two Bodhisattvas. "

The temple is one of the well-preserved cultural relic sites tourists can find in Beijing. Though renovations have been carried out over the years, it has luckily remained basically what it was when built in 1068 during the Liao Dynasty (916-1125). At the time it was called the Clear Water Court (Qingshuiyuan). Then it was renamed Spring Temple because of the sacred spring inside it. It was formally changed to the present name in 1428 during the Ming Dynasty (1368-1644), when the temple became the royal backyard for the imperial court. Since then the temple has been regarded with the highest reverence. many emperors including Emperor Qianlong, and Empress Dowager Cixi in the Qing Dynasty (1644-1911) even wrote about the temple. Although weathered by almost one millennium of rain and wind, the grandeur of the four-row complex remains undiminished.

The Mahavira Hall (*Daxiongbaodian*—Daxiong means a powerful warrior with dauntless courage, an honourable title for Sakyamuni), the main hall of the temple, is 3. 5 metres high and 18 metres deep. Sakyamuni, founder of Buddhism, sitting in the middle of the hall, is flanked by 20 standing Zuntian statues, a sort of Bodhisattva, each carved with different gestures and facial expressions.

Amitabha Hall where the statue of Amitabha sits. The relief sculpture of the Goddess of Mercy, or Guanyin, is said to be one of the top sculptures of ancient China. The smiling goddess sits on a blooming lotus flower propped by sea waves. Her right hand holds a bird in the traditional lotus gesture. The big halo behind Guanyin is portrayed in a golden sea of red and green ribbons. The sea palace, the dragons, the fairies and the stones protrude to form a three-dimensional picture. The sculpture appears so dramatic that tourists cannot help but marvel at the creator's talents one millennium ago. On the horizontal inscription board of the Amitabha Hall, is the Emperor Qianlong's inscription: *Dongjingdengguan*, meaning whether moving or not, a pious follower should observe the rules of faith all the time. Empress Dowager Cixi also left her words in the temple, *Miaolianshijie*, or the lotus world. Legend has it that the tale of the magnolia tree is the most famous. In spring, there are numerous blossoms on the old tree and the fragrance spreads all over the mountains and valleys. The petals are said to be the biggest ones in Beijing. The giant gingko tree is over 1, 000 years old. In autumn, the leaves all turn yellow, another attraction of the temple. The Lingguan Spring trickles down into a pond in the temple. The water is crystal clear, cool and sweet. Drinking it will refresh the spirit of tourists. The most incredible sight in the temple is the trees. A pine tree grows between the trunks of an old Chinese wisteria; and a cypress has rooted itself in a rhombus parvifolia. No scientific explanation can support the phenomenon. Local people put it down to the celestial location of Dajue Temple, or the Feng Shui or "Wind and Water Belief" — a system of dragonology, a "science" using the shape of nature objects such as rivers, hills, and trees. It was possible to choose the desirable sites for tombs, houses, and even cities. It was also able to foretell the fortunes of any community family or individual according to the spot selected. People believed in the past that a geomancer was able to counteract evil influence by good ones and to save whole districts from devastation by floods, pestilence, and so forth. On the very top of the temple, a pagoda built in the Liao Dynasty is embraced by a cypress and a pine tree, as if they are guarding the pagoda.

Hongluo Temple
红 螺 寺

The Hongluo Temple (tradition has it that two spiral shells gave out red light in the evening) is located at the foot of the Hongluo Mount 7 kilometres northwest of Huairou District. It was first built in the Tang Dynasty (618-907). Its original name was Daming (Great Brightness) Temple, and was then changed to Zifu (Fortune Supple) Temple in the Ming Dynasty.

Covering an area of 16. 6 acres, the Hongluo Temple is the biggest temple in the northern area of Beijing. The temple is divided into 5 courtyards. The central courtyard, taking Shanmen (the entrance of the temple), Tianwangdian (Hall of Heavenly Kings), *Daxiongbaodian* (Hall of Mahavira), and the Meditation Room as axes together make up 3 halls: namely, the Hall of Teaching Buddhist Scripture and two accompanying halls in the east and west sides. The eastern courtyard consists of a guestroom and dining rooms. The western courtyard comprises of Abbot's Cell and Shifangtang. The eastern back yard consists of Yanshoutang (the room for prolonging life), with the Monk's Hut in the north and an arena for practicing Qigong in the south. In the far west is the tower yard, which consists of the Ash Room for monks, the monk pagoda and the Pagoda of the Spiral Shell. The temple was the Holy land of Buddhism at that time. Here was also the birthplace of Jinghua Qigong. Many senior Buddhist monks were trained and practiced here. There is an account of thirteen founders in the book entitled Nian Song Yi Gui. Their twelfth founder was Hongluo Zifuxingongdashi, or Great Master of Zifuxinggong. The temple was a resident temple in which Buddhist monks were engaged in advanced studies, and abbots were cultivated for other temples.

The thirtieth founder of Yinguangdashi, the Great Master of Yinguang had also taught here. Therefore the senior Buddhist monks from Japan and Southeast Asian countries often went on a pilgrimage and studied Buddhist scripture here. The temple was deeply honoured by the emperors of the past ages. The temple was rebuilt many times. Emperors even came here to burn incense and prostrate themselves before the statue of the Buddha. The temple was therefore quite well known both at home and abroad.

Surrounded by hills dotted with pines and cypresses in thousands of different and graceful shapes, the temple is a place of quiet contemplation and is tastefully laid out. There is a Zhen Zhu Quan (the Spring of Pearl) in the west where the spring water is green and transparent and the rising bubbles are said to be like pearl. In the south, visitors can go boating, swimming and fishing in the Hongluo Reservoir. There are towering old trees in the yard and among them Chinese wisteria adopted by pine trees. Male and female ginkgoes and green bamboo are said to be the "Three Matchless Sceneries" in Beijing. The Hongluo Temple has been listed as one of the important cultural relics to come under Beijing Municipality protection. It has now a sacred place to sightsee after several years of successful renovation.

Memorial Hall of Beijing New Culture Movement
北京新文化运动纪念馆

The building was built in 1918 at Shatan, central Beijing, and quickly became known as the "Red Building" because it was built with red bricks. It used to be the former home of Peking University, or Beida in downtown Beijing, birthplace of the patriotic May 4th Movement of 1919. Offices in the building that formerly belonged to Chinese revolutionary pioneers including Mao Zedong, Li Dazhao, have been restored and opened to the public in late 2001. The Red Building has played a significant role in much of China's modern history. In 1918, when Mao Zedong first came to Beijing, he was an assistant in the library of Peking University. Revolutionary figures like Chen Duxiu and Li Dazhao, and cultural masters Lu

Xun, and Cai Yuanpei and Hu Shi all worked in the same space at various times. The building also witnessed the birth of China's first Communist group, before the foundation of the Communist Party of China. On May 4, 1919, about 3,000 students from over 10 universities in Beijing gathered on the north side of the building before marching to Tian'anmen Square to begin China's democratic revolution. Several government departments, which settled in the buildings in the 1950s, including the State Bureau of Cultural Heritage, moved out earlier in 2001 to make way for the building's opening to the public. Great efforts have been made to avoid damaging or changing the building's exterior and interior structures, including a ban on installing air conditioners in the offices. The Memorial Hall opened to the public in April 2002 after it refurnished.

Ancient Bell Museum of the Great Bell Temple
大钟寺古钟博物馆

The Great Bell Temple is located on the western outskirts of Beijing. It houses the largest bell in China. The bell was also named Yongle Bell after Ming Emperor Yongle who ordered it be cast about 600 years ago.

According to a recent test by the Chinese Academy of Sciences, its loud and clear sound reaches up to 120 decibels and can be heard 50 kilometres away in the depth of night.

Music experts of the Chinese Acoustics Institute have found its tone pure, deep and melodious with a sprightly rhythm. Its frequency ranges from 22 to 800 hertz.

The bell is known as China's "King of Bells," which is 6.94 metres high, 3.3 metres in diametre and 46.5 tons in weight.

Engineering Institute studied the bell and described the technique as "ground pit casting with a pottery clay coated mold."

According to the specialists, the clay mould had been put in a pit in the ground and the molten metal poured in at one stretch through two holes on the top of the mould. An ultrasonic examination of it found very few sand-holes. To achieve such a precise calculation, accurate timing and huge heating system were needed.

The experts also found the bell's metal, a perfect bronze alloy—80.54 per cent copper, 16.4 per cent tin and 1.12 per cent lead. Even when struck hard, it produces a fine sound.

But the most difficult part of the casting was the Buddhist sutras inscribed over the entire surface of the bell both inside and out. There are more than 230,000 Chinese characters inscribed on it.

The third Ming Emperor Yongle took power in 1403 after a coup known in Chinese history as the Jingnan (Pacification) Coup. Legend has it that, feeling guilty, he tried to atone for his misdeeds by having the great bell cast with 17 sutras.

He hoped to "divert public indignation by striking the bell," according to an "Ode to the Great Bell" inscribed on the tablet erected during the reign of Qing Emperor Daoguang. The tablet still stands by the side of the bell.

The bell was originally kept in the Imperial Longevity Temple. Shipping the bell from the foundry to the temple was a big problem, since there was no vehicle or machine that could handle it. A ditch was dug along the way, and water was fetched from newly sunk wells to make an ice route in winter. Placed on a huge sleigh, the giant bell was hauled to its destination by oxen. In 1733 the bell was moved from the Imperial Longevity Temple to the present site.

In addition to the Yongle Bell, 31 other bronze bells from the Song, Yuan, Ming and Qing dynasties are also on display outside the temple.

At present, the museum is devoted to ancient bells. It is China's first bell museum set up in 1985. The museum features a display illustrating the evolution of Chinese bells and the history of Chinese metallurgy. The bells on show have been collected from all over China. Some of the bells were moved here from the temples in Beijing.

Most of the bells are made of bronze, and the oldest was cast 700 years ago. The most famous of all is the great bell, which gave the temple its name. The exhibition was opened in 1986. By the beginning of 1992, the museum already collected 418 bells from both at home and abroad and there are another 96 bells, which are reproductions.

474

On June 27, 1997, an epigraphic tocsin 警世钟 cast by Dalian Daqing Metal Corporation Ltd. found the way to the Ancient Bells Museum of Beijing Grand Bell Temple. An over 400-word epigraph was inscribed on the bell, which records the history of British occupation on Hong Kong and embodies the Chinese people's determination to restore it.

Museum of the Chinese People's Anti-Japanese War
中国人民抗日战争博物馆

Located near the Lugou (Marco Polo) Bridge in the southwestern suburb of

Beijing, the Chinese People's Anti-Japanese War Museum was opened to the public in October 1987. The construction of the museum was begun on July 7, 1986 and was completed in early July 1987. Occupying an area of more than 20, 000 square metres, the museum has three exhibition halls with pictures, documents and artifacts showing the outbreak of the war, the attacks of Japanese troops against Chinese troops and civilians, the accomplishments of leaders of both the Chinese Communist Party and the Kuomingtang and their troops, and the foreign friends who helped China win the war. The museum was built with the funds donated by Shanghai Municipality, Guangdong, and Hubei provinces, as well as financial allocation from the State and Beijing.

The War of Resistance Against Japanese Aggression has a very important place in China's modern history. It marks a significant turning point in the historical development of the Chinese people from decline to vitalization. It was the first time that China won a complete victory over imperialist aggression, and for the first time China participated in a worldwide war against fascism as an important ally and made big contributions to the victory of the war.

A sculpture, "The Awakening Lion, " stands outside the entrance of the museum, symbolizing the spirit of the Chinese nation.

According to statistics, during the Japanese aggression against China more than 35 million Chinese people died or wounded. According to rate calculation 比值计算 in 1937, China's direct economic loss reached US$ 100 billion caused by the Japanese aggression, and indirect economic loss stood at US$ 500 billion. These figures were released by the Xinhua News commentator in commemoration of 60th anniversary of the July 7, 1937 Luguoqiao (Marco Polo Bridge) Incident.

The Sculpture Garden 雕塑园

Bronze sculpture, cobbled paths, towering monuments and columns of pines give an aura of grave serenity to the monument and sculpture garden, a memorial to Chinese people's triumph in the War of Resistance Against Japan (1937-1945). After five years (1996-2000) in the making, the garden opened to public on August 16, 2000 in Beijing. Located in the Fengtai District, the garden encompasses 20 hectares and cost 315 million yuan (US$38 million). Five hundred and fifty families were moved out to make way for the garden. Inside the 22, 500-square-metre sculpture area, 38 works of traditional Chinese bronze remind visitors of the solemn, stirring war. The sculptures are divided into four theme groups according to the different stages of the war. Japanese troops invaded China in 1937. By the end of the war in 1945, more than 35 million Chinese

475

people had been killed and wounded. The central square covers 2, 500 square metres, and the monument bears President Jiang Zemin's autograph. The 15-metre-high copper monument is made of granite and smashed tank ruins, which symbolize Chinese people's determination to rout invaders and protect world peace. The sculpture area radiates paths to the rest of the garden, connoting the Chinese people's desire to beat the Japanese invaders.

Beijing Natural History Museum
北京自然历史博物馆

Founded in 1958, the Beijing Natural History Museum is the largest in China. With an exhibition floor space of 3, 600 square metres, the museum is located at Tianqiao, close to the Temple of Heaven.

The museum is divided into four exhibition halls: flora, fauna, ancient animals and mankind. There are about 10, 000 fossils, specimens and models on display.

With a large number of archaeological finds and materials concerning anthropology, paleoanthropology, and anatomy, the hall of mankind tells how human beings came into existence and gradually developed. Visitors see models of Yuanmou Man in Yunnan, Lantian Man in Shaanxi, Peking Man, Dingcun Man in Shanxi, Upper Cave Man in Beijing, Homo habilis in Africa, Java Man in Indonesia, Neanderthal Man in Germany, and Cro-Magnon Man in France. "Origin of Man" is currently on exhibition in the museum. Three hundred photos, 800 exhibits, paintings done by celebrated artists and precious specimens vividly illustrate the evolution of man and the complete process of human life, from embryo and birth to growth and death. Exhibits from foreign countries are also on display in the museum. They were sent by the American Museum of Natural History in New York, the British Museum, the Musè National d'Histoire Naturelle in France, the Carolina Biological Supply Company in the US, and Beppu University in Japan.

In the hall of ancient animals most impressive is a complete dinosaur fossil, Hechuansaurus, the largest found so far in China. The giant creature, measuring 22 metres long and 3. 5 metres high, is a herbivore. Another big dinosaur fossil (Yongchuansaurus, a carnivorous animal), 4 metres high and 9 metres long, lived between 60 million and 20, 000 years ago. A fish fossil (Himalayasaurus), found in the Himalayas, proves that the mountains, including Qomolangma (Mount Everest), were once an expanse of sea. Footprints of dinosaurs have been studied by anthropologists all over the world. The footprints of different dinosaurs found in China are exhibited in the museum. They are important in studying the animal's behaviour as well as earth's evolution.

Stone Forest, fossil trees hundreds of millions of years old create a forest of sorts in front of the Beijing Natural History Museum. These fossilized trees, 0. 3 to 1. 2 metres in diameter, were discovered in Northeast China's Liaoning Province. They now occupy 100 square metres in the yard of the museum. One of the trees turned into an arch during the fossilization process. The round trunk became flat and crooked with an uneven diameter. It clearly shows the process of fossilization—from wood to silicon or agate.

Beijing Stone Carving Art Museum
北京石刻艺术博物馆

Established in 1980 and opposite the new National Library, the Beijing Stone Carving Art Museum covers an area of 15, 000 square metres. It is an open-air museum, which possesses more than 1, 200 artifacts, 620 of which are on display.

The museum has seven exhibition sections. They are synthetic stone carvings, stone tablets marking merits and virtues, epitaphs, books of stone rubbings, steles of temples and monasteries, tablets of guild halls and artistic stone engravings. The synthetic section displays 32 artifacts, which demonstrate the characteristics of stonecarving in Beijing, both in shape and content. The merit virtue tablets show the severe social estate system in Chinese feudal society. Inscriptions on the tablets mark the merits and virtues of some famous ministers and officials of the Ming and Qing dynasties (1368-1911). They are also valuable for research of historical figures.

The museum is located at the site of the Five Pagoda Temple. The temple and pagodas were built between 1403 and 1413 when an eminent Indian monk named Pancha Charma came to China and presented to the third Ming Emperor Yongle five gold Buddhas and designs for the pagodas. Emperor Yongle ordered the construction of the Diamond Seat Pagoda Vihara in honour of the Indian monk. It was completed in 1423.

Among the pagodas of the same style still standing in China, this is the oldest and the most exquisite. The architectural style with five pagodas on a platform (the Diamond Seat) was modelled on the Buddha Gaya in Bihar,

India, where Buddha is said to have attained enlightenment.

Standing 15 metres high, all the five pagodas were built with bricks inside and covered with slabs of blue and white granite outside. Smooth engraving made the stone carvings exceptional work of arts of the Ming Dynasty. The Indian style pagodas, the carvings and the unique traditional Chinese architecture are combined to make the building a brilliant example of the successful amalgamation of foreign culture into Chinese architecture and engraving.

The temple has sustained some damage over the centuries. Part of the pagodas were bombarded by the Allied Forces of the Eight Powers in 1900 and the damage is still evident.

Yanhuang Art Museum
炎黄艺术博物馆

Located in the northeastern part of Beijing, Yanhuang Art Museum completed in 1991, occupies an area of 3.75 acres. With four storeys in all (one is underground), the museum has a height of 20 metres. It is characterized by its distinctive colours, shapes and integration of various architectural makeup. The funnel shaped roof incorporates and unifies modern life, traditional culture and various architectural characteristics from all over the country. The roof's function and contour suit the needs of both an art gallery and a museum.

In order to eliminate interference from reflective light, architects have designed special windowless walls. Under the sunshine, the purple roof appears solemn, while the walls and ground have the elegant colour of granite. As a result, the different colours of the building form a sharp contrast to one another.

Beijing University Sackler Archaeology and Art Museum
北京大学赛克勒考古艺术博物馆

The Bijing University Sackler Archaeology and Art Museum opened on December 11, 1992. Located on the campus of Beijing University, the 4,000-square-metre museum is made of a main building, east and west halls, a rear hall and a central yard. Dr Sackler donated US$ 4 million to build the museum.

There are more than 10, 000 art treasures in the museum, including wares made of stone, pottery, bone, jade, bronze, and porcelain, ancient coins, paintings, garments and musical instruments.

Arther M. Sackler was a noted American pharmacologist, philanthropist and collector of art treasures. During the 1930s he donated funds to aid China's anti Japanese struggle. In order to support the study of ancient Chinese relics and to protect them, Sackler also donated funds to build the Sackler Fine Art Gallery in Washington D. C. and the Sackler Museum at Harvard University.

China Red Sandalwood Museum
中国紫檀木博物馆

Located adjacent to Resources Hotel along the Beijing-Tongzhou Expressway in the east Beijing, red sandalwood carving lovers now have a rare opportunity to look at some masterpieces. A unique exhibition of carvings is being held at the China Red Sandalwood Museum in Beijing. It is the first exhibition of its kind in the world. Organized by Fu Wah Furniture Enterprise Co Ltd., the show is part of a series of activities celebrating the 50th birthday of the People's Republic of China. More than 1,000 pieces of red sandalwood carvings are on display at the museum. They include some replicas of carvings that existed in the imperial palaces in the Ming (1368-1644) and Qing dynasties (1644-1911). From the theme to the selection of materials, from the design to the carving, this collection can be considered exceptional. Chen Lihua, the curator of the museum said that the project of a red sandalwood museum was born 10 years ago. It came from a desire to protect and promote an art that has a history of more than 1,000 years.

Construction of the museum started in 1998 and was completed in 1999. The museum was opened to the public on September 17, 1999. The museum was built at a cost of about 200 million yuan (US$24 million).

National Museum of Modern Chinese Literature
中国现代文学博物馆

National Museum of Modern Chinese Literature at a cost of 150 million yuan (US$18 million) is a three-storey building capturing the splendour of traditional Chinese architecture: red walls, latticed windows and sloping roofs. Unlike most Chinese ancient buildings, the museum is decorated with blue roofs and white window frames, which gives a jolt of colour to the typically somber style of the city's museums. Covering an area of 15,000 square metres, the museum includes exhibition halls, a library and a multi-functional centre. The museum also spared little expense to create a place that would stand out and compare to the leading museums in China. All the statues and paintings in the museum are works by China's most famous artists. Even the hand-shaped door handles of exhibition rooms are pieces of art — they are bronze sculptures made into the hand mould of Ba Jin in 1996, one of China's greatest writer and the museum's honorary director. Three displays will remain fixtures at the museum: "Development of Modern Chinese Literature," "Memories of Literature Giants" and "Donation of Writers." Some of the exhibits, to a certain extent, are antiques. These include the original scripts, letters, diaries and photos which cannot be found elsewhere. The display, "Memories of Literature Giants, in the first exhibition hall, highlights the accomplishment of several distinguished writers like Lu Xun (1881-1936), Lao She (1899-1966) and Bing Xin (1900-1999). In the middle of the exhibition hall is the replica of Lu Xun's residence, which is called the "father of modern Chinese literature." His story *A Madman's Diary* is considered first story written in modern Chinese. The classic Chinese literature by Lao Zi and Confucius were written in literary Chinese, which is quite different from the spoken language. But literature drastically changed during an intellectual revolution, referred to as the New Culture Movement, which took place the early 20th century. Many of the new intellectuals, such as Lu Xun, held up for critical scrutiny in nearly all aspects of Chinese culture and tradition ethnic groups. The writers abandoned the classic language and chose to write in modern Chinese. As one of the most influential figures in the movement, Lu Xun had produced great literature, mainly including three collections of stories and 17 collections of essays. The exhibits of Lu Xun's residence are fairly simple: a desk of faded colour with the passing years and a plainly decorated bed. The enormous black-and-white portrait of Lu Xun is no doubt the focus of the exhibition.

Besides Lu Xun, the museum also pays tribute to Lao She, another great Chinese writer. many photos featuring Lao She's most successful dramas are on exhibition. His signature drama "Teahouse" tells the story of the ups and downs of a traditional Chinese teahouse and portrays the life of several small characters. The play reflects the painful changes in China from the 1890s to the 1940s. It has become a classical repertoire on China's stage and the first Chinese drama to tour in other countries since the founding of the People's Republic of China in 1949. Lao She had been admired and studied internationally. In 1999, scores of scholars from all over the world gathered in Beijing to commemorate the 100th anniversary of Lao She's birth. Some of Lao She's works have been published in foreign languages, like "The Quest for the Love of Lao Lee, ""Camel Xiangzi (The Rickshaw Boy)" and "Teahouse." Equally important, the exhibits donated by Bing Xin's family might bring up memories of this prominent writer and children's novelist, who died of heart failure early 1999. Her books have been widely used in primary schools for generations. they include "For Small Readers, " "Little Tangerine Lamp" and "Ode to Cherry Blossom. " The exhibits include dozens of letters from her readers who talk about their goals, their studies and their education while talking with Bing Xin. Her broad sense of love and sympathy for the family and nature and her love for the motherland had influenced generations of Chinese children. The exhibition of "Development of Modern Chinese Literature" showcases the most significant events in China's literature over the past 150 years. Literature had played a significant role in the history of China since early 20th century. This is true both in the warring periods before the founding of the People's Republic of China and the reform and opening-up in the 1980s and 1990s.

The third show mainly presents the 70-odd literary collections donated by famous Chinese writers and preserved by the museum since 1985. In addition to the three shows, the library is now open to the public, where interactive computer systems provide specific information of the museum. Since the new museum was completed in 1999, it has drawn increasing attention in Beijing. The architecture is sure to become a new landmark of the city.

Beijing Constabulary Museum
北京警察博物馆

Situated on Dongjiaominxiang in downtown Beijing, with 2,000 square metres of floor space for the exhibition, Beijing Constabulary Museum, highlights more than 7,000 exhibits relating to the police collected from China and overseas, with the oldest items being from the Han Dynasty (206 BC-AD 220). About 1,500 police-related items are on display at the museum, some of which are being shown to the public for the first time. The displayed objects, photos and models give a full picture of public security development in Beijing, the criminal system and police weapons, equipment and investigation, ranging from the Han Dynasty (206 BC-AD 220) till now. In the municipal bureau's 50-year-history, 58 policemen died at their posts, and their names are engraved on a wall in the museum.

The museum is devoted to the development of professional policemen and the history of China's public security undertakings, opened to public on August 1, 2001.

Beijing Shisanling Waxworks Palace of the Ming Dynasty
北京明十三陵蜡像宫
（about 34 kilometres from the city）

Located in the northwest of Changping District seat and leading to the Ming Tombs and the Great Wall, the Beijing Shisanling Waxworks Palace of the Ming Dynasty was completed and opened to the public on August 28, 1994. Construction lasted only 18 months. The Waxworks Palace is a pleasant place to visit, to shop, to dine and to be entertained. It covers an area of 19,000 square metres with a total floor space of 30,000 square metres. It is divided into 26 lifelike scenes with 374 figures.

With the exquisite art of waxworks and the modern technology of sound, light, and video it reproduces the major historical events of the 16 emperors of the Ming Dynasty spanning 276 years, from 1368 to 1644. The Palace is the largest in scale and the best in artistry of any waxwork museum of its kind in China. It gives visitors a historical review of the political, economic, cultural and folklore vicissitudes of the Ming Dynasty as well as an artistic treat.

The Waxworks Palace is under Sino-Belgian management. The total cost of its construction was 150 million yuan (RMB) or US$ 17.5 million.

482

Beijing Museum of Ancient Architecture
北京古建筑博物馆

Established in 1991, the Beijing Museum of Ancient Architecture is the only museum in China to exhibit China's architectural cultural tradition in an all-round and systemic way. The museum is housed in the imperial sacrificial architectural complex located in Xianlong Temple or the Altar of the God of Agriculture （先农坛）, southern Beijing. The architectural complex, with a history of some 500 years, glistens under the sunlight as the miniature of the colorful culture of China. Over the years, the museum has been collecting, studying and exhibiting the cultural heritage expressed in ancient Chinese architecture, arousing the interest of international and domestic professionals and the public. Mr Ieoh Ming Pei 贝聿铭, a famous architect of Chinese origin, once paid a visit to the museum. The museum exhibited the cream of the ancient Chinese architecture to the worldwide architects during the XX UIA Congress in 1999. The museum held a large exhibition entitled Road of China's Architectural Culture featuring traditional Chinese architecture; academic symposiums on traditional architectural design concepts and culture aimed at the 21st century, and related cultural activities. These are geared to show the age-old traditional Chinese architecture, its rich contents, and positive impact of traditional Chinese architectural culture on architectural development in the future. The museum expects more extensive and profound dialogue on the Chinese and foreign architecture, and is ready to make due contribution to expanding foreign exchanges.

The Altar of the God of Agriculture used to be the site of imperial sacrifice dedicated to the cult of Shennong, the Holy Farmer (a legendary ruler, the 2nd of the Three August Ones 三皇, supposed to have invented the plough and discovered the curative virtues of plants). The altar is located in the southern part of the city, directly to the west of the Temple of Heaven. It encompasses 300 hectares (741. 3 acres). The Altar itself, which faces south, is 1. 5 metres high and occupies an area of 15. 6 square metres. The hall to the north houses the sacred tablets and is provided with a platform for "observing the harvest." According to the rites of the Qing Dynasty (1644-1911), on the day of the spring equinox as fixed by the lunar calendar, the emperor would come here to sacrifice to the sacred tablet of Shennong. Following this ceremony, the emperor would plough several furrows of land with his own hands and retire to the observation platform to watch the princes, ministers and a representative group of common people finish the task. Legend has it that the emperor's plowing "set an example of industry to his subjects, thus dignifying the toil of the meanest agricultural laborer." The area also contains an Altar to the Year God 太岁殿 for carrying out sacrifices to the planet Jupiter and auxiliary halls on the east and west for carrying out sacrifices to the Deities of the 12 Lunar Months (Yuejiangshen).

After the founding of the Republic of China in 1912, the main hall was turned into a Temple of Loyalty in memory of the 72 martyrs who died in an uprising at Huanghuagang in Guangzhou, Guangdong Province. Here there is also a dressing room where the emperor changed into the ceremonial robes worn during the sacrifices; a divine granary for storing the five grains used in the ceremony; and the Palace of Celebrating Completion 庆成宫, where the Ming emperors carried out their pre-sacrificial fast.

Temple of Successive Emperors
历 代 帝 王 庙

Located near Fuchengmen in Xicheng District, the Temple of Successive Emperors, one of Beijing's three imperial temples, that was built in 1531 in the Ming Dynasty with an area of 21, 000 square metres, will be revamped. A key state-level protected cultural relic, the temple was used in the Ming (1368-1644) and Qing (1644-1911) dynasties to offer sacrifices to 188 successive emperors, 79 persons who had rendered outstanding service, ancient heroes and forefathers of the Chinese such as Fuxi 伏羲 (a legendary ruler of great antiquity, the first of the Three August Ones 三皇, credited with the invention of hunting and fishing and the domestication of animals), Yan and Huang (Yandi and Huangdi—or the Yellow Emperor —, two legendary rulers of remote antiquity) and outstanding emperors. The temple has been used as a school since 1949.

With the support of the bureau, Xicheng District, which is where the temple is situated, will restore it to its original splendor. The school has been moved out of the temple and it will be open to the public in 2003. The district has spent 8 million yuan (US$965,000) on renovation work on the temple since 1994. The project is an important part of the bureau's plan to spruce the area up for the new millennium.

The 62.5-square-kilometre area within Beijing's Second Ring Road (which is where the city wall and moat used to be), the original city area, will be the main focus of the protection plan.

Dongyue Temple
东 岳 庙

Located in Chaoyangmenwai Dajie, Dongyue Temple was first built in 1319 during the Yuan Dynasty (1279-1368). The temple consists of three parts, including main courtyard, east courtyard and west courtyard, encompassing 4.73 hectares (11.696 acres) with more than 600 room-units. It used to be the largest temple of Zhengyi Tao in North China. With the elapse of time, the temple had been dilapidated. After the founding of New China the temple was occupied by a school and government offices. Since 1995, it was taken back, and serves as Beijing's one and only folklore museum, where one may not only appreciate colourful, traditional handicrafts, but also buy them. The collection includes embroidered cloths, local Chinese dolls, traditional flowers, ceramics and pottery, as well as local opera performance tickets and program sheets. The temple itself is worth a close look, for the architecture of dynasties from the Yuan to the Qing (1279-1911) can been seen, and numerous statues of the immortals have been restored inside the temple.

The Chaoyang District Government allocated more than 30 million yuan (US$3. 6 million) in revamping this ancient temple and it has taken on a completely new look.

Ancient Laoshan (Old Mountain) Tomb
古代老山汉墓

Located in Laoshan in the western part of Beijing, the tomb is about 10 kilometres from the Forbidden City at the city's centre. The Laoshan area was a settlement site of great import during the Han (BC 206-AD 220) and Jin dynasties (AD 265-AD 420), and some relics from the Jin Dynasty were found there in the 1960s. The elevation at Loashan is about 130 metres.

In October 1999, local residents reported to the police that several men were piling dirt on a slope clearing. Police officers tracked them down and found seven men had been digging into the slope every day at midnight. Two months later, officers Li Ping and Li Liwen of the Babaoshan Police Station ventured into the channel, which was about 20 metres long, filmed its interior and removed some charcoal dust. Archaeologists confirmed that the charcoal was the protection layer above an ancient tomb. At 3 am on December 23, 1999, the diggers went to the slope again, only to fall into the hands of laws. The leader of the suspects, Dong Fusheng, later told the police that they had studied the landscape of the area for a few years and finally decided on the location. After a preliminary survey, archaeologists from the Beijing Cultural Relics Research Institute and the Beijing Cultural Relics Bureau started excavation in late February 2000. The most important finding was a small part of the *huangchangticou* 黄肠题凑, a square wall of cypress beams surrounding the coffin chamber. This was a unique burial custom reserved for emperors and local kings of the Western Han Dynasty (206 BC-AD 23). Outside the coffin walls, there was another set of walls, about 16 metres long and 13 metres wide. Based on the height of the *huangchangticou*, the coffin room was about 3 metres high. This discovery was another strong proof of the tomb owner's identity. The initial findings included dozens of pottery tiles from the Western Han Dynasty. Clearing the bushes and trees, archaeologists removed a chunk of earth 14 metres deep to reach the layers of charcoal and rammed earth above thick wood boards, which were believed to be the tomb's true ceiling. Although the tombs appeared to cover an area of 19.5 metres long and 16 metres wide, deeper excavation showed it actually 16 by 13 metres, much smaller than the area covered by the rammed earth. To the northeast of the tomb lies dozens of stone slabs which were out of order. Two rows of cypress column lined the north and south ends of the tomb. This layout was new to the Western Han tombs and indicated that the tomb construction ended abruptly, possibly due to the unexpected change of the owner's social position. Both the shape and the size of the tomb suggested that this for a king from the Western Han Dynasty.

Laoshan is situated at a unique place with many interesting finds. Not far to its east is the famous Babaoshan Revolutionary Public Cemetery, where rest the country's most prestigious figures since 1949. Between the two hills, a small tomb from the late Western Jin Dynasty (AD 265-AD 317) was discovered in 1965. The owner of the tomb is the wife of Wang Jun, a cruel and an ambitious landlord from the Beijing area. Among the few relics recovered was a silver bell decorated with eight small musicians. In 1982, at about 1 kilometre west of Laoshan, construction workers stumbled on the tomb of an anonymous high-ranking official from the late Western Han Dynasty. Many of the damaged relics were ceramics. The latest discovery at Laoshan brought much greater expectation to archaeologists, and the Beijing media have been speculating about its treasures since its dramatic discovery. The most daring guesses focus on two precious items, the *huangchangticou* and the *jinluyuyi*, jade clothes sewn with gold thread. The top part of *huangchangticou* found at Laoshan is slightly rotten but experts still retain great hope for it, as it might be another intact example after the first one discovered in 1973 at Dabaotai of the Fengtai District 15 kilometres southwest of downtown Beijing. Before 1973, archaeologists only knew that *huangchangticou* was a special mark from the Western Han Dynasty reserved for emperors and prestigious local kings. The mystery was unveiled through an unexpected discovery at Dabaotai. the excavation site holds two tombs, one for a king whom most experts agree was Liu Jian (ruled 73 BC-45 BC), head of a Guangyang Kingdom. The other tomb is for his wife, but it was burnt long ago and little remains exist. The underground palace of Liu Jian measures 23. 2 metres long and 18 metres wide, much bigger than the tomb at Laoshan. The most important find there was a square wall of tight-laid cypress beams around the coffin. Archaeologists finally understood that the yellow-brown beams cut out of cypress trees were the so-called *huangchang* (yellow intestine) and *ticou* means the way the beams were laid—with the head pointing inward to the chamber. These hard beams still retained the scent of cypress when they were exhumed. The 15, 880 beams made a 3-metre-high pile. At 90 centimetres long, most square beams measured 10 centimetres on each of the four sides.

Among the five tombs with *huangchangticou* found so far in China, this one is the most intact and offers clues to many historical labyrinths. The use of wooden coffins reached its pinnacle during the Western Han Dynasty. During the following Eastern Han Dynasty (AD 25-AD 220), stone slabs with carved pictures ascended the stage. With a wooden cover, the cypress wall had been effective in absorbing dampness and air, but neither the wall nor the five layers of wooden coffins inside protected Liu Jian from thieves. Archaeologists discovered the remains of the king lying outside the coffin, with an obvious rope mark on the neck. Thieves apparently burglarized him before the body decayed. From a few broken jade pieces on the ground, experts judged that Liu Jian may have donned a jade coat.

During the Han Dynasty, emperors and local kings wore jade coats upon death in the belief that this unique stone would safeguard their body and soul. Although many jade coats were discovered in China, those intact threaded with gold are scarce. Most were made with silver, copper or in some rare instances, silk threads connecting small jade squares. Before the Eastern Han Dynasty (AD 25-AD 220), the burial system was not as strict. Some local kings also used gold threads to make jade coats. The first intact ones ever discovered were from the tombs of Liu Sheng, king of the Zhongshan Kingdom and brother of Emperor Wudi (reigned 140 BC-86 BC), and of his wife, Dou Wan. The excavation of their tombs started in 1968 at Mancheng in Hebei Province about 120 kilometres southwest of Beijing. The two jade coats respectively used 2, 498 and 2, 160 pieces of jade with 1, 100 and 700 grams of gold thread.

On December 26, archaeologists from the Beijing Bureau of Cultural Relics confirmed that an ancient tomb existed in the area. Archaeological workers began to excavate the tomb on January 17, 2000, under the authority of the State Bureau of Cultural Relics. In early April 2000, the shape of the outer coffin appeared after the earth in the tomb had been removed. "*Ticou,*" which consists of piles of wooden poles and was used only by members of the royal family to protect their coffins, was also discovered in the tomb chamber. From May 2, 2000, workers began to build a 36-metre-long canopy over the site to protect it from the weather. After the construction was completed at the end of July of the same year, workers started to excavate the inner parts of the tomb chamber. A skeleton, which was later discovered to be that of a 35-year-old man 1. 61 metres tall, was also found in the front chamber of the tomb. Experts said that the man could be either a robber or the main inhabitant of the tomb who ended up in that position after being pulled out of the coffin by robbers.

A live broadcast of the opening of the ancient Laoshan Tomb of the Han Dynasty (206 BC-AD 220) was cancelled when the tomb was confirmed to be empty. Experts believe that grave robbers had taken most of the relics in the tomb. A previous live show of digging part of the tomb attracted a large audience, but few cultural relics were found. To date, more than 40 imperial tombs from the Han Dynasty have been exhumed across China, and some rare artifacts from these tombs have greatly helped research into the era.

PLACES TO VISIT

第四部分　参观单位

Peking (Beijing) University
北 京 大 学

Peking (Beijing) University, commonly called Beida, was founded in 1898 under the edict of Emperor Guangxu (1875-1908) as one of the major attempts to restore the declining Qing Dynasty (1644-1911). Its history is closely related to that of the development of modern China's politics, ideology, culture and sciences. Yan Fu and Cai Yuanpei who were China's famous educationists and ideologists, Mao Zedong, Li Dazhao and Chen Duxiu who were founders of the Chinese Communist Party, and Lu Xun who was China's great writer and chief commander of the Chinese New Culture Movement, either taught or held offices here. Ding Wenjiang studied geology at Beida before becoming a modern Chinese pioneer, using new techniques to survey the entire territory of China. Zhu Guangqian was the first to introduce Western aesthetics to China. Ma Yinchu (1882-1982), who worked as a professor and dean of the economics department in 1915 and once served as president of Beijing University in the period 1951 to 1960, devised in detail the family planning scheme, which is now an important policy in Chinese society. During the Chinese Democratic Revolution, Beijing University played a very important role in opposing old culture, in advocating science and democracy, and in disseminating Marxism. The University was also the cradle of the anti-imperialist and anti-feudal and May 4th Movement which took place in 1919.

Since the founding of the People's Republic of China, the University has implemented the Party's policy and carried out a systematic transformation of the educational system, of the teaching contents and teaching methods, and achieved great progress and development in all respects.

The task of Beijing University is to train research workers and college teachers in liberal arts, natural sciences and social sciences, to carry out scientific research projects and to make contributions to the development of national economy, science and civilization of China.

In the years from 1949 to 2001, nearly 120, 000 undergraduates and graduate students have graduated from this university. They are now scattered throughout the country, the bulk of whom have become the backbone in the industrial, agricultural, scientific, educational and cultural fields.

During this period, scientific research activities were in full swing and numerous results achieved were reaching advanced standards in the country.

Total synthesis of bovine insulin with full biological activity was first achieved by our research workers in collaboration with those of the Institute of Biochemistry and the Institute of Organic Chemistry under the Academia Sinica. In accordance with the policy of "Letting a hundred flowers blossom and a hundred schools of thought contend," extensive academic studies and discussions were carried out, resulting in a number of important achievements and publications, such as An Outline of Chinese History and History of Chinese Literature.

There are 29 departments in the University, among them 14 departments are of natural and applied sciences and 15 departments are of liberal arts and social sciences. In addition, there are two independent teaching and research groups on Marxism Leninism, offering courses of common requirement such as philosophy, political economy, history of the Chinese Communist Party, English and physical education. To strengthen scientific research, 31 institutes and 18 research centres have recently been set up. The University published two learned journals: Peking University Academic Journal (Natural Science Edition, Bimonthly) and Peking University Academic Journal (Social Science Edition, Bimonthly).

The University offers a four-year curriculum for undergraduates and a two-to-three-year curriculum for the Master Degree programme, and two to three years more for the Doctor Degree programme.

In 2001, the student body totalled 20,000, including over 1,000 postgraduates. Besides, there are 500 foreign students from over 60 countries. The number of teachers and research workers amounts to nearly 4,000, of whom 950 are professors and associate professors. The campus occupies an area of 150 hectares, with a building space of 430,000 square metres. The library has a collection of more than 5.3 million volumes of books, with 2,400 seats in 16 reading rooms. Besides, there are 20 department reading rooms.

Affiliated to the University are an instrument factory and an electronic instrument factory, both of which serve the needs of teaching and scientific research and undertake the trial production or production of certain products. The University Publishing House and Press publish textbooks, teaching materials and scientific monographs of all kinds for faculty members, students and the general reading public.

In recent years, the University has undergone a process of restoration and readjustment in its academic work, and has made important progress in the transformation of the admission system, in the improvement of the quality of teaching, and in strengthening of scientific research and international academic exchanges. The University is striving to become both a centre of education and a centre of scientific research so as to contribute positively to the transformation of China into a powerful modern socialist country which is highly democratic and highly cultured.

University Relics

In 2001, the State Council issued the fifth national cultural relics protection list. Among the 40-plus important historical sites, four are on University campuses. This is the first time that universities have entered the cultural relics protection list. The four sites are the Yanyuan architecture around Weiming Lake at Peking University, the early buildings of Tsinghua University in Beijing, the old site of Dongbei University in Shenyang of Northeast China's Liaoning Province, and the early buildings of Wuhan University in Central China's Hubei Province. The candidate sites' representation of the best of the architecture and culture of their time was a chief criterion for making the list. The buildings of Peking University were typical of the architecture of the early 1900s; the other universities on the list had been influenced by Western styles while keeping the Chinese traditions. Over 1,300 universities and institutions of higher learning across China applied for the list. But the four winners secured recognition with their fame and historic significance. In addition their buildings offer material to some architecture researchers. The State Council has declared 1,286 cultural relic sites under State protection. The number is quite small compared to China's long history. In Egypt and India, there are tens of thousands of cultural relic sites protected by the governments.

Beida Merges with Medical School

Beijing University and Beijing Medical University merged officials of the two schools announced on April 3, 2000. Beijing Medical University was absorbed into Beijing University, which is commonly known as Beida, giving it a medical school. The two universities in their new roles will complement each other in promoting the development of inter-disciplinary courses and in accelerating the dissemination of the schools' research findings.

In his congratulatory letter, President Jiang Zemin said that the merger of the two leading universities is a positive development for Chinese higher education. Leading universities should be keys for implementing the strategy of "revitalizing the country through science and education." He encouraged the new Beijing University and other universities to work harder for the nation's prosperity and development.

Beijing University boasts a rigorous and diligent academic style. Beijing

Medical University is well-known for training many medical specialists and contributing to the nation's medical and health advances.

Academic Degree System 学位制

In 1981, China instituted the system of bachelor's, master's and doctoral degrees, in the 10 fields of philosophy, law, literature, history, economics, education, science, engineering, agriculture and medicine. The Academic Degree Committee of the State Council which directs the awarding of degrees nationwide, has empowered institutions of higher learning and the relevant research institutes to establish degree evaluation committees, and to implement the actual work of conferring degrees.

More Foreign Students 外国留学生

Since receiving its first group of 33 foreign students from Eastern Europe in 1950, China has accepted 350,000 students from 160 countries over the past 50 years. Among those 350,000 students, more than 80,000 enjoy Chinese Government scholarships, while the remaining 270,000 are self-supported. Subjects chosen by foreign students range from the Chinese culture to medicine, engineering, the science and agriculture.

Foreign students studying or intending to study in China can hope to enjoy a better campus environment, as the country has pledged to further improve teaching and living conditions. The 356 colleges and universities that have been approved to take overseas students will be given more freedom to recruit foreign students. Colleges and universities with adequate teaching conditions may teach students in both Chinese and the students' mother tongues. They can also co-operate with overseas education institutions to develop learning programs for foreign students. Colleges and universities have been called on to improve their accommodations and other services for foreign students.

Beijing University Library 北京大学图书馆

Beijing University Library, the oldest and one of the largest libraries in China was founded in 1902 and was China's earliest centre for advocating Marxism and other modern progressive thought. Li Dazhao, one of the founders of the Chinese Communist Party, was head of the library from 1918 to 1922. The Beijing chapter of the Communist Party was organized in Li's office in 1920. The library collection is more than 5.3 million volumes, including 2.7 million books in Chinese; 1 million books in more than 20 foreign languages, plus newspapers and magazines. Its collection also includes over 160,000 rare volumes in Chinese and other languages, some of which date back 1, 000 years. Its collection is increasing at a speed of 100, 000 volumes a year.

A new library was completed at Beijing University in May 1998. It has a floor space of 27, 000 square metres and contains 3 million books. The University has Asia's biggest college library, with a total floor space of 50, 000 square metres, 4, 500 reading room seats and more than 7 million books. The new library features traditional Chinese architecture. The latest electronic equipment and automatic systems have been installed to offer a comprehensive modern service to readers. Construction of the library started in June 1996. Total investment amounted to 100 million yuan (US$12 million), including US$ 10 million donated by Li Ka-shing, a Hong Kong entrepreneur.

According to statistics, there are 2, 535 public libraries above county level in China. Each year these libraries receive 360 million people.

Beijing Medical University 北京医科大学

Beijing Medical University (College), one of the oldest medical schools in China, was founded in 1912, when it was named the Capital Medical School. Later it was merged with other schools of liberal arts and sciences to form Beijing University. Before 1949, there were only three departments: the Department of Medicine with a small sized hospital of 134 beds; the Department of Dentistry and the Department of Pharmacy. More than 1, 000 students graduated over a period of nearly 40 years, and many of them are now well-known scientists and professors across the country.

In 1952, it became an independent college and rapidly grew into one of the leading medical colleges in China. At present, there are five departments:

Basic Medical Science, Medicine, Public Health, Oral Medicine and Pharmacy, and a senior nurse school. Students come from all parts of the country and are well selected. In the last 5 decades after 1949, more than 16, 000 graduates have left the college to serve in health care centres of different levels. The teaching staff now consists of 470 professors and associate professors, 950 lecturers and attending doctors as well as 700 assistants, as against 138 teachers and doctors before 1950. There are nearly 2, 500 students, including 90 from foreign countries, mostly from the third world, as well as 550 postgraduates. To meet the needs of medical care and the training of medical and health personnel, the college has established 4 affiliated hospitals (2, 000 beds) and one teaching hospital (600 beds), covering all major medical services.

Beida Opens New School 北大新开设教育学院

On October 25, 2000, the 100-year-old Beijing University announced the opening of its School of Education, which is described by top university officials as a major step in the development of the world-renowned university. The school, which will only recruit students and researchers for master's degrees and doctorates, will focus on research on education theories and their application, education management, the analysis of education policy and the development of human resources. It will also provide consulting services to the central government. When conditions are mature, the school will set up the research centre on Internet-based education technologies.

The Chinese government is determined to speed up the development of education. It announced a strategy in 1995 "to revitalize the country through science and education."

Edgar Snow (1905-1972)

Born in Missouri, USA in 1905, Snow graduated from the Missouri School of Journalism and travelled to China as a stowaway to report on revolution and change, which he did with idealism and personal fervor. Edgar Snow first came to China in the summer of 1936 when he met Chinese leader Mao Zedong in Bao'an, temporary capital of the Chinese revolution in Northwest China's Shaanxi Province. Four months of painstaking observation and interviews with Mao Zedong not only dispelled Show's previous misgivings about China and gave birth to *Red Star Over China*, but also cultivated their life-long friendship. An intimate friend of Mao Zedong, Snow came to China again in 1939, and in 1965 and 1969 when he stood with Mao Zedong on the balcony of Tian'anmen Rostrum for the National Day celebration. With honest accounts of the Chinese revolution, Mao Zedong and his people, *Red Star Over China* has so far been translated into more than 20 languages and is considered to be the first book to introduce the Chinese revolution to the western world. For his efforts, Snow was at first received as a popular and insightful author. But later he was so vilified for helping to "lose China" that he "felt like an Ishmael in his own country" and he described himself as "a grain of wheat sandwiched between two blackboards" when talking about his experiences under McCarthyism in the 1950s. Snow spent the last years of his life in self-imposed exile in Switzerland and died there on February 15, 1972, just four days before US President Richard Nixon left on his historic trip to China. According to Edgar Snow's wishes his ashes were divided between the grounds of Weiming Lake in Peking University in China and the shores of the Hudson River in the United States. Snow was an American journalist/writer who made outstanding contributions to the cause of Sino-American understanding and friendship, still occupies a fond corner of the collective Chinese heart. "The basic facts of Edgar Snow should be made widely known to new generations both in the United States and in China," remarked Israel Epstein at the ninth Edgar Snow Symposium held on October 18, 2000 by China Society for People's Friendship Studies. Epstein is a member of the Standing Committee of the Chinese People's Political Consultative Conference and the vice-chairman of the society. He added: "It has become fashionable, almost habitual in the American media to cast China in an unflattering light." Refusing to buy media shadings, the Edgar Snow Memorial Fund has, since it was founded in 1974, insisted on creating opportunities for Americans to learn more about China, said Nancy K. Wilson, vice-president of the fund. Although Edgar Snow died long ago, the friendship between China and the United States, which he helped engender, is still growing and gaining in significance in today's turbulent global context, said Huang Hua, chairman of the society.

A new biographical feature film "Mao Zedong and Edgar Snow" was shot at a cost of about 5 million yuan (US$625,000). The three-hour film was produced by Changchun Studio, Jiangxi Film Studio and Jiujiang Yangtze Film Studio. The film was awarded a special prize by the jury in the Fifth China Changchun Film Festival late 2000, and was well received by audiences attending the Eighth Beijing Film Festival of University Students in April 2001. Since late 1995, scriptwriter Li Chao has been traveling across the country to get materials for the project, interviewing more than a hundred veteran Chinese soldiers and foreigners now living in China, including Israel Epstein and wife of Dr George Hatem, all friends of Snow. Song Jiangbo and Wang Xuexin from the Changchun Film Studio directed the film. The film "Edgar Snow and Mao Zedong" recaptures the 35-year-long friendship between Edgar Snow and the late Chinese leader Mao Zedong.

497

Tsinghua University
清华大学

Tsinghua (Qinghua) University is a comprehensive university incorporating science, engineering, liberal arts and management departments with special stress on engineering. Founded in 1911, the University is situated around a beautiful villa of the Qing Dynasty in the northwestern suburbs of Beijing.

Known for its limpid pools and verdant trees, which is the original meaning of the word "Tsinghua," the University now has a campus area of more than 520 hectares (1,300 acres) and over 700,000 square metres of floor space.

In its early days, it was called Tsinghua School, a school for sending students to further their studies in the United States. In addition, students recommended by other Chinese universities for advanced studies in America were also, after examinations and training, sent under a subsidization program in the name of Tsinghua School. During the 1920s, it was reorganized into the National Tsinghua University. After the War Against Japanese Aggression broke out in 1937, it moved to Kunming in Yunnan Province, and together with Peking University and Nankai University, was merged into the Southwest Associated University. However, Tsinghua University returned to its original campus in Beijing in 1946 with five constituent colleges: Arts, Law, Science, Engineering and Agriculture.

From 1911 to 1948, Tsinghua University trained a large number of outstanding scholars and scientists who became 2,687 graduates and 1,976 junior and senior preparatory students during the period.

After New China was founded in 1949, a nation-wide reorganization of higher education institutions were carried out in 1952 to meet the needs of the country's reconstruction. Some departments of Tsinghua University were merged with the departments of other higher education institutions, and the University became a multi-disciplinary university of engineering.

During 1950s departments related to new and developing sciences and technology were set up in Tsinghua University, which were rather early among universities in China. They include Nuclear Engineering, Electronics, Computers and Automatic Control, etc., and the self-dependent way of personnel training for those new branches of science was paved. By 1960s, the University had an enrollment of more than 10,000, and completed more than 100 important research projects urgently needed in national construction.

A number of prominent branches in the University reached or approached relatively advanced levels.

Between the mid-1960s and 1970s, the University suffered serious disruption from the cultural revolution, but quickly recovered and was rectified in late 1976. Now the university has 4 schools, 26 departments, 27 research institutes, 6 multi disciplinary centres, 95 laboratories and about 10 factories and workshops for teaching and research, with more than 300 faculty members and research staff and over 12, 500 students (including 10, 427 undergraduates, 2, 030 graduates and 97 foreign students) involving 150 various Degree Study Programmes as well as 687 R & D projects.

Besides, international academic exchange and technical co-operation have also been greatly increased in recent years.

Four schools: Graduate School, Continuing Education School, Sciences School and Economic Management School.

In April 1999, Qinghua University announced re-establishment of its Law School, which was closed 47 years ago. It is a significant event in the history of Qinghua University. Legal construction is very important for China's socialist modernization process, and the Qinghua Law School will nurture excellent legal talents for China. The re-establishment of the Law School is a crucial step in Qinghua's efforts to transform itself into a first-class university the world over. The University set up its Law School in 1928, and it was incorporated within other universities in 1952.

Higher Learning Centre

A research centre for higher learning in Qinghua University in Beijing went into operation on October 3, 1999. Aiming to enhance basic science research and train specialized talents for the 21st century. The centre has provided a favorable climate for the academic studies of mathematics, physics chemistry and biology. The centre has also invited some domestic and overseas scholars to work as researchers as full-or part-time professors. It has offered good working and living conditions for those scholars.

Qinghua University Merges with Arts College

Qinghua University officials unveiled the sign for the University's College of Arts and Crafts College on November 20, 1999 and Qinghua University have merged to improve engineering and industrial design; the merger should also elevate teaching in environmental arts, indoor decoration, and auto design.

Qinghua University Beat Cambridge in Boat Race

Qinghua University rowing team beat Britain's Cambridge University during the Sino-British boat race on Beijing Kunyu Canal on August 20, 2000. The nine-member Qinghua team clocked 6 minutes 45. 5 seconds to beat their counterparts, whose time was 6 minutes 53. 7 seconds, in the 2, 100-metre race. The race was the first of its kind between the two universities, the most famous academic institutions of their respective countries. The event attracted thousands of spectators.

Tsinghua to Celebrate its 90th Anniversary

Tsinghua University, whose alumni number among the highest ranks of government and industry in China, celebrated its 90th anniversary with a grand celebration on April 29, 2001. The prestigious school has spent nine decades contributing much to the nation's educational structure as well as to its science and technology achievements. More than 100, 000 students have graduated from the university since its founding. Known as "the cradle of Chinese engineers," the University has an enviable life of alumni featuring distinguished scientists who have lived up to the slogan "reviving the country by relying on science and technology." Thirty per cent of the members of the Chinese Academy of Sciences and 20 per cent of those in the Chinese Academy of engineering graduated from Tsinghua University. Equally noticeable is its large roster of high-profile alumni who steer China at different levels. From within the seven-member Politburo Standing Committee alone, Premier Zhu Rongji and Vice-President Hu Jintao once studied there. Zhu also serves as dean of Tsinghua's School of Economics and Management. Established in 1911, Tsinghua University, first named "Tsinghua Xuetang," developed from a preparatory school for students who would later be sent by the government to study in US universities into a prestigious Chinese university.

Today, the University has more than 7, 100 faculty and staff, and over 20, 000 students, including 12, 000 graduates, 6, 200 master's degree candidates, and 2, 800 doctorial candidates. The University has 11 schools and 44 departments offering master's degrees.

Medical School

Tsignhua University set up its School of Medicine on October 25, 2001, with Wu Jieping, member of the Chinese Academy of Sciences and the Chinese Academy of Engineering, appointed as the first dean. The new school has three departments: medical sciences, pharmacy and biomedical engineering. The establishment of the School of Medicine would help Tsinghua become a world-renowned comprehensive university.

Beijing Foreign Studies University
北京外国语大学

Established in 1941, Beijing Foreign Studies University (BFSU) celebrated its 60 anniversary on September 22, 2001, is known as home and abroad as the "Cradle of Diplomats." The University is one of the key foreign studies universities of China, large numbers of foreign languages taught, and many international links. It also serves as a national base for research in foreign language teaching and international studies. The University provides a wide range of education programs in foreign languages studies, including advanced training of professional translators and interpreters. In 1996, the University became a member of the state-sponsored 211 Programme, which comprises 100 major universities in China that will receive special support for development in the new century. There are now more than 60,000 graduates from the University, working in all parts of the world, active in fields such as foreign affairs, economics and trade, finance, media, education and academia. Among the graduates of the University are 230 Chinese ambassadors and over 400 counselors to foreign countries. Most of the interpreters for the state leaders are also graduates of the BFSU. Almost all the translators and simultaneous interpreters from China working for the United Nations are graduates of the University.

Known for its quality and achievements in foreign languages, the University continues to make new explorations and is transforming itself into a comprehensive university with multi-lingual and multi-disciplinary education for different levels in order to meet the challenges of China's reform and opening-up and its fast economic development. The University has a long tradition of academic research and has established a number of research institutes in different fields of studies, such as the National Research Centre for Foreign Language Education, a key national research centre in social sciences and humanities. As a leading university in foreign language studies, the University has a very strong faculty, with members in different fields of studies with diversified educational backgrounds and of a proper mix of academic and age stratification. The University has been actively engaged in extensive, comprehensive and in-depth international exchanges and co-operation. The Univeursity receives many delegations and visitors from foreign countries including government officials, diplomats, education specialists and other social activists. World leaders including former German Chancellor Helmut Kohl, former Australian Prime Minister Robert Hawke and Swedish Prime Minister Goran "Pearson" have visited the University. Meanwhile, professors and researchers from overseas are also invited to lecture at the university. It has invited 2,600 people from overseas up to the present. The University is carrying out reforms on its eight schools, nine departments and 12 research centres to ensure that its graduates have multiple skills as well as languages. The university has regular educational exchanges with more than 160 universities and col-

501

leges in 45 countries and regions in the world.

At present, more than 270 universities and colleges offering foreign language programmes.

Beijing Normal University
北京师范大学

Founded in 1902, Beijing Normal University is among the long standing teacher training colleges and universities in China. It is one of the key institutions of higher learning in China. Its main task is to train, for our country, middle school and college teachers characterized by all-round, i. e. moral, intellectual, and physical development, administrative personnel for educational work, scientific research workers, and workers in the fields of theories.

The University has a glorious revolutionary tradition. Its teachers and students played an important role in the student movements before 1949.

Li Dazhao, a leader of the Communist Party of China in her early days and a pioneer in the revolution, once taught at the University. During those years he propagated Marxism and disseminated scientific and cultural knowledge. Lu Xun, the chief commander of China's New Cultural Revolution, was a professor of the University from 1920 to 1926.

Since 1949 construction and development of the University have been very much in the thoughts of the Central Committee of the Party. The Chinese characters for the name of the University, and those for that of the first of its affiliated middle schools, which serve as their respective insignia, were written by Chairman Mao. Officials were sent by Chairman Mao to find out how things were at the University. In 1952, colleges and universities throughout the country were reorganized. The University was considerably enlarged by its union with Furen University (the Catholic Furen University) and by having incorporated into it the Department of Education of the Chinese People's University and that of Yanjing University (Today's Beijing University.) Originally housed in a building in the centre of the city, it was moved to its new premises in Beitaipingzhuang which covers an area of 66 hectares (163. 1 acres). Since then, it has begun a new period of development for the University.

502

The University has at present thirteen departments. They are Departments of Education, Philosophy, Political Economy, Chinese Language and Literature, History, Mathematics, Physics, Astronomy, Chemistry, Biology, Geography, Physical Culture and Foreign Languages (divided into three sections: English, Russian and Japanese). It has over 1, 200 teachers and scientific workers, and many foreign teachers from various countries also take part in the teaching work. To promote international cultural and academic exchange and to strengthen its contact and friendship with the academic circles of other countries, the University sends some learned and competent teachers abroad every year for study or programme work or on a study tour, and scholars from other countries are invited to give lectures in the university.

The University has, in addition, several institutes, namely, the Institutes of Marxism-Leninism, Mao Zedong Thought, Education, Studies of Education in Foreign Countries, History, Soviet Literature, Low Energy Nuclear Physics, and Modern Educational Technology. It also has three affiliated middle schools, an experimental primary school, and an experimental infant school, where teachers and students of the University do practical work in their study of primary and secondary education. The University edits and publishes periodicals for national circulation such as Journal of Beijing Normal University (Natural Science), Mathematics Bulletin and Foreign Languages in Schools. The University library comprises over 2 million volumes (of which about 300, 000 are in foreign languages) and over 6, 000 periodicals (of which about 2, 400 are in foreign languages). The University Library is an important means of education for the whole country.

The University admits undergraduates, post graduates and research students. The whole course of study for undergraduates covers four years, and that for postgraduates or research students two to four years.

It has at present an enrolment of over 5, 000 undergraduates and over 300 postgraduates and research students. Admission is granted on the basis of merit, each candidate is judged by his performance in the examinations which are conducted under the government's centralized supervision, and by the criterion of all-round i. e. moral, intellectual, and physical development.

The successful candidates live and study in the University, and enjoy free tuition, board and lodging, and medical care. Apart from specialized subjects, the undergraduates are required to take courses such as Marxist- Leninist political economy, philosophy, the history of the Communist Party of China, pedagogic, English or Russian and physical training. Upon graduation, all the students are assigned jobs by the government.

Now, the teachers and students, administrative staff and workers of the University, united as one, study and work hard for the realization of China's modernization programme and for the training of qualified professionals and the production of fruits of scientific research.

The Central University of Nationalities
中央民族大学

China is a unitary and multi-national country. Apart from the Hans, there are 55 minority nationalities. They account for 8.41 percent of the total population. (according to 2000 census, population of Chinese mainland reached 1.26465303 billion, of whom 106.465303 million are minority people and are distributed widely over 50 to 60 percent of the total area of the country)

The Chinese government has paid much attention to training cadres from the minority people. Early in 1941, during the Anti-Japanese War, an institute of nationalities was set up in Yan'an to bring up minority cadres to serve the Chinese revolution. After 1949 a dozen and more such institutes were established in Beijing and elsewhere for training minority cadres.

The University was established in 1951 by the central government aiming to educate officials and various professionals for the country's 55 ethnic groups. Over the past 50 years, more than 60,000 officials and various academics have graduated from the University. Most of them have become part of the backbone of different fields in minority regions. Many of them have become top officials in central government and provincial governments.

On June 14, 2001, Premier Zhu Rongji made the remarks when he inspected the Central University of Nationalities, which was celebrating its 50th anniversary. He called for more efforts to develop education for national minorities, which is vital to promote the economic development in minority regions and strengthen the harmony of various nationalities in the country.

Beijing Language and Culture University
北京语言与文化大学

Founded in 1962 as the Higher Preparatory School for Foreign Students, the school was renamed Beijing Language Institute in 1964 by order of the late Premier Zhou Enlai. In June 1996, with the approval of the State Education Commission, the school was designated as Beijing Language and

Culture University. The school specializes in teaching foreign students Chinese language and culture and it is the only one of its kind. The school received its new name on September 10 in a ceremony to mark Teachers' Day. From 1962 to 1995 the University made remarkable achievements, turning out 40, 000 foreign students from 150 countries and regions. The University is reforming its programmes in an attempt to improve teaching standards, scientific research and efficient school management. The changes are designed to improve the University's overall strength and create a hub for teaching Chinese as a foreign language and popularizing Chinese culture by the year of 2000. It also tries to expand the education of the Chinese and Chinese culture, and to improve overseas co-operation. Today, about 4, 000 international students and 1, 000 Chinese are enrolled each year in the University, which is nicknamed the "mini-United Nations."

Haidian University
海淀走读大学

Established in 1984, Haidian University is a private higher vocational school assisted by both private and government cash. Students who graduate from here not only have a state-recognized adcemic qualification, but also have comprehensive professional skills and are capable of solving practical problems. Statistics show that graduates from the university have a high employment rate. Among 1, 000 who graduated in 1999, 97% were employed, the fifth highest number among Beijing's 66 universities and colleges. Among 1, 094 graduates in July 2000, 98% got jobs. Haidian University is highly praised as its graduates have shown remarkable professional competence. Some graduates have become key people in domestic enterprises, joint ventures and institutions. The Education Ministry has decided to make the University a pilot school for higher vocational education in China.

As few financial aid from private financial groups, the school's finances come mainly from tuition fees. The University has managed to be successful in the market economy by deepening educational reform and setting up a vigorous management system. It has set up specialist subjects to meet market demand and has invited excellent teachers to it in order to improve teaching quality. In the past, people thought high-tech belonged to research sectors, not to higher vocational fields, which basically aimed to train professionals in the industrial and economic fields. This caused a serious inconsistency between education and market demand for high-tech,

505

leading to a lack of competent high-tech professionals. Therefore, training these professionals is considered to be urgent in view of the coming knowledge-based economy.

When setting up specialist subjects, the University put an emphasis on three elements: one is location. Located in Zhongguancun High-tech Zone, the forefront of the knowledge-based economy, the school is required to produce more high-tech oriented professionals. The second element is that it must have a vision when deciding what to specialize in. the third is that the school must take China's entry into the World Trade Organization into consideration, when more international professionals will be wanted. Haidian University has set up its teaching programmes according to the needs of students' possible future posts. Higher vocational education demands that students possess more theoretical knowledge and use it to solve practical problems. In this way it is different to middle vocation education.

The University takes advantage of the high-density of colleges and universities in the surrounding area to enhance its teaching quality and to help the school's development. It uses both full-time and part-time teachers who are experienced and outstanding in their work. Among them more than 50 % are professors or associated professors from China's famous universities such as Qinghua University, Beijing University, People's University, Beijing Space University, University of Science and Technology and Beijing Language & Culture University.

Boasting 92 specialties, the University has 14,013 students, making it the largest higher vocational school. Its four campuses are respectively located in Xueyuan Lu, Yongfeng town, Weigongcun in Haidian District and Xihongmen Town in Daxing District, encompassing 26.68 hectares and a building area of 100,000 square metres. Since the founding of the university, more than 10,000 of its students have graduated and 18,000 trainees have been trained, all becoming important forces in Beijing's economic construction.

The University owns 12 training schools such as the College of Science and Engineering, the Economic Administration College, the Information College, the International Language and Culture College, the Biotech College, the Traditional Culture College, the Art College, the Application Technology College, the Modern Technological Service College and Zhongguancun Training School.

The University has established business relationships with foreign institutes of higher learning from the United States, Canada, Australia, Germany, Switzerland, Japan and the Netherlands. The academic credits of students are mutually recognized. Its enrolment scale and graduates' employment rate have ranked in the top ten among colleges and universities in Beijing.

Always exploring and reforming, the University constantly aims to improve its teaching quality and educational management. At present the University features:

1. A State recognized diploma, full-time classes in school. Besides choosing their own jobs after graduation, graduates may be recommended by the school and get employment guidance and assistance to find jobs.

2. Teachers are excellent and mainly from first-class universities such as Qinghua University and Beijing University.

3. Advanced management and good learning style. The content of each class is closely linked to every other class. Emphasis on combining theory with practical problem solving abilities.

4. Advanced market-oriented profession specialists, which are comprehensive and flexible in order to cater to the development of Beijing.

As the new millennium has approached, the University is marching towards its goal—a cradle of application professionals.

Education Reform Underlined

The central government is calling on education departments at all levels to improve education systems to create a healthier climate for students. Educators should instill students with the spirit of patriotism and collectivism, teaching children not only to excel academically, but also morally. President Jiang Zemin's recent speech called on society to pay more attention to education and youngsters' mental and physical health. Jiang's speech is the guiding line for the reform of the education system. Teachers should have excellent teaching skills and serve as moral examples for their students.

To ensure the healthy psychological development of students, educators should help promote family-based education to help parents educate their children. By ignoring students' psychological needs, improper education techniques used by some teachers and parents have put heavy pressure on children today. The education system should be reformed, allowing schools and parents to communicate more freely with children.

507

The Central Academy of Fine Arts
中央美术学院

Established in 1918, the Central Academy of Fine Arts (CAFA) is the first national art school in China. It was given its current name in 1950.

Currently it has departments and programmes in Chinese painting, oil painting, printmaking, mural painting, sculpture, design art, history, computer, art and folk art. For decades, the school was based in a small compound adjacent to downtown Beijing's Wangfujing area, which is now the city's most prosperous commercial area. The limited space and worn facilities of the downtown campus were not up to meeting the school's growing demand, which had enjoyed increasing international recognition. During the feverish economic boom of 1994, the school moved out of the downtown campus to give way to real and commercial estate development. The controversial move incited some debate over whether art should give way to the economy. The school found a temporary home in a factory in eastern Beijing's Jiuxianqiao. In September 2001, it moved its own new campus located in the northeastern part of the city's Huajiadi.

The reform of the art education system in an era of information and economic globalization seems more urgent. Like in the rest of the world, Chinese higher art education is facing new challenges as the future of art becomes more and more uncontrollable and the boundary of art more blurred. The Central Academy of Fine Arts used to focus mainly on pure art. In the future it should pay more attention to art design to meet the demands of modern society. After opening a design department, the central academy is planning to establish a design school in the near future, which will train both art designers and design administrators. Of course it is important to put the aesthetics of pure art into the education and practice of design. That should be an advantage of the central academy. Against the background of globalization, it is necessary to stress humanistic concern and to develop an art education system with Chinese characteristics. Veteran architect, Wu Liangyong 吴良墉, designed the new campus for the Central Academy of Fine Arts. Claimed to be the world's largest art school, the new campus is spread out more than 7.6 hectares (18.78 acres) of floor space. The first phase of the project included construction of offices, dormitory buildings, sports facilities, a library, a function hall, a sculpture and plaster gallery, an outdoor theatre, and a multimedia studio. Space has also been left for an art museum and a design school to be built during the second phase of construction. According to architect Wu Liangyong, the buildings have been designed in gray, a typical colour of traditional elegant design of the traditional Chinese academy, a higher-learning institution popular in the Song Dynasty (960-1279). Wu Liangyong, a professor, of Tsinghua University, wanted to combine Western and modern elements in his design since modern technology is such an integral part of artistic creation and education in the modern age. The sculpture studio is

508

equipped with mechanical lifting facilities for the production of large-sized sculptures. The design and photography departments are equipped with the most advanced computers, camera and other high-tech equipment.

Experimental Kindergarten in Fengtai District
丰台区实验幼儿园

Located in Fangzhuang, the Experimental Kindergarten in Fengtai District was established in 1984. The kindergarten takes in more than 200 children (their age ranges from 3 to 6 years old) who are divided into 6 classes, namely, junior class, middle class and senior class. It boasts 34 teachers, of whom 50 per cent graduated from Pre-School Department of Beijing Educational School, Art Education Department of Beijing Normal University, and Beijing Dance College, and some of the teachers have engaged in literature and art work for quite a number of years. The kindergarten offers day care and week care services. Some of the children stay during the day, and are picked by their parents after work or by their grandparents in the afternoon. All the children have three meals a day and take a nap after lunch. They have two periods in the morning and are free playing around in the afternoon.

Three teachers are assigned to each class, two in charge of teaching and one baby-sitting. They teach the Chinese language, music, physical culture, arithmetic and all sorts of games. All the kindergartens in Beijing are either run by the State or by factories, neighbourhood committees and townships, and a few of them are privately owned.

The kindergarten is equipped with such amenities as a clinic, a data room, and a dance room. Each class is equipped with piano, audio-visual equipment, and the kitchen is equipped with modern cooking machinery as well.

Currently, China boasts about 110,000 kindergartens with an enrolment of more than 18 million pre-school children.

There are 120 million migrant workers, most of whom are farmers, seeking jobs in urban areas around the country and school-age children are estimated to be 2.4 – 3.6 million. There are three choices for these children's education, to drop out of school, to go to local public schools after paying big sums of extra fees and to go to less expensive private schools for children of migrant workers. Most migrant workers choose the third option for their children. Governments in urban areas should attach due importance to offering migrant workers' children equal access to education with local children.

509

Shougang (Capital Iron and Steel) Group
首 钢 集 团

Located in western Beijing, the Shougang Group was set up in 1919 and has a history of over 80 years. Before 1949 it was called iron and steel plant, but produced only iron. The total output of pig iron turned out before 1949 came to 286,000 tons, equivalent to less a month's output now. Since the founding of the People's Republic of China, the group has undergone constant expansion and reconstruction, and has been gradually turned into a comparatively complete iron and steel complex. Besides steel and iron, Shougang is involved in 12 other sectors, such as mining, machinery, electronics, building, shipping, foreign trade and finance. The Shougang NEC Electronics Co Ltd, a joint venture between Shougang Group and Nippon Electric Co of Japan, manufactures more than 50 million large integrated circuits annually, which help China's electronic technology reach the sub-micron level. The Shougang Motorman Robot Co Ltd was the first of its kind in China to produce large industrial robots. A subsidiary of Shougang, which was established in Yantai of Shandong Province, manufactures air conditioners with advanced technology and equipment. The product was widely used in domestically produced sedans, light vehicles and mini cars. The group also actively purchases foreign economic co-operation. It has undertaken more than 10 technological engineering projects in India and Zimbabwe. Its bulk cargo fleet, with 1 million-ton capacity, has transported various kinds of cargo for more than 60 countries and regions and has docked in more than 160 ports around the world. For years, Shougang has made environmental affairs one of its top concerns under pressure from the government and the public. As the largest source of liquid and gas emissions in the capital, it has been urged to show responsibility towards the community's interests. The group invested 421 million yuan (US$51 million) into 156 environmental projects from 1995 to 1998. By August 1999, the group has assets of more than 58 billion yuan (US$7billion). Its annual sales income both at home and abroad stands at 35.4 billion yuan (US$4.3 billion).

As immensely large State-owned enterprise and a trial unit for modern enterprise systems, Shougang Group was listed in the top 10 iron and steel corporations in China with 8 million tons of steel production annually. It turns out more than 3 million tons of SG-brand wire rods and 2 million tons of screw steels annually, making up one-fourth of China's building steel products market. The group set up a modern enterprise system at the end of 1999, as planned by the Central Party Committee, the State Council and the Beijing municipal government. Shougang will give key emphasis on the development of high-tech industries, while not expanding the iron and steel production in the coming years.

Nowadays, the group has 83 member companies, operating in 18 provinces, municipalities and autonomous regions as well as the Hong Kong Special Administrative Region.

The group has a total of 211, 000 workers and staff members. Its total assets reached 57. 9 billion yuan (US$6. 76 billion).

More than 100 foreign artists staged performances for over 1, 000 Chinese workers of the Capital Iron and Steel Company (CISC) in late September 2001. Workers gathered to watch colourful song and dance performances by folk artists from seven countries, including France, Finland, Belgium and Malaysia. The clean environment, fresh air, and blooming flowers impressed the foreign artists at the premises of the company, which used to be one of the city's major polluters. The company has invested a total of 906 million yuan (US$109. 42 million) to carry out 189 environmental improvement projects over the past five years. In the next five years, the funds earmarked for this purpose will reach 1. 25 billion yuan (US$150. 9 million).

In 2001, thousands of visitors thronged to the Beijing Capital Iron and Steel Company, which has transformed itself a heavy polluter to a garden-style manufacturing plant. Visitors can see how iron and steel are produced in an environmentally sound process while enjoying the picturesque location of the factory. This is more persuasive than advertisements.

China Rehabilitation Research Centre
中国康复研究中心

Located in the Majiapu area outside the south 3rd Ring Road of Beijing, China Rehabilitation Research Centre covers an area of about 100, 000 square metres, of which 80, 000 square metres are for the construction of the first stage. Its construction started in April 1986, and was completed in October 1988. It went into full operation in April 1989.

The Centre is affiliated with the China Disabled Persons' Federation. It is a comprehensive research institute established in China. It provides disabled people with overall rehabilitation. Also it is an educational institution for training rehabilitation professionals for the nation.

The Centre has been identified as the key project of China Second Five Year Plan, and was established under the investment of the Chinese Government, international gratis aid, and the funds raised by the China Fund for the Handicapped. The domestic input was about 100 million yuan (US $27 million) At the same time, the Japanese Government donated 3. 88 billion yen (US$3 million), the former Federal Republic of Germany provided US$ 2. 36 million, and the Canadian Government offered technical assistance which valued US$1. 3 million. In addition, the Centre also received support from USA, Hong Kong, and others.

The Centre adheres to the principle of overall rehabilitation and takes clinical rehabilitation treatment as the basis of its research work. Combining modern education, society, and engineering, the Centre comprehensively utilizes the modern science, technology and traditional Chinese medicine for the rehabilitation of the handicapped.

It also conducts clinical, technical and basic research in order to explore and develop new methods to solve the typical and complicated problems manifested by its patients in the process of rehabilitation. It also hopes to investigate and develop new diagnostic techniques and therapeutic measures which are expected to be valuable to dissemination.

The Centre will take full advantage of overseas technical aids to develop appropriate training programme for rehabilitation professionals in this country.

The Centre will establish extensive professional contacts with its colleagues abroad in order to set up a stable information network which will disseminate information to the rehabilitation circle in the nation.

The Centre's main research projects in recent years are traumatic paraplegia, amputation, hemiplegia, cerebral palsy, and poliomyelitis sequel. However, its current research focus is on the rehabilitation of traumatic and hemiplegia from cerebral vascular accident.

512

The Centre wishes to establish broad contacts and co-operation with individuals and units of other countries and join hands to work together to contribute to the development of rehabilitation programmes for the handicapped both at home and abroad.

China National Children's Centre in Beijing
北京中国儿童中心

China National Children's Centre is located in Guanyuan in the western part of Beijing. The Centre covers an area of 80, 000 square metres, with a floor space of 9,900 square metres. It was opened to youngsters in 1982.

The Centre's main attraction is the "balloon bike" in the Science and Technology Hall. As a young enthusiast pedals, air is pumped into a balloon.

The harder you pedal the higher the balloon rises. Another fascination is the multi-image mirror. As you enter an equilateral room formed by three mirrors, you are greeted by a thousand faces, all your own! Such interesting activities arouses curiosity about science and technology.

South of the Science and Technology Hall is the Art Hall. On both sides of the corridor hang prize winning works from the national children's painting exhibition such as: "I am as Tall as the Sun," "Wu Song, the Tiger Slayer," and "My Family." These unique compositions are colorful and imaginative.

There is also a cinema with a seating capacity of 600. South of the Art Hall is a reading room with a collection of 10,000 volumes where youngsters can choose their favourite books.

West of the Art Hall is a "China Scenes" Room decorated by the Central Experimental Theatre and the China Opera and Ballet Theatre. Amidst melodious music, children find themselves under tall coconut palms on the banks of the Ten Thousand Spring River on Hainan Province or at the foot of Guilin's wonderful peaks near the Lijiang River. When they walk into the inner room, they enter a world of ice and snow. As they travel through "China Scenes" a sense of patriotism swells in their hearts.

Along with a table tennis room and a video-recorder room, there is an exercise room where a group of eight or nine-year-old children are often found "somersaulting" under a coach's guidance. In the background, a brilliant porcelain mural depicts these and other sports events.

A cockpit of a model plane is located in the courtyard. This is a gift from the people of Shanghai which gives the occupant a feeling soaring to the sky.

513

Hancunhe, a Model Among Villages
韩 村 河

Hancunhe's fame has spread far and wide. As a model village in the suburbs of Beijing, it is well-known in China for its profitable construction company and high-tech farming, which have brought high incomes to its residents. Through generations of experience, local villagers realized that traditional farming could only meet their most basic needs. To get ahead financially, they had to industrialize and provide better services to the market. In 1978, Hancunhe started its first business, a construction team working on contract projects. Then local villagers earned most of their incomes building homes and offices in the capital. That team developed into the Hancunhe Construction Group Corporation in 1994. The corporation which now consists of 22 firms with 96 construction teams and 12,000 workers, makes more than US$7 million a year. The village also puts strong emphasis on modern farming techniques. The village has invested 20 million yuan (US$2.41million) in developing a vegetable garden where foreign varieties of vegetables are grown. The garden is also open to tourists. An orderly place of clean streets and modern homes, the village has built more than 500 apartments and 20 multi-storey buildings. Villagers pay only 10 per cent of the cost, about 30,000 yuan (US$3,614), for housing under a six-year installment plan. The rest is subsidized by the construction company. In the residential area, entertainment and service facilities, such as parks, swimming pools, cinemas, supermarkets, banks and post offices, have also been built to enrich village life.

The Evergreen Township
四季青乡

The Evergreen Township is located in Beijing's western suburbs near the Summer Palace. It is named "Evergreen" because it supplies fresh vegetables to the city's residents all the year round.

The township covers an area of 72.6 square kilometres with 2,400 hectares of cultivated land. It has 13,000 households with 46,000 people, more than 26,000 of them are able bodied.

The township mainly grows vegetables, but also has a forestry programme, breeds livestock, does sideline production and runs a fishery. It is a joint agricultural, industrial and commercial undertaking.

The township is a collectively-owned unit which was merged from six advanced agricultural producers' co-operatives in 1958. To keep track of growing production the township has become the basic accounting unit since 1978.

Under the township there are eight vegetable growing production brigades, two grain production centres, an agricultural experimental centre, a farm machinery repair station, a fruit and forestry company, an animal husbandry and native produce company, an industrial company, a construction company and a service centre.

Responsibility System 责任制

The system of responsibility in agricultural production is a form of management adopted for the collective economy. It offers a diverse and flexible organization of labour and payment methods which are popular among the farmers. This system was widely introduced in China's rural areas after 1979.

The general practice is to reduce the size of the labour groups in the production team, which is currently the basic accounting unit in the countryside and which is in charge of 20 to 30 households. A group formed voluntarily by several peasant households, individual farmer households or individual farmer regularly make a contract to undertake a certain production task with the production team. According to the terms of the contract, the contractor has certain rights and responsibilities. He is paid for his actual work and will be awarded for over fulfilling production target and will compensate for reduced production, so as to ensure more pay for more work. The farmers are bound to honour the time set in the contract but is free to arrange his own work schedule. This represents a change from the customary practice of the past in which the team leader directed daily production and the system of payment by the day regardless of the amount or efficiency of the work.

Even though the system of fixing output quotas based on households or individuals has been adopted, the public ownership of the means of production will not change. The farmers only have the right to use, not to buy, sell or transfer, the land, farm machinery and farm tools, and irrigation facilities, owned by the production team. The production team can retain a certain amount of the accumulation funds and use them to develop production, improve public welfare and help those families with financial difficulties.

Since the Third Plenary Session of the 11th Party Central Committee held in December 1978, the Party has adopted flexible rural economic policies, raised the government buying prices of agricultural and sideline products, relegated decision making power for agriculture to the grass roots level and reaffirmed the principle of "to each according to his work" so as to overcome absolute equalitarianism.

Generally speaking, there are two different categories: the system of responsibility in output quotas; the system of responsibility in production task.

Between 1979 and 1983, China made the dramatic transition from an agriculture system dominated by large collective farms to a more mar-

515

ket-oriented agriculture dominated by small family-run farms. Under such a system, despite farmers having been given their own contracted land, the distribution of products was still collectively managed. The situation did not improve until the household contract responsibility system was introduced in the early 1980s. Under this system, farmers assumed the responsibility for their own grains or losses. Nonetheless, while the household responsibility system granted each family more autonomy in production and distribution, industrialization in the rural areas is still lagging behind.

Township 乡

The establishment of township to take over the governmental functions of communes began in 1982 in keeping with a decision of the fifth session of the Fifth National People's Congress. It is regarded as one of the two most important economic reforms in rural areas. The other is the production responsibility system based on the principle of more earnings for more work. By the end of 2001, 20, 374 towns and 19, 341 townships had been established as against 2, 176 towns and 52, 534 townships in 1979 throughout China.

People's Communes, totalling about 54, 000, were first introduced in 1958. They had been rural grassroots units of power ever since, integrating governmental administration with economic management. The integration weakened political and administrative functions of grass root units, even though communes did at a certain stage contribute to rural economic progress. The great changes in rural areas in the last few years made commune administrations ill suited to present production practices and harmful to further development of the rural economy. Before 1977, the communes tried to control everything, ranging from Communist Party organization matters to farming plans, but nothing was done effectively. Over concentration of power naturally led to economic stagnation.

516

The separation of political and economic functions has made it possible for the Party township committees to concentrate on purely Party affairs, ensuring that the Party's political policies are implemented. As a result, civil administration is becoming the township government's responsibility, while farmers are making their own production and marketing decisions.

A township government usually consists of about 40 persons holding office for a three-year term. They are mainly concerned with all round planning of the local economy, taxes, markets, disaster, relief, public security, welfare and health, culture, and education.

There are also about 700, 000 village committees in China. These are self-management mass organizations.

China now has about 127. 6 million hectares (315. 3 million acres) of cultivated land, according to a research report on the development and utilization of China's arable land resources. More than 80 million hectares (197.68 million acres) of China's 127.6 million hectares of farmland are not irrigated in 2001. The research was done by the institute of agricultural regions under the auspices of the Chinese Academy of Agricultural Sciences. The report predicts that China's grain output increased by 50 million tons by 1996, and 90 million tons by 2000 so long as the potential of cultivated land is tapped. The output of cotton and oil bearing crops is also likely to rise by a big margin by the end of this century.

The research gives a classification of arable land in the country based on topography and regional distribution and makes an overall evaluation and analysis on land quality and quantity. The area of low yield land is almost double that of high yield which is 28.5 million hectares, only one fifth of the total. The report studies problems in the utilization of land. For example water resources and labour are not being fully used, multiple cropping needs further improvement and some land is seriously polluted.

According to the report, China should strengthen the management of arable land by formulating appropriate laws and regulations. Meanwhile, it calls for intensive and careful cultivation on the limited land available together with exploration of new land in a planned and orderly manner.

Villagers' Committee 村民委员会

Like neighbourhood committees in urban areas, the villagers themselves control villagers' committees. Their major tasks are to set up committees for people's mediation, public security, public affairs and social services in their areas, to mediate civil disputes, to help maintain public order and to convey the residents' opinions and demands and made suggestions to the people's government. There are more than one million villagers' committees in China's rural areas. Villagers' committees, China's basic rural autonomous organization, are not only in charge of land management (land, though distributed to each household, is collectively-owned), but also responsible for education and the public health of the villagers.

Fangzhuang Residential District
方 庄 住 宅 区

Located seven kilometres southeast of central Tian'anmen Square, the Fangzhuang Residential District covers an area of 369 acres with a to-

517

tal floor space of 2. 66 million square metres. It is one of the largest residential projects in Beijing.

The district is divided into four parts by two thoroughfares crossing at its centre. Together with a circular road linking the four parts, they provide the traffic system for the district. The public service buildings such as shops, a post office, cinema and restaurants are arranged mainly along the west-east thoroughfare, while along the north-south road there is a 30-metre-wide green belt on each side. The green belts are designed to shield traffic noise from the residential buildings behind them. The northwest quarter is the district's public activities centre. It contains the main department store, the sports and cultural activity centre and the largest park in the district. On the north side of the northeastern quarter are two groups of residential buildings, 22 to 28 floors high, arranged in two serpentine lines. These two lines of high buildings have a large green space between them. The centre of the district's southwestern part is a circular area of green land surrounded by 10 to 25-storey apartment buildings in four groups. To the south of this area of green is a circular-shaped 30-storey apartment building. The ground floors of these buildings are all designed for public use.

The main elements of the district's southeastern section are four groups of tall apartment buildings. Each group contains five or six buildings linked by a large terrace. The terraces are, in fact, one-storey public service buildings and part of them are used as garages. These terraces and the roof gardens are linked by several overpasses. Residents can easily walk from one garden to another.

The district's circular drive connects the four parts' main green areas. Green areas make up 60 per cent of the district. Each of them projected 76, 000 residents, in 21, 300 households, has 2. 8 square metres of green land. The district's largest garden is in the northwest quarter with about 15 acres around the cultural activities centre. The central part of the garden is an area of curving lawn. Its northeastern part is dominated by Chinese flowering crabapples, while the southeast mainly boasts Chinese roses.

In the northeast quarter, the major green land between the two lines of tall apartment buildings covers about 20, 000 square metres. Its ground is naturally undulating and dominated by various ornamental trees such as pagoda trees, maple and ginkgo. They create changing scenes with different colours in different seasons.

The green environment is designed in various styles according to the buildings. Among the residential buildings, there are also some with two or three storeys, clustered with 10-storey buildings besides those with more than 20 storeys. Therefore, the green areas also vary, in a natural style, symmetrical style and courtyard style. In the southeastern quarter, trees are planted densely around the four roof gardens on the terraces. Shrubs and flowers dot the lawn.

The district also has its own public services. It has its own recreational and cultural activities' centre, stadium, hospital, a central heating system and gas pipes. Each of its quarters has its own middle schools, primary schools and kindergartens.

The apartments are divided into three standards according to their sizes, interior facilities, and decorations in order to suit the demands and incomes of different residents. Most of the apartments are designated for private purchase.

In the late half of 1998, the residential district was extended to the east, and another 86 hectares (215 acres) of land is included into the district, making a total of 584 acres of land in the district. It has become the largest residential district in Asia.

Beijing-based Fangzhuang Sports Park, designed by Beijing Municipal Development Group, opened to the public on December 22, 2000. It is the first large sports park building in the district in Beijing. The park, in the south of the city, encompasses 30, 000 square metres and includes an indoor tennis court, two basketball courts, a 6-line track, a football field, and a gymnasium. The park was built in answer to the National Fitness Programme which urges Chinese citizens to improve their health.

Neighbourhood Committees 街道委员会

China's neighbourhood committees, urban counterparts to the villagers' committees, have become deeply rooted since their 1952 founding.

In Beijing alone, there are more than 3, 200 such committees, with about 25, 000 officially appointed workers. Early in 1954, two years after the first neighbourhood committee was set up in China, the State promulgated a regulation ensuring the legal position of the committees. The Constitution of the People's Republic of China passed in 1982 reiterated the fact that neighbourhood committees are the mass organizations of self-management at the grass-roots level.

Since their birth, the committees have contributed to society by mediating civil disputes, helping to maintain public order, conveying residents' opinions and demands, and making suggestions to the people's government.

In accordance with these functions, sub-committees for public security, welfare, people's mediation, family planning, and public sanitation have been set up. One distinguished achievement of such committees is people's mediation, in which family or neighbourhood disputes are mediated to avoid legal action. These committees are also credited with the cracking down on criminal cases. In addition, the committees offer various kinds of services to ease the problems of residents in making clothes, repairing bikes, and looking after children.

Beijing Arts and Crafts Factory
北京工艺美术工厂

The Beijing Arts and Crafts Factory is a multiple product handicraft factory in Beijing. It was built in 1960. At present, the factory has a staff of 1,300, of whom 700 are women. The main products of the factory are traditional Chinese crafts like jade carving, ivory carving, lacquerware carving, cloisonné, dough figurines and wax ware in a dozen or so varieties. In addition, they also produce wooden stands and brocade caskets for their art products. The products are mainly for export and are sold to more than ninety countries and regions in the world.

Handicraft art in China has a long tradition. The carving of jade and ivory dates back to 3,000 years ago. While cloisonnè has a history of more than 500 years.

Before 1949, handicraft art was done by individual craftsmen using backward methods. Life was so hard for them that their art was in a state of stagnation in 1948. After 1949, under the leadership of the Party and the people's government, small co-operatives were organized in 1952 and handicraft art was restored and developed rapidly. Later, the factory was formed by the amalgamation of three co-operatives. They have inherited, reformed and developed the traditional arts, giving them new life and creating a large variety of products. For example, the vase which depicts the development of China's steel industry follows the design of the Ming and Qing dynasties. Handicrafts showing China's socialist construction or friendship with the people of other countries have also been produced, such as "The Nanjing Yangtze River Bridge," "The Launching of a 10,000 Ton Freighter," "The Flowers of Friendship Bloom Among Table Tennis Players," and "A Tour to the Great Wall." They are all large ivory carvings. "A Tour to the Great Wall" depicts an excursion of the foreign friends to the Great Wall. It symbolizes that the friendship between the Chinese people and people of the world is as everlasting as the Great Wall.

520

Several pieces are based on famous buildings in the world, such as the Eiffel Tower in Paris, the Pyramids of Egypt, the Korean Qianlima and the Leaning Tower of Pisa. Sometimes, they combine the skills of different kinds of arts in a single item. For instance, "The Dragon and Flower Incense Burner" is a combination of filigree, jade and lacquer carving on the main body of a cloisonne article. They have made some progress, yet there are still problems to be tackled. The quality of some of their products is not up to the standard and the artistry needs to be improved. To serve the people of China and the world better, they are doing their best to make further improvements based on the comments and suggestions from customers both at home and abroad.

Beijing Cloisonné Factory
北京景泰蓝厂

Cloisonné is a famous traditional enamel ware, known as the "Blue of Jingtai" in China, with a history of over 500 years. It was so called because "blue" was the typical colour used for enameling and "Jingtai" was the reign title of the 7th Ming Emperor. Enamel ware became very popular during the emperor's reign (AD 1450-AD 1456). There is a great variety of products, such as vase, jar, bowl, plate, box and ashtray. They are brilliant in colors and splendid in design. Cloisonne is one of the famous arts and crafts of Beijing.

The making of cloisonné requires rather elaborate and complicated processes; base hammering, copper strip inlay, soldering, enamel filling, enamel firing, polishing and gilding. The products are featured by excellent quality. The skill and workmanship have been handed down from the Ming Dynasty. Quite a number of new varieties have been created. It enjoys a high reputation both at home and abroad. They are mostly for export.

Built in 1956, the cloisonné factory is the biggest in China with 6 workshops and 1, 800 workers. They work 5 days a week and 8 hours a day, and enjoy free medical treatment. Men retire at the age of 60, women at 55. After retirement, they can get a pension according to their working age. The factory runs a kindergarten and a nursery.

The "Beijing Enamel Brand" cloisonné wares are made in this factory. They take up over 70 percent of cloisonné wares produced in China. With a registered trade mark Jingfa, the products won an honorable title of renowned product in Beijing in 1975. They were conferred the title of "top

521

quality product" by the Ministry of Light Industry in 1979, and again won
the prize of the National Hundred Flower Golden Cup in 1981. In the factory there is a gift shop for visitors.

Cloisonné-Making 景泰蓝制作

The first step is body making. The material used for making the body is
copper, because copper is easily hammered and stretched. This step requires a sound judgement in shaping and uniformity of thickness and
weight. It is in fact the work of the copper smith. The only difference is
that when an article is well shaped, the copper smith's work is finished,
whereas the cloisonné craftsman's work is just on the start.

The second step is filigree soldering. This step requires great care and
high creativeness. The artisan adheres copper strips onto the body. These
strips are of 1/16 inch in diameter and of lengths as the artisan desires.
The strips or filigree thus adhered make up a complicated but complete
pattern. The artisan has a blueprint in mind and he can make full use of
his experience, imagination and aesthetic view in setting the copper strips
on the body.

The third step is to apply the color which is known as enamel filling.
The color or enamel is like the glaze on ceramics. It is called *falang*. Its
basic elements are boric acid, saltpeter and alkaline. Due to the difference
in the minerals added, the color differs accordingly. Usually one with
much iron will turn grey, with uranium, yellow, with chromium, green,
with zinc, white, with bronze, blue, with gold or iodine, red. In time of
filling, all the colors, ground beforehand into minute powder and contained
in plates, are placed in front of the workers and are then applied to the little compartments separated by filigree.

The fourth step is enamel firing. This is done by putting the article,
with its enamel fillings, to the crucible. After a short moment, the copper
body will turn red. But after firing, the enamel in the little compartment
will sink down a bit. That will require a refilling. This process will go on
repeatedly until the little compartments are finally filled.

The fifth step is polishing. The first polish is with energy. Its aim is to
make the filigree and the filled compartments even. The whole piece is a-
gain put to fire. Polish once more with a whet stone. Finally, use a piece
of hard carbon to polish again so as to obtain some luster on the surface of
the article.

The sixth step is gilding. This is done by placing the article in fluid of
gold or silver. Add electric current. The exposed parts of the filigree and
the metal fringes of the article will be smoothly and evenly gilded.

522

After that, the metal part of the article will not get rusty. Then the article will again undergo another electroplating and a slight polish.

Beijing Carpet Factory
北 京 地 毯 厂

Beijing Carpet Factory has been developed into what it is today from a carpet producers' cooperative. It had only a few scores of workers in the early years after 1949. The factory now has over 2, 100 workers and staff members, of whom 55 per cent are women. It produces more than 40 varieties of products, including carpets of traditional Beijing style, artistic designs and floral patterns.

The workers and staff members of the factory have made great efforts to inherit and develop the traditional arts in carpet weaving. At the same time, they have renovated and replaced some old equipment and technique, which were low in working efficiency but high in labour intensity, such as cleansing and dyeing of woolen yarn. They have also replaced hand-operated scissors. All this has greatly improved the quality of the products and the efficiency in production.

Beijing Carpets 北京地毯

China is famous for carpet making which dates back to about 3, 000 years ago. The people of Beijing learned this craft from the Tibetans in the Qing Dynasty. The demand for Tibetan carpets was so pressing that more and more craftsmen came to the capital city and settled down. Thus the carpet industry flourished.

Of all the carpets made in Beijing, the "Temple of Heaven" brand carpets are among those highly acclaimed in the world market. Their craftsmanship and designs are superb and outstanding due to the craftsmen's great efforts to combine traditional folk art with modern technology.

Nowadays, Beijing produces many carpets, each of which has its own feature both in design and quality. Carpets with motifs symbolizing Happiness and Longevity are always popular. There are those with distinctive, mythical motifs such as dragons, phoenixes and unicorns, while some others are modelled after ancient Buddhist themes.

In 1903, Beijing carpets won the first prize in the International Exposition held in the United States for the novelty of their designs, fine craftsmanship as well as durability. At present, Beijing is still upholding this fine tradition.

523

The art of carpet-making is now being further perfected by new designs and ever-improving technology in spinning, dyeing, weaving, cutting and washing.

Carpet-Making 地毯制作

There are three steps in carpet making: designing, weaving, shearing and clipping.

Designing: Pattern designing of a carpet has a direct bearing on the quality and value of the product. Chinese carpet designs are mainly drawn from the decorative patterns in architecture, that is the patterns on beams and window frames. Things in nature inspire some designs. The latter is typified by the Chinese floral pattern. In general, such design patterns confirm to the ideas and style of Chinese classical art. Contemporary ideas have found their way into carpet designing in recent years, adding to the artistic value of Chinese carpets.

Weaving: Wool must be carefully selected, classified, combed and rid of any impurity before it is spun into yarn. The yarn is then dyed in different colors as dictated by the design patterns. Delicate workmanship is needed for the weaving process. A carpet is usually hand-done by four workers weaving in unison. They must weave uniformly to ensure that the pattern and shape of the carpet come out evenly and undistorted. These carefully hand-done carpets can stand wear and tear. They can be washed and exposed to sunlight without fear of its colours fading.

Shearing and Clipping: Once woven, a carpet is sheared and clipped so that the design pattern stands out in relief. It is then bathed in a special solution and dried, which adds to the lustre of the carpet.

524

The Capital Gymnasium
首 都 体 育 馆

The Capital Gymnasium is the largest gymnasium in China. It was begun in May 1966, and was finished and opened to the public in March 1968. It is 122 metres long, 107 metres wide and 28. 8 metres high, with a total floor space of 30, 000 square metres. The horizontal steel frame is 99 by 122 metres. There are in the gymnasium a competition hall, three training rooms and a number of lobbies for spectators.

The competition hall is 88 metres long and 40 metres wide. Table tennis, badminton, basketball, volleyball and gymnastic contests can be held and ice hockey and skating performances can be organized all the year round. It is big enough to hold 24 ping-pong tables and is installed with a large automatic scoreboard.

There are more than 18, 000 seats; some of which are movable or partly movable and can slide inward to enlarge the sporting ground. In the gymnasium there are also press rooms, rooms for radio and television transmission and international telephone booths, through which sports news can be promptly conveyed throughout China and to other parts of the world. It was designed and built by the Beijing Municipal Architectural Design Institute.

Chaoyang Gymnasium
朝 阳 体 育 馆

Elliptical in shape, the Chaoyang Gymnasium is 96 metres long and 66 metres wide. It was built for the volleyball games in 1990 Asian Games. Covering an area of 3. 5 acres, its steel cable supported roof has two arching bridges suspended from two thick steel cables. The building's overall look is somewhat like a liner sailing under a suspension bridge.

The gymnasium can hold an audience of 3, 200. And its inside ground level is 4. 5 metres below ground level. Skylights here create daylight conditions. After the Asian Games, the gymnasium is used for basketball, badminton, ping-pong and seven person handball matches. Apart from these, the gymnasium can also host various kinds of performances.

Beijing Friendship Store
北京友谊商店

Beijing Friendship Store, with various kinds of goods and good service, is located in Jianguomenwai Street. Ever since the store started business, it has had the honor of receiving the heads of the governments, diplomats in China, non-governmental bodies, tourists, overseas Chinese, compatriots from Taiwan, Hong Kong and Macao. Thus the store has helped to expand exchanges and enhance friendship between the Chinese people and the people of other countries. It has also helped the overseas Chinese to get a deeper understanding of New China.

Available in the store are jewelry, precious stones, ivory and jade carvings, ceramics, carpets and rugs, embroideries and paintings, carved lacquerware, cloisonné, the four treasures of the study, writing brush, ink stick, ink slab and paper ancient-style furniture, fur coats, garments,

525

shoes and hats, cotton and woolen goods, silk articles, hand-drawn table cloths, knitwears, cosmetics, general merchandise, cigarettes, wines, canned food, tremella, ginseng, deer antlers, Chinese patent medicine, and imported articles, totalling more than 90,000 kinds.

Among the above, there are some rare treasures such as porcelain of Jingdezhen, jewelry of Beijing, silk product of Suzhou, tea of Fujian, ginseng of Northeast China, glossy ganoderma of Mount Taishan, and Cordyceps sinensis of Sichuan.

Various kinds of handicraft articles with motif of scenic spots, historical sites and Chinese stories, fairy tales and pictures with the meaning of good luck bring people the artistic treat of beauty. For the convenience of customers, the store has had more than 30 services added these years.

The main services are:

1. International and domestic consignment business: the store renders postal services, consignment by sea, land and air, and sees to insurance formalities.

2. Purchase by post: if the guest wishes to purchase from the store, just write to the store and the store will do its best to meet his or her requirements.

3. Processing and repairing: to process and repair different kinds of jewelry according to the Customer's requirements.

4. Currency exchange: foreign currencies can be changed right at the store for your convenience.

5. Services of garments-making, laundry, dyeing and purchase.

6. For customers' refreshments, Coffee & Cold Drink Hall in the store serves perfectly cold and hot drinks and pastries.

To cope with the development of tourist industry in China, and for the convenience of customers, the store will expand its business scope so as to supply customers with even more commodities of novel and excellent texture.

Beijing Antique Store
北 京 古 玩 店

Liulichang Street has its name originated from the kilns that had been set up to make glazed tiles and bricks in the 13th to 17th centuries when the Yuan (1279-1368) and Ming (1368-1644) dynasties had their respective capital built in Beijing. By the time of the mid-18th century during the reign of Emperor Qianlong of the Qing Dynasty (1644-1911), the street,

Beijing Antique Store 北京古玩店

Name	Branch
Bogu Zhai 博古斋	Original Chinese Calligraphy & Paintings 63 East Liulichang Tel: 6303-0146
Moyuan Ge 墨缘阁	Modern Chinese Calligraphy & Paintings 61 East Liulichang Tel: 6303 – 3338
Hongguang Ge 虹光阁	Original Chinese Calligraphy & Paintings 96 East Liulichang Tel: 6303-1951
Yungu Zhai 韵古斋	Original Bronzes, Stones & Ceramics 80 East Liulichang Tel: 6303-0954
Cuizhen Zhai 萃珍斋	Bronzes, Stones & Ceramics 17 West Liulichang Tel: 6303-0954
Yunyu Zhai 韫玉斋	Imitated Antiques 108 East Liulichang Tel: 6303-3338
Zhenhuan Ge 振寰阁	Bronzes, Stones & Other Artifacts 70 East Liulichang Tel: 6303-0004
Dunhua Zhai 敦华斋	Original Ceramics 66 East Liulichang Tel: 6303-3848
Qingyun Tang 庆云堂	Original Stone Rubbings 20 West Liulichang Tel: 6303-1209
Guanfu Zhai 观复斋	Original Stone Rubbings 22 West Liulichang Tel: 6303-0023
Yueya Tang 悦雅堂	Antique Export Branch under Special License 90 East Liulichang Tel: 6303-0020

lined with curio, calligraphy and painting stores became prosperous. Busy with cultural activities during the past 200 years, this old street has taken on a completely new look after reconstruction and looks more splendid.

Beijing Antique Store is located right here in this very ancient cultural street. The store consists of eleven branch shops, Bogu Zhai, Moyuan Ge & Hongguang Ge handle original works of calligraphy and paintings by famous Chinese scholars and painters of different times and embroideries as well; Yungu Zhai, Cuizhen Zhai, Yunyu Zhai, Zhenhuan Ge & Dunhua Zhai deal mainly in bronzes, stones, ceramics and cloisonné, as well as ivory, wood and bamboo carvings, etc.; Qingyun Tang & Guanfu Zhai sell rubbings from different dynasties, paper, writing brushes, ink stones and ink sticks of different times, and seals made by famous seal engravers; Yueya Tang operates as the country's exclusive licensed dealer of the most ancient works of art.

For the convenience of the customers, the store provides foreign exchange, packing, shipping and mail services. Simple and convenient are

527

the processes involved.

Business Lines 营业范围

Original Ceramics; Ancient Bronze, Cloisonné & Enamel Wares; Gold, Silver & Lacquer Wares; Ancient Coins; Jadeite, Jade and Glass Wares; Carvings of Bamboo, Wood & Ivory, Hardwood Furniture; Ancient & Modern Chinese Calligraphy & Paintings; Silk Tapestry and Embroidery; Round and Folding Fans; Stone Rubbings, Seals and Seal Imprints; Paper, Brushes, Ink Sticks and Ink Stones, etc.

Jigu Ge 汲古阁

"Jigu Ge" in Beijing is a shop with more than 50 years' experience in the reproduction of antiques and historical relics for export and selling to tourists.

At "Jigu Ge," there are many experts in restoring historical relics and in making reproductions, with their excellent traditional Chinese expertise. They also provide restoration and reproduction services to museums in China and overseas for historical relics like bronze wares, earthenwares, stone rubbings, ancient murals, imitations of ancient paintings, high quality ink stones, etc.

The products are sold to countries in Asia, Europe, Africa, America and Australia. Because of the vivid appearance and reasonable prices, the products have gained popularity in these countries.

The store provides services of packing and shipping.

Beijing Economic and Technological Development Area (BDA)
北京经济技术开发区

528

Located near the entrance of the Beijing-Tianjin-Tanggu Expressway, the Beijing Economic and Technological Development Area (BDA) is an international, standard industrial park. It is 7 kilometres away from the city centre and 16.5 kilometres from Tian'anmen Square. It is also just a 25 minutes drive from the Beijing Capital International Airport and a 90 minutes drive to Tanggu Port. It is an ideal place to invest and develop.

BDA can take advantages of large cities' resources such as talent, information, capital and market because of its easy access to the city centre. Meanwhile it does not have as much pollution and traffic as those in the city centre. However, investors can still enjoy the most favourable policies because BDA is one of the State-level economic and technology development zones. For years, BDA has given key emphasis to ecological and sustainable development of the area, which enables the area's environment to be better than city suburbs and centre. More than 114,000 trees, bushes and flowers have been planted in the area, which help create fresh air and a clean environment. Greenery covers one-third of BDA's total area. The first phase of BDA covers 15 square kilometres. A total of 7.3 billion yuan (US $879 million) has been invested in the area's fixed assets, which includes 2 billion yuan (US$240 million) invested in land development and public facilities. The relatively perfect public facilities have created favorable conditions for luring foreign investments. So far, BDA has finished the construction of 930,000 square metres of buildings, 45 kilometres of roads and 208 kilometres of pipes. It has also finished construction of a power substation, a telecom bureau, water supply system and gas and heating systems. Public facilities such as a post office, international hospital, restaurants and a golf course have been completed and in work. BDA has the right to approve the establishment of firms with registered capital of less than US$30 million. Approximately 10 bureaux, including the planning bureau, land bureau, construction bureau and economic development bureau, have been established in the area. The customs office, finance department, taxation bureau, public security bureau, banks and other relative departments have also set up branches in the area.

Beijing First Social Welfare Institution / Beijing Senile Illness Hospital
北京市第一福利院 / 北京市老年病医院

Beijing First Social Welfare Institution, an institute unit set up by Beijing Municipal Government for the senior citizens, is the first senile illness hospital bringing the medical treatment, recuperation, rehabilitation into an integral whole which was approved by Beijing Public health Bureau. In 1994, it was nominated as one of the first lot of "Second Grade" welfare institutional unit by the Ministry of Civil Affairs.

Established formally on May 3, 1988, the institution now covers a construction area of 20,000 square metres (including the senility medical recovery building) and owns 450 bed spaces. It mainly accepts the single senior citizens living in Beijing, who have difficulties in living out their lives at home. The aged people from Hong Kong, Macao, Taiwan, overseas Chinese and other patients with various senile illnesses are being welcomed as well.

Located in a quiet and tasteful environment shaded by trees, perfuming flowers and plants, the institution is divided into rehabilitation zone, medical zone, and security zone. The institution owns fairly adequate medical recovery facility and has a group of medical staff with therapy of combining traditional Chinese and Western medicine. The institution is also equipped with treatment room, painting and calligraphy room, reading room, entertainment room for the seniors enjoying themselves and recovering, a full set of logistic care system.

Adhering to the principle of laying equal stress on both recovery and medical treatment, the institution devotes evey effort to the study and treatment of the senile illness. Experienced with many years of clinical practice, it continues approaching the new technology and method of curing difficult and complicated senile illness through activities of specialists' consultation, academic exchanges and science study item. It has accumulated the experiences in respect of treatment, nursing and recuperation of the senile cardiovascular diseases and obtained curative effect.

To serve the seniors wholeheartedly is the aim of the welfare institution. "Love, patience, care, enthusiasm, and consideration" is the service policy of the institution. It keeps up the professional spirit of adoration, contribution, unity, enterprise, and carries out standard management, superior service to create an area of long-life paradise for the older people to convalesce, cure, enjoy, and play a role.

TRAVEL INFORMATION

第五部分　旅游资讯

Dining

珍馐美味

Beijing Regional Celebrated Cuisines
北京著名的地方风味

Chinese cuisine is renowned all over the world for its appearance, aroma, and flavour. Its unique style of preparation, cooking and presentation can be traced to the beginnings of Chinese history more than 5,000 years ago. As the capital of China for Jin, Yuan, Ming and Qing dynasties (1115-1911), Beijing developed its own unique cuisine incorporating the best features of different regional styles. Beijing cuisine reached its present form in the imperial kitchens of the Qing Dynasty (1644-1911). Among the most famous dishes or styles which found their way from the imperial court to public restaurants are Court Cuisine, Beijing Roast Duck, Tan Cuisine, Mongolian Hot Pot, and Barbecued Meat.

Court Cuisine 宫廷菜肴

Court Cuisine, as the name suggests, consists of dishes once prepared exclusively for the imperial family. Every dynasty in Chinese history had an "imperial kitchen" to prepare meals for the emperor and his consorts. The dishes were not only meticulously prepared, but also included rare and expensive foodstuffs, such as bear's paws, birds' nests, sharksfins, venison, sea cucumbers, duck webs and other delicacies of land and sea. The Court Cuisine of today is based on the dishes prepared by the Qing imperial kitchens but further developed ever since.

There are several restaurants in Beijing where it is available: The "Imitation Imperial" Restaurant in Beihai Park, and the Pavilion for Listening to Orioles Restaurant in the Summer Palace and some other restaurants featuring the court cuisine.

Fangshan (Imitation Imperial) Restaurant is located on Qionghua Islet with a hill behind and a lake in front. You enter Beihai Park by the east gate, cross a bridge, turn right and walk along the lakeside for 5 minutes, you will get to the restaurant. The restaurant offers a picturesque view. There are 11 halls, large and small, which can accommodate a total of 250 people. All the dishes and desserts are imitations of imperial cuisine. Its dishes are carefully prepared and beautifully served. The taste is subtle and clear. The textures are crisp and tender. The restaurant is also famous for its delicate pastries, including pea flour cakes, kidney bean flour rolls, miniature corn cakes and sesame seed buns with minced meat filling. These pastries originated among the ordinary people of Beijing and there are interesting stories about how they were introduced to the Qing court. For instance, the corn cakes found their way into the court in 1900 when the Allied Forced of Eight Imperialist Powers occupied Beijing. On her flight to Xi' an, 1, 200 kilometres by railway, Empress Dowager Cixi was so hungry that she ate a corn cake, a staple food much that upon her return to Beijing she ordered the imperial kitchen to make corn cakes for her. But the chefs, afraid that ordinary cakes might be too rough for Cixi to eat, made miniature cakes with finely-ground corn flour and white sugar instead.

The Pavilion for Listening to Orioles Restaurant used to be a theatre in the Summer Palace where the Empress Dowager used to enjoy opera and music. The name implies that the imperial music was as beautiful as the singing of orioles. After 1949, it was changed to a restaurant. It is divided into eight dining rooms of various sizes in two courtyards and can seat up to 500 customers at one time. During busy season, there are three sittings for lunch in the restaurant: 11: 30 am; 12: 40 pm; 13: 30 pm.

The menu is based on the Imperial Cuisine, and the experienced chefs can prepare more than 300 dishes and pastries from the Ming and Qing imperial recipes.

Beijing Roast Duck 北京烤鸭

Beijing Roast Duck is prepared from specially-bred Beijing crammed duck with a unique roasting process which gives it a perfect combination of colour, aroma and taste, a crisp thin skin, and a mouth-melting, and delicious flavour.

Beijing Roast Duck dates back 300 years, and originated in the imperial kitchens of Jingling (today's Nanjing).

534

Beijing's first restaurant which served roast duck was started by Yang Quanren, who arrived in Beijing from nearby Ji County, Hebei Province, to establish a business in 1835. Yang opened a stall to sell roast chickens and ducks on Beijing's Qianmen (Front Gate) Street during the mid-19th century. On July 18, 1864, he had saved enough money to buy a grocery at Number 24 Roushi(Meat Market) Street—today, the busy avenue that stretches south from Qianmen. Calling his shop Quanjude (Repository of All Virtues), Yang began to sell ducks he roasted in a special hanging oven that had formerly been used in the palace kitchen to cook whole piglets. His process involved filling the dressed ducks with boiling water, tying them tightly with sorghum fibres, and then hanging them to roast. during the cooking, they were constantly roasted, resulting in a dish with crisp skin, tender and delicious meat.

On the side he offered stir-fried duck liver, a steamed egg custard made with duck fat and a duck bone soup. Customers began to flock in and Yang soon set up a restaurant on the site. This technique was invented by an imperial kitchen chef more than 600 years ago.

Before 1949, Beijing Roast Duck was an expensive dish enjoyed only by the rich. Today's Beijing duck restaurants are crowded with ordinary people every day.

In 1954, a branch was opened in Xidan. Another branch started in 1959 at Shuaifuyuan just off the Wangfujing Street. The original restaurant was also expanded, but was still not large enough to cater to all those insisted on eating Beijing Roast Duck. To meet the demand, a seven-storey building covering an area of 15,000 square metres was constructed at Hepingmen on West Qianmen Street, which opened for business in May 1979. The restaurant has 41 dining halls of varying sizes and can seat up to 3,000 customers at a time. The banquet hall can accommodate 400 people, and about 1,000 roast ducks are served each day. Hepingmen is the first restaurant in China which serves only one main dish to occupy a seven-storey building.

The chefs in the restaurant can make more than 30 kinds of cold dishes and 50 hot dishes—all using ducks as the main ingredient. The ovens for roasting the ducks have changed from the old hanging type to gas, electric and even automatic machines. Toady, a duck order can be roasted automatically in several minutes. The ducks are now sold in halves, thirds or even smaller quantities.

There are many Beijing Roast Duck restaurants in the major cities of the world, such as Belgrade, Tokyo, London, New York, Los Angeles, San Francisco, Indonesia, Singapore and Hong Kong. But Beijing Roast Duck is the real McCoy in Beijing because the ducks themselves are raised in a special way on the outskirts of the Capital City.

Beijing Duck is roasted in a specially constructed oven, which is square outside, has a crescent-shaped door, and is round inside, where there are two racks for hanging the ducks for roasting. Underneath is the fire pit where hardwood such as date, peach and pear are used as fuel. These give plenty of heat with little smoke and impart a fruity fragrance.

The duck is basically roasted by the heat reflected through the oven to the roof and sides of the oven. This way of roasting makes the outside well-done and the inside tender, the skin crisp, and meat savoury.

To prepare the duck for roasting, the stomach is emptied and air pumped in. Then it is brushed with a maltose solution and dried in an airy place. The carcass is plugged, half-filled with hot water; the duck is then ready to be hung for roasting. The crucial point of roasting is the fire and timing. Too short a time means that the duck is underdone and the skin browned unevenly; too long a time makes the meat tough and the skin dry. Experienced chefs are able to regulate the heat and turn each duck to maintain the right temperature. Generally speaking, veteran chefs use their experience to watch colour, temperature and timing to accurately judge the degree of doneness. When the duck has turned golden brown, with the gravy inside becoming clear and transparent, it means it is ready to serve. It takes 5 years for chefs to learn to roast the duck, but 15 years to master the technique which is today a special branch of cookery science in China.

Beijing Roast Duck is one of the famous specialties in the city. It is prepared from a 2-month-old white Beijing Duck. When it is roasted and steamed for about 45 minutes, the duck is ready for serving, the whole duck is carried to the table on a platter, and the chef will often make an appearance to display his culinary creation. The skin is cut into small pieces, which are then served to the guests. The slices of golden skin are eaten by wrapping them inside thin pancakes or in sesame cakes which are dipped in a sauce of chopped scallions.

Tan Cuisine 谭家菜

Tan Cuisine originated in the household of Tan Zongjun, a bureaucrat of the late Qing Dynasty. Very particular about their food and drink, Tan Zongjun and his son Tan Zhuangqing would pay high fees to hire skilled chefs to cook at their home. In this way the Tan family created a cuisine based on Guangdong cuisine, one that incorporates the best elements of many other regional styles. The private dinner parties given at the Tan house gradually made their cuisine famous. After the fall of the Qing Dynasty, the then impoverished Tan opened a small restaurant, and thus Tan dishes found their way into society and became a Beijing specialty and an element of home-style cooking in Beijing households.

Tan Cuisine has three main features which we may note as follows:

1. Balance of sweet and salty. The cuisine is both sweet and salty, balancing northern and southern styles. There is a saying that "southerners have a sweet tooth, and northerners crave salt," but Tan dishes manage to satisfy both.

2. Soft cooking. The dishes are well-cooked, well-flavoured and soft and so are considered suitable for older people as well as those much younger.

3. Purity of natural ingredients. This type of cooking pays special attention to the natural flavours of the ingredients. Therefore, gourmet powder

536

and other such seasoning are rarely used. Two of the most popular dishes in Tan Cuisine are steamed chicken with mushrooms and duck with crab meat.

At present, Tan Cuisine is only offered at the Beijing Hotel, and Tan Mansion Restaurant (谭府大酒家)at the Xizhimen Overpass.

Mutton Hot Pot 涮羊肉

Mutton Hot Pot (a. k. a. Rinsed Mutton) is a Muslim specialty. All the year round, the family, relatives, and friends would gather round the fire and eat in intimacy and warmth. It has now spread to people of all nationalities including foreign diplomats and overseas visitors in Beijing and become one of the capital's most celebrated dishes. The hot pot used to be a brass pot with a wide outer rim around a chimney and a charcoal-burner underneath. Nowadays electric pot is used. Water containing mushrooms and dried shrimps is boiled in a pot. Thin pieces of raw mutton are cooked with chopsticks in a self-service pot of boiling water. Diners dip thin slices of raw mutton into the water, where the meat cooks rapidly. The cooked slices are then dipped into a sauce. This cooking method ensures that the meat is both tender, and tasty. Cabbage, noodles and pea starch noodles are gradually added to the boiling water, which becomes a very rich broth drunk at the end of the meal.

The piquant sauce is individually mixed by each diner from an array of more than a dozen condiments such as sesame paste, glutinous rice wine or Shaoxing (Zhejiang Province) rice wine, fermented (preserved) bean curd, salted Chinese chive-flowers, soy sauce, chili oil (paste), shrimp sauce (paste), rice vinegar, chopped chives (green onion), sesame oil, salt, sweet pickled garlic, salted leek buds, chopped scallions, flower-pepper oil and minced coriander; mixed together, often with the addition of a raw egg, and the flavour harmonizes surprisingly well. Only raw meat, vegetables and seasoning are provided, and the diners cook and serve themselves. This makes for a rather active meal. Rinsed Mutton has a history of more than a thousand years, when beef, chicken, fish, shrimp, pork were also cooked in hotpots. Covering an area of 1, 200 square metres, the new Donglaishun (Success Comes from the East) Restaurant can serve 350 customers at one time. Because of its reputation, the restaurant had established 96 chain restaurants by May 2002 in 24 provinces, autonomous regions and municipalities throughout China.

Barbecued Meat 烤肉宛

Barbecued Meat is a Manchu dish which has now become a Beijing specialty. More than 300 years ago it was the custom for Qing officials in Beijing to go on picnics in the hills around the capital on the Double Ninth

537

Festival (the ninth day of the ninth month of the lunar calendar). They would bring with them boiled beef or mutton, various seasonings and garnishes, and an iron pan for re-cocking the meat. In some attractive spot they would build a fire, heat the pan over it and sear the cold boiled meat in the pan. The seared meat was then dipped into soy sauce and mashed garlic before being eaten. This dish was gradually introduced into restaurants. About eight years ago, the recipe was changed to make the meat more palatable: raw beef or mutton was cut into thin slices and marinated before searing. This kind of barbecued meat then became very popular.

The animals are raised in Dachang, Hebei Province, where mutton and beef are of high quality and very tender. Mr Wan Jinting and Wan Jinfu, the 7th generation of the Wan family pay particularly attention to the cutting and barbecuing. It is extremely important to have choice cuts of meat for this dish. The preparation of mutton for barbecuing is similar to the procedure for Rinsed Mutton decribed above. The beef comes from a four-or-five-year-old animal weighing 150 kilograms or more, but only some twenty kilograms of meat from the lion and chunk are used. The meat is trimmed and frozen before being cut into strips 16 cm long and 4 cm wide, which are then cut across the grain into three slices. The meat is marinated in a mixture of soy sauce, crushed ginger, wine, shrimp paste, sesame seed paste, rice vinegar and chopped coriander. The meat slices are then seared over high heat on a special barbecue grill 66 cm in diameter. The meat is very tender and has a unique flavour and aroma.

There are several famous Barbecued Meat restaurants in Beijing. Examples of these are the Kaorouji (Barbecued Meat Quarter), which opened for business in 1686, is picturesquely situated on the banks of the Shichahai (Lake of Ten Monasteries) north of Beihai Park just inside Di'anmen. It is also known for its fried lambs' tails, fried Gansu duck and mutton or prawn shashlik. The Mufeng Barbecued Meat Restaurant, formerly known as the Barbecued Meat Garden, is located near Xuanwumen in the south-western part of the city (the Muslim centre of Beijing) and is over one hundred years old. A new Barbecued Meat Restaurant was opened in Zhongguancun in July 2002.

Red Mansions Banquet 红楼宴

Generally speaking, in famous literary works, none excels the classic novel *A Dream of Red Mansions* written by Cao Xueqin (?-1763) in the description of gourmet or table delicacies. With regard to the more than 400 characters of the Ning Mansion and the Rong Mansion, the book gives spectacular details of banquets, big or small, seasonal delicacies, tonics of four seasons, fine pastries, gruel, soups, noodles and top quality wines as

538

well. The description of these delicacies is not only closely linked with the characterization and plot of the monumental works, but also gives a complete account of the colours, smells and tastes of the delicacies, making countless devoted readers of the book in the past and at the present regret being unable to savour in person the delicious food described by Cao Xueqin.

Today, this dream has come true. The chefs of Yangzhou Xiyuan Hotel, Yangzhou Guesthouse and the Cooking Department of the Commercial Training School of Jiangsu Province have prepared and served a large "Red Mansions Banquet" which has been highly praised by scholars researching into the work of *A Dream of Red Mansions* and Chinese and foreign customers for the colour, smell, taste, pattern, and utensils of the dishes.

Entering the "Red Mansion Hall" of the aristocratic ambiance of the Qing Dynasty, diners feel as if in the Grand View Garden described in the book. On the luxurious and elegant painted table there is an array of silver wares; waitresses dressed up in the style of "slave girls in the Red Mansions" are waiting respectfully to welcome diners.

The first course of the banquet is a dish for pleasing the eyes with the name of "Grand View," featuring "beautiful landscape" and "peacocks" and "butterflies," all exquisitely carved and vivid. The overture is cold dishes of the style of Jia family, with the names of "Gold Hairpin and Silver Thread," "Jadeite Feather Dress," "Grain-Picked Goose Duck's Heart," "Rouge Dried Goose Meat," "Delicious Tomato Dried Fish," which are appetizing and during which customers may enjoy tea and chat with each other. When the main dishes of the Ning Mansion and the Rong Mansion are served, the banquet enters its theme. The first course is "Celery Sprout on Snow", implying two Chinese characters "Xue" and "Qin" which are corresponding to "snow" and "celery." On the glittering "white snow" made of egg white are scattered green celery sprouts in addition to soft dried goose meat, which are very delicious. "Southern Wine Duck Series" is a dish made of domestic duck, wild duck and quail, which are thoroughly cooked with high quality Shaoxing wine, winning the warm applause of guests. Served next one by one are pheasant claws, pigeon eggs, snow flake bean curd... The most unique dish is "Pearls in Old Clams." The "pearls" made of the meat of whitefish or grouper are hidden under the shell of a turtle and are stewed with slow fire with specially chosen condiments. The dish is tasty and its smell is excellent, with wonderful feeling in the mouth. It is said that this was a famous dish once prepared by Cao Xueqin himself.

Following the main dishes are "Happy Red Court fine pastries" (Happy Red Court is the living quarters of Jia Baoyu, the leading male character

539

in the book). These pastries can be called the re-emergence of the theme of the Red Mansion food. *"qingwen stuffed bun"* (*stuffed bun wrapped by the thin* of soy bean milk,) *"tianxiang* lotus root,"	"happy jiaozi" (dumplings,) "jujube paste and yam cake,"	"bean curd thick soup,"	"aromatic rice gruel,"	"gingko soup"... Every course of pastries or refreshment and every soup is exquisite and fantastic. The guest is indeed reluctant to eat them up, but s/he is also unwilling to miss any one of them. Guests will also have the pleasure of enjoying the "Qionghua Flower Wine," "Tribute Spring Tea," and the like, which were presented to the imperial court and beloved by the sisters of the Grand View Garden. This will add to the interest and charm of the banquet.

"Red Mansions Banquet" is extremely elegant in appearance and unparalleled in taste, and every course has its own story. Customers can eat while chatting and enjoying the sights. It is a harmony of gourmet delights and culture and an enjoyment for the senses and the mind. It will be a great pleasure, just like in the dreamland.

Beijing's Time-Honoured Brands 北京老字号

The Legend of Smelly Bean Curd 臭豆腐的传说

A young man from Anhui Province named Wang Zhihe came to Beijing nearly 300 years ago to take the imperial examination. But he failed the exams the first time. Determined to take them again, Wang set up a small tofu mill to finance his continued stay in Beijing, but his business did not go very well. Then, one hot day in summer, Wang Zhihe cut his surplus fresh tofu into small pieces and dried it to eat the next day. He put some salt and Chinese prickly ash onto the tofu to preserve it, and put it into a jar. However, he forgot all about his jar of tofu until several months later. When he opened it a strong smell came out. The snow-white tofu had turned dark green. Not wanting to throw it away, Wang plucked up courage and tasted a little. And to his surprise, the smelly tofu tasted great. Following closely on his experience, he asked some neighbors to try it. They love it and asked Wang to make more.

Wang Zhihe never did pass the examinations. But he made loads of money selling tofu and eventually set up a smelly tofu shop. In the late Qing Dynasty when Empress Dowager Cixi came to power, its reputation soared. The down-to-earth dish finally started to appear in recipe books and it was put on the imperial menu. The new food caught on and across the country smelly tofu producers mushroomed.

In 1949 the Beijing municipal government brought together the local urban producers and set up the Beijing Smelly Tofu Factory. And, of course, the smelly tofu brand was called "Wang Zhihe."

Tianfuhao Braised Pork Leg 天福号酱肉

With a history of nearly 300 years, the Tianfuhao Braised Pork Leg is famous cooking meat in Beijing. The upper part of the pig's leg is used. The leg is first cooked for an hour in boiling water with salt, ginger, and cooking wine. Then it is taken out, washed in cold water, and put into stock from which the fat has been skimmed off, and braised until it is well done.

In 1738 a man named Liu Deshan opened a cooked meat shop with his son, and named the store Tianfuhao. They had to take turns to cook during the night. One night, when his son was on duty, he was very exhausted and fell into sleep. When he woke up, he found that the pork was over-done and the stock had become thick sauce. He managed to remove the meat, sold it when it got cold. An officer happened to buy the pork and found it very delicious. The following day he came back again for more such pork. Finally, the father and the son changed their way of cooking and specialized in this kind of pork, and their business became flourishing.

McDonald's 麦当劳餐厅

Located on the corner of Wangfujing Street, the busiest shopping street, McDonald's opened its first restaurant in May, 1992 in Beijing. It is a joint venture between McDonald's Corporation and the General Corporation of Beijing Agriculture, Industry and Commerce. The restaurant has a seating capacity of 700 people and employs a local staff of nearly 1,000. About 95 percent of its food and packaging is supplied in China, including beef, chicken, fish, potatoes, lettuce, and various beverages. McDonald's opened its first China outlet in 1990 in the southern city of Shenzhen near Hong Kong.

Kentucky Fried Chicken 肯德基

541

Located at Qianmen (Front Gate), the Kentucky Fried Chicken (KFC) Restaurant with a seating capacity of 505, was the first of its kind, opened in China by the Beijing Kentucky Company, a joint venture between China and the US Kentucky International Corporation. It was opened on November 12, 1987. At the very beginning, some people doubted whether it was successful or not. A year later at the end of 1988, turnover and profits were surprisingly double the planned figures and more. Ever since the KFC restaurants in China have been snowballing bigger and bigger. By the end of 2001, Kentucky Fried Chicken (KFC) has increased its outlets in 121 cities in China to 475 since its first restaurant opened in Beijing in 1987.

It plans to open another 120 new outlets in 2002. And McDonald's boasts 377 outlets in 67 cities in China.

Transportation
交　　通

Trains Depart from Beijing 北京始发列车
(Effective from October 21, 2001)

Trains Depart from Beijing Railway Station
北京站始发列车时刻表

No. of Train 车次	Dep. Time 发车时间	Terminal 终点站	Arr. Time 抵达时间
T509	07:30	Qinhuangdao 秦皇岛	10:23
K339	12:40	Jiamusi 佳木斯	11:22
2537	13:00	Tonghua 通化	06:51
4495	13:12	Qinhuangdao 秦皇岛	18:12
K265	14:10	Mudanjiang 牡丹江	11:28
T237	18:11	Harbin 哈尔滨	07:33
T17	18:20	Harbin 哈尔滨	06:49
T271	18:40	Jilin 吉林	07:34
1467	19:48	Jiagdaqi 加格达奇	21:30
2549	21:10	Anshan 鞍山	06:39
K53	22:15	N.Shenyang 沈阳北	07:25
K95	22:38	Fushun 抚顺	08:28
T121	23:44	Changchun 长春	10:37
4411	04:12	Tianjin 天津	05:55
7061	06:27	Tianjin 天津	09:33
T531	08:05	Tianjin 天津	09:24
T533	08:45	Tianjin 天津	10:13
1301	09:42	Manzhouli 满州里	18:42
T535	10:14	Tianjin 天津	11:28
T11	10:22	N.Shenyang 沈阳北	19:27
4419	10:30	Tangshan 唐山	14:23
T537	11:30	Tianjin 天津	12:44
T523	12:30	Qinhuangdao 秦皇岛	17:42
T539	13:45	Tianjin 天津	14:14
T541	13:53	Tianjin 天津	15:12
K215	14:20	Tumen 图们	15:50
K543	15:10	Tianjin 天津	16:29
T47	16:00	Qiqihar 齐齐哈尔	07:31
T545	16:10	Tianjin 天津	17:29
T547	16:52	Tianjin 天津	18:11
K27	17:25	Dandong 丹东	07:28
T71	17:30	Harbin 哈尔滨	06:19

No. of Train	Dep. Time	Terminal	Arr. Time
T225	18:48	Dalian 大连	06:42
T551	19:10	Tianjin 天津	20:29
T225	18:48	Dalian 大连	06:42
T551	19:10	Tianjin 天津	20:29
T553	19:46	Tianjin 天津	21:00
T59	20:30	Changchun 长春	06:55
T81	21:30	Dalian 大连	07:02
2589	21:57	Jinzhou 锦州	06:35
K19	22:50	Moscow 莫斯科	18:34
K39	22:50	Qiqihar 齐齐哈尔	19:21
K39	22:50	Tulihe 图里河	08:33
2597	07:38	Jinan 济南	13:09
K45	09:03	Fuzhou 福州	19:42
T35	13:30	Jinan 济南	18:00
1461	15:18	Shanghai 上海	12:27
2547	15:30	Yantai 烟台	06:41
T31	15:50	Hangzhou 杭州	07:30
1425	16:30	W. Nanjing 南京西	10:04
T85	17:01	Suzhou 苏州	06:54
2539	17:11	Qingdao 青岛	07:26
T21	18:00	Shanghai 上海	08:00
T13	18:08	Shanghai 上海	08:08
T109	19:00	Shanghai 上海	09:00
T63	19:20	Hefei 合肥	07:00
T103	20:00	Shanghai 上海	10:00
2565	20:08	Xuzhou 徐州	07:20
T65	20:40	W. Nanjing 南京西	08:24
2517	21:33	Weihai 威海	13:40
T25	22:10	Qingdao 青岛	07:57
K51	22:20	Rizhao 日照	12:30
K101	23:10	Wenzhou 温州	05:30
2549	21:10	Anshan 鞍山	06:39
K53	22:15	N. Shenyang 沈阳北	07:25
K95	22:38	Fushun 抚顺	08:28
T121	23:44	Changchun 长春	10:37
K3	07:40	Erlian 二连	20:39
K23	07:40	Erlian 二连	20:39
K43	11:42	Lanzhou 兰州	16:17
K43	11:42	Jiayuguan 嘉峪关	21:59
4433	11:35	Chawu 茶坞	12:53
K263	21:20	Baotou 包头	11:10
4437	22:58	Datong 大同	07:15
T235	05:14	E. Guangzhou 广州东	05:13
T123	20:30	E. Guangzhou 广州东	20:35
T521	14:40	Shijiazhuang 石家庄	17:45
7155	06:58	Chengde 承德	14:12
K711	07:20	Chengde 承德	11:18
2251	13:22	Dandong 丹东	11:25
7153	16:28	Chengde 承德	23:17
4413	23:23	Chengde 承德	04:32

Trains Depart from Beijing West Railway Station
北京西客站始发列车时刻表

Train No.	Dep. Time	Terminal	Arr. Time
1481	05:28	Hankou 汉口	21:28
T91	06:15	E. Guangzhou 广州东	05:23
K707	06:36	Shijiazhuang 石家庄	09:52
T511	07:35	Shijiazhuang 石家庄	10:20
T79	08:10	Wuchang 武昌	21:02
2567	08:43	Hanzhong 汉中	13:36
T525	09:00	Handan 邯郸	13:22
K219	09:50	Shijiazhuang 石家庄	13:16
T97	10:06	E. Guangzhou 广州东	09:31
T97	10:06	Kowloon 九龙	13:10
T5	10:51	Nanning 南宁	17:03
T515	11:01	Shijiazhuang 石家庄	13:41
K117	11:10	Panzhihua 攀枝花	07:40
K267	12:58	Huaihua 怀化	16:39
T29	13:28	Shijiazhuang 石家庄	16:08
K49	13:56	Yichang 宜昌	09:16
T29	13:46	Guangzhou 广州	12:46
T513	14:30	Shijiazhuang 石家庄	17:08
T57	14:55	Zhengzhou 郑州	21:54
T145	15:10	Nanchang 南昌	13:48
T151	15:28	Xining 西宁	20:39
T7	16:00	Chengdu 成都	19:18
T55	16:10	Xi'an 西安	06:16
K157	16:20	Zhanjiang 湛江	07:44
K183	16:30	Nanyang 南阳	08:46
2505	16:43	Shiyan 十堰	15:12
T1	17:00	Changsha 长沙	08:38
T41	17:12	Xi'an 西安	06:45
T231	17:25	Xi'an 西安	07:26
T519	17:38	Handan 邯郸	22:06
2101	17:47	Luoyang 洛阳	07:12
T75	18:00	Lanzhou 兰州	18:16
1389	18:23	Chongqing 重庆	05:04
K703	18:38	Yuncheng 运城	09:52
T37	18:53	Wuchang 武昌	07:00
T77	19:30	Hankou 汉口	07:31
K9	19:40	Chongqing 重庆	21:06
T61	20:00	Kunming 昆明	15:17
K185	20:10	Hengyang 衡阳	18:33
T69	20:20	Urumqi 乌鲁木齐	19:59
2089	20:43	Xinyang 信阳	10:02
2519	21:10	Hancheng 韩城	13:49
K717	21:50	Taiyuan 太原	07:10
T29	22:20	Guangzhou 广州	21:00
T87	22:30	Guiyang 贵阳	06:20
K179	22:39	Zhengzhou 郑州	06:31
1363	20:50	Chengdu 成都	08:28

Train No.	Dep. Time	Terminal	Arr. Time
1487	08:10	Zhengzhou 郑州	20:20
K307	10:00	Xiamen 厦门	20:24
4487	11:05	Shijiazhuang 石家庄	17:23
1453	12:15	Nanchang 南昌	07:30
K105	13:58	Shenzhen 深圳	20:05
1427	14:10	Anqing 安庆	08:53
1409	17:20	Hefei 合肥	08:35
T167	18:00	Nanchang 南昌	07:50
1621	18:18	Fuyang 阜阳	05:40
1625	20:03	Ganzhou 赣州	19:55
T107	20:30	Shenzhen 深圳	20:28
1483	00:14	Baotou 包头	14:02
K713	10:10	Datong 大同	16:27
4439	12:31	Zhangjiakou 张家口	16:17
K177	13:40	Yinchuan 银川	09:39
K217	19:37	Baotou 包头	08:44
K89	20:40	Hohhot 呼和浩特	07:20
K705	23:29	Datong 大同	06:20

Trains Depart from Beijing South Railway Station
北京南站始发列车时刻表

Train No.	Dep. Time	Terminal	Arr. Time
1714	03:53	Baotou 包头	17:53
K237	07:00	Baotou 包头	20:51
7115	07:31	Zhangjiakou 张家口	12:57
1455	07:48	Hohhot 呼和浩特	19:24
4447	13:26	Zhangjiakou 张家口	17:45
4473	13:56	Datong 大同	20:58
4443	14:53	Zhangjiakou 张家口	19:31
4415	17:18	Zhangjiakou 张家口	21:37
K273	22:46	Baotou 包头	11:52
2141	23:08	Wuhaixi 乌海西	18:23
4453	00:19	Chengde 承德	05:40
1713	03:11	N.Shenyang 沈阳北	22:50
K275	08:34	Hailar 海拉尔	13:25
2189	16:32	Ulanhot 乌兰浩特	13:10
1457	19:19	Tongliao 通辽	08:50
2559	21:33	Chifeng 赤峰	07:15
7095	06:37	Taiyuan 太原	20:41
7197	17:47	Laiyuan 涞源	23:20
4509	07:11	Dezhou 德州	12:19
1503	16:41	Lianyungang 连云港	07:32
K255	04:54	Ningbo 宁波	05:06
4471	14:31	Dezhou 德州	19:41
K127	05:00	Changchun 长春	17:50
4457	06:37	Qinhuangdao 秦皇岛	11:40
7059	13:39	Fengrun 丰润	17:30
2143	06:11	Tianjin 天津	08:02

Train No.	Dep. Time	Terminal	Arr. Time
4427	14:06	Tangshan 唐山	18:15
K125	00:38	Xi'an 西安	17:14
4441	01:14	Shijiazhuang 石家庄	05:20
4451	04:03	Shijiazhuang 石家庄	08:15
7063	08:14	Baoding 保定	11:40
4459	09:32	Taiyuan 太原	19:43
2163	15:27	Changzhibei 长治北	06:13
2553	20:52	Zhengzhou 郑州	06:42
4407	22:58	Handan 邯郸	04:56

The Fourth Nationwide Speed-up 火车第四次提速

Trains on five trunk railway routes such as Beijing to Kowloon in Hong Kong; Wuhan to Chengdu; Wuhan to Guangzhou; Hangzhou to Zhuzhou and Harbin to Dailian saw a new round of speed increases in October 2001. The combined length of these five routes is 6,713 kilometres. By the end of October 2001, a trip by train travelling 2,372 kilometres from Beijing to Shenzhen along the Beijing-Kowloon Railway takes less than 24 hours, compared with the previous 30 hours. The Ministry of Railway will launch another two nationwide speed-ups, one in 2003 and the second in 2005. The schedule also indicates that a total of 28 railway routes, adding up to more than 20,000 kilometres, will be upgraded during the three nationwide speed-ups over the next five years, thus being able to handle trains travelling at speeds between 120 kilometres to 140 kilometres per hour. Passengers from Beijing, Shanghai and Guangzhou will have easy access to any part of the country with the fast railway network in 2005. Railways used to be the biggest monopoly in long-distance transport. In recent years, however, some of its former clients have been lured away to the airways and highways. China experienced three upgrades to its railway in 1997, 1998, and 2000, raising train speeds along a number of major railways to 120 kilometres an hour from 60 kilometres an hour. The Ministry of Railway hopes to keep its share of the trade by increasing train speeds and upgrading services. China's total rail network is expected to reach 75,000 kilometres by 2005.

Public Transportation in Beijing 北京的公共交通

Bus and trolley stops are ideally located for passengers. There is a bus stop every 5 or 6 hundred metres in the urban areas and every one kilometre in the suburbs. At present, Beijing has more than 400 bus and trolley bus lines. One and two-digit numbers are for urban bus lines, three-digit numbers beginning with "1" (such as 101, 102, 103, 104, 105) are for trolley bus lines and managed by the Trolley Bus Company; three-digit numbers beginning with "3" (such as 331, 332, 333, 334, 335) are suburban bus lines. Also, buses of three-digit numbers beginning with "2" (such as 203, 204, 205, 206, 207) mainly run from 12: 00 pm to 05: 00 am the next morning. Buses of three-digit numbers beginning with the number of "8" (such as 801, 802, 803) are air-conditioned. And the traffic lines beginning with the number "9" are mainly suburban ones and managed by the Public Bus Company's enterprises, where the monthly ticket is not used. Apart from buses and trolley buses, there are also mini-buses in the main streets and tourist places which conveniently stop wherever passengers wave. In Qianmen, Beijing Railway Station, Dongzhimen, Yongdingmen, Zhaogongkou and Lianhuachi, there are long-distance buses to outer suburbs, such as Hebei, Shandong, Inner Mongolia, Shanxi, Shaanxi, Henan and Jiangsu provinces, etc. There are more than 8, 000 buses and trolley buses in operation in Beijing.

Since early October 1997, public buses in Beijing have been extended their routes and their running time to help ease the strain brought on by increasingly crowned traffic. The city government has designated a special lane for the public buses on Chang'an Boulevard, one of the busiest in the Chinese capital, efforts have been made to open new routes and extend operation time. Public bus routes have been extended to 197 of the city's newly-built residential quarters and nine suburban districts and counties. In the past, bus service closed at 11 pm in the city and 7pm in the suburbs. Operating time has been extended to 12 pm and 9 pm respectively.

There are more than 60, 000 taxis in Beijing and the round-the-city circle line subway (23. 6 kilometres) and east-west subway line (also called Underground Chang'an Boulevard) from Sihuidongzhan to Pingguoyuan (Apple Orchard) totaling 31 kilometres long as well. Construction of 13. 5-kilometre east-west subway from Bawangfen to Fuxingmen started in June 1989. The subway opened to traffic on September 28, 1999 to mark the 50th anniversary of the founding of the People's Republic of China. Per ride (flat rate) on the subway costs 3 yuan. The subway under Tian'anmen is 13 metres deep.

Also there are at present more than 4, 000 mini buses in operation in the Capital City.

Expressways in Beijing 北京的高速公路

(figures below are listed in descending order)

Beijing	to	Harbin	1,400 kilometres
Beijing	to	Tongzhou	18. 6 kilometres
Beijing	to	Taiyuan	515 kilometres
Beijing	to	Kaifeng (Beijing section)	42 kilometres
Beijing	to	Shijiazhuang	270 kilometres
Beijing	to	Tianjin & Tanggu	142 kilometres
Beijing	to	Changping via Great Wall to Chadaocheng	69. 98 kilometres
Beijing	to	Shenyang	658. 33 kilometres
Beijing	to	Badaling	69. 98 kilometres
Beijing	to	Shanghai	1, 262 kilometres

Capital Intl. Airport Exp.   19 kilometres
(Capital Airport to Sanyuanqiao)

The Inner Second Ring Road 内二环   23. 6 kilometres

The outer Second Ring Road 外二环   32. 7 kilometres (opened to traffic in September 1992)

The Third Ring Road 三环   48 kilometres (opened to traffic in 1994 with 52 bridges)

The Fourth Ring Road 四环   65. 3 kilometres (with 147 bridges on it, opened to traffic in June 2001)

The Fifth Ring Road 五环   94. 5 kilometres (15. 2 kilometres opened to the traffic in September 2001)

The Sixth Ring Road 六环   188 kilometres (26. 5 kilometers from Tongzhou to Majuqiao 通马段 (通州至马驹桥)opened to traffic, 100 kilometres per hour); 22 kilometres from Tongzhou to Huangcun

Seventh Ring Road 七环   440 kilometres

Beijing—Miyun Expressway   69 kilometres

The Beijing Municipal Government has officially named the Fourth Ring Road the "Olympic Boulevard." The boulevard has eight-lanes with 147 flyovers to connect with the major streets of the city. The construction of three streets— Deshengmenwai, Xizhimenwai and Xueyuanlu — in northwestern Beijing to connect the Second, Third and Fourth Ring roads were finished in June 2001. The three roads have been designed without traffic lights to speed up traffic flow and ease the city's transportation pressure. Guang'an Avenue, the third major east-west street in the city, opened to traffic in July 2001. Parallel to Chang'an Boulevard and located in southern Beijing, the Guang' an Avenue has promoted the development of southern Beijing, which has lagged behind the rest of the city. Transportation is always a challenge for any city. By 2007, a fairly sophisticated transportation network will be completed. The five ring roads with linked expressways, the newly built city rail and the Olympic subway will contribute to an efficient transport system.

Built an average of 2. 5 kilometres away from the city's Third Ring Road, the new road boasts a total length of 65. 3 kilometres, including 147

548

overpasses of various scales. Its designed hourly speed is 80 to 100 kilometres, much higher than that of the city's other two ring roads—55 to 65 kilometres per hour.

Seven expressways in and out of Beijing 进出北京的七条高速公路：

1. Jingjintang (Beijing-Tianjin-Tanggu) Expressway 京津塘(北京－天津－塘沽)高速公路 (Beijing section: 37.6 kilometres)
2. Jingshi (Beijing-Shijiazhuang) Expressway 京石(北京－石家庄)高速公路 (Beijing section: 45.6 kilometres, construction of the expressway began in 1986 and completed in November 1993, taking 7 years to complete; it was the first of its kind ever built in Beijing; The first expressway from Bonn 波恩 to Coln 科隆 in Germany was built in 1932 in the world; The first expressway from Shanghai 上海 to Jiading 嘉定 was built in 1988, taking three years to build)
3. Capital Intl. Airport Expressway 首都机场高速公路 (19 kilometres)
4. Badaling Expressway 八达岭高速公路 (69.98 kilometres)
5. Jingtong (Beijing-Tongzhou) Expressway 京通高速公路 (18.6 kilometres)
6. Jingha (Beijing-Harbin) Expressway 京哈(北京－哈尔滨)高速公路 (Beijing section: 31.9 kilometres)
7. Jingshen (Beijing-Shenyang) Expressway 京沈高速公路 (Beijing section: 39.8 kilometres)
8. Beijing-Kaifeng Expressway from Beijing's southern part (Yuquanying) to Gu'an Bridge of Hebei Province totalling 42.65 kilometres; the section, costing 2.71 billion yuan (US $326.5 million), and opened to traffic in June 2001. 京开高速公路

The Ten China Highways in and out of Beijing 进出北京的十条国道

No. of Highway	Total length (km)	Beijing section (km)	Exit Point/Termination
China Highway 101 (Beijing-Chengde Rd.)	240	123.4	Dongzhimen / Chengde 东直门／承德
China Highway 102 (Beijing-Harbin Rd.)	1,400	31.9	Chaoyangmen / Harbin 朝阳门／哈尔滨
China Highway 103 (Beijing-Tianjin-Tanggu Exp.)	140	37.6	Fenzhongsiqiao / Tanggu 分钟寺桥／塘沽
China Highway 104 (Beijing-Fuzhou Rd.)	2,300	47.2	Yongdingmen / Fuzhou 永定门／福州
China Highway 105 (Beijing-Zhuhai Rd.)	2,600	47.2	Yongdingmen / Zhuhai 永定门／珠海
China Highway 106 (Beijing-Guangzhou Rd.)	2,500	44.6	Yuquanying/Guangzhou 玉泉营／广州
China Highway 107 (Beijing-Shenzhen Rd.)	2,600	50	Guang'anmen / Shenzhen 广安门／深圳
China Highway 108 (Beijing-Kunming Rd.)	3,200	139.5	Fuxingmen / Kunming 复兴门／昆明
China Highway 109 (Beijing-Lhasa Rd.)	3,900	119	Fuchengmen / Lhasa 阜成门／拉萨
China Highway 110 (Beijing-Yinchuan Rd.)	1,300	98.8	Deshengmen / Yinchuan 德胜门／银川
China Highway 111 (Beijing-Jiagdaqi Rd.)	2,050	166.9	Dongzhimen / Jiagdaqi 东直门／加格达奇

Note: China Highway 104 and 105 coincide in Beijing section. Only 10 highways start from Beijing. These 11 China Highways within the boundaries of Beijing total 813 kilometres, of which there are 5 highways in the mountainous area, totalling over 400 kilometres.

因 104 国道和 105 国道的北京段重合，故北京的国道数量实际上有 10 条。这 11 条国道在北京境内总长 813 公里，其中 5 条是山区公路，长 400 余公里。

Light Rail in Beijing 北京的轻轨铁路

Beijing's urban traffic congestion has been greatly eased thanks to the launching of the city's light rail project. The initial tracks of Beijing's first light railway line were laid down on October 1, 2001. Started in October 2000, construction of the light rail began at the Huilongguan (a residential area encompassing 8.5 million square meters and home to 230,000 residents) East Station in the Huilongguan residential areas in northern Beijing's Changping District. The light rail stretches from the Huilongguan East Station to Xizhimen in the west, a communications hub, and Dongzhimen in the east. Construction of the light rail has been divided into two sections. The western section of Beijing's light railway, from Huilongguan to Xizhimen was finished in May 2002 and the eastern section from Huilongguan to Dongzhimen was completed by September 2002. With 16 stations, the 40.9-kilometre light rail opened to traffic before October 2002. The decibel levels in areas around the railway meet with the national standard. To reduce the noise caused by the trains, each track has been fused with another to make the railway line free of cracks and special acoustic celotex boards have been set up at Zhongguancun, the site of the Chinese Academy of Sciences and in residential areas. Since most of the basic infrastructure work was completed on the western section in July 2001, including the viaduct construction, railway stations, and rail-bed construction, the railway line inches towards completion at a speed of 1.2-1.25-kilometres per day. The urban railway goes through the Zhongguancun Science and Technology Park in Haidian District, which is also home to dozens of universities and research institutions. Thanks to the light rail, the time required neighbourhoods to central Beijing has been markedly cut, with Xizhimen and Dongzhimen, the two terminal stations of the railway, connecting with the ring subway and many public transportation lines, and will invite more people to move out of downtown districts. With an investment of 6.6 billion yuan (US$780 million), the railway line is the most environmentally friendly, convenient and comfortable in the Capital City. The light rail transoports more than 14,000 commuters per day and can serve more than 28,000 passengers in the future.

Xizhimen and Dongzhimen, the two terminal stations of the railway, connect with the ring subway and many public transportation lines. The traffic flow is more convenient for passengers. Construction of the railway has promoted the real estate market to heat up in areas around the line, especially in Huilongguan and Xisanqi.

Design of another light rail in Beijing is completed and construction will begin soon. The section light rail system will start from Sihui East Station in the east to Tongzhou District in Beijing's eastern suburb.

According to the latest plan, the rail network includes 13 lines, with a total length of nearly 400 kilometres. Twenty cities in China are preparing for the construction of subways or light railways.

Taxi in Beijing 北京的出租汽车

In a bid to upgrade the city's taxi industry, Beijing has its first joint-venture taxi company. Beijing-based Jinjian Taxi Company and Delgo Taxi Management Company from Singapore have agreed to establish the first taxi company in the city. The joint venture has an initial investment totaling 250 million yuan (US$30.2 million) and 3,300 taxicabs. Delgo is a large taxi company in Singapore that owns 5,000 cabs, occupying one-third of the total number in Singapore. It is also the first company who applied Benz as taxicabs in Singapore. According to China's relevant regulations, a Sino-foreign joint venture taxi company must pay its cars in China. The cars may be made in China or imported. For imported cars, tariffs might be reduced or cancelled. Besides using high-grade cars, the company will equip the cabs with global positioning system and attach more importance to driver training. The joint venture keeps the brand of Jinjian, since it has established a high reputation in Beijing. The Chinese part, Beijing Jinjian Taxi Company, is one of the famous branded taxi ventures in Beijing. It has 3,500 cabs of various models. Delgo has set up joint ventures in Guangzhou, Shanghai and Shenyang. As the capital, Beijing has a large population and is visited by many people for business or travel. Its taxi transportation industry is under great pressure for better services and hardware equipment. The Beijing municipal government had decided to foster more big taxi companies with better services and equipment, and phase out small, bad-performing ones. The government will reduce the number of taxi operating companies from more than 800 to just 200 by restructuring, mergers, and granting licenses. It is aiming to establish 20 brand-name operating companies, which run 40,000 brand-name taxicabs. The city now has a total of 67,000 taxis run by 80,000 taxi drivers, accounting for

12 per cent of the city's ground transportation. In the next six years, all of Beijing's taxis will be equipped with global positioning systems (GPS), which help the taxi drivers to make good use of the geographical information to find their costumers and to find different locations. By 2008, 80 per cent of Beijing taxis will use natural gas, a clean energy, to reduce the city's air pollution. The municipal government is considering the gradual phase out of Xiali taxis, a relatively low-grade car, to brighten the city's look.

Reappearing of Pedicabs in Beijing 北京人力车

In Beijing today, there are more than 5,000 public buses, about 600 trolley buses, and nearly 70,000 taxis. But they have not fully taken the place of pedicabs. There are now over 500,000 registered pedicabs in the Capital City now.

Most pedicabs begin work late at night after regular buses stop. Or they go out early in the morning before the first buses pull out of their terminals. Only a few night buses and taxis share business with the pedicabs during those hours. Slowly and smoothly, the pedicabs ride on the streets, and the passengers really can see the sights. Therefore, in the day, some tourists would like to take a pedicab. There is another reason why pedicabs are sometimes at a premium. Beijing is an ancient city famous for its vast number of tiny hutong narrow alleys behind the broad streets and avenues. A taxi seldom bothers to go into these *hutongs*. When it does, the taxi finds the alleys leading nowhere. A pedicab is useful on such occasion. To most pedicab drivers, whom were born Beijingers, the *hutongs* zigzag to everywhere. A pedicab is able to take the passenger to places deep in the alleys unmarked on maps.

Pedalling a pedicab is a lucrative job. It attracts many unemployed young people and retired workers. Even a few state factory workers resigned from their jobs and become self-employed drivers, in spite of their ensured salaries and welfare subsidies. They can make a fortune out of pedaling a pedicab. The drivers are usually warm-hearted towards their customers. In the early 1950s, there were 100 pedicab service stations with more than 5,000 drivers, most of them carrying freight. Because of a lack of public buses, pedicabs were once a major means of passenger transport in Beijing too. In 1960s, more than 1,000 pedicab stations were set up in urban district for round-the-clock service. Pedicabs were banned as an example of a "man-exploiting-man" phenomenon during the Cultural Revolution from 1966 to 1976. Motorized rickshaws replaced pedicabs, but they soon were dismissed because of air pollution and noise.

The pedicabs reappeared in the late 1970s and have shown no sign of disappearing from the scene again. Sometimes, people can see that overseas tourists enjoy the city by sitting on pedicabs.

Bicycle 自行车

There are now about 1, 500 million bicycles in the world, of which 470 million bicycles in China represent about one third of the total number of bicycles in the world.

For every 100 families there are 160 bicycles in cities in China and 80 bicycles per 100 families in rural areas. No wonder people in the world unanimously acknowledge that China is the kingdom of bicycles.

As for the innovator of the world's first bike, people have different views, and no final conclusion has yet been reached on this matter.

Historical records show that during Qing Emperor Kangxi's reign (1662-1722), Hung Luzhuang, a skillful craftsman, made a hand-operated, self-walking bike. In 1790, a French person produced a "wooden horse" which many people think is one of the world's first bicycles. In 1800, a Russian manufactured the world's first bike with metal chain drive. By 1839, an Englishman invented a bike with pedals fixed on the wheels. But the bike was made of wood. Inventions relating to the bike have reached more than 15, 000 in the world.

At present, the manufacture of bicycles is in its prime period. Bikes with different styles are produced one after the other.

A clown of the Swiss Circus produced a 14-centimetre-long mini-bike, which created the world's smallest record. It is said that he himself "rode" the bike and travelled around the city of Zurich.

Two German people manufactured a world's biggest bike. Its wheel was as tall as a man. The Danish people produced the world's longest bike, which could carry 35 people to ride on it. The Chinese acrobats have created a world's record with 19 acrobats on a bike, while one acrobat rides the bike all the other 18 performers with their arms stretched out to form beautiful and graceful patterns.

Of course, the most important use of bicycle is the means of transportation. Apart from China, bicycles are the chief means of transportation in many Asian countries and in Africa. And in some cities in Europe and North America, there are bicycle-lovers.

Nowadays, because of traffic jams, waste gas and sound pollution of cars, which pose a serious threat to the health of people in advanced countries, and more people realize the superiority of bicycles. Some men of insight predict that the real prime of bicycles is not now but in the near future.

Why Are There so Many Bicycles in Beijing?
北京为什么有这么多自行车

It is a very good question. Well, let me try and explain. Beijing has the advantage of being very flat. It is easy for people to ride bikes to go to work, to shop or to visit their relatives.

Many big factories and research institutes are located on the outskirts of the city. So many people have to commute from their homes to their place of work, and transport is simpler by bike.

Beijing is one of the ancient capitals in China. The layout of the inner city that is within the Second Ring Road is like a chessboard. The alleys or narrow streets are more convenient for bikes than for buses or trolley buses.

Since the Third Plenary Session of the 11th Party Central Committee of the Communist Party of China, the policy of opening to the outside world in 1978 has greatly improved the living standards of the Chinese people. More and more people from other parts of China come to this capital city to work, to travel, to visit their relatives or to do business. Nowadays, there are about 3. 5 million transients from all over China everyday in the city. In 2001, more than 2. 8 million foreign travellers, compatriots from Hong Kong, Macao, and Taiwan came to Beijing for a visit. This aggravated traffic jams in the city.

In 1949, public transport in the city of Beijing depended upon 5 buses and 49 tramcars, and about 30, 000 rickshaws. Since then, the city government has done a tremendous amount of work to improve traffic facilities. According to the latest statistics, there are about 100 million bicycles in Beijing (8. 63 million bikes in Tianjin, 6. 5 million in Shanghai, and 430, 000 in Chongqing—a hilly city), over 3, 000 public buses, over 500 trolley buses and two subways totaling 54 kilometres in length. Many streets have been widened, and a large number of overpasses and underpasses have been built in the last 20 years. But all these cannot meet the needs of the explosive population in Beijing. Traffic jams happen quite often in the daytime. During rush hours, people usually say, it is faster to go to work by bike than to go to work by bus.

Furthermore, to ride a bike is good exercise and helps people stay healthy. China is a developing country and at this stage there are very few cars. They are beyond the average person's income. Traffic will become quite chaotic when there are more cars and more bicycles.

Trolley buses were the first form of public transportation in China. They first appeared in Beijing in December 1904 and later in Shanghai. But until the 1940s trolley buses remained unpopular with the municipal governments—because of the difficulties in setting up power lines and building the tracks. The belated spreading of public forms of transportation resulted in the popularization of rickshaws and bicycles. All Chinese bicycles were imported in the early days. At first, it was the foreigners who brought bicycles into the concession zones. Later when it was thought fashionable to ride a bike, Chinese began taking to them.

The first Chinese cyclist, Ding Boru, was an employee at the foreign-run Tianjin customs. As a wealthy young compradore, Ding was exposed to all kinds of foreign goods. After buying a bike in 1900, he cycled to work every day instead of taking a sedan chair. He was criticized by sedan-lovers who said he was blindly worshipping foreign things. But the bicycle intrigued most inhabitants. And soon bikes became very popular. At the end of the Qing Dynasty (1644-1911), a large number of bicycles were imported by the upper classes. Bikes only became part of the ordinary street scene in the late 1930s when imported bicycles were sold at bargain prices. Shop assistants, office workers and students were soon pedaling around.

From rickshaws through trolley bus to bicycle—this is how China embarked on its modernization course.

Electric bicycles—which run on battery-operated motors—are winning over riders of ordinary pedal-pushing bikes because of their speed and convenience. They were first manufactured in 1980s in China, but sales fell flat because there was no specially made battery for these bikes. Today, thanks to improvements in battery quality, the electric bikes are easy to manage and gaining in popularity. There are now more than 100 electric bicycle producers in China. The industry turned out 310,000 such bicycles in 2001, compared with 150,000 in 1999 and 60,000 in 1998. Japan is another large producer of such bicycles in the world, with total production reaching 180,000 in 2001, up from 100,000 in 1998. Although China is one of the largest producers of electric bikes in the world, its number of large-scale manufacturers is actually quite small. According to a survey of 51 major Chinese electric bike makers, only six churned out more than 10,000 electric bikes in 2000 and 10 produced between 5,000 and 10,000 only. Electric bikes are still new in China. Time is needed for people to become familiar with them and accept them. Each bike's price of between 2,000 yuan (US$240) and 3,000 yuan (US$360) is still expensive for ordinary citizens. Today, there are more than 470 million bikes in China. If electric ones replace 1 percent, the market will be very large. And if the battery is further improved and the prize is reduced, Chinese people will not be able to resist buying the latest cycling invention.

A City Without Any Bicycle 没有自行车的城市

Believe it or not! There is a city without any bicycles in the "Kingdom of Bicycles" in China. The city is Suifenhe, a small border city in Northeast China's Heilongjiang Province. There are no residents that either ride or own bicycles. No stores there sell bicycles either. The reason is simple the mountainous terrain is not favorable for bicycles. The city, with a population of 20, 900 and covering an area of 460 square kilometres, is surrounded by hills. And it is hard to find a large plot of flat land in either the urban or suburban areas. A special fleet of taxis, all green colored Beijing jeeps, serves residents and visitors.

This is unusual in a country with a total of nearly 500 million bicycles. And each year, China produces over 40 million bicycles. The city of Suifenhe bears another unique feature — its road and street signs, store names and public facilities are written both in Chinese and Russian. The city shares 26 kilometres of border areas, the city has attracted many investors, businessmen and visitors from both at home and abroad. Nearly all salesmen and private businessmen bargain or negotiate business in Russian. The majority is self-taught in the language.

Beijing-Tianjin-Tanggu Expressway 京、津、塘高速公路

Construction of an expressway between Beijing and the port of Tanggu via Tianjin started in 1987, and the Beijing-Tianjin section of the expressway, which was one of China's key projects for the Seventh-Five-Year Plan period (1986-1990), was completed in August 1990. The end of 1991 finished the rest of it.

The expressway runs 142. 7 kilometres between Beijing and Tianjin, and is 26 metres wide. The 151. 6 kilometres four-lane road is designed for traffic operating at speeds up to 120 kilometres per hour. The expressway, capable of relieving one third of the loads carried by the Beijing-Tianjin-Tanggu Railway and accommodating 25, 000 vehicles a day, has improved transportation between Beijing and Tianjin. And it has bolstered trade in North China.

Foreign and Regional Airlines Offices in Beijing
外国和地区航空公司驻京办事处

Name	Telephone
Aeroflot (SU)	65002412/65002980
Air France (AF)	65881388
Air Macau (NX)	65063505
Alitalia (AZ)	65067163
All Nippon Airways (NH)	65909191
Asian Airline (OZ)	64681118

British Airways (BA)	65124070
Canadian Airlines Intl LTD (LP)	64649168
Chosnminhang Korean Airways (J)	65323981
Dragonair (KA)	65182533/65183450
EI AI Israel Airlines (LY)	65974514
Ethiopian Airlines (ET)	65050314/65050315
Finnair (AY)	65127180/65127181
Interflug (IF)	65006678/65127181
Indonesian Airlines (GA)	65052901
Iranair (IR)	6512 4840/4945/65002255 ext. 3710
Japan Airlines (JL)	65053775/65130888
Korean Airline (KE)	84538888
Lufthansa German Airlines (LH)	64653500/64654488
Malaysia Airlines (MH)	65052681
Mongolia Airlines (OM)	65014544
Northwest Airlines (NW)	65053505
Pakistan Intl. (PK)	65051681/65051682
Philippine Airlines (PR)	65127180/65050136
Polish Airlines (LO)	65050136/65052288 ext. 102
Qantas (QF)	64673337
Royal Brunei 文莱皇家航空公司	65055073 ext. 3
SAS (SK) Scandinavian Airlines	85276100
Singapore Airlines (SQ)	65052233
Swissair (SR)	65125425
Tarom (RO)	65323552
Thai Airways Intl. (TG)	64608899
United Airlines (UA)	64631111

Shopping
购　　物

557

Wangfujing Commercial Area 王府井商业区

After a construction face-lift, the 700-year-old Wangfujing (the Well of the Prince's Mansion) Street or Golden Street, one of China's oldest and most famous commercial areas, was meant to be well-known in the world through the renovation, look brand new to people on September 11, 1999 when it opened to the public. The Wangfujing Street lives up to its glorious past, but with a new look. To give it a new look they completely got rid of the street's poor infrastructure at a price of over 1 billion yuan (US$120. 5 million). The new infrastructure can sustain the commercial area of 300 square metres to run smoothly for 50 years, with specially designed supplies of electricity, water, gas, communications and transportation. Along the 810-metre-long street are over 200 shops. A 60-member clean-up team for a single commercial area might have been remarkable in scale in Beijing, but expecting them to keep 500, 000 visitors, the estimated average daily volume of visitors in the area; to keep the area clean was just unrealistic. The new street can also provide convenience for pedestrians and motorists alike. Take the transportation as an example. Gone for good are the old days of narrow streets jam-packed with people. The area has no problems at its entry and exit even with a half million people and 1, 020 vehicles. Also, in spite of being modern and new, the renovated Wangfujing Street has retained its traditional cultural atmosphere. The street is a kind of beauty perfectly combining tradition, modernity, culture and commerce. With a group of sculptures depicting the lives of the people of Beijing in the old times was established before the modern Sun Dong An Plaza, a 70-square-metre relief sculpture recalling the operation of the 12 old famous shops in the area was set on the southern wall of the Women's Department Store. Also the ancient well, from which the street got its name, was also symbolically restored.

The street came into being in the Yuan Dynasty (1279-1368) more than 700 years ago. Wangfujing Street is said to have received its name in the Ming Dynasty more than 500 years ago. One of the emperors was said to want all his 10 brothers to build their mansions in the place now known as Wangfujing so as to make it easy for him to keep a wary eye on them for fear that they might pose a direct threat to him. Therefore, the street was then named Shiwangfu, meaning mansions for 10 imperial brothers. Nowadays, the street is one of the busy shopping areas in Beijing. There are more than 200 shops on the 810-metre-long street from Nankou of Wangfujing to Jinyu (Goldfish) Hutong (Lane). Tourists love to go shopping here. Within 8 years from 1992 to 1999, 1 billion yuan (US$120 million) was spent on renovating the whole Wangfujing Street, and shops with more than 1. 8 million square metres of all kinds of buildings along the street. According to statistics, before 1992, the highest flow of visitors numbered 450, 000 every day in Wangfujing Street. Every day about 200, 000 shoppers came to Beijing Department Store, but later, about 50, 000 came to do shopping at Beijing Department Store. To change the situation, the Beijing Municipal Government decided to restore all the shops and the street so that they can attract more people to come to the street reputed as a "golden street" by the people of Beijing.

Wangfujing Street has presented a shining new face after the second phase of its extension project was completed on September 11, 2000. The traffic conditions in the Wangfujing area have been greatly improved thanks to the construction of new roads, such as the Department Store West Road, running parallel to Wangfujing, and the expansion of old ones like Dengshikou Xijie Street, which runs perpendicular to Wangfujing. More than 330 public and private buildings have been removed to make way for roads, trees and lawns. Donghuamen night fair, the centre of the street, has received a face-lift and serves as a food court for visitors. The 340-million-yuan (US$41 million) project aims to make Wangfujing Street the capital's biggest shopping centre. The street has been extended from 810 metres to 1,150 metres (Wangfujing Nankou to Dengshi Xikou), and expanded to include shopping, entertainment, tourism and business. According to the practices of developed countries, places for entertainment and tourism should occupy half of the commercial centre as a whole; Wangfujing was brought up to this standard after renovation. The Jinyu (Goldfish) Hutong on the east side of the street has been turned into an avenue of hotels and restaurants, while a back street on the west side has been built into a street of snack bars and was reopened to the public on September 11, 2000.

The Oriental Plaza has a 100,000-square-metre shopping centre. Wangfujing area has become the city's central business district because of its easy access to major roads, high land prices and high density of retail and service business, as well as its high degree of population flow. Nowadays, the Wangfujing area has been formed naturally in the city's centre, in much the same way as most central business districts have sprung up in other international cities.

At present, there are five major commercial areas such as Wangfujing commercial area, Xidan commercial area, Dazhalan commercial area, Longfusi commercial area and Chaoyangmenwai commercial area.

559

Xidan Commercial Area 西单商业区

Xidan's commercial street has stretched 1,300 metres from the Xidan crossroads to Xisi, with a width of 70 metres. A group of corridors has been built between various shops, business centres and office buildings, and has become a hub for clothes vendors, as are the two underground floors in the Xidan subway station. The New Xidan Street is mainly composed of special shops with famous brands and stores for high-tech products, including computers, software and telecommunication-related commodities. The street concentrates on the development of entertainment, recreation, and food, and drinking sectors. It is one of the major shopping centres in the western part of Beijing. What strong appeal Xidan offers to consumers is the bustling commercial atmosphere. The area has been transformed from a traditional commercial marketplace into a comprehensive commercial area bringing catering, entertainment, culture, tourism, finance, hotels, real estate and telecommunications together with commerce at the core. Xidan Food Market, the Snack Centre, the Kangle Sports Centre and the National Product Sales Centre will be built in Xidan commercial area in the next five years. The lighting system has been upgraded and more greener land added.

At present, there are eight large markets in the area, including Xidan Market, Xidan CVIK Store, Xidan Shopping Centre, and Zhongyou Department Store. Xidan Market ranked first in Beijing for several years in a row in terms of annual sales. It is one of China's top five large markets in terms of sales volume. Xidan Market received 500, 000 consumers during the four holiday weeks of the year.

Some Shopping Centres in Beijing 北京的购物中心

Name	Add.	Tel.	Business Scope
Beijing Department Store	Wangfujing Dajie	65126677	Comprehensive
Beijing Duty-Free Shop	15 Fuxingmenwai Dajie	68010414	Comprehensive
Beijing Antique Shop	64 Dong Liulichang	63036596	Antiques
Beijing Arts & Crafts Dept.	Wangfujing Dajie	65127965	Arts & crafts
Beijing Drawing Shop	289 Wangfujing Dajie	65138413	Paintings & calligraphy
Biluochun Tea Shop	142 Wangfujing Dajie	65254722	Teas
China Bookstore	115 Dong Liulichang	65258351	Books & journals
Dong'an Market	Wangfujing Dajie	65258351	Comprehensive
Friendship Store	17 Jianguomenwai Dajie	65003311	Comprehensive
Guiyou Shopping Mall	5A Jianguomenwai Dajie	65011177	Comprehensive
Hongsheng Musical Instrument Store	225 Wangfujing Dajie	65253797	Chinese & Western musical instruments
Jianhua Leather & Fur Store	192 Wangfujing Dajie	65250801	Mink fur
Liubiju Pickle Shop	Liangshidian Jie, Dazhalan, Qianmen	63034278	Pickles
Lisheng Sports Service Centre	201 Wangfujing Dajie	65250581	Sports articles
Longfu Building	95 Longfusi Jie, Dongsi	64014433	Comprehensive
Muslim Building	Wangfujing Dajie	65138287	Comprehensive

Name	Add.	Tel.	Business Scope
Maolong Commercial Company	10 Building, Jianguomenwai Dajie	65002559	Arts & crafts
Neiliansheng Footwear Store	34 Qianmen Shangye Dajie	63012038	Cloth shoes
Rongbaozhai Studio	19 Liulichang, Xuanwu Dist.	63035279	Paintings & stationery
Ruifuxiang Silk & Cloth Store	5 Dazhalan Jie, Qianmen	63035313	Silk & satin
Shengxifu Hat Store	156 Wangfujing Dajie	65251196	Hats & shoes
Tongrentang Pharmaceutical Store	Dazhalan Jie, Qianmen	63014883	Chinese medicine
White Peacock Arts Service Centre	Dongbei Binghe Lu, Deshengmenwai	62011199	Arts & crafts
Xidan Shopping Mall	Xidan Beidajie	66024695	Comprehensive
Yuanlong Embroidery & Silk Store	15 Dongjie, Yongneizhongli, Chongwen Dist.	67012854	Silk and satin

Beijing Mall—the largest shopping mall in Beijing 北京最大的购物中心
Beijing Mall, to date the largest shopping mall in Beijing, laid its foundation on November 30, 2001 in the southeast area of the capital. Neighbouring the Beijing-Tianjin-Tanggu Expressway, Beijing Mall encompasses 36.62 hectares (90.49 acres) with a planned building area of 600,000 square metres. Developed by Beijing Dadi Investment Co Ltd, the total investment is estimated at 3.3 billion yuan (US$397 million). The Mall is composed of three parts — for shopping, entertainment and recreation—and will open for business on National Day (October 1) holiday in 2003.

Hotel Accommodations
住　宿

Some Star-Rated Hotels in Beijing
北京部分星级饭店
(in Chinese alphabetic order)

Five-Star Hotels ★★★★★	Telephone	Fax
Beijing Hotel 北京饭店	65137766	65137703
The St. Regis Beijing 北京国际俱乐部饭店	64606688	64603299
Beijing Wangfujing Grand Hotel 北京王府井大饭店	65221188	65223816
The Great Wall Sheraton Hotel 长城饭店	65905566	65905398

Hotel New Otani Changfugong 长富宫饭店	65125555	65139810
Jade Palace Hotel 翠宫饭店	62628888	62561447
Diaoyutai State Guest House 钓鱼台国宾馆	68591188	68590997
Diaoyutai Hotel 钓鱼台大酒店	68590996	68590997
Grand Hotel Beijing 贵宾楼饭店	65137788	65130049
Radisson Plaza State Guest Hotel 国宾酒店	68005588	68003308
Beijing International Hotel 国际饭店	65126688	65129972
Holiday Inn Crowne Plaza 国际艺苑皇冠假日饭店	65133388	65132513
Overseas Chinese Prime Hotel 华侨大厦	65136666	65134248
Imperial City Hotel 皇城大饭店	63091991	63091988
Swissotel Hong Kong Macau Center 港澳中心瑞士酒店	65012288	65012501
Jing Guang New World Hotel 京广新世界饭店	65978888	65973333
The King Wing Hot Spring Hotel 京瑞大厦	67668866	67655858
Kunlun Hotel 昆仑饭店	65903388	65903158
Tianlun Dynasty Hotel 天伦王朝饭店	65138888	65137866
The Palace Hotel 王府饭店	65128899	65129050
Shangri-La Hotel Beijing 香格里拉饭店	68412211	68418005
New Century Hotel 新世纪饭店	68492001	68491107
Hilton Hotel 希尔顿饭店	64662288	64653073
Kempinski Hotel 凯宾斯基饭店	64653388	64653366
China World Hotel 中国大饭店	65052266	64612502

Four-Star Hotels ★ ★ ★ ★

Olympic Hotel 奥林匹克饭店	62176688	62172861
Poly Plaza Hotel 保利大厦	65001188	65010268
Paragon Hotel 宝辰饭店	65266688	65274060
Grand View Hotel 大观园酒店	63538899	63539189
Debao Hotel 德宝饭店	68318866	68334571
Oriental Garden Hotel 东方花园饭店	64168866	64150638
Guangzhou Mansion 广州大厦	66078866	66085998
Traders Hotel 国贸饭店	65052277	65050818
Sino-Swiss Hotel 国都大饭店	64565588	64565678
Peace Hotel Beijing 和平饭店	65128833	65126863
Henan Plaza 河南大厦	67751188	67745691
China Resources Hotel 华润饭店	65572233	65585668
Hotel Beijing-Toranto (Jinglun) 京伦饭店	65002266	65002022
Holiday Inn Downtown Beijing 金都假日酒店	68338822	68340696
Jianguo Hotel 建国饭店	65002233	65002871
Gloria Plaza Hotel-Beijing 凯莱大酒店	65158855	65158533
CATIC Plaza Hotel 凯迪克大酒店	64940959	64941288
Holiday Inn Lido 丽都假日饭店	64376688	64376237
Landmark Towers 亮马河大厦	65906688	65903513
Celebrity International Grand Hotel 名人国际大酒店	64981166	64960909
Minzu Hotel 民族饭店	66014466	66022120
Capital Hotel 首都大酒店	65129988	65120309
CVIK Hotel 赛特饭店	65123388	65123537
Radisson SAS Hotel 皇家大饭店	64663388	64653181

Beijing Continental Grand Hotel 五洲大酒店	64915588	64910107
Fragrant Hills Hotel 香山饭店	62591166	62591762
The Beijing Mandarin Hotel 新大都饭店	68319988	68322136
Xinqiao Hotel 新侨饭店	65133366	65125126
Millenium Hotel 新时代大酒店	63578888	63574001
Xiyuan Hotel 西苑饭店	68313388	68314577
Yanshan Hotel 燕山大酒店	62563388	62568640
Vision Asia Hotel 亚视金朗大酒店	65132288	65136810
Jinjiang Asia Hotel 亚洲锦江大酒店	65007788	65008001
Friendship Hotel 友谊宾馆	68498888	68498866
Zhaolong Hotel 兆龙饭店	65972299	65972288
Central Garden Hotel 中苑宾馆	62178888	62174728
CCECC Plaza 中土大厦	63266666	63260788
China Travel Service Tower 中旅大厦	64622288	64612502
Zhongyu Century Grand Hotel 中裕世纪大酒店	63954908	63989999

Three-Star Hotels ★ ★ ★

Badaling Hot Spring Holiday Village 八达岭温泉度假村	69142277	69186869
Beijing Gorge Hotel 北京峡谷宾馆	69661888	69662666
Beiren Hotel 北人大酒店	67716600	67714176
Beiwei Hotel 北纬饭店	63012266	63011366
Paragon Hotel 宝辰饭店	65266688	65274060
Chains City Hotel 城市宾馆	65007799	65007787
Chongwenmen Hotel 崇文门饭店	65122211	65122122
Daxin Hotel 大兴宾馆	69242356	69258899
Dongfang Hotel(New Building) 东方饭店(新楼)	63014466	63044801
New Ark Hotel 方舟宾馆	65947733	65935294
Fengzeyuan Hotel 丰泽园饭店	63186688	63084271
Guohai Hotel 国海饭店	65137799	65123686
Guomen Hotel 国门路大饭店	64378866	64374322
Guangming Hotel 光明饭店	64678822	64677682
Hadamen Hotel 哈达门饭店	67112244	67116865
Hepingli Hotel 和平里大酒店	64275577	64221869
Huangyuan Hotel 皇苑大酒店	68413388	68414327
Huabei Hotel 华北大酒店	62028888	62027196
Huadu Hotel 华都饭店	65971166	65971615
Overseas Chinese Hotel 华侨饭店	64016688	64012386
Huineng Grand Hotel 惠能大饭店	63496688	63451924
Jingduyuan Hotel 京都苑饭店	65291166	65291886
Jingmin Hotel 京闽饭店	67326699	67320650
Golden Leaf Hotel 金叶大厦	65013322	65082499
Golden Era Hotel 金世纪大酒店	67782255	67753886
Jin'an Huangdu Hotel 金安皇都大酒店	65155588	65158616
Lingnan Hotel 岭南饭店	68412288	68414392
Miyun Yunhu Holiday Resort 密云云湖度假村	69943931	69944190
Media Hotel 梅地亚中心	68514422	68515255
Nanyueyuan Hotel 南粤苑宾馆	63714466	63716231

Nuolin Hotel 诺林大酒店	63540399	63542677
Jianguo Hotel 建国饭店	63016688	63013883
Qiaoyuan Hotel 侨园饭店	63038861	63844709
Qilu Hotel 齐鲁饭店	66180966	66180969
Qiran Hotel 奇然大酒店	63532288	63544886
Ritan Hotel 日坛宾馆	65125588	65128671
Great Hall of People Hotel 人民大会堂宾馆	66071188	63095893
Commercial Business Complex 商务会馆	63292244	63292140
Shengtang Hotel 盛唐饭店	62564305	62563092
Sihuan Hotel 四环宾馆	68185599	68211346
Taishan Hotel 泰山饭店	62919988	62911066
Taiwan Hotel 台湾饭店	65136688	65136896
Tiantan Hotel 天坛饭店	67112277	67143132
Tianzhao Hotel 天兆大饭店	65080088	65021859
Winterless Hotel 温特莱大酒店	65032416	65032415
Tibet Hotel 西藏大厦	64981133	64978751
Xijiao Hotel 西郊宾馆	62322288	62311142
Beijing Rainbow Hotel 新北纬饭店	63012266	63011366
New World Courtyard Hotel 新世界万怡酒店	67181188	67081808
Xinxing Hotel 新兴宾馆	68166688	68514669
Yashi Yinya Hotel 银亚大酒店	68152288	68280459
Yanjing Hotel 燕京饭店	68536688	68537531
Yanxiang Hotel 燕翔饭店	64376666	64376231
Yuanfang Hotel 远方饭店	64225588	64222376
Ocean Hotel 远洋酒店	65228888	65229564
Yuexiu Hotel 越秀大饭店	63014499	63014609
Yulong Hotel Beijing 裕龙大酒店	68415588	68413108
Grand Hotel 圆山大酒店	62010033	62019893
Bamboo Garden Hotel 竹园宾馆	64032229	64012633
Exhibition Centre Hotel 展览馆宾馆	68316633	68347450
Ziyu Hotel 紫玉饭店	68411188	68411355

Star-Rated Tourist Apartments (Villas) 星级公寓(别墅)

Dongzhimen International Apartment ★★★★ 东直门国际公寓

Guangming Hotel ★★★★ 光明饭店

Jinyu Mansion ★★★★ 金玉大厦

Yong'an Hotel ★★★ 永安宾馆

Songyu Apartment ★★ 松榆公寓

564

Entertainment
娱 乐

Peking (Beijing) Opera 京剧

Peking Opera, the unique theatrical synthesis of song and dance, acting and acrobatics, was originally a form of local theatre in North China, but its popularity has now spread throughout China. Like most Chinese local operas, it is truly a comprehensive art combining stylized acting with singing, acrobatics, and colorful costumes. It has become the most popular and influential of more than a hundred kinds of dramatic forms on the Chinese stage.

Peking Opera began to emerge in its present form more than 200 years ago to the time of Qing Emperor Qianlong (1736-1795). On his frequent hunting expeditions in south-central China, Emperor Qianlong developed an interest in the local operas. In 1790, to celebrate his 80th birthday, he summoned opera troupes from different localities to perform for him in Beijing. Four famous troupes from Anhui Province remained in Beijing after the celebrations, and the vigorous clear tunes of Anhui Opera gradually replaced *Kunqu* Opera, which had been popular in the palace and among the upper classes in Beijing. In 1828, a Hubei troupe came to Beijing and often performed together with the Anhui troupes. These two types of singing blended on the same stage and gradually gave birth to a new genre, which came to be known as Beijing Opera. Therefore, Beijing Opera has incorporated the best elements from operatic forms.

In the early part of the 20th century, millions went to the opera house—more like a teahouse or a variety theatre—and largely through the acting genius of the late Mei Lanfang (1894-1961), Peking Opera even influenced Western artists such as British Film Artist Charles Spencer Chaplin (1889-1977)卓别麟(林), and German playwright and poet Bertold Brecht (1898-1956)布莱希特.

The singing in Peking Opera is highly stylized but its variations of rhythm and pitch enable the performer to express the thoughts and emotions of different characters in different situations. Recitatives may be in dialogue and monologue form; either a special kind of musical speech, *yunbai* (spoken parts in Peking Opera where the traditional pronunciation of certain words is slightly different from that in current Beijing dialect), or standard spoken Chinese, *jingbai* (parts in Peking Opera spoken in Beijing dialect or capital vernacular) may be employed. Acting in Peking Opera encompasses a set range of movements, gestures and expressions. Every movement or pose, such as stroking a beard, setting a hat straight, swinging a sleeve or lifting a foot, has its own "formula" or pattern, which has been reduced to its essentials and perfected.

The art of illusion is one of Peking Opera's most important characteristics, expressed through techniques of exaggeration and concentration. It is said that Peking Opera performers conquer time and space. Backdrops and stage props are kept to a minimum; often a table and two chairs in front of a big curtain is regarded as sufficient. The three dimensional stage props of modern Western drama are seen as superfluous or even as an encumbrance. The performers use gestures and body movements to represent actions such as opening and closing a door, going up or down a building or a mountain, and embarking, disembarking or travelling by boat. A decorated whip represents a horse, a paddle, a boat and two pennants embroidered with wheels of a carriage. When an actor walks in a circle, it means he has gone on a long journey. Four generals and four soldiers signify an army and fighting in the dark through dance and acrobatics on a brightly lit stage. By such techniques, passed down and developed by generations of performers, Peking Opera has made it possible to transform a small stage into the whole universe.

Stringed and wind instruments are used for the musical accompaniment to Peking Opera, but even more characteristic as the percussion instruments—gongs and drums of different sizes and types, and castanets made of padauk wood and bamboo. The most important stringed instrument is the *jinghu* (a kind of two-stringed fiddle) followed by the *erhu* (also a two-stringed fiddle), plus some plucked instruments such as *yueqin* (a kind of mandolin with four strings). The stringed instruments are played in unison but do not practice Western-style harmony.

The character roles in Peking Opera are finely differentiated according to age and disposition. Female roles are called *dan*, male roles are *sheng*, clowns are *chou*. Roles characterized by the use of different patterns of facial make-up which distinguish a rough, frank character from a cruel or sinister one are called *jing jiao* or *hua lian* (painted faces); the audience knows from the colours and patterns what kind of character is being portrayed. For instance, <u>red</u> signifies loyalty and courage, <u>yellow</u> signifies fierceness, <u>white</u> usually signifies villainy and <u>black</u> signifies honesty and straightforwardness. Spirits, monsters, immortals and Buddhas are often identified by gold and silver. There are different performing styles also for each of these role types, including different styles of singing.

The elaborate and gorgeous costuming of Peking Opera is one of its special characteristics. They are based on the style of the Ming Dynasty costume, with much use of deep red, deep green, yellow, white, black and blue. Strongly contrasting colors are freely used, and embroidery in gold, silver and colored thread. They are strict rules for costumes based on rank character and life-style. The stage props are decorated and beautified versions of their real-life counterparts, and are often works of art in themselves.

The plot-development of Peking Opera does not conform to the general pattern of other types of drama. In modern theatre and drama, the struggle between heroes and villains is gradually developed, and the final outcome is left to the end. But in Peking Opera, the heroes and villains revealed as soon as they appear on the stage. The audiences for Peking Opera, have gone beyond the desire to know the outcome: they are already familiar with the plots about the Monkey King, Xiang Yu the Conqueror, the women generals of the Yang family. It is rather the magic of the performance itself and the skilful techniques of the singing, dancing and acrobatics, which attract them. For this reason the same piece can be seen over and over again without boredom. The first performer to introduce Beijing Opera abroad was the famous *dan* actor Mei Lanfang (1894-1961), who went to Japan in 1919, to the United States in 1929 and the Soviet Union in 1935. In 1932, another famous Peking Opera, Cheng Yanqiu, made a tour of Europe and gave performances and lectures. Since 1949 Peking Opera troupes have made frequent trips abroad, to places such as Japan, Europe, Latin America, the United States and Africa. Today Peking Opera has won high praise throughout the world.

Recently, traditional opera has undergone something of a renaissance and there are performances nightly in Beijing. Overseas tourists should not miss the opportunity to see one, even though tourists will be baffled by much of it. Most operas are based on folk mythology or classical literature, but don't worry about the plots (even many Chinese have difficulty following the archaic language and the words of songs are usually screened at the side of the stage to assist audiences). What impresses the audience most is the sumptuous costumes and make-up and the acrobatic battle scenes (like circus performers, opera artists are rigorously trained from early childhood.) Everything in the opera has significance—from the embroidery on a robe indicating the wearer's rank to the pattern and colour of his make-up, expressing character. As in other Asian dance forms, gestures, even of fingers and eyes, are all-important. And mime is a key element. Very few people are used and it is up to the actor to show, by lifting a foot that he is going through a doorway, or by waving a whip that he is riding a horse.

Swords and staves will be brandished and twirled at breakneck speed in flight sequences without the actors ever touching one another. For the aficionados, it is the singing that matters (old timers talk of "listening to" rather than "watching" an opera,) but the lengthy arias may seem strange to ears raised on Western harmonies.

Likewise the harsh, percussive sounds of the orchestra, which sits on one side of the stage and is led by an "*erhu,*" or two-stringed Chinese fiddle.

Among the most famous Peking Operas are "the Monkey King," "the Drunken Beauty," "the White Snake," "Crossroads," " a Fisherman's Revenge," and "Strategy of an Unguarded City." But for the newcomer, program of excerpts featuring the highlights of two or three operas is recommended, since entire performance may prove a little much to take at one setting.

Theatres regularly presenting Peking Opera include Chang'an, Liyuan at Qianmen Hotel, and Hunan Guild.

Beijing International Amateur Peking Opera Festival
北京国际京剧票友演唱会

It was held from July 7 to 11, 2000. The festival brought 79 performers from the Chinese mainland, Hong Kong, and Taiwan, as well as from Japan, the Republic of Korea, the Philippines, Russia, India, Sweden, Morocco, Sudan, and the United States to demonstrate their love for, and mastery of, the ancient Chinese performance art. Mei Baojiu, the son of Mei Lanfang, the greatest 20th century master of Peking Opera has been deeply involved in Peking Opera for the whole of his life. During the festival, he served as one of the adjudicators of the show. This Peking Opera Festival stimulated amateur activities and ensured that this essential aspect of the traditional Chinese culture will survive into the future.

Mei Lanfang and His Museum

Mei Lanfang (1894-1961), a greatest artist who devoted most of his life and energy to Peking Opera, won his name for his creative performances, especially in playing *dan*, the role of young women. The Mei Lanfang Museum was set up in 1983. It is a typical *Siheyuan*.

(1) A compound, with houses around a courtyard, was where Mai Lanfang spent his last 10 years with his family. The main courtyard keeps its original style and design. In the exhibition room, photos, objects, and the charts are shown to explain Mei Lanfang's artistic life.

(2) A quadrangle is a compound with rows of rooms built in the four directions so that a square inner courtyard is formed at the centre. Old Beijing inhabitants used to call it *Sihefang* — (*Sihe* means "surrounding from all directions")

(3) *Piaoyou* 票友—a passionate Peking Opera buff

The Four Grand Masters of Peking Opera 京剧四大名旦

The history of male actors play in female roles could be traced back to the folk performing arts spreading along the Yellow River and Yangtze River a thousand years ago, which were refined and developed in practices that reached the present level of artistic interpretations. In recent years, the

568

most famous male actors contributing greatly to Peking Opera are: 4 grand masters: Mei Lanfang (1894-1961), Shang Xiaoyun (1899-1976), Xun Huisheng (1899-1968), Cheng Yanqiu (1904-1958); 4 masters: Li Shifang, Zhang Junqiu, Mao Shilai, and Song Dezhu. Owing to the changes in history, China does not cultivate male actors anymore. 中国京剧史上四大名旦(男旦)：梅兰芳、尚小云、荀慧生、程砚秋；四小名旦：李世芳、张君秋、毛世来、宋德珠。这些艺术家为中国的京剧艺术做出了卓越的贡献。

Peking Opera Glossary 京剧术语

The ma' e impersonator must now, as then, learn how to walk naturally and gracefully. The older feminine roles for instance—called *laodan* (the role of an old woman in traditional opera) parts, in which mothers and aunts, dowager queens and other elderly ladies were impersonated—had always to be done in so slow and dignified a manner that it is said that actors could not consider themselves perfect until they could hold a brush between their knees and walk about without letting it fall. Women's roles of maid servants and the like, wearing gaudy costumes, are called *huadan* (one of the main divisions of the *dan* or female role in traditional opera—traditionally the role for a woman of questionable morals, notably a coquettish maid servant or an amorous young woman, bold, seductive, and charming; great emphasis being placed on acting), and women clown parts *caidan* (the feminine counterpart to the *chou* role, or female comedians—portraying a shrew, a dangerous woman, or the ever-present matchmaker, all comic, lowly, and mean) or *choudan* (comic role—one of the four main roles in traditional opera, the other three being *sheng* 生 (male role—one of the four main roles in traditional opera, the other three being *dan*, *jing*, and *chou*; *Sheng* can be subdivided into *Laosheng*, *Xiaosheng*, and *Wusheng*,) *dan* 旦, and *jing* 净; recognized by the patch of white paint around the eyes and nose, sometimes outlines in black, and representing foolish, awkward, or stingy people, though not necessarily evil ones).

Among actors there are several well-defined categories in which they move. For instance, the *sheng* are the actors of the chief male roles. This category is subdivided into older men with beards (*Laosheng or Xusheng*), young men (*Xiaosheng*), the scholar officials (*Wensheng*), and the army men (*Wusheng*). These last have to be specially trained as their fighting includes much high-grade acrobatic work, which demands a very fine degree of co-ordination. The scholar officials (*Wensheng*) have to bring to their roles all the dignity, poise and good manners possible, and the young lads (*Xiaosheng*) must sing in a high falsetto to convey an impression of extreme youth.

569

Next to the *Sheng* actors are the *Dan* players who perform the women's roles. These too have their subdivisions: the *Laodan* who are the elderly, dignified women; the *Qingyi* who are the middle aged and somberly dressed matrons; and that most exciting of female roles, the *Huadan*, the women who have more acting than singing to do. Then there are the *Guimendan* who represent the innocent young women still kept at home. Then there are the *Daomadan*, the tough, hard-riding, fighting women like the famous female warrior Hua Mulan or the woman leader of a rebellion.

The *Jing* actors play the parts of adventurers, heroes, bandits or other tough-natured people. The *Chou* are the clowns; their task is the same as that of the Western clown—to keep the audience laughing and to improvise quips at the right moment to break the tension in some serious play.

Other characters are the *Mo* or *Fumo*—a kind of *Sheng* but not so imposing; perhaps an old servant or a barbarian general or some other minor character. Then there are the *Fujing* who are minor *jing* characters; these are perhaps not only fierce and tough but also somewhat ridiculous, or at any rate, hardly heroic.

Moustaches and beards also have special significance. The beard divided into three indicates the righteousness and integrity of the wearer. A short moustache shows that the wearer is somewhat crude and rough, and those, which sweep upwards belong to tricky, slippery fellows.

Perhaps the most fascinating study in connection with stage costume is that of the painted faces of the actors. Masks are won usually only when animals are represented—tiger, wolf, pig, bear and so on. The art of painting the face, however, has been very highly developed; and each painted face has a special meaning to the knowledgeable theatergoers.

The Sheng 生 can be divided into *Laosheng*, *Xiaosheng*, *Wawasheng* and *Wusheng* in traditional opera.

Laosheng 老生 is one of the main divisions of the male role in traditional opera (the *Laosheng* actor is always bearded and represents a man of maturity and integrity, e. g. a middle-aged scholar, magistrate, a statesman, etc.)

Xiaosheng 小生 is one of the main divisions of the *Sheng* or male role in traditional opera (representing young students, scholars, or warriors; *Xiaosheng* actor never wears a beard and speaks and sings in a mixture of high falsetto and tenor).

Wawasheng 娃娃生 a subdivision of the *Xiaosheng* role in traditional

570

opera, representing loud-voiced boys.

Wusheng 武生 is one of the main divisions of the *Sheng* or male role in traditional opera (portraying military heroes, high-ranking generals, and heroic outlaws; the *Wusheng* actor being majestic in bearing and skilled in Acrobatic performance, swift movement, and agile play with weapons).

The Dan 旦 is female role (one of the four main roles in traditional opera, the other three being *sheng, jing, chou*;) The *Dan* is again subdivided into *Qingyi, Huadan, Wudan,* and *Daomadan (Laodan).*

Qingyi 青衣 is one of the main divisions of the *Dan* or female role in traditional opera (portraying faithful wives, chaste women, and maidens in distress or poverty but noble in character).

Huadan 花旦 is one of the main divisions of the *Dan* or female role in traditional opera (traditionally the role for a woman of questionable morals, notably a coquettish maid servant or an amorous young woman, bold, seductive, and charming; great emphasis being placed on acting.)

Wudan 武旦 is one of the main divisions of the *Dan* or female role in traditional opera (representing a military maiden, a princess of martial character, or a woman bandit; combining the most charming feminine virtues with those of masculine character).

Daomadan 刀马旦 Sword-and-horse *dan*—a subdivision of the *Wudan* role (portraying horse-women and female warriors, who wear tight-fitting clothes, twirl weapons, and perform acrobatic feats).

Laodan 老旦 is the role of an old woman in traditional opera.

Jing 净 painted-face role 大花脸 (one of the four main roles in traditional opera, the other three being *sheng, dan* and *chou,* so called from the variety of intricate and startling patterns in brilliant colors painted on the faces of the players; The *jing* or painted-face actor represents a man of general, a minister, a brigand, or a demon, singing and speaking in a full raucous voice rising to protracted enunciation of tremendous volume).

Chou 丑

comic role 三花脸，即丑角 (one of the four main roles in traditional opera, the other three being *sheng*, *dan* and *jing*; recognized by the patch of white paint around the eyes and nose, sometimes outlined in black, and representing foolish, awkward, or stingy people, though not necessarily evil ones); comedian; clown; three-flower face 三花脸 (another name for *chou*, presumably from the outline of the white patch on the face).

Peking Opera Face Patterns 京剧脸谱

Face patterns represent a unique make-up art of the traditional Chinese dramatic form. They follow a set mode in composition, sketching and colouring.

Face patterns date far back in history. Ancient Chinese entertainers sometimes wore masks known as "dummy faces." Mask-wearing dancers of the Sui and Tang dynasties and the non-human impersonators of the Yuan operas further promoted their popularity. In time, following the development of the opera and the needs of the performances, the mask was replaced by the painted patterns. At first only red, white and black colours were used for decoration, while the bolder colours were reserved for demons and monsters and outlaws, and only the eyebrows and sockets were painted. It was not until the Ming Dynasty that a fairly complete gallery of face patterns took shape. The Peking Opera face patterns were developed on the basis of the Hubei and Anhui operas, and by borrowing from the *kunqu*, *yiyang* and *bangzi* operas.

Only male characters, especially the *jing*, or "painted face," wear face patterns. They make up exaggerating the most typical characteristics of the roles they play in mental outlook, moral character, sentiment, appearance, age and status. As soon as an actor steps onto the stage, his painted face gives a clear concept of his character-loyal or traitorous, good or evil. The audiences have long accepted such expressions. In general, *red* stands for loyalty and uprightness; *purple*, courage and resolution; *black*, toughness and irascibility; *yellow*, brutality and scheme; *White*, treachery and machination; *gold and silver*, mythical figures. Different characters are represented with their faces painted with ingenious patterns in different colors.

The dominant colour and the minutely executed patterns highlight the character without imparting a sense of confusion.

Flowery-face role 花脸—a popular name for *jing* 净 (so called from the elaborate facial painting)

Kunqu Opera 昆曲

Kunqu Opera first appeared in the Kunshan area of what is now Jiangsu Province, and became popular across the country in the Ming (1368-1644) and early Qing (1644-1911) dynasties, long before the birth of Peking Opera and other local operas. Emperors, officials, intellectuals and the populace appreciated them as an integral part of their leisure. *Kunqu* Opera gave birth to a dozen Chinese local operas, including Peking Opera. As *Kunqu* Opera catered more to the highbrow tastes of royal families and intellectuals, it gradually lost favour with the common masses. During the "cultural revolution" (1966-1976), it became nearly extinct.

After the turmoil of that time, *Kunqu* Opera was still loved by modern intellectuals, who, like their ancient counterparts, were intoxicated by its art, a perfect combination of literature, poetry, dance, music and local opera. Nowadays, young people prefer almost any other form of entertainment to *Kunqu* Opera. Films, videos, games, pop music, disco and karaoke, all are better than what they see as old-fashioned and dull. *Kunqu* Opera has a very small, but very devoted audience.

Kunqu was the origin of many traditional Chinese operas, including the Peking Opera. It is also famous for its poetical and refined dialogues and elegant and gentle movements. In spite of its charms, *Kunqu* Opera is facing difficulties, which can be seen in its dwindling audiences. Some performers are even seeking to change their careers for better incomes. Currently, China has six *Kunqu* Opera theatres with only 600 practitioners. Thus, China is taking measures to protect and revitalize Kunqu Opera. The government will build more theatres for audiences and performers. The United Nations has joined the Chinese Government in strengthening protection of the 600-year-old *Kunqu* Opera. A senior United Nations Educational, Scientific and Cultural Organization (UNESCO) counselor, Sevastian Veg, came to China on July 25, 2001 to discuss with Chinese officials ways to protect and develop the opera. Veg inspected the Beijing-based Beifang *Kunqu* Opera Theatre and Jiangsu *Kunqu* Opera Theatre to get first-hand knowledge about the current status of the opera. UNESCO is co-operating with the Chinese authorities to revitalize the *Kunqu* Opera. UNESCO has consulted with local governments on the latter's 10-year plan aiming to bring more audiences to *Kunqu* Opera. Veg said UNESCO has helped local governments to preserve the operas' cultural heritage in the form of a fund-in-trust sponsored by United Nations mem-

573

bership countries. UNESCO listed *Kunqu* Opera in a catalogue of 19 "oral and intangible heritages" of the world on May 18, 2001.

The seven-act *Kunqu* Opera, features Yang Yuhuan, a tragic heroine who lived in the Tang Dynasty (618-907). Emperor Xuanzong's favourite concubine, she was said to have been forced to commit suicide by the emperor. But there is another version of the story, which says that with the help of Japanese statesman Abeno Nagamaro, Yang Yuhuan escaped death and fled to Japan, and eventually settled down there. She played the role of cultural ambassador, promoting understanding and exchanges between the two countries. The creative opera includes orchestra, music, opera, dance and drama for the first time.

"Ban Zhao 班昭," a six-act *Kunqu* Opera, which follows the life of Ban Zhao (c AD 49-AD 120), a female historian of the Eastern Han Dynasty (AD 25-AD 220). Born into a family of historian, Ban Zhao loved to read books in her formative years. After her father and brother died, she carried on their work of writing history books. For years she worked hard without enjoying normal family life—she married, but her husband left her because he could not bear to marry a woman who wrote all day long. But Ban Zhao persevered until she finished her works in her 70s, dying in solitude. In "Ban Zhao," large sections of spoken dialogue are used, striking a great contract with *Kunqu* Opera classic like "Peony Pavilion" and "The Romance of West Chamber." Actually, like any other opera, *Kunqu* Opera is made up of four parts—songs, dialogue, acting and martial arts. But over the past century, dialogue has been neglected with the introduction of spoken drama because it is commonly believed that one feature that distinguishes the two dramatic forms is the use of dialogue. Dialogue is certainly quite differently expressed. While a spoken drama requires an everyday, realistic style, dialogue in *Kunqu* Opera rhymes and is literary, making it quite hard to understand for the untrained, modern ear. Unlike traditional *Kunqu* Opera, "Ban Zhao" has more dialogue than songs. Instead of promoting the plot, songs are used as a way of expressing inner feelings. In "Ban Zhao," the dialogues have more functions. They are not only used to explain the plot, but also to express feelings at critical moments when a monologue or a song would take too long. At the opera's climax at the end of the fourth act, Ban Zhao sings no songs to express her shock, pain and anger on hearing about the death of her beloved husband, who no longer loves her. All is conveyed by the short sentence: "Give me back my husband." Over the past few decades, Chinese operas have generally been regarded as a highly formulated art form, which means that the true inner feelings of the characters have been neglected for the sake of exterior movements.

Theatres in Beijing 北京的剧场一览表

Name	Telephone
Beijing Theatre 北京剧院	64911228
Beijing Exhibition hall Theatre 北京展览馆剧场	65903377
Beijing Workers' Club 北京市工人俱乐部	63529574
Beijing Recreational Centre 北京康乐官	64993434
Beijing Workers' Gymnasium 北京工人体育馆	65024558
Beijing Century Theatre 北京世纪剧场	64002927
Beijing Concert Hall 北京音乐厅	66057006／66055812
Theatre of Beijing Youth Palace 北京青年宫剧场	66152241
Beijing Qiseguang Children's Theatre 北京七色光儿童剧场	84022285
Small Theatre of Beijing People's Art Theatre 北京人民艺术剧院小剧场	65250123
Beijing International Club 北京国际俱乐部	65322188
Beijing Night City 北京之夜文化城	65272814 ／ 65272815
Poly Theatre 保利剧院	65131039
Chang'an Grand Theatre 长安大戏院	65101308 ／ 65101309
Chang'an Small Theatre 长安小剧场	65101155ext. 116
Chang'an Club 长安俱乐部	65229988
Chaoyang Theatre 朝阳剧场	65072421／1818
Big Tower Magic Theatre 大铁塔梦幻剧场	65812750 ／65814122
Grand View Garden Theatre 大观园戏楼	63519025
Universe Theatre of Dongcheng Children's Palace 东城区少年官天地剧场	65023984
Concert Hall of the National Library 国图音乐堂	68419220 ／ 68485462
Gongwangfu Grand Theatre 恭王府戏楼	66157671
Guo'an Theatre 国安剧院	62026328
Hanlin Peking Opera 翰林京剧	63519025／63037979
Huguang Guild Hall 湖广会馆	63518284
Haidian Theatre 海淀影剧院	62558026
The Art Salon of Holiday Inn Crowne Plaza	65125063
Royal International Club 皇家国际俱乐部	68338888
Capital Club 京城俱乐部	64672225
Jinfan (Golden Sail) Concert Hall 金帆音乐厅	65250615
Laoshe Teahouse 老舍茶馆	63036830
Theatre of the Youth Palace 青年官剧场	66152211
Grand Theatre of the Cultural Palace of Nationalities 民族官大剧场	6602277
Minzu Concert Hall 民族音乐厅	64919081
Liyuan Theatre 梨园剧场	63016688ext. 8867
People's Theatre 人民剧场	66181634
Capital Gymnasium 首都体育馆	68313926
Capital Theatres 首都剧场	65250996
Century Theatre 世纪剧院	64660032 ／ 64664805
Universal Theatre 天地剧场	64169893
Wansheng Theatre 万胜剧场	63037449
Zhengyici Theatre 正乙祠戏楼	63033104

Concert Hall in the Zhongshan Park 中山音乐堂	66057006 / 6559828
Small Theatre of the Central Experimental Drama Theatre 中央实验话剧院小剧场	64031109
Black Chamber of Central Academy of Drama 中央戏剧学院黑匣子剧场	64035626
Concert Hall of Central National Troupe 中央民族乐团音乐厅	64919081
Zhonghe Theatre 中和剧院	63037083
The Forbidden City Concert Hall 紫禁城音乐厅	65598285

Some Golf Clubs and Golf Courses in Beijing
北京部分高尔夫俱乐部和高尔夫球场

Name	Tel.
Beijing Golf Club 北京高尔夫俱乐部	8947 0005 / 8947 0108
Chaoyang Guangjitang Golf Club 朝阳广济堂高尔夫俱乐部	6500 1149 / 6501 8584
Country Golf Club 乡村高尔夫俱乐部	6940 1111 / 6940 2020
Beijing International Golf Club 北京国际高尔夫俱乐部	6076 2288 / 6076 1111
Grand Canal Club 大运河俱乐部	8958 3058 / 8958 2288
Xiaoling Mini Golf Course 晓玲迷你高尔夫球场	6358 8814 / 6355 2929

In China, there are now 100 golf courses in operation. Their business is not satisfactory.
Note: The word "golf" is a combination of abbreviation of green 绿色, oxygen 氧气, light 阳光, foot 步履. What a coincidence!

Others
其 他

Main Medical Centres in Beijing
北京主要的医疗机构

Name	Specialized field	Tel.
P.U.M.C. Hospital	Gynecology & obstetrics, internal secretion	65127733
Beijing Hospital	Comprehensive	65126611
Beijing Tongren Hospital	Otorhinolaryngology, ophthalmology	65129911
Beijing Chinese Medicine Hosp.	Internal diseases	64010761
Beijing No.1 Hosp. for Infectious Diseases		64211031
Sino-Japanese Friendship Hosp.	Comprehensive	64222592
Beijing Friendship Hosp.	Urology, thoracal surgery, tropical diseases	63032011
Beijing Stomatogical Hospital	Stomatology	68329355
Beijing Children's Hosp.	Pediatrics	68523596
Xiyuan Chinese Medicine Hosp.	Chinese medicine treatment	62563344
Beijing Jishuitan Hospital	Burn, orthopedics	66028351
Beijing Tiantan Hospital	Neuro surgery	67016611
BJ Traditional Chinese Medicine	Chinese medicine treatment	67689938
Fuwai Hospital	Cardiovascular diseases	68314466
Beijing Tumor Hospital	Tumor	67781331
Plastic Surgery Hospital	Plastic surgery	68202233
Beijing Xuanwu Hospital	Internal neuro treatment	63012835
Beijing Emergency Medical Centre	Emergency treatment	120 / 66014433
Asia Emergency Centre Beijing Off. (China World Trade Centre)	Emergency treatment	65053521
Intl. SOS Emergency Centre, Beijing Office Emergency Treatment	Room 438, Kunlun Hotel	65003419

Commonly-Used Hotline Telephone Directory
常用热线电话

China International Country Code Number	0086
Beijing City Code Number	010
Local Telephone Information	114
Time Check	117
Medical Emergency	120
Weather Information	121
Traffic Emergency Call Service	122
EMS and Floral Service	185
Mobile Phone Subscriber Service	1860
Civil Aviation Information Inquiry	2580
Air Ticketing Service	2581
Commercial Information Service	2583
Railway Information Inquiry	2585
Exit Inquiry Service	64078237
Taxi Hotline	68351150
148 Law Inquiry Hotline	63890148
Service Centre Inquiry	63153408
Mayor Hotline	65128080
Train Ticket Booking Telephone	63217188
Beijing Tourist Hot line	65130828
China Consumers' Association	63011234
China International Travel Service Head Office	66053822
China Youth Travel Service	65243388
China Merchant International Travel Service	65975280
Beijing China Travel Service	65941133
China Peace International Travel Service	65611635
China Travel Service Head Office	65140830
China Comfort Travel Service Head Office	65940885
China Women Travel Service	65262244
Beijing China International Travel Service	65157515
Capital Airport Inquiry	64563604/3605/3606
Beijing Railway Station Booking Office	65127378/65127354
	65634512/65634622
Beijing Railway Station Inquiry	51059999
Beijing West Railway Station Booking Office	63214215/63216253
	63216273/63246810
Beijing West Railway Station Inquiry	63210114
Capital Taxi Company	65138893
Tourist Bus Company	64363452
Beijing Taxi Company	68312288
Overseas Chinese Affairs Agency of the State Council	64040331
Hong Kong and Macao Office of the State Council	68315014
Taiwan Affairs Office of the State Council	63098946

Overseas Chinese Affairs Office, Beijing Government	65124589
Beijing Taiwan Affairs Office Inquiry	65125309
Expatriates Management & Visa Department of	65253102
the Beijing Public Security Bureau	

Climate in Beijing 北京的气候

Month		Jan	Feb	Mar	Apr	May	Jun	Jul	Aug	Sep	Oct	Nov	Dec
Average Temperature (℃)		-4.6	-2.1	4.7	13.0	19.9	23.6	25.8	24.4	19.1	12.2	4.3	-2.5
	High	10.7	15.5	22.6	31.1	36.6	38.9	39.6	38.3	32.3	29.3	23.3	13.5
	Low	-22.8	-17.6	-12.5	-2.4	3.7	11.2	16.1	12.3	4.9	-1.4	-11.6	-18.0
Precipitation(mm)		2.6	7.7	9.1	22.4	26.1	70.4	196.6	243.5	69.3	21.2	7.9	1.6
Wind Speed (m.p.s.)		2.4	2.7	3.0	3.3	2.8	2.2	1.7	1.6	1.8	2.1	2.2	2.5

Four Seasons	Winter	Spring	Summer	Autumn	Winter
	26/ 10-31/ 3	1/ 4-25/ 5	26/ 5-5/ 9	6/ 9-25/ 10	26/ 10-31/ 3
	160 days	65 days	95 days	45 days	

Brutal Heatwave Scorches the People of Beijing (July 24, 1999)

On July 24, 1999, Beijing's daytime temperature reached 42.2 degrees centigrade, the hottest day recorded in half a century. In the history of Beijing, 42.6 degrees centigrade was recorded on June 15, 1942. The capital suffered a similar heatwave from June 24 to July 2, 1999. It broke a record set in 1942 when the maximum temperature exceeded 35 degrees centigrade for nine consecutive days.

Beijing's Double Emblems
北京的市树、市花

Beijing became the first Chinese city to adopt two trees and two flowers as its emblems.

The Chinese scholar tree 国槐 and the oriental arborvitae 柏树, and the Chinese rose 月季 and chrysanthemum 菊花, were approved as the city's representative trees and flowers at the closing session of the Municipal People's Congress on March 12, 1987.

Over the past few years, local residents participated in the citywide search for appropriate trees and flowers after a proposal by the municipal government.

These trees and flowers have all been long time residents of the Chinese scholar tree, which has strings of thin leaves and fragrant white flowers, as a symbol of happiness, and the oriental arborvitae, an evergreen tree of the pine family, as a symbol of longevity.

1980s Top Ten Buildings in Beijing
北京20世纪80年代十大建筑

The newspapers "Beijing Daily" and "Beijing Evening News" in the late half of 1987 sponsored a Beijing wide poll to select the top ten buildings constructed in the Chinese capital in 1980s. The results of the poll were disclosed on April 28, 1988. The top ten edifices are:

1. National Library of China 中国国家图书馆
2. China International Exhibition Centre 中国国际展览中心
3. Central Colour Television Centre 中央彩色电视中心
4. Beijing Airport Terminal 首都机场候机楼
5. Beijing International Hotel 北京国际饭店
6. Daguanyuan (Grand View Garden) 大观园
7. The Great Wall Sheraton Hotel 长城饭店
8. China Theatre 中国剧院
9. Memorial Hall for the War of Resistance Against Japanese Aggression
   中国人民抗日战争纪念馆
10. The Subway Station at Dongsi Shitiao 地铁东四十条车站

The poll was based on 224, 500 ballots cast by the people in different walks of life in Beijing. The National Library of China was nominated 173, 046 times.

These ten buildings were considered "architectural breakthroughs" that reflect China's reforms and opening to the outside world.

The awards were announced at a press conference in Beijing on April 28, 1988.

1990s Top Ten Leading Structures in Beijing
北京20世纪90年代十大建筑

579

Sponsored by Beijing Municipal Planning Committee, Beijing Municipal Construction Committee, Beijing Municipal Planning Association, Beijing Daily, Beijing Evening News, and Beijing TV Station, a list of the ten leading structures in Beijing in the 1990s disclosed on May 15, 2001. The results were produced by a survey of 630, 000 Beijing citizens, the Beijing Youth Daily reported. The top ten leading structures are as follows:

1. The Central Radio and Television Tower 中央广播电视塔
2. The National Olympic Sports Centre and Asian Games Village 奥林匹克体育中心亚运村
3. The New World Centre 新世界中心
4. The Exhibition Hot House of Beijing Botanical Garden 北京植物园展览温室

5. The New Capital Library 首都图书馆新馆
6. The New Library of Tsinghua University 清华大学图书馆新馆
7. The Office Building of Foreign Languages & Research Publishing House 外语教学与研究出版社办公楼
8. The Beijing Henderson Centre 北京恒基中心
9. Beijing Sun Dong An Plaza 北京新东安市场
10. Beijing International Financial Centre 北京国际金融中心

Beijing's Gates 北京的城门

Nine inside, seven outside, four in the Imperial City is a phrase used by Beijing residents since the Ming Dynasty (1368-1644) as an aid to remembering the number of gates in the walls of their city.

Nine Inside 里九城门

Gate of Exalted Literature (Chongwenmen) 崇文门
South-Facing Gate (Zhengyangmen) 正阳门 or Front Gate (Qianmen) 前门
Gate of Universal Prowess or Gate of Occult Might 宣武门 (Xuanwumen)
Mound Formed Gate 阜城门 or Gate of Just Rule (Pingzemen) 平则门
Western Gate 西直门 (Xizhimen) or Gate of Harmony & Righteousness (Heyimen) 和义门
Gate of Virtuous Triumph (Deshengmen) 德胜门
Gate of Peace and Stability (Andingmen) 安定门
Eastern Gate (Dongzhimen) 东直门 or Gate of Upholding & Benevolence (Chongrenmen) 崇仁门 Gate Facing the Sun (Chaoyangmen) 朝阳门 or Gate of Uniformity & Affinity (Qihuamen) 齐化门

Seven Outside 外七城门

Eastern Informal Gate (Dongbianmen) 东便门
Broad Canal Gate (Guangqumen) 广渠门
Left Gate of Peacefulness (Zuo'anmen) 左安门
Gate of Eternal Stability (Yongdingmen) 永定门
Right Gate of Peacefulness (You'anmen) 右安门
Gate of Universal Peace (Guang'anmen) 广安门
Western Informal Gate (Xibianmen) 西便门

Four in the Imperial City 皇城四门

Gate of Heavenly Peace (Tian'anmen) 天安门
Gate of Earthly Peace (Di'anmen) 地安门
Gate of Eastern Peace (Dong'anmen) 东安门
Gate of Western Peace (Xi'anmen) 西安门

On a tour of Beijing, visitors learn about the different functions of old Beijing's nine city gates, the meaning of the saying "east for the wealthy, west for the noble, north for the poor, and south for the lowly."

Each of the 20 gates had its own function & has left many interesting stories.

Zhengyangmen was the pass emperors used for travel to the Temple of Heaven for worshipping ceremonies. Only the imperial sedans and carriages were allowed to use the gate, while funeral ceremonies and carriages were forbidden to pass here.

The most popular carts passing **Chongwenmen** were those carrying liquor, as distilleries were then located in the south and east of the city.

<u>Chaoyangmen</u> was the gate of grain since it linked transportation between the Forbidden City and Tongzhou (present-day Tongzhou District). Tongzhou was the beginning of the Grand Canal (1974 kilometres in distance) linking Beijing and Hangzhou in Zhejiang Province. Tribute grain from the south was shipped to the capital on the canal. Warehouses were built close to Chaoyangmen. Today's Nanmencang, Beimencang, Xintaicang and Lumicang were used to store rice in the past.

<u>Xizhimen</u> was the water gate named for its position as the gateway to Jade Spring Hill, which was the source of the imperial drinking water.

Gates were also connected with walls which were used to defend Beijing. On top of the wall, special facilities in the shape of sawtooth were built to shield arrows and other reasons. Other facilities included blockades that prevented soldiers from falling down the wall. Building the walls was a costly project. It was once reported that more than 40 million bricks and great quantities of earth, lime and timber were used to wall the city.

Nowadays, Beijing's city walls have all been demolished. Only a few gate towers are left. The Old Beijing Mini Landscape Park presents a complete picture of the 20 city gates and walls, although in a scaled down version.

The great architect Kuai Xiang 蒯祥 of the Ming Dynasty adopted Chinese astrology when he built the city. In the theory, the number Nine represented the divine Heaven, the number Five the dragon and the Earth in the middle of the Universe. Under such a theory, Kuai Xiang constructed nine gates, five fortresses and a platform in the shape of the Chinese character Earth in the middle of the palace. The design symbolized the emperor's divinity of both the Nine and the Five.

From the modern point of view, Beijing's arrangement of the axis thoroughfare and four lakes of Nanhai (South Sea or Lake), Zhonghai (Middle Sea or Lake), Beihai (North Sea or Lake) and Houhai (Rear Sea or Lake) are shaped like two dragons raising their heads rivaling for a pearl. We see the dragon and alarming pearl motif often repeated in ancient Chinese ceramics and elsewhere in the artifacts of Chinese antiquity. It is symbolic as well as artistically fanciful and articulated design.

The Eight Scenic Spots of Yanjing (Old Name for Beijing)燕京八景

Yanjing is the former name of Beijing. Referring to the eight attractions Emperor Qianlong (1736-1795) of the Qing Dynasty celebrated in his poetry, the Eight Scenic Spots are as follows:

Qiongdao Chunyin (Jade Islet Spring Shade / Jade Islet in Shady Springtime) 琼岛春阴

It is a tablet on the eastern hill side of Jade Flower Islet in Beihai Park. Springtime clouds and fog used to float around the forested islet, completely shading it.

Yuquan Baotu (Leopard Leaping the Fountain of Yuquan) 玉泉趵突

It erupts from a cave at the foot of Yuquan (Jade Spring) Mountain in the western suburbs of Beijing. Spring water winds from the "cave's" mouth where Yuquan is inscribed around the mountain, inspiring the name Yuquan Cuihong (Yuquan Falling Rainbow).

Taiye Qiufeng (Autumn Wind of Taiye 【Pool of Great Secretion】/ Autumn Winds on Taiye) 太液秋风

It is a tablet in Shuiyunxie Pavilion located on the eastern bank of Zhonghai Lake at Jiniaoyu Bridge's southern end. Composed of Beihai and Zhonghai lakes, Taiye Lake offers a breadth of fresh air within the city proper.

Jimen Yanshu (Fog Tree of Jimen / Trees in the Mist at Ji Gate) 蓟门烟树

It is a tablet that stands on the relic of Xitucheng (West Earth Wall) just outside Xizhimen near Xueyuanlu Road in western Beijing.

Xishan Qingxue (Sunny Western Hills after Snow / Sunny or Snowy Days of Western Hills) 西山晴雪

It refers to the Fragrant Hills, the section of the Western Hill closest to the city. The Fragrant Hills are beautiful in any season. Snow covers the hills during the winter while aromatic flower bloom during the spring and summer; in autumn, a palette of red, orange and yellow leaves decorate the hillsides.

Lugou Xiaoyue (Morning Moon over Lugou Bridge / Moon over the Lugou Bridge at Dawn) 卢沟晓月

It refers to a steel erected at Lugou Qiao (Marco Polo Bridge). The name Morning Moon over Lugou Bridge refers to Emperor Qianlong's poem celebrating the bridge. The 485 lion statues perch on the bridge's balustrades seem to be playing with each other under a full autumn moon.

Jintai Xizhao (Sunset of Jintai / Golden Terrace in the Glow of the Setting Sun) 金台夕照

It refers to the tablet once erected in an eastern suburb of Beijing. When King Yanzhao of the Spring and Autumn Period (770 BC-476 BC) sought a truly virtuous person, he built a platform on which he placed piles of gold; thus, the platform became known as "Jintai" or "Gold Platform."

Juyong Diecui (The Great Wall Surrounded by Lush Greenery at the Juyong Pass / Layers of Green Mounts Near Juyong Pass) 居庸叠翠

It refers to a tablet originally erected at the southeast part of Juyong Pass. With only a narrow gorge connecting the north and south sections, the mountain area near Juyong Pass is very perilous. However, a view from the foot of the gorge up toward the mountains offers a bird's eye view of wild flowers and rolling green hills.

The Vicissitudes of the City Proper and Its Administrative Area in Beijing 北京市区及行政区域的变迁

The circumference of the city proper had been expanded from Qinghe in the north to Nanyuan in the south, and from Dingfuzhuang in the east to Shijingshan in the west. The city proper of Beijing had a circumference of 750 square kilometres.

Year	City Proper (Sq. Kilometres)	Administrative Area (Sq. Kilometres)
1949	108.9	707
1957	192.1	
1965	273	
1975	290.8	
1980	346	
1990	1,040	16,800

Profiles of Beijing's Districts and Its Counties
北京的区、县介绍

Beijing is one of the four municipalities directly under the leadership of the Central People's Government. It is divided into 16 districts and 2 counties, of which 4 are urban districts (Dongcheng, Xicheng, Chongwen and Xuanwu), 4 suburban districts (Chaoyang, Haidian, Fengtai and Shijingshan), 8 outlying suburban districts (Mentougou, Shunyi, Tongzhou, Fangshan, Changping, Pinggu, Huairou and Daxing) and 2 suburban counties (Miyun and Yanqing). The city has 36 towns, 253 townships, 4,432 villagers' committees, 3,753 residents' committees and 101 neighbourhood committees.

Dongcheng (East City) District 东城区
Covering an area of 24.7 square kilometres, the district is divided into 10 neighbourhood committees with a population of some 600,000. The renowned commercial streets Wangfujing and Dongsi are situated here. The Beijing Railway Station is located within the district.

Xicheng (West City) District 西城区
Encompassing 30 square kilometres, the district is divided into 10 neighbourhood committees with a population of about 750,000. Zhongnanhai (Central South Sea), the seat of the Party's Central Committee, is located within the district. Xidan commercial district and financial institutions are concentrated in the district as well. The Forbidden City, Beihai Park, the Round City, and Dr Sun Yat-sen's Park are also located within this district.

Its GDP was 19. 5 billion yuan (US$2. 3 billion) in 2000, up 13. 4 per cent on the previous year.

Xuanwu District 宣武区

Occupying an area of 16. 5 square kilometres, it is divided into 8 neighbourhood committees, with a population of some 550, 000. It is the birthplace of modern Beijing city proper, with many old names in business and age-old architectures. Commercial business is flourishing.

Chongwen District 崇文区

Covering an area of 15. 9 square kilometres, the district is divided into 7 neighbourhood committees with a population of 410, 000. The old Beijing commerce, service industry and light industry, special arts and crafts industry are well-developed in the district. Famous centuries-old brand shops are located in it.

Chaoyang District 朝阳区

The Chaoyang District, honoured as a diplomatic window and the window of international exchange for Beijing, is the biggest urban district, as well as one of the most modernized parts of Beijing. Encompassing 470. 6 square kilometres, and located north of Jianguomenwai Avenue between the city's Eastern Second Ring and Eastern Third Ring and the Fourth Ring roads, Chaoyang District is divided into 21 neighbourhood committees and 24 townships with a population of 2. 3 million. It is the largest district of the capital city. The district is an important non-staple food production base and important industrial district. More than 98 per cent of the foreign embassies, representative offices of the United Nations, news agencies and 62 per cent of the city's five-star hotels are located in the district. Capital Airport, Workers' Stadium, and Asian Games Village and etc., are concentrated in this district. In 2000, GDP in Chaoyang District reached 48 billion yuan (US$5. 9 billion). The district is home to more than 60 per cent of the foreign business agencies in Beijing, 3, 000 foreign companies and 167 international agencies.

584

Furthermore, Datun and Wali areas in the north will be the location of the 12. 15-square-kilometre Olympic Park in 2008 and they will be the centre of exhibitions and sports in the future.

Haidian District 海淀区

Covering an area of 426 square kilometres, the district is divided into 17 neighbourhood committees and 11 townships with a population of 1. 44 million Famous high-tech industry and institutions of higher learning are located in the district. Its rural area is Beijing's non-staple food production base. Its western mountainous area is one of the Beijing's famous fruit production bases.

Fengtai District 丰台区

Covering an area of 304. 2 square kilometres, the district is divided into 13 neighbourhood committees and 6 townships with a population of 790, 000. The district is Beijing's southwestern gateway. Most trains coming and going pass through the district. Fengtai District is also famous for " kingdom of vegetables" and good reputation for "township of flowers. "

Shijingshan District 石景山区

Covering an area of 81. 8 square kilometres, the district is divided into 9 neighbourhood committees and an agricultural committee with a population of 300, 000. It is Beijing industrial district. It is rich in water resources and Yongding River passes through it.

Fangshan District 房山区

Encompassing 1, 866. 7 square kilometres, it is divided into 3 towns, 29 townships and one neighbourhood committee with a population of 760, 000. Its mountainous area makes up 60 per cent. With many rivers, the district is 45 kilometres away from the city centre. Famous for places of historic interests, the district produces snow-white marble, chestnuts, persimmons, Beijing white pear, and hongxiao pear. Within its boundary, there are some large-scale enterprises.

Mentougou District 门头沟区

Occupying an area of 1, 331. 3 square kilometres, the district is divided into 18 townships and 5 neighbourhood committees with a population of 270, 000. The district is a mountainous area with more than one hundred peaks, and mountainous area occupies 96 per cent of the total area of the district. It is rich in coal, limestone, and granite; Its local products include rose, day lily 黄花, twigs of the chaste tree (used for weaving baskets, etc.)荆条, wild jujube 酸枣, mushrooms, and Beijing white pear.

Tongzhou District 通州区

Covering an area of 870 square kilometres, the district is divided into 11 towns, one district with 12 townships and 28 neighbourhood committees with a population of 600, 000. Since ancient times, Tongzhou District has been the eastern gateway of Beijing, communications hub and strategic points. At present, the district is the biggest satellite city of Beijing.

Shunyi District 顺义区

Covering a total area of 980 square kilometres, the district is divided into one town, 28 townships with a population of 540, 000. It is 30 kilometres from Dongzhimen. Within its boundary is plain, with crops growing in the fields and it is named "granary of the Capital. "

Changping District 昌平区

Covering an area of 1, 430 square kilometres, the district is divided into one district, 3 towns and 26 townships, one state-run farm, one special tourist zone with a population of 430,000. It is 34 kilometres from the city centre. Changping is renowned for tourist scenic zone with numerous scenic spots and tourist facilities. Within its boundary it is rich in natural resources, mineral products, and rural products.

Daxing District 大兴区

Approved by the State Council, Daxing became a district on April 30, 2001. Encompassing 1,012 square kilometres, Daxing District is divided into 1 district, 9 towns and 18 townships with a population of 520,000. It is a plain district and one of satellite cities of Beijing. Panggezhuang is famous for water melon both in Beijing and Tianjin.

Huairou District 怀柔区

Covering an area of 2,557.3 square kilometres, the district is divided into 7 towns and 14 townships with a population of 260,000. It is 50 kilometres from the city centre. Ninety per cent of the district is mountainous and it is home to chestnuts. Other fruits include walnuts, haw, sweet pear, *ya* pear, and apricot kernel.

Pinggu District 平谷区

Covering a total area of 1,075 square kilometres, the district is divided into 21 townships with a population of 380,000. Most of the area is occupied by mountains. Its mountain products include walnuts, chestnuts and apricot kernel. Within its boundary it is rich in natural resources, and gold ranks first in the outskirts of Beijing.

Miyun district 密云县

Occupying an area of 2,335.6 square kilometres, the county is divided into 2 towns and 22 townships with a population of 420,000. It is 75 kilometres from the city centre. Built in 1958, Miyun Reservoir is one of the largest reservoirs in North China. Within its boundary it is plenty of mountain products (such as haws, chestnuts and walnuts).

586

New airport attracts tourists Villagers of the Hedouyu Village in Eastern Beijing's Pinggu District pooled 3.5 million yuan (US$422,705) recently and established an airport near the famous Jingdong (east of Beijing) Great Karst Cave. Approved by related authorities, the airport, along with a Chinese-made 12-person Yun-5-B aircraft, will be used to start air tourism in the area. Each air tour will take 10 minutes. Formed 1.5 billion years ago, the cave had long been known as a major tourist attraction of the district.

Yanqing County 延庆县

Covering a total area of 1,980 square kilometres, the county is divided into 25 townships with a population of 270,000. The county is mountainous with many rivers passing through it. The county features apples, shrimps, haws, chestnuts and apricot kernels.

Where Does Beijing Time Come From?
北京的时间来自何方

Beijing time, the standard time measurement for nearly 1. 3 billion Chinese people, does not come from Beijing. It comes from Shaanxi Observatory, China's only time-sevice centre, which is operated by the Chinese Academy of Sciences.

Located in Pucheng County, Shaanxi Province, Northwest China, the observatory's four 208-metre iron towers are surrounded by guards and high walls. Before 1949, Chinese time relied on the United States Navy Observatory. In the early 1950s, China's time service was provided by the Shanghai Astronomical Observatory via Zhenru International Telecommunication Station of the Ministry of Posts and Telecommunications. Due to inadequate facilities and equipment, and an unsuitable geographical position—Shanghai is too far east of the centre of the nation—the country's time service was not accurate. The late Chairman Mao Zedong said that China must have her own standard time. On March 26, 1966, the State Council held a special conference, chaired by the late Premier Zhou Enlai, which approved the plan to set up China's standard-time service centre. Project 326 began and the number eventually became the code name for the time-service centre. Once the plan was approved, the first task was to select the location for the centre. It needed to be constructed in an open area where the sun was positioned directly overhead at 12: 00 pm. sharp. By 1970, the China BPM short-wave time-service station was completed. The station started providing standard Beijing time on December 15, 1970. Since then the time-service centre has consistently provided the accuracy needed by high tech space-age industries, and scientific organizations in China. In accordance with international practice, a country's standard time is determined by the time zone in which the country's capital is located. Since China stretches across five time zones, the time-service station had to be built in the centre of the nation. China Central Television Station and Central People's Broadcasting Station adjust their clocks according to the standard time frequency reported by the Pucheng Time Service Centre, and they provide the people of Beijing with the correct time.

Shaanxi Observatory and the State telecommunication department plan to cooperate with foreign partners to manufacture a time-measurement device that can directly receive the time signals from the observatory, and check the time automatically and avoid making even the smallest of errors. In the near future, people will get their time directly from the observatory via this device, and they will no longer have to rely on the service provided by TV and radio stations.

Offices of Organizations of the United Nations System
联合国组织系统驻京办事处

United Nations Development Program UNDP   65236871   65675543
United Nations Fund for Population Activities (UNFPA)
65323733   65323734   65323735   65323736
65323737   65323738   65323739   65323730
WORLD FOOD PROGRAMME (WFP)
United Nations Children's Fund (UNICEF)
65323131   65323132   65323133   65323134   65323135
United Nations High Commissioner for Refugees (UNHCR) 65321647
Food and Agriculture Organization of the United Nations (FAO)
65323835   65322836   65322837   65321345
World Health Organization (WHO)   65323731   65322359

Waterway Project in Beijing 北京的水系工程

Waterway project kicked off on April 20, 1998, and took two years to complete. The northern half of the waterway, running between the Summer Palace and Bayihu Lake, was finished in summer 1999, and pleasure boats took to that waterway in July 1999, becoming an instant hit. And the southern half runs from Bayihu Lake to Gaobeidian, which was finished in August 2000. The entire length of the waterway project totals 44 kilometres between the Summer Palace of the north of the city and Gaobeidian in the south of the city. The total budget was 336 million yuan (US$ 40. 5 million). It has created a new tourist attraction—pleasure boating through the ancient capital.

The southern half of the waterway is progressing, officials have found it difficult to connect the two channels, which hinder the city's plans to build the waterway into a new tourist attraction here in the capital. As a historical city and political and cultural centre of China, Beijing used to be abundant in clear rivers and beautiful lakes. Seven locks are needed to enable pleasure boats to travel all the way through downtown Beijing, with the terrain of Beijing sloping down from northwest to southeast like a staircase.

Downtown Waterway Reopened

Beijing's renovated downtown waterway was opened to the public again on

April 8, 2000 after a winter's rest, beginning another round of bustling activity for the spring and summer season. Regarding tourists's complaints about the shortage of ship tickets and the stuffy air inside ships in 1999, the Beijing Capital River Basin Tourism Development Incorporation said it has increased the number of ships from 8 to 21, all of which are air-conditioned, to correct the problems. Besides, the planned wrap-up of the city's renovation of the downtown waterway will enable the pleasure boats to travel 44 kilometres in 2000, instead of 19 kilometres in 1999.

Modern Village Agricultural Park 现代农村农业园

Inspired by people demands to return to nature, Beijing Glorious Land Agricultural High-tech Park has built a modern village agricultural park, which is located in suburban Haidian District of Beijing, to welcome visitors. Every day there are more than 500 visitors and most of them are students, agricultural insiders and holidaymakers. The model park consists of a family farmland area and a section for leisurely sightseeing. Visitors can learn how to plant crops, purchase vegetables and flowers, or eat "green food" in the park's restaurant. The agricultural park encompasses about 4 hectares (9. 88 acres), in which more than 200 independent units are located within an area of 1 square kilometre. In the sightseeing section, peaches, apples, grapes, hawthorns, flowers and plants are grown. In the modern helio-greenhouse are flowers for all seasons of the year. In 2000, the park earned 10 million yuan (US$1. 2 million) from the sightseeing business. The revenue was much higher than the average income of most parks in Beijing. The park's successful experience indicates that ordinary visitors should not be isolated from high-tech parks, which educate as well as provide a means for relaxation. Apart from sightseeing, research on crop planting and stockbreeding is the park's leading activities. To ensure safety, the park has strengthened quarantine procedures before visitors enter the stock raising area.

SCENIC SPOTS WITHIN ONE DAY'S JOURNEY FROM BEIJING

第六部分　北京周边地区旅游景点介绍

Hebei Province
河 北 省

The Eastern Qing Tombs 清东陵

(the UNESCO on the World Cultural Heritage List inscribed both the Eastern Qing Tombs and the Western Qing Tombs on the night of November 29, 2000 in Cairns, Australia, at the 24th Session of the World Heritage Committee of the United Nations Educational, Scientific and Cultural Organization)

In Zunhua County, Hebei Province, some 125 kilometres east of Beijing, lies a group of imperial tombs of the Qing Dynasty. It is known as the Eastern Tombs because there is another group, the Western Tombs, located in Yixian County, southwest of Beijing. It is the largest and most complete group of imperial tombs in China, covering an area of 48 square kilometres. It includes 15 tombs for five Qing emperors, their empresses and concubines. The tombs for the emperors and empresses are decorated with yellow glazed-tiles. The tomb area is screened by mountains to its north and set off by evergreen pines and cypresses. It is said that the first Qing Emperor, Shunzhi, chose the site on a hunting trip.

The emperors who were buried here are Shunzhi (Xiaoling), Kangxi (Jingling), Qianlong (Yuling), Xianfeng (Dingling) and Tongzhi (Huiling). Altogether 5 emperors, 14 empresses and 136 imperial concubines were buried here, including the notorious Empress Dowager Cixi.

The Eastern Qing Tombs were first built in 1663, following the model of the Ming Tombs. Xiaoling, the tomb of the first Qing emperor is the most elaborate of all. A huge archway stands before the Big Red Gate. Inside the gate is the Stele Pavilion with a stele inscribed with an account in Manchu and Chinese of the accomplishments of Emperor Shunzhi. A 12-metre-wide "way of the spirit," paved with bricks and lined by stone statues of animals and figures, leads from the archway to the tomb of Emperor Shunzhi.

There are ways that branch off to the right and left, leading to the other tombs which are different in size and elaborateness.

To the west of Xiaoling is Yuling, the tomb of Emperor Qianlong. His reign lasted for 60 years and his tomb is among the most splendid ones with a floor space of 327 square metres.

The underground palace of his tomb is composed of three chambers with

four stone gates, in the shape of Chinese character "zhu" meaning
"ruler." It is famous for its fine marble carvings on the walls and ceilings.
Most notable are the eight bodhisattvas, four devarajas, small Buddhas and
Buddhist sutras carved in Sanskrit and Tibetan languages.

The tomb of Empress Dowager Cixi, Dingdongling, is the most magnificent. The carving on the ramp leading up to the Hall of Eminent Favour
shows a dragon and a phoenix playing with a pearl, but in a reversed pattern: the phoenix above the dragon. The marble balustrade is carved with
dragons and phoenixes amidst clouds and waves.

The columns in the main hall are decorated with coiling dragons in gold
leaf, the inner walls of the side halls are covered with designs of bats
(symbolizing good luck) and the Chinese character "longevity."

Now the underground palaces of the tombs of Emperor Qianlong and
Empress Dowager Cixi are open to the public.

Sun Dianying 孙殿英 (1889-1947), a warlord, looted the tomb of the
Empress Dowager in July 1928. He closed the tomb grounds under the
pretext of using it for military maneuvers and, with the help of his troops,
opened the tomb of Cixi and stole the treasures.

Empress Dowager Cixi spent a fabulous amount of money to build a
mausoleum for herself long before her death. Its total cost came up to 72
tons of silver.

The peculiar interest is that Empress Dowager Cixi's tomb mound is
bare. It is because that before she passed away she ordered that her tomb
mound must be bare. Therefore the earth piling up her tomb mound was
roasted. Firstly water could not sink into the tomb for the purpose of protecting it. Secondly, it had no grass nor trees grown on her tomb mound,
visitors would not have had the chance to sit on it. Empress Dowager Cixi
did not want people to sit on her tomb mound.

594

The Western Qing Tombs 清西陵

Situated in Yixian County of Hebei Province, 130 kilometres southwest of
Beijing, the Western Qing Tombs are the eternal sleeping chambers for 4
emperors, 3 queens, and 69 princes, princesses and imperial concubines
of the Qing Dynasty. Walled on all sides by green hills, the tombs nestle
comfortably on a large plain.

The entire area of some 800 square kilometres of hilly land is covered by
more than 20,000 ancient pines and cypresses, shading the winding paths
between the tombs.

It was the custom in feudal China for each dynasty to have its royal
burial ground where emperors, empresses, concubines, princes and

princesses were buried together. Why did the Qing Dynasty have two separate tomb sites when the others had one?

When Yongzheng, the third emperor of the Qing Dynasty (1723-1735), ascended the throne, he actually selected Jiufengchaoyang Mountain as his burial ground within the boundary of the Eastern Qing Tombs. But the minister in charge reported that the tomb site was not an ideal place, for the area was not grand and had poor soil. Folklore says that Emperor Yongzheng was an egocentric and mealomaniac person. He did not want to take a less conspicuous place among the Eastern Qing Tombs after the best sites had been taken by his grandfather and father. Hearing this Emperor Yongzheng gave it up and ordered that another tomb site be chosen for him. Other people say that Emperor Yongzheng did not dare to be buried beside his father since he distorted the late emperor's testament and usurped the throne. Court officials were dispatched across the country.

One of them returned claiming to have discovered in Yixian County "the most blessed site under the sun." Gratified, Yongzheng ordered his tomb built there, despite the unwritten rule forbidding separate burial plots within one imperial family.

Construction of his tomb began in 1730 and was completed in 1737, laying the foundation for what is now called the Western Qing Tombs. Flanked by other tombs, Tailing, the tomb of Emperor Yongzheng, is the biggest and earliest building.

A five-arched bridge leads to its entrance. After crossing it, tourists will see three imposing stone archways in the south, east and west. They are exquisitely carved with mountains, rivers, flowers and animals. They form a vast square, north of which is the red gate that was the entry to the tomb complex. Once through the gate, officials dismounted and proceeded on foot. Otherwise, they would be executed.

At the end of the Sacred Way, a 2.5-kilometre-long road covered with brick and stone slabs and shaded by pines and cypresses, is the huge Great Stele Hall. Inside the hall there are two stone turtle-like animals supporting inscriptions in both Chinese and Manchu, praising Emperor Yongzheng's virtue and merits.

Outside the hall stand four ornamental columns carved out of white marble. On top of them sit four *wangtianhou*, meaning fairy animals. They were regarded as offspring of the dragon. Two of the columns face the tomb, and other two have their backs to it. One pair is asking the emperor not to forget his ancestors and to frequent the place; the other is persuading him not to be too sorry for his ancestors and to go back home to attend to important state affairs.

Crossing a stone bridge with seven arches, a road lined with huge stone sculptures of men and animals leads to the spectacular Long'en Hall (Hall of Boundless Benevolence). It houses the spirit tablets of Emperor Yongzheng and his consort.

Sacrificial ceremonies were held here every year during the Qing Dynasty. Behind is the Soul Tower, which carries a tall stone tablet engraved in Chinese, Manchu and Mongolian. It says that the coffin of Emperor Yongzheng is in an underground palace under a tumulus behind the tower. And one of his consorts and a concubine were buried with him.

When Emperor Yongzheng died in 1735, his son and heir, Emperor Qianlong, issued an order whereby any later emperor must be buried in the Western Qing Tombs if his father was buried in the Eastern Qing Tombs, or vice versa, thus maintaining a balance between the Western Qing Tombs and the Eastern Qing Tombs.

Like the Eastern Qing Tombs and the Ming Tombs, the Western Qing Tombs are the culmination of Chinese imperial tomb architecture. The local authorities used to believe that it had been broken into, but not long ago an excavation team discovered that it was actually intact, although there were traces of digging and hacking on the granite wall blocking the entrance of the underground palace. Obviously, the thieves had been stopped there.

The excavation team didn't get through that wall either. After much consultation with the government, it was decided that for the moment the underground palace be left alone until adequate means have been found to handle the excavation and preservation.

One kilometre west of Tailing lies Changling, the tomb of Emperor Jiaqing. He reigned from 1796 to 1820. The tomb was built in 1803. On the whole, the architectural style of Changling is very similar to that of Tailing. But the rammed earth platform atop the underground palace is larger. The floor of its main hall, Long'andian (the Hall of Boundless Benevolence), is covered with yellowish stone plates that have natural violet patterns reflecting an exquisite brilliance throughout the hall.

Of all the Western Qing Tombs, perhaps Muling, the tomb of Emperor Daoguang (1821-1850) comes closest to fantasy. Emperor Daoguang should have had his tomb in the Eastern Qing Tombs under Qing Emperor Qianlong's rule. Immediately after he took the throne, he did order his tomb built in the Eastern Qing Tombs, then the family plot. After seven years' hard work, the tomb was completed. One of his queens was buried inside. One night, Emperor Daoguang had a nightmare in which he saw his late queen struggling in a stormy ocean and crying for help. After he woke up the next morning, the troubled emperor personally went to the tomb and found to his terror that its underground palace was flooded and that the coffin of the queen was half submerged in water. The emperor was very angry and ordered it to be destroyed. Officials involved in the construction were either demoted or punished.

In 1832 when Emperor Daoguang went to pay respect to his ancestors buried in the Western Qing Tombs, a second family site, he was greatly impressed by the place and chose it as the site of his tomb. Legend has it that Emperor Daoguang thought that his underground palace in the Eastern Qing Tombs had been flooded because of water-spewing dragons disturbed by construction. He fancied that if dragons were put up onto the ceiling, he could avoid another flood by burying hundreds of dragons inside his "Hall of Boundless Benevolence," thus pleasing the God of Rain dragon. Therefore, more than 1,000 carpenters were recruited all over the country, and carved many wooden dragons in the ceiling of the Hall of Boundless Benevolence of the tomb, making it different from other tombs.

Nowadays, the ceiling is a dragon world. There are 712 dragons carved in high relief out of a kind of fragrant wood called *nanmu*, a kind of cedar, there are exuding bright clouds which are also carved out of the same kind of wood, but in low relief, in the background. Entering the hall, you can still smell the fragrance of the wood.

Another feature of Muling is a tall three-gate archway made of glazed tiles. Flanked by old pine trees, the archway leads to the main part of the tomb, with the dragons and phoenixes on the archway reflecting gold in the sun.

The smallest and also the most recent tomb in the Western Qing Tombs is that of Emperor Guangxu who reigned from 1875 to 1908. Unlike the tomb of his ancestors, Guangxu's tomb was built one year after his death, thus lacking the towering pavilions and stone sculptures decorating his ancestors' tombs. The only interesting part of this tomb, Chongling, is the underground palace. The tomb was robbed in 1938 during wartime. It now contains the coffins of Emperor Guangxu and his consort but no funeral objects. Excavated in 1980, now it is an eternal testimony to the incredible craftsmanship of the Chinese workers at the beginning of the 20th century.

The last emperor, Aisin Gioro Puyi, who reigned from 1909 to 1911, was buried in Babaoshan Cemetery of Beijing after he died of cancer in 1967.

The Eastern and Western Imperial Tombs of the Qing Dynasty

Tomb	Emperor	Reign Title	Reign Period
Eastern Tombs			
Xiaoling	Aisin-Gioro Fulin	Shunzhi	1644-1661
Jingling	Aisin-Gioro Xuanye	Kangxi	1662-1722
Yuling	Aisin-Gioro Hongli	Qianlong	1736-1795
Dingling	Aisin-Gioro Yizhu	Xianfeng	1851-1861
Huiling	Aisin-Gioro Zaichun	Tongzhi	1862-1874
Western Tombs			
Tailing	Aisin-Gioro Yinzheng	Yongzheng	1723-1735
Changling	Aisin-Gioro Yongyan	Jiaqing	1796-1820
Muling	Aisin-Gioro Minning	Daoguang	1821-1850
Chongling	Aisin-Gioro Zaitian	Guangxu	1875-1908

The Mountain Hamlet to Flee the Heat or Mountain Manor for Avoiding (Escaping) the Summer Heat 承德避暑山庄 (including a profile of Chengde 包括承德概况)

The Imperial Travelling Palace, also known as the Chengde Lodge (Chengde Ligong), derives its name from the Warm Spring (Requan) situated in the northeast Hebei Province about 250 kilometres (155 miles) away from Beijing. The area is also known as Bishushanzhuang (Mountain Hamlet to Flee the Heat or Mountain Manor for Avoiding the Summer Heat) due to its location among lush, tree-covered mountains and its pleasant temperatures in summer, which average 19. 3 ℃ in the hottest months of the year.

598

Chengde is one of the 24 famous historical and cultural cities and one of the 44 major scenic spots in China. Chengde administers the city district and Chengde County, with a total area of 4, 442 square kilometres and a population more than 800, 000. Encircled by mountains and with brooks and streams running right through the city, Chengde has a beautiful scenery and a pleasant climate. It is here that the austere, elegant Chengde Mountain Hamlet to Flee the Heat, the magnificent "Eight Temples Beyond the Great Wall" or "Eight Outer Temples") and the strange hills and crags combine to make Chengde a city of scenic and historical interest with a special and rational layout, as well as a world-renowned bustling tourist attraction.

In the late period of the primitive society, the Chinese ancestors began to live and farm in this region. The urban areas started gradually to expand with construction of the Chengde Mountain Hamlet to Flee the Heat and the Eight Temples Beyond the Great Wall. From 1703 to 1861 (Qing Emperors Kangxi, Yongzheng, Qianlong, Jiaqing, Daoguang and Xianfeng), the Mountain Hamlet to Flee the Heat served as a place of important political activities of the Qing Dynasty and the secondary political centre for the Qing imperial court. For this reason, Chengde boasts of a wealth of cultural relics and ancient buildings.

Lying in the city and dotted with scenic wonders, the splendid Mountain Hamlet to Flee the Heat possesses a scenery characteristic of both North and South China, earning for it the reputation of "incorporating all the beautiful sceneries under the sun in a single park." The Eight Temples Beyond the Great Wall are sublime and spectacular, each having a style of its own.

Within the city area, mountains stand side by side. The general configuration of the earth's surface around the city is peculiar, belonging to the typical Yardan landform which is rarely seen in North China. The abundance of strange peaks and grotesque rocks with which nature has endowed Chengde is a constant source of marvel for tourists both at home and abroad.

Chengde belongs to the temperate continental climate; its annual average temperature ranges from 8. 8 ℃ to 24. 4 ℃ in the hottest month in summer. Being a basin, it is cool in summer and mild in winter. With moderate rainfall and few sandstorms, it is not only an ideal summer retreat but also an enjoyable place for people to spend their winter. Flowers bloom throughout the year.

Chengde has long been famous for its special local products. its wide choice of preserved and fresh fruit and unique game food are welcomed by tourists both at home and abroad.

After New China was founded, great changes have taken place in terms of industry, agriculture, city construction, science and culture and environment protection in Chengde. Although it is visited by tens of thousands of people each year, it still retains remarkable tracts of wildness and provides habitat for some of our most magnificent animals—reindeer and hares.

The Chengde Mountain Resort

The Chengde Mountain Resort (Bishushanzhuang) or literally "Mountain

Hamlet to Flee the Heat" in the northern part of the city was the biggest garden of the imperial family in the Qing Dynasty (1644-1911).

In order to consolidate the unity of the multi-national state and pacify the frontier areas, Emperor Kangxi, the second Emperor of the Qing Dynasty, made many inspection tours in North China. During his inspection tours, he found that Chengde with its proximity to the capital of Beijing was beautiful in scenery and pleasant in climate. Therefore, in 1703 he decided to have a summer resort built here. Construction of the project was completed in 1790 lasting 87 years. Within the Mountain Resort, there are more than 20 building complexes scattered throughout the park, consisting of more than 100 individual halls, pavilions, studios, pagodas and terraces. Each of these complexes has its own poetic name. Every year both Qing Emperors Kangxi and Qianlong spent about six months enjoying the cool and handling government affairs here. Because the Qing rulers could not accustom themselves to Beijing's hot dry summers and sought relief by travelling north of the Great Wall. After the Qing Dynasty was overthrown in 1911, the Mountain Hamlet to Flee the Heat had been left in disrepair. Since 1949, New China has listed it as a major historical monument under the state protection and allocated a large sum of money to have it restored. Nowadays, it has taken a completely new look and become a bustling tourist destination.

The Mountain Resort covers an area of 5, 640, 000 square metres or 5. 64 square kilometres — 2. 16 square miles — (twice the size of Summer Palace in Beijing) and the wall enclosing it is as long as 10 kilometres. The Mountain Resort is divided into two parts — the palace area and the garden area. The entire scenery creates an effect often seen in traditional Chinese landscape paintings. Rows upon rows of pavilions and halls bejewel the whole resort, and temples and nunneries dot the deep valleys and tree-clad, undulating mountains.

In the southern part of the lake area are the palace buildings where the Qing emperors lived, conducted state affairs and held grand celebrations. The main buildings are: Zhenggong (Front Palace), Songhezhai (Pine-Crane Hall), Donggong (East Palace) and their annexes. Tourists on their way to the Front Palace have to pass through Lizhengmen (Gate of Beauty and Righteousness). Just inside is Wumen (Meridian Gate) with a horizontal tablet engraved with the golden characters for "Mountain Hamlet to Flee the Heat" in the calligraphy of Qing Emperor Kangxi (1662-1722). The courtyard is paved with gray bricks and luxuriant old pines are grown here and there, surrounding the environment with a serene and solemn atmosphere. The main hall of the Front Palace is Danbojingchengdian (Hall of Frugality and Placidity), also known as *Nanmu* Hall because it was built of the fine-grained fragrant hardwood called *nanmu*. This kind of *nanmu* can give off an unusual scent reputed to repel mosquitoes in summer. This simple and graceful-looking structure is exquisitely decorated, with superbly engraved ceilings and partitions. It is here that the Qing emperors once received court ministers and foreign envoys. *Sizhishuwu* (Literary of The Four "Knows"*)is a place where the emperor would relax before and after holding ceremonies, and only the most important members of the Qing court were permitted to come to have audience with him. In the courtyard outside, ancient cypresses still flourish and their leaves stay green year-round.

The Lake Area 湖区

The lake area is the key scenic spot of the Mountain Resort. Of the 72 scenic wonders named by Qing Emperors Kangxi and Qianlong, 31 are in the lake area. With winding banks, the lake area has a maze of islets linked by causeways and small bridges. The entire place presents a typical South China scene when a breeze rustles the willow trees along the shore and the lotus, reeds and water chestnuts sway over the schools of fish swimming leisurely in the water. Boat-riding on the lakes, tourists will find their eyes insufficient to take in so many beautiful sights that greet them. The triple Lake-Centre Pavilions located in the eastern end of the lake area are perched on a stone bridge and their reflections in the water are a feast for the eye. *Wenyuanshizilin* (Graceful Lion Garden), linked to the triple

---

* The Four "Knows" — Heaven knows, the gods know, I know and you know — refers to the upright behaviour of an official in the Han Dynasty (206 BC-AD 220). Yanpozhishuangdian (Hall of Cool Mists and Ripples), the emperors' bed chamber, is the place where Qing Emperor Xianfeng passed away on his sickbed in 1861. Yunshanshengdilou (Hall of the Panorama of Cloud-Covered Mountains) is the last structure of the Front Palace. The skillfully arranged rockeries serve as the staircase leading visitors to the tower, where, looking north, visitors can get a bird' s eye view of the lakes and hills ahead. The Pine-Crane Hall resembles the Front Palace in architectural layout. It consists of six buildings which are connected by a winding corridor in an integrated whole. The garden-like place was once the residence of empress dowagers. The Pine Soughing Valley stands majestically on a tree-covered hill, overlooking the lakes. Qing Emperor Qianlong named its main hall Ji' entang (Hall for Remembering Kindness) to commemorate his study sessions here with his grandfather, Qing Emperor Kangxi. This hall used to be the place where Qing Emperor Kangxi received officials and read and made comments on the memorial submitted by them. The East Palace originally had six buildings, but they were all damaged by fire before 1949.

The buildings in the palace area are unique in style, quite unlike other gorgeous palaces. Their foundations just like those of ordinary people' s houses, they are simply furnished, unembellished, austere and elegant, harmonizing well with the simplicity of the whole Mountain Resort.

Lake-Centre Pavilions by a causeway, is unique in style. To the east is an islet called Jinshan (Golden Hill). The towers and pavilions are strung out along the shore orderly, connected by a winding corridor. Climbing up the three-tier hexagonal tower and gaze at the hills and lakes far and near, tourists will feel as if they are surrounded by traditional Chinese landscape paintings. In the central part of the lake area is Yuesejiangsheng (Hall of Moonlit River), where Emperors Kangxi and Qianlong used to study Confucian classics. Here the environment is quiet and fresh and green with lotus fragrance and willows. Ruyizhou Islet (so named for its similar shape to the Chinese ornamental object *ruyi**is the biggest one in the lake area. Looking to the north, visitors will find Yanyulou (House of Mist and Rain) perched on Qingliandao (Green Lotus Islet). When it rains, the hills and trees are shrouded in mist—a wonderful sight. It is here that Qing Emperor Qianlong used to read and watch the clouds and rain. In the western part of the lake are Fangyuanju (Aromatic Garden Residence) and other four scenic spots. The buildings here are small and exquisite and scattered here and there along a winding dyke, adding charm to the entire area.

A Vast Expanse of Grassland 广袤的旷野 To the north of the lake area is a vast plain covered with luxuriant grass and trees, where reindeer and hares often roam about. The park is laid out entirely in the Mongolian style, whisking tourists to a typical Mongolian grassland. Wanshuyuan (Garden of Ten Thousand Trees) has a crouching tablet inscribed with the garden's name in the calligraphy of Emperor Qianlong. It is here that Emperor Qianlong received Mongolian princes, the Panchen Lama of Tibet and the British special envoy, George MaCartney. Not far northeast from the garden is Yongyousi (Temple of Perpetual Blessing), the family temple of Qing emperors, inside of which is an imposing stupa, 66 metres high, with a dazzling gilded copper top. Whenever Emperor Qianlong came to the Mountain Resort, the first thing he did was to come here to offer sacrifices. In the west lies Wenjinge (Knowledge Imparting Hall) which, built in the style of the Tianyige Pavilion in Ningbo, Zhejiang Province, was a book repository of the Qing ruling house.

Picturesque Mountains and Tranquil Valleys 山秀谷幽 The northwestern part of the Mountain Resort is all wooded mountains, steep crags

602

---

* *ruyi* 如意, a good luck sceptre, was developed from a back scratcher, originated from the Eastern Jin Dynasty (AD 317-AD 420). The sceptre is about half a metre long and made of metal, stone, bone, jade, coral or lacquer, etc. It was given as a gift and served as a symbol of good wishes for the prosperity and longevity of the recipient. Ruyi means: "May your wish come true."

and deep valleys, where the scenery varies from season to season. Here, 44 scenic spots, each with a style of its own, were built during the reigns of Emperors Kangxi and Qianlong. Walking along the zigzag mountain paths to the accompaniment of the soughing of the wind in the pines, the chirping of birds and the murmuring of the streams and tourists will be transported into a haven of peace, far removed from the din and turmoil of the world. About 500 metre west from Lishuyu (Pear Tree Valley) lies Lihuabanyuegou (Pear Blossoms and Moonlit Ditch). The scenery is especially enchanting in spring time, when myriad of blooming pear trees emit intoxicating aroma and the moon shines through a thin veil of clouds. On top of a mountain northwest of the resort is Simianyunshanting (Cloud and Mountain-Encircled Pavilion). Standing in the pavilion, tourists will feel as if they are surrounded by clouds and mist, and on fine days, they can view the peaks and clouds some 50 kilometres away. North from Zhenziyu (Hazel Dale) is Chuifengluozhaoting (Pavilion of the Hammer Peak in the Glow of the Setting Sun), where, in the depth of winter, tourists' eyes will be greeted by a spectacular northern China scene as they gaze south at the snow-capped mountains in the distance.

Grotesque Peaks and Quaint Crags 奇山异石 With its peculiar landform, Chengde is noted for its odd-shaped peaks and crags. Qichuifeng (Sledgehammer Peak) is 38-metre-high solitary pinnacle which stands on a meandering ridge five kilometres to the northeast of Chengde City. The pinnacle, shaped like an inverted sledgehammer, looks ominous, with one end pointing skyward and the other end overlooking a precipitous cliff, and when viewed from afar its solitariness is shown off an advantage against the surrounding peaks tinged red by the glow of a setting sun. On the summit of a southern mountain, just across a valley, is Hamashi (Flog Crag) which is like a frog with its head rearing in the pose of making a jump. On the eastern bank of the Wulie River is Luohanshan (Arhat Hill), so named because it looks like an arhat sitting meditation on the riverside. On a height south of the city is the sky-piercing Sengmaoshan (Monk's Headgear Peak) which takes its name from its shape. Fifteen kilometres west are two grotesque pinnacles rising sheer from the ground like two pagodas. Shuangtashan (Twin Pagoda Hill), quite by coincidence, is crowned with a tumble down pagoda erected in the Liao Dynasty (916-1125). In addition, there are Guangrenling (Broad Benevolence Ridge), Chaoyangdong (Sun Cave), etc., forming the "Ten Scenic Wonders of Chengde" noted for their sublimity, oddness or tranquillity. More interest is that a lot of legends and myths are attributed to these scenic spots, adding mystery to the landscapes of the city.

603

Eight Outer Temples or Eight Temples Beyond the Great Wall 外八庙

Outside the walls of the Chengde Imperial Travelling Palace, temples in the Tibetan, Han and Mongolian styles are found scattered among the nearby hills. Built on a larger scale than any of the temples in Beijing, they are collectively known as the Waibamiao (Eight Outer Temples or Eight Temples Beyond the Great Wall), because they were administered by eight different departments and located outside the Chengde City. In fact, there were 12 large-scale groups of temples, seven of these had been destroyed or damaged, leaving only 5 are still standing. The temples reflect artistic characteristics of the Han, Tibetan and Mongolian nationalities.

Construction of these temples began in 1713 by the second Qing Emperor Kangxi and was completed in 1780 by the fourth Qing Emperor Qianlong lasting 67 years. To consolidate the unity of China's multi-national state, the Qing Government adopted the policy of "ruling according to their customs" towards the Mongolian, Tibetan and other minority nationalities and constructed a number of temples with distinctive styles in line with their religious beliefs. Imposing, elegant and exquisite, these temples combine the essence of the architectural art of many nationalities. The Eight Outer Temples and the Mountain Hamlet to Flee the Heat are a foil to each other. The Eight Outer Temples are the crystallization of the blood and sweat of the Chinese labouring people. They not only shine with the radiance of the brilliant Chinese culture but also bear witness to the unity and development of China's multi-national state.

Those five remaining temples are as follows:

Temple of Universal Tranquillity 普宁寺

Situated to the north of the Mountain Helmet to Flee the Heat, the Temple of Universal Tranquillity was built in 1755 by Qing Emperor Qianlong in pursuance of Emperor Kangxi, his grandfather's policy of "control through conciliation" and in commemoration of his victory in suppressing the rebellion of the upper strata of the Junggar people in Xinjiang. The temple consists of many magnificent halls and laid out in apple-pie order, covering an area of 23,000 square metres. Its front half follows the layout of the Buddhist monasteries of the Han people. The Grand Hall of the Buddha is characteristic of the ancient architecture of the Han people. Its rear half is based on the Buddhist concept of the world as manifested in the sacred place of Tibetan Lamaism, the Sameye Monastery. The 36.75-metre-high Hall of Mahayana and its surrounding terraces, halls and Lamaist pagodas with their peculiar layouts bespeaks the unique style of the Tibetan plastic arts. The huge wooden image of the Buddha in the Hall of Mahayana is a rare image of its kind (free wood such as pine, cypress, elm, fir and linden are used for carving the giant Buddha). With an exact height of 23. 511 metres towering up through the building's five storeys, known as the Goddess of Mercy (Guanyin) with a thousand hands and a thousand eyes, the wooden Buddhist figure with golden paint measures nearly 10 metres around the waist and weighs about 110 tons. Well-proportioned and magnificent, this Buddha is one of the largest wood sculptured Buddhas still existing in China. Each of the Buddha's fingers on its 42 arms is thicker than an average person's leg. On the head of the statue stands a smaller image, 1. 2 metres tall, which according to tradition represents Guanyin's teacher Amitabha. His position on top of Guanyin's head denotes the high esteem in which he was held. In the first half of 1999, the Buddha was listed in the Guinness Book of Records as the tallest statue of its kind in the world. The figure, which was carved in 1755, is made of 120 cubic metres of wood, enough to build a four-storey house. The Central Research Institute for Relics Protection and the Prospecting and Designing Institute under the Ministry of Construction measured its exact height, 27. 21 metres.

The Hall of the Great Vehicle is surrounded by a number of smaller halls and white terraces which are arranged in a mandala pattern, representing the structure of the universe. The hall itself symbolizes Mount Sumeru, the centre of the Buddhist universe, and surrounding it are the "four greater continents" and the "eight lesser continents."

Renovation of the famous wooden statue of Avalokitesvara in the Temple of Universal Tranquility was started in late 1998. The project's implementation was divided into two stages. During the first stage, high-technology methods were used to steam-clean the Buddha which towers 22 metres and has 42 arms with an eye on each palm. Modeled on a Tibetan temple, the Temple of Universal Tranquility is a key relics site under State protection. In 1994, it was evaluated worthy of the World Cultural Heritage List together with the other historical interests in Chengde, where the famous Imperial Summer Resort is located.

Putuozongsheng Temple 普陀宗乘之庙(亦称小布达拉官)
The Temple is also known as the Lesser Potala. Built within more than 4 years from 1767 to 1771, the temple is situated north of the Mountain Resort. Putuozongsheng is modeled on the Potala Palace in Tibet, therefore it is also named "Lesser Potala Palace." The entire temple covers an area of 220, 000 square metres. It was built by Qing Emperor Qianlong to cele-

brate his 60th aniversary (the Emperor's 35th reign), empress's 80th anniversary (the Emperor's 36th reign) and to host the upper strata personages of the minority peoples from Mongolia, Qinghai, and Xinjiang who came to join in his birthday celebrations. The temple has a special artistic value. A crystallization of the style and characteristics of ancient Tibetan architecture, the temple is made up of 50 Buddhist halls, scripture-reciting halls, monks' living quarters, red terraces, white terraces topped with one or five pagodas and glazed ceremonial arches which rise and fall with the mountain slopes in a variable rectangular disposition. The red terrace is 42.5 metres high and 59.7 metres in width. It is the main structure within the temple and imposing. The temple compound is tranquil and peaceful where stand tall pines, cypresses and rockeries, adding solemnity to the ambient atmosphere.

The Temple of Sumeru Happiness and Longevity 须弥福寿之庙
Encompassing 37,900 square metres, the temple was constructed by Qing Emperor Qianlong in 1780 after the model of the Tibetan Trashilhunpo (Tashilunbu) Monastery at Xigaze (Shigatse) and its name is a direct translation of the Tibetan name "Temple of Complete Happiness and Longevity." The year 1780 was the 70th birthday of Emperor Qianlong, therefore the celebrations were held on a larger scale than usual. This temple was specially built in Tibetan style as a temporary residence (or travelling palace) and scripture-teaching place for the Sixth Panchen Lama in 1780 when the latter travelled all the way from Xigaze to Chengde to offer birthday celebrations to Emperor Qianlong. The temple contains both the layout of Tibetan palace buildings and the special features of ancient Han people's architecture, making it a rare specimen of the combination of the styles of ancient Han and Tibetan architecture. It takes on added elegance and splendor with its imposing halls, red walls, glittering gilded roofs, gold dragons poised as if ready to spring, glazed pagodas, luxuriant woods and unique rockeries.

The Temple of Pacifying the Outlying Areas or The Temple of Consolation for People from Afar 安远庙
Constructed in 1764, Anyuan Temple, an imitation of Ili Temple in Xinjiang is situated due east of the Mountain Hamlet to Flee the Heat. Previously in 1759, more than 6,000 people of the Dashidawa clan (达什达瓦部) of the Junggar tribe (准噶儿) in Xinjiang migrated to the former Rehe Province (Chengde being its capital before its abolition as a province after 1949). Because their Gu'erzha Temple 固尔扎庙 on the northern bank of the Ili River in Xinjiang had been destroyed during a war, Qing Emperor Qianlong had a similar temple built in Chengde for their worship, naming

it Anyuansi. The temple roofs are covered with black glazed tiles. Serving as a foil to green mountains, blue sky and white clouds 在青山、蓝天和白云的衬托下, the temple looks more magnificent and solemn with religious atmosphere. It is said that in the concept of Buddhism, black colour represents the Buddhist Nirvana Mountain (Nirvana 涅槃 means "of Buddhist monks or nuns"pass away 圆寂). Buddhists believe that they will achieve charitable and pious deeds 功德圆满 after death and will not suffer re-birth and re-death nor they will get suffering of samsara (transmigration 轮回). At the same time, in Buddhism black color is emblematic of a strong wind, which can help the sailing boat to accelerate its speed and get to the shore of the Land of Ultimate Bliss 极乐世界 as soon as possible. Another saying goes: black colour stands for water. The Ili Temple was destroyed by fire and the Anyuan Temple is topped with black colour, which is symbolic of water covering the roofs of the temple. 象征有水压顶。

The Temple of Universal Happiness 普乐寺

Encompassing 24,000 square metres, the Temple of Universal Happiness (also known as Round Pavilion 圆亭子) was erected in 1766 when upper strata personages from the Mongolian and the northwestern tribes came to pay respects to Qing Emperor Qianlong for the stability and peace in northwestern region of China. The main building, the Pavilion of the Brilliance of the Rising Sun (旭光阁), is noted for its caisson ceiling and unique wooden mandala, the only one of its kind in China outside Tibet. The temple's outer walls were once topped by eight colourful glazed-tile pagodas built on lotus flower pedestals, but nowadays only one of them still stands. Legend has it that they are said to symbolize the lotus flowers that appeared at every step taken by Sakyamuni, founder of Buddhism, when he was very young.

Average annual frost-free period is 158 days. First frosting day usually falls on September 30.

Annual Mean Temperature (℃) in Chengde

Jan	Feb	Mar	Apr	May	Jun	Jul	Aug	Sep	Oct	Nov	Dec
-9.2	-5.8	1.9	11.4	18.5	22.2	24.4	22.9	17.3	10.0	0.7	-7.5

Scheduled Train

If you wish to visit Chengde by train, take Tourist Train No. 225 at Beijing Railway Station. The train leaves the railway station at 07:29 and arrives at Chengde at 12:10 or you take Train No. 591/593 leaving the railway station at 13:28 and arriving at Chengde at 18:32.

Star-Rated Hotels in Chengde

Name	Star-Rate	Add.	Tel.	Fax
Yunshan Hotel Chengde 承德云山饭店	3	6 East, Nanyuan Road, Chengde, Hebei Province, China	(0314) 2026171	2024551
Chengde Guest House for Diplomatic Missions 承德外交人员宾馆	3	Middle Wulie Road, Chengde, Hebei Province, China	(0314) 2021970	2021980
Huilong Hotel Chengde China 中国承德会龙大厦	2	Railway Road, Chengde, Hebei Province, China	(0314) 2085367	2082404
Chengde Yurt Spend One's Holidays Village 承德避暑山庄蒙古包度假村	2	East Entrance, Wanshu Park, Summer Resort, Chengde, Hebei Province	(0314) 2162710	2163094
Qiwang Building 承德绮望楼宾馆	2	1 East Road, Bifeng Gate, Chengde, Hebei Province, China	(0314)2022196	2021904
Chengde Guest House 承德宾馆	2	33 Nanyingzi Stree, Chengde, Hebei Province, China	(0314)2023157	2021341
Chengde Guest House (South Building) 承德宾馆(南楼)	1	Nanyingzi Street, Chengde, Hebei Province, China	(0314)2022551	2021341

Travel Agency

Chengde China International Travel Service 承德中国国际旅行社
Add: 6 East Nanyuan Road, Chengde, Hebei Province, China
Tel: (0314) 2026418 / 2026827　Fax: 2027484

An Introduction to Qinhuangdao 秦皇岛市概况

Many residents in Beijing and Tianjin would like to go to Beidaihe, a seaside resort along the Bohai Sea some 300 kilometres northeast of the Beijing to escape the summer heat and damp nights of July and August. Since it has been used as a summer resort by the royal family of the Qing Dynasty (1644-1911) and then, a century ago, by foreign communities in Beijing and Tianjin, Beidaihe has grown into a popular folks' destination to kill off the unbearable hot days. In fact, Beidaihe is so well-known that many Chinese people think Qinhuangdao is a district of Beidaihe, not the opposite.

Shanhaiguan is another district of Qinhuangdao. Shanhaiguan is known for its rich historic and natural attractions such as Laolongtou (Old Dragon's Head), Yansai Lake and Jiaoshan Mountain. Shanhaiguan has always been an important corridor between northern and northeastern China and has witnessed many battles over the centuries. Strategically located between the mountains and the sea, the area got its name from its geographical location. Built upon the eastern starting point of the Great Wall, Shanhaiguan is one of a few Chinese cities with a complete city wall.

There are about 70 places of interest in Shanhaiguan. Laolongtou, the First Pass Under Heaven, Jiaoshan Mountain and Yansai Lake are must-see sites.

Laolongtou is the eastern starting point of the Great Wall, about 20 metres run into the sea. In ancient times, people used to refer to the Great Wall as a giant dragon and this is how it got is name. First built in 1381 during the Ming Dynasty (1368-1644), Laolongtou was bombarded by the Allied Forces of the Eight Imperialist Powers in 1900 and was not restored until 1987. The First Pass Under Heaven, built at the same time as Laolongtou, is an important strategic point and is the first pass on the eastern end of the Great Wall, hence the name. The two-storey gate tower is 12 metres high and 23 metres wide. From its top, tourists can have a breaktaking view of the Bohai Sea to the south and of the Great Wall snaking its way up amongst the mountains on the northern side. The tower also holds an exhibition of ancient weapons. Sculptures of a few dozen generals who were once stationed there complete the visit.

A three-kilometre walk along the Great Wall will bring tourists to the Jiaoshan Mountain, the highest peak in the Qinhuangdao area. Tourists can take the bus to the foot of the mountain and from there a cable car will bring them all the way right up to the top, known for its jiao (horn) shaped rocks.

Yansai Lake is the only major site not directly connected to the Great Wall. Located 9 kilometres northwest of Shanhaiguan, the lake is 15 kilometres long and more than 60 metres deep, and threads its twisting way between two mountains. By boat, tourists can enjoy different precipices towering along the lake shores. Cypress and pine trees covering the mountains are mirrored on the lake. Those who have visited Guilin's Lijiang River or the Three Gorges of the Yangtze River are bound to experience the same feelings of wonder as they pass along the lake.

Pleasure-seekes can have access to a lot of beaches in the district of

Shahaiguan, though the most convenient ones are possibly the two alongside Laolongtou, each extending 200 metres wide and about 4 kilometres long. The water is reasonably clean, the beach smooth, the sands fine and the tides gentle.

Following are the star-rated hotels in Qinhuangdao area. Tourists make hotel accommodation reservation in advance before going to Beidaihe for summer retreat.

Star-Rated Hotels in Qinhuangdao 秦皇岛星级饭店

Name	Star-Rate	Add.	Tel.	Fax
North Star Holiday Village 秦皇岛北辰度假村	3	20 Wenti Road, Qinhuangdao, Hebei Province, China	(0334)8051083	8051263
Qinhuangdao Great Wall Hotel 秦皇岛长城酒店	3	202 Yanshan Stree, Qinhuangdao, Hebei Province, China	(0335)3061666	3061075
Qinhuangdao Cindic Hotel 秦皇岛信谊大酒店	3	Yingbin Road, Qinhuangdao, Hebei Province, China	(0335)3062243	3062254
Jinshan Hotel 秦皇岛金山宾馆	3	4 Dongsan Road, Beidaihe, Hebei Province, China	(0335)4041338	4042478
Foreign Trade Hotel 河北外贸秦皇岛宾馆	2	30 Youyi Road, Qinhuangdao, Hebei Province, China	(0335)3414605	3423754
Xiadu Hotel 夏都宾馆	2	48 Hongqi Road, Haigang Dist., Qinhuangdao, Hebei Province, China	(0335)3035115	3035108
Haiyue Mansion 秦皇岛海岳大厦	2	159 Yingbin Road, Qinhuangdao, Hebei Province, China	(0335) 3065760	3063943
Qinhuangdao International Seamens' Club 秦皇岛国际海员俱乐部	2	37 Haibin Rd., Qinhuangdao. Hebei Province, China	(0335) 3031441	
Beidaihe Youyi Guest House 北戴河友谊宾馆	2	1 Yingjiao Rd., Beidaihe, Qinhuangdao, Hebei Province, China	(0335) 4041945	4041945
Nandaihe Holiday Villa 中化南戴河度假村	2	Youyi Road, Nandaihe, Qinhuangdao, Hebei Province, China	(0335) 4050103	4050921
Yanyou Hotel Qinhuangdao 秦皇岛宴友酒店	2	N. Entrance, Lijiaoqiao, Wenhua Rd., Qinhuangdao, Hebei Province, China	(0335) 3032875	(0335) 3053260
Tiankai Hotel Qinhuangdao 秦皇岛天开大厦	2	121 Yingbin Rd., Qinhuangdao, Hebei Province, China	(0335) 3063455	3060090

Name	Star-Rate	Add.	Tel.	Fax
Qinhuangdao Yingbin Mansion 秦皇岛迎宾大厦	2	40 N. Wenhua, Qinhuangdao, Hebei Province, China	(0335) 3035200	3034765
Beidaihe Nite Hotel 北戴河尼特大酒店	2	Dongjing Rd., Beidaihe Dist., Qinhuangdao, Hebei Province, China	(0335) 4043739	4042032
Qinhuangdao Yanbin Hotel 秦皇岛燕滨大酒店	2	Southern Tip, Yingbin Rd., Qinhuangdao, Hebei Province, China	(0335) 3063128	
Qinhuangdao Hotel 秦皇岛宾馆	2	2 Wentao Rd., Haigang Dist., Qinhuangdao, Hebei Province, China	(0335) 8051642	8051646
Qinhuangdao Seaview Hotel 秦皇岛海景大酒店	2	55 B Dongshan St., Haigang Dist., Qinhuangdao, Hebei Province, China	(0335) 3093118	3034959
Qinhuangdao Port Hotel 秦皇岛港口宾馆	2	27 Haibin Rd., Qinhuangdao, Hebei Province, China	(0335) 3093141	3098641
Qinhuangdao Tianma Hotel 秦皇岛天马大酒店	1	380 Yanshan St., Qinhuangdao, Hebei Province, China	(0335) 3070288	3061658

Swimming there is a romantic experience—especially under the moonlight—with Laolongtou and the Great Wall as a marvelous background. Motor-boating and horse-riding services are available and shower facilities are provided.

All trains bounding to Northeast China stop at the Shanhaiguan Railway Station. Unlike the Beidaohe Railway Station which is 10 kilometres away from the beach area, the Shanhaiguan Railway Station is located directly in town. The trains are air-conditioned and riding is about three and a half hours from Beijing Railway Station to Shanhaiguan.

Anji (Zhaozhou) Bridge 安济(赵州)大桥

Zhaozhou Bridge, spanned over the Jiaohe River in Zhaoxian County, Hebei Province, designed and built by Li Chun 李春 from 590 to 608 during the Sui Dynasty (581-618), has stood the tests of earthquakes, floods and traffic for nearly 1,400 years. It is the world's oldest single-arch stone bridge still in use today. To protect this monument, a parallel bridge was constructed in 1980s. The main arch of the old bridge has a span of

37. 35 metres and the total length of the bridge is 50. 84 metres. The two minor arches at each end are known as open spandrel arches, spanning 3. 81 metres and 2. 85 metres respectively. They not only improve the general look of the bridge but also help reduce its weight and thus lighten the load on the bridge's foundation. In times of flood, the minor arches join the main one to facilitate the passage of the current, thus weakening its impact on the body of the bridge itself. This bridge has been universally acknowledged as a model in the world history of stone arch bridge with its delicate technology, scientific design and beautiful structure.

Travel Agency 旅行社

Name	Add.	Tel.	Fax
Qinghuangdao International Travel Service	124 West Section, Yanshan Street, Haigang Dist. Qinhuangdao, Hebei Province, China	(0335) 3607354/3602875	(0335) 3602872
Beidaihe International Travel Service	4 Third Road of the East Beach, Beidaihe, Hebei Province, China	(0335) 4041748	(0335) 4031890

Shanxi Province
山　西　省

Yungang Grottoes in Datong 大同云冈石窟

612

〔Yungang Grottoes in Datong, Shanxi Province was added to the list of World Heritage by United Nations Educational, Scientific and Cultural Organization (UNESCO) in December 2001〕

With the wide spread of Buddhism in China in the second century AD, grotto art was introduced to China from India, developing rapidly in this century after the fourth century AD. Grottoes were carved in cliff faces in various places, particularly in North China. The best-known among them are the Dunhuang Grottoes in Gansu Province, the Longmen Grottoes in Henan Province and the Yungang Grottoes in Shanxi Province. These are three major treasure troves of Buddhist art in China.

Located 16 kilometres west of Datong City, Yungang Grottoes are hewn out of cliffside in a honeycomb pattern, stretching for 1, 000 metres (one kilometre) from east to west. The Grottoes were built more than 1, 500 years ago in the Northern Wei Dynasty (386-534). The huge project got underway around 460. Within four decades (453-495), a thousand grottoes and some one hundred thousand Buddhist statues were completed together with large numbers of niches and colourful decorations. Nowadays, more than 51, 000 statues remain, the largest being 17 metres high and the smallest only few centimetres. Whether massive or tiny, all are meticulously carved. Yungang Grottoes is one of the largest group grottoes in China and also a world-famous art treasure.

Apart from the Buddhist statues there are multiple niches on the wall of the stone chambers and these are embellished with sculpture of Flying Apsaras, Buddhist episodes, edifices, flowers and other quaint designs. These are beneficial to the study of ancient Chinese architecture, sculpture, costumes, art, painting, carving and musical instruments.

Of the existing 53 grottoes, 21 are spacious and divided into three distinct groups: the eastern, middle and western. The eastern group (Grottoes 1 to 4) contains mainly pillars and Buddhist statues; the middle group (Grottoes 5 to 13) and the western group (Grottoes 14 to 21) are the most splendid. Tourists usually begin their tour with the middle group. On entering the first cave tourists are greeted by the 17-metre-tall Buddha carved out of solid rock. The figure is seated in a dignified posture, its facial expression often startling viewers when it comes into view finally from the fourth level of the cave walkway, for its head nearly touches the ceiling. The ear measures 3. 1 metres, the foot 4. 6 metres and the middle finger 2. 3 metres. The walls and ceilings are filled with sculptured niches containing graceful small Buddha and Flying Apsaras images. Grotto No. 6 is the most magnificent. Also known as the "Grotto of Sakyamuni," it is dominated by a huge square pillar about 15 metres high. The walls of the grotto are covered with sculptures of Buddhisattvas, Buddhas and Flying Apsaras. Especially attractive are the 20-odd carvings in relief on the four sides of the pillar, depicting scenes from the life of Sakyamuni (founder of Buddhism) from birth until his attainment of Nirvana. One impressive sculpture describes Sakyamuni parting from his favourite horse when he left home. The atmosphere of Grotto No. 12 is made lively by sculptures of fairies dancing on the ceiling and walls. Of these, the most captivating is a group carved on the northern wall. Some play flutes, while others beat drums. Then there are those playing the pipa, a 4-stringed lute. The conductor of this orchestra is depicted on the opposite wall. Each figure appears very alive and vigorous, all attention on the music. These sculptures shed much light on ancient Chinese musical instruments and their use. The

613

western group of caves consists of Grottoes No. 16 to No. 20. These are the earliest of Yungang's remaining grottoes. They are oval in shape and each contains a statue of Buddha 13 to 16 metres high. The most spectacular of the five is Grotto No. 18. In its centre is a tall image of the Buddha with a round pillar-shaped body. The upper part of the Buddha is clothed in a stone robe on which the sculptor has carved 1,000 tiny Buddha images. The varied postures and facial expressions of these tiny sculptures are extremely exquisite.

Carved on the eastern wall of the grotto is a smiling goddess with a bottle in her hand. She is leaning slightly forward as though she is about to leave the wall and fly down to share her bottle with the mortals below.

For many centuries, nature and human being caused much damage to the Yungang Grottoes. According to the statistics, 1,400 Buddhist statues were stolen and shipped out of China by foreign plunderers. Quite a number of those remain are missing their heads and limbs.

Since the founding of the People's Republic of China, both the central government and local government have done much to renovate and protect the Yungang Grottoes. Cracked caves and statues have already been reinforced and chemical means have been tried out to deal with weathering. To further protect the Yungang Grottoes, a new highway has been constructed to bypass the Yungang Grottoes.

The Nine-Dragon Wall 九龙壁

The Nine-Dragon Wall in Datong City was erected as a screen in front of the prince residence of the 13th son Zhu Guidai of the First Ming Emperor Zhu Yuanzhang in 1392 in the Ming Dynasty. The prince residence was destroyed by war in the end of the Ming Dynasty and only the Nine-Dragon Wall remains. The wall is 45.5 metres long, 8 metres high and 2.02 metres thick. There are four nine-dragon screens (walls) in China, the other two are in Beijing, and the newly-built one is in Nanning, Guangxi Zhuang Autonomous Region. The Nine-Dragon Wall was used as a decoration and was supposed to ward off evil spirits.

Mount Wutai 五台山

With a perimeter of 250 kilometres, Mount Wutai is one of the four famous Buddhist shrines in China. It enjoys the same popularity as Mount Emei in Sichuan Province, Mount Putuo in Zhejiang Province, Mount Jiuhua in Anhui Province. The five platform-shaped peaks, the East, West, South, North, and Central Platforms formed Mount Wutai. The area inside the five peaks is called Inner Wutai and that outside Outer

Wutai. At the East Platform (Sea-Viewing Peak 望海峰), tourists can observe sunrise; at the West Platform (Hanging Moon Peak 挂月峰), tourists can enjoy the full moon in mid-autumn when the scenery is fascinating; at the South Platform (Brocade Peak 锦绣峰), tourists can mount the summit of the peak in summer and look around into the distance, where the scenery is enchanting; the elevation of the North Platform (Yedou Peak 叶斗峰) is the highest—3,058 metres, being the roof of North China, and is snow- and ice-capped all the year round, looking magnificent; at the Central Platform (Verdant Rock Peak 翠岩峰), huge rocks covered by moss appear radiantly green under sunshine like seething dragons, hence the name "dragon-seething rocks." The area of Mount Wutai features rising and falling ridges and peaks, crisscross gullies and ravines, river valleys, luxuriant forests and interlocking basins and mountains.

More charming is the unique climate at Mount Wutai. At the coldest spots ice does not melt all the year round; at fairly cold places, it snows in September and thaws in April the following year; at the warmest places, rivers do not freeze and there is no frost the year round. At Mount Wutai the difference in humidity is very great. As the climate here is cool even in mid-summer, Mount Wutai is also known as Cool Mountain. The unique climate brings about unique scenery. Climbing up the summit of North Platform, tourists see peaks completing with one another for beauty among seething clouds. Sometimes, it rains heavily at the foot of the mountain, but the sun shines atop the summit; spring is very much in the air at the base, while the summit is covered with snow and ice. Climbing up the mountain on a fine day, tourists will find a colourful semi-circular halo appearing by their sides. The halo is about three metres high and about two meters wide, composed of red, orange, yellow, green, blue, and purple belts. One's shadow and movements will be reflected in the halo (a bright circle of light, as around the sun or moon in misty weather). It is the reflection at Mount Wutai of the meteorological feature also known as the "Emei Halo."

Mount Wutai, the Buddhist shrine, is said to be the place where Manjusri Buddha was consecrated. During the period AD 58 to AD 75, Emperor Ming Di sent an envoy to go on a pilgrimage to India for Buddhist scriptures. After returning to the homeland, the envoy built the White Horse Temple at Luoyang and, in the following year, built a temple at Mount Wutai. Legend has it that the peak to the west of the town of Taihuai resembled Divine Vulture Mountain in India, the newly built temple was named the Tafu Temple of the Divine Vulture, which is today the

615

Temple of Revelation. In the following years, more and more temples were constructed at Mount Wutai during the Northern Wei, Northern Qi, Sui, and Tang dynasties until the end of the Qing Dynasty (1644-1911). According to historical records, there were more than 300 temples during the heyday of Mount Wutai. However, due to social vicissitude, the temples at Mount Wutai experienced several rises and falls. Today, there are still 39 temples remaining in Inner Wutai and 8 temples in Outer Wutai, making a total of 47 temples. Among the temples at Mount Wutai, Nanchan Temple 南禅寺, the Temple of Buddha's Halo 佛光寺, the Temple of Revelation 显通寺, Dagoda Temple 塔院寺, Buddha Summit 菩萨顶, Shuxiang Temple 殊像寺, Bishan Temple 碧山寺, Dragon Spring Temple 龙泉寺, Nanshan Temple 南山寺, Jinge Temple 金阁寺, Zhenhai Temple 镇海寺 and Dailuo Summit 黛螺顶 are the most influential. The above-mentioned temples are not only magnificent and exquisite in structure, but also preserve large quantities of valuable cultural relics and art works of Buddhism. The coloured sculpture and mural of the Tang Dynasty, the white marble carvings of the Qing Dynasty, the jade Buddha of Myanmar and Huayan Scripture Pagoda are all unique in China.

Cool and tranquil, Mount Wutai is a famous summer resort. To know, you must go.

Pingyao——One of the World Cultural Heritage Sites
平遥

Pingyao, a well-known ancient city in Shanxi Province, will relocate over 20,000 residents out of the city in the period 2002 to 2006 to better protect this World Cultural Heritage site. The city was built 2,000 years ago. It has well-preserved the ancient city walls, residences, government offices, and stores of the Ming (1368-1644) and Qing (1644-1911) dynasties. It was therefore the United Nations Educational, Scientific and Cultural Organization (UNESCO) inscribed the city on the World Cultural Heritage list in 1997. Encompassing 2.25 square kilometres, the city has a population of 45,000. To restore the original outlook of the ancient city, the local government has decided to relocate residents in the downtown area. At the same time, the city government has made great efforts to improve the local environment. Thirty polluting enterprises around the city will be closed, with 30 chimneys and more than 400 coke furnaces being demolished at the same time.

Tianjin Municipality
天 津 市

Tianjin, the major industrial and commercial city in North China, is just one and half-hours' drive from Beijing. It is a municipality directly under the Central Government and it is an open seaside city. With the Haihe River and the Grand Canal crossing in its centre, the city enjoys convenient communications not only on land and in the air but also on water. The Tianjin New Harbour, built in 1952, is the largest artificial seaport in North China, serving as Beijing gateway to the sea. The biggest container quay has been built here. The Water Park, located southwest of the city, is the city's one of the most attractive sites. The azure green water and the tiny boats can be enjoyed together with other pretty views. The city's carpets, colour clay figures and New Year paintings from Yangliuqing are famous for their exquisiteness. Goubuli steamed stuffed buns and Guifaxiang fried dough twists are two of the city's famous snacks.

The places and snack we recommend include: Solitary Joy, the Panshan Mountain, Yangcun Mini World, the Yangliuqing New Year Pictures and Goubuli steamed stuff buns.

Solitary Joy (Dule) Temple 独乐寺

Located in Jixian County, 113 kilometres from Tianjin City, the Solitary Joy Temple, also known as the Big Buddha Temple, was first constructed in the Tang Dynasty (618-907) and rebuilt in 984 in the Liao Dynasty (916-1125). Dule means exclusive happiness. Legend has it that when An Lushan 安禄山 (?-757, a general of the Tang Dynasty) rebelled against the emperor, he held a meeting here at the temple before going to war and he gave the temple its present name because he wanted happiness exclusively for himself instead of sharing it with the people. The temple consists of an entrance gate, the 23-metre-high Guanyin (Avalokitesvara or Goddess of Mercy) Pavilion and the chambers on the east and west sides. The gate, the roof of which has five ridges and four slopes, is China's extant oldest. The pavilion, built in 24 different systems of brackets inserted between the top of a column and a crossbeam, is the cream of China's extant high-rise pavilions of wooden structure. On top of all this, it stands formidable despite 28 major earthquakes. Inside the pavilion is a 16-metre-high clay statue of Avalokitesvara, or the Goddess of Mercy, beautiful in shape and enchanting in mien, a rare treasure among clay sculptures following the style of the Liao Dynasty (916-1125).

Panshan Mountain 盘山

Panshan Mountain is located 12 kilometres to the northwest of the Jixian County seat. It is renowned for its beautiful landscape in China. The mountain is an extension of Yanshan Mountain with an average elevation of 500 metres. Its peak towers nearly 1, 000 metres, Historically, it was reputed as "No 1 Mountain in East Beijing." According to historical records, from the 2nd century onwards, many celebrated emperors of China such as Li Shimin (599-649; reigned 626-649) of the second Tang Emperor, Kangxi (reigned 1662-1722) and Qianlong (1736-1795) of the Qing emperors paid visits to this mountain and there are still preserved here many inscriptions by illustrious figures in Chinese history. The scenery of Panshan Mountain is always beautiful through the year because apart from the elegant mountains and cliffs, it is covered with deep foliage. The mountain has five peaks, such as Guayuefeng 挂月峰, Zigaifeng 紫盖峰, Zilaifeng 自来峰, Jiuhuafeng 九华峰 and Wujianfeng 舞剑峰; eight rocks 八石 such as Hanging or Suspending (Xuankong) Rock 悬空石, Shaking (Yaodong) Rock 摇动石, Sun (Liangjia) Rock 晾甲石, General (Jiangjun) Rock 将军石, Wood-clamping (Jiamu) Rock 夹木石, Skylight (Tianjing) Rock 天井石, Frog (Hama) Rock 蛤蟆石, and Python (Mang) rock 蟒石; 72 monasteries and Taoist temples and 13 exquisite pagodas and pavilions, terraces, buildings and towers. They are comparable to the Wutai Mountain in Shanxi Province, which also has five peaks. Therefore, it is also known as the East Wutai Mountain. The best scenery of the Panshan Mountain is the pine forests at the top 上盘之松, the strange rocks at the middle 中盘之石 and the streams at the foot of the mountain 下盘之水为三盘之胜. The mountain is some fifty kilometres in circumference. Visitors can find an attraction at almost every step and a lot of attractions have interesting legends about them. It has been opened to public since 1979.

618

Yangcun Mini World 杨村小世界

Situated in the west of Yangcun Township of Wuqing District, Tianjin, the Yangcun Mini World is 80 kilometres from Beijing to the north and each 30 kilometres apart from Tianjin to the south and Langfang to the west.

The Yangcun Mini World boasts the world famous and typical sceneries, historic spots, architecture and art of different countries, according to a certain proportion to miniature within one garden. The garden is a large-scale comprehensive amusement park with its appropriate cultural recreational activities and service trades.

It encompasses 32 hectares of land. The entire garden constitutes according to the natural plate lectonics of the earth with sceneries scattered reasonably, strewn orderly mountains alternating with rivers, and combining movement with quietude. The 1,134 sceneries of more than 80 countries are miniature within one garden according to 1:1 and 1:50 relative proportion. A part of the water region of over 13.33 hectares (32.93 acres) is reserved for growing lotus and fish raising. In the water visitors can cruise round "the world" on the yacht of Columbus. Visitors can also row boat in "the Atlantic" and go angling in "the Indian Ocean." The world famous bridges reflecting amid the lakes and mountains connect the five continents and four oceans in the garden as a whole. The narrow paths are full of twists and turns between sceneries with shades of green trees. All these fully realize the organic combination of the garden being of the East and West.

The 113 points of interest in the garden can be typically summed up into the following categories:

1. The historic spots of ancient culture—the Great Wall of China, the Pyramid of Egypt, etc.
2. The example of modern architecture—The Eiffel Tower of France, the Sydney Opera House of Australia, etc.
3. The essence of world sculpture—the 100-metre sculptured corridors, etc.
4. Religious temples and churches—cathedral of St. Basil Blazhenny of Russia, the Great Golden Pagoda of Rangoon, Myanmar, etc.
5. The famous natural scenes—Mount Fuji of Japan, Mount Rushmore National Memorial of USA, the scenes of Latin America, etc.
6. The scientific scenes of the world—the Greenwich Clock of U.K, the Monument of Equator of Ecuador, etc.
7. Folk custom and folkways of different countries—windmill of Holland, the natives dwelling house of New Zealand, etc.

In the garden, visitors can not only review the human history and learn the modern culture but also amuse oneself and mould one's temperament. The recreational spots with the attractions of foreign countries such as Hampton Forest Labyrinth, the Doll Museum of Finland, the Mini Golf of Germany, the Amusement Town of Lisbon of Macao and the Children's World, the Future World, the Lucky Cave, the Water Paradise, the Pavilion of Magic, etc. will bring you boundless joy.

Yangliuqing New Year Pictures 杨柳青年画

Yangliuqing is a small town in the western suburbs of Tianjin. New Year

Pictures workshops appeared there at the end of the Ming Dynasty (1368-1644), employing people to paint, cut wood, print and mount pictures. During the Qing Dynasty (1644-1911), "Yangliuqing" became China's most famous kind of woodblock picture. At its heyday, most people living in the town and in the surrounding 32 villages were engaged in the business. They produced more than 20 million pieces a year. As well as maintaining the sincerity of traditional folk paintings, the Yangliuqing pictures also absorbed the characteristics of traditional Chinese "realistic" painting and paid close attention to the details of the figures. The coloring used the different effects of "soft colours (gentle, clear and sometimes pinkish)" and "hard colours (strong, deep and pure)." Yang liuqing pictures use both process printing and hand drawing for colour. The themes range from the dignified Door God (whose pictures were often pasted on the front door of a house as a talisman in old China), chubby children and elegant ladies, to scenes from ancient novels and folk tales. The images are vivid and colorful. Larger sized woodblock pictures are a specialty of the Yangliuqing pictures.

"*Goubuli*" Stuffed Bun (*Goubuli* Dumpling) 狗不理包子

Near the end of the 19th century, Yuan Shikai (1859-1916), a warlord, bought some *goubuli* buns in Tianjin to present them to Empress Dowager Cixi (1835-1908). The name of stuffed buns became astonishing within the Imperial Palace and the shop was officially named the Repository of Virtue. But people still called the *goubuli*— "stuffed buns shop."

In 1916, Gao Guiyou, owner of the shop, passed away and was succeeded by his son, Gao Jinming. The *goubuli* stuffed buns were then in their heyday and branch shops had been set up in the city. In 1947, the shop was run by a grandson, Gao Huanzhang. In 1952, some troubles came to Gao's family and the shop operations were suspended. In 1956, the Tianjin Municipal Government decided to reopen the shop.

The *goubuli* stuffed buns have a history of over 100 years. They were named after former owner Gao Guiyou, whose pet name was *goubuli*.

The *goubuli* stuffed buns are popular because they use only choice materials and are exquisitely prepared. They are well-known in China and in some foreign countries. A shop of Tianjin "*goubuli*" stuffed buns has been opened in Beijing, and they have been introduced to Japan. The trade fair held in Koba, Japan in March 1981, invited a chef from Tianjin to make the *goubuli* stuffed buns. It was a smashing success.

Star-Rated Hotels in Tianjin 天津星级饭店 （Area Code 022）

Name	Star-Rate	Tel.	Fax
Sheraton Tianjin Hotel 喜来登大酒店	5	23343388	23358740
Tianjin Huanbohai Intl. Hotel 天津环渤海国际酒店	5	28208787	28208484
Dickson Hotel 帝城大酒店	4	28364888	28365018
Holiday Inn 假日饭店	4	26288888	26286666
Geneva Hotel 津利华大酒店	4	28352222	28359855
Hyatt Regency Tianjin 凯悦饭店	4	23301234	23311234
New World Astor Hotel 利顺德大饭店	4	23311112	23321128
The Crystal Palace Hotel 水晶宫饭店	4	28356888	28358886
Teda International Hotel 泰达国际酒店	4	25326000	25326216
Teda Central Hotel 泰达中心酒店	4	25206666	25206665
View Hotel 北方宾馆	3	25311301	25311322
Cairnhill Hotel 金禧大酒店	3	27351688	27354784
Golden Sail Hotel 金帆大厦	3	25326666	25324504
The Caesar Palace Hotel 凯撒皇宫大酒店	3	23375995	23374922
Park Hotel 乐园宾馆	3	28309818	28302042
Longfeng Hotel 龙凤酒店	3	24310148	24313416
Victory Hotel 胜利宾馆	3	25345833	25344570
Sports Hotel 体育宾馆	3	23915800	23916271
Tianjin Grand Hotel 天津宾馆	3	28359000	28359822
Sinta Hotel 先达大酒店	3	23388558	23388558

621

Name	Star-Rate	Tel.	Fax
Friendship Hotel 友谊宾馆	3	23310372	23310616
Yucheng Intl. Hotel 裕城国际大酒店	3	23312000	23308816

Part Seven

OLYMPICS & SPORTS

第七部分　奥林匹克运动会和体育运动

The History of the Olympic Games
奥林匹克运动会历史

In 1896, when the Olympic flame was kindled and the modern Olympic Games began in Athens, Greece, 285 athletes—all men—representing thirteen countries competed in nine sports for crowns of wild olives.

From July 19 to August 5, 1996 nearly 11,000 athletes—including some 3,800 women—representing 197 countries and regions competed in 26 sports for a total of 1,933 medals. Obviously, the Olympic Games have come a long way in the last hundred years. Still, one thing has not changed: the Olympic Games continue to capture the human imagination by embodying the duel principles of excellence and sportsmanship.

The 1996's Olympic Games were held in Atlanta, Georgia of the United States. That was the fourth time the United States hosted the Olympics; in 1904, the Games were held in St. Louis, and in 1932 and 1984, they were held in Los Angeles. The Atlanta Games signified the first time the Olympics have been held in the southern region of the United States. The birthplace of Dr Martin Luther King Jr., and the first major city in the South to elect a black mayor, Atlanta demonstrated a commitment to the ideals the Olympics represent. About 40,000 volunteers—mostly Atlanta's —worked together for months, even years, to stage these Games in the spirits of friendship and co-operation.

In 1996, some 3.5 billion people—two-thirds of the earth's population watched the Olympics on television. On the archery field and in the swimming pool, on the track and in the gymnasium, athletes redefined the limits of the human body. As we admire the efforts of Olympians from both our own and other countries, perhaps we too will "dream dreams no mortal ever dreamed before." And even as we do, the eternal Olympic flames or competition, fair play, friendship, peace and unity will continue to light our way in the future.

China's Olympic History
中国奥林匹克史

China's road to participation in the Olympics was a long and winding one. Like other significant events running through China's modern history, Chinese Olympic history is not only a story of the country's athletic ability, but also the development of national strength. It is full of twists and turns, pain, and, finally joy.

Some people say China's Olympic history started at the very first Olympic Games in 1896, during the latter part of the Qing Dynasty (1644-1911) was ruled by Empress Dowager Cixi (1835-1908). Upon receiving an invitation from the International Olympic Committee (IOC), nobody at her court knew what "Olympics" meant. When she was eventually told it was a sport meet, including running events, she burst out laughing and said: "Well, we may send some of our eunuchs who are running the court so well. They are good runners." This might be a mere story about the unpopular dowager. It remains a mystery as to whether the Qing court actually received a letter of invitation from the IOC at all. In order to find an answer to this question, Lu Enchun, a coach with the Chinese gymnastics team, once went to the Imperial Palace in Beijing to look into the Qing archives. He was completely at sea among the piles of documents.

Gu Bingfu, former director of the China Sports Museum, made a similar effort from a different angle in 1995 when he visited the Olympic Museum in Lausanne. The only answer he got from the keeper was that not every country was invited to the first Olympics. In 1922, Chinese diplomat Wang Zhengting was elected onto the IOC. It was then that the IOC formally recognized a sport organization in China. It is stipulated in the Olympic Charter that only an organization recognized by the IOC may enter competitors for the Olympic Games.

It was not until 1932, when the 10th Olympic Games were held in Los Angeles, that China was invited for the first time to send athletes. Four years before this, at the Ninth Olympics in Amsterdam, China had been invited to send an observer to attend the opening ceremony—a man named Song Ruhai. In addition, an overseas Chinese, He Chaohua, registered to take part in a cycling race on behalf of the motherland. Unfortunately, he was injured and hospitalized, but he is still considered the first Chinese Olympian.

In his "Chinese History of Sports over the Past Century," Professor Wu Wenzhong confirms that China was first represented by Song Ruhai at the Olympic Games in 1928 and that he acted as an observer. Song also recorded this in his book "The World Games."

No delegation worthy of the name was sent to the Olympics until 1932. Even then, the Chinese Government had no real intention of taking part. The Japanese had occupied Northeastern China and set up the puppet state of Manchukuo. They attempted to send a promising athlete, Liu Changchun, to the games to represent the puppet regime in order to give it credibility as a country. But the patriotic-minded athlete made a statement in the newspaper "L' Impartial, " refusing to represent Manchukuo at the Olympics. Meanwhuile, General Zhang Xiuliang (1901-2001) exposed the Japanese aggressors' scheme and declared that he would sponsored Liu Changchun to the Olympics to represent China. He announced at a graduation ceremony at the Northeastern University that Liu and his coach Song Junfu would participate in the 10th Olympic Games on behalf of China. Although eliminated in the preliminary heats of the 100m and 200m sprints, clocking 11. 1 and 22. 1 seconds respectively, Liu, as the first Chinese athlete to appear at the Olympics, paved the way for China's future participation in the global sports event.

China's participation in the 10th Olympic Games in 1932, though by only one athlete, aroused more worldwide attention than the Chinese Government had expected. At the time, the government felt a little uneasy about how the public would react to the fact that just one man should represent the most populous country. In 1935, one year before the 11th Olympics, it set aside a special fund for Olympic preparations, choosing the best athletes and opening up a number of training classes. A delegation was organized, consisting of 69 competitors for athletes, swimming, basketball, football, weightlifting, boxing and cycling; 39 observers and nine traditional Chinese wushu (martial arts) masters. In addition, 150 journalists and visitors accompanied competitors to Berlin at their own expenses. At the Olympics, the martial arts demonstrators went to Denmark, Sweden, Czechoslovakia, Hungary, Austria and Italy, where they were warmly received as envoys of the Chinese people and highly acclaimed for their performances with bare hands or using ancient weapons such as swords, cudgels and spears. Some of the performers later became well-known masters, professors, or leaders of national organizations, including Zheng Huaixian, the late president of the Chinese Wushu Association. The observers, who were PE teachers and scholars, spent more than six weeks in Europe, and they visited sports facilities, studying sports management and physical training in schools and colleges—a study tour that proved very useful for their work after their return to China. As far as the Olympic competition was concerned, Chinese athletes failed to collect a single medal. All were eliminated in the preliminaries except for Fu Baolu in the pole vault, holder of the then national record of 4. 015m. his best performance fell below 4m at the Games. Afterwards, he joined the air force and was killed during the War of Resistance Against Japan (1937-1945).

No Olympic Games were held for the 12th and 13th Olympiads because of the Second World War. In 1947, China started preparations for the

627

14th Olympic Games for the next year. Selective trials and intensive training were held for the 10, 000m, 400m, marathon, 400m hurdles, 100m freestyle swimming, 1, 000m cycling, basketball and football. But the Olympic delegation received no more than US$ 25, 000 from the government, with a deficit of US$ 70, 000-80, 000 to be collected by the delegation itself. Part of the funds was raised at home. To make up the balance, the basketball and football teams played 15 and 32 matches respectively collecting gate money during a four-month tour to Hong Kong, Saigon, Manila, Bangkok, Singapore, Rangoon and Calcutta, before they arrived in London in late July——just in time for the Olympic Games. To cut down on expense, it is said that the delegation brought its own food amounting to 4 tons for 48 people. Though the results in competitions were quite disappointing——without a single point to the delegation's credit, the efforts the Chinese athletes had made were considered remarkable. Take Lou Wen'ao for instance. He was a deaf-mute and took part in the 10, 000m and marathon, during which he developed blisters all over his feet because he wore a pair of ordinary shoes made of rubber soles and cloth uppers. The Chinese basketball team was placed 18th among the 23 participating squads. The Chinese cyclist, He Haohua, was at one point second in his race, but fell from his bike near the finish to dash his hopes for a medal. Despite their poor performances and hardship, the Chinese Olympians never forgot the British people's friendship towards them——as expressed in the children's hunt for their autographs, the Londoners' invitations to their homes and the royal reception at Buckingham Palace. This spoke of an international understanding so important for the establishment of a peaceful society after the Second World War and following a 12-year break for the Olympics.

With the founding of the People's Republic of China in 1949, the Olympics received greater attention. The Chinese Olympic Committee (COC) decided to take part in the 15th Olympic Games to be held in Helsinki in 1952. A problem arose when some of the former COC members who had fled to Taiwan with the Kuomintang authorities claimed to the International Olympic Committee (IOC) that they, rather than the COC, should represent China at the Games. It was not until July 17, just two days before the opening of the event, that IOC passed by vote a resolution to invite the Chinese mainland's COC to the Olympics as China's sole representative. The COC received the resolution and a cable of invitation from the organizing committee on July 18. There being no proper air transport available, it was impossible to fly the Chinese delegation from Beijing to Helsinki for the opening ceremony. Although delayed, the Chinese athletes arrived at the Olympic village and hoisted the red five-star national flag for the first time in Olympic history, which as pointed out by China's late Premier Zhou Enlai, was a great victory in itself. In 1954, at its 49th session in Athens, the IOC adopted a resolution on the official recognition of the Chinese mainland's COC and decided to invite China to take part in the 16th Olympic Games to be held in Melbourne in 1956. But then something unexpected happened. On the list of IOC members there appeared two Chinese National Olympic Committees, Some people in the IOC had, regardless of the resolution passed at the 49th session, placed Taiwan on the list. The Chinese delegation, which was in Guangzhou and ready to depart for Melbourne, simply lodged a protest and withdrew from the Olympics. China did not participate in the following Games until the IOC Executive Board passed in 1979 a resolution on the reinstatement of the Chinese mainland to the IOC, while the Olympic Committee in Taiwan could only use the name "Chinese Taipei Olympic Committees." China immediately decided to participate in the 13th Winter Olympic Games to be held in Lake Placid, USA, in February 1980, and in the 22nd Olympic Games to be held in Moscow in August the same year. China sent 28 athletes to the United States—for the first time to a winter Olympics—to compete in speed skating, figure skating, the biathlon and cross-country and alpine skiing. It was also represented at the following three winter Olympics. Owing to the Soviet Union's invasion of Afghanistan, the COC and Chinese athletes, though fully prepared, boycotted the 22nd Moscow Olympics in their struggle against hegemony and in defense of Olympic principles.

With the restoration of the Chinese Olympic Committee's lawful seat on the IOC and of the Chinese sports delegation's right to participate in the Olympics, Chinese athletes went to Los Angeles Games as China's first full participation in a Summer Games. Chinese shooter Xu Haifeng won the first LA gold in the men's pistol event, with the medal awarded to him by IOC President Juan Antonio Samaranch himself. As the first Olympic gold ever collected by a Chinese in Olympic history, it was called "a breakthrough"—an event that brought great joy to the whole Chinese nation. All in all, China earned 15 gold, 8 silver and 9 bronze medals and was placed fourth in the medals table. Since then, Chinese athletes have been regular participants of the Olympic Games. They have shed tears at their losses and shared laughter at their triumphs. At the 27th Olympics held in Sydney, Australia, in 2000, China emerged as one of the biggest winners, taking home a total of 28 gold, 16 silver and 15 bronze medals.

Olympics 2008
奥林匹克运动会 2008

Ten (10) cities in the world wanted to stage 2008 Olympics.

Ten cities submitted letters to the International Olympic Committee expressing interest in bidding for the 2008 Summer Olympics. So far, Bangkok, Istanbul, Havana, Osaka, Paris, Beijing, Seville, Toronto, Kuala Lumpur and most recently Cairo had already filed their candidatures with the IOC. The 10 cities were one short of the record 11 which began the bidding process for the 2004 Summer Games, won by Athens. IOC president Juan Antonio Samaranch said in October he believed as many as 13 countries might nominate cities for the 2008 Games. Buenos Aires, Cape Town and Rio de Janeiro had also expressed interest but had yet to file official notice at the IOC's Lausanne headquarters.

Beijing was the early favourite. The Chinese capital lost out on the 2000 Games to Sydney by only two votes. The host city was selected at the IOC Congress in Moscow in September 2001.

Cities, which met the midnight deadline, will attend an information meeting with the IOC on February 24, 2000.

More Sports Facilities for Olympic Games
为奥运会大量新建体育设施

Beijing is poised to build a colossal sporting and exhibition centre to help the campaign for hosting the 2008 Summer Olympics. The centre site is around the Asian Games Village near the Fourth Ring Road and its main premises will cover 405 hectares (1, 212. 5 acres). One stadium and nine gymnasiums will be set up in the centre to meet the demands of hosting the Olympics. The Beijing Municipal Government is seeking plans and designs from home and abroad. Bidders are required to submit their ideas before July 11. Beijing is chasing the 2008 Olympic along with nine other cities: Istanbul, Havana, Osaka, Seville, Toronto, Paris, Bangkok, Cairo, and Kuala Lumpur.

Chronicle of Beijing's Bid for Olympic Games in 2008
北京申办 2008 年奥运会年代记

- On November 25, 1998, Beijing presented its application for the 2008 Olympic games to Chinese Olympic Committee.
- On April 7, 1999, the International Olympic Committee (IOC) accepted

the application from Beijing.

- On September 6, 1999, Beijing founded the Beijing 2008 Olympic Games Bid Committee.
- On February 2, 2000, the Beijing Bid Committee's logo, motto and website are officially launched.
- February 24, 2000, the IOC held a joint conference for all the applicants and released the new bidding process. Meanwhile, the IOC also gave out a questionnaire of 22 questions to each of the applicants.
- June 20, 2000, answers to the questionnaire are submitted to the IOC.
- On August 28-29, 2000, the executive committee of the IOC announced the candidates, from a list of 10 bidding cities, in Lausanne. Beijing was one of the five candidates on the list with Paris, Toronto, Osaka, and Istanbul.
- September 1, 2000, IOC sets up the evaluation commission to assess the five candidate cities and their capability to host the Games.
- September 6, 2000—Signature of the Candidature Procedure.
- September 9, 2000, Chinese President Jiang Zemin writes to IOC President Juan Antonio Samaranch to express the Chinese Government's support of Beijing's bid.
- September 13, 2000, Sydney—The IOC Executive Board draws lots to determine the order of Candidate City presentations, etc.
- September 15, October 1, 2000, Sydney—Games of the XXV11 Olympiad, 2000. China wins 28 gold medals and ranks third on the medal board.
- September 25, 2000, Sydney—Information meeting between the IOC and the Candidate Cities.
- December 13, 2000, Lausanne—Ten-minute presentation by each of the Candidate Cities to the IOC Executive Board.
- January 17, 2001—Submission of Candidature file to the IOC. Mid-February to mid-April 2001—Visits of the IOC Evaluation Commission to the Candidate Cities.
- February 20-25, 2001—IOC Evaluation Commission visits Beijing to inspect the city's capacity to host an Olympic Games.
- May 15, 2001—Report by the IOC Evaluation Commission to the Executive Board, Beijing's bid is appraised as "excellent." The report says that Beijing would stage an "excellent Olympic Games." Designation by the IOC Executive Board of Candidate Cities to be submitted to the IOC session for election.

July 13, 2001, 112th IOC Session, Moscow—Beijing was elected as the Host City of the Games of the 29th Olympiad in 2008.

Ten Reasons Why Beijing Should be Venue for the 29th Olympic Games 北京申办第 29 届奥运会的十大原因

1. China Is the World's Most Populous Country. Boasting one fifth of the world's total population, including 400 million youngsters, yet China has never had the chance to host an Olympics. An Olympic event in Beijing will spread the Olympic message to more people and increase the popularity of Olympic sports.

2. Solid Economic Strength Beijing is a rapidly developing city. The GDP of Beijing had reached US$24 billion, an average GDP per capita of more than US$2, 000.

3. Remarkable Sports Results China came fourth in the last two Olympics medal tables. Chinese athletes have won 1, 317 world championships, breaking 1. 026 world records.

4. Social and Political Stability Beijing has one of the lowest crime and traffic death rates among the world's cities. The city can guarantee safety and security during major sports events.

5. Splendid Culture The city of Beijing was built 3, 045 years ago (1045 BC), and has been the capital of China for more than 800 years.

6. Rich Experience in Holding Big Sports Games Beijing successfully played host to the 11th Asian Games in 1990 and the Sixth Far East and South Pacific Games for the disabled in 1994. It will host the 21st World Students Games in 2001.

7. A Beautiful Olympic Park Beijing will build a 1, 215-hectare Olympic Park in northern Beijing. It will include an 80, 000-seat stadium, 14 gymnasiums, an athlete village and an international exhibition centre. Surrounded by a 760-hectare forest and green land, this area is a perfect place for athletes to achieve their best performances.

8. First-Class Communication, Traffic, Hotels and Other Public Utilities Beijing boasts 344 star-rate hotels accommodating 400, 000 people. Capital Airport can receive 35 million passengers annually, and air routes link the city with 54 cities in 39 countries.

9. All-out Support from the State Government Premier Zhu Rongji says the Chinese Government will do its best to support the bid for the Olympic games, and will create a good bidding environment on May 8, 2000.

10. Strong Support from the People According to a poll, 94. 6 per cent of Beijing citizens (12. 8 million) support the bid for the 2008 Games.

New Roads Expected to Speed Up Traffic 交通畅通工程

A new subway, highway and a light railway will improve traffic flow through Beijing in time for the city's 2008 Olympic Games bid. Priorities would be given to four main areas in the next bid phase, including improvements in the traffic system. Many people the world over held Beijing as a firm favourite city among the five candidates for the 2008 Olympics on August 28, 2000 from a list of 10 bidding cities by the International Olympic Committee. Other finalists include Osaka, Toronto, Paris and Istanbul. The traffic congestion will be greatly eased by these measures. When it is completed, the traffic will be greatly improved and it will contribute a lot to the bid programme. According to the committee's plan, the No 5 Route Subway, which runs parallel to the city's axis, is scheduled to reach the Olympic Green — the main venue for hosting the Games. The subway will become one of the main transport routes in the capital city when the passenger number reaches 440 million a year. The 5th Ring Road and the light rail across the city are currently being built. Together with the north Fourth Ring Road, the routes will send tens of thousands of athletes to the Olympic Village when Beijing becomes the host of the Games in 2008. Other roads linking to the Village will be re-built and extended to meet the demand for staging the Games.

Greener Beijing for Great Olympic 绿色北京迎接新奥运

According to the plan drafted by the Beijing Municipal Government, during the next seven years, the city authorities will put 46 billion yuan (US $5.75 billion) into air improvement. In 1999, 10 billion yuan (US$1.25 billion) was invested in the same area. Priorities would be given to air condition and the money will mainly be sued to control exhaust emissions, dust storms, coal fumes and to plant more trees. By 2008, the air quality will mostly reach above-average standards set by the municipal government. Air quality will be of a good standard nearly half of the time by that time. To fight against urban pollution is one of the top priorities for Beijing, one of five candidates for the 2008 Games. The city launched a bid in the early 1990s to host 2000's Olympic Games, but Sydney piped Beijing at the post by just two votes. The ambitious environmental plan was part of the city's efforts to become the 2008 Olympic hosts. According to government statistics, 1-2 per cent of the nation's gross domestic product (GDP) was invested in environment protection, though this is not high enough to prevent the environment from getting worse. The goal of the current plan is to raise the amount of money spent on the environment to as much as 4.5 per cent of GDP. Forty per cent of the city into green space through the plan and the water shortages in the city won't be a problem. The city's water recycling system should guarantee water supplies. Key

633

projects in the plan include building a boulevard flanked by 100-metre wide green spaces. The 2008 bid would help the city make great environmental progress. People in Beijing will benefit from the Olympic bid even if we lose it. That is why we support it.

Beijing's environmental condition is expected to improve greatly in the seven years prior to the Olympics to fulfill the city's "Green Olympics" promise. A dozen environmental experts from the country's leading academies and institutes including the Chinese Academy of sciences, Peking University, Tsinghua University and the Chinese Institute of environmental Science, began a review of the Beijing's 10th Five-Year (2001-2005) Plan on ecological protection on July 23, 2001. The municipal government plans to allocate 4 to 5 per cent of its annual gross domestic product (GDP) to environmental protection projects, according to the draft plan. By the end of 2007, the city's vegetation coverage will be greatly increased with tree coverage in mountainous areas reaching 70 per cent and coverage on plains exceeding 25 per cent, according to the plan. Green spaces in urban areas in the city will total 125 square kilometres. Beijing's "Green Olympics" blueprint hails harmony between human beings and nature, which is a key focus in the city's environmental plan over the next five years. The plan should be a long-term project, which takes into consideration the proper use of energy, natural resources and land, convenient and efficient communication and an adjustment in the industrial structure. Over the next five years, the Beijing municipal government will invest more money in environmental protection projects. Industrial pollution will be reduced greatly and more basic environmental protection facilities will be built in the near future. The city's environmental condition has already been improved; its air quality has been substantially upgraded in the last two years. The air quality level in Beijing attained a Grade Three or better for over 300 days in 2000, according to statistics from the Beijing Environmental Protection Bureau.

634

It is predicted that the tourism industry in China, especially in Beijing, will be further enhanced as a result of Beijing's winning the right to host the 2008 Olympics.

Update of Sports Facilities 更新体育设施

Construction of sports infrastructure is a vital factor in the bid for the 2008 Olympic Games. As one of the five cities competing to host the 29th Olympics, Beijing is busy rebuilding its existing venues and planning to build new ones. A number of major sports sites in Beijing are being renovated, including the Capital gymnasium, The Workers' Stadium, the

Workers' Gymnasium and the National Sports Centre. The facilities in many stadiums and gymnasiums in Beijing fall below the international level that they should reach for the Olympic Games, the world's largest meet. The renovations are mainly concentrating on updating the telecommunication systems in the sports venues. Advanced TV broadcast systems will also be available. The locker rooms are also to be improved and work is to be done on such systems and their ventilation systems.

As well as the existing sites, some new sports facilities will be built in the next seven years. Among these new constructions, the Beijing International Exhibition and Sports Centre is set to be of the first magnitude. The centre will be located at the north end of the Zhongzhoulu, the axis of the ancient city of Beijing. It will be an extension of the axis, which boasts many famous historical sites, such as the Forbidden City, and the Drum Tower. The new center will follow the architectural style of ancient Chinese buildings and will be symmetrical in design. Work on the building's blueprints started in March 2000. Public companies were invited to bid for the project in late March 2000. In just three months, 26 Chinese and foreign designing companies including those from the United States, France and Australia, handed in 16 designs. The sponsoring departments then invited 10 famous Chinese architects and three foreign authorities to form a jury to select the best design from the 16 presented. According to an agreement reached by the sponsors, the design that received at least half the jury's votes was to become the first prize winner. But unfortunately, none of them got enough votes. After four days' strict appraisal, two designs, one Chinese and one American, won second prize and three others received the third prize, but the first prize remained vacant. As such, the Beijing Architectural Designing Institute and the Beijing Institute of City Planning and Design were assigned to design the construction plan. They have just finished a preliminary design for the centre, which will cover an area of 405 hectares (101. 25 acres). About half of the total area will be taken up by water and greenery. The centre will consist of four major parts: large sports facilities, a 400, 000-square-metre exhibition centre, a 200, 000-square-metre trade centre and hotels and related facilities. The sports facilities will include an 80, 000-seat stadium, five gymnasiums, an athlete's village and a press centre. The Beijing 2008 Olympic Games Bid Committee handed in the preliminary plan for the Beijing International Exhibition and Sports Centre to the International Olympic Committee on September 10, 2000. The Beijing Municipal Government also intends to build a theme park—the Olympic Green, which will extend north to embrace the 760-hectare(1, 900 acres) Wali Forest Park and will include the

50-hectare (125 acres) Chinese Nationalities Museum in its southwest corner.

The Previous Venues of Olympic Games
历届奥运会举办城市

Sequence 次序	Year 年	Host City 举办城市
The 1st	1896	Athens of Greece
The 2nd	1900	Paris of France
The 3rd	1904	Saint Louis of the United States of America
The 4th	1908	London of Great Britain
The 5th	1912	Stockholm of Sweden
The 6th	1916	Berlin of Germany (not held due to World War I)
The 7th	1920	Antwerp 安特卫普 of Belgium
The 8th	1924	Paris of France
The 9th	1928	Amsterdam of the Netherlands
The 10th	1932	Los Angeles of the United States of America
The 11th	1936	Berlin of Germany
The 12th	1940	Helsinki of Finland (not held due to World War II)
The 13th	1944	London of Britain (not held due to World War II)
The 14th	1948	London of Britain
The 15th	1952	Helsinki of Finland
The 16th	1956	Melbourne of Australia
The 17th	1960	Rome of Italy
The 18th	1964	Tokyo of Japan
The 19th	1968	Mexico City of Mexico
The 20th	1972	München of Germany
The 21st	1976	Montreal of Canada
The 22nd	1980	Moscow of the former Soviet Union
The 23rd	1984	Los Angeles of the United States of America
The 24th	1988	Seoul of the Republic of Korea
The 25th	1992	Barcelona of Spain
The 26th	1996	Atlanta of the United States of America
The 27th	2000	Sydney of Australia
The 28th	2004	Athens of Greece
The 29th	2008	To be held in Beijing of China

Glossary of Olympiad (Olympic Games / Olympics)
奥林匹克运动会术语

Acrobatics; Acrobatic gymnastics 技巧
Angling 钓鱼
Arch bowls 十柱槌球游戏
Archery 射箭
Aquaplane 滑水板运动
Auto race 汽车大赛
Badminton 羽毛球 (Mixed doubles event 混双)

Bandy 水上曲棍球
Baseball (Softball)棒球 / 垒球
Basketball 篮球
Billiards 台球
Basque game of pelota 巴斯克回力球戏
Big wave riding 巨浪冲浪运动
Board games 棋类
Bocci 地掷球
Body building 健美
Bowling 保龄球
Boxing 拳击
Breaker 水浪／击浪
Bridge 桥牌
Canoeing and yachting 船艇
Canoeing 皮划艇
Carrier pigeon 信鸽
World chess 国际象棋
Chinese chess 中国象棋
Chinlon 藤球
Competitive rhythmic gymnastics; Rhythmic competition gymnastics 艺术体操
Codeball 弹球
Codeball in the court 墙弹球运动
Codeball on the green 草地弹球运动
Court hand-ball 墙手球
Cricket 板球
Croquet 槌球
Curling 掷冰壶
Cycling 自行车赛
Decathlon 十项全能运动—An athletic event in the modern Olympic Games consisting
    often events: 100-metre race, long jump, putting the shot, high jump, 400-metre
    race, 110 metre hurdles, discus, pole vault, throwing the javelin, and 1, 500-metre
    race.(十项全能运动—田经比赛中男子全能项目之一,比赛分两天进行:第一天顺
    序为 100 米、跳远、铅球、跳高、400 米;第二天为 110 米高栏、铁饼、撑竿跳高、标
    枪和 1 500 米。)
Discus 铁饼
Diving 跳水
Men's (10 m) springboard preliminary round 男子(十米)跳水预赛
Dry skiing 滑旱雪
Equestrian sports 马术
False start 抢跑
Faustball (fistball) 拳球运动
Fencing 击剑
Figure skating 花样滑冰
Fives 壁手球
Football 足球
Gliding 滑翔运动

637

Gobang 五子棋

Golf 高尔夫球

Gorlutke (Gorokea) 高路克（俄罗斯的一种击木桩竞技运动）

Gymnastics 体操

Handball 手球

Hockey 曲棍球

(110m)Hurdles men (110 米) 高栏

Ice hockey 冰球

Ice-yacht 冰上驶帆

Jack 靶球

Jai alai (peluta) 回力球运动

Judo 柔道（Women's judo 78-kilograms category or class 女子柔道 78 公斤级）

Kabaddi 卡巴迪

Lacrosse 兜网球／曲棍网球

Marathon Race 马拉松—A long-distance race, named after the battle of Marathon (490 BC), the result of which was announced at Athens, Greece by an unnamed courier who fell dead on his arrival, having run nearly 23 miles. This runner is sometimes cited as Pheidippides (or Philippides), who actually ran from Athens to Saparta to seek help against the Persians before the battle. In the modern Olympic Games, the marathon race was standardized in 1896, the distance being standardized at 26 miles 385 yards or 42 kilometres and 195 metres (or 42, 195 metres) in 1924.

Men's horizontal bar 男子单杠

Men's parallel bars 男子双杠

Men's pole vault 男子撑竿跳

Martial arts 武术

Military pentathlon 军事五项运动

Modern pentathlon 现代五项运动

Motor boat race 快艇竞赛

Motor racing 汽车运动

Motor cycling 摩托车赛

Mountaineering 登山运动

Netball 简易篮球

Orienteering 原野健行

Paddle tennis 板网球

Parachuting 跳伞运动

Pentathlon 五项全能运动—An athletic contest of five events, usually the jump, javelin throw, 200-metre race, discus throw, and 1, 500-metre flat race. In the ancient Olympic Games the contest consisted of running, jumping, throwing the discus and javelin, and wrestling. (五项全能运动—田经比赛中全能运动之一，男子五项一天比赛完，顺序为跳远、标枪、200 米、铁饼和 1500 米。女子现代五项分两天进行：第一天为 100 米低栏、铅球、跳高，第二天为跳远、800 米。)

Peso pallo 芬兰式棒球

(50km) Race walk men（男子 50 公里）竞走

Rodeo 骑野马

Roller hockey 滑旱冰

Roller skating (Rugby) 橄榄球

Rowing 赛艇

Sambo 桑勃／摔跤

(Quadruple) Sculls women 女子（四人）双桨

Sepak Takraw 藤球

Shooting 射击

Speed skating 速度滑冰

Skateboarding 滑板

Skibobbing 雪犁

Skiing 滑雪

Soft Tennis 软式网球

Softball 垒球

Springboard 跳水

Squash 墙网球

Sumo 相扑

Surf riding (Surfing) 冲浪运动

Swimming 游泳

Synchronized 10 metre (3 metre) platform men
男子双人 10 米 (3 米) 高台跳水

Synchronized swimming 花样游泳

Table tennis 乒乓球 Bigger balls 大球 (40 mm to former 38 mm)

Take (or Complete) a grand slam in the sport—winning at the World Championships,
　　the World Cup and the Olympics 中国乒乓球大满贯（瑞典的 Jan Ove-Waldner 瓦
　　尔德内尔、刘国梁、孔令辉 2000 年 9 月 25 日）；世乒赛、世界杯、奥运会冠军

Takraw 塔阔球（泰国）

Taekwondo (Men's 58kg) 跆拳道（男子 58 公斤级）

Tennis 网球

Ten part routine; Trampo lining 蹦床运动

Tchout Ball 巧固球

Thailand boxing 泰拳

Track and field 田径

Travel by canoe 乘轻舟旅游

Triathlon 铁人三项

Triple jump 三级跳远

Underwater sports 水下运动

Uneven bar 平衡木

Volleyball 排球 (libro 自由人）

Water polo 水球

Water skiing 滑水

Weightlifting 举重

Women's balance beam 女子平衡木

Women's floor exercise 女子自由体操

Women's pole vault 女子撑竿跳

Wrestling 摔跤

Wushu 武术

Yachting 帆船

Terms of Football 足球术语

Assistant referees 助理裁判员

Back 后卫

Ball handling 控制球;运球

Ball playing skill 控球技术

Bicycle kick; over-head kick 倒钩

Block tackle 正面抢截

Body check 身体阻挡

Brazilian formation 巴西队阵型;4-2-4 阵型

(To) break through; to beat 带球过人

(To) break up an attack 破坏一次攻势

(To) break loose 摆脱

Bully 混战（特指球门前）

Centre half back 中卫

Centre forward; centre 中锋

Clean catching（守门员）跳球抓好

Clearance kick 解除危险的球

Chest-high ball 平胸球

Chesting 胸部挡球

Close-marking defense 盯人防守

Close pass; short pass 短传

Close-range shot 近射

Consecutive passes 连续传球

(To) control the midfield 控制中场

Corner ball; corner kick; corner 角球

Deceptive movement 假动作

(To) disorganize the defense 破坏防守

Diving header 鱼跃顶球

Draw 打平（平局）; The football game wended in a draw. 这场足球最后踢平了。

Dribbling 盘球

Fair charge 合理冲撞

(To) fall back 退回

Finger-tip save（守门员）托救球

Flank pass 边线传球

Flying header 跳起顶球

Football; soccer 足球

Football field 足球场

Football team 足球队

Footballer; football player 足球运动员

Forward 前锋

Four backs system 四后卫制

Four-five-one formation 4-5-1 阵型

Four-three-three formation 4-3-3 阵型

Four-two-four formation 4-2-4 阵型

Free kick 任意球

Goalkeeper 守门员

Goal kick 球门球

Grazing shot 低射；贴地射门
Groundball; grounder 地面球
Hand ball 手球
Half-way line 中线
Half back 前卫
Header 头球
High lobbing pass 高吊传球
Inside left 左后幺
Inside right 右后幺
(To) intercept 截球
Kick-off circle 中圈
Kick-off 开球
Left back 左后卫
Left half back 左前卫
Long drive 远射
Midfield 中场
Miss-hit 未射中
Offside 越位
Open football 拉开战术
Outside left right 左边锋
Outside right forward 右边锋
Off-side trap 越位战术
(To) pass the ball 传球
Penalty kick; spot kick 点球
Points 积分
Red card 红牌（表示判罚出场）
Referee 裁判员
Referee's ball 裁判员抛球
Right back 右后卫
Right half back 右前卫
Rolling pass; ground pass 滚地传球
Scissor pass 交叉传球
(To) score the World Cup's first golden goal 打进世界杯第一个金球
(To) set a wall 筑人墙
(To) set the pace 掌握进攻节奏
(To) shoot 射门
Slide tackle 铲球
Spot pass 球传到位
Shoot-on-sight tactics 积极的抢射战术
Striker 前锋；攻击手 / hat-trick 帽子戏法

The team finished second in its group with two wins and one loss.
该队以两胜一负的成绩取得小组第二名。
The outcome of the game is a foregone conclusion. 这场比赛胜负已定。
(To) take the penalty 罚点球
(To) take a pass 接球
Three-six-one formation 3-6-1 阵型

641

Time wasting tactics 拖延战术

Total football 全攻全守战术

(To) trap 脚底停球

(To) win or lose in a match is temporary while friendship between the contestants is lasting.

比赛的胜负是暂时的,友谊是永久的。

Triangular pass 三角传球

Throw-in 界外球

Victory hangs in the balance. 这场比赛胜负未定。

Volley pass 凌空传球

(To) ward off an assault 击退一次攻势

Win 胜

Wing play 边锋战术

Yellow card 黄牌(表示警告)

Sporting History Rooted in China
中国的体育史根深蒂固

Chinese sports have a long history and a profound influence over world sports, and demonstrate the great intelligence of the Chinese people from various ethnic groups. During the Xia (2070 BC-1600 BC), Shang (1600 BC-1046 BC) and Zhou (1046 BC-221 BC) dynasties, sports had three main functions: education, military training and entertainment. During the Qin (221 BC-206 BC) and Han (206 BC -AD 220) dynasties, as well as the Three Kingdoms (AD 220-AD 280), ancient Chinese sports entered a period of growth as China evolved as a feudal society. With the unified empires of the Sui (581-618) and Tang (618-907) dynasties bringing social stability, the development of sports took a great stride forward. Cultural exchanges between China and its neighbouring nations resulted in reciprocal influences. Many Chinese games, including wushu—or Chinese kungfu—and go, or encirclement chess, spread overseas while foreign disciplines such as acrobatics enriched Chinese sports. During the Song (960-1279), Liao (916-1125), Jin (1115-1234) and Yuan (1279-1368) dynasties, sports got a big boost and started to aim at health and entertainment. In the Ming (1368-1644) and Qing (1644-1911) dynasties, techniques and skills had largely been improved and sports began to attract many people. Ancient Chinese sports have survived despite wars and changes of dynasties. The Chinese sporting culture is a product of the input of many ethnic groups across the country, from Han people in Central China to nomadic tribes in the northern grasslands and the ethnic groups in southern China. The development of ancient Chinese sports has been unique, mainly because of its long history, lively activities and popularity. Ancient Chinese sports have played a vital role in the development of world

642

sports and made a valuable contribution to the Olympic Movement. As one of the oldest sporting activities, archery can be traced back as far as the Paleolithic age, some 280, 000 years ago. The use of the bow and arrow was very popular as both a sport and a hunting activity. Since the introduction of guns in the Song and Yuan dynasties in the 12th and 14th centuries, the significance of archery in military use weakened, while its use in competition and entertainment strengthened. Modern archery has recently developed using traditional archery techniques. Football, also called cuju in ancient Chinese literature, is believed to have originated in China before the Warring States Period (475 BC-221 BC). Drawings of football games have been found on stone and brick paintings and even on seals, indicating that there were many forms of football games, some similar to present day matches, other resembling dances. Games on horseback, or polo, are a combination of horsemanship and ball games. They can be dated back to the Three Kingdoms Period (AD 220-AD 280). The golden time of polo occurred during the Tang Dynasty (618-907). Athletics can be considered one of the main components of modern sports, and was one of the oldest and most popular sporting activities in ancient China. During the Song (960-1279) and Yuan (1279-1368) dynasties, running became one of the major military training activities. Running competitions were held each in the Yuan Dynasty (1279-1368). Wrestling, called jiaoli or xiangpu in ancient Chinese, also had its roots in early Chinese history. In the Tang Dynasty (618-907), the Xiangpu House was set up at the imperial palace in order to train wrestlers for competitions. Water and ice sports, including swimming, diving, boat racing and skating, were very popular in ancient China. Many Ming (1368-1644) and Qing (1644-1911) dynasties paintings featuring skaters can be found indicating that ice sports were also part of traditional Chinese physical activities.

Great Victory Ends Years of Dreaming

多年的梦想终于迎来了伟大的胜利

As Juan Antonio Samaranch, president of the International Olympic committee (IOC), announced Beijing as the host for the 2008 Summer Olympic Games in the World Trade Centre in Moscow, wild cheers and hearty applause ever Olympic Games for the world's most populous nation. Beijing won in a landslide victory in the second round ballot with 56 votes from 105 voting IOC members, ahead of Toronto with a distant 22, Paris 18 and Istanbul 9. Osaka, which received six votes, was eliminated in the first round. It was a rather quick victory compared with the last two votes in 1993 and 1997 when the winner only came out in the last round.

President Jiang Zemin, Premier Zhu Rongji, Chairman of the Standing Committee of the National People's Congress Li Peng and other Chinese leaders also joined the joyful crowd in Tian'anmen Square and the Chinese Millennium Monument, sharing with them the joy of victory.

President Jiang Zemin sent a letter to IOC President Samaranch on the early morning of July 14 to show respect for his contribution to the Olympic movement and extend thanks to the IOC members. President Jiang Zemin said that the Chinese Government and people will go all out to support Beijing and make the 2008 Olympic Games an event that "carries forward Olympic spirit, promotes world peace and promote friendship among peoples all over the world."

More than 180 billion yuan (US$21. 7 billion) will be poured into utilities projects, including the improvement of the public transport network, urban landscaping and the removal of shabby neighborhoods, while over 46 billion yuan (US$5. 5 billion) will be designated for environmental cleanup and US$1. 6 billion on 22 Olympic venues after a landslide victory on July 13, 2001.

Beijing will further invest and build its fifth and sixth ring roads, following on the heels of the completion of the Fourth Ring Road in June 2001. Meanwhile, Beijing's expressway construction will experience a 200 per cent increase, from the existing 200 kilometres to 600 kilometres.

Forty-five billion yuan (US$5. 4 billion) will be invested to improve Beijing's environment, including the adjustment of energy structures, restructuring of its industrial layout, protection of urban water and the improvement of garbage disposal. Other investment will involve the capital's information system and housing.

In the next 5 years, Beijing will also finish renovating more than 9 million square metres of old houses, and the per capita living floor space will rise to 18 square metres.

Cultural and historical sites in this ancient capital will also be better protected, with the injection of 1. 73 billion yuan (US$208 million) from a special fund.

Statistics from the Beijing 2008 Olympic Games Bid Committee indicate that the sports event could bring a budget income of US$1. 6 billion, with a surplus of at least US$ 16 million after deducting budget expenditures. Although it will not be a big sum of money, it indicates the readiness of Chinese to help others who need our help. Actually, China has helped build over 50 stadiums in dozens of foreign countries in Asia, Africa, and Latin America in the past 36 years while sending many Chinese coaches to improve local sports training. As a result, IOC President Juan Antonio

Samranch flew to Beijing and awarded the Chinese Government the Olympic Cup in April 1986. In this same spirit, the Olympic torch will travel through Tibet, along the Yangtze River, the Yellow River, the Great Wall, to Hong Kong, Macao and Taiwan before coming to Beijing. this route touches all 56 ethnic groups of the Chinese nation. Even before reaching China, the torch's path allows the most people ever to share the happiness, the vision of peace and glory of the Olympic Games.

The Olympic Games will create 2 million jobs in Beijing, particularly in areas of environmental protection, high-tech, infrastructure and management.

The endeavour could add 10 billion yuan (US$1.2 billion) to Beijing's gross domestic product per year and impact the economy for at least 12 years.

Just as the Olympic Games will foster global interest in the charm of the Chinese ancient capital of Beijing, visitors and athletes from around the world also will have the opportunity to experience the splendour of five other Chinese cities chosen as sub-venues for the 2008 Olympic Games. The 2008 Olympic Games will take place in 37 competition venues, with another 58 venues provided for training.

Qingdao in East China would feature a sailing centre, and soccer matches would be played in East China's Shanghai, North China's Tianjin and Qinhuangdao and Northeast China's Shenyang. The choice of these venue sites, design and construction of the venues will best present the concept of a "Green Olympics," "High-tech Olympics" and "People's Olympics." With facilities already under construction, the five cities, each with unique scenic attractions, are ready to provide enjoyable and safe accommodations for Olympic guests in 2008.

International Marina 国际小船停泊港

Known as a "pearl on the Yellow Sea," Qingdao is surrounded on three sides by water, with Laoshan Mountain as a backdrop. Qingdao's red-tiled roofs and verdant foliage complement its picturesque setting. Its fine beaches, pleasant climate and popular beer brewery make it wildly appealing to tourists. Qingdao, which has the finest aquatic sports centre in Asia, is well known for water competitions. Thus it is no surprise that the International Sail-boating Association judged that Qingdao is capable of becoming the site of the sailing contest for hosting the 2008 Olympics.

Oriental Pearl 东方明珠

The great metropolis of Shanghai is ready to host key soccer matches in 2008 at its magnificent 80,000-seat Shanghai Stadium. Shanghai, one of the world's most popular cities, boasts an intriguing, unique blend of Chinese and Western influences. As one of the favourable Chinese cities for foreign tourists, the city on the Huangpu River is modern, sophisticated and lively.

Communications Hub 交通枢纽

Soccer is simply a tradition in Tianjin. The city has raised many distinguished players for the national team. An easy one-hour train trip from Beijing; Tianjin is bounded on the east by Bohai Sea, and the Yanshan Mountain on the north and the Hebei Plains on the south and west. This commercial hub is already hard at work preparing for the 2008 Games. In March 2002 Tianjin began construction on a new sports stadium that will cost 800 million yuan (US$96 million). The stadium is to be completed by the end of 2003. The Tianjin Crystal Palace Hotel, a five-minute ride from the stadium, will host the world's soccer athletes.

Beach Resort 海滩避暑胜地

With 126 kilometres of coastline, the famed tourist city of Qinhuangdao on the Bohai Bay will offer soccer players exquisite scenery and a breath of fresh seas air. The city started in July 2001 to build its largest sport venue, the Qinhuangdao Stadium. It will cost 300 million yuan (US$36 million) and will be built in 2002. The International Seaside Resort, just 3.5 kilometres from the stadium, will house the athletes and the media.

Hometown of Soccer 足球之乡

Soccer fans from Shenyang, a famed "hometown of football" in China, are overjoyed by the prospect of the city becoming an Olympic venue. Shenyang, the largest industrial city in Northeast China, stands at the junction of key north-south and east-west rail routes, making it a major communications and transportation centre for the region. The 42,000-square-metre Wulihe Sports Stadium will be a soccer site for 2008.

APPENDIX

第八部分 附 录

The Administrative Regions in China
中国行政区域划分

Province 省 (23)	Provincial Capital (省会)	Area Code 区号
1. Anhui 安徽	Hefei 合肥	(0551)
2. Fujian 福建	Fuzhou 福州	(0591)
3. Gansu 甘肃	Lanzhou 兰州	(0931)
4. Guangdong 广东	Guangzhou 广州	(020)
5. Guizhou 贵州	Guiyang 贵阳	(0851)
6. Hainan 海南	Haikou 海口	(0750)
7. Hebei 河北	Shijiazhuang 石家庄	(0331)
8. Heilongjiang 黑龙江	Harbin 哈尔滨	(0451)
9. Henan 河南	Zhengzhou 郑州	(0371)
10. Hubei 湖北	Wuhan 武汉	(027)
11. Hunan 湖南	Changsha 长沙	(0731)
12. Jilin 吉林	Changchun 长春	(0431)
13. Jiangsu 江苏	Nanjing 南京	(025)
14. Jiangxi 江西	Nanchang 南昌	(0791)
15. Liaoning 辽宁	Shenyang 沈阳	(024)
16. Qinghai 青海	Xining 西宁	(0971)
17. Shaanxi 陕西	Xi'an 西安	(029)
18. Shandong 山东	Jinan 济南	(0531)
19. Shanxi 山西	Taiyuan 太原	(0351)
20. Sichuan 四川	Chengdu 成都	(028)
21. Taiwan 台湾	Taibei 台北	(00886 – 02)
22. Yunnan 云南	Kunming 昆明	(0871)
23. Zhejiang 浙江	Hangzhou 杭州	(0571)

Autonomous Region 自治区（5）

24. Guangxi Zhuang 广西壮族　　Nanning 南宁　　　　（0771）

25. Inner Mongolia 内蒙古　　　Hohhot 呼和浩特　　（0471）

26. Ningxia Hui 宁夏回族　　　Yinchuan 银川　　　　（0951）

27. Xinjiang Uygur 新疆维吾尔　Urumqi 乌鲁木齐　　（0991）

28. Xizang（Tibet）西藏　　　　Lhasa 拉萨　　　　　（0891）

Municipality 直辖市（4）

29. Beijing 北京　　　　　　　　　　　　　　　（010）

30. Chongqing 重庆　　　　　　　　　　　　　（023）

31. Shanghai 上海　　　　　　　　　　　　　（021）

32. Tianjin 天津　　　　　　　　　　　　　（022）

Special Administrative Region 特别行政区（2）

33. Hong Kong 香港（established on July 1, 1997）　　（00852）

34. Macao 澳门（established on December 20, 1999）　　（00853）

Tour Guides Basics in China
导游人员的基本素质

1. Smile. You are on a tour!
2. Never say "no" to a tourist.
3. Comply with tourist reasonable requests immediately.
4. Take personal responsibility to get the answers to tourist's questions.
5. Greet tourists with a warm welcome and wish our departing tourists a warm good-bye and invite them back.
6. Use the tourist's name wherever possible.
7. Wear an immaculate uniform at all times, including your nametag.
8. Escort tourists rather than point out directions to another area of a place.
9. Be knowledgeable of China to answer tourist's inquires.
10. Use proper telephone etiquette.
11. Know your role in an emergency situation.
12. Notify your superior immediately of assistance you may have.
13. Develop (make) a buddy system during a tour.

The Chinese Chronology
中国历史年代表

Name of Dynasty 朝代	Period 年代	Seat of Capital 都城
Xia Dynasty 夏	2070 BC – 1600 BC	Yangcheng (E. Dengfeng, Henan) 阳城 (河南登封东)
Shang Dynasty 商	1600 BC – 1046 BC	Bo (S.Caoxian, Shandong) 亳 (曹县南)
Zhou Dynasty 周	1046 BC – 256 BC	
Western Zhou 西周	1046 BC – 771 BC	Gaojing (W. Xi'an) 镐京 (陕西西安西)
Eastern Zhou 东周	770 BC – 256 BC	Luoyi (Luoyang, Henan) 洛邑 (洛阳) (夏,商,西、东周是最早建都的地方)
Spring & Autumn Per. 春秋	770 BC – 476 BC	
Warring States 战国(1)	475 BC – 221 BC	
Qin Dynasty 秦	221 BC – 206 BC	Xianyang (Shaanxi) 咸阳 (陕西)
Han Dynasty 汉		
Western Han 西汉(2)	206 BC – AD 23	Chang'an (Xi'an, Shaanxi) 长安 (西安)
Eastern Han 东汉	AD 25 – AD 220	Luoyang (Henan) 洛阳 (河南)
Three Kingdoms 三国		
Wei 魏	AD 220 – AD 265	Luoyang (Henan) 洛阳 (河南)
Shu Han 蜀汉	AD 221 – AD 263	Chengdu (Sichuan) 成都 (四川)
Wu 吴	AD 222 – AD 280	Jianye (Nanjing, Jiangsu) 建业 (今江苏南京)
Western Jin 西晋	AD 265 – AD 316	Luoyang (Henan) 洛阳 (河南)
Eastern Jin 东晋(十六国)		
Eastern Jin 东晋	AD 317 – AD 420	Jiankang (Nanjing) 建康 (南京)
东晋(十六国)(3)	AD 304 – AD 439	
Northern & Southern Dynasties 南北朝	AD 420 – AD 581	
Southern Dynasties 南朝		
Song 宋	AD 420 – AD 479	Jiankang (Nanjing) 建康 (南京)
Qi 齐	AD 479 – AD 502	Jiankang (Nanjing) 建康 (南京)
Liang 梁	AD 502 – AD 557	Jiankang (Nanjing) 建康 (南京)
Chen 陈	AD 557 – AD 589	Jiankang (Nanjing) 建康 (南京)
Northern Dynasties 北朝		
Northern Wei 北魏	AD 386 – AD 534	Pingcheng (Datong, Shanxi) 平城 (山西大同)
Eastern Wei 东魏	AD 534 – AD 550	Ye (Southwest Linzhang, Hebei) 邺 (河北临漳西南)

651

Name of Dynasty 朝代	Period 年代	Seat of Capital 都城
Northern Qi 北齐	AD 550 – AD 577	Ye（Southwest Linzhang，Hebei）邺（今河北临漳西南）
Western Wei 西魏	AD 535 – AD 557	Chang'an（Xi'an）长安(今西安)
Northern Zhou 北周	AD 557 – AD 581	Chang'an（Xi'an）长安(今西安)
Sui Dynasty 隋	AD 581 – AD 618	Daxing（Xi'an）大兴(今西安)
Tang Dynasty 唐	AD 618 – AD 907	Chang'an（Xi'an）长安(今西安)
Five Dynasties & Ten Kingdoms 五代十国		
Five Dynasties 五代	AD 907 – AD 960	
Later Liang 后梁	AD 907 – AD 923	Bian（Kaifeng）汴(今河南开封)
Later Tang 后唐	AD 923 – AD 936	Luoyang，Henan 河南洛阳
Later Jin 后晋	AD 936 – AD 946	Bian（Kaifeng）汴(今河南开封)
Later Han 后汉	AD 947 – AD 950	Bian（Kaifeng）汴(今河南开封)
Later Zhou 后周	AD 951 – AD 960	Bian（Kaifeng）汴(今河南开封)
Ten Kingdoms 十国	AD 902 – AD 979	
Wu 吴	AD 902 – AD 937	Yangzhou，Jiangsu 江苏扬州
Southern Tang 南唐	AD 937 – AD 975	Jinling（Nanjing）金陵(江苏南京)
Wu Yue 吴越	AD 907 – AD 978	Hangzhou，Zhejiang 浙江杭州
Chu 楚	AD 907 – AD 951	Changsha，Hunan 湖南长沙
Min 闽	AD 909 – AD 945	Changle（Fuzhou，Fujian）长乐(今福建福州)
Southern Han 南汉	AD 917 – AD 971	Guangzhou，Guangdong 广东广州
Former Shu 前蜀	AD 903 – AD 925	Chengdu，Sichuan 四川成都
Later Shu 后蜀	AD 933 – AD 965	Chengdu，Sichuan 四川成都
Jingnan（Nanping）荆南	AD 924 – AD 963	Jingzhou，Hubei 荆州(今湖北)
Northern Han 北汉	AD 951 – AD 979	Taiyuan（Shanxi）太原(山西)
Song Dynasty 宋	960 – 1279	
Northern Song 北宋	960 – 1127	Kaifeng（Henan）开封(河南)
Southern Song 南宋	1127 – 1279	Lin'an（Hangzhou）临安(今杭州)
Liao Dynasty 辽（契丹）	907 – 1125	Huangdu（Bairin Zuoqi，Inner Mongolia 皇都(今内蒙巴林左旗)
Western Xia 西夏	1038 – 1227	Xingqingfu，（Yinchuan，Ningxia）兴庆府(今宁夏银川)
Jin Dynasty 金	1115 – 1234	Zhongdu(today's Beijing)中都(今北京)
Yuan Dynasty 元	1279 – 1368	Dadu（Beijing）大都(今北京)
Ming Dynasty 明	1368 – 1644	Yingtianfu 应天府（Nanjing）、Beijing
Qing Dynasty 清	1644 – 1911	Beijing 北京
Republic of China 中华民国(4)	1912 – 1949	Nanjing 南京
People's Republic of China 中华人民共和国	Founded in 1949	Beijing 北京

Ming Dynasty（1368-1644）明朝

Dynastic Title（Dihao）	Name	Reign Title（Nianhao）	Period
Taizu 太祖	Zhu Yuanzhang 朱元璋	Hongwu 洪武	1368-1398
Huidi 惠帝	Zhu Yunwen 朱允炆	Jianwen 建文	1399-1402
Chengzu 成祖	Zhu Di 朱棣	Yongle 永乐	1403-1424
Renzong 仁宗	Zhu Gaochi 朱高炽	Hongxi 洪熙	1425
Xuanzong 宣宗	Zhu Zhanji 朱瞻基	Xuande 宣德	1426-1435
Yingzong 英宗	Zhu Qizhen 朱祁镇	Zhengtong 正统	1436-1449
Daizong 代宗	Zhu Qiyu 朱祁钰	Jingtai 景泰	1450-1456
Yingzong 英宗（resumed government）	Zhu Qizhen 朱祁镇	Tianshun 天顺	1457-1464
Xianzong 宪宗	Zhu Jianshen 朱见深	Chenghua 成化	1465-1487
Xiaozong 孝宗	Zhu Youtang 朱祐樘	Hongzhi 弘治	1488-1505
Wuzong 武宗	Zhu Houzhao 朱厚照	Zhengde 正德	1506-1521
Shizong 世宗	Zhu Houcong 朱厚熜	Jiajing 嘉靖	1522-1566
Muzong 穆宗	Zhu Zaihou 朱载垕	Longqing 隆庆	1567-1572
Shenzong 神宗	Zhu Yijun 朱翊钧	Wanli 万历	1573-1620
Guangzong 光宗	Zhu Changluo 朱常洛	Taichang 泰昌	1620（29 days）
Xizong 熹宗	Zhu Youxiao 朱由校	Tianqi 天启	1621-1627
Sizong 思宗	Zhu Youjian 朱由检	Chongzhen 崇祯	1628-1644

Qing Dynasty（1644-1911）清朝

Dynastic Title（Dihao）	Name	Reign Title（Nianhao）	Period
Taizu 太祖	Aisin-Gioro Nurhachi 爱新觉罗努尔哈赤	Tianming 天命	1616-1626
Taizong 太宗	Aisin-Gioro Huang Taiji 皇太极	Tiancong 天聪	1627-1635
		Chongde 崇德	1636-1643
Shizu 世祖	Aisin-Gioro Fulin 福临	Shunzhi 顺治	1644-1661
Shengzu 圣祖	Aisin-Gioro Xuanye 玄烨	Kangxi 康熙	1662-1722
Shizong 世宗	Aisin-Gioro Yinzhen 胤祯	Yongzheng 雍正	1723-1735
Gaozong 高宗	Aisin-Gioro Hongli 弘历	Qianlong 乾隆	1736-1795
Renzong 仁宗	Aisin-Gioro Yongyan 渥琰	Jiaqing 嘉庆	1796-1820
Xuanzong 宣宗	Aisin-Gioro Minning 旻宁	Daoguang 道光	1821-1850
Wenzong 文宗	Aisin-Gioro Yizhu 奕𬣞	Xianfeng 咸丰	1850-1861
Muzong 穆宗	Aisin-Gioro Zaichun 载淳	Tongzhi 同治	1862-1874
Dezong 德宗	Aisin-Gioro Zaitian 载𣉢	Guangxu 光绪	1875-1908
(no dynastic title)	Aisin-Gioro Puyi 溥仪	Xuantong 宣统	1909-1911

Note: (1) During this period, seven powerful states co-existed such as Wei 魏, Zhao 赵, Han 韩, Qi 齐, Qin 秦, Chu 楚 and Yan 燕.

(2) Including Wang Mang who established Xin Mang Dynasty（AD

8-AD 23). During this period, large-scale peasant uprising broke out and peasant regime was set up. In AD 23 Xin Mang Dynasty was wiped out. In AD 25 Eastern Han Dynasty was established. 包括王莽建立的"新"王朝(公元 8 年 -23 年)。王莽时期,爆发大规模的农民起义,建立了农民政权。公元 23 年,新莽王朝灭亡。公元 25 年,东汉王朝建立。

(3) During this period of Eastern Jin Dynasty (AD 317-AD 420) in northern China, there co-existed successively 16 kingdoms (AD 304-AD 439) as follows: 这时期,在我国北方,先后存在过一些政权,其中有:

Name of Dynasty	Period	Seat of Capital
Han (Former Zhao) 汉(前赵)	(AD 304 – AD 329)	Pinyang (NW Linfen, Shanxi) 平阳(山西临汾西北) Chang'an (now Xi'an) (迁)长安(今西安)
Chang (Cheng Han) 成(成汉)	(AD 304 – AD 347)	Chengdu (Sichuan) 成都(四川)
Former Liang 前凉	(AD 317 – AD 376)	Guzang (Wuwei, Gansu) 姑臧(甘肃武威)
Later Zhao (Wei) 后赵(魏)	(AD 319 – AD 351)	Xiangguo (Xingtai, Hebei) 襄国(河北邢台) Ye (SW Linzhang, Hebei) (迁)邺(河北临漳西南)
Former Yan 前燕	(AD 337 – AD 370)	Longcheng (Chaoyang, Liaoning) 龙城(辽宁朝阳) Ji (SW Beijing) (迁)蓟(今北京西南)
Former Qin 前秦	(AD 350 – AD 394)	Chang'an (now Xi'an) 长安(今西安)
Later Qin 后秦	(AD 384 – AD 417)	Chang'an (now Xi'an) 长安(今西安)
Later Yan 后燕	(AD 384 – AD 407)	Zhongshan (Dingzhou, Hebei) 中山(河北定州)
(Western Yan * 西燕)	(AD 384 – AD 394)	Chang'an (now Xi'an) (初)长安(今西安) Changzi (Shanxi) (迁)长子(山西)
Western Qin 西秦	(AD 385 – AD 431)	Yuanchuan (Gansu) 苑川(甘肃)
Later Liang 后凉	(AD 386 – AD 403)	Guzang (Wuwei, Gansu) 姑臧(甘肃武威)
Southern Liang 南凉	(AD 397 – AD 414)	Xiping (Xining, Qinghai) 西平(青海西宁) Ledu (Qinghai) (迁)乐都(青海)
Southern Yan 南燕	(AD 398 – AD 410)	Guanggu (Shandong) 广固(山东)
Western Liang 西凉	(AD 400 – AD 421)	Dunhuang (Gansu) 敦煌(甘肃) Jiuquan (Gansu) (迁)酒泉(甘肃)
Xia 夏	(AD 407 – AD 431)	Tongwan (Shaanxi) 统万(陕西)

Name of Dynasty	Period	Seat of Capital
Northern Yan 北燕	(AD 407 – AD 436)	Longcheng (Hebei) 龙城(河北)
Northern Liang 北凉	(AD 401 – AD 439)	Zhangye (Gansu) 张掖(甘肃)
(Dai * 代)	(AD 315 – AD 376)	Pingcheng (Inner Mongolia) 平城 (内蒙古)

* Western Yan and Dai were not included in the 16 kingdoms, hence the 16 king doms in the Chinese history. 历史上称十六国。

(4) 1912-1949
1912-1916 Yuan Shikai 袁世凯 (1859-1916)
1916-1917 李元洪 (1864-1928)
1917-1918 冯国璋 (1857-1919)
1918-1922 徐世昌 (1855-1939)
1922-1923 李元洪 (1864-1928)
1923-1924 曹锟 (1862-1938)
1924- 段琪瑞 (1865-1936)
1924-1927 第一次国内革命战争
1927-1949 蒋介石(1887-1975)

The First Civil Revolutionary War

After the death of Dr Sun Yat-sen in 1925, the Kuomintang gradually split up and the right wing, represented by Chiang Kai-shek, usurped the leadership of the party. But because of the political and organizational work done by the Communist Party, the tide of revolution continued to grow. After wiping out the counter-revolutionaries in Guangdong, the revolutionary forces began the Northern Expedition in 1926. Supported by the broad masses, the revolutionary army defeated the Northern Warlords and occupied central and south China. The worker-peasant movement grew rapidly throughout China. Seeing that the warlord government was tottering under the blows of the revolutionary forces, the imperialist powers started looking for a new agent. Finally, they chose Chiang Kai-shek who was then Commander-in-Chief of the National Revolutionary Army.

Ignoring the resolute opposition of the Kuomintang's left wing represented by Song Qingling (Madame Sun Yat-sen), the Kuomintang controlled by Chiang Kai-shek (1887-1975) and Wang Jingwei (1883-1944) betrayed the policy of Kuomintang-Communist Co-operation and the anti-imperialist and anti-feudal programme laid down by Dr Sun Yat-sen and turned its guns against the revolutionary people led by the Communist Party. In April 1927, Chiang Kai-shek staged a counter-revolutionary coup and carried out a massacre of communists and other revolutionaries just at a time when speedy victories were being won in the Northern Expedition.

Then he established his "national government" in Nanjing.

Researchers Have Made Breakthrough in Documenting Early Chinese History

In 1996, a State project was launched to determine the chronology of early Chinese history in the Xia (2070 BC-1600 BC), Shang (1600 BC – 1046 BC) and Zhou (1046 BC-256 BC) dynasties. The project aimed to draw a clear, and coherent picture of China's strenuous beginnings. On November 10, 2000, the initial research results after nearly five years' strenuous work made public.

Chinese ancestors who lived 3,000 years ago left a huge puzzle for their descendants to work out before leaving this world. The puzzle is made up of scrambled clues from scattered writings and oral legends but there are some missing pieces as well. For five years, more than 200 Chinese historians, archaeologists, astronomers, physicists and other scholars have put their heads together to sort the puzzle out and develop a chronology of early Chinese history. The project, which has won a special research grant from the Ministry of Science and State Administration of Cultural Relics, is known as the Chronology of Early Chinese History in the Xia, Shang and Western Zhou dynasties. After five years' work, the researchers announced on November 9, 2000 in Beijing that they had achieved initial research results, discovered many missing pieces and sorting out some of the puzzle. According to Li Xueqin, the chief historian leading the project, the scholars have been able to ascertain that the earliest Chinese dynasty, the Xia, existed for about 470 years between 2070 BC and 1600 BC. The Shang Dynasty, which followed the Xia, is now divided into the earlier (1600 BC-1300 BC) and the later periods (1300 BC-1046 BC), according to researchers. The years of the reigns of the 12 monarchs of the later Shang Dynasty and all the 13 monarchs of the Western Zhou Dynasty (1046 BC-771 BC) have been ascertained. Above all, researchers have been able to pinpoint the years when King Wu waged a decisive battle against the last king of the Shang Dynasty and put himself on the throne in what became the Western Zhou Dynasty. The year 1046 BC was the year when ancient Egypt, in the Tanite 21st Dynasty (1085 BC-945 BC), was losing control of its Asiatic empire; when successive kings of the 2nd Dynasty of Isin (c. 1156 BC-1025 BC) in Babylonia were trying to stem the disintegration of their empire; and when India was about to enter the later Vedic period (c. 1000 BC-500 BC) to witness ever more cultural prosperity.

The initial research results indicated that the earliest ascertained period in Chinese history goes back more than 1,200 years than previously thought. But it has been a daunting and hard task to solve the puzzle and

656

see the overall historical picture. Sima Qian (135 BC-87 BC), a great historian who lived in the Western Han Dynasty (206-BC-AD 23), delved into historical record, visited areas where great events documents in earlier annals were said to have taken place and talked with people who were elderly and learned. But he still found it difficult to sort out the puzzle before the year 841 BC, when the 10th king of the Western Zhou Dynasty was forced to give up his rule to two respected royal dukes after widespread uprisings in the country. A systematic and scientific approach to sorting out the historical puzzle was designed. After examining the existing clues and broken pieces, they divided the work into nine research branches and 44 topics. Individual research accomplishments in the fields of history, archaeology, astronomy, mathematics and physics since early on in the 20th century provided a solid foundation for the project. In five years, archaeologists conducted or expanded scientific excavations at some 15 sites in Henan, Hebei, Shanxi and Shaanxi provinces and Beijing as well. The researchers have harvested many relics that relate to monarchs in the Shang and Western Zhou dynasties. Although only a few pictographs have been found inscribed on bronze ware from tombs of the Xia Dynasty, more than enough ruins and relics now prove the existence of the Xia Dynasty. The historians have also studied the dates engraved on 60 bronze containers, which were once used in the Western Zhou Dynasty. The dates became important clues for ascertaining the chronology of the kings in the periods. Meanwhile, philologists have searched nearly 400 ancient Chinese annals and collected written records, and gathered "clues" recording astronomical events and indicating the locations of earlier dynastic capitals. During their research, astronomers looked at celestial phenomena that happened thousands of years ago, especially the solar and lunar eclipses Chinese ancestors recorded piously in ancient classics that were often associated with important political events such as ascension of a king or the demise or defeat of another king. By correlating the astronomical data with the modern calendar, they helped create a rough time framework for kings in the later period of the Xia and Shang dynasties. Physicists from Beijing University and the Institute of Archaeology of the Chinese Academy of Social Sciences also joined the project. They collected samples from human bones and tiny parts from animal bones bearing the earliest Chinese characters, the *jiaguwen* (oracles bones), all unearthed from tombs proven to belong to the Shang and Western Zhou dynasties. They then conducted scientific carbon dating via radiocarbon dating equipment and an accelerator for the time frame of the historical periods. For each of the years, the researchers first determined that results from historical records, archaeological evidence, astronomical calculations and carbon dating techniques tallied and correlated before putting the ascertained piece into the chronological puzzle.

The new chronology of early Chinese history is by no means the first in Chinese history. Liu Xin 刘歆 (? -AD 23), a historian, founder of the school studying classical Chinese writings and an astronomer, wrote the first chronology of Chinese history in the later years of the Western Han Dynasty (206 BC-AD 23). Despite the achievements, the researchers involved in the project agreed that the bigger puzzle about the political, social and economic development of the early Chinese dynasties is far from complete.

Units of Weights and Measures
度量衡单位一览

1 *chi* = 1/3 metre = 1.0936 feet
1 *li* = 1/2 kilometre = 0.3107 mile
1 *mu* = 1/15 hectare = 0.1644 acre
1 tael = 50 grams = 1.7637 ounces
1 *jin* = 1/2 kilogram = 1.1023 pounds
1 *dan* = 50 kilograms
1 *sheng* = 1 litre = 0.22 British gallon
1 *dou* = 10 litres = 2.2 British gallons
1 metre = 3 *chi* = 3.2808 feet
1 kilometre = 2 *li* = 0.6214 mile
1 sq. km. = 4 sq. *li* = 100 hectares = 0.3861 square mile
1 sq. metre = 9 sq. *chi* = 10.7636 sq. feet
1 hectare = 15 *mu* = 2.4711 acres
1 kilogram = 2 *jin* = 2.2046 pounds
1 metric ton = 2,000 *jin* = 0.9842 British ton
1 cubic metre = 27 cubic *chi* = 35.3147 cubic feet
1 pound = 16 ounces = 453.6 grams
1 *mu* = 666.7 square metres
1 yard = 0.9144 metre

Renminbi—Chinese Currency
人民币—中国货币

Chinese currency is called Renminbi (R. M. B.), and is issued by the People's Bank of China. The basic unit of Renminbi is the **yuan** and the subsidiary units are the jiao and fen. A **yuan** is divided into 10 **jiao** and a **jiao** is equal to 10 **fen**. **Yuan** and **jiao** are issued notes and fen in coins. **Yuan** notes are in denominations of 1, 2, 5, 10, 50, and 100: while **jiao** notes are in denominations of 1, 2, and 5.

The State Council announced that China issued new notes for its Renminbi **yuan** currency beginning on April 27, 1987, including for the first time denominations greater than 10 **yuan**.

The new notes are in nine denominations of one **jiao**, two **jiao**, five **jiao**, one **yuan**, two yuan, five **yuan**, 10 **yuan**, 50 **yuan**, and 100 **yuan**.

Ten **fen** equals one **jiao** (also known as **mao**). Ten **jiao** equals one **yuan**. At present, Renminbi notes also exist in one **fen**, two **fen** and five **fen** denominations. The lager bills are printed in Braille to assist the blind. Decided in 1980, the designs for the new **yuan** notes are as follows:

● The front of the one-**yuan** note features portraits of representatives of the Yao and Dong ethnic minority groups, and the back design is of the Great Wall of China.

● The front of the two-**yuan** note features portraits of representatives of the Uygur and Yi ethnic minority groups, and the back design is a scenic spot in South China.

● The front of the five-**yuan** note features portraits of representatives of the Tibetan and Hui ethnic minority groups. The back shows the Wu Gorge on the Yangtze River.

● The front of the 10-**yuan** note features portraits of a farmer and representatives of the Han and Mongolian peoples. The design on the back shows Mount Qomolangma (Mt. Everest).

● The front of the 50-**yuan** note features portraits of a worker, a farmer and an intellectual. The back shows a scene in Hukou, a scenic spot on the Yellow River.

● The black and blue 100-**yuan** note features on the front side, portraits of the late Chinese leaders Mao Zedong, Zhou Enlai, Liu Shaoqi, and Zhu De, and the back side is an image of a peak in the Jinggang Mountains, a former revolutionary base in Jiangxi Province. The note also bears a watermark of the late Chairman Mao's portrait.

China is for the first time issuing its Renminbi **yuan** currency in 50- and 100-**yuan** notes.

Both the old and the new Renminbi are recognized as legal tender having the same value. This is not a drastic financial reform, but a move designed to meet the needs of a growing market-oriented economy.

Economic reforms began in 1979 have brought dramatic changes to the

659

economy and to the people's everyday life. A much greater volume of goods and services are involved under the emerging planned socialist market economy. There is much more traveling by sales-people, by purchasing agents of State-owned and collective enterprises and by individual entrepreneurs in towns and country. Consumer durable are entering Chinese homes at a rapid rate. All this has led to public awareness of the inconvenience and risk of having to carry big bundles of cash in small denominations for business transactions. Economists and laymen have been urging in the press that instruments of credit such as personal checks, installment buying, letters of credit and even credit cards should be introduced more widely to meet the needs of expanding socialist market economy.

The introduction of credit, while undoubtedly facilitating business, could result in unhealthy expansion of the volume of money in circulation. The government and China's financial institutions recognize the need to develop the expertise and acquire the experience to handle such a sophisticated financial setup. Moreover, the ordinary consumer needs to learn how to use credit wisely and avoid it pitfalls.

The move is part of the effort to further improve China's monetary system and make money circulation and accounting easier to suit the nation's economic development.

The Issue of Renminbi "No 5"

The People's Bank of China (PBOC) began to issue the fifth version of renmibi banknotes on October 1, 1999. The new series includes eight categories, 100 **yuan**, 50 **yuan**, 20 **yuan**, 10 **yuan**, 5 **yuan**, 1 **yuan**, 5 **jiao** and 1 **jiao** notes. The 100-**yuan** bill was launched on October 1, 1999 and others followed. China's political stability, sustained, fast and healthy economic development contributed to a ripe time for the issue of the new currency version. China's fourth version of renminbi bills, which began to be circulated on April 27, 1987, has its shortcomings and "is not invulnerable to counterfeiting" and is not meeting perfectly the needs of ATMs.

Being the first to have been designed and printed independently by the PBOC with international advanced note-making technology, the new version has much higher anti-counterfeiting features.

Pictures, watermarks and numbers on the new version are larger than the previous ones and more easily recognizable to users.

The Issue of 20-Yuan Note

The People's Bank of China began to issue the second group of the fifth version of renminbi on October 16, 2000. The new version includes paper currency with face value of 20 **yuan** (US$2. 40 and two coins with face value of 1 **yuan** (U$0. 12) and 1 jiao (US$0. 012) respectively. The obverse side of the brown 145-millimetre-long and 70-millimetre-wide 20-**yuan** paper note has the portrait of the late Chairman Zedong, with the words "People's Bank of China" in Chinese, as well as a flower-and-plant design. The diameter of the white 1 **yuan** and 1 jiao coins is 25 millimetres and 19 millimetres respectively. The observe sides of the coins have the words "People's Bank of China" in Chinese, 1 **yuan** and 1 **jiao** in both Chinese and Chinese phonetic lettres, as well as the year they are issued.

Silver Coins Commemorate Festival

The People's Republic of China issued silver 10-**yuan** coins on September 5, 2001 to commemorate the Mid-Autumn Festival. The coin, which is legal Chinese currency, features the legendary Moon Palace, the name of the People's Republic of China and the title of the year on the front side. The back shows blooming flowers and a full moon along with the denomination. The silver coin contains 1 ounce of pure silver. It is round with a diameter of 40 millimetres and is worth about US$1. 20.

Twelve Animal Years
十 二 生 肖

In addition to a 12-month yearly cycle, the Chinese have a 12-year cycle, designated by animal signs.

Year of the Rabbit	1903	/15	/27	/39	/51	/63	/75	/87	/99	/2011
Year of the Dragon	1904	/16	/28	/40	/52	/64	/76	/88	/2000	/2012
Year of the Snake	1905	/17	/29	/41	/53	/65	/77	/89	/2001	/2013
Year of the Horse	1906	/18	/30	/42	/54	/66	/78	/90	/2002	/2014
Year of the Goat	1907	/19	/31	/43	/55	/67	/79	/91	/2003	/2015
Year of the Monkey	1908	/20	/32	/44	/56	/68	/80	/92	/2004	/2016
Year of the Rooster	1909	/21	/33	/45	/57	/69	/81	/93	/2005	/2017
Year of the Dog	1910	/22	/34	/46	/58	/70	/82	/94	/2006	/2018
Year of the Pig	1911	/23	/35	/47	/59	/71	/83	/95	/2007	/2019
Year of the Rat	1912	/24	/36	/48	/60	/72	/84	/96	/2008	/2020
Year of the Ox	1913	/25	/37	/49	/61	/73	/85	/97	/2009	/2021
Year of the Tiger	1914	/26	/38	/50	/62	/74	/86	/98	/2010	/2022

Eight Democratic Parties in China
中国八大民主党派

Revolutionary Committee of the Kuomintang

The patriotic and democratic members of the former Kuomintang founded two organizations—the Sanminzhuyi (the Three People's Principles) Comrades' Federation and the Kuomintang Association for Promoting Democracy—in 1945 and 1946 respectively. On January 1, 1948 the organizations joined together to form the Revolutionary Committee of the Kuomintang. The majority of its members are former Kuomintang members and those who have historical connections with the Kuomintang in the cultural, educational, health and financial fields.

China Democratic League

In September 1944, the China Democratic League grew out of the China League of Democratic Political Organizations, which had been set up in 1941. Its members are mostly intellectuals working in the fields of culture, education and science.

China Democratic National Construction Association

Founded in December 1945, its members are mainly former industrialists and businessmen and intellectuals connected with them.

China Association for Promoting Democracy

This Association was established in December 1945 and is composed mainly of teachers and staff of primary and middle schools and people working in the fields of culture and publications. The China Association for Promoting Democracy has now 65,000 members.

Chinese Peasants' and Workers' Democratic Party

Its predecessor was founded in August 1930. In February 1947, this committee changed its name into the Chinese Peasants' and Workers' Democratic Party. Most of its members work in the fields of public health and medicine.

China Zhi Gong Dang

It was formerly an organization formed by some members of the Hongmen

662

Zhi Gong Tang (Party for Public Interest) among compatriots in Hong Kong and overseas Chinese. In 1946, the China Zhi Gong Tang resumed its activities in Hong Kong and later moved its headquarters to Guangzhou. Most of its members are returned overseas Chinese and their relatives. The Zhi Gong Tang now has 15, 663 members and has set up 16 provincial-level organizations.

Jiu San Society

The Society grew out of the Democratic and Science Society — a political organization of people in the academic circles. To commemorate the victories of the War of Resistance Against Japan and the worldwide anti-fascist war, the society changed its name to the Jiu San Society on September 3, 1945. Its members are mostly noted scientists and technologists. Jiu San Society now has 68, 440 members and set up provincial-level Chongqing Municipal Committee and a group of municipal-level and grass-root organizations.

Taiwan Democratic Self-Government League

Founded in November 1947, its members are mainly natives of Taiwan Province who live on the mainland of China.

The term democratic parties refers to the eight other parties apart from the Communist Party, which take part in the Chinese People's Political Consultative Conference (CPPCC) as part of the patriotic untied front led by the Chinese Communist Party.

Formed and gradually developed before the founding of the People's Republic of China, the democratic parties originated mainly in the national bourgeoisie, urban upper petty bourgeoisie and also among intellectuals and other patriotic personages. In the struggle against imperialist aggression and for people's democracy, these parties have a long history of co-operation with the Chinese Communist Party. This was seen even back in their founding days when they took an active part in the country's democratic patriotic movement as the revolution progressed. In answering the Communist Party's call for convening a new People's Political Consultative Conference, they participated in the preparatory work of the conference from May 1948 to early 1949. It was at this meeting that the "Common Programme of the CPPCC" was adopted, the Central People's Government elected and the founding of the People's Republic of China proclaimed. In its relations with these democratic parties, the Communist Party of China follows the policy of "long-term co-existence and mutual supervision 长期共存,互相监督" and "showing utter devotion to each other and sharing honour and disgrace 肝胆相照,荣辱与共." It respects their political freedom and equality and organizational independence as granted by the Constitution. Since the founding of the People's Republic of China, the democratic parties have conscientiously taken part in consultation on important issues concerning the State, united and encouraged their members and people they associate with to actively take part in all fields of work and practice self-education and ideological remolding in combination with their professional studies and practice. Many representative figures from the democratic parties have been elected deputies to the people's congresses at all levels, in addition to many who hold responsible positions in the standing committees of the people's congresses and people's governments and economic, cultural, educational, scientific and technological departments. The democratic parties have also grown in membership, with local and primary organizations set up in most of the country's provinces, centrally administered municipalities, and autonomous regions and in many large and medium-sized cities.

With their number increasing to more than 30 million in 2000 from less than 50,000 before the founding of the People's Republic of China in 1949, intellectuals play a crucial part in the modernization and revitalization of China. The term "intellectuals" refers to all those who have had middle school or higher education and those with similar educational levels. They include university and middle school teachers and staff members, university and middle school students, primary school teachers, professionals, engineers and technicians, among whom the university and middle school students occupy an important position.

China's Housing Reform
中国的住房改革

A detailed housing reform plan for departments and institutions under the central government and the Central Party Committee was announced on August 26, 1999. And thus China put an end to its welfare housing distribution system in 1999. A commercialized housing distribution system has replaced the former system. Under the plan, departments and institutions under the central government and Central Party Committee are expected to cease welfare allocations of housing built since the end of 1998. In principle, all other cities drew up a similar plan before the end of September 1999.

China adopted a welfare distribution system long ago. State and work units built housing and distributed it to their employees as a kind of welfare. Employees paid a symbolic rent. The reform requires that all housing should be sold to employees at at-cost prices. In principle, new economy housing and older housing, except low-rent housing for low-income families, have been sold rather than rented to employees. Residential housing built by work units, of which construction began before the end of 1998, have been sold to employees at at-cost prices—about 1, 450 yuan (US$175) per square metres. The same applies to commercial housing bought by work units completed before the end of 1999. Employees whose housing was inadequate in relation to their ranks or lengths of service or who did not have housing was able to apply for subsidies when buying homes. The amount of subsidies were calculated principally in accordance with their basic salaries, ranks and lengths of service. Work units established special accounts for their employees. Employees could use the subsidies when they bought homes upon approval by their work units. Unfortunately, ordinary families in large cities could hardly afford a housing unit even with the help of housing subsidies, because the prices of commercial housing were too high. Take Beijing for instance, the average price for a 60-square-metre housing unit was about 360, 000 yuan (US$43, 373), while the average annual income of an ordinary family was less than 24, 000 yuan (US$2, 892). To create effective housing demand, China had to open a secondary housing market. Relatively low prices of secondary housing (usually 1, 000-2, 000 yuan or US$120-US$240 per square metre lower than the new housing at the same location) would not only help spur housing sales, but would also help balance housing prices. The Ministry of Construction released a regulation in May 1999, announcing that public housing bought by individuals, who had legal property rights, could be traded on the secondary housing market. But public housing in the following categories might not be sold:

1. Housing purchased at prices below levels set by the State during housing reform and where the owner has not made up the difference.
2. Housing of which the floor area and amenities exceed State norms, and the owners have not paid for the extras as required.
3. Housing that is to be relocated or torn down for construction.
4. Housing where property rights are owned by multiple proprietors, which can only be sold with the agreement of all owners.
5. Mortgaged housing, for which creditors have not given written permission for the sale.
6. Housing should not be sold if the sale means the former owners will face new financial difficulties.

In order to provide further guidance for the market, the Ministry of Construct announced another regulation in July 1999, clarifying housing property rights in transactions. State officials and employees own housing property rights "upon buying public housing at at-cost prices." They can then go to the secondary housing market if they want to sell their homes or exchange them for something more spacious. The regulations will go a long way towards creating an active housing market, stimulating housing purchase and eventually boosting growth in gross domestic product.

Information of Application for Residence Permit, Its Extension or Alteration by Aliens Working in Joint Ventures, Co-operative and Foreign Wholly-Owned Enterprises in China

三资企业外籍人员申请居留证

1. Aliens and their family members in joint ventures, co-operative and foreign wholly-owned enterprises in China should hold the Visa Z to enter China and apply to the Administration of the Beijing Municipal Public Security Bureau.
2. When applicants apply for residence permits, the following documents and certificates should be presented:
   a. The duplicate and the photocopy of the *Business License* issued by Bureau of Industry and Commerce Administration (the photo-copy will be handed in).
   b. *Employment Certificate* issued by the Department of Labour (Address: 5 Yongdingmennei Xidajie, Xuanwu District. Tel: 63018339.
   c. *Health Certificate* issued by Beijing Health and Quarantine Bureau (Address: 20 Hepingli Beijie. Tel: 64274239)
   d. Two recently-taken, bare-headed and full-faced photographs (two-inch size).
   e. *Aliens Residence Application Forms* filled out with the seals of the host enterprises.
3. When applicants apply for the extension of residence permits or alteration of working units, the following certificates should be presented:
   a. The duplicate of the *Business License* and the *Employment Certificate* issued by the Department of Labour for application for the extension of residence permit.
   b. Alien's Application Form for Visa or Certificate filled out with the seals of the host enterprise.

666

c. The former *Employment Certificate*, the document certifying the termination of his/her work issued by his/her previous unit, the duplicate and the photocopy of the new *Business License* as well as new *Employment Certificate*(the photocopy will be withdrawn) from the present working unit for application for alteration of working enterprises.

d. Alien's Application Form for Alteration of Visa or Certificate filled out with the seals of the host enterprise.

Information on Application for Residence Permit, Its Extension or Alteration by Foreign Experts in Cultural and Educational Sector, Teachers, Experts of Science and Technology, Professional Technical Personnel and Other Employees

外国文教专家、外籍教师、科技专家、专业技术人员及其他工作人员申请居留证、居留证延期或变更须知

1. Foreign Experts in Cultural and Education Sector, Teachers, Experts of Science and Technology, Professional Technical Personnel and Other Employees should hold the Visa Z to enter China and apply for, within thirty days of entry, residence permits at the Division of Aliens Administration of the Beijing Municipal Public Security Bureau.

2. When applicants apply for residence permits, the following documents should be presented:

    a. *Foreign Expert Certificate*(photocopy will be handed in), and *Alien's Application Form for Residence Permit* filled out with the seal of the institution.

    b. *Health Certificate* issued by Beijing Health and Quarantine Bureau (Address: 20 Hepingli Beijing. Tel: 64274239).

    c. Two recently-taken, full-faced and bare-headed photographs (two-inch size).

3. When applicants apply for extension of residence permit or alteration of working units, the following documents should be presented:

    a. Renewed *Foreign Expert Certificate for application for extension for* residence permit.

b. *Alien's Application Form for Renewal of Visa or Certificate* filled out with the seal of the host institution.

c. Documents certifying the termination of his/her work issued by his/her previous unit and the new *Foreign Expert Certificate* issued by his/her present working unit for alteration of working unit.

d. *Alien's Application Form for Alteration of Visa or Certificate* filled out with the seal of the host unit.

Information on Application for Residence Permit, Its Extension or Alteration by Aliens Working in the Representative Offices of Foreign Enterprises in China and Their Family Members

外国长驻代表机构中的外籍工作人员及家属办理居留证、居留证延期或变更须知

1. Aliens working in the representative offices of foreign enterprises in China and their family members should hold the Visa Z to enter China and apply for, within thirty days of entry, residence permit to the Division of Aliens Administration of the Beijing Municipal Public Security Bureau.

2. When applicants apply for residence permits, the following documents and certificates should be presented:

   a. *Working Card* of the permanent representative office of foreign enterprises in China issued by the Department for the Administration of Industry and Commerce as its photocopy (photocopy will be handed in).

   b. *Employment Certificate* issued by the Department of Labour and its photocopy (photocopy will be handed in). Tel: 63018339.

   c. *Health Certificate* issued by Beijing Health and Quarantine Bureau. Tel: 64278734.

   d. Two recently taken, bare headed and full-faced photographs (two inch size).

   e. *Alien's Application Form for Residence Permit* filled out with the seal of the host enterprise.

3. When applicants apply for extension of residence permits or alteration of working units, the following documents should be presented:

   a. *Working Card* and *Employment Certificate* for application for extension of residence permit, (photocopies will be handed in).

b. *Alien's Application Form for Renewal of Visa or Certificate* filled out with the seal of the host enterprise.

c. Documents certifying the termination of his / her work issued by his / her previous enterprise. *Working Card* and *Employment Certificate* issued by the present working unit for application for alteration of working units (photocopies will be handed in).

d. *Alien's Application Form for Alteration of Visa or Certificate* should be filled out with the seal of the host enterprise.

Time Difference Between Major Cities in the World
世界主要城市时差

(12 o'clock Noon, Greenwich Mean Time)

City	Local Time	City	Local Time
Beijing 北京	20.00	London 伦敦	12.00
San Francisco 旧金山	04.00	Conakry 科纳克里	12.00
Mexico City 墨西哥城	06.00	Accra 阿克拉	12.00
Guatemala City 危地马拉城	06.00	Bamako 巴马科	12.00
Havana 哈瓦那	07.00	Dakar 达喀尔	12.00
Panama City 巴拿马城	07.00	Algiers 阿尔及尔	12.00
Bogota 波哥大	07.00	Brazzaville 布拉柴维尔	13.00
Lima 利马	07.00	Tirana 地拉那	13.00
Washington 华盛顿	07.00	Stockholm 斯德哥尔摩	13.00
New York 纽约	07.00	Vienna 维也纳	13.00
Caracas 加拉加斯	07.30	Warsaw 华沙	13.00
Santiago 圣地亚哥	08.00	Rome 罗马	13.00
Buenos Aires 布宜诺斯艾利斯	09.00	Prague 布拉格	13.00
Montevideo 蒙得维的亚	09.00	Paris 巴黎	13.00
Reykjavik 雷克雅未克	11.00	Geneva 日内瓦	13.00
Budapest 布达佩斯	13.00	New Delhi 新德里	17.30
Belgrade 贝尔格莱德	13.00	Bombay 孟买	17.30
Berlin 柏林	13.00	Dacca 达卡	18.00
Sofia 索非亚	14.00	Rangoon 仰光	18.30
Damascus 大马士革	14.00	Phnom Penh 金边	19.00

City		Local Time	City		Local Time
Ankara	安卡拉	14:00	Bangkok	曼谷	19:00
Cairo	开罗	14:00	Ulan Bator	乌兰巴托	19:00
Capetown	开普敦	14:00	Djakarta	雅加达	19:30
Bucharest	布加勒斯特	14:00	Singapore	新加坡	19:30
Helsinki	赫尔辛基	14:00	Manila	马尼拉	20:00
Baghdad	巴格达	15:00	Irkutsk	伊尔库斯克	20:00
Nairobi	内罗毕	15:00	Pyongyang	平壤	21:00
Dar es Salaam	达拉斯萨拉姆	15:00	Tokyo	东京	21:00
Moscow	莫斯科	15:00	Osaka	大阪	21:00
Teheran	德黑兰	15:30	Canberra	堪培拉	22:00
Karachi	卡拉奇	17:00	Wellington	惠灵顿	24:00
Colombo	科伦坡	17:30			

A List of Overseas and Domestic Travel and Tourism Development in China

中国海外和国内旅游发展情况一览表

m. = one million

Item / Year	Inbound tourists 入境人数	Foreign currency earning US$ 100 m. 外汇收入 亿美元	Hotels 全国饭店 (家)	Rooms 房间数	Domestic tourists 100m. by turnstile count 国内旅游 亿人次	Domestic tourism receipt (100 m. yuan) 国内旅游收入 (亿元)	Total tourism rec. (100 m. yuan) 旅游总收入 (亿元)	Intl. travel agency 国际旅行社	Dom. travel agency 国内旅行社
1978	1,809,200	2.6	137	15,539					
1979	4,203,901	4.5	150	17,149					
1980	5,702,536	6.2	203	31,788					
1981	7,767,096	7.85	296	41,251					
1982	9,477,005	8.4	362	51,625					
1983	12,852,285	9.4	371	59,588					
1984	12,852,185	11.3	505	76,994					
1985	17,833,097	12.5	710	107,389	2.4	80			
1986	22,819,450	15.3	974	147,479	2.7	106			

670

1987	26,902,267	18.6	1,283	184,710	2.9	140			
1988	31,694,804	22.46	1,496	220,165	3.0	187			
1989	24,501,394	18.1	1,788	267,505	2.4	150			
1990	27,461,821	22.2	1,987	293,827	2.8	180			
1991	33,349,761	28.45	2,130	321,116	2.9	200			
1992	38,114,945	39.47	2,354	351,044	3.3	250			
1993	41,536,943	46.83	2,552	386,401	4.1	860			
1994	43,684,456	73.23	2,995	406,280	4.5	950			
1995	46,386,500	87.33	3,720	486,100	6.29	1,375.7			
1996	51,127,500	102.00	4,418	594,200	6.39	1,638.0			
1997	57,588,000	120.74	5,150	675,000	6.44	2,112.7	3,112.2		
1998	63,478,400	126.02	5,782	765,000	6.94	2,391.18	3,438.4	1,171	4,773
1999	72,790,000	140.99	7,035	889,400	7.19	2,831.00	4,002.4	1,256	6,070
2000	83,443,900	162.24	10,481	948,200	7.44	3,175.54	4,519.0	1,128	7,725
2001	89,012,90	177.92			7.84	3,522.36	4,995.0		
2002									
2003									
2004									
2005									
2006									
2007									
2008									

Overseas Tourism Development in Beijing
（Since 1978）

北京的海外旅游发展情况一览表

Year	Total Arrivals (10,000) by turnstile count 人次	Number of Hotels	Number of Rooms	Foreign Currency Receipt（US $ 100 million）
1978	18.70	11		1.00
1979	25.20	13		1.50
1980	28.60	24		1.20
1981	39.40	35		1.17
1982	45.70	39		1.32
1983	50.90	41		1.42
1984	65.70	50		1.68

Year	Total Arrivals (10,000) by turnstile count 人次	Number of Hotels	Number of Rooms	Foreign Currency Receipt (US $ 100 million)
1985	93.60	64		3.21
1986	99.00	71		4.56
1987	108.10	76		5.45
1988	120.40	79		6.75
1989	64.50	107		4.65
1990	100.40	155		6.75
1991	132.10	203		8.50
1992	174.81	234		10.76
1993	202.75	232		12.49
1994	203.00	249		20.09
1995	206.90	247		21.80
1996	218.90	255		22.52
1997	229.80	297		22.50
1998	220.10	308		23.80
1999	252.39	375		24.96
2000	282.09	407	84,000	27.68
2001	285.80	506		29.50
2002				
2003				
2004				
2005				
2006				
2007				
2008		c.900	c.170,000	
2009				
2010				
2011				

Star-rated hotels in Beijing (in 2001)

5-Star   21
4-Star   34
3-Star   141
2-Star   181
1-Star   45

Foreign Embassies in Beijing
外国驻华使馆及电话

(in an alphabetic order)
（按汉语拼音字母顺序排列）

Name	Add.	Tel.
A		
阿富汗伊斯兰国大使馆 Embassy of the Islamic State of Afghanistan	东直门外大街 8 号	65321582
阿拉伯联合酋长国大使馆 Embassy of the United Arab Emirates	塔园外交人员办公楼	65322112
阿拉伯埃及共和国大使馆 Embassy of the Arab Republic of Egypt	日坛东路 2 号	65321825
阿塞拜疆共和国大使馆 Embassy of the Republic of Azerbaijan	塔园外交人员办公楼	65324614
阿尔及利亚民主人民民共和国 Embassy of the Democratic People's Republic of Algeria	三里屯路 7 号	65321231
阿尔巴尼亚共和国大使馆 Embassy of the Republic of Albania	光华路 28 号	65321120
阿根廷共和国大使馆 Embassy of the Republic of Argentina	三里屯东 5 街 11 号	65321406
阿曼苏丹国大使馆 Embassy of the Sultanate of Oman	亮马河南路 6 号	65323692
安哥拉共和国大使馆 Embassy of the Republic of Angola	塔园外交人员办公楼	65326968
安提瓜岛和巴布达大使馆 Embassy of Antigua and Barbuda	东长安街	65137788-9188
爱沙尼亚共和国大使馆 Embassy of the Republic of Estonia	凯宾斯基饭店	64653388
爱尔兰大使馆 Embassy of Ireland	日坛东路 3 号	65322691
奥地利共和国大使馆 Embassy of the Republic of Austria	建国门外秀水南街 5 号	65322061
澳大利亚大使馆 Embassy of Australia	三里屯东直门外大街 21 号	65322331/7
埃塞俄比亚联邦民主 共和国大使馆 Embassy of the Federal Democratic Republic of Ethiopia	建国门外秀水南街 3 号	65325258
B		
保加利亚共和国大使馆 Embassy of the Republic of Bulgaria	建国门外秀水北街 4 号	65321946

673

白俄罗斯共和国大使馆 Embassy of the Republic of Belarus	日坛东一街	65326505
巴西联邦共和国大使馆 Embassy of the Federative Republic of Brazil	光华路 27 号	65322881
巴林国大使馆 Embassy of the State of Bahrain	塔园外交人员办公楼	65325025
巴基斯坦伊斯兰共和国大使馆 Embassy of the Islamic Republic of Pakistan	东直门外大街 1 号	65322504
巴勒斯坦国大使馆 Embassy of the State of Palestine	三里屯 3 街 2 号	65321361
巴布亚新几内亚大使馆 Embassy of Papua New Guinea	塔园外交人员办公楼	65324312
贝宁共和国大使馆 Embassy of the Republic of Benin	光华路 38 号	65322741
比利时王国大使馆 Embassy of Belgium	三里屯路 6 号	65321801
冰岛共和国大使馆 Embassy of the Republic of Iceland	亮马河大厦	65321736
博茨瓦纳共和国大使馆 Embassy of the Republic of Botswana	塔园外交人员办公楼	65927795
玻利维亚共和国大使馆 Embassy of the Republic of Bolivia	塔园外交人员公寓	65325751/5
布隆迪共和国大使馆 Embassy of the Republic of Burundi	光华路 25 号	65323074

C

朝鲜民主主义人民共和国大使馆 Embassy of the Democratic People's Republic of Korea	建国门外日坛路	65321186
赤道几内亚共和国大使馆 Embassy of the Republic of Equatorial Guinea	三里屯东 4 街 2 号	65323679

D

多哥共和国大使馆 Embassy of the Republic of Togo	东直门外大街 11 号	65322202
丹麦王国大使馆 Royal Danish Embassy	三里屯 5 街 1 号	65322431
德意志联邦共和国大使馆 Embassy of the Federal Republic of Germany	东直门外大街	65322161

E

厄立特里亚国大使馆 Embassy of Eritrea	塔园外交人员办公楼	65326534
厄瓜多尔共和国大使馆 Embassy of the Republic of Ecuador	建国门外公寓 11 号楼 12 号	65323849
俄罗斯联邦大使馆 Embassy of the Russian Federation	东直门北中街 4 号	65322051

F

法兰西共和国大使馆	三里屯东 3 街 3 号	65321331
Embassy of the Republic of France		
芬兰共和国大使馆	塔园外交人员办公楼	65321817
Embassy of the Republic of Finland		
菲律宾共和国大使馆	秀水北街 23 号	65321872
Embassy of the Republic of the Philippines		

G

刚果共和国大使馆	三里屯东 4 街 7 号	65321658
Embassy of the Republic of the Congo		
刚果民主共和国大使馆	三里屯 5 街	65323224
Embassy of the Democratic Republic of the Congo		
古巴共和国大使馆	建国门外秀水南街 1 号	65326568
Embassy of the Republic of Cuba		
哥伦比亚共和国大使馆	光华路 34 号	65323377
Embassy of the Republic of Colombia		
圭亚那合作共和国大使馆	建国门外秀水东街 1 号	65321337
Embassy of the Cooperative Republic of Guyana		

H

哈萨克斯坦共和国大使馆	三里屯东 6 街 9 号	65326183
Embassy of the Republic of Kazakhstan		
大韩民国大使馆	国贸中心	65053171
Embassy of the Republic of Korea		
荷兰王国大使馆	亮马河南路 4 号	65321131
Royal Netherlands Embassy		

J

加拿大大使馆	东直门外 19 号	65323536
Embassy of Canada		
捷克共和国大使馆	建国门外日坛路	65326902
Embassy of the Czech Republic		
柬埔寨共和国大使馆	东直门外大街 9 号	65321889
Royal Embassy of Cambodia		
吉尔吉斯共和国大使馆	塔园外交人员办公楼	65326458
Embassy of the Kyrgyzstan Republic		
加蓬共和国大使馆	光华路 36 号	65322810
Embassy of the Republic of Gabon		
加纳共和国大使馆	三里屯路 8 号	65321319
Embassy of the Republic of Ghana		
几内亚共和国大使馆	三里屯西 6 街 2 号	65323649
Embassy of the Republic of Guinea		
津巴布韦共和国大使馆	三里屯东 3 街 7 号	65323795
Embassy of the Republic of Zimbabwe		

K

卡塔尔国大使馆	塔园外交人员办公楼	65322231
Embassy of the State of Qatar		
科特迪瓦共和国大使馆	三里屯北小街 9 号	65323572

675

Embassy of the Republic of Cote d'Ivoire

科威特国大使馆	光华路 23 号	65322182
Embassy of the State of Kuwait		
喀麦隆共和国大使馆	三里屯东 5 街 7 号	65321828
Embassy of the Republic of Cameroon		
肯尼亚共和国大使馆	三里屯西 6 街 4 号	65323381
Embassy of the Republic of Kenya		
克罗地亚共和国大使馆	三里屯东三街外交公寓	65326241
Embassy of the Republic of Croatia		

L

老挝人民民主共和国大使馆	三里屯东 4 街 11 号	65321224
Embassy of the Lao People's Democratic Republic		
黎巴嫩共和国大使馆	三里屯东 6 街 51 号	65322197
Embassy of the Republic of Lebanon		
莱索托王国大使馆	塔园外交人员办公楼	65326842
Embassy of the Kingdom of Lesotho		
大阿拉伯利比亚人民社会主义		
民众国人民办事处	三里屯东 6 街 3 号	65323666
The People's Bureau of the Great Socialist		
People's Libyan Arab Jamahiriya		
利比里亚共和国大使馆	塔园外交人员办公楼	65325617
Embassy of the Republic of Liberia		
卢旺达共和国大使馆	秀水北街 30 号	65322193
Embassy of the Republic of Rwanda		
卢森堡大公国大使馆	内务部街 21 号	65135937
Embassy of the Grand-Duchy of Luxembourg		
立陶宛共和国大使馆	塔园外交公寓	65324421
Embassy of the Republic of Lithuania		
罗马尼亚大使馆	日坛路东 2 街	65323442
Embassy of Romania		

M

美利坚合众国大使馆	秀水北街 3 号	65323831
Embassy of the United States of America		
孟加拉人民共和国大使馆	光华路 42 号	65322521
Embassy of the People's Republic of Bangladesh		
缅甸联邦大使馆	东直门外大街 6 号	65321425
Embassy of the Union of Myanmar		
马达加斯加共和国大使馆	三里屯东街 3 号	65321353
Embassy of the Republic of Madagascar		
马来西亚大使馆	东直门外大街 13 号	65322531
Embassy of Malaysia		
马里共和国大使馆	三里屯东 4 街 8 号	65321704
Embassy of the Republic of Mali		
马耳他共和国大使馆	塔园外交人员公寓	65323114
Embassy of the Republic of Malta		
马其顿共和国大使馆	三里屯外交公寓	65326282

Embassy of the Republic of Macedonia
马绍尔群岛共和国大使馆　　　　塔园外交人员办公楼　　　　65325904
Embassy of the Republic of the Marshall Islands
蒙古国大使馆　　　　秀水北街 2 号　　　　65321203
Embassy of Mongolia
毛里求斯共和国大使馆　　　　三里屯外交公寓办公楼　　　　65325695
Embassy of the Republic of Mauritius
毛里塔尼亚伊斯兰
共和国大使馆　　　　三里屯东 3 街 9 号　　　　65321346
Embassy of the Islamic Democratic Mauritania
摩洛哥王国大使馆　　　　三里屯路 16 号　　　　65321796
Embassy of the Kingdom of Morocco
莫桑比克共和国大使馆　　　　塔园外交人员办公楼　　　　65323664
Embassy of the Republic of Mozambique
摩尔多瓦共和国大使馆　　　　塔园外交人员公寓　　　　65325494
Embassy of the Republic of Moldova
墨西哥合众国大使馆　　　　三里屯东 5 街 5 号　　　　65322574
Embassy of the United Mexican States
秘鲁共和国大使馆　　　　三里屯外交人员办公楼　　　　65323719
Embassy of the Republic of Peru
N
尼泊尔王国大使馆　　　　三里屯路西 6 街 1 号　　　　65321795
Royal Nepalese Embassy
尼日利亚联邦共和国大使馆　　　　三里屯东 5 街 2 号　　　　65323631
Embassy of the Federal Republic of Nigeria
南非共和国大使馆　　　　燕莎中心　　　　651914
Embassy of the Republic of South Africa 64
南斯拉夫联盟共和国大使馆　　　　三里屯东 6 街　　　　65323516
Embassy of the Federal Republic of Yugoslavia
纳米比亚共和国大使馆　　　　塔园外交人员办公楼　　　　65324810
Embassy of the Republic of Namibia
挪威王国大使馆　　　　三里屯东 1 街 1 号　　　　65322261
Royal Norwegian Embassy

P
波兰共和国大使馆　　　　日坛路 1 号　　　　65321235
Embassy of the Republic of Poland
葡萄牙共和国大使馆　　　　塔园办公楼　　　　65323497
Embassy of the Republic of Portugal
R
日本国大使馆　　　　日坛路 7 号　　　　65322361
Embassy of Japan
瑞典大使馆　　　　东直门外大街 3 号　　　　65323331
Embassy of Sweden
瑞士大使馆　　　　三里屯东 5 街 3 号　　　　65322736
Embassy of Switzerland

S

塞浦路斯共和国大使馆 Embassy of the Republic of Cyprus	塔园外交人员办公楼	65325057
沙特阿拉伯王国大使馆 Royal Embassy of Saudi Arabia	三里屯北小街1号	65324825
斯里兰卡民主社会主义 共和国大使馆 Embassy of the Democratic Socialist Rep. of Sri Lanka	建华路3号	65321861
塞内加尔 Embassy of the Republic of Senegal		65322646
塞拉利昂共和国大使馆 Embassy of the Republic of Sierra Leone	东直门外大街7号	65321222
索马里共和国大使馆 Embassy of the Somali Republic	三里屯路2号	65321752
苏丹共和国大使馆 Embassy of the Republic of the Sudan	三里屯东2街1号	65323715
苏里南共和国大使馆 Embassy of the Republic of Surinam	京伦饭店	65002266
斯洛伐克共和国大使馆 Embassy of the Slovak Republic	日坛路	65321531
斯洛文尼亚共和国大使馆 Embassy of the Republic of Slovenia	建国门外3号楼53号	65326356

T

塔吉克斯坦共和国大使馆 Embassy of the Republic of Tajikistan	塔园外交公寓	65322598
泰王国大使馆 Royal Thai Embassy	光华路40号	65321903
土库曼斯坦大使馆 Embassy of Turkmenistan	塔园外交人员办公楼	65326975
土耳其共和国大使馆 Embassy of the Republic of Turkey	三里屯东5街9号	65322650
坦桑尼亚联合共和国大使馆 Embassy of the United Republic of Tanzania	三里屯亮马河南路8号	65322394
突尼斯共和国大使馆 Embassy of the Tunisian Republic	三里屯东街1号	65322435

W

文莱达鲁萨兰国大使馆 Embassy of Brunei Darussalam	三里屯外交人员办公楼	65324094
乌兹别克斯坦共和国大使馆 Embassy of the Republic of Uzbekistan	三里屯北小街7号	65326305
乌干达共和国大使馆 Embassy of the Republic of Uganda	三里屯东街5号	65321708
乌克兰大使馆 Embassy of Ukraine	三里屯东6街11号	65326359
乌拉圭东岸共和国大使馆 Embassy of the Oriental Republic of Uruguay	塔园外交人员办公楼	65324445

委内瑞拉共和国大使馆 Embassy of the Republic of Venezuela	三里屯路 14 号	65321295

X

新加坡共和国大使馆 Embassy of the Republic of Singapore	秀水北街 1 号	65323926
新西兰大使馆 Embassy of New Zealand	日坛路东 2 街 1 号	65322731
希腊共和国大使馆 Embassy of the Republic of Hellenic	光华路 19 号	65321317
匈牙利共和国大使馆 Embassy of the Republic of Hungary	三里屯东直门外大街 10 号	65321431
西班牙大使馆 Embassy of Spain	三里屯路 9 号	65321986
阿拉伯叙利亚共和国大使馆 Embassy of the Syrian Arab Republic	三里屯东 4 街 6 号	65321372

Y

也门共和国大使馆 Embassy of the Republic of Yemen	三里屯东 3 街 5 号	65321558
大不列颠及北爱尔兰联合 王国大使馆 Embassy of the United Kingdom of Great Britain & Northern Ireland	光华路 11 号	65321961
印度共和国大使馆 Embassy of the Republic of India	日坛东路 1 号	65321856
印度尼西亚共和国大使馆 Embassy of the Republic of Indonesia	三里屯外交人员办公楼	65325488
伊朗伊斯兰共和国大使馆 Embassy of the Islamic Republic of Iran	三里屯东 6 街 13 号	65322040
伊拉克共和国大使馆 Embassy of the Republic of Iraq	建国门外秀水北街 25 号	65323385
亚美尼亚共和国大使馆 Embassy of the Republic of Armenia	塔园外交公寓	65325677
以色列国大使馆 Embassy of Israel	国贸中心西办公楼	65052970
越南社会主义共和国大使馆 Embassy of the Socialist Republic of Viet Nam	光华路 32 号	65321155
意大利共和国大使馆 Embassy of the Republic of Italy	三里屯东 2 街 2 号	65322131

Z

约旦哈希姆王国大使馆 Embassy of the Hashemite Kingdom of Jordan	三里屯东 6 街 5 号	65323906
乍得共和国大使馆 Embassy of the Republic of Chad	光华路 21 号	65321925
赞比亚共和国大使馆 Embassy of the Republic of Zambia	三里屯东 4 街 5 号	65321554
智利共和国大使馆 Embassy of the Republic of Chile	三里屯东 4 街 1 号	65321641

About the Author
作 者 简 介

Résumé

1998	Retired
1995	Consultant of China Civil International Tourist Corporation (Hereafter abbreviated to CCITC)
1989-1994	President of CCITC
1987-1988	Vice President of CCITC
1986-1987	Assistant President of CCITC
1984-1986	Deputy Chief of Tourism Administrative Division of Beijing Tourism Bureau
1980-1983	Vice Section Chief of Beijing Branch of China International Travel Service (Hereafter abbreviated to CITS)
1965-1979	English-speaking interpreter for Beijing branch of CITS
1965	English-speaking interpreter for CITS Head Office
1960-1965	Majoring in English in Nanjing University, one of key universities in China
1938	Born in Liyang, Jiangsu Province

Activities

	Led more than 800 foreign delegations and tour groups since 1965
1978	Visited Romania, Cypress, Syria, Jordan, Kuwait, Pakistan and Nepal with the Chinese Acrobatic Troupe—the top acrobatic troupe in China, worked as an English-speaking interpreter
1985	Visited Washington D. C. and New York for Beijing Economic & Trade Exhibition held in Washington D. C., was in charge of tourism hotels, and ancient architecture section for the exhibition
Apr. 1986	Senior guide for People to People Emergency Services Delegation led by Dr Grady P. Bray
Jun. 1986	Senior guide for the American Academy of Forensic Sciences Delegation led by President Dr Don H. Mills
Oct. 1986	Senior guide for Measurex Group led by Dr David A. Bossen
Aug. 1987	Organizer & senior guide for U. S. / China Joint Session on Trade, Investment & Economic Law (850 participants including delegates and guests) Senior guide for Post Conference Programme No 4 (153 people) of the session
Oct. 1987	Senior guide for Litton Group from the U. S. A.
Apr. 1988	Senior guide for People to People Arson Investigation Delegation led by Mr John Primrose
May 1988	Senior guide for People to People Aviation Safety Delegation led by Vice Admiral Donald Engen
Sep. 1988	Senior guide for the U. S. / Japan Bilateral Session Post Programme led by Mr Donald F. Pitts (judge of the Superior Court) sponsored by People to People

Sep. 1988	Senior guide for Public Safety Communication Delegation led by Mr Robert Tall sponsored by People to People
Dec. 1988	Was chosen as one of the outstanding guides in Beijing by Beijing Tourism Administration
Mar. 1989	Organizer and senior guide for China/ E. E. C. Symposium on Legal & Practical Aspects of Investment in China 300 people from 18 countries
May 1989	Senior guide for CSI (Customers Satisfaction Initiative) Awards from England (175 people)
Jan. 1989	Visited San Francisco, Seattle, Spokane, New York, Austin, San Antonio, Houston, Los Angeles, was in charge of promoting travel to China Part-time teacher for Jingdu (Capital City) Tourism Personnel Training Centre, Beijing Tourism College, several travel agencies both in Beijing and other cities in China
Mar. 1990	Senior guide for (America) Young Electric Sign Company (Incentive Group, 64 people) led by Michael I. Young
Apr. 1990	Organizer & senior guide for APLA 4th General Assembly & Conference on "Trade Friction & Its Solution of Asia — Pacific countries with the U. S. Market (145 delegates)
Apr. 1990	Appointed by the National Tourism Administration of the People's Republic of China for setting examination paper for the Second National Guide Examination.
1990	Chief organizer and senior guide for Asia-Pacific Lawyers Association General Assembly Meeting (185 people) held in Beijing
May 1990	Chief organizer and senior guide for the 14th World Mining Conference (699 delegates from 70 countries and regions) held in Beijing
May 1990	Was awarded an honourable certificate for making outstanding contributions to the successful convocation of the 14th World Mining Congress held in Beijing on May 14-18, 1990 issued by the Chinese leading Group of the 14th World Mining Congress, and the Science and Technology Committee of P. R. China
Oct. 1990	Was invited to be part-time Associate professor of travel agency management by the President of the Beijing Second Foreign Language Institute (China Tourism University)
Nov. 1990	Senior guide for American Taichi Centre Seminar from Chicago
Nov. 1990	Was awarded the title of associate professor of English by the government
Jan. 1991	Visited San Francisco, Seattle, Spokane, Minneapolis, Chicago, New York, Houston, Austin and Los Angeles Was invited to give lectures on tourism, agriculture, & family planning in China at St. Edwards University, U. S. A. Was invited to be interviewed on tourism in China for 45 minutes by Mr William Crawsord in the Studio of KLRU TV Station of the University at Austin, USA.
Jun. 1991	Senior guide for World Affairs Council Silk Road Tour led by Mr Thomas B. Gold and Mrs. Kimberley Weichel
Jul. 1991	Senior guide for the US Torosian Cycling Delegation (52 participants), sponsored by People to People, rode 250 miles in 2 weeks, from Beijing

681

	to Nanjing to Shanghai triumphantly
Apr. 1992	Senior guide for the US Torosian Cycling Delegation, 35 delegates, sponsored by People to People, rode approximately 280 miles in 2 weeks, from Beijing to Nanjing to Shanghai triumphantly
Jun. 1992	Senior guide of the US Keith Bird-Watching Delegation, 73 participants, sponsored by People to People, watched 233 species of Chinese birds in 2 weeks, from Beijing, Changchun, Baicheng, Xianghai Nature Reserve, Xining, the Bird Island, Xi'an (Lishan Mountain) and Shanghai (Fengxian coastal area)
May 1993	Was invited to be professor of Tourism Department of Nankai University
Oct. 1994	Senior guide for Intl. Amusement Parks and Attractions Delegation led by Mr Joseph M. Meck, President of its Association
Oct. 1994	Was appointed member of the Technical Committee of National Tourism Standardization by the State Technical Supervisory Administration
Oct. 1994	Senior guide for the US Child Care Providers Delegation sponsored by People to People
Oct. 1994	Senior guide for the Chicago Conciliation Delegation led by Dr Barbara Amodio.
Nov. 1994	Senior guide for Intl. Food Science and Technology Delegation led by Dr "Ted" Hood sponsored by People to People
Nov. 1994	Was invited by Horwath International for Annual Meeting held in mid-November 1994 – China World Hotel, Beijing, to give lectures on the Forbidden City, the Great Wall, the Temple of Heaven and the Summer Palace (for 100 female guests)
Oct. 1995	Senior guide for the US Economic and Social Concerns for the Elderly Delegation led by Dr Daniel Thurs (45 delegates), sponsored by People to People
Oct. 1995	Senior guide for the US and Canada Crafts Business and Trade Delegation led by Ms Donna Robertson
1998	Was listed *who's who* in Changzhou area
Jan. 1999	Was appointed as Senior Vice President of Beijing Bei Ao Intl. Travel Service
Apr. 1999	Visited Hong Kong
Jun. 1999	Was in charge of the XX (UIA) The International Union of Architects Congress Beijing'99 (over 2,000 participants from more than 100 countries and regions)
Sep. 1999	Was in charge of the reception of "Inspecting and Learning Groups" (600 people) from 14 provinces, autonomous regions and municipalities of the Sixth National Games of Nationalities' Traditional Sports; Was awarded an honourable certificate issued by the Organizing Committee for making outstanding contributions to the successful convocation of the Sixth National Games of Nationalities' Traditional Sports

Professor Zhu Qixin is recognized by many as China's leading expert on travel and tourism and has devoted considerable study to the arts and cultural heritage of his native

China. A graduate of Nanjing University, one of China's key universities, Professor Zhu majored in English and is the author of numerous books on travel and tourism.

In 1992, Professor Zhu, taught at the China Travel and Tourism University, and was a Professor at Nankai University. He has prepared and certified many of China's leading National tour guides and was appointed by the National Tourism Administration of the People's Republic of China to set the examination papers and standards for the National Guide Examination. He has been appointed by the National Tourism Administration of China to give lectures on Tourism Reception Management and Quality Control Management for China's general managers and deputy managers in the travel industry throughout China. In early 1995, China Technical Supervision Administration appointed Professor Zhu as China National Technical Standardization Committeeman on Travel and Tourism.

Since his early days as an English-speaking interpreter for the Head Office of China International Travel Service (CITS) and Beijing branch of CITS, where he acted as the English-speaking guide for China's top acrobatic troupe on their visits to Romania, Cypress, Syria, Jordan, Kuwait, Pakistan and Nepal, Professor Zhu's career has spanned nearly 40 years of active service of high responsibility in China's travel and tourism industry. In 1985, he was in charge of tourism, tourism hotels and the ancient architecture section of the Beijing Economic and Trade Exhibition in Washington, D. C. and has visited the United State several times and has taught there.

As Vice Section Chief of the Beijing branch of China International Travel Service, as Deputy Chief of Tourism Division in Beijing's Tourism Administration, and variously as Assistant President, Vice President, Director and President of China Civil International Tourism Corporation (CCITC), and Professor Zhu has received well in excess of 800 foreign delegations and VIP tour groups in China, and has been the chief organizer and senior guide for such international conferences in China as the 14th World Mining Congress (Beijing), the APLA 4th General Assembly and Conference on Trade Friction and Its Solution in Asia-Pacific Countries with the US and EC Market, the US/China Joint Session on Trade, Investment and Economic Law, and the Asia-Pacific Lawyers Association General Assembly Meeting, XX UIA Congress Beijing '1999, among others.

Professor Zhu has led and researched award-winning trips throughout China on a wide range of imaginative professional and educational journeys including the US Keith Bird-watching Delegation in which 73 participants watched and recorded the habits of 233 species of Chinese birds in remote and scenic areas of China, and the US Torosian Cycling Delegation in which Professor Zhu personally rode a triumphant 280 miles throughout China visiting historical spots and returning intact to Beijing. For many years he has been the chief organizer and advisor to the People to People Citizen Ambassador Programme on their visits to China. In November 1994, Professor Zhu was invited by Mr Werner E. Rotach, Chief Executive Officer of Horwath International to give presentations on prime sights such as the Summer Palace, the Great Wall and the Forbidden City to the accompanying persons at the annual meeting held in Beijing.

In early 1999, Professor Zhu was specially invited as Senior Vice President of Beijing Bei Ao Intl. Travel Service and was in charge of the XX UIA (International Union of Architects) Congress Beijing '1999 (2,000 participants from more than 100 countries and regions).

In September 1999, Professor Zhu was authorized by the World Tourism Organization (WTO) through UNDP based in Beijing to translate the Tumen River Area Development Program (a brochure "The Tumen River Area—New Horizon in Travel") into Chinese.

Books and Newspapers for Reference for the Sights of Beijing
参 考 用 书

Books

- Liu Junwen, ed., *Beijing China's Ancient and Modern Capital* (Foreign Language Press, 1982)
- Zhou Shachen, ed., *Beijing Old and New*, (New World Press, 1984)
- *Information Office of Beijing Municipal Government*, *Beijing Official Guide* (Latest Revision '99)
- The Editorial Department of New World Press, and the English Language Service of Radio Peking, *Sixty Scenic Wonders in China* (New World Press, 1980)
- *Dictionary of China's Sights* (Lexicographical Work Publishing House, 1981)
- 99' *Cihai* 辞海—a reprinted dictionary in a reduced format—published by Shanghai Lexicographical Work Publishing House
- *A Tourist Guide to Chengde* (1984)
- Angus Maciver, Robert Gibson, *The New First Aid in English* (1978)
- *A Guidebook to Exit-Entry* (1999)
- Rewi Alley, Peking Opera (1984)
- Mai Yangzhen, *Quadrangles of Beijing* (1994)
- Executive Office, China Tourist Hotel Star-Rating Committee, National Tourism Administration, *China Star-Rated Hotels* (1997-1998)
- Gong Dan, *Food and Drink in China*—A Visitor's Guide (1986)

Newspapers

- *China Daily* (Beijing, 1981-)
- *Beijing Evening News*
- *China Tourism News* (Beijing)

责任编辑：谭　燕

设　　计：吴　涛

摄　　影：王文波　小　石等

图书在版编目(CIP)数据

北京名胜游览/朱歧新编．—北京：中国旅游出版社，
2002. 7

ISBN 7 – 5032 – 2005 – 8

I. 北… II. 朱… III. 旅游指南—北京市—英文
IV. K928. 91

中国版本图书馆 CIP 数据核字(2002)第 040934 号

书　　名：北京名胜游览

编 著 者：朱歧新

出版发行：中国旅游出版社

　　　　　　(北京建国门内大街甲九号　邮编：100005)

印　　刷：北京 1201 工厂

版　　次：2002 年 7 月第 1 版

　　　　　2003 年 3 月第 2 次印刷

开　　本：850 毫米 × 1168 毫米　1/32

印　　张：22

字　　数：560 千

印　　数：5001 – 10000 册

审 图 号：京 S(2002)023 号

定　　价：43. 00 元